For Ruth Peterson and Sybil Nisenholz

Series Editorial Assistant: Carol Craig
Production Administrator: Annette Joseph
Production Coordinator: Holly Crawford
Editorial-Production Service: Grace Sheldrick, Wordsworth Associates
Text Designer: Denise Hoffman
Manufacturing Buyer: Megan Cochran
Cover Administrator: Linda K. Dickinson
Cover Designer: Suzanne Harbison

Copyright © 1991, 1987 by Allyn and Bacon
A Division of Simon & Schuster, Inc.
160 Gould Street
Needham Heights, Massachusetts 02194

Library of Congress Cataloging-in-Publication Data
Peterson, J. Vincent.
    Orientation to counseling / J. Vincent Peterson, Bernard
Nisenholz. — 2nd ed.
        p. cm.
    Includes bibliographical references and indexes.
    ISBN 0-205-12809-2
    1. Counseling.   2. Counselors.   I. Nisenholz, Bernard.
II. Title.
BF637.C6P45   1990
158'.3—dc20   90-47297
                                                                CIP

Printed in the United States of America
10 9 8 7 6 5 4 3 2 1   96 95 94 93 92 91

Credit: (pp. 7–8): From *The Therapeutic Relationship: Foundations for an Eclectic Psychotherapy,* by C. H. Patterson. Copyright © by Wadsworth, Inc. Reprinted by permission of Brooks/Cole Publishing Company, Monterey, California 93940.

Orientation to Counseling

SECOND EDITION

J. Vincent Peterson
Indiana University, South Bend

Bernard Nisenholz
California State University, Northridge

Allyn and Bacon
Boston   London   Toronto   Sydney   Tokyo   Singapore

AUGUSTANA UNIVERSITY COLLEGE
LIBRARY

Contents

Foreword   ix
Preface   xi

SECTION ONE   *The Helping Relationship*

1   Focus on the Counselor   3

Differences between Effective and Ineffective Helpers   4
Describing the Effective Counselor   5
Helping as a Way of Life   19
Counselor Education   20
Summary   20
Questions and Activities   21

2   Focus on the Helping Relationship   23

Characteristics of Clients   23
How People Become Clients   24
The Therapeutic Alliance   25
The Helping Process   30
Summary   45
Questions and Activities   46

3   Focus on Developing Respons/ability: The Learning of Counseling Skills   47

The Counseling Relationship—Core Conditions   47
Stage I—Attending Skills   48
Stage II—Exploration Skills   58
Stage III—Understanding   66
Stage IV—Action   77
Stage V—Termination   81
Summary   83
Questions and Activities   84

4   Focus on Using Skills: Conducting an Inner-View   85

Setting the Stage: The Environment   85
Counselor Characteristics and Behaviors   87
Conducting the First Session   88
Summary   94
Questions and Activities   95

SECTION TWO   *Professional Orientation*

5   Focus on the Origins and Scope of the Field of Counseling   99

Origins   99
The Field of Counseling   104

Further Discussion of the Dimensions of Counseling   109
Summary   118
Questions and Activities   120

6 Focus on a Career in the Helping Professions   121
The Mental Health Field Hierarchy   121
Credentialing   123
The Market for Counselors   127
Professionalism   131
Ethical and Legal Issues in Counseling   137
Summary   142
Questions and Activities   143

7 Focus on Selected Counseling Specialties   145
Generalist or Specialist   145
Guidelines for Selecting a Counseling Specialty   147
Selected Specialty Areas   148
Consultation   158
Human Resource Development in Business and Industry   162
Summary   165
Questions and Activities   166

8 Focus on the Problems of Becoming and Being a Counselor: Stress Management and the Prevention of Burnout   167
Stress and Burnout Defined   167
Causes of Burnout in Counseling Training   170
Causes of Counselor Burnout   172
Stress Management—Preventing Burnout   174
Summary   179
Questions and Activities   180

9 The Responsibility of the Counselor in the Greater Society   182
The Social Context of Change   182
Precedence for Social Commitment   183
Obstacles to Professional Involvement   185
Values and Priorities   186
Incomplete Evidence   186
Emotional Factors   186
What Can We Do?   187
Summary   190
Questions and Activities   191

SECTION THREE   Foundation Areas in Counseling

10 Focus on Theory in the Practice of Counseling   195
What Is a Theory?   195
Why Have a Theory?   196

Major Theoretical Approaches   202
Counseling Theory—A Paradigm Shift   211
General Systems Theory—Applications for Counseling   215
Developing a Personal Approach to Theory   218
Summary   219
Questions and Activities   219

11 Focus on Selected Theoretical Approaches to Counseling and Psychotherapy   220

Person-Centered Counseling   221
Gestalt Therapy   228
Transactional Analysis   231
Cognitive-Behavioral Counseling   234
Rational-Emotive Therapy   238
Transpersonal Counseling   240
Wholistic Counseling   245
Summary   248
Questions and Activities   248

12 Focus on Group Work   250

Origins   250
Types of Groups   252
Why Work with Groups?   254
Therapeutic Forces in Groups   256
Stages of Group Development   258
Leadership Styles and Functions   263
Group Leadership Techniques   264
Group Approaches   268
Problems and Issues in Group Work   268
Summary   269
Questions and Activities   270

13 Focus on Family Counseling   271

What Is a Family?   271
Family Life Cycle   272
Family Counseling   273
Theoretical Approaches   281
Family Counseling Techniques   287
When Is Family Counseling Needed?   289
Marriage/Relationship Counseling   290
Summary   293
Questions and Activities   294

14 Focus on Career and Lifestyle Counseling   295

Historical Perspective   295
Terminology   297
Does Career Counseling Differ from Personal Counseling?   298

Career Counseling Theory   299
Career Counseling Strategies   306
Trends   309
Summary   311
Questions and Activities   312

SECTION FOUR   General Foundations

15 Focus on Human Growth and Development for Counselors   315

Growth and Development of the Whole Person   316
Areas of Development   318
Summary   338
Questions and Activities   339

16 Focus on Cross-Cultural Approaches to Counseling   340

Background   341
Culture and Cultural Pluralism   341
Stages in the Development of Cross-Cultural Awareness   343
Barriers in Cross-Cultural Counseling   344
Problems and Issues in Cross-Cultural Counseling   350
A Multicultural Approach to Counseling   352
Summary   355
Questions and Activities   356

17 Focus on Assessment of Individuals   357

Background   357
Purposes of Individual Assessment   358
Diagnosis   359
Different Theoretical Approaches to Assessment   363
Assessment Techniques   366
Assessment Guidelines   374
Assessment Standards   375
Summary   376
Questions and Activities   376

18 Focus on Research in Counseling   378

Types of Counseling Research   378
Methods of Research   379
Problems in Encouraging Research   381
Problems in Conducting Research   382
Incongruencies between Practice and Research   384
Solving the Problems of Conducting Counseling Research   385
Summary   387
Questions and Activities   387

SECTION FIVE   *The Synergistic Counselor*

19 Epilogue   391

Who the Counselor Is   391
What the Counselor Can Do   392
What the Counselor Knows   392
Summary   393

Appendix   395

Ethical Standards of the American Association for Counseling and Development   395

Bibliography   404

Author Index   425

Subject Index   428

Foreword

A wide variety of introductory texts in counseling is available. The trend has been toward larger and heavier books. In part, this has been the result of the proliferation of counseling from secondary schools to elementary schools, rehabilitation agencies, mental health agencies, drug and alcoholism treatment centers, and other settings. Whereas in the past introductory texts focused on counseling in secondary schools, authors now want to produce a text appropriate for an introductory course that includes students preparing for all these areas. It can be argued that it would be desirable for each of these groups to have its own introductory text, as indeed is usually the case for rehabilitation counselors.

A second factor contributing to the voluminosity of introductory texts is the attempt to include all of the areas and topics covered in an entire master's program. Reviewers fault authors for omitting any topic considered to be an element in a master's program and for failing to provide detailed coverage. The result is an unwieldy book loaded with topics and details that are considered in depth in other courses, leading to excessive repetition that is wasteful of time and boring to students.

There is, then, a need for an introductory text that is clearly introductory—one that introduces the student to the broad field of counseling and provides an orientation to counseling as a generic profession. While including the major areas of counselor preparation in a master's program, such a book would not attempt to treat in detail all areas covered in other courses, such as tests and measurements, or theories of counseling and psychotherapy, or techniques and skills.

Peterson and Nisenholz have produced such a book in *Orientation to Counseling,* Second Edition. Its coverage is broad and comprehensive, including a number of areas not found in other texts. The focus on the counselor as a person offers the student an excellent opportunity to evaluate himself or herself as a potential counselor.

This focus and the personal, clear, and highly readable writing style make this book eminently suitable for graduate and undergraduate students considering a career in the helping professions. Accuracy and scholarship are not sacrificed for readability. There is no other introductory text that I know of so appropriate for graduate and undergraduate students. It provides an excellent orientation to the field of counseling.

C. H. Patterson
University of North Carolina, Greensboro
(1987, 1991)

Preface

The field of counseling is dynamic. In the few years since the publication of the first edition of *Orientation to Counseling,* we have witnessed a number of changes. These changes include the addition of two divisions (gerontology and marriage and family counseling) to the American Association for Counseling and Development (AACD), development of student assistance programs, the publication of a revised edition of the *Diagnostic and Statistical Manual of Mental Disorders* (DSM III–R), increased interest in spirituality in counseling, and almost a doubling of the number of states that now license professional counselors.

Orientation to Counseling, Second Edition, includes information on all of these changes and more. Before preparing the second edition we reviewed introductory counseling courses. We asked the directors of counseling programs at more than 400 universities to send us a copy of the syllabus for their introductory counseling courses. We received more than 125 syllabi from campuses across the country. One finding became clear from our review of the syllabi: There is no consensus as to how the introductory course should be taught. There is a wide divergence of approaches with regard to almost every variable investigated, including the use of textbooks, type of assignments, methods of evaluation, and the nature of the content to be presented.

Many instructors initiate their courses with a discussion of the history of counseling; others begin with a discussion of counseling theories; some start with the teaching of counseling skills; and others begin with a study of the role of the counselor. This second edition of *Orientation to Counseling* presents the material so it can be applicable to a number of differing views as to how an introductory course should be designed.

We have maintained the basic structure of the first edition by placing the initial focus on counselors—who they are, what they are able to do, and what they know. However, instructors who desire to begin with the origins of counseling might assign Section Two to their students at the outset. Other instructors wishing to begin with the variety of theories found in counseling might make their first assignments from Section Three of the book. A decided strength of this edition is the flexibility with which it can be used with a wide variety of instructional approaches. The accompanying instructor's manual offers additional suggestions for the teaching of an introductory course.

Some of the most extensive changes in this second edition are in the area of counseling theory. We have taken the general systems approach out of the "Counselor of the Future" section and now include it as an integral part of the present approach to theories. We believe that systems theory is a major approach that counseling students need to consider from the onset of their study of the field. We also have added a chapter describing a variety of theoretical approaches to counseling, including approaches that might be considered on the cutting edge of the field—transpersonal counseling and wholistic counseling (see chapter 11). These latter approaches illustrate the diversity of the field and indicate how practitioners are increasing their awareness of the personality dimensions of the clients with whom they work as well as including ecological factors. We note the definite trend away from working with only the affective domain, or specific behaviors, or thoughts. We emphasize a more integrative systems approach to working with individuals, families, and other human organizational structures.

Orientation to Counseling, Second Edition, provides a perspective of the growth of the profession with a presentation of a time-line illustrating the development of the counseling field. This time-line dramatically illustrates the ever-growing and expanding nature of this dynamic field (see chapter 5).

Orientation to Counseling, Second Edition, also contains a new chapter related to the responsibilities of the counseling professional to the greater society (see chapter 9). As counselors, we influence the world around us. We should be aware not only of the impact we have in working directly with our clients but also of the effect we can have when we go beyond. Again, looking at clients' concerns from a systems approach as well as from a prevention perspective, counselors must become aware of and involved in issues beyond the counseling relationship. The time to develop an active approach to dealing with these larger societal concerns is at the beginning, when students are first becoming involved in the field. Early student reaction to this new chapter has been very positive.

Another major change is the addition of questions and activities to the end of each chapter. An important way to make material more meaningful is to become actively involved with the content as quickly as possible. Readers are therefore encouraged to pursue as many of these questions and activities as possible.

Other changes in this edition of *Orientation to Counseling* include the updating of content in all chapters, the combining of two chapters on skill development into one chapter (chapter 3), and the addition of an epilogue.

The basic objectives of the first edition remain unchanged. These objectives include developing a book that students will enjoy reading; one that will not just provide information, but will also involve them in the material and provide a comprehensive, but not necessarily encyclopedic overview of the field of counseling. Our ultimate objective remains to have students be able to make a clearly thought-out decision about whether to continue their education in the field of counseling. We hope their decision will be the result of their involvement with the content and related experiences presented in *Orientation to Counseling.*

A major feature we retain is the relationship of the areas presented to the content areas in most master's level counseling programs, including all programs accredited by the Council for Accreditation of Counseling and Related Educational Programs (CACREP), the accrediting arm of AACD. Accordingly, the sections of the book also correspond, in general, to the content areas identified by the National Board for Certified Counselors (NBCC) for the certifying of professional counselors. Many candidates for the NBCC examination report that this book is an excellent study guide. We are pleased with the favorable evaluations received from our toughest critics, the students who have purchased and read the book. We hope that any revisions will enhance what we believe is an already valuable resource.

We carry forward to this second edition of *Orientation to Counseling* our practice of avoiding sexist language and we continue to use the terms *counseling* and *psychotherapy* interchangeably. Also, we choose to spell *wholistic* with a *w* to emphasize the broad, encompassing nature of the term.

Acknowledgments

We express our appreciation to the following people for their assistance in the preparation of this edition: Thomas V. Trotter, University of Idaho, Michael Spretnjak, and Geri Stone. Our thanks also go to our students for their valuable feedback. We also appreciate the encouragement and support received from Ray Short, series editor at Allyn and Bacon, and Carol Craig, series editorial assistant at Allyn and Bacon, and the superb editorial efforts of Grace Sheldrick, Wordsworth Associates. All have contributed significantly to the quality of this book.

The Helping Relationship

CHAPTER 1

FOCUS ON _____

The Counselor

Who makes an effective counselor?
Is simply liking people enough?

Welcome to the field of counseling! Whether you are beginning an extensive formal program of counselor education—one that could involve periods of formal and informal study for the rest of your working life—or you want an overview of the field, you will find this a fascinating field of study.

To begin, the field of counseling is growing, both in size and scope. There are increasing numbers of counselors, and they are finding an ever-widening choice of counselor-related occupations. In addition to learning the necessary knowledge and skills, you will encounter controversies, colorful personalities, and a variety of ethical and legal issues. Throughout your studies you will find that counseling is a highly personal field dedicated to helping individuals and groups solve personal problems.

Because counseling is such a personal field, we believe that a good place to begin is with the study of the characteristics of counselors: who they are, what they know, and what they can do. Chapter 1 highlights the personhood of the counselor, and chapters 2, 3, and 4 demonstrate how a fully functioning counselor initiates, develops, and concludes a therapeutic relationship.

In these early chapters we encourage you to begin to think about whether counseling is the appropriate field for you, and, if it is, to make an early commitment to become the best possible counselor. One way to do this is to do more than just read the chapters in this book. Get involved with the material. Consider how the facts and ideas relate to you personally. The questions and activities at the end of each chapter can help facilitate your involvement. Take advantage of the opportunity and begin now to develop a positive professional attitude (PA) to the counseling profession.

Most of us believe we can be helpful to others. With that idea in mind, an increasing number of people are entering the counseling field. Many are interested in remediation and rehabilitation. They want to help what might be called the casualties of the system: the discouraged, the disturbed, and the disturbing. Others are interested in prevention and in helping people to learn and use skills and attitudes that will help them avoid or forestall debilitation. Still others enter the field to help others attain the highest level of human potential.

Those who enter the field of counseling as students may already have training and experience in the helping professions, perhaps as teachers, nurses, or clergy. They often stay with their original profession on completion of counselor training and use their newly acquired knowledge and experience to enhance their work. Many students enter graduate-level counselor education programs from a variety of educational backgrounds, ranging from art to zoology. They strive to develop high degrees of knowledge and skill in a field that can lead to a broad variety of employment opportunities as well as provide a springboard for advanced training.

Some job titles currently held by graduates of counselor education programs include mental health counselor, organizational development consultant, personnel development trainer, school counselor, and nurse counselor. These seemingly different occupations have much in common. They are all concerned with what has been labeled " 'the people problem'—helping people achieve more effective relationships between themselves and others or with the world in which the live" (Combs, Avila, & Purkey, 1971, p. 4).

Does being a nice, caring person ensure success as a counselor? Is it enough to like people and to have a desire to help them? Does the completion of a required course of study guarantee that a counselor will be a positive influence when working with people? What changes, if any, will a counseling student need to experience as part of the educational process? This chapter deals directly with these issues and more as we explore the world of the counselor.

DIFFERENCES BETWEEN EFFECTIVE AND INEFFECTIVE HELPERS

People from all walks of life use a variety of what they believe to be helping behaviors in their interactions with others. However, the results of many interventions are often less than helpful, and subsequent statements such as "I was only trying to help" are hardly comforting.

What is even more discouraging is that sometimes interventions by trained professionals can be harmful rather than helpful. Carkhuff (1983) reports that "we have found that all helping and human relationships may be 'for better or for worse.' The effects depend upon the helper's level of skills in facilitating the helpee's movement through the helping process toward constructive helping outcomes. These responsive and initiative helping skills constitute the core of all helping relationships" (p. 272).

The conclusion that helping professionals can hurt as well as help was arrived at in a circuitous fashion. During the 1950s several investigators charged that counseling and psychotherapy did not make a difference (Eysenck, 1952; Levitt, 1957). These investigators found that people in control groups, those not assigned to therapists, gained as much, on the average, as those who were seen by professional practitioners. Approximately "two-thirds of the patients improved and remained out of the hospital a year after treatment, whether they were treated or not" (Carkhuff, 1983, p. 259).

Closer study of professionally treated clients, however, indicated that the results of therapy covered a broader range in this sample than was found in groups of potential clients who did not receive therapy. Analysis of the results of therapy on clients of the professional therapists indicated that some clients got significantly better and some got worse. Counseling and psychotherapy did, in fact, make a difference; however, the disturbing conclusion was that the effect could be either helpful or harmful.

The most significant finding on the effectiveness of professional therapists was that the helpful and harmful effects could be accounted for largely by the levels of functioning of the helpers on certain interpersonal dimensions, such as the ability to listen with understanding. Therapists who offered high levels of the identified interpersonal dimensions facilitated the process of positive movement of their clients. The clients of therapists who offered low levels of the same dimensions stayed the same or got worse (Carkhuff, 1983; Rothstein, 1989).

These findings have been confirmed by experimental studies in which the variables were controlled (Carkhuff & Alexik, 1967; Holder, Carkhuff, & Berenson, 1967; Piaget, Berenson, & Carkhuff, 1968). The findings have also been generalized to other areas of helping and human relationships: parent–child relations (Carkhuff & Pierce, 1976) and teacher–student relations (Aspy & Roebuck, 1977). In a study of leadership ability in groups, Lieberman, Yalom, and Miles (1973) found that a combination of caring and meaning attribution behaviors were directly related to positive outcomes, whereas other behaviors such as high emotional stimulation led to negative results.

> In general, the overall conclusion of these studies is that the "less knowing" persons (clients) will move toward the levels of functioning of the more knowing persons (helpers) over time, depending on both the extensiveness and intensity of contacts. Helpees of high functioning helpers get better on a variety of process and outcome indices, while helpees of low level functioning helpers get worse. (Carkhuff, 1980, p. 216)

DESCRIBING THE EFFECTIVE COUNSELOR

What then are the attributes of a high functioning counselor? A number of studies conducted during the past 30 years have investigated the relationship between personality characteristics and effectiveness in counseling. The results have been consistent: there are no inherent personality characteristics—not even IQ—that correlate with successful counseling (Rowe, Murphy, & DeCsipkes, 1975).

However, as noted, a definite correlation exists between the skill or functioning level of the helper and effective counseling. Specific interpersonal skills that have been identified include communicating empathy, respect, concreteness, confrontation, self-disclosure, and immediacy (Rothstein, 1989; Truax & Carkhuff, 1967). In a review of research related to a variety of helping professionals including teachers, school counselors, counselors-in-training, and clergy,

Combs (1986) found that the helper's belief system is a significant factor in being an effective helper.

Combs found five areas of belief that appear to discriminate between good and poor helpers:

1. Good helpers have the belief that it is the personal meaning of another person that is what is important, not external, behavioral data. They believe in being sensitive and empathic.
2. Good helpers have very positive beliefs about people, seeing them as dependable, able, and trustworthy.
3. Good helpers have a positive belief in self. They have a good self-concept, confidence in their abilities, and a feeling of oneness with others.
4. Good helpers have strong beliefs about purposes and priorities. Beliefs held about the purposes of society, helping, and relationships influence their goals and their interventions.
5. Good helpers have strong beliefs about appropriate methods for helping. Research has not indicated any specific methods that discriminate between effective and ineffective helpers. It appears that it may well be the values and beliefs that the helper has about the methods used that make the difference. (pp. 56–58)

Overall, in recent years emphasis in the field has shifted from the counselor's personality to educating counselors to perform particular behaviors, skills, or interactions (Rothstein, 1989; Rowe et al., 1975). Ford (1979) suggests that training efficacy can be maximized by selecting trainees with high initial proficiency levels in specified target skills.

Furthermore, in studying any profession there is always a concern about what the professional knows. This question is of particular importance in the helping professions because we place a high value on self-knowledge as well as on externally acquired knowledge. Thus, in describing effective counselors, we are concerned with who counselors are, what they know, and what they can do.

Who the Counselor Is: Personal Characteristics

One commonly desired outcome of counseling is to help clients become more self-actualizing, or more fully functioning, or more closely approximating their highest levels of potential. If this is a goal for clients, some counselor educators (e.g., Carkhuff & Berenson, 1977) believe that it should be an objective for counselors as well. If counselors are to help a client become more fully functioning, it is reasonable to suggest that counselors also be involved in the process. Counselors may not be able to help anyone progress beyond the point that they themselves have attained.

In a quest to determine what was special about individuals who were functioning at high levels, Maslow (1956) studied healthy people who were judged to be using personal resources in highly effective ways. The following 14 character-istics as summarized by Patterson (1985) were found generally to describe Maslow's subjects, with no subject necessarily rating high on all of the character-istics.

Characteristics of the Self-Actualizing Person

1. *More efficient perception of reality and more comfortable relations with it.* This includes the detection of the phony and dishonest person, the accurate perception of what exists rather than the distortion of perception by one's needs. Self-actualizing people are more aware of their environment, both human and nonhuman. They are not afraid of the unknown, and can tolerate the doubt, uncertainty, and tentativeness accompanying the perception of the new and the unfamiliar. . . .

2. *Acceptance of self, others, and nature.* Self-actualizing persons are not ashamed of their human nature, with its shortcomings, imperfections, frail-ties and weaknesses. Nor are they critical of these aspects of other people. *They respect and esteem themselves and others.* Moreover, they are honest, open, genuine, without pose or facade. They are not, however, self-satisfied, but are concerned about discrepancies between what is and what might be, in themselves, others, and society. . . .

3. *Spontaneity.* Self-actualizing persons are not hampered by convention, but they do not flout it. They are not conformists, but neither are they anti-conformist for the sake of being so. They are not externally motivated or even goal-directed—rather their motivation is the internal one of growth and development, the actualization of themselves and their potentialities. . . .

4. *Problem-centering.* Self-actualizing persons are not ego-centered, but focus on problems outside themselves. They are mission oriented, often on the basis of a sense of responsibility, duty, or obligation rather than of personal choice. . . .

5. *The quality of detachment; the need for privacy.* The self-actualizing person enjoys solitude and privacy. It is possible for him to remain unruffled and undisturbed by what upsets others. He may even appear to others as asocial. . . .

6. *Autonomy; independence of culture and environment.* Self-actualizing per-sons, though dependent on others for satisfaction of the basic needs of love, safety, respect, and belongingness, ''are not dependent for their main satis-factions on the real world, or other people or culture or means-to-ends, or in general on extrinsic satisfactions. Rather, they are dependent for their own development and continued growth upon their own potentialities and latent resources.'' (Maslow, 1956, p. 176)

7. *Continued freshness of appreciation.* Self-actualizing persons repeatedly, though not continuously, experience awe, pleasure, and wonder in their everyday world.

8. *The mystic experience; the ''oceanic feeling.''* In varying degrees and with

varying frequencies, self-actualizing persons have experiences of ecstasy, awe and wonder with feelings of limitless horizons opening up, followed by the conviction that the experience was important and valuable and had a carry over into daily life. . . .

9. *Gemeinschaftsgefühl.* Self-actualizing persons have a deep feeling of empathy, sympathy or compassion for human beings in general. This feeling is unconditional, in that it exists along with the recognition of the existence of negative qualities in others which provoke occasional anger, impatience, and disgust. . . .

10. *Interpersonal relations.* Self-actualizing people have deep interpersonal relations with others. They are selective, however, and the circle of friends may be small, usually consisting of other self-actualizing persons. They attract others to them as admirers or disciples. . . .

11. *The democratic character structure.* The self-actualizing person does not discriminate on the basis of class, education, race, or color. He is humble in the recognition of what he knows in comparison to what could be known, and he is ready to learn from anyone. He respects everyone as potential contributors to his knowledge, but also just because they are human beings.

12. *Means and ends.* Self-actualizing persons are highly ethical. They clearly distinguish means from ends and subordinate means to ends.

13. *Philosophical, unhostile sense of humor.* [Self-actualizing persons have a] spontaneous, thoughtful [sense of humor,] intrinsic to the situation. Their humor did not involve hostility, superiority, or sarcasm. . . .

14. *Creativity.* [Self-actualizing persons were all found] to be creative, each in his own way. The creativity involved here is not the special talent creativeness. It is a creative potentiality inherent in everyone but usually suffocated by acculturation. *It is a fresh, naive, direct way of looking at things.* (Patterson, 1985, pp. 39–41)

Self-actualizing persons are involved with people and issues in the real world. They are not selfish or self-centered, but they have the self-assurance and confidence of persons who know who they are and how they relate to other people.

> Self-actualizing people are, without one single exception, involved in a cause outside their own skin, in something outside of themselves. They are devoted, working at something, something which is very precious to them—some calling or vocation in the old sense, the priestly sense. They are working at something which fate has called them to somehow and which they work at and which they love, so that the work–joy dichotomy in them disappears. (Maslow, 1971, p. 43)

The importance of having self-actualizing characteristics has been confirmed partially, at least, by Combs (1986). He found that beliefs helpers hold about themselves and others and their purpose were significant factors in the counseling relationship. Counselors have the responsibility to monitor and evaluate their self-actualization efforts in order to better help others in their quest for self-actualization (Pietrofesa, Leonard, & Van Hoose, 1978). Self-actualization is a process; it is not expected that counselors will be self-actualized, but rather that they are aware of where they are in the process and what they need to do to move toward their goal.

Additional Characteristics of Counselors

Some additional characteristics that are important in becoming a counselor include personal energy level, risk-taking ability, tolerance of ambiguity, authenticity, trustworthiness, and capacity for intimacy. Again, there is no strong correlation between a given characteristic and effectiveness as a counselor. Nevertheless, an awareness of the following characteristics may help to promote a better understanding of the counseling process itself.

Level of Personal Energy.

Counseling on a full-time basis in a school or agency could mean, in a given week, conducting 15 to 20 or more intensive 50-minute counseling sessions, staffing several case conferences, handling a number of brief crisis cases, attending a variety of meetings, and completing paperwork, among other duties. What is vital in a schedule like this is that for each counseling session counselors must be able to attend to clients totally, with full reservoirs of energy. Passive, nonenergetic counselors are not as likely to inspire the trust and confidence of clients that more dynamic, energetic counselors might generate (Cormier & Cormier, 1985).

Attending to the client includes being able to set aside such things as personal issues and thoughts about the previous client, which takes much energy and strength. Counselors who are not able to maintain this high energy level can burn out. A prospective counselor who has a high energy level to begin with, or who can develop and maintain a personal strength-building program, will be better prepared for both the rigors of a counselor training program and a career in counseling. Both physical and mental strength need to be maintained (see chapter 8). Carkhuff and Berenson (1977) suggest that "only those who are physically robust and live fully from a high level of energy are potential sources of nourishment and may be entitled to confront" (pp. 199–200).

Risk-Taking Ability.

Counseling involves taking risks, including being rejected as a helper, being confronted with a client who is hostile or who presents a problem that a counselor is totally unprepared for or not trained to handle, and having to confront a client directly without knowing how this action will be perceived. Much of the risk in counseling involves the use of helper behaviors that may be new or may not have been used often enough for the counselor to have a reasonably high comfort level.

Counseling often includes confronting a client in a caring way, a skill that involves a high level of risk and energy. For many people, confronting another person is one of the riskiest of interpersonal behaviors. In many counseling situations, however, it is not until the client's inconsistent thoughts, feelings, and behaviors are confronted that the real work of counseling and change begins. Yet confrontation is anxiety-provoking, because the client's response is unpredictable. Confrontation can lead to a potentially fruitful yet unpredictable period of interaction that is uncomfortable to those who like to be prepared for any possible outcome and who literally work from a script.

Additional risks in helping include the first meeting with a client, or a group, and handling crisis cases such as potential suicides or homicides. One major function of counselor education is to provide the knowledge and skills necessary to help make such encounters less of a risk. Ultimately, as Gilbert Wrenn (1983) warns us, counselors must take risks both professionally and politically, or risk entering new fields of work.

Tolerance of Ambiguity.   The tolerance of ambiguity has been defined as the capacity of a counselor "to tolerate the uncertainty of not knowing exactly what the client really wishes to discuss until a relationship is established which will allow the process of counseling to continue" (Pietrofesa et al., 1978, p. 105). Pietrofessa and his colleagues stress the importance of tolerance of ambiguity in counseling by noting research evidence indicating that a significant relationship exists between tolerance of ambiguity and the effectiveness of counselor responses. Being able to weigh the meaning of a client's statements carefully may result in more accurate, effective responses.

The field of counseling is filled with ambiguities. There are no standardized diagnostic procedures guaranteed to determine quickly the exact nature of each client's problem, and there are literally hundreds of ways to approach clients and their problems. Furthermore, a basic premise of many theoretical approaches to counseling is that it is up to clients to take responsibility for the ultimate solutions to their problems. Counselors, therefore, cannot simply prescribe a proven antidote for problems the way a medical doctor might prescribe penicillin for a case of bronchitis. Counseling is a field that is basically as much art as it is science, and it generally tends to attract practitioners who are comfortable in this type of ambiguous setting.

Authenticity.   Authentic counselors do not hide behind roles or defenses. They are congruent, with verbal and nonverbal messages conveying the same meaning. They are genuine, sincere, and honest. Being authentic and congruent indicates "a cohesiveness among one's values, attitudes and beliefs—it represents psychological health and well-being" (Pietrofesa, Hoffman, & Splete, 1984, p. 215).

Being authentic includes being able to self-disclose. This ability is of particular value in helping counselors learn about themselves. It also may be a factor in the counseling process itself. It is therefore an area of particular concern for prospective counselors. Do they have the capacity to self-disclose? Do they want to develop this ability? Are they able to self-disclose comfortably at a relatively deep level? Some persons may be able to tell many stories and yet not disclose much if anything about themselves. Self-disclosure, like other behaviors, can be carried to the extreme where, for example, the client ends up counseling the counselor.

Trustworthiness.   Strong (1968) has described counseling as a social-influence process in which counselors strive to establish a power or influence base by virtue of first being perceived by clients as trustworthy, attractive, and expert or competent. Then, when the power base is established, counselors can use that power to influence clients to do whatever is necessary to manage their lives more effectively (Cormier & Cormier, 1985; Egan, 1986). Trustworthiness is described here; expertness or competence are discussed later in this chapter. Attractiveness is discussed in chapter 4 as part of a description of an initial interview.

Trust is a vital element in any meaningful relationship, and it is of particular importance in counseling relationships. What is important according to Strong (1968) is the clients' perception of the counselor as being trustworthy. Being trustworthy can mean being able to keep personal information confidential; being reliable in word and deed; having power, but not misusing it in any way; and being willing and able to work to understand the client (Egan, 1986).

Initial trust often comes as a result of the role of counselor, a role generally regarded as trustworthy by society; a reputation for honesty, perceived sincerity and openness, and lack of motivation for personal gain (Strong, 1968). Once a relationship has been established, the counselor's behavior contributes to the ongoing development and maintenance of trust. Behavior that contributes to trustworthiness includes consistency in words and action, nonjudgmental acceptance of client disclosures, and a feeling of active involvement (Cormier & Cormier, 1985).

Capacity for Intimacy.   A counseling relationship can be one of the most intimate personal relationships. Clients share their most personal thoughts and feelings, often telling counselors things they have never told anyone else. Counselors communicate deep levels of acceptance and understanding, make caring confrontations, and often share their own personal thoughts and feelings. The capacity for nonpossessive intimacy on a regular basis is an attribute that some people seem to have naturally and some never seem to attain. Most people, however, can learn to develop their capacity for intimacy in order to be able to be psychologically close to a client at the depths of an existential crisis.

Counselors who have difficulty with intimacy may fear being vulnerable and the possibility of being rejected. Associated with these feelings may be a fear of closeness and affection. Counselors with these fears may create excessive emotional distance in counseling relationships and avoid challenging or confronting clients when appropriate (Cormier & Cormier, 1985). Chapter 4 further elaborates on this characteristic and the skills related to it.

What the Counselor Knows:
External and Self-Knowledge

Two basic types of knowledge concern a prospective counselor: external knowledge and self-knowledge.

External Knowledge

External knowledge is learned from books, lectures, audio- and videotapes, and listening to others. Although there is little demonstrated relationship between the ability to show high levels of knowledge on tests and effectiveness in counseling, there is a legitimate expectation for sufficiently high levels of external knowledge. Entrance requirements into graduate school, specific course requirements, exit requirements—which may include comprehensive written or oral examinations, and the relatively recent requirement of the successful completion of a standardized national examination for counselor certification—all speak to the need for the counselor trainee to have a strong external knowledge base.

In general, areas of knowledge in which overall mastery is expected include an understanding of the profession itself, the helping relationship, group dynamics, human growth and development, counseling theory, career development, social and cultural foundations, appraisal of individuals, and research and evaluation. The areas noted are the general areas covered in the National Counseling Certification Examination. Further elaboration of each area is presented in subsequent chapters. In addition to being knowledgeable, counselors need to have a desire to learn, be intellectually curious, and know what is happening to clients as they progress through counseling (Cormier & Cormier, 1985).

Knowledge of Self

A large amount of external knowledge needs to be mastered, but all of it is insignificant compared to an in-depth knowledge of oneself. When working with clients who are concerned about the meaning of life, the making of moral and ethical decisions, and dealing with values and value judgments, it is essential that counselors know and are comfortable with themselves. The importance of the self, and how one alters self-knowledge, are described in the next section.

Self as Instrument

> *A person's self is the sum total of all he can call his. The self includes, among other things, a system of ideas, attitudes, values, and commitments. The self is a person's total subjective environment; it is the distinctive center of experience and significance. The self constitutes a person's inner world as distinguished from the outer world consisting of other people and things.*
>
> Jersild (1952, p. 9)

> *The use of the self by the therapist is an integral part of the therapeutic process and it should be used consciously for treatment purposes.*
>
> Satir (1987, p. 23)

Simply stated, the basic tool counselors have at their disposal is themselves (Combs et al., 1971; Bugental, 1987). Pens, paper, tests, tapes and tape recorders, art materials, film, toys, and computers might be used at various times by counselors. However, these ancillary materials play a small role in the helping professions. Counselors must be willing and able to use all of their personal resources. Are they able to observe the total person with their eyes, ears, and intuitive senses, picking up nonverbal as well as verbal cues, noting, for example, inconsistencies among tone of voice, body posture, and verbal content? Do they have the energy to be able to enter the world of troubled clients and work within that framework to help bring about change? Are they open and comfortable enough to be able to self-disclose in an appropriate manner? Are they disciplined enough to be able to help clients become specific in stating their concerns? Are they willing to take the risks involved in confrontation? Finally, are they able to put all of these skills together to develop direct, mutual communication (intimacy)? Are they in the process of growth or in the process of deterioration?

The growth-deterioration process illustrated in Figure 1.1 does not mean that changes in a person are exclusively one way or the other, or that a counselor should never have any negative experiences. In fact, some therapists, such as Rollo May (1984), suggest that we often can best relate to the suffering of others from our personal experiences with pain. Due to varying conditions and circumstances, there will probably always be movement up and down the growth–deterioration continuum. In general, however, it would be anticipated that the prevailing tendency of a person's becoming and being a counselor would be toward growth rather than deterioration.

To Know Oneself

And seek not the depths of your knowledge with staff or sounding line. For self is a sea boundless and measureless. Say not, I have found the truth, but rather, I have found a truth.

Gibran (1923, p. 61)

The ancient command of Socrates to "know thyself" is of particular importance to counselors. Because our thoughts and feelings about ourselves can directly influence how we interact with clients, it is necessary to have full knowledge of ourselves. Self-knowledge, according to Weinstein and Alschuler (1985), consists of descriptions, predictions, and management of one's inner experiences. In attaining self-knowledge, we also need to consider the terms *self-concept,* an indicator of what we think about ourselves, and *self-esteem,* an indicator of how we feel about ourselves (Hamachek, 1985). How do we go about the process of knowing ourselves? What initially sounds deceptively simple is indeed most difficult to do.

Some initial stage setting may be helpful. The first step is to acknowledge that the universe "is infinite and any assumptions or beliefs that we hold concerning its reality are subject to question" (Hulnick, 1977, p. 71) and further, "in the province of the mind there are no limits" (Lilly, 1972). In effect then, nothing is impossible. Believing that something is impossible will ensure that one will never experience it. It does not mean that the event could not happen with another person.

The second step toward self-knowledge is to be open to experience.

GROWTH

Level 5

Creative Counselors

Self-actualizing, spontaneous, maximally
effective in promoting positive change in
self and others

↕

Level 4

Personally Effective

Potent, chronically constructive, promoting
positive change

↕

Level 3

Minimally Effective

Situationally distressed, marginal/support
system, capable of change and constructive
action

↕

Level 2

Disturbed

Neuroses, chronic negative patterns, resistant
to change

↕

Level 1

Severely Disturbed

Psychoses, ingrained destructive patterns,
immune to change

DETERIORATION

FIGURE 1.1   Levels of Growth and Deterioration: Where Helping Professionals May
Be Functioning *(Table adapted from:* Beyond Counseling and Therapy *by Robert R.
Carkhuff & Bernard G. Berenson. Copyright © 1967 by Holt, Rinehart & Winston, Inc.
Adapted by permission of CBS College Publishing)*

We begin to pay close attention to what is going on within ourselves and our environment. At this point, we discover a strange awakening, and we begin the descent
into our inner world. We take risks; we attempt to express ourselves in spite of our
fears. Now, we may even wonder whether we were wise to have begun this journey,
but something deep within will not let us turn back. We have tasted a finer substance,
and we muster the quality of heart-felt courage and proceed in the face of fear. We

> plunge downward into the very blocks themselves. We experience and confront our resentment, our low self-esteem, our alienation, our bitterness, our unforgiving attitudes, but now we no longer pretend that they are not a part of us. We realize that we *are* like that, and we do not like what we see. (Hulnick, 1977, p. 1)

The third step is self-disclosure.

> I have to be free and able to say my thoughts to you, to tell you about my judgments and values, to admit to you my failures and shames, to share my triumphs, before I can really be sure what it is that I am and can become. I must be able to tell you who I am before I can know who I am. And I must know who I am before I can act truly, that is, in accordance with my true self. (Powell, 1969, p. 44)

Hearing your thoughts spoken out loud, perhaps even clarifying them as you speak, and receiving feedback from others are often revealing and rewarding. This actually is one possible outcome offered to justify the hundreds of hours teenagers spend talking on the telephone. Sharing ideas, perceptions, and feelings with significant others is a helpful way to self-understanding and the clarification of beliefs and values. This is one reason that some counselor education programs advocate that counseling students participate in therapy while pursuing a degree, a requirement we strongly support.

Related to step three is step four. Step four is to be open to others and to know them. Sydney Harris (1981) suggests that there is a paradox in this whole process of knowing oneself: "We can only know ourselves through knowing others and we can only know others through knowing ourselves" (p. 6). Niebuhr (1955) supports this when he says that "the self cannot be truly fulfilled if it is not drawn out of itself into the life of the other" (p. 31). It is difficult to know yourself by focusing only inward or by reflecting on how other people respond to your thoughts and feelings. We gain much more from discovering ways in which we are similar as well as different from others. Not only is this ability to reach out to know others necessary for self-understanding, but it is also vital to the counseling process.

Another way to know more about oneself is to determine how you view others. What people see and describe "in the behavior of others is frequently a projection of their own drives, fears, and needs" (Hamachek, 1985, p. 137).

The fifth step is to release ourselves from previously held assumptions and misconceptions "by *forgiving ourselves* for having created them in the first place" (Hulnick, 1977, p. 71). Through this process we become aware of what we believe and value. As we work through the distortions and misconceptions we have, we release energy, making it easier to be open to new experiences and to know ourselves at a deeper level.

> *The successful release is often experienced as a "lightening" of body weight and the lifting of a great burden from one's shoulders. Now, we can understand and feel empathy or compassion since we have confronted our own pain.*
>
>   Hulnick (1977, p. 71)

Finally, to tie these five steps together, it is helpful to keep a journal. Keeping a journal is a form of self-disclosure; however, it is often not shared with others. Thoughts, feelings, descriptions of experiences, stories, poems, records of dreams, doodles, and drawings—all can be kept in a journal. In fact, attending special journal writing workshops can help maximize the use of this vehicle. A journal is significant not only for the record of growth that it provides, but also because our written expressions are sometimes different, often in subtle ways, from our verbalizations. We can again learn more about who we are. Cormier and Cormier (1985) state that ''it is just as important to keep track of our own personal growth as it is to keep track of what technique or change program we are using with a client. Otherwise we run the risk of behaving incongruently in our relationships with clients'' (p. 13).

Knowing oneself and directly appreciating the unlimited potential one has are crucial in applying the self-as-instrument concept. One is then free to take risks and to use one's total person in the helping relationship. Both the left (cognitive, rational) side of the counselor's brain and the right (intuitive, affective) side are engaged. The body is used to demonstrate attentiveness, and the voice is used as a tool to communicate awareness of the client's feeling level. Above all, the counselor would communicate authenticity. The helping relationship becomes a total experience for the counselor's complete self.

What the Counselor Can Do: Helping Skills

What we can do may be, as Carkhuff (1983), Rothstein (1989), and others suggest, a major factor in effective helping. A person may be attractive and trustworthy and have a high level of knowledge and self-awareness and yet be ineffectual in helping other people solve problems. For a few, the skills of helping may come naturally; for most people, however, it takes a great deal of study and practice to develop all the necessary skills at a high level. With these skills, expertise and competence (Egan, 1986; Strong, 1968) are clearly established. Expertise can be inferred by noting a person's title, seniority, diplomas, certificates, licenses, and reputation; however, it is the counselor's actual behaviors that ultimately determine competence.

The specific skills such as empathic listening and self-disclosure (discussed earlier as being effective in counseling) are described in detail in chapters 3 and 4. Interpersonal skills that assist in developing a helping relationship can be classified under three headings: attending, responding, and initiating. Attending behaviors serve to involve the client directly in the helping process. They include such skills as maintaining eye contact, using proper body language, and following verbally without changing the subject. Attending skills are generally seen as prerequisites to subsequent skills (Carkhuff, 1983; Egan, 1986; Ivey & Simek-Downing, 1980).

Responding behaviors are useful in helping the clients explore and clarify their problems. These behaviors include responding with accurate empathy, clarification, specificity of expression, and reflection of meaning. These behaviors also include being able to listen and respond directly to the client's feelings as well as to the content expressed.

Initiating skills include probing, self-disclosure, confrontation, and direct mutual communication. The skills of initiating are helpful when working in the problem-solving or action phase of counseling.

An Example of a Counselor Functioning in a Counseling Relationship

The following excerpts from two counseling sessions conducted by Carl Rogers (Meador & Rogers, 1984, pp. 167–168) demonstrate how a counselor uses all three areas—who the counselor is, what the counselor knows, and what the counselor can do—in working with a client. Rogers is working with a nontalkative client named Jim: *

Client: No. I just ain't no good to nobody, never was, and never will be.

Counselor: Feeling that now, hm? That you're just no good to yourself, no good to anybody. Never will be any good to anybody. Just that you're completely worthless, huh?—Those really are lousy feelings. Just feeling that you're no good at *all*, hm?

Who counselor is: Risk-taking
What counselor can do: Empathic responding

Client: Yeah (muttering in low, discouraged voice) that's what this guy I went to town with just the other day told me.

Counselor: This guy that you went to town with really told you that you were no good? Is that what you're saying? Did I get that right?

What counselor can do: Clarifying

Client: M-hm.

Counselor: I guess the meaning of that if I get you right is that here's somebody that meant something to you and what does he think of you? Why he's told you that he thinks you're no good at all. And that just really knocks the props out from under you. (Jim weeps quietly) It just brings out the tears.

What counselor can do: Reflection of meaning; empathizing

(Silence of 20 seconds)

Client: (rather defiantly) I don't care though.

Counselor: You tell yourself you don't care at all, but somehow I guess some part of you cares because some part of you weeps over it.

What counselor can do: Confronting discrepancy

(Silence of 19 seconds)

---

*Reproduced by permission of the publisher, F. E. Peacock Publishers, Inc., Itasca, Illinois. From Betty D. Meador and Carl L. Rogers, "Person-Centered Therapy." In Raymond J. Corsini, *Current Psychotherapies*, third edition, 1984, pp. 167–168.

Counselor: I guess some part of you just feels, "Here I
am with another blow, as if I hadn't enough blows like
this during my life when I feel that people don't like
me. Here's someone I've begun to feel attached to and
now *he* doesn't like me. And I'll say I don't care. I
won't let it make any difference to me—but just the
same the tears run down my cheeks.

*What counselor
can do: Empathiz-
ing*

Client: (muttering) I guess I always knew it.

Counselor: Hm?

Client: I guess I always knew it.

Counselor: If I'm getting that right, it is that what
makes it hurt worst of all is that when he tells you
you're no good, well shucks, that's what you've always felt about yourself. Is that the meaning of what
you're saying? (Jim nods slightly, indicating agreement.) M-hm. So you feel as though he's just confirming what—you've already known. He's confirming
what you're already felt in some way.

*What counselor
can do: Reflection
of meaning*

(Silence of 23 seconds)

Counselor: So that between his saying so and your
perhaps feeling it underneath, you feel just about as
no good as anybody could feel.

*What counselor
can do: Empathiz-
ing*

(Silence of 2 minutes, 1 second)

Counselor: (thoughtfully) As I sort of let it soak in and
try to feel what you must be feeling—it comes up
sorta this way in me and I don't know—but as though
here was someone you'd made a contact with, someone you'd really done things for and done things
with. Someone that had meaning to you. Now, wow!
He slaps you in the face by telling you you're just no
good. And this really cuts *so* deep, you can hardly
stand it.

*What counselor
can do: Empathiz-
ing; Responding
to feelings*

(Silence of 30 seconds)

Counselor: I've got to call it quits for today, Jim.

*Who counselor is:
Openness*

(Silence of 1 minute, 18 seconds)

Counselor: It really hurts, doesn't it? (This is in response to his quiet tears).

*What counselor
can do: Empathiz-
ing*

(Silence of 26 seconds)

Counselor: I guess if the feelings came out you'd just
weep and weep and weep.

Empathizing

(Silence of 1 minute, 3 seconds)

Counselor: Help yourself to some Kleenex if you'd
like—can you go now?

*Who counselor is:
Caring*

(Silence of 23 seconds)

Counselor: I guess you really hate to, but I've got to
see somebody else.

Self-Disclosing

(Silence of 20 seconds)

Counselor: It's really bad, isn't it?   *Empathizing*

(Silence of 22 seconds)

Counselor: Let me ask you one question and say one   *What counselor*
thing. Do you still have that piece of paper with my   *knows: Client*
phone numbers on it and instructions and so on? (Jim   *depressed; poten-*
nods.) O.K. And if things get bad, so that you feel real   *tial of suicide;*
down, you have them call me. 'Cause that's what I'm   *keeps communica-*
here for, to try to be of some help when you need it. If   *tion lines open*
you need it, you have them call me.

Client: I think I'm beyond help.

Counselor: Huh? Feel as though you're beyond help. I   *What counselor*
know. You feel completely hopeless about yourself. I   *can do: Empathiz-*
can understand that. I don't feel hopeless, but I can   *ing; Self-*
realize that you do. Just feel as though nobody can   *disclosing*
help *you* and you're really beyond help.

(Silence of 2 minutes, 1 second)

Counselor: I guess you just feel so, so down that it's   *Empathizing*
awful.

Note how Rogers integrates his skills, personal characteristics, and knowledge so expertly and fluently.

HELPING AS A WAY OF LIFE

Carkhuff and Berenson (1977) indicate that "helping is as effective as the helper is living effectively," and that a person entering the field of counseling enters it as a way of life. Supporting what has been discussed above, they suggest that the helper has to be a whole person, one who is in the process of becoming a self-actualizing person. They indicate that

> only the fully functioning whole person has the right to be a helper, for only he or she lives in society yet is able to see society through the eyes of its victims; and only he or she can discriminate between the good and the bad. Those counselors and therapists functioning below this level have no right to offer themselves as helping agents and models. The fact is that most counselors and therapists cannot successfully meet the circumstances with which their helpees are failing to cope. The interaction between such a helper and his helpee can be nothing more than a fraud. (p. 246)

Counselors living as whole persons believe deeply that even major adversities will not destroy their inner core. They are willing to take and will even seek risks. Impoverished persons carefully avoid all major risks, working from the personal belief that if they do not they would not survive. Anyone who expects to help others cope with the vicissitudes of life needs to be able to demonstrate that capacity as well.

To become a counselor is to adopt a way of life; anything less would be to play a game, enact a role, be phony. Helping is not something that takes place in an arena where the latest techniques are used in a demonstration of skill in manipulating less than whole clients. One cannot assume the role of the helper for eight hours and then become oneself again and hope to be effective.

COUNSELOR EDUCATION

If counseling as a profession is a way of life that can best be undertaken by persons who are self-actualizing or in the process of becoming fully functioning, whole people, what implications does this have for the selection and education of counselors/helpers?

We begin with students already committed to becoming fully functioning, whole persons. Rothstein (1989) suggests that students should be selected with regard to their ability to function at a high level in interpersonal skills. The student must be open to and committed to personal, constructive change. Counselor education is not and should not be merely a vehicle to attain legitimacy for present beliefs and practices. Some counselor candidates believe that everything they are already doing is satisfactory, but that they need a degree or certificate to make them legitimate. These people tend to be less open to personal change and, through their influence in the educational setting, negatively influence other students. Even though counselor education involves personal growth, it should not be seen as a substitute for personal therapy.

The curricular emphasis in counselor education programs, according to Rothstein, should be on the enhancement of therapeutic, facilitative functioning. Because of the importance of the counselor's belief system, Combs (1986) would like to see less emphasis on learning how to counsel and more on *"becoming a counselor."* To develop "a broad, accurate, personally relevant, internally consistent, and appropriate system of beliefs about self, others, purposes, and desirable ways of relating to the world, both in and out of personal practice," counselor education programs should provide a wealth of opportunities for interaction with clients as well as "continuous immersion in a process of exploration of ideas and discovery of personal meanings" (p. 59).

In the final analysis, the purpose of counselor education is to involve qualified students in a lifelong learning process that can be transmitted to their clients. The effective counselor education program should be designed to develop the belief systems and the helping skills repertoires necessary to help students grow and enable them to work effectively with a variety of clients and problems.

SUMMARY

People enter the field of counseling from a variety of backgrounds with the general objective of helping people live more effectively with themselves and others. As graduates, counselors work in areas ranging from problem prevention to remediation and treatment. To become an effective counselor, caring and having concern for people are helpful, but not sufficient. Effective counselors can be distinguished from ineffective counselors by their belief systems and by the nature and quality of the relationship skills used; other personal characteristics do not seem to correlate, either positively or negatively, to being an effective counselor. Clients of ineffective counselors become worse, whereas clients of effective counselors improve.

A major premise notes that it may be difficult, if not impossible, to help a client beyond the point at which you, the counselor, are. As part of the description of who the counselor is, the characteristics of the self-actualizing person have been presented as something for counselors to be personally aware of as they work to help others become more fully functioning. Other counselor characteristics, such as having a high level of personal energy, being willing and able to take risks, having a tolerance of ambiguity, and a capacity for intimacy, and being perceived as authentic and trustworthy, indicate what might be expected of practitioners in the field, but they do not guarantee success in the field.

What the counselor knows is also important. Counselors are expected to have both external knowledge learned from outside sources and self-knowledge attained from enhanced personal awareness. The self-as-instrument concept, with the person of the counselor being the most effective tool in the counseling relationship, has been presented along with methods to better know and understand oneself.

What the counselor can do is of primary importance. Expertise or competence in the execution of attending, responding, and initiating skills determines a counselor's effectiveness.

A transcript of a portion of an actual counseling session was presented, with notations of what the counselor was demonstrating through his actions, who the counselor is, what he knows, and what he can do.

Developing the characteristics and the skills necessary to be an effective helper needs to be seen as part of a total way of life, with the counselor making what amounts to a lifetime commitment to education and personal growth.

QUESTIONS AND ACTIVITIES

1. *Keeping a Journal.* Keeping a personal journal is an individual discipline that can be a rich source of insight. Purchase a notebook in which to record what you learn from reading this book and from class participation. You can also include reactions to other aspects of your life, such as dreams, interactions with friends, and such events as an earthquake. From time to time, review your journal entries. You might choose to share parts of your journal with a trusted friend. See Hugh Prather's *Notes to Myself,* (Lafayette, CA: Real People Press, 1970), for an example of a published personal journal.

2. What does it mean to you to use your self as an instrument in counseling? Could you become a good counselor without doing this? What attitudes and behaviors of yours might you have to change to use this concept?

3. Where would you place yourself on the scale in Figure 1.1? Are you moving up or down the scale? Check out your perceptions with significant others in your life. If the premise is true that you would have difficulty helping someone get beyond where you are, how far might *you* expect to help clients grow?

4. Which characteristics of a self-actualizing person present the greatest challenge to you personally?

CHAPTER 2

The Helping Relationship

*What causes people to seek help from others
and what happens when they do?*

This chapter examines the many aspects of the helping relationship and the developmental process of helping. Having considered the counselor as the major instrument in the helping relationship, we turn first to a description of the other part of the relationship—the client who comes for help, voluntarily or involuntarily. This description is followed by a discussion of the other characteristics of the helping relationship as it relates to counseling.

CHARACTERISTICS OF CLIENTS

Persons who seek help often do so out of desperation. Usually they have tried to relieve their troubled feelings in numerous ways but have not been successful. Jerome Frank (1978) states that

> despite the diversity of complaints, most persons who seek or are brought to psychotherapy, suffer from a single condition that assumes protean form, and all psychotherapies counteract this condition. As a first approximation this condition may be termed demoralization. . . . Demoralization ensues when a person is unable to cope with a life situation that he and those about him expect him to be able to handle. (p. 10)

Often clients feel overwhelmed by feelings of pain, anxiety, helplessness, and hopelessness. No options seem to be open. Clients appear to have lost control of their lives. According to Ivey and Simek-Downing (1980),

> clients usually come for counseling because they have some degree of decisional conflict and because they are blocked in their behaviors, thoughts and feelings. The client frequently has unfinished business and needs to broaden his perspective, break old behavior patterns, develop new behaviors, and choose fulfilling alternatives. (p. 29)

The problem presented does not necessarily represent objective reality, but it is reality for the client. Lankton (1980) states, ''How else could clients be coming into our offices with descriptions of pain, frustration, and limitations when other people find the world exciting, open-ended, and availing nothing but choices? It is not the 'world' itself that dictates unhappiness, it is each person's *version* of it'' (p. 17). Clients coming for counseling often seem to be wearing blinders that prevent them from perceiving the options that would make their lives richer or would at least give them hope that life could be better. The desire for relief of anxiety and pain and a faint feeling of hope motivate clients to seek therapy; it is this feeling of hope that the counselor draws on and encourages.

Initially, the expectation of clients is that the counselor can do for them what they cannot do for themselves. Perhaps the counselor can make sense out of their confusion, provide insight and meaning to their problem, and then provide the solutions. However, the trained counselor realizes that only clients can take responsibility for their own lives. With the counselor as a catalyst, clients must discover and implement their own solutions. Ineffective counselors, in their eagerness to help, often jump in and attempt to give advice, try to relieve the client's pain, and make things all better. They fail to realize that counseling is a process, actively involving both the client and the counselor. A relationship must be established and the problem clearly defined and understood before action is taken toward a solution.

HOW PEOPLE BECOME CLIENTS

There are three ways by which people become clients:

1. *Self-initiated action.* A person experiences discomfort, often by clearly acknowledging a specific problem. He or she knows of the existence of professionals trained in counseling and has a basic feeling of trust in their abilities. Such self-referred clients tend to have the greatest chance for success because they already have some information about the general counseling process. They are also motivated by their pain. The probability of seeking counseling is greatest if a person associates with people who know and value counseling (Kadushin, 1969).
2. *The recommendation of others.* A person may recognize that he or she has a problem, but may not be able to identify it or know where to go for help. Significant others in a person's life may not only help the person identify the problem but may also make suggestions or recommendations as to where to seek help. Because much of this advice may be contradictory and all of it is externally derived, the client does not generally have as high a motivational level as one who is self-referred (Kadushin, 1969).
3. *Coercion.* A person may be sent for counseling by legal or social coercion. A judge may give a drunk driver a sentence of 6 months of counseling, or a teacher may send an acting-out child to a counselor for help. Business orga-

nizations may also require psychological help for an employee as a condition of continued employment. Involuntary referrals are probably the most difficult cases a counselor faces because the client is not there by choice and therefore has little personal motivation to change any behavior. However, counselors can still be effective with these clients.

Having personal problems is a universal human affliction; however, being able to receive professional help in solving these problems is often a matter of social and economic status. Schofield (1964) found that psychotherapists prefer clients who fall into the YAVIS syndrome—young, attractive, verbal, intelligent, and successful. The geographical distribution of mental health care professionals, with one-half of the psychiatrists in the United States located in five states, and how these professionals select their clients to fit their preferences (Albee, 1977) suggest that contemporary mental health treatment has largely become the province of the white and the wealthy. Recent federal government cutbacks in the support of social service agencies and programs tend to support this conclusion.

THE THERAPEUTIC ALLIANCE

The counselor is the most important element in the helping relationship; the next most important element is the therapeutic alliance, or working relationship, between the counselor and the client. Without this working relationship, little can be achieved. This relationship is so prominent that the effectiveness of counseling can, in large part, be correlated to its degree of development. Ultimately, the counselor's initial and ongoing objective is to establish the core conditions of trust and respect so that a therapeutic alliance can be established whereby both the counselor and the client work together to achieve mutually established goals. Once these core conditions have been established, they must be maintained. Any ongoing personal relationship has to be nurtured; this is especially crucial in the case of the therapeutic alliance. With the exception of the personal and psychological health of the counselor or the life and safety of the client, the relationship between the counselor and the client takes precedence over any other aspect of counseling. A review of 85 studies of the outcomes of psychotherapy reported in the 1985 Annual Review of the American Psychiatric Association indicated that psychotherapy that showed the strength of the alliance between the client and the counselor was a better predictor of therapeutic success than the specific kind of therapy, the qualities of the therapist, or the kind of client (Goleman, 1985).

Having an effective therapeutic alliance does not mean that there is an absence of tension or an avoidance of conflict in the relationship. On the contrary, an effective therapeutic alliance is one in which confrontation can and does occur and can be satisfactorily worked through.

A counselor's tasks, then, are to establish the relationship, to monitor it, and to enlist the client's assistance in keeping the alliance strong. As with any alliance, it involves a mutual responsibility for maintenance. As Rosenblatt (1975) puts it:

> I want to assist you, individuals, persons, to become whole, to integrate . . . your lives. To do this, I need assistance from you, from the individual himself. You become my teacher and I become your student, to learn who you are, how you live your life. We become partners in an open-ended, free wheeling venture to get to know each other, to assist each other. You permit me to practice my skills, to exercise my strength as a person, to feel good about my abilities, you help me pay the bills. I help you complete unfinished business from your past, to fill in the holes or gaps in your sense of yourself, to learn, to grow, to have a second chance to be reborn, to live. (p. 3)

Counselors, through their training and awareness, usually notice and respond to cues that might indicate difficulties in the relationship; however, clients may do so as well. Some cues noted by the counselor may be quite obvious, such as regularly missing appointments; others may be subtle, perhaps a change in the client's tone of voice. One or two such cues may be coincidental, but a pattern should be brought to the attention of the client and clarified. In general, however, as in most interpersonal relationships, focusing and dwelling on negative aspects of the relationship can be destructive. As a rule it is more productive to nourish the strengths of the relationship in positive ways; for example:

> **Counselor:** "We have really been successful in coming up with several good ways that you might use to help you get better grades."

Inner-Viewing versus Interviewing

Just as there are different ways that a person may become a client, there are different approaches that a counselor can use in establishing a therapeutic alliance with a client. Many authors of books and articles on counseling talk about the counseling interview and the interviewing of clients. Using the terms *interview* and *interviewing* actually mislabels and confuses the counseling process for counselor trainees, clients, and perhaps even for experienced counselors. Counselors have been plagued for years with the problem of how best to describe what it is they do when they work with individual clients. Relabeling the terms used in referring to what counselors do would be a major step in improving communications with all involved.

The conventional wisdom regarding the concept of an interview has one person, in some form of authoritative position, asking a variety of questions of another person, perhaps taking notes or otherwise recording the transaction; for example, a prospective employee interviewing for a job, or a reporter interviewing a state department official about foreign affairs. However, this conventional conceptualization of an interview, when applied to working in a helping relationship such as counseling, can have negative effects. If this description is followed, it requires the counselor to be able to come up with a steady flow of meaningful questions that are supposed to get right to the heart of the problem. When the questions do not succeed at this, the counselor (interrogator) draws further on his or her resources in an effort to come up with more, or at least some, successful questions. If questioning continues to be unproductive, the client may be perceived as resistant, and the counselor may be seen as ineffectual.

Even when successful, the result of such an approach is that the overall focus of the session is not on the client, but on the counselor and the effectiveness of his or her questioning skills. This approach also tends to set a norm for the counseling sessions themselves, with the counselor being expected to initiate and determine the content and nature of the interaction, and the client taking little responsibility for what happens during the sessions.

It is true that this type of questioning/interrogating interview can occur in legitimate helping relationship settings (e.g., a counselor using reciprocal inhibition [Wolpe, 1958], or a social worker taking a case history); however, most current theories and approaches to counseling do not put a great deal of emphasis on the interrogative expertise of the counselor. Patterson (1974), in fact, is quite direct when he states that "questioning by the therapist has little place in counseling or psychotherapy" (p. 112). It is our position that questions, if used selectively and timed appropriately, can have an important role in the counseling process. However, the counselor-trainee should be encouraged to learn to tune in to the client as directly as possible without the use of questions and to try to understand accurately what the actual problem is from the client's point of view. This is an important concept, because each of us experiences the world differently, and we operate as if this experience is indeed reality. The client who hides under the bed, believing that someone from another planet is searching for him, operates out of his experience of the world. For him this experience is reality, and from this experience, he perceives the world and makes his choices in terms of behavior. In addition, the world around us and the words we use to describe it are not the same. The counselor's task is to try to get an "inner-view" of the world of the client. Once the counselor is in touch with this inner-view he or she is then better able to work with the client to help change the attitude or behavior in question.

Questioning is the primary tool used in interviewing, but inner-viewing requires that the counselor focus more on the client, using a variety of skills including attending behavior, active and passive listening, and self-attending. Authors of articles and books on helping interviews do include discussions of these and other related skills; however, because these skills are presented in a context of conducting an interview and all that the term connotes, the importance of noninterrogative skills in the total context of counseling is not always easily grasped by the counselor-trainee.

It is therefore important at the beginning of counselor education to talk in terms of the counseling or helping "session" and the counselor's ability to establish a helping relationship and to attain an accurate inner-view of what the client is experiencing. It is difficult to know how a client can be helped if this kind of inner-view is not attained. This process would closely resemble what Egan (1986) calls "advanced accurate empathy." For example:

> **Client:**   I really like my teacher. Everybody in the whole school admits that she's about the best. She makes English and history come alive, not like the others. But still I can't talk to her the way I'd like to.
>
> **Counselor:**   You really like her and are glad that you are in her class, but, Jim, it seems that you are a bit resentful because she doesn't show you much personal attention. (Egan, 1975, p. 137)

Another way to look at the difference between interviewing and inner-viewing is through the use of the diagrams in Figures 2.1 and 2.2. In interviewing (Figure 2.1), the counselor is represented by a figure with a given cognitive-emotional configuration, or set. The client, who is experiencing a problem, has a different cognitive-emotional set. Counselors using a predominantly interrogative interviewing approach attempt to determine the nature of the client's cognitive-emotional condition through what might be a systematic approach, but what is more often than not hit-or-miss questioning (step 1). Other interventions may also be used, with the ultimate desired outcome being a change in the client's attitude or behavior (step 2).

The inner-viewing approach (Figure 2.2) is a process that begins with the counselor, who has a particular cognitive-emotional makeup or set, meeting a client who has a different cognitive-emotional set (step 1). The counselor, using systematic observation, listening, and responding skills, works to enter the phenomenological field of the client. Entering that phenomenological field requires that the counselor project himself or herself so as temporarily to experience reality as the client does, to crawl into the client's skin and feel and perceive at one

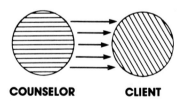   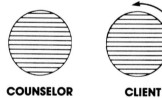

COUNSELOR   CLIENT   COUNSELOR   CLIENT

Step 1.   A. Client comes with   Step 2.   Client changes as a
      cognitive-emotional   result of counselor's
      set different from that of   questions (and other
      counselor.   external interventions).

      B. Counselor questions
      client.

FIGURE 2.1   Interviewing Model *(V. Peterson & B. Nisenholz, [1984] "Inner-Viewing vs. Interviewing: An Approach to Aid Counselors-in-Training Develop Greater Empathy Skills,"* New Jersey Journal of Professional Counseling *47[1]: 27–28).*

COUNSELOR   **CLIENT**

Step 1.   Client comes with
cognitive-emotional
set different from that
of counselor.

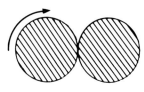

COUNSELOR   **CLIENT**

Step 2.   Counselor, using specific
attending and responding
skills, works to understand
perspective of client.

COUNSELOR   **CLIENT**

Step 3.   Using skills such as
responding with accurate
empathy, counselor enters
client's phenomenological
field.

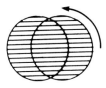

COUNSELOR   **CLIENT**

Step 4.   Working within the
phenomenological field
of the client, changes in
thought, attitude, and
behavior occur as a result
of counselor's use of a
variety of skills.

COUNSELOR   **CLIENT**

Step 5.   Termination occurs when the
goal of the client is attained.
Note that as the relationship
ends, the client is not a copy
of the counselor; also, the
counselor does not return to
being exactly the way he or she
was before the encounter occured.

FIGURE 2.2   Inner-Viewing Model *(V. Peterson & B. Nisenholz, [1984] "Inner-Viewing vs. Interviewing: An Approach to Aid Counselors-in-Training Develop Greater Empathy Skills,"* New Jersey Journal of Professional Counseling *47[1]: 27–28).*

with client. Most important, the client becomes the judge of how successfully the counselor is inner-viewing. If the client does not experience the counselor as having entered his or her phenomenological field then he or she has not (steps 2 and 3). Working within the client's phenomenological framework, the counselor can help the client help himself (step 4). The counselor and client then terminate the relationship (step 5).

It is important to point out that the counselor does not necessarily return to step 1 exactly, because in a meaningful interaction with a client, both participants would be affected. Also, the client does not become a carbon copy of the counselor.

What is most important about using the inner-viewing approach is that it requires counselors, being skilled and psychologically healthy, to be flexible and open from the beginning. They work in every way to enter the clients' phenomenological field and then work from there to help clients solve their own problems. This approach requires a significant amount of involvement and skill on the part of the counselor. Once this is understood, it is easier to appreciate what a demanding job being a successful counselor is. The inner-viewing steps are an integral part of the stages of the helping process, as described next.

THE HELPING PROCESS

There are different ways or models of describing the counseling/helping process. The term *process* can be defined as the characteristics of the ongoing counselor/client relationship—the therapeutic alliance—as it develops over time. Counseling is a continuous process; however, to study the elements of counseling directly, most models divide the process into stages. In each stage of the process certain skills, attitudes, and strategies on the part of the counselor are prominent. Initially, for example, relationship-building skills and the engendering of hope are prominent; then skills that facilitate client insight and awareness become important. Decision-making and action strategies follow these, and finally, the skills involved in terminating the relationship. (The process may be recycled or the skills involved in terminating the relationship may be used.) Although there are similarities in all of the models, there are differences in emphases and approaches. Presented here is a five-stage model of the counseling process based on the work of Carkhuff (1983), Egan (1982), Ivey (1983), Hansen, Stevic, and Warner (1986), and Brammer (1979) (Figure 2.3).

There are decision points between each stage of the counseling process (Figure 2.4). These are points at which, for various reasons, counseling might be terminated before the total process is complete.

The model suggests three kinds of client change: perceptual-emotional, rational, and behavioral. With the use of this model, counselors have a framework from which to function and a means to evaluate where in the process they are as well as to evaluate the process itself. The stages in the model are similar to those

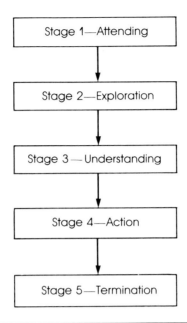

FIGURE 2.3 The Helping Process

in human development in that they are flexible and overlapping, yet each step must be passed through successfully if counseling (growth) is to be effective. If counselors are not competent, they will not be able to move through the stages, becoming stuck in whatever stage they are unable to perform. As a result, every time they try to move ahead, they will be blocked by their failure to complete the necessary tasks of some previous step. They will be forced to return to that previous stage and encounter it successfully in order to move ahead again in the process.

The stages apply to both short-term and long-term therapy, and they are applicable to virtually all theoretical approaches to psychotherapy. Different theories do, however, place greater emphasis on certain stages; for example, behavioral therapists stress stages one, two, and four, whereas Gestalt therapists stress stages one, two, and three.

There is no time element implicit in the description of these stages. Theoretically and actually, it is possible to work through all five stages in one session of 50 minutes or less. It could also take several years, depending on the nature and depth of a given problem. Upon satisfactory resolution of a problem, the entire process may be recycled to work through additional concerns.

The guidelines presented in this model are broad enough for neophyte counselors with significant differences in personality and skill levels to use as a base when they begin the process of developing personal approaches to the establishment of therapeutic alliances.

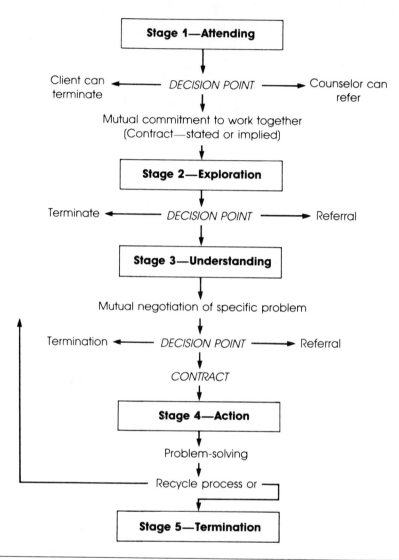

FIGURE 2.4   The Helping Process

Stages of the Helping Process

The five stages of the helping process are (1) establishing a relationship—a brief initiating, attending period; (2) an exploratory period; (3) an understanding stage; (4) an action stage; and (5) termination. The stages are described in terms of the counselor's and the client's characteristics, behaviors, and experiences in each stage. Table 2.1 gives a general outline of the interaction that takes place during the helping process.

TABLE 2.1 Counselor and Client Characteristics and Behaviors during the Five Stages of the Helping Process

Stage I—Attending

Client	Counselor
Checks out procedures	Provides working environment
Tests relationship	Clarifies process
Is cautious	Attends to client and self
States concerns	Observes, listens, accepts client
Presents problem	Gives client space to state concerns
	Is nonjudgmental

Stage II—Exploration

Client	Counselor
Begins to explore	Establishes trust
Experiences counselor as helper	Shows concern and caring
Is less defensive	Gives empathic responses
Sees problem becoming clearer	Communicates respect and warmth
Attains greater awareness of feelings and concerns	Acknowledges client feelings
Becomes aware of self-destructive behaviors	Responds to client feelings
	Focuses on here and now
Becomes aware of problems in the here and now	Gives feedback
	Mild confrontations
Is more self-disclosing	Helps client personalize meaning
	Summarizes

Stage III—Understanding

Client	Counselor
Takes responsibility for problems	Helps client personalize problem
Strengthens commitment	Deals with intensified levels of feeling
Identifies discrepancies	Uses advanced levels of empathy
Develops insight	Confronts, self-discloses
Confronts impasse	Directs, interprets, probes
Experiences release of energy	Uses immediacy
May terminate on identification and understanding of problem	

Stage IV—Action

Client	Counselor
Puts ideas and insights into action	Helps generate and evaluate alternatives
Further clarifies thoughts and feelings	
Sets goals, implements plan, and evaluates actions	Helps client decide on an alternative to test
If goals not met, revises plan; if goals met, moves to new problem or toward termination	Gives encouragement
	Gives feedback to client on results of activity

(continued)

TABLE 2.1 Continued

Stage V—Termination

Client	Counselor
Evaluates gains	Helps complete unfinished business
Acknowledges changes	Assesses client readiness for ending
Works with loss of relationship	counseling
Plans beyond relationship	Gives feedback, affirmation
	Reviews process
	Arranges for follow-up

The following is a brief discussion of the dynamics of each stage of the helping process along with a description of the nature of the involvement of the counselor and the client at each level.

Stage I—Establishing a Relationship/Attending

The first stage of the counseling process begins when the client and the counselor first meet (e.g., in the office waiting room), and start the process of becoming acquainted.

> And so the two strangers meet. They look at each other, sniff the air between them. Their invisible antennae gently stretch out, tentatively probing, and gingerly assessing. Their intuitions working consciously and far below consciousness, take stock. One silently thinks, "Is this someone I can believe in? Someone I can trust with my secrets, my guilts, and shames, my tender and deep hopes for my life, my vulnerability?" The other wonders, "Is this someone I can invest in? Someone I can stand by in pain and crisis? Someone I can make myself vulnerable to? What surprise may this person bring forth, and what may that surprise trigger within me?" (Bugental, 1978, pp. 27–28)

Once the first session is over, the client and helper must decide whether or not to go ahead. How much of a commitment are they willing to make, if any? Can they work with each other? If client and helper feel positive toward each other, it still does not ensure a genuine relationship: the client must trust the helper enough to bare his or her innermost emotions, concerns, and secrets. The helper must be ready to accept the client as an individual who is capable of changing and growing and not be frightened by the client's anxiety. A bonding must be formed, and a respect for each other must be maintained.

Because of clients' failure to own their problems, the initial problems presented are often not the real problems. For example, a college student might enter therapy complaining that his classes are boring, he feels anxious, he has difficulty concentrating, and he is failing his courses even though his previous academic achievement has been quite high. Initially, he may ask for help in concentrating and reducing anxiety so that he can pull his grades up and satisfy his parents. He might blame his professors, or the institution. As the relationship develops, the problem begins to change. The student begins to realize that he is going to college in this major only to satisfy his parents. He would like to be in a different major or perhaps even travel and work for a while. His parents oppose this. The problems now are his difficulty in finding separateness from his parents and developing an inner locus of evaluation.

This first stage is generally quite brief, perhaps lasting from only a couple of minutes to one session or so, with the participants' meeting and quickly sizing up each other. Social amenities take place here as well as general housekeeping procedures, such as discussing things like the length of sessions, and fees. A formal case history, if required, would be part of this stage. Here, clients begin to tell their stories, with counselors' attending fully to all of the clients' messages.

Stage I—Client Process.   Clients entering therapy are concerned not only about their plight, but also about how much they should reveal. What secrets should be kept? It is not uncommon that the presenting problem is not the major problem. The client is often concerned with: What will the counselor be like? Will counseling take a long time? Will the counselor really understand and accept me? The counseling process for the client may, in fact, begin when the appointment is made. Between the time the appointment is made and the appointment itself, much work is done by clients as they rehearse, and on occasion even write out, what they plan to discuss with the counselor.

If the client has any questions or concerns about the procedures and process, he or she might ask them at this point. It is in the best interest of the client and of the relationship for the client to have as clear an understanding as possible about the counseling process. In particular, it is vital for the client to know that it is not a magical process, where something is done to or for him or her by the counselor. At some point, either at the request of the counselor, or spontaneously, the client may begin to talk about why he or she came for counseling.

Often, the first session is like the first round in a boxing match, in which both fighters are trying to figure out each other's approach, testing each other out, and being somewhat cautious. It is the start of what some helpers have described as a journey in which both client and helper engage each other, invest in each other, and learn from each other.

As the first stage unfolds, clients start to explore their problems. They become more open and self-disclosing with the counselor and begin to reduce their defensiveness and resistance. They experience the counselor as a responsive, understanding person.

Stage I—Counselor Process.   After introducing themselves and taking care of procedural matters, depending on their personal approach or the guidelines of their agency, counselors may ask questions regarding background information. In some settings, a separate intake interview is scheduled to go over procedures and to attain a case history before actual counseling begins. Other agencies request that a client come in 15 to 20 minutes early to fill out a detailed information form prior to the first session. Counseling time is not taken up, then, with generally routine questions.

From the beginning, counselors work to establish trust based on openness and honesty of expression. They use themselves as instruments in order to attend fully to the client. This means that counselors have to be aware of what is going on inside themselves as well as the client. Initially they give clients space to state their concerns. They allow clients to initiate topics, following them verbally and nonverbally as appropriate. They attempt to develop a learner stance toward clients in order to be open to the clients' experience of their existence. In doing so, counselors observe, listen, and experience clients without judging or evaluating. Counselors strive to be attuned to all the messages clients are trying to convey. By doing this, counselors gather vital information necessary to acquire a full picture of the client's world without necessarily asking questions. Gradually, through their attitudes and behaviors, counselors establish credibility as understanding, responsive, and trustworthy persons.

The first stage of the counseling process is a relatively brief one, as stated previously, lasting from only a few minutes to almost an hour. It consists mainly of helping clients become comfortable enough to begin expressing their concerns and expectations from counseling. The stage is concluded when counselors begin to make substantive interventions, such as responding empathically, clarifying, or summarizing.

It is possible that clients may spend most of the first session elaborating on their problems with a minimum of verbal or nonverbal responses by the counselor. In such cases, the counselor's summary, or other intervention, at the end of the first session would then signal the end of the first stage of the helping process and start the beginning of the second stage.

Stage II—Exploration

In the first stage of the counseling process, the emphasis is on establishing an environment in which clients can comfortably tell their story with the counselor learning how clients experience and perceive their world. The counselor has accumulated a basic picture of who the client is, what the client needs and wants, and how help could be given. The major focus in Stage II is on the strategies and techniques needed to bring about a fuller exploration of the nature of the client's basic concerns.

Stage II—Client Process.
In this stage clients increase their level of exploration and self-disclosure. They move from surface structure to deep structure and gradually acquire a greater awareness of the depth of their feelings and the nature of their concerns. Ivey and Simek-Downing (1980) refer to *surface structure* as the immediate sentences the client uses to share thoughts, feelings, and perceptions, and *deep structure* as the words, thoughts, and perceptions that underlie the surface-structure sentences. The client becomes more oriented to the present in regard to his or her problem. He realizes, for example, that it is not only that his bad breaks as a child are causing his problems now, but how he continues to use these bad breaks to keep him from taking responsibility. He begins to become

aware of the incongruities of his thoughts, feelings, and behaviors, and of how many of his behaviors may be self-defeating. He experiences the counselor as someone who will be there with him at deeper levels, and he becomes less defensive and more open. In the process the nature of the problem becomes clearer. As trust in the counselor increases, the presenting problem may be phased out and another, perhaps more serious, problem may emerge.

Stage II—Counselor Process.   The specific counselor process goals for this stage include facilitating client exploration of problems and feelings in order to increase the client's self-awareness, focusing on the immediacy of the client's problems, maintaining and enhancing the relationship, using selected strategies as interventions to facilitate further exploration, dealing with feelings that impede progress toward selected goals, providing encouragement for the client to face himself or herself at deeper levels of understanding, and making a further commitment to the counseling relationship.

Stage II—Decision Point.   Sometimes clients feel a cathartic relief as they work through the exploratory stage and become better able to verbalize their feelings. They might believe that their problems are now solved and therapy is no longer needed. Some counselors refer to this phenomenon as a "flight to health." Often there is a reluctance on the part of the client to face the pain and discomfort that might come from further exploration, and there is a fear of what the dark side of his or her personality might be like. However, some clients feel even worse as they work through their painful self-confrontations. They may become confused and discouraged. Perls (1969) called this "the point of impasse in therapy." It is the point at which clients are dissatisfied with their old ways of behaving, but are unable to find self-support for change. As a result, clients implode, or go into themselves. They experience fear of the unknown. They have been comfortable with their old behaviors even though these behaviors do not serve them well any more. They begin to worry whether other people will still accept them if they change, or whether they will like themselves. As a result, clients may wish to terminate the relationship. Counselors need to pay attention to their feelings and those of the client in this situation. It may be necessary to terminate the relationship if the counselor is also uncomfortable, perhaps by making a referral to another counselor. On the other hand, the counselor might provide the necessary encouragement at this point for the client to continue exploration to deeper levels. Further information on this phenomenon is provided in this chapter under the section on resistance.

Stage III—Influencing New Understanding

Stage three focuses on using insights and awareness in order to allow clients to personalize their contributions to the problems they are facing and thereby to set the stage for them to begin to take action in order to resolve those problems.

Stage III—Client Process. This stage is characterized by clients' awareness of the personal involvement needed for changing and specific knowledge of what needs to be done. Clients realize that they are responsible for their behavior and for changing it. They let go of their defenses and filters and concretely experience their role in their problems. They decide to confront the impasse and make a leap of faith. They strengthen their commitment to their goals in counseling and allow themselves to experience their repressed feelings and any remaining unfinished business. As a result, clients become more congruent in terms of feelings, attitudes, and behaviors. There is an increased awareness of self and the external world. Clients experience a different perception of the meaning of their problems in their present existence. Clients mourn their "old selves," which may have served them well through much of their life but are no longer appropriate with their new perceptions and awareness.

As clients complete this mourning they become calmer and more at peace. They begin more freely to experience all aspects of themselves, redirecting their energy away from keeping themselves rigid and safe to being freer and more alive.

Stage III—Counselor Process. Counselors must feel competent to deal with a client's intensified levels of feelings. They may still need to offer some encouragement, support, and positive reinforcement as a client strengthens a commitment to change. In addition, they must be able to offer an advanced level of accurate empathy, high-level confrontation, and authenticity as a client works through the impasse. They might use interpretation or perhaps summarize the client's process. Finally, as the client achieves clarity and feels freer, counselors must be able to provide an accurate reflection of meaning in describing the client's problem.

Usually, with the increased intensity of interaction in the relationship that develops in this stage, certain strong feelings, which may have been developing earlier on the part of the client toward the counselor and vice versa, may become noticeable. These conditions, commonly called "transference" and "counter-transference," are discussed separately in this chapter.

Stage III—Mutually Agreed on Problem. The conclusion of the understanding stage, Stage III, is reached when the client has clearly defined his or her problem, and it is fully acknowledged by the counselor. Without this point clearly attained, any action steps would generally be doomed to failure. One reason some counseling is not effective is that problem-solving and other action steps have been taken before a problem has been clearly defined and before there was a commitment to change on the part of the client.

This agreement can be considered a "therapeutic contract" (Gottman & Lieblum, 1974). A contract reduces ambiguity and minimizes unrealistic expectations of therapy and of the counselor. It activates the therapeutic alliance and brings the client into full involvement in the process. The contract may include a limit on the number of sessions and may stipulate the types of treatment and evaluative procedures to be used. Ultimately, the total therapeutic contract includes the payment of fees, appointment schedules, and cancellation procedures.

Many therapies, such as Gestalt, or person-centered, may end with Stage III as far as the formal helping relationship or therapeutic alliance is concerned. The client, as a result of significant work in the exploration and understanding stages, has had his or her problem clearly defined and, with the insights gained, makes changes as necessary. Insight therapists often find that when the problem has been clarified, the client gets an "Aha!" experience, saying in effect, "That's it and I know what to do about it. People have been telling me for years."

Stage IV—Facilitating Action

Although some therapies consider the therapeutic process completed when insight and awareness have been achieved, many therapies, particularly the cognitive-behavioral approaches, move into a fourth action-oriented stage. The primary element necessary for moving into Stage IV is having a mutually agreed on problem as a result of the exploration and understanding stages.

Stage IV—Client Process.
Clearly defining the problem leads directly into action. In this stage of the counseling process, clients have the opportunity to learn and further clarify their thoughts and feelings, to practice new behaviors, to formulate alternative actions, and to make decisions and carry them out. It is important in this stage that plans and goals are selected, tested, and evaluated.

Stage IV—Counselor Process.
The counseling relationship in this stage is more of an adult-to-adult relationship than in any of the preceding stages. Decision-making skills come to the forefront. Counselors help clients examine the array of potential solutions and make a commitment to action based on evaluating solutions and their possible consequences. Counselors support and encourage clients as they test solutions in their home environment. They attempt to reinforce client action, and in the process make themselves more and more dispensable. If necessary, counselors help clients return to earlier stages if further clarification of the problem is needed. Finally, both client and counselor assess whether the goals of counseling have been met. Accomplishments are summarized, and progress is evaluated.

Plans for terminating and for how the client will continue alone are formulated; however, the whole process may be recycled to work on another problem. Many counselors begin to wean their clients by scheduling more time between counseling sessions.

Stage V—Termination

The fifth stage is characterized by summarizing and wrapping up any unfinished business and saying goodbye. Usually the door is left open for possible follow-up or for work on other problems.

Terminating is generally not a major problem if the other stages of the counseling process have been worked through successfully. Clients are usually ready to leave, and they often begin the terminating process before the counselor does. However, some clients have difficulty letting go and attempt to bring up new issues in order to prolong the relationship. Counselors also have to be able to let go when the need for this type of relationship has been met. One method used by a counselor to make the final parting less abrupt, and yet stress its finality, was to have a closing ceremony, in which client and counselor toasted each other with a nonalcoholic beverage.

Stage V—Client Process.   As part of the termination process the client may learn how to conclude a temporary relationship successfully and how to appraise its worth. Unfinished business, if any, should be identified and planned for, and follow-ups, if any, should be scheduled. Also, a final recapitulation of the entire process on the part of the client can be most helpful, to acknowledge and internalize the gains made as a result of counseling.

Stage V—Counselor Process.   An important part of the termination process is to prepare the client for the ending of the relationship. In time-limited therapy, the date of the final session is known from the onset. In other cases, however, some notice needs to be given at least one or two sessions prior to the final session. Efforts also need to be made by the counselor to assist the client in working through the process of the loss of the relationship, just as earlier the client had to grieve the loss of self-destructive behaviors.

The counselor may add to the client's recapitulation, if appropriate, and affirm the changes made and the client's responsibility and involvement in the process. Finally, negotiations may be made for follow-up sessions if mutually desirable.

Dynamics That May Hinder the Helping Process

Even though the counselor may have a solid understanding of the helping process and be generally proficient in the skills necessary in different stages of the process, there are still interpersonal dynamics that can interfere with, or even prevent, the process from being completed. Some of these dynamics are resistance, transference, and countertransference.

Resistance

Resistance occurs when the client uses his or her defense system in a way that opposes the purpose of change. Resistance is common in all forms of counseling and is not necessarily a totally negative dynamic. The noted hypnotherapist Milton Erickson (1964) has suggested that resistance "is a vitally important communication on the part of [clients'] problems and often can be used as an opening into [their] defenses" (p. 8).

Resistance can take many forms. Otani (1989) has identified and classified 22 different forms of client resistance into 4 major categories. The first category deals with the quantity of the clients' responses, such as talking continuously, being silent, or giving only very brief responses. The second category refers to the content of the clients' responses. Here, you might find a great amount of small talk, intellectual talk, preoccupation with the past or future, and rhetorical questions.

The third category of resistance deals with the style of the clients' responses. This category is comprised of response patterns in which the client manipulates the manner of communicating information to the counselor. Specific forms of resistance in this category include discounting, in which the client tends to say "Yes but . . ." to everything the counselor offers; setting limits on topics that can be discussed; blaming others and refusing to take personal responsibility; trying to second-guess the counselor; trying to please the counselor; acting seductive; making false promises, such as promising to do a homework assignment and not following through; and bringing up important issues just before the close of counseling sessions.

In the fourth category, the client breaks basic counseling rules. Resistant behaviors in this category include not being punctual, missing appointments, delaying or refusal of payment, and making improper requests of the counselor, such as asking for rides or attempting to borrow money.

Resistance occurs because significant learning about oneself can be quite threatening to individuals. Rogers (1951) states that "any experience which is inconsistent with the organization or structure of self may be perceived as a threat, and the more of these perceptions there are, the more rigidly the self-structure is organized to maintain itself" (p. 515). It is inevitable that helpers encounter resistance during the helping process. If there were no threats or conflicts in terms of the client's concerns and problems, the client would be relaxed and open to awareness in the first place, and there would be no need for the process of therapy. So as destructive and as energy consuming as they might be, resistance tactics give a client some measure of protection. Resistance tactics do allow for survival and often become creative forces in a difficult environment.

There is, indeed, a paradox that is part of many helping relationships, when a client comes for assistance with a personally difficult situation and then proceeds almost immediately to resist making any personal changes that could improve his or her circumstances. It is not difficult to appreciate that clients do not necessarily come for help thinking in terms of their having to change themselves. It is more likely that the client believes that what is necessary to feel better is for *other* people to change *their* behavior.

Usually clients use resistance at an unconscious level; this is often manifested by an ambivalence toward being helped. Clients want help, relief, and peace of mind, but they believe that they are being threatened. They may have to change an attitude or behavior that has served them well for many years, one that they have become secure with. Some clients perceive a change as a death of some part of them. At the same time, clients must make a leap of faith, having had little experience in the world with their new attitudes and behaviors. Significant others in their lives are also used to the old personality characteristics. Will they still accept them? Will they let them change? It is this unknown void that is anxiety provoking, and the closer clients approach the void, the more chance there is for resistance.

Fritz Perls, the originator of Gestalt therapy, believed that all resistance represented the client's refusal to be self-supportive and, in fact, to grow up. He urged counselors to explore the gain or payoff the client received from his resisting. Brammer and Shostrom (1982) defines the kind of resistance described above as "internal." Internal resistance is a tendency of the organism to retreat from perceived threat, usually painful attempts to explore or alter patterns of behavior or of core personality structure. Clients are no longer pleased or comfortable with their old selves. They may want to give up or alter their patterns of behavior, but self-support is not yet forthcoming. There is a fear of changing.

Sometimes clients begin to express feelings or share deeper information too fast. They then feel vulnerable and judged and begin to resist. In another form of internal resistance, clients offer a rationalization or simple explanation in order to resist awareness or further exploration of a situation.

External resistance is clients' reactions to cues outside themselves. In most cases this would be to the counselor. Carl Rogers (1951), among others, believes that external resistance grows out of poor technique on the part of the counselor. Rogers maintains that resistance is not a necessary, inevitable, or desirable part of the helping process. He believes that resistance comes from counselor's attempts to shortcut or accelerate the helping process. This would be analogous to a situation in which an overly directive counselor immediately begins to work in Stage IV, problem-solving, skipping the first three stages.

Another form of external resistance has to do with clients' readiness to deal with counselors. They may be confused by the counselor's role or by the helping process. They may expect an instant cure and become disappointed when it is not forthcoming. The counselor should lay the proper groundwork and develop a structure so that clients will be clear as to what happens in the helping relationship.

Counselor Resistance. Counselors themselves can often manifest resistance. Some counselors, for example, may become anxious when their clients move deeply into very emotion-laden concerns. As a result, such counselors may change the topic, or, in some other way, interrupt the client's continued exploration.

Counselors may also resist because they dislike their clients, lack necessary skills, or have failed to come to terms with certain issues in their own lives. Some counselors may have problems centered around power and control issues. Others may have difficulty establishing the closeness or intimacy necessary to help a client work through an existential problem.

Methods of Handling Resistance. In the various theoretical approaches, resistance is treated somewhat differently. Perhaps the greatest differences exist among the psychoanalytical, humanistic, and behavioral approaches. The psychoanalytical method of dealing with resistance involves interpreting and analyzing clients' resistance as to its presence, purpose, ramifications, historical origin, and present dynamics. Resistances are gradually worked through until clients become less and less resistant. Among the humanistic approaches, person-centered therapists work at reducing threat in the counselor-client relationship so that clients will more readily confront themselves. Existentialists sensitively confront and point out the resistances. Gestaltists view resistance as a creative force rather than as something to be broken down, and they also focus on the resistance by pointing out how clients avoid unpleasantness. Rational emotive therapy (RET) adherents view resistance as a failure to face reality by seeking magical solutions. RET counselors challenge their client's need for a magical solution. Behavioral counselors might make subsequent therapy sessions contingent on clients' exhibiting nonresistant behavior and demonstrating that by completing their therapeutic homework assignments.

Generally, counselors might ignore mild resistances, lower the anxiety level of a client through humor or diversion, reflect the resistant feeling to the client, point out the resistance, challenge it, interpret its dynamics, or consider a variety of different approaches for responding to the client. Resistance can be handled on a continuum from completely ignoring it to direct confrontation. Resistance patterns serve as useful cues in learning about the helping process and about both client and counselor personality patterns.

Transference

Transference is the phenomenon in which the client reacts to the therapist, not objectively as a real person, but as a virtual reincarnation of a parent or another significant figure from the client's past. More generally, transference is used to label any feelings the client expresses toward the counselor. As people move from childhood to adult life, they carry with them many feelings, values, and attitudes that take the form of fixed patterns of behavior that manifest themselves during certain interpersonal situations. For example, an adult man who may have been intimidated by a harsh, punitive father may respond to all authoritarian men in the same way he did as a little boy awaiting punishment for a misdeed. Thus, present reality is always distorted. In therapy the client expects to be treated by the therapist in ways similar to ways the client was handled by previous authorities. Transference can occur in all helping relationships but is more predominant in psychotherapeutic counseling because of the deeper intensity of the relationship.

Transference is a cornerstone of Freudian therapy. Freud discovered that, if not interfered with, the client inevitably projected feelings and attitudes from the past into the therapeutic situation. Occasionally, these transference reactions become so intense that clients actually live through, with the therapist, some of their earlier traumatic experiences. Freud called the development of these exaggerated transference reactions "transference neurosis." He believed that these reactions would enable the client to adopt new, more mature, and appropriate behaviors facilitated by an accepting, more permissive authority figure, the therapist.

There is disagreement regarding the necessity of inducing the transference relationship. Some neo-Freudians, as well as humanists and behaviorists, pay more attention to here-and-now problems. They believe that personality change can occur without the client's regressing to infantile neurosis. In fact, many counselors consider the outbreak of transference behaviors a sign of bad therapy.

Depending on the theoretical point of view then, the effect of transference in a helping relationship may range from being a helpful, necessary part of the process to a harmful phenomenon. Most non-Freudian approaches to counseling tend, generally, to minimize the importance of the phenomenon.

Countertransference

The counterpart of the client's transference is often referred to as *countertransference*. This has to do with the counselor's personal emotional response to the client. Generally, in psychoanalytical terms, it is reserved for situations in which the client's behavior invokes in the counselor conflicts relating to unresolved situations in the counselor's life, causing the counselor to respond to the client in a nonobjective way. However, countertransference does not have a precise standard definition, even among psychoanalysts. It is generally agreed, however, that the phenomenon is not beneficial to the helping process. It could be considered as another example of resistance on the part of the counselor.

Brammer and Shostrom (1982) view countertransference as "conscious and unconscious attitudes of the counselor toward real or imagined client attitudes or overt behavior" (p. 227). Under this definition countertransference could be an expression of humanness, a genuine response to the client, or a counselor's projections.

Watkins (1985) identifies four patterns of countertransference behaviors: overprotective, benign, rejecting, and hostile. Overprotective behaviors include cushioning statements with many qualifiers in order to soften their impact; preventing clients from experiencing unpleasant emotions such as anxiety, hurt, or guilt; and talking in a very low voice in order to shield the client from verbal stimulation. In using benign behaviors, the counselor creates a benign, bland counseling atmosphere in which the positive is accentuated and the negative is avoided as much as possible. This behavior is often used because the counselor has an intense need to be liked by the client or is frightened by any displeasure or anger on the part of the client.

Rejecting countertransference behavior involves aloofness and coolness on the part of the counselor in an effort to create considerable separateness between the counselor and the client. Often the counselor is fearful of client demands and of becoming responsible for the client's welfare. The counselor becomes intimacy-phobic. Finally, hostile behaviors might be used by counselors who are fearful of being like their clients and adapting behaviors that are personally detestable. Hostile behaviors include verbal abuse of various kinds such as curtness, or bluntness, missing or coming late to appointments, and enjoying the turmoil of clients' experience.

It is of utmost importance that counselors be aware of their own values and feelings. The counselor is not, and should not be, neutral and removed from forming any close contact with the client in order to prevent countertransference. Values and feelings are transmitted both overtly and covertly in any interpersonal relationship. Unless counselors have a deep awareness of their own values and feelings, their behavior toward clients can have a negative impact. In addition, counselors must be certain that clients are free to make their own choices and even reject counselors' values if clients so desire. In cases in which clients know the counselors' values, the counselor should make it known to the client that these values are not necessarily the ones that are best for the client, or the ones that the client should follow.

The most effective weapon against countertransference is counselor awareness and growth. Video- or audiotaping counseling sessions in order to analyze counselor responses is highly recommended. It is also recommended that counselors undergo their own psychotherapy and participate in growth groups. A counselor can also seek out supervisory assistance from counselor educators, field supervisors, and/or colleagues.

SUMMARY

The primary reasons that clients seek counseling are discouragement and the inability to cope. People generally become clients in one of three ways: self-initiated action, the recommendation of others, and by coercion. Once they have come for counseling, the therapeutic alliance can be developed and the counseling process can unfold. A distinction has been made between the counseling terms *interview* and *inner-view,* and between an interview and a counseling session. These differences were related to the counseling process itself, which was described in terms of a synergistic model.

The counseling process begins with developing the basic helping relationship or therapeutic alliance. The counselor's task in developing the alliance includes establishing and monitoring the relationship and enlisting the client's help in maintaining it. The stages of the counseling/helping process were described, beginning with attending, followed by exploration, understanding, action, and termination. A description of client and counselor behavior during each of the stages was presented.

The counseling process is often impeded by the dynamics of resistance on the part of both the client and the counselor, transference on the part of the client, and countertransference on the part of the counselor. Each of these factors was described along with its negative effects. Guidelines for working with and minimizing these factors were developed.

QUESTIONS AND ACTIVITIES

1. How open are you to change? How do you show resistance in your interpersonal relationships? What do you fantasize would happen if you were to let go of your resistances? How do you feel about expecting clients to change when you, yourself, may be reluctant to do so?

2. What issues in your life might result in your becoming involved in countertransference with a client? How might you recognize the phenomenon? What might you do about it?

3. Are you aware of examples of transference in your observations of interactions with other people? Share examples with your classmates.

4. Counselors are confronted with a wide variety of clients: people who may have abused family members, or may be drug addicts and/or AIDS victims, or may have different ethnic and cultural backgrounds, for example. With which type of clients do you believe you would have the most difficulty working? How would you expect to deal with a case in which you knew that you were likely to be judgmental or otherwise biased against the client?

FOCUS ON

Developing Respons/ability: The Learning of Counseling Skills

What ways of responding to a client are particularly helpful in establishing and maintaining a counseling relationship?

THE COUNSELING RELATIONSHIP— CORE CONDITIONS

There are hundreds of approaches to counseling and psychotherapy, and the adherents of each claim to be successful. One review of almost 400 studies indicates that counseling and psychotherapy can be effective and that theoretical differences are not significant (Smith, Glass, & Miller, 1980). There are no known cases of practitioners abandoning their particular counseling approach in favor of another approach that has been proven to be demonstrably superior. The availability of all these approaches can be confusing to the beginning counselor. Where does one begin? Does it make a difference what approach a counseling student learns?

It is helpful to note that there is at least one area that almost all counseling and consulting approaches have in common: the initial establishment of a relationship, creating rapport. To assist a client in making attitudinal and behavioral changes, it is generally acknowledged that the counselor needs to take some time to develop what Carl Rogers (1957) identified as the core conditions for establishing a relationship. As the research cited in Chapter 1 indicates, the counselor's ability to develop and implement the skills related to the core conditions may determine whether the counselor is helpful or harmful. These core conditions, initially labeled *empathy, genuineness,* and *positive regard,* have been elaborated upon by theorists and researchers in the field (Brammer, 1985; Combs & Avila, 1985; Carkhuff, 1987; Danish & Hauer, 1973; Ivey, 1988; Egan, 1986; Gazda, Asbury, & Balzer, 1984). This elaboration was undertaken to clarify often vague and general terms for the purpose of training beginning students in the establishment of a helping relationship.

Chapter 3 describes those skills that have been demonstrated as important in establishing and maintaining the helping relationship. Competent implementation of these skills by the counselor allows the client to move successfully through the five stages of the counseling process.

Although these various skills may be associated with one stage more than another, the skills can be used whenever an individual counselor deems them to be appropriate. Also, different theoretical approaches may call for different patterns of skill use. It should be emphasized that the skills for attending and exploration are important throughout the counseling process and not just in the first two stages.

In studying all of the helping skills, the emphasis is on learning to respond effectively to a client as well as on learning to initiate interventions. Developing the ability to respond effectively is, in effect, the study of how to conduct an inner-view rather than an interview. The ability to use a broad repertoire of responses skillfully is one way of distinguishing a skilled counselor from a nurturing layperson.

STAGE I—ATTENDING SKILLS

The counselor's behaviors in Stage I of the counseling process are critical. If the behaviors are inappropriate there may be little or no opportunity to use additional skills. The basic skills of Stage I are attending skills, in terms of attending to the client as well as to the counselor, and the skills of using encouragers and silence.

Before counselors can really help anyone, they have to be able to get involved with the other person. They do this through a systematic process of paying attention.

A good helper is a perceptive helper. He attends carefully to the other person and listens to both his verbal and his non-verbal messages. He clarifies these messages and acts constructively on the results. He is also in touch with his own thoughts and feelings and how they interact with those of the client. (Egan, 1975, p. 56)

How the counselor attends to the client can have a great deal of influence on the client. Attending to another person is by itself highly reinforcing. People work hard to arrange situations so that others will pay attention to them. Effective attending is vital to establishing the helping relationship in that from the beginning it demonstrates that the counselor is interested and caring. The behavior of effective attending tends to put demands on the client. "If I am with you fully, invest myself in you, and work with you, all of this demands a response on your part" (Egan, 1975, p. 65). If a counselor is afraid of making any demands on the client, this fear would probably show up first in his or her attending behavior.

Counselors attend in at least three important ways: physical attending, psychological attending, and self-attending. Physical attending refers to the posture, eye contact, and the general position that counselors take with regard to the client. Psychological attending refers to the ability to tune into the nonverbal as well as the verbal messages of the client. Self-attending refers to the ability of counselors to be open, relaxed, and centered—to tune into their own awareness.

A client who is coming for help from someone who is probably a total stranger is often extremely sensitive to the cues emanating from the counselor. An ambivalent client may use a counselor's nonattending behaviors as a reason to terminate the relationship after the first session. A client may, of course, decide to terminate the relationship early for a variety of other reasons even though the counselor's attending behavior was superb. The point here is that the effective counselor has an attending response repertoire that quickly forms the foundation for a solid helping relationship. From the beginning, he or she deliberately strives to avoid behaviors that would be detrimental to the relationship.

Physical Attending

Building on the "self as instrument" concept, there are specific things that the counselor can do to adopt a posture of involvement with a client, to be physically attentive. Regardless of what problem a client may present, the counselor is expected to be able to control and modify his or her own behavior appropriately. Some specific guidelines for effective physical attending are as follows:

1. Have no physical object between you and the client. An object such as a desk places a clear and often large physical barrier between you and the client. Even executives of major corporations recognize this, and when they really want to become involved in helping someone they will come out from behind their desks and work with the person face to face.
2. Maintain a comfortable working distance. In general, being too close to a person while attempting to facilitate a therapeutic relationship is not very helpful; neither is being too distant. Many individual and cultural differences are involved here; however, a distance of about three to five feet between persons in a sitting position is usually suitable.
3. Face the other person directly. The posture that demonstrates the most involvement is facing the person squarely (Carkhuff, 1983; Egan, 1986). This is a dimension, however, where one should begin carefully. Squarely facing very shy or very disturbed persons, or persons from different cultural backgrounds, is often perceived as threatening behavior. In cases such as these, it is often helpful to begin by facing the client at an angle of about 15 degrees off center so that both the counselor and the client can more comfortably look away at times. As the relationship develops, a more direct face-to-face posture can be taken.
4. Establish eye contact. The counselor should initiate and maintain eye contact with the client. Again, this is to be done initially with some discretion. Direct, sustained eye contact can create discomfort in the shy person and can be perceived negatively by people from different cultural backgrounds. In general, the idea is to try to establish eye contact while also scanning the

client's face and body for other nonverbal cues. At times when the relationship and the interaction are particularly intense, there generally are long periods of sustained eye-to-eye contact, the degree of which is not in the immediate awareness of either of the participants.

5. Maintain an open-position posture. Crossed arms and crossed legs are often signs of lessened involvement. An open posture is a sign that the counselor is open to what the client has to say and open to communicating directly to the client. It is a nondefensive position.

6. Lean toward the other. This is another "sign of presence, availability, or involvement" (Egan, 1975, p. 65). One might lean forward as much as 10 degrees when attending from a standing position and as much as 20 degrees when attending from a sitting position.

7. Remain relatively relaxed. Relative relaxation says to the client, "I am comfortable with you."

8. Keep breathing. Being aware of your breathing is important here. People who are anxious tend to virtually stop breathing. Maintaining a regular deep breathing pattern will help you attain an appropriate state of relaxation.

The counselor's personal concern with the establishment of all of the conditions listed above will naturally bring about some tension. However, if the counselor is one

> who is living effectively, and is relatively comfortable with involvement and intimacy, he will be relatively relaxed, even in the attending position described. The helper who is relaxed, although intense and hard working, can give himself the space he needs in order to listen and respond fully. . . . The helper who is tense and tight will almost inevitably infect his client with his own malaise. (Egan, 1975, p. 66)

Psychological Attending

Counseling is usually portrayed as a predominantly verbal activity when actually it is much more than that. The counselor can be effective even though the client may not have told him specifically what the problem is. The process does not depend on a continuous stream of words; for example, a client, while trying to describe a problem to a counselor may in the process be silent and mentally be sorting out issues without overtly discussing them. To be totally with another person, to attend to a client psychologically, incorporates appropriate physical attending along with systematic observation and listening.

Psychological attending helps to provide the counselor with a full picture of the client's world without interfering in the counseling relationship as psychological tests and other assessment devices could. Clients project every part of their existence in the way they talk, move, dress, act, look, feel, and think. If counselors can see and hear with all of their senses, they will discover much that will be vital to their understanding of a client's world.

Observing

Perhaps as important as any other skill is the counselor's skill of observation. Even before appropriate attending behavior is established or the client begins to speak, the counselor can begin to make observations. As a person enters a room and takes a seat, observations of his or her general energy level can be made in four specific areas: grooming, posture, body build, and nonverbal expressions (Carkhuff, 1983). Grooming cues include appearance of clothes, hair, hands, including fingernails, and face.

Nonverbal cues to note initially are speed of movement, facial expressions, gestures, and head and eye movements (Carkhuff, 1980). The authors have found that greeting their clients with a handshake before each session is an important source of data. Table 3.1 depicts some nonverbal behaviors and their possible effects or meanings.

Cues about posture include persons' carriage as they walk and sit; whether they lean forward when interacting or sit with their head drooping. Body-build characteristics to be observed include abnormalities in weight and muscle tone.

There are three reasons for the counselor to make observations. First, the observations "provide a basis for making helpful behavior descriptions" (Loughary & Ripley, 1979, p. 117). These skillfully made observations provide a data base to enable counselors to understand clients and their problems, as well as to determine change. Thus, counselors will not be relying only on clients' verbal messages. Some practitioners, in fact, claim that the nonverbal messages are more accurate than the verbal ones (James & Jongeward, 1971). Second, these observational data can also be useful in providing accurate information that enables counselors to confront clients on the inconsistencies and contradictions between their verbal and nonverbal behaviors in the later stages of counseling. Third, observing helps in the identification of feelings. The ability to tune into and deal with a client's emotional condition is in many cases much more productive than focusing on clients' words. Words deal with the *what* or content of clients' messages. According to Mehrabian (1971), most people pick up only about 7 percent of a message from the content, whereas 38 percent is picked up from such things as tone of voice, volume, and speed of talk; and 55 percent is picked up from facial expressions and other body language An effective counselor should be able to describe behavior accurately.

> Observations and any inferences made from them must be considered to be hypotheses which need to be confirmed or denied over time by the helpee's behavioral and verbal expressions. Observations should not be taken as a valid basis for making snap judgments about a person. (Carkhuff, 1980, p. 53)

Some inferences that might be made on the basis of observations relate directly to the client's levels of functioning and could significantly affect the way the counselor interacts with the client. A counselor working to develop empathy with a client might particularly notice and match the client's energy and emotional levels. For example, a counselor would not emit a high energy level with

TABLE 3.1 Inventory of Nonverbal Behavior

Nonverbal Dimensions	Observed Behaviors	Description of Conselor-Client Interaction	Possible Effects or Meanings
Paralinguistics	Whining or lisp	Client is complaining about having a hard time losing weight; voice goes up like a whine.	Dependency or emotional emphasis
Face	Eyes strained; furrow on brow; mouth tight	Client has just reported strained situation as a child. Then client sits with lips pursed together and a frown.	Anger or concern; sadness
Eyes	Staring or fixation on person or object	Counselor has just asked client to consider consequences of a certain decision. Client is silent and gazes at a picture on the wall.	Preoccupation, possibly rigidness or uptightness
Mouth	Open mouth without speaking	It has been a long session. As counselor talks, client's mouth parts slightly.	Suppression of yawn—fatigue
Arms and hands	Arms folded across chest	Counselor has just initiated conversation. Client does not respond verbally; sits back in chair with arms crossed against chest.	Avoidance of interpersonal exchange or dislike
Total body	Facing other person squarely or leaning forward	Client shares a concern and faces counselor directly while talking; continues to face counselor while counselor responds	Openness to interpersonal communication and exchange
Distance	Moves away	Counselor has just confronted client; client moves back before responding verbally.	Signal that space has been invaded

enthusiastic and rapid speech with a client who has low energy level and very slow, deliberate, and possibly stammering speech. The ways in which clients attend in a counseling situation give a significant amount of data about their physical, emotional, and intellectual levels. These same levels of functioning are appropriate to you as a counselor. How do they fit you now? How do they fit when you are in a helping situation?

Listening

Listening is a special type of observing. In this case the focus is on observing the verbal expressions of the client. As we have seen, much preparation is necessary in terms of physical and psychological attending to the client before we get to the core of helping: listening to the client's problem. It is a simple axiom that one cannot usually help others unless their problem is understood, and in order to find out what the problem is, it is necessary to listen well.

Developing the skill of total active listening takes much effort and practice. Many people are selective, even lazy listeners, listening only for praise or criticism. Some people do not listen at all. Listening is a skill that we need as students, employers and employees, family members, and especially as friends, yet few persons have had systematic training in listening. The basic conditions for active listening follow.

Resist Distractions. Use your ability to be a selective listener. Stay with the client in spite of temptations to respond to various external cues. We have all experienced social situations that required the use of our powers of selective listening in order to stay with a conversation in spite of major distractions. Use this same skill in the helping relationship.

Keep the Focus on the Client. If you are observing appropriately and attending physically, this should follow. Beginning counselors, and experienced ones at times, can become so concerned with what they are going to say that they simply do not listen to everything that the client says. To assist in keeping the focus on the client it is helpful for the counselor to do 5 things:

1. Adopt an attitude of acceptance of what the client says. This includes taking the position of being nonjudgmental even though the client may be presenting very controversial or shocking material to you.
2. Listen to the tone of voice. The "music" often tells more than words do. A client could be describing a very logical straightforward problem, but the voice could have a whiny, helpless quality about it. On the other hand, a person who presents a very serious, personally devastating problem may not be aware of the personal strength that his or her voice communicates.
3. Listen for cues to clients' feelings. In many cases, it is more important to first help clients communicate their emotions before effective work with the cognitive components of their problems can be done. Sometimes working with the emotional content may be all that the counselor need do.

4. Listen for common cognitive and emotional themes that are continually repeated, often in different ways (Carkhuff, 1985).
5. Listen for generalizations, deletions, and distortions.
   a. *Generalizations:* Clients often avoid being specific and inaccurately represent their real experiences through generalizations. "People push me around," for example, is a generalization because the noun "people" fails to identify anyone specifically. We know that *all* people do not push a client around. The real experience may be, "My father pushes me around." Here something specific is identified in the client's experience (Harman & O'Neill, 1981).
   b. *Deletions:* Another way that clients present their experiences inadequately is by leaving things off or deleting them. When a client says, "I'm frightened," that person is not including what or whom he or she is frightened of. The result is a communication with missing parts.
   c. *Distortions:* "By distortions, we refer to things which are represented in the client's model, but are twisted in some way (limiting) her ability to act and (increasing) her potential for pain" (Bandler & Grinder, 1975, p. 51). For example, a person may distort all critical messages with the response, "I'm not lovable," or "I'm incapable." This personalizing of critical messages prevents the person from learning anything of value from outside feedback.

      Another type of distortion is the transformation of verbs into nouns. As a result, an ongoing process becomes distorted into a thing or event, and the individual loses choices. The task of the counselor is to reverse the distortion in order to reconnect the individual with the possibility for action. To do this the counselor transforms the noun back into a verb in his or her response.

      Example 1:

      Client: "I don't get any respect."
      Counselor: "You are aware of how others might respect you."

      Example 2:

      Client: "I regret my decision."
      Counselor: "And you also seem to keep yourself from redeciding."

Obviously, beginning counselors will not be able to listen for and become aware of all aspects of client communication. What is important is to be aware of the complexity and difficulty of high-level active listening and strive to attain the experience and supervision necessary to develop these skills fully.

Self-Attending

Many counselors learn the skills of physical and psychological attending and yet still seem to lack something. Bernie Nisenholz reports an incident that happened to him that brings this point home:

I was working with a client who had been seeing me on an individual basis for a few months. I had experienced a difficult day and was feeling tired both emotionally and physically. However, I decided to see my client since my work day would be complete at the conclusion of the session. I imagined that I would have no difficulty once the session began. About ten minutes into the session my client suddenly stopped her line of exploring, looked quizzically at me, and stated, "I somehow don't feel that you're really listening to me today like you usually do." I realized that she was correct. I had been deluding myself into believing that I was really attending to her. After all, I was utilizing *all* the attending skills. However, it was purely mechanical, almost robot-like. I was attending to her, but not to myself, and as a result something significant was missing. (personal report)

Self-attending is the process in which counselors are attuned to what goes on within themselves, prior to, during, and after the therapeutic relationship, and when appropriate, sharing their findings with their clients. Without the ability to attend to self, a significant factor may be lacking in a counselor's effectiveness.

Baldwin (1987) states that the person of the counselor always impacts the therapy, and when the counselor denies this impact, a key element of therapy is left out of his or her awareness. A similar point of view is reflected by Satir (1987):

If I, as a therapist, am denying, distorting, projecting, or engaging in any other form of masking, and am unaware of my own internal stirrings, I am communicating these to those around me no matter how well I think I am disguising them. (p. 21)

Existentialists often refer to the quality of being really there in the client/counselor relationship as "presence." From the existentialist point of view, then, one of the most important skills is the ability of counselors to facilitate the client's presence as well as their own. Burnout, an indicator of high levels of stress, can also be noted early, and preventive action can be taken if the counselor is skilled in self-attending.

The Process of Self-Attending

For full effectiveness, counselor self-attending needs to occur before, during, and after the counseling session.

Pre-Session Self-Attending

The process of self-attending should begin before the session itself. At least a few minutes should be scheduled before seeing a client to enable the counselor to be appropriately prepared. In addition to self-attending behaviors, many counselors also use this time to review notes of previous sessions and treatment plans related to the upcoming client.

In-Session Self-Attending

Having been trained to focus solely on the client, counselors can experience feelings of guilt if they find themselves focusing on things going on inside of them rather than within their clients. However, as previously illustrated, avoiding this awareness may be detrimental to the helping process. What is important is for counselors to have a way to systematically attend to themselves during a counseling session and to be able to relate their awareness to the relationship, disclosing when appropriate. This process is similar to the tasks of truck drivers, which are primarily to be aware of highway conditions in order to complete their runs successfully and also to be aware of any internal dynamics such as fatigue, hunger, and irritability that may affect the outcome of their trip.

Post-Session Self-Attending

When a session is completed, it is important that the counselor again do some self-attending. Counseling is difficult and intense work; a systematic practice of attending to one's self after each session is helpful in reducing personal stress as well as preventing burnout. Much of this could be done while writing or dictating notes on the session itself.

Here again, it is important to do a breathing, centering relaxation activity, this time to release any residual tensions and to help clear the mind for the next session or activity. If counselors find themselves having trouble relaxing and are unable to attend to the clients and themselves effectively, these are significant indicators that their personal stress level is very high and should be dealt with directly.

The final step is to take leave of the case and move on to the next activity. Again, it is important for counselors to note any difficulties they have in separating themselves from their client's case.

It is essential that the use of any or all of these self-attending skills be brief and direct. Counselors need to be aware that the more time they use to focus on themselves, the less time they have to focus on their clients' concerns. Self-attending does not mean being self-conscious; it means being self-aware and trusting in that awareness.

Responding as Part of Attending Behavior

For the most part, physical attending, psychological attending, and self-attending require little verbal initiating or responding on the part of the counselor. In a few rare cases, paying close attention to another person by using the skills described may be all that is necessary to be of significant help to that person. However, in most cases it will be necessary to make some specific responses as well as to initiate interaction. The skilled counselor has a broad repertoire of responses at hand. Once clients have summoned the courage to come and talk to someone about their problems, they will often let loose with a torrent of stored-up thoughts and feelings. In such cases the counselors do not really have to say much but may need only to attend and express what Ivey (1988) calls "encouragers."

Encouragers

Encouragers are the many verbal and nonverbal ways a counselor has to encourage the client to continue to talk about thoughts, feelings, and behaviors without having to ask a battery of questions. Encouragers include such things as "um-hum," repetition of one or two of the client's words, nods of the head, and hand gestures. Much physical and psychological attending behavior can be classified as responses to the client in this category.

Using encouragers helps the counselor tune in to what the client is communicating. When used correctly, the client maintains control of the session by talking about what he or she wants to discuss and yet is forced to elaborate, explain, and take a more in-depth look at the problem. Examples of "encouraging" responses include:

1. "Tell me more"; "Go on" (perhaps accompanied by an appropriate hand gesture).
2. "Um-hum"; "Uh-huh" (often accompanied by a nod of the head).
3. "And . . ."; "Then . . . ?", "So . . . ?"; "Oh . . . ?"
4. The repetition of the last few words or one or two key words; ". . . he yelled at you."
5. "Give me an example"; "for instance . . ."
6. "And to you, that means. . . . ?"

Encouragers are accompanied by a great deal of attending behavior and have considerable power and importance, particularly in initial helping sessions. Using encouragers keeps the focus on clients and on what they want to deal with and minimizes the counselor's influence as to the direction of the session. Their use also results in more unstructured data for the counselor to attend to.

Responding with Silence

Silence as a response can often be very powerful. It can have much the same effect as that of an encourager such as "Go on" or "and then. . . ." Silence keeps the focus on the client and allows the client rather than the counselor to direct the content of the sessions. Goodman (1984) found that significant changes in the helping relationship occurred when the length of silence or pauses between utterances was increased even if only by a fraction of a second. "The major effect . . . was one of feeling less crowded or being allowed to speak freely" (pp. 278–279). Crowding the client, making no or very short pauses, and interrupting tends to reduce the disclosure of personal feelings.

> When the time between responses is expanded, the discloser naturally feels invited to take time to reply, to delve more deeply into what he or she feels, and to try to express it to an uncrowding listener. (Goodman, 1984, p. 279)

If the material discussed after a silence broken by the client is repetitious, then a verbal response of some sort is usually required. In sessions where client or counselor both are talking continuously, there is not much time for the absorption of material gained. Silence can help meet this need, especially at times when some significant learning appears to be taking place. Silence can help these changes become a lasting part of the client's behavior.

STAGE II—EXPLORATION SKILLS

The skills used in the exploration stage of the counseling process build on the attending skills of Stage I. Exploration skills include responding with primary-level accurate empathy, reflecting meaning, summarization, and responding with respect and genuineness.

Responding with Empathy

When a client begins to tell his or her story and is encouraged by attending behavior, it is usually important for the counselor to "communicate to the client what it is that he understands of the client's perspective of the world" (Egan, 1975, p. 73). The closer the counselor's response to the client's ideas and feelings, the more accurate the empathy. Before actually beginning the work of helping a client solve a problem, it is important that both the counselor and the client have a common understanding of what the problem really is. If the counselor and the client do not have this common understanding they may end up working on no problem at all. This could result in a termination of the relationship, with the counselor saying that the client was "resistant," and the client considering the counselor inept.

There may, of course, be the circumstance in which the client does not have a clearly identified problem even after a number of counseling sessions have taken place. The client may simply need to communicate with another person and may remain more or less in the exploratory stage throughout the relationship. This, too, needs to be understood and communicated empathically.

Accurate empathy is important for another major reason. Often a client will approach a counselor with a safe, presenting problem, a problem that is not too threatening. The client, in fact, may use this presenting problem to develop a feeling of the trust level that the counselor is able to generate before the client brings up the real problem. If the empathic responses are accurate, the client's real problem, whether the initial presenting problem or not, will more likely be dealt with. Most important, the counselor's empathic understanding enables the client to become his or her own counselor and growth enhancer.

Developing Empathy

Empathy is the skill of being able to get inside the skin of the other person, "to look at the world through the perspective or frame of reference of the other person and get a feeling for what the other's world is like" (Egan, 1975. p. 76). Empathy involves being able to enter into and understand the other person's thoughts and feelings accurately as if the counselor were this other person or to walk in the world of this other person. According to Egan (1986) only a person highly sensitive to the thoughts and feelings of others can achieve empathy. Bozarth (1984) proposes that the concept of empathy is idiosyncratic. Idiosyncratic empathy emphasizes

> (1) the transparency of the therapist in relationship to the other person; (2) the person-to-person encounter in the relationship; and (3) the intuition of the therapist. The basic premise is that the role of the . . . therapist is that of being transparent enough to perceive the world nonjudgmentally, as if the therapist were the other person, in order to accelerate the formative tendency of the other person toward becoming all that he or she can become." (Bozarth, 1984, p. 69)

A counselor using idiosyncratic empathy might respond with metaphor, other imagery, or personal reaction.

Personal reaction may take the form of what is often called process empathy, that is, focusing on nonverbal messages. Counselors do not necessarily focus on all the client processes of which they are aware. Generally, counselors will attempt to help clients acknowledge and express processes that have to do with the here and now relationship of the client and counselor. For example, a counselor might notice that the client is squirming in her seat as she tries to explain how she erred in judgment. He might respond to the squirming by attending to the client's sense of embarrassment: "I sense how difficult it is for you to tell me this."

Responding to Content

Clients continually communicate who they are by how they respond—the tone of their voice, the words used, the speed of their speech, and their nonverbal behaviors. When experiencing this inner-view, counselors must be able to communicate to their clients what has been picked up regarding feelings and the thoughts, behavior, and experience that underlie those feelings. It isn't enough to say "I understand"; clients need to know what it is that is understood.

In learning to communicate understanding of what has been said it is helpful to begin by focusing on the content and to reflect this back to the client.

Client: "It looks pretty bleak to me. I don't see any way out of this situation. I've about given up."

Counselor: "From your perspective things really seem hopeless."

In responding to a client, it is important that the response not be perceived as a rote parroting of a statement. There are, however, occasions (as mentioned in the discussion of encouragers) when the restatement of just a word or two can be helpful in allowing the client to continue to explore the nature of the problem in a productive way.

When there appears to be a natural break in the client's verbal communication, or when the client begins to be repetitive without adding new content or feelings, the counselor may make a response that lets the client know exactly what has been heard.

> **Counselor:**   "I've heard you say that you feel discouraged because someone else received the promotion you feel you deserved."

Once responding to content has become comfortable, it is important to move on and to practice responding to feelings using the same format.

> **Client:**   (wringing her hands): "I can't get control of things. I think I have everything handled well and then things just fall apart."
> **Counselor:**   "You feel really frustrated because everything you work for does not go right."

The statement above might be considered a carefully worded paraphrase. It describes the person's feelings and also cites a cause for these feelings. The client, hearing such a statement, is able to acknowledge it as being correct, correct it if it is erroneous, or simply continue from that point in the exploration of thoughts and feelings.

If the statement is incorrect, the counselor can clarify what was misstated and then restate the initial statement as corrected:

> **Counselor:**   "You feel scared because you think you are losing control."

Virtually all problems have a feeling component. It is often the emotional content that is most difficult to work with both from the client's and the counselor's point of view. Our society generally does not encourage the free and open expression of emotions, so clients often have a difficult time expressing the emotions that may literally be tying them up in knots. The counselor may have an equally difficult time trying to communicate in words the emotions that he or she sees the client struggling with.

When trying to describe feelings, it is particularly important to avoid statements such as, "You feel *like* you've taken on too much responsibility" or "You feel *that* you've been put in the wrong class." Statements beginning with "you feel like . . ." and "you feel that . . ." tend to describe thoughts or beliefs rather than emotions. Note this in the client's speech as well. "I feel like going home" is not dealing directly with an emotion. This is more an example of a person's representational mode of speech than of an emotional condition.

In order to come up with words or phrases that are interchangeable with the feelings of the client rather than parroting words, Carkhuff (1980) suggests the following helpful approach: If you have a general impression of what the client is expressing, ask yourself: "When I feel (*general feeling*), how do I feel?" If the client's term was "lonely," you could ask yourself, "how do I feel when I feel lonely?" Some of your responses might be "sad," "dejected," perhaps even "scared." You might check these out to see if they fit. Some words might be dismissed because they clearly are not applicable; others might need modification by the client. For example:

Client: "Well, when I'm feeling lonely I'm not really scared, but I do get a little frightened that maybe I'll never have any friends at this school."

Table 3.2 contains a list of general categories of both positive and negative feelings, along with different levels of intensity within each category. In terms of developing basic empathy, it is helpful for the counselor to communicate at least at the same general level of intensity as the client. In studying the list in Table 3.2 you may add words and phrases to each level presented. To communicate at all levels, the counselor must be able to recognize feelings and their level of intensity, as well as have a well-developed "feeling" vocabulary to be able to communicate perceived emotions.

Reflection and Empathy

Counseling professionals often have equated reflection with empathy. Carl Rogers adopted the term *reflection* as a way of helping the counselor to be empathic and to check whether the counselor is understanding the client. Empathy is a process by which the counselor enters the client's existence. Reflection is a technique that may aid in the process (Bozarth, 1984). Reflection, in and of itself, does not guarantee counselor empathy.

Reflection of Meaning

In helping clients explore the nature of their problems, it is useful to ascertain the meaning that is attributed to events and situations in clients' lives. As Frankl (1959) has pointed out, events in and of themselves are neutral; it is people who ascribe meaning to them. A summer thunderstorm can mean joy and hope for a farmer and sadness and discouragement for a baseball player.

As clients continue to communicate verbally and nonverbally, it is essential that the meaning of the various messages be ascertained in order to help. Clients could continue to talk without any direction, which may provide cathartic relief; however, some feedback is generally helpful. As counselors work to communicate empathy with clients, they are primarily reflecting the thoughts and feelings that they have picked up with all of their senses. With all of the data collected, the counselor may or may not get a sense of what the messages mean to the client.

Counselor: "I sense that it is very important for you to be the best in your class."

Counselor: "Being divorced is quite confusing. On the one hand it means having a lot of freedom that you say you've never had, and yet on the other hand you are now very lonely."

TABLE 3.2 Categories of Feelings

Relative Intensity of Words	Feeling Category				

Mild Feeling	*Anger*	*Conflict*	*Fear*	*Happiness*	*Sadness*
	Annoyed	Blocked	Apprehensive	Amused	Apathetic
	Bothered	Bound	Concerned	Anticipating	Bored
	Bugged	Caught	Tense	Comfortable	Confused
	Irked	Caught in a bind	Tight	Confident	Disappointed
	Irritated	Pulled	Uneasy	Contented	Discontented
	Peeved			Glad	Mixed up
	Ticked			Pleased	Resigned
				Relieved	Unsure
Moderate Feeling	*Disgusted*	*Locked*	*Afraid*	*Delighted*	*Abandoned*
	Hacked	Pressured	Alarmed	Eager	Burdened
	Harassed	Torn	Anxious	Happy	Discouraged
	Mad		Fearful	Hopeful	Distressed
	Provoked		Frightened	Joyful	Down
	Put upon		Shook	Surprised	Drained
	Resentful		Threatened	Up	Empty
	Set up		Worried		Hurt
	Spiteful				Lonely
	Used				Lost
					Sad
					Unhappy
					Weighted

Intense Feeling				
Angry	Ripped	Desperate	Bursting	Anguished
Boiled	Wrenched	Overwhelmed	Ecstatic	Crushed
Burned		Panicky	Elated	Deadened
Contemptful		Petrified	Enthusiastic	Depressed
Enraged		Scared	Enthralled	Despairing
Fuming		Terrified	Excited	Helpless
Furious		Terror-stricken	Free	Hopeless
Hateful		Tortured	Fulfilled	Humiliated
Hot			Moved	Miserable
Infuriated			Proud	Overwhelmed
Pissed			Terrific	Smothered
Smoldering			Thrilled	Tortured
Steamed			Turned on	

Note: The context in which words such as these are used may result in shifting their intensity as well as changing the category in which they are used. Words are listed here only to suggest the range of options available to the helper seeking to identify feelings of the client. From *Helping Relationships and Strategies*, by D. E. Hutchins and C. G. Cole © 1986 by Wadsworth, Inc. Reprinted by permission of Brooks/ Cole Publishing Company, Pacific Grove, California 93950.

Through the process of reflecting the meaning as perceived by the counselor, the client's thoughts and feelings may become clarified, which then leads to the next counseling stage—actually understanding the nature and scope of the problem. In considering the importance of meaning, Frankl (1959) suggests that the greatest human need is for each of us to have a core of meaning and purpose in our life.

Even though Carl Rogers never included it as such when he described the core conditions for a helping relationship, responding to meaning probably should be considered as one of the fundamental conditions. It definitely is a characteristic of Rogers's counseling approach (see transcript, chapter 1). Rogers's approach is often characterized as predominantly paraphrasing and reflecting feelings, "however, *meaning* plays an even more important part in his overall thinking and conceptualization" (Ivey, 1983, p. 136).

Yalom (1985), in describing his landmark study of group leadership (Lieberman, Yalom, & Miles, 1973), reported that two leadership functions, caring and meaning attribution, had a direct relationship to positive outcomes: *"The higher the caring and the higher the meaning attribution, the higher the positive outcome"* (p. 502). Caring includes such factors as offering support, affection, praise, protection, warmth, acceptance, genuineness, and concern. Meaning attribution includes clarifying, translating feelings and experiences into ideas, providing a cognitive framework for change, explaining, and interpreting. Both caring and meaning attribution were critical; however, neither alone was sufficient to ensure success. Yalom's conclusion is that "the Rogerian factors of empathy, genuineness and unconditional positive regard thus seem incomplete; we must add the cognitive function of the leader" (p. 502).

Reflection of meaning in the exploration stage "focuses on the client's frame of reference even if the meanings and values are unclear." As a result of reflection of meaning "clients search for deeper ideas underlying their statements and behaviors and learn to interpret their experience from their own frame of reference" (Ivey, 1980, p. 137).

Summarization Responses

Summarizations, a form of empathic responding, are used to pull together material in a counseling session over a period of time, from a few minutes, to an entire session or to several sessions. Generally, the counselor summarizes selected key concepts and dimensions as accurately as possible, for the client. A request to determine the degree of accuracy may be added to the summary statement.

Counselor: "You've started several times in the last few minutes to talk about how angry you feel toward your mother, but each time you've wandered off on a different topic. You seem to want to deal with this anger toward your mother, but it is awfully difficult to stay with it. Does that fit?"

Counselor: (at the end of the session): "You began the session today working on trying to feel better about yourself. And you really have worked hard. You've been able to come up with several things that you already appreciate about yourself as well as a couple of things you want to feel better about—such as your grades. You've made a plan to build yourself up and to stop putting yourself down. You've shown a lot of strength and determination as you've done this, and it really feels as though you are serious about following through on your plan. Is that all pretty accurate?''

Counselor: "In each of the last three sessions now you've begun with a different problem, each time coming up with ways of solving your problem; yet you don't seem to follow through on any of these ideas. Now you bring in another new problem when it is not clear whether or not we're finished with the previous ones."

Summarization is important to help keep a client moving, to add more data to what has already been given, and to provide some structure and direction to what may seem to be a casual, random conversation. Accurate summarization is, in fact, an empathic response and, like responding to feelings or reflecting meaning, can be considered a specialized subskill of the greater skill of responding empathically.

Responding with Respect and Genuineness

Rogers and others who have studied the core conditions of the counseling relationship have described two additional factors, which have been labeled *respect* and *genuineness*. Research reported by Truax and Carkhuff (1967) indicates that these conditions are identifiable and helpful. However, generally they are included as part of other responses and as an integral part of the counselor's presence in the relationship rather than as specific verbal responses in and of themselves.

Respect initially was called "unconditional positive regard" by Rogers (1957), indicating that the counselor's caring for the client and willingness to work with him or her were not dependent on any specific behavior on the client's part. The client does not have to try to please the counselor. Other terms used to describe this attribute are *prizing, valuing,* and *nonpossessive warmth.*

Expressions of warmth, caring, and unconditional acceptance usually come in the manner in which a counselor speaks or acts rather than from any given specific verbal response. For example, a counselor silently hands a client a box of tissues as he or she struggles with a very sad situation.

Genuineness was initially called *congruence* by Rogers (1957) when he described the condition. Counselors who are communicating genuineness are indicating that they are not just mirrors or blank screens, but open, honest, sincere persons who are directly involved in the relationship. They are real persons in a real encounter (Patterson, 1974), not phonies playing a role.

According to Rogers, being congruent means that the external communication of the counselor matches internal experiences. While the quality of genuineness may be communicated along with other responses such as empathy, it could be given as a specific response using self-disclosure as described under attending behavior. Self-disclosure is indeed one way of communicating genuineness, because it does involve the communication of external and internal experiences of the counselor.

STAGE III—UNDERSTANDING

After working through the first two stages of the process, the client, in the third stage, focuses on a specific problem. The counselor's responses help in clarifying the nature of the problem. The object of the third stage is to have the counselor and the client understand fully the nature of the client's concerns, culminating in a contract to take action on a mutually agreed on problem.

Responding with Advanced Accurate Empathy

Egan (1986), in his approach to skill training, makes a distinction between levels of empathy. Basic empathy, as described in Stage II, is the communication of the understanding of the client's surface feelings and meanings. This is a major component of the first stage of the counseling process. Advanced accurate empathy, a skill generally found in the second stage of the process, goes beyond the surface, to reach feelings and meanings that are buried, hidden, or in other ways not attainable by the client. The advanced empathy response enables the client to see the need for action and helps him or her attain a more objective frame of reference. It is with advanced accurate empathy that the counselor is able to put together both stated and unstated material.

Carkhuff (1987) uses the term *personalizing* to describe this type of additive response. Carkhuff maintains that when we accurately add to clients' expressions, we are helping them understand where they are in relation to where they want or need to be (p. 128). Personalized, empathic responses can acknowledge the meaning or the significance described experiences have for the client, the feelings related to the problem, and the goal itself. A response format for making a personalized, empathic response is as follows: "You feel _____ because you cannot _____ and you want to _____" (Carkhuff, 1987). An example of this type of response is: "You feel angry because you cannot resolve your differences with your mother and you want to learn how to work things out with her." Advanced accurate empathy or personalizing helps clients:

1. See the bigger picture. ("Your problem doesn't seem to be just with your geometry class, you seem to be having trouble with almost everything connected with school.")
2. See what is expressed indirectly. ("I think I'm hearing you say that you are more than disappointed—perhaps even angry.")
3. See the logical conclusions of what has been said. ("Do I hear you say that, since you have lost all enthusiasm for school, you'd like to drop out, at least for a while?")

4. Open up areas that are only hinted at. ("You've brought up sexual matters a number of times. My guess is that sex is a pretty touchy issue with you—but pretty important, too.")
5. See what may have been overlooked. ("I wonder if it's possible that some people take your wit too personally, that they see it as sarcasm rather than humor?")
6. Identify themes. ("You've mentioned several times, in different ways, that people you don't know make you uncomfortable and even frighten you. Is that the way you see it?")
7. Fully own feelings and behaviors. ("I'm not sure whether or not you are saying that you actually do want to court her.")
8. Connect seemingly unrelated topics. ("I'm wondering if there isn't some relationship between your poor grades, the difficulty you are having in getting dates, and the arguments you are having with your parents.")

Advanced empathy or personalized responses, as illustrated above, might be considered hunches based on a fair amount of data gleaned through stages of the counseling process, which when shared with clients help them see a problem more clearly. The counselor should include some indication of tentativeness when expressing advanced accurate empathy or other responses that might be seen as challenging to clients, so that clients will not take those responses as accusations. Clients should feel comfortable enough to be able to disagree with the counselor's response (Egan, 1986).

The following example illustrates the difference between basic level and advanced accurate empathy.

> **Client:** "I'm having a lot of problems with my parents. Just because they're paying for my college education, they want to control everything I do—like who I should date, where I should go, even what courses I should take. I don't know how to break free of them and be my own person."

Counselor responses:

a. Basic empathy:
   Counselor: "You're really angry with your parents for trying to control you when you would like to make your own decisions."
b. Advanced accurate empathy:
   Counselor: "I hear you wanting to stand on your own two feet and be responsible for yourself. It seems that you are not only angry with your parents, but also at yourself for still having to be dependent on them."

Too Much Accurate Empathy?

In responding to a client, the counselor may give what he or she considers an accurate description of the person's emotional state and find that the client rejects it cold. The counselor could work with the client to come up with a statement that is more acceptable and might also make a mental note of the first statement. It is here that the counselor observes that empathy, if it is extremely accurate, closely resembles a form of confrontation. It could be that the counselor is responding accurately to expressed or implied feelings that the client has not fully allowed himself or herself to acknowledge or accept.

Counselor: "It seems to me that you're saying that you hate your mother."

Client: "No, I love my mother. You're not supposed to hate your mother."

If the counselor has picked up an accurate feeling that is rejected by the client, it will quite likely be one of the themes that recurs. The recurring theme can be responded to in the description given the client. If the feeling is accurate, the client may be more likely to acknowledge it when confronted with it the second or third time it occurs. However, if the response is not accepted even though it is a recurring theme, it is not the duty of the counselor to browbeat the client or force an interpretation on him or her.

Responding with Concreteness

If the client's statements are general and abstract, the counselor, in responding, tries to work for greater specificity or more concreteness. This "helps the client become more specific, [helping] him move from vagueness to clarity and focus upon reality, upon the practical; thus he is helped to move from feeling to action" (Patterson, 1974, p. 108). Giving concrete responses in the early stages of the relationship helps to keep the counseling process moving. If the client is allowed to continue to make only general statements, the process will stagnate. Examples of concreteness follow:

Client: "I'm really confused. I don't know what to do with my life. I've thought all along that I wanted to be a doctor, but now I know my grades are so bad that I would never be admitted to any medical school. I have a number of other options, but I'm not sure those are what I really want to devote my life to."

Counselor: "It seems that you've recently become aware of how your previous plans are not going to work out and you are at a loss as to what direction to take now."

Clearly, this kind of general, abstract response will not help the client focus on the specifics of the problem. Compare it with the following concrete response to the same client statement:

Counselor: "You seem to be sure that your goals will not be met if you do not get a medical degree, and that doesn't seem likely at this point. What isn't clear to me is the exact nature of the goals to which you are striving.''

Responding with Self-Disclosure

Self-disclosure, as a specific skill, refers to counselors' sharing personal information about themselves. These revelations may be similar or different from those of the client. Self-disclosure also includes personal statements about counselors' ideas, values, attitudes, and experiences.

What happens in the counseling relationship must be for the benefit of the client and must be related to a counseling goal. Self-disclosure must not be done simply to make the counselor feel better. When used effectively, counselor self-disclosure can be a model for client disclosure. It can set a comfortable atmosphere for client self-disclosure and exploration. When self-disclosure is used too often, the focus tends to shift to the counselor rather than remaining on the client. Clients also may view counselors who self-disclose inappropriately as phony or manipulative. In such cases the helping process is blocked. When self-disclosure is used too sparsely, it may hinder client disclosures, or clients may view the counselor as being aloof. A middle ground based on clinical experience is most effective.

Most effective counselor self-disclosure responses consist of ''I'' statements that are on a feeling level in the here and now and are made in direct response to statements made by the client so that they are close to what the client is currently experiencing. Some clients can be threatened or frightened away by counselors' self-disclosures. Therefore, counselors need to understand their clients quite well so that self-disclosure will be effective. This suggests that most counselor self-disclosure is most appropriate in the later stages of the counseling process. Counselor self-disclosure can also lead to or become part of confrontation and immediacy interactions. Examples of appropriate self-disclosure are:

1. **Client:** ''I'm not sure you can understand how painful it is for me, and how abandoned and empty I feel since my wife has left me.''
   Counselor: ''I *can* sense your pain, hurt, and feeling of loneliness perhaps even more than you realize since I have gone through a similar experience when my husband found another woman.''
2. **Client:** ''I can't tell you how much I've gotten out of counseling. You've helped me get through a very tough time.''
   Counselor: ''I really appreciate your openness and the way in which you have decided to take charge of your life. I have learned a great deal from you.''

Responding with Confrontation

When counselors give a confrontation response, they are essentially describing discrepancies they have observed in a client's behavior. There are three broad categories of confrontation responses:

1. Communicating perceived discrepancies between the client's expression of what he is and what he wants to be (real self vs. ideal self);
2. Communicating perceived discrepancies between the client's verbal expressions about himself (awareness or insight) and his behavior, either as it is observed by the counselor or reported by the client; and,
3. Communicating perceived discrepancies between the client's expressed experience of himself and the counselor's experience of him. (Carkhuff, 1969, p. 191)

An observant counselor, using skills such as those described above may attain sufficient data to make any or all of the three types of confrontation responses from the very beginning of the relationship. However, direct confrontation early in the helping process is not always productive. Therefore, counselors should be tentative and cautious in making early confrontation responses. "Premature direct confrontation may have a demoralizing effect on an inadequately prepared helpee" (Carkhuff, 1969, p. 93). Examples of possible early confrontation responses are: "It seems to me that you're saying two different things," or "I'd like to check something out here—a few minutes ago you said A and now you are saying B and I'm sort of confused." These are in effect clarification statements, and in the later stages of the helping relationship, these statements, if appropriate, would be more direct and to the point.

Confrontation is threatening to both counselors and clients. Often, counselors are people who want to be liked and who do not want to do anything that would cause anyone to get angry or unhappy with them. One way of assuring that clients will not get upset is never to confront them. Clients usually do not like to feel uncomfortable, and being confronted directly with distortions, deletions, or discrepancies in behavior is likely to raise levels of discomfort. A change in behavior, however, rarely takes place without some discomfort. Often the ultimate choice clients have to make is whether they are more uncomfortable with their present behavior than they would be if they changed it. Often, clients would rather just talk about how bad they feel than put themselves through a process of change that would possibly ease their problem. Ironically, not confronting clients could leave them frustrated with the counseling process.

Confrontations are crucial to the counseling process. As Patterson (1974) points out, "direct communications precipitate an awareness of a crisis in the client that, when faced, leads to movement to higher levels of functioning. The goal is to enable the client to confront himself and when desirable, others" (p. 76). According to Carkhuff, confrontation is indeed essential to life itself. *"Confrontation of self and others is prerequisite to the healthy individual's encounter with life"* (Carkhuff, 1969, p. 93). Counselors who protect clients by not confronting them appropriately are not being helpful and are probably also protecting themselves.

In addition to being aware that appropriate confrontation is important for client growth, it may be helpful for the counselor to realize that confrontation need not be limited to negative distortions, deletions, or discrepancies. Confrontation also can be used to describe assets and resources that are discounted or unrecognized.

Counselors using the core conditions at high levels use confrontation more frequently than do low-level functioning counselors, according to research findings. Significantly, high-level counselors confront their clients more often with their assets and resources than with their limitations. Low-level counselors do the reverse (Patterson, 1974, p. 77).

To confront someone in a therapeutic way is to respond with a very high level of empathy. The counselor has heard a person so well that he or she is aware of some distortion in the client's perception of the world or observed some discrepancies in behavior. The counselor then responds to the client, describing what has been observed. Although the possibility of unpleasant connotations exists, a confrontation response can be one of the most helpful of all the responses. In the final analysis, it may be helpful to acknowledge that the entire helping process is confrontation (Egan, 1975).

In the following dialogue, the counselor avoids a confrontation with the client. This dialogue also illustrates a lack of openness and honesty on the counselor's part which suggests that instances of avoidance of client confrontations may be included in the discussion of genuineness.

> **Counselor:** "I think it is very important to be completely open and honest with each other."
> **Client:** "Well, how do I seem to you; how do I come across when you listen to me?"
> **Counselor:** "Well, er, um, . . . I like you. You're a nice person."
> **Client:** "Don't equivocate!"
> **Counselor:** "Maybe we need to get to know each other better."
> **Client:** Maybe."

The next example illustrates a high level of confrontation. Note that it is difficult to distinguish this from a high level of empathy.

> **Client:** "All the way over here, I kept wondering what I would talk about. I still don't know what to say."
> **Counselor:** "You seem to be groping for something to work on."
> **Client:** "I suppose that I could talk about my mother, but I seem to be handling the situation better."
> **Counselor:** "I get the feeling that you would like me to direct you."
> **Client:** "I wouldn't mind. I'm always initiating things. Maybe you can do it today. Is that OK?
> **Counselor:** "It's OK that you ask; however, I would rather you struggle with it."
> **Client:** "You're mean. Why won't you?"
> **Counselor:** "I won't take responsibility for you. I believe that you are perfectly capable of taking responsibility for yourself."

> **Client:** "You seem to have a whole lot more faith in me than I have in myself. I wait for my mother to direct me too, and then get angry when she does."

The following dialogue, in which the client is faced with an unrecognized or unaccepted strength, illustrates a positive confrontation.

> **Client:** "I must seem like a real victim with all my maladies. Do I come across like a victim to you?"
>
> **Counselor:** "I know that you seem to be running into a series of problems, and although I don't see you as coping with them very well right now, I really don't experience you as a victim. You seem too sensitive and in touch with your feelings."
>
> **Client:** "I really don't feel like a victim, but somehow. . . ."
>
> **Counselor:** "You don't like being seen as a victim."
>
> **Client:** "I don't want people to feel sorry for me."
>
> **Counselor:** "You seem to be afraid that people wouldn't like you if you honestly express your feelings."

Responding with Immediacy

Immediacy is "the ability to explore with another what is happening in their relationship" (Egan, 1986, p. 232). Immediacy is perhaps the deepest level of a counseling relationship. It is nonsexual intimacy, what theologian Martin Buber (1958) has called the "I-Thou" relationship. It is an experience best friends can have, and one that some people never seem to have.

Responding with immediacy or "direct mutual communication" (Ivey, 1971; Ivey & Authier, 1978), in effect, integrates all of the other types of responding. Effective immediacy includes a high level of empathy, respect, and concreteness. It is a special case of self-disclosure. The disclosure of the counselor's view of the relationship can be perceived by the client as being confronting, which it is. When a counselor makes an immediacy response, the relationship itself is brought directly into the helping process. An immediacy response can, therefore, be powerful. Such responses, which build as they do on all of the others, tend to be most effective in the later stages of the counseling process.

Because direct mutual communication is not common to many clients, it can be a threatening and demanding experience. Being aware of this, counselors work cautiously and tentatively, assisting clients in learning more about themselves without unduly frightening them. In some cases the essence of a client's problem may be a fear of intimacy and the vulnerability that accompanies it. The client may use previously successful approaches to sabotage the establishment of such a relationship. Examples of immediacy follow.

> **Client:** "I'm not sure I should continue these sessions. I don't feel I'm getting anywhere. You—they don't seem to be helping me. I don't get the feeling you are very concerned."

>**Counselor:**   "You're pretty discouraged and feel like quitting and giving up trying."
>**Client:**   "Yeah . . . it doesn't seem worthwhile to continue."

Here, the counselor ignores the client's feelings and focuses on the general reaction of discouragement. Contrast this with the following dialogue, where the counselor responds with a high level of immediacy to the client's confused feelings of aggression. Note the elements of empathy and confrontation in the counselor's response.

>**Client:**   "I'm feeling sort of low. I couldn't get out of bed this morning. I had some bad news last night. Don't know how to deal with it. I almost forgot our appointment. Anyway, I did apply for that job we had talked about. That was before my car broke down."
>**Counselor:**   "I'm really feeling lost. You're jumping around from one thing to another, and I'm having a hard time following you. I am aware that you are feeing depressed about something but are not ready to share it. Like there isn't enough trust in our relationship at this point."

Responding Using Interpretation

Interpretation responses are perhaps the most controversial of all the various types of responses. Interpretation can be defined as an attempt to impart meaning about a client's behavior based on the counselor's observations and knowledge. The goal of this approach to interpretation is to increase the client's insight or awareness regarding his or her behavior. The various therapeutic approaches used in counseling employ interpretation to one degree or another. It might be appropriate to recognize that interpretation exists in all therapies and to place its use on a continuum from implied and tentative to direct and active (see Table 3.3).

   Person-centered counselors (see chapter 11) point out that there is no evidence for the effectiveness of interpretation responses. They also note that interpretation switches the focus from the client's frame of reference, fosters resistance, and places the therapeutic responsibility on the counselor. However, Brammer and Shostrom (1982) point out that even reflections of feelings, which person-centered counselors emphasize, are in themselves conservative interpretations because counselors must select, from the material given to them, those feelings which they deem important. The counselor's experience and knowledge greatly influence what material is responded to. A high-level reflection of feeling adds more meaning to a client's statement.

   Fritz Perls, the founder of Gestalt therapy, declared that interpretation is a therapeutic mistake (Perls, 1969). However, one technique in Gestalt therapy is called "feeding the client a sentence."

>   In listening to or observing the patient, the counselor may conclude that a particular attitude or message is implied. He will then say, "May I feed you a sentence? Say it and try it on for size. Say it to several people here." He then proposes his sentence,

TABLE 3.3 Continuum of Interpretation

Client Is Source	Counselor Is Source Client Is Problem Solver	Counselor Is Source
Implied, Tentative Counselor is slightly in front of client.	Counselor is ahead of client but client appears ready to handle feedback and make sense of it.	*Direct, Active* Counselor makes elaborate and in-depth theoretical explanation.
Counselor goes slightly beyond what the client can recognize as part of his or her communication to counselor. Counselor picks up nuances and implicit meanings from client. Client is the primary source.	Interpretation presented as guess or hunch. Client is discoverer and ifnds own truth with counselor's assistance.	Cleverly guides client toward truth. Counselor is expert.
Person-centered counselling	Gestalt therapy Adlerian counseling	Psychoanalysis

and the patient tests out his reaction to the sentence. Typically, the counselor does not simply interpret for or to the patient. Although there is obviously a strong interpretative element here, the patient must make the experience his own through active participation. If the proposed sentence is truly a key sentence, spontaneous development of the idea will be supplied by the patient. (Levitsky & Perls, 1970, p. 148)

An approach such as Gestalt therapy discourages interpretation and uses it only in an indirect way. The psychoanalytic approach, on the other hand, places heavy emphasis on skillful interpretation as a cornerstone of the therapeutic process.

In any event, making an interpretation is a delicate operation. It can easily confuse the client, who has been taking initiative and responsibility in the relationship, to hear the counselor take a more authoritative role. Interpretation is most effective if the counseling relationship has been developed so that there is a high degree of trust and security between client and counselor.

If interpretations are used, they should be used selectively and phrased tentatively. Interpretations are for the benefit of clients, not to show the astuteness of counselors. Clients need to determine whether an interpretation fits or makes sense. In spite of using all of the skills described above, counselors may not be able to enter the client's world. A good interpretation must enable clients to understand themselves or their problems more clearly and as a result encourage them to act more effectively.

Responding Using Probes and Questions

As discussed in chapter 2, the use of questions in counseling sessions is controversial. It has been suggested that counseling can be done effectively without their use. However, even though there is little evidence on the effectiveness of using questions in counseling, many counselors and most theoretical approaches use question-asking as a counseling technique. Therefore, if questions are to be used, are some types of questions better than others? Are questions more appropriately used at certain stages of the counseling process? And, how do probes differ from questions?

Probing.   A probe is a response that attempts to seek information or to provoke further response along a certain line (Porter, 1950). Probing responses usually take the form of a direct or indirect question. There are also probes that are commands or directives, such as "Tell me more" or "Go on." These open-ended probes are especially helpful during the earlier stages of the counseling process, but they are useful in all stages.

Questioning.   In general, as the counselor works to establish the therapeutic relationship and to understand the client's world during the first three stages (attending, exploration, and understanding), direct questioning is usually not as effective as the various responses described above. During the third stage and throughout the action phase (Stage IV) of the counseling process, the use of questions becomes most effective.

After the initial intake session, when some specific questions are necessary, the use of questions should be minimized. This is essential in order to facilitate the client's exploration and understanding of his or her own thoughts and feelings. Such a procedure avoids the usually unproductive pattern of the counselor asking the questions and the client doing nothing but waiting for the next question. Instead of the focus being on the client, it is on the counselor, with the counselor feverishly trying to come up with the question that will break the case wide open. The session becomes a form of inquisition. An environment is established in which the counselor is clearly the authority, the expert. The client may then expect that once the questions are over, the expert will have the proper solution to the problem.

Clients take very little responsibility in that type of situation, and even when satisfactory solutions are found, they do not learn to solve their own problems. The next time they are stuck they must seek out another authority. However, when questions are called for, it is important to know the types of questions to ask (direct or indirect) and the effectiveness of each type.

Direct versus Indirect Questions.   Direct questions are to the point, without any ambiguity or vagueness. The indirect question, like the "commanding" probe above, usually has no question mark at the end. However, it is generally clear that a query is being made and that an answer is expected. Such queries can be presented without ambiguity. The indirect questions are more open in nature, giving the client more room to respond and to give direction to the session content. Examples of direct and indirect questions are:

Direct: "How is your new school?"
Indirect: "I wonder how your new school seems to you."
Direct: "What is your opinion about getting an abortion?"
Indirect: "I wonder what some of your thoughts are on abortion."
Direct: "Your divorce is almost final. How do you feel about it?"
Indirect: "I'll bet you've got a lot you'd like to talk about since your divorce is almost final."
Direct: "Isn't it hard to do everything you have to do with four little kids to take care of?"
Indirect: "I'd be interested in hearing how you manage to do everything with four young children."

Types of Direct Questions.   Open, noncued questions that give no indication of the correct response can be helpful in uncovering affective and cognitive material that has not been brought out in any other way; for example, "What are your feelings about school?" With an open question the client is free to respond in any way. Open questions usually begin with "How," "What," "Could," "Would," or "Why?" (see Table 3.4).

TABLE 3.4 Types of Direct Questions

Exploratory Open, Non-cued Questions	*Exploratory Closed, Non-cued Questions*	*Nonexploratory Closed, Cued Questions*
How did you feel about what Bob said?	Did you feel hurt by what Bob said?	You didn't let Bob's remark get to you, did you?
What did you feel when your mom walked in?	Were you scared when your mom walked in?	When your mom walked in, you were scared to death, weren't you?
Will anyone go with you to the game?	Are you coming with us?	You're going to come with us, aren't you?
Opens doors to communication. Communicates to the respondent that the questioner wants to hear about whatever the respondent wants to say. A wide range of responses possible.	Closed because this type of question often results in simple yes or no responses with no elaboration.	Blocks open communication. Cues a desired answer; makes it difficult for respondent to give a truthful response if the truth is in opposition to the questioner's desires.

Wilson, Lopis, and Radke (1978), p. 69.

How and what questions solicit facts and gather information. They can also focus on client process or emotion, thus developing greater client self-awareness. For example, a counselor might ask a client, "How do you stop yourself from asking for what you want?" or "What does it do for you to act like a child?" "Could" or "would" questions facilitate client self-exploration. An example is, "Could you share some of your fears about getting married?" With an open question the client is free to respond in any way. "Why" questions generally produce reasons, excuses, explanations, or intellectual history. They can also lead to client defensiveness and are rarely recommended by any theoretical orientation.

Closed, noncued questions limit the client to either affirmation or denial (see Table 3.4). To answer the question, "Do you like school?" the client needs answer only "yes" or "no." The closed question can be useful if there is some particular information the client has not voluntarily disclosed (for example, "Are you married?"); however, if this approach is continued, the focus of the session is controlled by the questions rather than by what the client wants to work on.

A third type of question, the closed, cued question, clearly blocks communication. Built into the question is the cue to the desired answer; for example, "People who are really honest wouldn't lie, would they?" Often the cues are found both in the tone of voice and the expressions on the counselor's face as well as in the words themselves. This type of question has little known therapeutic value for a client.

STAGE IV—ACTION

Action, or problem-solving, is the next to the last stage of the counseling process. It is followed by termination. In many cases, clients who have successfully completed the exploratory and understanding phases of the helping relationship will have an "Aha!" experience. They are able to say, "I now know what the problem is *and* what I have to do to solve it. Thank you!" Such clients may have spent a great deal of time working on their problems before coming to see a counselor. They may have already received much advice from family members and friends and, therefore, have many ideas to work with once the exact nature of their problem is understood and accepted. In these cases, the action stage of counseling takes place within the clients themselves without further intervention by the counselor. In other cases, clients may go through the understanding stage and realize that any problems they had were dealt with already; or perhaps they may become aware that they had no specific problems, but rather were troubled by existential issues such as finding meaning in their lives.

Stage IV action skills focus on directives and problem-solving methods. Counselors may take charge and give directives, in effect telling the clients what to do, or they may assist clients in putting their ideas and insights into some form of action through the use of problem-solving techniques, with the clients' taking the burden of responsibility for the decisions made.

Directives

Directives are the instructions given to the client during the counseling session. They tell the client what to do, and they play a major role in some theoretical approaches, such as Gestalt therapy and behavioral counseling. Directives may consist of guiding a client through a fantasy exercise or relaxation activity, urging repetition of certain key phrases, giving homework assignments, or directing a role-playing situation. As with questioning, appropriateness of timing is important in the use of directives. Open-ended probes and giving directions for a breathing exercise may be offered at any stage in the counseling process. However, homework and advice-giving, if they are to be effective, have a better chance when given in the latter stages of the process.

Behavioral counseling practitioners use direct intervention in the solving of problems as a regular practice (see chapter 11). For example, they may develop desensitization hierarchies and relaxation programs for students who have test anxiety.

Advising

Advising is a form of directive, which, grossly or subtly, indicates what the client should do. Advising may be appropriate as long as it is tentatively suggested with no strings attached and is not perceived as a demand.

> **Advice (inappropriate):** "You should divorce your husband."
> **Advice (appropriate):** "I really would like you to look at other alternatives—would you be willing to do that?"

Giving advice is often fruitless because there is seldom any suggestion that a counselor can offer a client that the client hasn't already thought of and rejected. Counselors who want to avoid feelings of rejection tend to give advice sparingly, if at all. A helpful guideline in giving advice is never to give any advice for which you are not willing to accept full responsibility.

Before offering appropriate advice for resolving a given problem, it is often helpful to find out what clients have already considered and then add not one but at least two suggestions to those ideas. With this approach, even clients who have not thought of any solutions on their own will still have a minimum of two solutions from which to choose. The decision is then theirs rather than one imposed on them by the counselor.

Homework Assignments

Homework assignments can be viewed as a special type of advice-giving. Assignments are used as part of many therapeutic approaches for a number of reasons, including putting into practice what was learned in the counseling sessions, practicing new behaviors, and keeping a record of selected activities. Depending on the theoretical approach of the counselor, homework assignments may be given as early as the first counseling session. Homework assignments, like other types of advice, are not always carried out by clients and as a result can become a source of frustration within the relationship.

Homework can also be used as part of bibliotherapy, where the client is instructed to read some relevant literature pertaining to his or her situation as a supplement to counseling. There are many popular and well-written self-help books on the market, often in paperback editions. Also, some biographies, autobiographies, fiction, and poetry can be therapeutic. Such material often gives hope, gives clients something to identify with, or provides meaning to their lives.

Problem-Solving Approaches

A number of specific approaches directly involve the client in the problem-solving process. As two of these problem-solving methods are presented, it will become apparent that all of the counseling skills described above are essential in the process of arriving at solutions.

The Method III Approach—T. Gordon

Thomas Gordon (1974), in working with parents, teachers, counselors, and others in the helping professions, has adapted the scientific method to counseling so that it can be used by virtually all populations to solve a variety of problems in a way in which everyone feels good. No solution is externally imposed on the participants. In Methods I and II, according to Gordon, either the counselor or the client is in control, and issues of manipulation and feelings of winning and losing are prevalent. Method III is seen as a ''no one loses'' strategy. Above all, it is an approach that the client can learn and use in subsequent problem situations. The six specific steps in Gordon's approach are as follows:

1. Determine the problem. This results from the exploration and understanding stages.
2. Generate possible solutions. This is a brainstorming step to come up with as many solutions as possible. No evaluation of ideas is involved at this step, so that as many different ideas as possible might be generated.
3. Evaluate possible solutions. This is the step in which the various solutions generated in the preceding step are evaluated and given priorities by the client. Ideas can be combined or expanded on as part of this step.
4. Make a decision on one possible solution. At this point the counselor encourages the client to commit to one solution and follow through on it.
5. Implement the decision. This is when the client actually puts the solution into operation.
6. Assess results. This is an important follow-up step necessary to determine success. If the solution wasn't successful, it might need to be modified and attempted again, or the client might have to move to a second possible solution. The process can be repeated until the final assessment is positive.

Reality Therapy—W. Glasser

William Glasser (1965) developed his problem-solving approach, reality therapy, while working with various client populations from regular school children to girls in a reform school. The basic steps in his approach are similar to Gordon's; however, Glasser adds a few interesting dimensions to the process.

Glasser's approach is essentially one of both counselor and client involvement. The first of eight steps in reality therapy is making friends. In this step, an atmosphere of acceptance and openness is developed through the use of active listening skills and attending behavior. The counselor must convey caring for and involvement with the client. This atmosphere must exist throughout the next seven steps. This corresponds to developing the relationship, as described in the previous chapter.

Once the relationship is established, the client, in step two, is asked, "What are you doing now?" and, in step three, "Is your behavior helping you?" The client is encouraged to make a value judgment about his or her own behavior. The openness created in the first step allows the client to communicate honestly and minimizes any feelings of being threatened by the self-judgment.

The fourth step is to encourage the client to make a plan aimed at some desired goal. The counselor may assist the client in formulating a plan by using Gordon's problem-solving steps, as previously described.

Obtaining a commitment to the plan is the fifth step. The client makes a personal commitment as well as a commitment to the counselor. This is often done by putting the plan and the commitment to the plan in the form of a contract that is signed by both client and counselor. The counselor, in Glasser's important sixth step, will not accept excuses if the commitment is broken. By accepting excuses, the counselor is admitting that he or she does not think that the client can do any better. If the person fails, a new commitment is made.

The seventh step is don't punish, but don't interfere with reasonable consequences. A client whose problem is excessive absences from work may make a plan that will decrease the frequency of absences. If the plan fails, the consequence may be that the client loses the job. The counselor would not intervene on the client's behalf, because losing the job is a reasonable, though unpleasant, consequence. Accepting the client's failure, however, is not a reasonable consequence. Regardless of how failure occurs, the client should be asked for a value judgment and a new plan.

In the eighth step, the counselor is admonished never to give up. The counselor's confidence in the client despite frequent breaking of commitments lets the client know that the counselor believes that the client *can* act differently.

In any of the eight steps, it may be necessary to go back to an earlier step in the process. The relationship may break down, and it may be necessary to go back to step one and begin again. Throughout the process, it may be helpful to the counselor to remember Glasser's basic premise: All actions are attempts at filling needs. The goal of reality therapy is to help people learn more responsible and effective ways of meeting their needs.

STAGE V—TERMINATION

The termination of individual counseling is a significant stage in the counseling process; however, little attention has been paid to it in the literature. Ward (1984) states that if terminating counseling is handled effectively, the counseling outcome can be maximized, and new client learnings and behaviors will more likely be maintained. If handled inappropriately, effective change is unlikely to occur, and the client may be discouraged from seeking further help when necessary.

When Is the Time to Terminate?

There is usually no ideal situation in which the client has resolved all past and present problems and has learned to handle new problems without difficulties when they arise. In discussing the time for termination, Zaro, Barack, Nedelman, and Dreiblatt (1982) state that

> the ending of therapy usually represents a compromise between hoped for changes and limitations arising from waning motivation, the subjective discomfort of being in therapy, its cost, and a variety of other factors. (p. 142)

Knowing when to terminate is often especially difficult for beginning counselors. Sometimes counselors make a premature decision to terminate when a client exhibits the flight-to-health phenomenon discussed in chapter 2. Sometimes they extend counseling long after it is productive. Clients or counselors who have individuation-separation or dependency-independency issues, or counselors who are ignorant of how or when to make a decision to end counseling, can create particular problems at this stage. It is hoped that counselors will have successfully resolved these issues before entering practice.

As the client successfully works through the stages of counseling, termination of the relationship begins to become an important issue. Clients often experience less need for counseling and make direct statements to that effect, or drop hints. For example, clients may speak of having made tremendous progress, or may share how they intend to solve a problem rather than ask the counselor to do it.

After reviewing the literature on the termination stage, Ward (1984) presents several client behaviors other than direct verbal statements that signal the approach of termination, including less intensity in counseling sessions, lateness, joking, intellectualizing, missed appointments, apathy, acting out, withdrawal, denial, expression of anger, mourning, feelings of separation and loss, dissolution, futility, impotence, dependency, inadequacy, abandonment, and regression to previous and less constructive behavior patterns. The client may engage in these behaviors in order to resist actually terminating. It is often difficult to end a close relationship. It is not uncommon for a client to manufacture new problems in order to remain in the counseling relationship. It may be necessary for the counselor to make the initial suggestion and then help the client to work through the issues relating to the termination process. The counselor must make an assessment of the client's readiness to terminate. If the client is ready, the counselor must then complete any unfinished business in the relationship with the client, aid the client in exploring feelings that arise during the termination process, and prepare the client for postcounseling self-reliance and transfer of learning.

Making the Decision to Terminate

Several antecedent areas can aid the counselor in making the decision to terminate. The primary area is whether the client has reached his or her therapy goals. Therefore, it is important that the counselor and client achieve an explicit understanding of the counseling goals in the beginning stage (Lanning & Carey, 1987). This is not always easy to do, as with clients who come to counseling with vague problems, such as general apathy or undefinable anxiety. In such cases, therapeutic goals are more difficult to define and progress more difficult to measure (Zaro et al., 1982). The counselor might also assess the client's coping ability, ability to relate intimately with significant others, capacity to enjoy life, productivity in work and career, increased valuing of self and others, rate of progress in reaching the goals of counseling, and confidence to live effectively without counseling (Ward, 1984). Usually, the termination stage is a continuation of the adult-to-adult mutual negotiations types of relationship begun in Stage IV.

Once the decision to terminate is made, counseling should not end abruptly. The process may require a number of sessions in order to obtain closure. Some counselors begin to meet their clients less frequently. During this stage, counselors make fewer interventions, and clients are encouraged to assume greater responsibility for the sessions. The counselor will help the client review progress from the beginning of the relationship. The counselor might go back and review a counseling session recorded early in counseling (Ward, 1984). The counselor gradually removes formal support and structure as the client demonstrates greater readiness to function on his or her own.

Completing Unfinished Business and Exploring Feelings

It is important that the counselor and client bring to closure any relationship issues through the discussion of feelings toward one another and toward the relationship. The goal is to bring about an appropriate ending in which everything that needs expression is expressed. Clients may summarize their reactions to the counseling process and to the counselor and provide feedback as to what was and was not facilitative (Ward, 1984). Clients might also be encouraged to explore any feelings regarding termination such as loss, grief, or abandonment. For termination to be completely successful, it is important that clients not deny or avoid such feelings. It is important that counselors be aware of their own feelings regarding the ending of counseling relationships. Students and interns especially should consult with their supervisors regarding all areas of termination.

Preparation for Postcounseling Self-Reliance and Transfer of Learning

The counselor can help the client formulate some specific strategies and plans for the transfer of learning from counseling to the client's everyday life situations. Ward (1984) suggests having the client make self-contracts concerning behavior after counseling has ceased, rehearsing new roles, renewing goal setting, using imagery to project future behaviors, and using counseling or feedback on the level of client functioning and issues that the client might anticipate later. Counselors can make it known to the client that the option of entering counseling again is acceptable and viable. Entering counseling again should not imply failure for the client.

SUMMARY

Skills vital to establishing the counseling relationship and working through the first two stages of the counseling process have been described. Attending skills (Stage I) relate to establishing rapport and being responsive to the client through the use of physical and psychological attending skills as well as counselors being tuned into themselves as part of the process. While the attending skills involve a lot of nonverbal responding to the client, including silence, the major verbal responses stressed in Stage I were encouragers to help the client continue to discuss a problem. Basic empathy is the major exploration skill presented in Stage II, along with several subskills.

Responding with empathy refers to the counselor's ability to understand and, more important, to communicate accurately to the client what the counselor understands. Reflecting feelings and meaning builds empathy and helps clients to clarify and be congruent. Summary statements help tie together key concepts over various periods of time (from current to previous sessions). They help provide structure and direction to the counseling process.

The responding and initiating skills associated with the latter stages of the counseling process have also been presented. These skills are important in helping the client move through the counseling process. They build on and are in addition to those skills of the earlier stages of the therapeutic alliance.

The skills of advanced accurate empathy, concreteness, self-disclosure, confrontation, immediacy, interpretation, and different types of probing techniques are part of the understanding stage of the counseling process. These skills are used to help focus and clarify the nature of the client's problem. Once the client clearly understands the problem, the client may already know what to do to resolve it. If not, the process moves on to the fourth stage, the action or problem-solving stage.

With a mutually agreed on understanding of the problem to be resolved, the counselor has a number of problem-solving approaches that can be used. The problem-solving approaches of Thomas Gordon and William Glasser are interactive methods in which the counselor works with the client to take responsibility for the generation of problem solutions and the implementation and evaluation of those solutions. A series of clarifying responses have been presented that may be useful in working with clients in both the understanding and action stages.

When the client has successfully pursued a course of action that results in the solving of the agreed on problem, another problem may be focused on, with the relationship returning to the exploration stage (Stage 2), or the movement may proceed toward the termination of the relationship. The preparation for and implementation of termination of the relationship involves a variety of the skills used in earlier stages, with the major new skill being knowing how to comfortably say goodbye to a person with whom one has developed a close relationship.

QUESTIONS AND ACTIVITIES

1. With which of the skills in chapter 3 are you most competent? Which ones need more development? Are there any skills that particularly give you difficulty, perhaps even scare you? Why do you think this is so? Discuss this in class.
2. Videotape a short conversation with another student. Play back the videotape and observe your physical and psychological attending.
3. Observe films or videotapes or listen to audiotapes of professional counselors working with clients. See if you can identify the various stages of counseling in each instance. Compare your findings with those of other students.

CHAPTER 4

FOCUS ON
Using Skills:
Conducting an Inner-View

What is the structure of a helping session?
What really happens?

It is important to learn the various helping skills necessary to the counseling process and to be able to apply these skills effectively in counseling sessions. Knowledge of these skills does not guarantee the successful conduct of helping sessions, but not knowing them can have a detrimental effect.

In chapter 2, when describing the first two stages of the counseling process, general guidelines for the development of a therapeutic alliance were presented. This chapter details some basic guidelines for conducting an actual counseling session. We deal primarily with the first session; however, a similar structure can be used for all subsequent sessions as well.

SETTING THE STAGE: THE ENVIRONMENT

In developing a successful helping relationship, there is no correct environmental setting. Effective work can be done while shooting a game of pool with a client in a day treatment center or while seated side-by-side on a transcontinental flight. When possible, however, counselors strive to set up the positive characteristics of their counseling setting, working to attain what Jerome Frank (1973) has called the ''placebo effect'' in the environment itself. A placebo has been defined as

> any therapy or component of therapy that is deliberately used for its nonspecific, psychological, or psychophysiological effect, or that is used for its presumed specific effect, but is without specific activity for the condition being treated. A _placebo,_ when used as a control in experimental studies, is defined as a substance or procedure that is without specific activity for the condition being evaluated. The _placebo effect_ is defined as the psychological or psychobiological effect produced by placebos. (Shapiro & Morris, 1978, p. 371)

The objective of this effort to structure the environment is to present conditions in such a way that the client will feel comfortable and reassured from the onset of contact with the counselor.

The office location plays a role in helping to establish the confidence clients need in order to be able to talk about an area of their lives in which they feel deficient or confused. For example, having an office in a relatively secluded part of a school building is preferable to one next to the school principal's office or adjoining the university commons area. There is still enough of a concern over the stigma of having mental health problems that many people needing help may not want to be seen entering or leaving a counselor's office.

The secretary's office and reception area should offer a feeling of warmth, comfort, and an overall feeling of confidentiality. This approach should be carried through to the counseling office itself, so that clients when seated would feel no more anxiety than they had prior to entering the office. Many practitioners decorate the walls of their offices with diplomas, licenses, and other certificates to enhance the placebo effect, suggesting that here is a place that is safe and secure with a practitioner who is highly qualified to provide the services desired. Such efforts enhance the expertness and competence of the counselor in the perception of the client (Cormier & Cormier, 1985, p. 46). It should be noted that in states where there is a licensure law, it is mandatory that the state license be prominently displayed.

Many professional offices have furniture that is deliberately designed to avoid a stark, institutional look. A desk, if present, is often set to the side of the room, not being used as a rule during a session other than for such things as administering a test instrument. Clients seem to work better if their chair is reasonably padded, but not overly stuffed. Clients seated in overstuffed sofas may feel almost too relaxed and may even get to the point at which they lose motivation to work on their problems. A recliner is used by many practitioners for specialized purposes, such as for giving instruction in relaxation techniques and for systematic desensitization purposes.

Another functional item that might be in an office is an easel with a pad of paper, or a chalkboard. These items are useful for times when the counselor or the client wishes to express something that cannot be easily expressed in verbal terms alone. Many counselors use such tools to clarify or explain aspects of the counseling methods they are using, to list alternatives in the problem-solving process, or, when working with families, to construct a family tree. Video and audio tape recorders are also useful tools whether the counselor is a student in training or a fully certified professional. In addition to being excellent instruments for helping professionals review sessions and improve their skills, tape recorded sessions have been used directly in helping clients work on their problems. For example, a portion of a session may be replayed immediately so a client can better note how whiny his voice is while he is trying to act forcefully, or a recording of an entire session can be sent home with a client so she can review the approach she took in solving a problem.

An important and necessary item in any counseling office is the ubiquitous box of tissues. The presence of the tissue box indicates to the client that the expression of emotions is acceptable in this setting and that there is permission to cry if desired. A clock, located strategically so that the counselor can see it without distracting the client, is helpful in controlling length of sessions.

Because the major instrument in helping is the counselor, there is little need for other office equipment or supplies. Too many furnishings or decorations can prove to be distracting rather than helpful. There are, of course, specialists who have certain requirements consonant with their specialty; for example, a group or family therapist will need space and furniture available to accommodate a large number of clients, and art and music therapists usually have fairly large space requirements along with a substantial amount of supplemental equipment and material.

The characteristics of the office setting, then, can play an important part in at least the initial stage of the counseling relationship. Once human interaction has taken place and the counseling relationship established, environmental conditions take on a significantly reduced role.

COUNSELOR CHARACTERISTICS AND BEHAVIORS

Facilitative counselor characteristics are described in chapter 1. Additional counselor characteristics that are applicable primarily to initial or early sessions include:

1. *Attractiveness.* The client's perception of the counselor in terms of likability, friendliness, warmth, and similarities in attitudes and background has been considered an important aspect of influence in counseling settings (Strong, 1968). Attractiveness is a nonspecific factor that may help in initial contacts, but is not a substitute for counseling skills (Cormier & Cormier, 1985; Patterson, 1985).

   One aspect of attractiveness is personal appearance. The counseling relationship is a professional one, so that generally high standards of grooming and dress are appropriate. However, it is difficult to set any uniform rules. For example, some male counselors in college counseling centers choose not to wear ties because they believe that this sets them on a level different from their clients and possibly provides a barrier to full and open communication. Also, counselors working with special populations such as juvenile delinquents or with modalities such as dance therapy tend to dress in ways appropriate to these conditions.

2. *Punctuality.* Being on time for an appointment communicates respect for the client. It is also an ethical and even a legal issue. It is part of fulfilling your contract with the client.

3. *Comfortable assertiveness.* Meeting a client for the first time affords the counselor an excellent opportunity to make contact with the client on three different levels: verbal, physical, and psychological.

a. Verbal. The counselor makes contact by greetings and the immediate use of the client's name; for example, "Good afternoon, Mrs. Johnson. Do you prefer to be called Carol or Carolyn?"
b. Physical. The counselor takes the opportunity to shake hands with all participants in the session.
c. Psychological. Nonverbal communication is established by direct eye contact.

Care should be taken to ensure that contact can be made at these three levels during the initial meeting because it may be helpful in collecting data about the client and for establishing norms for the relationship itself.

CONDUCTING THE FIRST SESSION

The nature of the first session may be dictated in part by what has preceded the actual meeting of the client and counselor. In most settings, there is usually some preliminary gathering of information about the client. This can range from having the client answer a few basic questions at the time an appointment is made to having the client come in for a preliminary session with a case manager, when a significant amount of preliminary data is gathered. If the session is one to which the client has been referred or if it is a counselor-initiated session as could occur in a school setting, the counselor would usually have a fairly extensive client file prior to the first contact.

In settings in which a precounseling interview is not possible or appropriate, it is generally good practice to have a newly scheduled client come to the counseling office about 15 minutes prior to the appointment time to fill out information forms (and insurance forms, if applicable). Many counseling offices provide the new client with a written description of the counseling process, specific policies regarding making and breaking appointments, and information about arranging for payment (if applicable). Such descriptions may include a discussion of confidentiality, noting instances in which the counselor cannot maintain confidentiality, such as in the case of actual or suspected child abuse. The basic principle behind this preliminary information gathering and dissemination is to allow as much of the counseling hour as possible for establishment of the therapeutic relationship. In ideal settings, counselors should have virtually all the preliminary information they need before the first session begins.

A description of the thoughts and feelings that can take place when the counselor and client first meet is presented in chapter 2. Here, we discuss how the counselor can influence what transpires in this first meeting.

Shertzer and Stone (1971) offer five general guidelines for an initial session: (1) establishing rapport (initiating the therapeutic alliance), (2) providing structure, (3) helping the client talk, (4) remaining alert to the client's feelings, and (5) closing the session smoothly. We add a sixth guideline: attending to the counseling process. Each area is examined in detail.

Rapport

Rapport has been described by Belkin (1975) as being established "when the counselor demonstrates an accepting, open attitude, when he shows interest in what the client has to say, and when he does everything in his power to make the client feel comfortable" (p. 296). This process obviously begins with the establishment of a comfortable environment and during the initial meeting of the client even before he or she comes into the office. This process continues throughout the session with virtually every verbal and nonverbal response of the counselor contributing to it. Using the responding skills described in chapter 3, the counselor will genuinely be communicating the respect and warmth that are so crucial in creating an atmosphere of acceptance and understanding.

In an opening session it may be helpful not to be too insightful or communicate too much understanding for the reasons Tyler (1969) describes:

> We must recognize that the people who consult us may have mixed feelings about being understood. They must be sure that understanding can in no way constitute a threat before they can welcome it. Many of us are afraid that someone will "see through us," uncovering our hidden weaknesses. We have put up strong defenses against this. Much of what we say, many of the things we do, are designed to hide rather than to reveal our underlying motives and traits. For this reason if it happens that the counselor shows by some penetrating remark that he has seen through a new client's defenses, the person may very well retreat in panic from the whole situation. It is only when he has become certain of a thorough-going unshakable acceptance that he can run the risk of trying to make his real feelings understood. (pp. 49–50).

Because developing the relationship is such a key component in the counseling process, counselors work with patience and sensitivity during an opening session for good reason. However, as with any set of guidelines, there are exceptions. A client who has already gone through much of the exploration process mentally may come for help. Although the initial encounter with the counselor would be a first session as we are describing, in reality the client may be ready to work at a deep level from the outset. Accurate, empathic listening will help verify this readiness.

Providing Structure

Because coming into a formal helping relationship is a new experience for most clients, an additional way to help establish rapport is to provide a brief description of what will transpire during the time the counselor and the client will be together. This description need not occur at the beginning of the session, except for one important instance—when a session will be tape recorded. Permission to tape record needs to be obtained at the start of the session and can be included as part of other information about the structure of the session. In the case of children under age 18, permission to tape record must be obtained from parents or guardians prior to the first session.

Some specific structural concerns counselors might want to present to the clients include the length of the session, the counselor's role, the topic of confidentiality, the possible number of sessions, and the recording of the session, if that is to be done. Provision should also be made for the client to be able to ask any questions related to the counseling process. Here is an example of how a practicum student began an initial session after the introductions were made:

> "Today, we're going to spend almost an hour together to work on whatever you would like to talk about. As I am a graduate student under supervision, I will be tape recording the session. My supervisor will be the only other person to listen to the tape, and her basic concern is to help me improve my responses to you. Are you clear as to this procedure and what we will do today? (Client responds: "Yes.") "I would like to have you sign this paper indicating that you are aware that the session is being taped." (Client signs document) "Thank you. OK, now, where would you like to begin?"

Providing structure enhances perceived counselor/client similarities and with that, increased interpersonal attractiveness. It also fulfills the ethical responsibility of informing clients of the purposes, techniques, and limitations of counseling (Cormier & Cormier, 1985, p. 53).

Helping the Client Talk: Open Invitation

The concluding question in the example above is a sample of what Ivey (1971) calls an open invitation to talk. Open invitations allow clients to select the subject matter and in effect begin to provide their own structure to the session. Asking a question is the most common way to begin a counseling session. This opening probe could range from a very closed, cued, direct question like "Would you like to tell me how you get along with your mother?" to a very open, non-cued, indirect statement such as "I'm interested in knowing what you want to work on today." The latter statement gives much more latitude to the client to give direction to the solution of the problem and keeps the session oriented in the present. This latter approach is clearly an open invitation to talk. Once the client has begun talking, the use of encouragers such as "go on" (see chapter 3) and empathic understanding responses will help the client continue to tell his or her story.

Remaining Alert and Responding to the Client's Feelings

When clients present their problems, it is easy for counselors to focus on the cognitive content and to become almost oblivious to the emotional content. Just being able to talk with someone can have a therapeutic effect, and to have that person (a counselor) tune into, understand, and accept both positive and negative feelings is even more therapeutic. It is in striving for an inner-view that the types of responses to clients' feelings presented in chapter 3 can be implemented at an appropriate level.

Responding to emotions, including those not necessarily stated in words, is an instance of the counselor's listening to the music and not just the words. This is often helpful; for example, "Even though you haven't said it, I can tell by the clenching of your fists and the sound of your voice that you are really quite angry!" It is possible that a client just needs to express and work through emotions in a given situation. The client may already know what action needs to be taken, but emotional issues need to be dealt with first. This possibility may account for a significant portion of the great number of one-session counseling relationships.

Attending to the Counseling Process

Conducting a successful inner-view involves more than attending and responding to clients and the statements they make. It is important to attend to the process of the session itself. Without direct awareness of what is happening during the session, the client and the counselor may drift aimlessly for the entire hour. The counselor, therefore, should mentally note what is happening during the session and communicate any observations to the client when appropriate. The use of internal and closing summaries are ways through which the counselor can communicate the nature of the counseling process during a session.

Internal Summaries

As the session progresses and the counselor uses various responding skills to help the client explore and understand a problem area, it is often useful for the counselor to build in an "internal" summary statement or two to help clarify and understand what has been going on in terms of both content and process. A common tendency of beginning counselors is to respond directly to each statement of the client, keeping a one-to-one relationship between the client's statements and the responses. To formulate an internal summary, the counselor should pull together the various thoughts, feelings, and behaviors that have been communicated. A summary may refer to patterns or themes, discrepancies and inconsistencies, or just help clarify a large amount of data from time to time during the session; for example, "You've just told me three good things that have happened to you today, and are you ever happy!"

A summary statement may be a useful response to help focus on feelings, especially if much of the material in the session has been cognitively oriented; for example, "You've described a whole list of things that have gone wrong for you, and you're really pretty upset." A response relating to the process of a particular session might be, "Every time we get close to some feelings of sadness or anger, you immediately change the subject."

Internal summary statements used at different times during a counseling session help provide some structure, if only to note that "I am paying attention to all that is happening here and will report my findings from time to time." In the initial session especially, this response can be of great help. The client may literally have stored up such great amounts of material (problems) in anticipation of the time that there would be an empathic listener that he or she may go off in different directions. Discussion of closing summary statements is included in the treatment of the termination process.

Significance of the Presenting Problem

Another benefit of attending to the process and using internal summary statements is to help keep track of the initial presenting problem. As mentioned previously, it is an interesting phenomenon in counseling that the initial problem presented at the beginning of the first session is often not the problem on which the client ultimately chooses to spend the bulk of the counseling time. The presenting problem can be a very "safe" one, one that friends and family would not laugh about if they knew that personal help was being sought, such as wanting to take a career interest inventory or needing to find some information about colleges. Such initial "needs" often serve as a smoke screen for more serious problems. The client uses this safe problem as a way of testing the counseling relationship and determining whether the counselor is to be trusted with more serious concerns. Many counseling centers that offer testing services find that the tests and inventories they offer serve to help the client safely begin the process of self-disclosing. If the relationship is comfortable, the client may talk about other concerns in addition to discussing the test results. In fact, in many instances the tests and their results are often ignored after the relationship becomes established and the real problem is disclosed.

Occasionally, a client presents a real problem that in effect is only one symptom of a greater problem. A client might complain of not having friends and want to learn ways to establish friendships, for instance. As the counseling process unfolds, the client discovers that the greater problem in establishing friendships is the fear of feeling vulnerable in close relationships. As expected, the presenting problem is usually the real issue, the one the client wants to resolve. Careful attending and accurate empathic responding will clarify this fact for both the counselor and the client.

Closing the Session

The process of closing a session begins with having a set time limit established, then giving a warning signal that the time limit is near, making closing summaries, and making arrangements for the next session.

Time Limits

Because a counseling session is a professional service, clear boundaries are necessary, an important one being the ending of the session. A session should be kept to a fairly strict time limit. A generally standard practice is a 50-minute hour for individual sessions with adults, down to 20- to 30-minute sessions with young children. Group and family counseling sessions may last from 1 ½ to 2 hours. The time limit should be clear to all concerned from the beginning of the first session. Having set a time limit, it is also important that the session be brought to a comfortable, gradual close rather than end it abruptly.

There are several reasons for maintaining a set time limit. First, 50 minutes of intense personal contact can be physically and psychologically draining on both parties. Second, if clients know that they only have a limited amount of time, they will see that the important issues are brought up. This, however, does not mean that a client will not test the established limits. It is not uncommon for a client to introduce a new but serious topic with just a few minutes left in the session. Fritz Perls (1969) once stated that the last 10 minutes of the therapeutic session often tend to be the most important. One reason for this is that the client, after struggling along with lesser feelings and thoughts, finally builds up the courage to move more deeply just as time is running out. This can become an unconscious manipulation that might force the counselor to give the client more time. Handled appropriately, it can be suggested that the new topic might be a good place to begin the next session. Counselors must be aware that both they and their time can be manipulated and that if a topic is crucial, it should surface before the end of the session. There does not seem to be any evidence that providing extra time in such cases is beneficial. What is often likely to occur if the counselor spends additional time and energy is that a pattern of extending the allotted time will become the norm in subsequent sessions. Crisis counseling cases such as working with a client who is contemplating suicide would be an exception to this format.

Warning Signal

As the end of the session draws near, it is helpful to give the client some indication of this fact, such as "We have about 10 minutes left." Within this final block of time the client can finish up a topic and not be allowed to pursue any new topics.

Closing Summaries

At the end of the session, it is helpful and instructive for the counselor to have the client give a summary of what has been learned or experienced. The counselor could initiate this by saying something like: "Since the session is almost over, I'm wondering if you could tell me what you learned or experienced as a result of our work together today." It is usually informative and interesting to hear what the client has focused on throughout the session. This is a major way of determining progress and, in effect, evaluating the session. It is also a way of helping determine what if anything might be done in the way of homework as well as providing material to be dealt with in the next session.

After the client has summarized, the counselor still has the opportunity for a final summary of the entire session. The counselor can just affirm what the client has said or add issues and decisions that the client may have overlooked.

Arranging for the Next Session

The final stage of the session is to see if the client wants to continue the relationship and to then establish the time and date. Some counselors are more direct and authoritarian in this regard, telling the client when the next appointment will be rather than negotiating it.

An open-ended approach to setting the next session and, in effect, giving greater responsibility to the client for determining when counseling will take place, would be to say something like: "Is this time and day convenient for you for our next session?" If the problem is not particularly urgent, for example, a college freshman who has a whole year to choose a major, the counselor could say something like, "Would you prefer that we meet next week or every other week?"

In crisis situations, one way of determining the client's feeling of crisis would be to say something like, "How often and when do you think we should meet?" As mentioned, the number of sessions can be established at the beginning of the first session. In all cases, counselors need to make the final determination as to dates and times based on their objective view of the problem and their schedules.

Performance Anxiety

Learning all of these skills and then trying to use them all during counseling sessions can lead some beginning counselors to experience performance anxiety—anxious feelings resulting from trying too hard to do everything perfectly. Counselors "with excessive performance anxieties are less effective because they are responding more to their own internal needs (to be helpful, competent, or liked) than they are to the client's need to be understood" (Teyber, 1988, p. 29).

Counselors can use the process of self-attending (described in chapter 2) to become aware of this performance anxiety phenomenon occurring and then can practice some of the stress management techniques (described in chapter 8) to help relieve anxiety. Taking the opportunity to practice the various skills repeatedly under supervision is the best way to be assured that you will perform with a minimum of performance anxiety in the counseling session.

SUMMARY

A detailed description has been presented of how to implement the skills presented in earlier chapters in conducting an inner-view. The emphasis here is on an initial counseling session with a concern for the physical environment and the conditions that help set the stage for a successful session. However, the process described here is applicable to subsequent sessions as well.

Counselor characteristics of particular importance during a first session include attractiveness, punctuality, and comfortable assertiveness. Personal appearance is an important factor, at least initially, becoming less of a factor as the relationship is established. Counselors should dress appropriately for the counseling settings and the clients with whom they work. They should keep appointments on time, make contact with the client physically by shaking hands, verbally through conversation, and nonverbally by establishing eye contact. These steps are part of the process of establishing rapport and beginning the development of the therapeutic alliance. The manner in which the counselor begins the session, the structure provided, including the setting of time limits, and the giving of open invitations for the client to begin talking, have been described. The counselor has been encouraged to notice and respond to the feelings and emotions the client is communicating as well as to the verbal content.

While counselors are being attentive to the verbal and nonverbal material presented by the client, they also learn to become aware of the counseling process itself. They note whether the presenting problem maintains its initial importance or whether the focus has shifted to another issue. The use of internal summaries to help keep the counselor and the client alert to the counseling process and the movement within the session has been described and encouraged.

The preparation for closing a counseling session successfully includes giving a few minutes' warning, inviting the client to note specific areas covered that were of particular importance, things learned, and perhaps actions that might be taken. The counselor then has the opportunity to make a final summary, reinforcing ideas and actions the client has offered and adding additional comments as appropriate. The arrangements for the next session (if any) are then made. The beginning counselor needs to be aware of performance anxiety in conducting a counseling session and to know how to manage such anxiety should it occur.

QUESTIONS AND ACTIVITIES

1. How is a person supposed to be able to focus on the client, attend to the counseling process, attend to one's self, and do a good job as a counselor? Which of these do you believe would cause you the most difficulty? What would you have to do to develop these particular skills?

2. In various settings, practice the skill of taking a genuine interest in another person using attending and responding skills. How easy is this for you to do? What are the consequences of this type of interaction?

3. Make an appointment to see someone for some type of help, something that you may have been putting off for some time, such as seeing a faculty advisor or going to a dentist. Upon meeting this person, be aware of the environmental setting and the characteristics of the helper, such as attractiveness, punctuality, the developing of rapport, and assertiveness. What characteristics seemed to be helpful in establishing a helping relationship and which tended to be counterproductive? Compare notes with other class members.

Professional Orientation

CHAPTER 5

The Origins and Scope of the Field of Counseling

*How did the counseling field develop
and what does it include?*

This chapter presents an overview of the development of the counseling profession. It then elaborates on the extensive nature of the current field of counseling.

ORIGINS

Counseling is both very old and quite new. The practice of one person helping another in dealing with the problems of living has been going on for centuries, usually in the form of family members, friends, or clergy assisting an individual. On the other hand, the practice of having an outsider, a professionally trained expert not necessarily affiliated with a religious institution, work with a person to resolve life's problems is a relatively recent phenomenon.

In the late 19th century, physicians like Jean Martin Charcot and Pierre Janet in France began treating mental illness with nonmedical techniques such as hypnosis. A physician named Sigmund Freud studied with Charcot but found that hypnosis was not satisfactorily treating his patients. Freud then began experimenting with what has been called a talking cure. Patients would free associate ideas and share their dreams, and then the therapist would provide his interpretations. The insights gained through this process were judged to be therapeutic. In large part, Freud's approach to therapy, called psychoanalysis, was a major factor in the development of psychiatry, the profession in which a medically trained person attains special training related to diseases of the mind.

Even though Freud's work provided a basis for working with human problems through the process of talking and the sharing of knowledge and information, psychoanalysis and psychiatry have generally had only an indirect influence in the development of the counseling profession. Many theorists influential in the development of the counseling field developed their ideas independently or in reaction to Freud rather than building directly on his work.

In the early part of the 20th century, the primary precursors of the field of counseling were the vocational guidance movement, the mental health movement, and the study of individual differences in conjunction with the development of psychometry (Whiteley, 1984). In large part, counseling developed from a nonmedical, nonpsychoanalytic point of view. The field has been subsequently influenced by a number of different movements and events, including group work, humanistic and learning theory, family therapy, and the two world wars (see Figure 5.1). The influences of these various sources of ideas, methodologies, and energy continue to make the counseling field one of the most dynamic, continuously developing forces in the human services field. As seen in the ever increasing scope of the counseling field (see Figure 5.1), counselors educated 20, 15, or even 10 years ago may have significant deficiencies when compared to counselors who have recently graduated.

The Influence of Vocational Guidance

Vocational guidance dates back to the turn of the century. The first guidance counselor was Jessie Davis, who began his service at Central High School in Detroit in 1898. The movement took hold with the work of Robert Parsons, who has been called the father of guidance. In 1908, Parsons established the Vocational Bureau of Boston to work primarily with improving the postschool placement of individuals. In 1909, Parsons published the landmark book, *Choosing a Vocation*. Subsequent developments in the vocational guidance movement are described in chapter 14.

The vocational guidance movement provided a cornerstone for the present counseling profession. In 1952, the National Vocational Guidance Association was one organization instrumental in funding the American Personnel and Guidance Association (APGA) (now the American Association for Counseling and Development). The guidance movement has been an important part of the American school system for many years. School counselors are still often referred to as guidance counselors. The Vocational Guidance Association became a subdivision of the larger association and is now known as the National Career Development Association.

The Influence of External Events

The field of counseling has been highly sensitive and responsive to national and world events, and the field has benefited in the process. For example, during the great depression the vocational guidance movement was strengthened because of the increased need for vocational information and job placement. Both World Wars I and II contributed to the development of the counseling field. Personnel needs in both wars required new and improved psychological tests and testing procedures, many of which are now fully incorporated into the counseling process. Attempts to meet the needs of disabled soldiers after World War II led to the establishment of counseling services for veterans, which included the development of group counseling procedures. Group work, however, did not make a

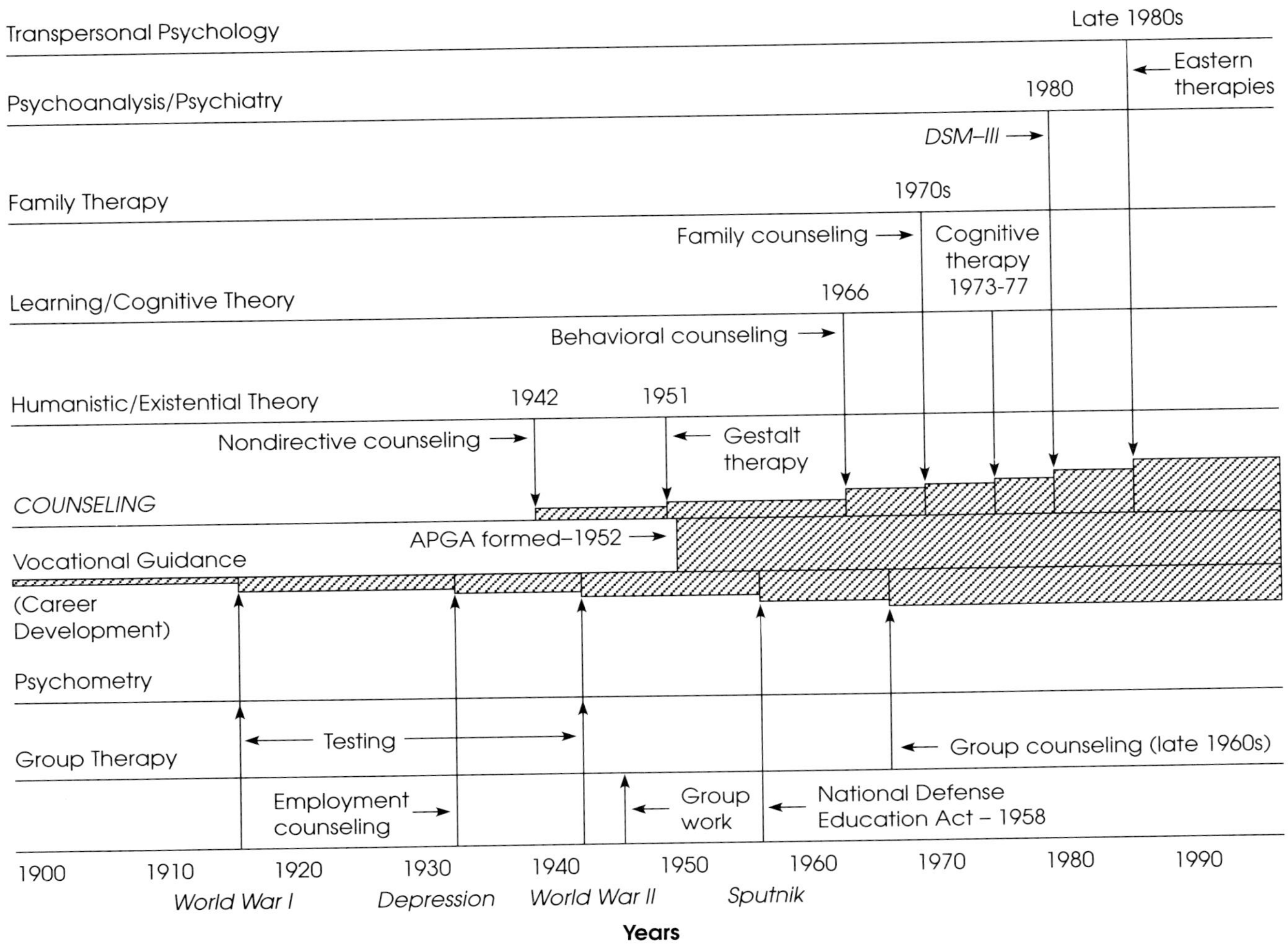

FIGURE 5.1 The Development of the Field of Counseling

Contributors to the Field of Counseling

major impact on the counseling field until the late 1960s and early 1970s. Russia's 1957 launching of the space satellite *Sputnik* led the U.S. Congress to enact the National Defense Education Act (NDEA), which significantly increased the numbers and the quality of training of school counselors.

The Influence of Theoretical Approaches

Early vocational guidance counselors were influenced by the trait factor approach, in which counselors first try to determine what characteristics or traits a person has and then try to match those factors with the specific factors required to perform certain occupations. Carl Rogers's 1942 book, *Counseling and Psychotherapy,* gave rise to a nonmedical, humanistic approach to personal counseling, with more of a focus on the client and the client's feelings than on characteristics and traits. Gestalt therapy, another humanistic approach, entered the field in the 1950s. In the 1960s, when the field of counseling experienced its greatest growth, behavioral therapy, a derivative of learning or behavioral theory, became influential. Cognitive therapy began making an increased impact in the 1970s and was often coupled with behavioral approaches to form cognitive-behavioral therapy. In the 1980s, there began to be greater influence on the field of counseling from the Eastern philosophies. These ideas, which first entered the American awareness during the 1960s, are currently encompassed by transpersonal psychology and include concern with the human spiritual side.

In terms of historical impact of theoretical conceptions on the field of counseling, the 1950s might be considered the decade of affect (and client-centered therapy); the 1960s, the decade of behaviorism (and behavior therapy); and the 1970s, the decade of cognition (and cognitive therapy) (Patterson, 1986, p. 562). The 1980s did not have a dominant theoretical influence, although transpersonal counseling, incorporating Eastern therapies did begin to make an impact.

The past decade has had more of a wholistic, eclectic emphasis, building on what had previously been developed. (Note that the spelling of wholistic is chosen deliberately to suggest a total, inclusive approach to the field.) Wholistic practitioners often incorporate much of what has been in vogue in the society, including an emphasis on health and wellness and new age ideas, such as dealing with the spiritual side of human behavior. Another dimension of the wholistic approach that was introduced in the 1970s and gained strength in the 1980s, is the systems perspective. This point of view suggests that a client does not have a problem in isolation. To help clients you have to understand the nature of the interactions they have with various aspects (systems) of their environment (see chapters 10 and 12).

Group and Family Therapy

Another major influence on counseling in the late 1960s and 1970s was group counseling. Group counseling had been used during World War II and before, but not until Carl Rogers's work with encounter groups was published in 1970 did group work become popular. Today, most theoretical approaches tend to favor working in groups rather than individual counseling if one has a choice.

Family therapy, which also had been developing after World War II, began to have an increasing impact on the counseling field in the late 1970s. The systems approach has been pursued extensively by family counselors, especially because the family is perhaps the most important system for an individual. Many counselors today will not see a client unless they are able to involve the client's family.

Psychiatry

As noted, counseling has developed without any major direct influence from the field of psychiatry; however, in recent years, psychiatry has begun to make an impact on the field of counseling. In the late 1970s and early 1980s, increased numbers of personnel trained as counselors became employed in a wide variety of community agencies. Because many mental health counselors working in agencies in which formal diagnoses are required for treatment plans and insurance payments, counselor education students must now become well-versed in the *Diagnostic and Statistical Manual, 3rd ed. revised* (DSM III–R) (American Psychiatric Association, 1987). The DSM, developed and published by the American Psychiatric Association, is now in its third revised edition, and a fourth edition is expected in the early 1990s. Mental health counselors now work with physicians, psychiatrists, and psychologists in a variety of settings to provide quality care, using the common language dictated by the DSM III–R. Because government agencies and insurance companies generally require some type of formal diagnosis before they will pay insurance claims, the use of the DSM III–R will increase.

The time-line in Figure 5.1 shows some forces that have shaped the field of counseling. Each external influence has expanded and enriched the field. What should be evident is that the field is in the process of continual development, incorporating ideas and strengths from related disciplines to become more comprehensive. Counseling is a field in which it is important to have a good overall background and to consider becoming a specialist in a given area, such as career counseling or marriage and family counseling.

This background leads to a more detailed discussion of the work of a contemporary counselor. The most common perception of a counselor is of a person talking in a one-to-one situation with a person who has a problem. This perception is ironic because not many trained counselors spend 30 to 40 hours a week seeing clients on an individual basis. Even counselors in mental health centers who practice individual counseling on a regular basis are usually limited to 20 to 25 sessions per week, a little more than half of a 40-hour week. This is not to suggest that trained counselors do not work at their jobs, but rather to indicate that the field of counseling is more complex and involved than merely working with clients one-to-one. A trained counselor may regularly provide different functions geared to a variety of goals, use a number of modalities and techniques, and serve a number of populations. The second part of this chapter describes the various functions, goals, techniques, and populations involved in the field of counseling.

THE FIELD OF COUNSELING

To describe the broad field that is open to the prospective counselor, it is helpful to use a model developed as a structural guide to the field. Morrill, Oeting, and Hurst's (1974) model of the dimensions of counseling intervention (Figure 5.2) "permits the identification and classification of a variety of counseling programs or counseling approaches and thereby serves as a means of categorizing and describing the potential activities in a variety of settings" (p. 355). The three primary dimensions described by the model are the intervention target, the purpose, and the method. Any intervention by a counselor has these three dimensions: a person or group at whom the intervention is aimed, a reason for the intervention, and a manner of carrying it out.

Target of the Intervention

Individual

Traditionally, the target of a counselor's intervention has been an individual client on a one-to-one basis. Recently there has been a growing emphasis on group counseling. To a great extent, group counseling is individual counseling within the context of a group, since there is usually no direct effort to change the group as a functional unit. Either one-to-one or in a group, the counselor's objective is to help the individual make changes as a result of new information, altered attitudes and perceptions, and the learning of new responses and skills.

Primary Group

Often the target of the counseling intervention is the primary group that most directly affects the individual. In the case of children, for example, a 5-year-old child may be seen on an individual basis; however, because the child's attitude and behavior are directly and continuously influenced by family members, it is unlikely that much lasting change can be affected without involving the members of the family as well.

> The *primary group* is the basic unit of social organization—that group (or groups) most influencing the individual. [They are] intimate, continuing personal associations on a face-to-face basis, determined by degree of intimacy rather than by proximity. (Morrill, Oeting, & Hurst, 1974, p. 356)

Families and peer groups are the basic primary groups. These groups have a significant impact on the behavior and attitudes of individuals in the group, and

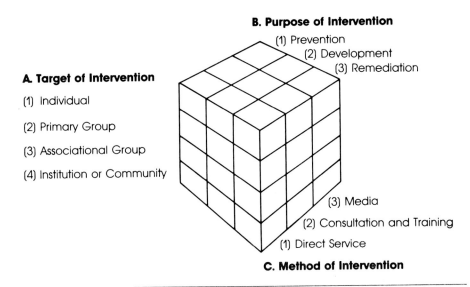

B. Purpose of Intervention
(1) Prevention
(2) Development
(3) Remediation

A. Target of Intervention

(1) Individual

(2) Primary Group

(3) Associational Group

(4) Institution or Community

(3) Media
(2) Consultation and Training
(1) Direct Service

C. Method of Intervention

FIGURE 5.2 Dimensions of Counseling Interventions (Adapted from *W. Morrill et al., "Dimensions of Counselor Functioning,"* Personnel and Guidance Journal *52 [6/ 1974]: 354–359. Reprinted by permission of American Association for Counseling and Development, publisher and copyright holder)*

vice versa. When working with primary groups, counseling interventions should include working on communication patterns and improving the interaction patterns and structural relations of the group.

Association Group

An association group is an organized group that may be based on chance or choice association. Such groups could be a social studies class, a Kiwanis Club, or a college fraternity. Members of these groups have similar interests or goals and are held together by some type of organizational structure. Possible interventions with associational groups include goal-setting and implementation strategies, developing communication skills, providing leadership training, and changing patterns of interaction.

Institution or Community

A community or institution as a target group differs from associational groups in that members are generally aware of being part of the institution or community but may rarely, if ever, attend any type of formal meetings. Neighborhoods, religious organizations, school systems, industrial concerns, cities, states, and even nations are examples of this target level. Modes of intervention could include "attempts to alter goals, communications, system linkages, power distribution, information flow, sections, and so on" (Morrill, Oeting, & Hurst, 1974, p. 357).

Purpose of the Intervention

The second major dimension presented in this model deals with the purpose of a given counseling intervention: (1) prevention of a potential problem, (2) development of skills to enhance personal abilities and potential, and (3) remediation of an existing problem. The scope of purpose presented in this dimension offers a greatly enlarged view of the purposes of counseling. Rather than being solely a reactive, remediating function, there is also ample opportunity for proactive or preventive counseling interventions to help prevent problems and to foster positive personal development.

Preventive Counseling

Prevention is concerned with identifying skills that are needed now or that may be needed in the future and providing a means for acquiring them. The intents are to anticipate future problems and to move to prevent them by providing individuals or groups with needed skills or by creating changes in the environment (Morrill, Oeting, & Hurst, 1974, p. 357).

As Albee (1977) has noted, not all of those who need care are able to obtain it, primarily for economic reasons. However, even though there are thousands of new psychotherapists being trained every year, there probably will never be enough to adequately help all of the people who need it, assuming that appropriate funding was available. Furthermore, remediation, if obtained, is not always successful. In the final analysis, the cost would be prohibitive even if such an approach was deemed desirable. Even now, the cost to society of having large numbers of people in various states of debilitation is staggering. Clearly, a different approach would seem to be necessary. It is this challenge that preventive counseling is trying to meet.

Prevention is usually proactive—initiating, anticipating, reaching out actively—and aimed at large groups of people rather than individuals, in anticipation of a debilitating life problem. Groups targeted for prevention programs are generally considered to be at risk, or susceptible to experiencing the disorder sometime in the near future. The primary objective is to present activities and programs that will prevent or at least minimize the incidence of a disorder in the population at risk (Conyne, 1983, p. 332). An example is drug abuse prevention programs for middle-school students.

Preventive programs may be offered directly by a counselor to a targeted group or they may be offered indirectly, through the use of media, for example. Much of the work that Ann Landers and Dear Abby do in the newspapers is preventive. A most important site for preventive counseling is in the schools (often under the label of guidance), where counselors provide information and organize and lead programs covering a variety of topics and approaches: sex education, communication skills, learning the skill of saying ''no,'' self-awareness, and career choice.

Well-designed premarital counseling and parenting classes for expectant parents can be very important in helping to prevent future problems, perhaps even for generations to come. In some cases, environmental or institutional changes can be designed, such as those that might be helpful in preventing trauma on the part of students as they move from middle school to high school life. Preventive approaches often put counselors in the position of being advocates for their client populations.

Developmental Counseling

Developmental counseling refers to "those programs designed to enhance the functioning and developmental potential of healthy individuals and groups" (Morrill, Oeting, & Hurst, 1974, p. 357). Developmental counseling focuses on helping clients achieve positive personal growth throughout the various stages of their lives. This could also be called life counseling. The current emphasis in this area can be noted by the recent name change of the major professional organization for counselors. The American Personnel and Guidance Association is now the American Association for Counseling and Development. Several divisions of the organization have also added the term *development* to their names (see chapter 6).

Developmental counseling involves working with children and adults who are not currently faced with a crisis or an otherwise incapacitating problem and helping them understand and know themselves better and accept themselves. The ultimate goal is to develop fully functioning, self-actualizing people.

According to Dinkmeyer & Caldwell (1970), the goals of developmental counseling for elementary school children

> are the development of self-understanding, awareness of one's potentialities, and methods of utilizing one's capacity. . . . This type of counseling, then, becomes personalized learning, not individualized teaching. The child learns not only to understand himself but to become ultimately responsible for his choices and actions. (p. 84)

The stages of individual development have been described by Piaget (1952), Havighurst (1953), Erikson (1963), Kohlberg (1971), and Sheehy (1976). Much developmental counseling takes place in schools as counselors help children prepare for and go through childhood developmental stages. Gazda (1984) has formulated an extensive development group counseling approach designed to help counselors facilitate the growth of their clients across seven basic areas of human development (cognitive, emotional, moral, ego, physical-sexual, psychological, and vocational). Recently there has been increased emphasis on providing developmental counseling services for adults. This has focused on such developmental stages as midlife and retirement (see chapter 15).

Comparison of Preventive and Developmental Counseling. Preventive and developmental counseling are similar in many ways. They are both designed for reasonably well functioning people who are not necessarily in any current psychological crisis. The processes used often tend to be proactive and educative in nature, featuring information-giving experiential activities, discussions, and homework.

Both types of counseling use similar activities and can be done individually and with groups. Preventive counseling, because it often focuses more on information giving, can be used with large groups.

Preventive counseling tends to focus more on individuals or groups identified as having or about to have problems. It also tends to be more topic- and skill-oriented, centering on topics such as drug awareness and decision-making skills. Developmental counseling deals more with prompting and encouraging positive growth for all, helping clients progress successfully through the developmental stages in their lives.

Developmental counseling works particularly well in small groups (8 to 12), which in the past may have been referred to as growth groups. On an individual basis, it might be seen as individual wellness counseling. Such counseling "is geared mainly for people who consider themselves emotionally and physically fit, yet seek to enhance their state of being. This growth-oriented approach to wellness is founded on self-responsibility. Each participant explores his or her unique path to wellness and, ultimately, peak performance" (Health and Lifestyle Center of Memorial Hospital, 1983, p. 3).

Both types of counseling can be seen as being preventive in nature. Both work to help individuals develop to their full potential and in so doing minimize the need for future counseling.

Remediation

Remediation is what most people refer to when they speak of counseling, therapy, or psychotherapy. Counseling interventions at the remediation level involve responding to an individual or group that has a felt need or problem usually involving psychological discomfort. In individuals this could include the full variety of personal, social, and vocational problems, whereas with groups it could be structural or organizational problems. The basic intervention strategy used at this level is what Pietrofesa, Hoffman, and Splete (1984) call "facilitative counseling." "Facilitative counseling is the process of helping the client to clarify a concern; then through self understanding and acceptance, to devise a plan of action and finally to act on it in a self-responsible manner" (Pietrofesa et al., 1984, p. 11). The term *facilitative counseling* describes well the process presented in the early chapters of this book.

Methods of Intervention

Basically, professional counselors can provide their various intervention strategies directly through face-to-face sessions with the client(s) or indirectly by consultation and training and the use of media. Each method is introduced here and discussed later in greater detail.

Direct Service

Traditionally, counseling services have generally been made directly to the client. A person or group immediately in distress needs the most expert skills, and any intermediary would be unsatisfactory. There are, however, limitations to the provisions of direct service in terms of cost, "both in money and in scarce professional time" (Morrill, Oeting, & Hurst, 1974, p. 358). Fees can be quite prohibitive, but even if money were no object there are not enough trained professionals to provide direct service to all in need. One inexpensive form of direct service is the telephone hotline service, available in many communities, which can help in crisis situations.

Consultation and Training

Consultation and training have become important approaches in elementary schools where trained counselors devote much of their time to consulting with and training teachers, primarily in preventive and developmental work. They also provide remediation. A major activity of many counselors in private practice is consulting with private business and industry and offering various training programs.

Media

The most indirect method of providing counseling services is through the use of media. In addition to newspaper articles and services such as Ann Landers, television and radio now offer counseling services, often as part of a talk show format such as the Donahue Show. Some radio shows encourage listeners with concerns to call in. Personal computer networks also are now dealing with personal problems, although professionally trained counselors are not necessarily involved. Here, the service would be direct, albeit generally very brief.

Packaged, programmed counseling materials on topics such as parenting are also available in workbook format, often using cassettes and film strips. Perhaps the most indirect method, but not necessarily the worst, is computer-oriented counseling. Some preliminary studies on self-help indicate that some clients would rather tell their troubles to a computer than to another human being. Counseling programs for use on home computers are available. Bibliotherapy, the use of books to help bring about therapeutic change, is perhaps the most successful example of providing counseling services by way of media. Self-help audio and videotapes are also very popular.

FURTHER DISCUSSION OF THE DIMENSIONS OF COUNSELING

The model describing the dimensions of counseling intervention presented here can be used to describe the broad scope of the counseling profession. By creatively combining the various dimensions, new and important ways of meeting the needs of our society can be provided. Also, further elaboration of each dimension provides added awareness of the breadth and depth of the field of counseling.

Target of Intervention

In 1957, the editor of the *Journal of Counseling Psychology* rejected an article on group counseling because "Counseling is a process [involving] two persons" (Morrill, Oeting, & Hurst, 1974, p. 6). As the previous description of the targets of counseling intervention indicates, the field of counseling has come a long way. Today, professionally trained counselors will as likely target their interventions toward one of the various types of groups as toward an individual. Even when the intervention is targeted toward an individual, it is highly probable that the individual may be participating in group counseling.

Individual/Group Counseling

The basic and most common form of counseling is individual. Most theoretical conceptualization and direct experience of counseling have resulted from one-to-one counseling beginning with, in large part, the work of Freud. Individual counseling still is dominant and is the basic modality used in training counselors.

A more recent phenomenon has been the expanded use of working in and with groups. Although there are a few examples of group work dating back to the early 1900s, group counseling did not really become a significant approach until the 1960s. In the 1960s there was a veritable explosion in group work ranging from systematic programs in group guidance to counseling groups designed around various theoretical approaches to sensitivity training and encounter groups.

From all of this activity has come a solid group-counseling base. One result has been that most practitioners in most major theoretical approaches emphasize and even prefer group counseling as opposed to individual counseling. Carl Rogers, with his person-centered approach, has been one of the pioneers in group work and has worked with various types of groups since the late 1960s.

Frederick Perls, the founder of Gestalt therapy, worked almost exclusively in group settings. The proponents of rational emotive, behavioral, transactional analysis, and reality therapy all emphasize the value of group work.

There are many reasons for preferring group counseling over individual counseling, including:

1. Cost: clients are charged less in a group than for individual sessions.
2. Practice: clients are able to try out new ideas and behaviors with a number of people in the group and receive immediate feedback.
3. Vicarious learning: there are more people to serve as models.
4. Efficiency: the counselor is able to serve more clients.
5. Universality: the client does not feel so alone with his problems. He may find others with the same, similar or even worse problems. (Yalom, 1975)

Individual counseling is more flexible to schedule and is preferred by some clients who do not want to compete with others for therapists' time as well as by clients who would not feel comfortable sharing their problems with others.

However, both types of counseling will continue to prosper because of their specialized features. Chapter 12 contains extended coverage of group counseling.

Family Counseling

A specialized type of group counseling, family counseling, came into its own in the 1970s. Developing from a number of different sources (Ackerman, 1966; Haley, 1971; Minuchin, 1974; Satir, 1967; Watzlawick, 1966), family counseling has emerged as one of the most powerful approaches to counseling. This is largely because, as indicated above, the family is seen as a primary group (see Figure 5.2).

A major drawback of both individual and group counseling is that clients may change their behavior, but when they return to the family, the family members may not be willing or able to accept the change. Clients may actually be forced back to their old behavior. Also, in many cases changes on the part of other family members, or in family structural or communication patterns, may be necessary to bring about changes in individual family members. See chapter 13 for extended coverage of family counseling.

Marriage Counseling

Marriage counseling can be seen as a specialized form of family counseling. Typically the husband and wife are seen together by the counselor in marriage counseling, although some counselors may also see each spouse individually as part of the process. Sometimes members of the expanded family may also be brought in if deemed appropriate by marriage counselors. Merle Ohlsen (1979) has developed a model for working with married couples in groups. A group generally consists of three or four couples.

Peer Group Counseling

Peer group counseling is a type of primary group counseling that is particularly helpful in working with adolescents. For many young people, the primary group shifts from the family to the peer group in early adolescence. At this point the peer group often has more influence than the family on the attitudes and behavior of the adolescent. Peer group counseling is often used in high school settings, in detention homes, and with young people on probation. Much of the work done with these groups may be remedial, but a significant amount of work may be preventive and developmental.

Another form of peer group counseling includes self-help groups such as Alcoholics Anonymous and Overeaters Anonymous. These groups typically consist of people with similar problems who gather together to help each other and themselves. Typically, no outsider serves as a counselor or leader.

Associational Groups

Counselor interventions with associational groups such as classes, clubs, and fraternities are primarily preventive and developmental, although there may be occasions when an organization or group may have difficulties significant enough to require remediation. Much of the work done at this level involves short workshops or longer term seminars centering on concepts such as human relations training, developing communication skills, leadership training, and organizational development.

Much work at this level is being conducted by professionals who are specifically trained in organizational development as opposed to having their primary training in counseling. In either case the specific intervention used may be similar or even identical. Large corporations often have professionals on staff who can provide preventive and developmental services to various subgroups within the organization.

Institution or Community

In working with the larger institution or community, the interventions are again generally preventive or developmental. As the groups become larger, it becomes increasingly difficult to use remediation approaches.

Most interventions described in relation to associational groups apply here. Again there is a great deal of emphasis on organizational development on an even broader basis. Community counseling has, in the last decade, become a major area of counselor activity. Much of the work here is concerned with implementation of services, interaction of the various community service agencies, short- and long-term planning, and research and evaluation.

Purpose of the Intervention

One way to describe the purposes of the various types of intervention is to use a continuum of psychological helping relationships ranging from guidance to training to therapy (see Table 5.1).

It should be noted from the outset that there are three basic intervention purposes: prevention, development, and remediation. These purposes are not distinct entities. As Table 5.1 illustrates, there is much overlap both in terms of process and content. Much developmental counseling is by its nature preventive, and if remediation is successful, future problems related to the target problem should be prevented.

Nevertheless, Table 5.1 offers a variety of ways to differentiate among the purposes of intervention. The left, or preventive, side of the continuum is mostly teaching/training; the right side is oriented more to therapy and treatment. From clients' points of view, however, if they are actively involved at any point along the continuum, they are learning about themselves and how to cope with life's problems. Fundamentally all interventions involve a teaching/learning component, and this component tends to function more effectively when a positive helping relationship has been established.

On the remediation side of the continuum, the terms *counseling* and *psychotherapy* are used. Over the years there has been extensive discussion regarding the differences between counseling and psychotherapy, and whether, in fact there *are* any differences. Patterson (1974), for one, has steadfastly maintained that the basic processes are similar, if not the same. A generally accepted difference between counseling and psychotherapy suggests that psychotherapists tend to have had a longer training period. They usually have a doctorate either in psychology or in medicine specializing in psychiatry, and as a result, they tend to deal with the more severe problems, particularly those requiring long-term therapy.

In actual practice, however, those distinctions have not always been maintained. Counselors and social workers may work with severely disturbed people, clients who often manifest dangerous pathological behavior. Psychologists and psychiatrists may devote professional time working with the so-called normal population. In either case, the actual techniques and therapies used may not vary much. The only area in which there is a clear differentiation in duties involves treatments that call for medication—only the psychiatrist can legally prescribe medications.

The purposes or goals of intervention on this continuum, then, are to help the person acquire knowledge and skills that will prevent future problems, to develop all aspects of the person's potential, and to teach needed coping skills. Although to some extent these appear to be distinct and separate purposes, the client and the counselor, in the process of working on any one of these goals, may serendipitously end up attaining secondary, perhaps unstated or even unrecognized, goals in one or both of the other areas.

Methods of Intervention

As indicated in Figure 5.2, the three primary methods of counseling are direct service, consultation and training, and media. Some elaboration of the scope of these methods follows.

Direct Service

Direct service in the counseling field has been characterized primarily by what might be called "talk therapy," where both the client and the counselor talk to each other and presumably listen as well. Chapters 10 and 11 describe basic theoretical approaches in counseling. In essence, these are all various forms of talking therapies even though their theoretical framework may vary significantly.

Over the years, a number of other direct-service modes have been developed. Even though the term *therapy* is often used in conjunction with these approaches, they generally are not able to meet many of the requirements of a complete theory of counseling as described in chapter 10. These modalities, therefore, are often used as an adjunct to a talk theory (e.g., combining art therapy with Gestalt therapy). Presented here is a partial listing of therapeutic modalities currently available. Special training, in many cases including an advanced degree, is appropriate for most of the following approaches.

TABLE 5.1 A Continuum of Psychological Helping Relationships

	Prevention	*Developmental*	*Remediation*
Descriptive Titles	Guidance Preventive counseling Training Teaching (subject matter instruction)	Developmental counseling Human relations training Organizational development groups T groups	Counseling Facilitative counseling Crisis counseling	Psychotherapy Therapy
Goals	To develop awareness: skill-building	To develop human potential	To develop client self-responsibility and commitment	To increase coping, change attitudes, behaviors
Time Orientation	Present (here and now)	Present	Present	Past, present, future
Time-Lines	Specific time span	Continuous (over life span)	Varies (short- to long-term)	Varies (could be brief, but more likely several months to several years)
Setting	Almost anyplace	Education, business, religion	Generally clinical—could be in other settings (e.g., milieu counseling)	Clinical

Activities of Counselor	Model, teach, information-giving, referral to other agencies	Aiding value clarification Teaching decision making	Attending, understanding, confronting, decision-making skills	Attending, understanding, confronting, decision-making skills
Clientele	Anyone	Anyone	"Normals"	Persons deficient in coping; disturbed or disturbing behavior
Possible Concerns	Drug awareness, self- and career awareness, sex education	Developing self-concept in elementary school Midcareer change Retirement planning Acceptance of death and dying	Educational, vocational Personal, emotional, and interpersonal problems Rehabilitation	Severe emotional and personality disorders

Art Therapy.   The use of various art media to help clients express themselves. Often thoughts and feelings that cannot be easily expressed verbally emerge when a client is able to work freely with art techniques.

Music Therapy.   Playing, singing, and listening to music can all be very evocative and can be used to help a client work through problems.

Body Therapies.   These include bioenergetics, dance therapy, and different types of massage. The muscles and tissues of the body, as well as the mind, remember things that happened to the person. Often deep-seated emotions can be expressed through the use of various physical activities.

Hypnotherapy.   Hypnosis has been used in the treatment of specific behaviors such as smoking cessation and weight-loss programs.

Phototherapy.   The use of phototherapy, both the taking of new pictures and the reviewing of old family pictures, can be a valuable adjunct to a number of theoretical approaches. The photos become a stimulus for communication during the counseling process.

Psychodrama.   A specialized structured approach used with a group in which a client uses other group members to work through family issues in the form of a play or skit.

Milieu Therapy.   The use of the client's natural setting to conduct counseling (e.g., counseling a teenager while shooting baskets on a playground).

Consultation and Training

Consultation and training may involve direct or indirect services depending on the targeted population. An example of an indirect service is a counselor consulting with teachers on the best way to present a drug abuse program to primary grade school children. A direct service would be providing a workshop on stress management techniques to office managers.

Consultation and training activities tend to be primarily preventive and/or developmental in nature. Usually, the consultant comes in response to a felt need on the part of the client. Occasionally, training programs in particular may be required of employees by their superiors.

Consultation usually consists of a one-to-one or a group relationship over a period of time. The initial meeting centers on goals and objectives to be attained, and subsequent meetings focus on the completion of those objectives.

Training generally involves providing skill-development opportunities to adults in a variety of personal and interpersonal areas. A major organization (American Society of Training and Development—ASTD) publishes journals and offers its own training programs for the training of trainers. Other nonuniversity organizations such as the National Training Laboratory (NTL) offer training and certification for trainers.

Training is usually offered in two basic formats: seminars and workshops.

Seminars.   Seminars are generally designed to be relatively small in size (18 to 20 people) so that there can be a significant degree of interaction between the counselor/trainer and each participant. They are usually scheduled for relatively long periods of time—one week or four weekends, for example.

Workshops.   Workshops are generally designed to work with small to large groups of people with little or no direct interaction by the counselor/trainer with individual participants. They are usually scheduled for short periods of time— one day, one weekend.

The key term in the area of training is *organizational development* (see chapter 7). Whether it is a government agency, a church, a school, or a business, it is likely that the organization will have any of a variety of organizational problems that may restrict its effectiveness and productivity. Many businesses and agencies are employing their own in-house organizational development experts to provide regular training services to their employees.

Media

As a vehicle of indirect counseling services, the various media provide valuable resources with which to help people. Most newspapers have daily columns geared to helping people cope with personal problems. Increasingly, counselors are appearing on radio and television shows speaking directly to problems of personal living. Other counselors give lectures and presentations to PTOs and service clubs as well as to the community at large. Others write books and produce audio and videotapes that provide valuable help for many people.

Application of the Field of Counseling Model

Three examples illustrating how the field of counseling model can be used with different applications of counseling techniques and theory are described briefly.

A program designed to train Navaho paraprofessionals to work with the developmental tasks of children and parents on a Navaho reservation fits the model as follows (see Figure 5.3): The target of the intervention was the family or primary group, the purpose of the intervention was developmental, and the methods of intervention by the professionals were consultation and training (Dinges, Yazzie, & Tollefson, 1974).

Crookston (1974) has proposed a design for an "intentional democratic community" (p. 382) to be developed for use in college residence halls. In this example, the counselor would work with an associational group (the members of the residence hall), providing a direct service in terms of group leadership, and

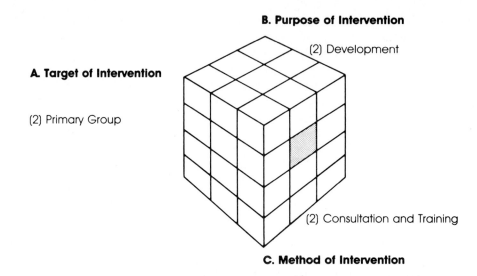

B. Purpose of Intervention

(2) Development

A. Target of Intervention

(2) Primary Group

(2) Consultation and Training

C. Method of Intervention

FIGURE 5.3   Sector or Counselor Functioning Cube Employed in Developmental Intervention for Navajo Family Mental Health *(N. Dinges et al., "Developmental Intervention for Navajo Mental Health," Personnel and Guidance Journal 52 [6/1974]: 390–395. Reprinted by permission of American Association for Counseling and Development, publisher and copyright holder)*

the purpose would be developmental, to help the residents become a community (see Figure 5.4).

Johnston (1974) created a college-level sex education program to help students deal with issues of sexuality and birth control (see Figure 5.5). Some direct service was offered in the way of lectures, and consultation and training were offered to develop discussion leaders and train a peer counselor. The overall purpose of the program was to prevent unwanted pregnancies and other sexual problems. Individuals desiring such help were the targets of the intervention.

SUMMARY

The origins and development of the field of counseling have been described, noting the field's direct roots in the vocational guidance movement of the early 20th century and how and when other external influences have contributed to and expanded the field.

A three-dimensional model has been presented to demonstrate the broad scope of intervention activities in which a trained counselor may become involved. The field of counseling presented incorporates three different dimensions: the target of the counselor's intervention, the purpose of the intervention, and the method of intervention.

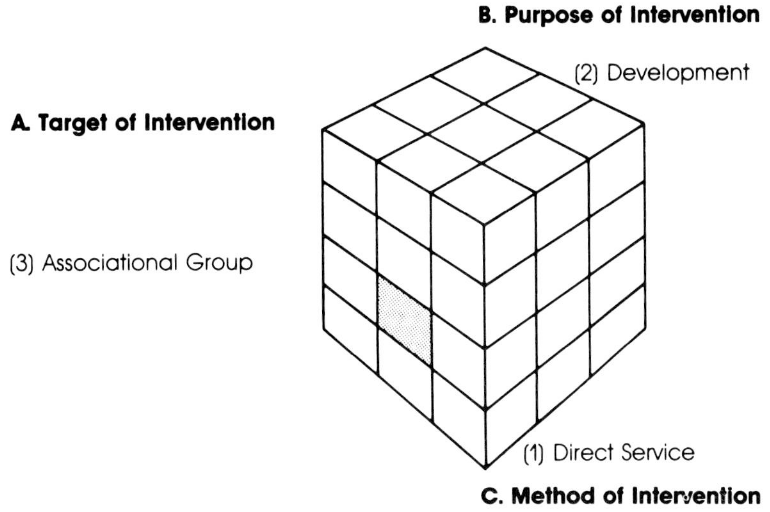

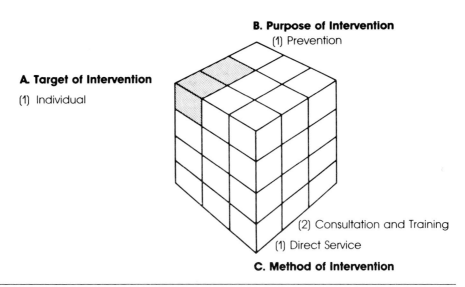

FIGURE 5.4 Sector of Counselor Functioning Cube Employed in Developing a Democratic Community in a College Residence Hall *(B. Crookston, "The Intentional Democratic Community in College Residence Halls,"* Personnel and Guidance Journal *52 [6/1974]: 382–389. Reprinted by permission of American Association for Counseling and Development, publisher and copyright holder)*

FIGURE 5.5 Sectors of Counselor Functioning Cube Employed in a Sexuality and Birth Control Outreach Program *(C. Johnston, "Sexuality and Birth Control: Impact of Outreach Programming,"* Personnel and Guidance Journal *52 [6/1974]: 406–411. Reprinted by permission of American Association for Counseling and Development, publisher and copyright holder)*

The target of the intervention includes (1) individuals, working in an one-to-one setting or in group settings; (2) primary groups such as family and peer groups; (3) association groups such as classes or fraternal clubs; and (4) institutions or communities.

The purposes of interventions include prevention, development, and remediation. Prevention interventions emphasize the anticipation of future problems and provide the information and skill training necessary to prevent the occurrence of problems. Developmental counseling takes into consideration all the developmental stages human beings go through during a lifetime and helps provide the training, knowledge, and support necessary to help people successfully encounter the various stages of life. The similarities among and differences between preventive and developmental interventions as well as between counseling and psychotherapy have been described.

Remediation is the providing of services to clients with specific problems, commonly referred to as counseling, therapy, or psychotherapy. The facilitative counseling responses described in chapters 2 through 4 of this book are illustrative of the specific interventions that occur as part of remediation.

The methods of intervention by which counselors provide their service include direct and indirect service. Direct service involves meeting with individuals or groups who have specific, immediate needs. A variety of different approaches may be used to provide direct services, including a broad spectrum of techniques such as art and music therapy. Radio and television call-in shows in which listeners can attain immediate responses to personal problems are another form of direct service. Direct service usually applies to remediation cases. Indirect services include consultation and training for individuals or groups who have more long-term needs, as in the areas of preventive and developmental work. Indirect services also include conducting workshops and seminars and working through the print and broadcast media. Packaged programmed materials in the form of books and audio- and videotapes also are available in most stores.

QUESTIONS AND ACTIVITIES

1. Much of the growth and development of counseling has come as a result of events outside of the field (e.g., World Wars I and II). What current events or forces in our society are you aware of that might eventually have an impact on the field of counseling? In what ways might you predict that the field will be affected?

2. As you think of your goals in the counseling field at this time, where on the cube (Figure 5.2) do your interests fit? What part(s) of the cube would have best represented your interests before entering this course?

3. List all the examples of counseling interventions provided in the media in your community, such as radio and television talk shows and newspaper advice columns. What is the quality of these interventions? What ethical problems are posed by these interventions?

CHAPTER 6

_____ *FOCUS ON* _____

A Career in the Helping Professions

What can I do with a counseling degree?

One major change in recent years in the field of counseling has been a change in emphasis of most colleges that offer master's degrees in counseling. Prior to the mid-1970s, the emphasis in most counselor education programs was primarily on the training of elementary and secondary school counselors. Throughout the 1980s, counselor education programs changed by adding direct training and often specialization in such areas as community counseling and marriage and family counseling (Hollis & Wantz, 1986).

With this shift in the nature and scope of counselor education, more counselor education students are choosing fields other than school counseling. This means that virtually all agencies and institutions that provide mental health services are potential sources of employment for counselor education graduates. Also, because counselor graduates tend to have strong backgrounds in human relationships and communication skills, they are often employed in business and industry in personnel, training, and development settings.

This change of emphasis from a specialization in school counseling to more generic training as a helping professional has been a quiet one not yet fully appreciated by professionals within the mental health field, much less by laypersons. Many people still think of a counselor as a school counselor rather than as a mental health counselor. The title *mental health counselor* was not included in the *1980 Dictionary of Occupational Titles,* and yet, in 1985, the Association of Mental Health Counselors was the largest subdivision in the American Association for Counseling and Development.

THE MENTAL HEALTH FIELD HIERARCHY

Within the mental health field is a hierarchy that is generally based on the academic degree and the length of training involved. This hierarchy is supported by government and insurance company policies. The hierarchy is headed by psychiatrists, followed by clinical psychologists, counseling psychologists, social workers, and counselors. Within the classification of counseling are a large number of specialties. These include career planning and placement counselors, marriage and family counselors, mental health counselors, pastoral counselors, employment counselors, nurse counselors, vocational rehabilitation counselors, school counselors, and substance abuse counselors. There are also specialists who work in areas such as probation, personnel, and training and development. At the bottom of the hierarchy are paraprofessionals, who have had a minimum of training, but who may work at positions such as serving on a suicide prevention switchboard.

Psychiatrists generally have the greatest amount of training; they are physicians who have specialized in the diagnosis and treatment of mental disorders. A psychoanalyst is, with a few exceptions, a psychiatrist who treats mental disorders using the ideas and approaches developed by Sigmund Freud.

Clinical and counseling psychologists usually have doctorates. All states now regulate the title of *psychologist* with the general stipulation that anyone using that title has to complete a licensure process successfully. In past years in some states, it was possible to qualify as a psychologist with a master's degree in psychology or a related field, but that is rarely the case now. Membership in the American Psychological Association (APA) is now limited only to holders of doctoral degrees in psychology. The differences between a clinical and a counseling psychologist are few. Both generally require the doctorate and an APA-accredited training program. There may be some differences in courses taken or internships completed. In practice, clinical psychologists often deal with the more serious mental and emotional disorders, but not necessarily exclusively.

Social workers usually have a two-year master's degree (MSW). They often serve as caseworkers, taking more direct action than a counselor or psychologist might take to alleviate or eliminate a client's problem.

Much distinctiveness of each group is not in the exclusive nature of what they do but is based more on political and economic considerations in terms of various agency, governmental, or insurance company regulations. For example, state regulations may require that certain human service functions at a nursing home be performed only by someone with an MSW. Insurance companies and the government play a major role in the maintenance of this hierarchy through their decisions as to which professionals may receive third-party payments (insurance or Medicaid payments for professional services). Psychiatrists generally qualify for all insurance carriers that provide mental health coverages, and clinical and counseling psychologists qualify in some instances. In many cases, psychologists, social workers, and counselors may be reimbursed for their services by a third party (government or insurance company) if their work is authorized and verified by a psychiatrist or a physician. There is currently a significant amount of lobbying going on at all levels on the part of psychologists, social workers, and counselors to have insurance companies and the government provide payment to all professionals who are qualified to provide mental health services.

CREDENTIALING

A major trend in the counseling field in the last decade has been the movement toward credentialing of professional counselors. This movement, while not universally accepted as necessary or even desirable, will in the long run do much to enhance the credibility of counselors. This will be noticeable particularly in terms of providing the professional identification necessary for being accepted for employment by other helping professionals and to place counselors in a better position to be eligible recipients of third-party payments from government agencies and insurance companies. There is, however, no evidence that licensure and certification result in more effective counselors. What is perhaps most important is that with this credentialing movement there are now mechanisms for at least assuring some minimum quality standards that should be of value in protecting the public interest.

Credentialing activities include licensure, certification, educational program accreditation, and the accreditation of counseling service agencies. Each of these services is defined and described separately.

Licensure

The licensure of professionals in any field is a state prerogative. Toward the end of the 1970s, a number of states began to pass legislation that led to the licensing of people deemed qualified to be named counselors. In most states at the present time there is little legal restriction on the use of the term. Many people in other fields such as sales use the term *counselor* in titles such as insurance counselor, financial counselor, and fashion counselor. In an attempt to separate the professionally trained mental health counselor from people who use the title indiscriminately, professionals in the field have lobbied their state legislators to develop a set of criteria and procedures for licensing counselors. States may have very specific legislation governing specific specialties within the field such as school counselors, alcohol and drug abuse counselors, and marriage and family counselors.

A major problem in developing licensure standards and procedures for mental health counselors is that there often is much resistance generated by other professionals, including psychologists, psychiatrists, and social workers, who view the licensing of counselors as direct threats to their territory. When the actual job descriptions and functions of a counselor are clearly detailed in a legislative bill, the results come perilously close to describing what psychologists, social workers, and psychiatrists do. Licensing of counselors, then, is seen as a threat to the livelihood of these other professionals.

Nevertheless, by 1986, 18 states had passed licensure legislation, and by 1990, counselors could attain professional licenses in 32 states. Licensure bills are now under consideration in most other states. It seems that although the process is very slow, eventually all states will have some form of licensure law for counselors. State licensure may or may not be reciprocal depending on the given laws.

Certification

Even though the prerogative to license belongs to the state, professional organizations can develop standards and procedures to certify professionals. Beginning in the late 1970s, the major professional organization for counselors, the American Association for Counseling and Development (AACD), led by one of its subdivisions, the American Mental Health Counselors Association (AMHCA), began the development of a national counselor certification procedure. While AMHCA was developing standards and procedures specifically for the certification of mental health counselors, the parent organization was developing a more global certification process.

There are now at least four ways that a professional counselor may be certified by the AACD, with various degrees of rigor required. The AACD offers the Nationally Certified Counselor (NCC), which requires an approved educational background and experience plus a written examination. The AMHCA offers the designation of Certified Clinical Mental Health Counselor (CCMHC), which also requires approved training and experience, a written examination, and the submission of a counseling work sample. The Commission on Rehabilitation Counselor Certification certifies rehabilitation counselors (CRCs), and a counselor may also attain certification as a Nationally Certified Career Counselor (NCCC). Certification may also be attained through meeting the requirements of other organizations such as the American Association of Marriage and Family Therapists (AAMFT).

Five benefits of certification (Messina, 1985; Stone, 1985) are:

1. *Professional identity.* Certification as an NCC identifies the individual as a professionally certified counselor and a distinctive professional within the mental health field; certification as a CCMHC, CRC, or NCC indicates that the individual is a specialist within the counseling profession.
2. *Visibility.* Certified counselors are listed in registers that are made available to mental health centers and to consumer, insurance, and medical organizations.
3. *Credibility.* Certification procedures are consistent with established national guidelines and are backed by an organization with a code of ethics and procedures for handling consumer ethical complaints.
4. *Flexibility.* Certification is considered to be of value to counselors who will be able to take the certification across state lines if they should move.

5. *Continued professional growth.* Because of recertification requirements, the skills of certified counselors will be kept current in order to better serve the consumer.

Accreditation

The accreditation of counselor training programs by professional organizations is another trend that developed in the 1970s. In the accreditation process, professional organizations establish standards for training professionals and then evaluate training institutions against the standards. Institutions that meet or exceed the standards are determined to be accredited. Students graduating from accredited institutions may receive benefits not given graduates of unaccredited schools, may be exempt from certain certification or licensure requirements, and perhaps are more employable.

The Association for Counselor Education and Supervision, a division of AACD, has developed an accreditation process for counselor education programs. This accreditation process is regulated by the Council for Accreditation of Counseling and Related Educational Programs (CACREP). CACREP evaluates school counseling, community counseling, and student personnel programs at the master's degree level and the doctor's degree in education programs. Numerous universities have gone through the accreditation process and are now accredited as approved counselor education programs. Beginning in 1985, students from nonaccredited programs had to have two years of approved experience after the completion of their degree before they could apply for certification as an NCC.

As seen from the description above, there is a link between the accreditation regulations and certification because essentially the same organization is determining the standards and procedures for both. Certification is easier to attain by students who are graduates of an accredited program. This link has been criticized as leading to programs that will be relatively static and noncreative. On the other hand, others argue that to be recognized as professionals it is important that accredited programs maintain and set standards and that certified practitioners are able to demonstrate adherence to those standards.

There is reason to believe that the overall trend of counselor licensure and certification will continue and that the levels of qualification will continue to be increasingly demanding. The general rule of thumb for a person entering the field is to apply for licensure or certification at the earliest possible time. Waiting even as much as one year may mean having to meet additional requirements.

Counseling Services Accreditation

The practice of certifying counseling centers and agencies dates back to 1962, but it gained momentum as the related credentialing activities have developed. The International Association of Counseling Services (IACS), a corporate affiliate of AACD, accredits community, junior, and technical college counseling centers, public and private counseling agencies, and university and college counseling centers in the United States and Canada. The basic purposes of certification efforts, conducted on a voluntary basis, are encouraging and assisting counseling service facilities to meet high professional standards, informing the public about competent and reliable services, and fostering communications among counseling services operating in a variety of settings (McDonough, 1985, p. 4).

For counseling practitioners to be considered professionals, the day may not be far off, as McDonough (1985) suggests, when they will need to be members of a professional organization such as AACD, be graduates of an accredited program, be licensed or certified, and also work in an approved counseling center or agency.

Continuing Education

As the counseling profession continues to develop, it becomes increasingly necessary for counselors to continue to pursue their educational training. Though most master's level counselor training programs are approximately 2 years long, programs cannot provide the depth of training and experience necessary for work in the many specialized areas of the field. Many students go on to pursue doctoral programs, generally in counselor education, counseling, or clinical psychology; others pursue specialized forms of training at one or more of a variety of private, nonuniversity institutes, such as one of the Gestalt Institutes, the Reality Therapy Institute, and the Adler Institute. Many of these training programs last approximately 2 years but are often offered in a way that will accommodate the schedule of a working professional; for example, they will meet for 2 weeks every 6 months with weekend meetings in between.

Continuing education on a regular basis is generally a requirement for maintaining a license or certificate. Such continuing education can usually be met in a variety of ways. Continuing Education Units (CEUs) can be earned by attending professional workshops, seminars, conferences, and conventions. Such opportunities are offered by universities, professional organizations, community agencies, and independent entrepreneurs at times and locations generally convenient to most professionals.

Professional conventions are held locally, statewide, regionally, and nationally. Often professional development institutes and seminars are offered in conjunction with major conventions. Continuing education not only meets certification and licensure requirements, but also has the potential of being tax deductible.

Reading professional journals is a common and inexpensive way to continue one's education. Such reading is an excellent way to keep up with the most current developments in the field. Books are also a vital way to keep up with the field, providing greater depth to a given topic. Even though CEUs are not given for reading journal articles and books, many employers expect their helping professionals to read one or more monthly journals on a regular basis and several books a year that are related to the field.

THE MARKET FOR COUNSELORS

Making predictions about the prospect of employment for trained counselors in either the near or distant future is risky at best. Nonetheless, it is a concern that every prospective counselor has, and it needs to be addressed directly.

Economic and Social Trends

There are basic trends in our society that are clearly evident and speak to this issue. There is a major trend in our economy in the direction of an increase in the service occupations and the information services in particular. John Naisbitt, in his book, *Megatrends* (1984), sees professionals such as group counselors, teachers, and social workers as being primarily information workers where knowledge is crucial and "the creation, processing and distribution of information is the job" (p. 5).

In 1950, only about 17 percent of Americans were employed in information jobs. In 1984, more than 65 percent were information workers. "In 1960 the approximately 7.5 million professional workers were the fifth largest job category and employed about 11 percent of the workforce. By 1981 that group had more than doubled to 16.4 million workers and made up almost 17 percent of the overall workforce (and almost half of those are women)" (Naisbitt, 1984, pp. 5–6).

This trend is expected to continue into the next century, according to the United States Department of Labor. Employment in the services sector of the U.S. economy is expected to rise 34 percent, making this sector the fastest growing of all the industry divisions. Specifically, within this sector, the Department of Labor has projected a demand for personnel trained in fields related to counseling to grow from 14 to 24 percent through the 1990s (U.S. Dept. of Labor, 1988). An exception to this trend may be in the area of private practice.

A second major social trend that may account for some of the increased need for counseling services is the changing nature of the family. The pattern of an extended family living together or in close proximity is experienced by only a small proportion of the U.S. population. At the other extreme, 25 percent of the households counted in the 1980 census are single-person families. Increasing numbers of individuals are living alone. A related trend is the ever-increasing number of single-parent families. This trend toward more isolation and alienation is a factor that often results in a need for the services of counselors and other helping professionals.

The range of human services now offered by business and industry constitutes a third major trend. Business and industry have made a strong commitment to human resource development, learning in large part from the success of the Japanese. Most changes involve greater employee involvement in decision making as well as in other aspects of corporate life. Helping both employers and employees function effectively in the work environment is a task handled capably by ever-increasing numbers of counselors who have specialized in human relations development and organizational development.

Business and Industry

In the past, counseling graduates have been employed in business and industry in personnel departments, engaged primarily in hiring and firing employees and in solving labor disputes. In recent years, the scope of such departments has changed. Now, personnel or human resource departments may offer career development services, Employee Assistance Programs, team-building workshops, and leaders for Quality Circles and may provide direction for Quality Work Life programs. The targets of these services are not only the assembly line employees, but all employees, starting with the company president.

Borrowing a term from the counseling field, Naisbitt, in *Megatrends* (1984) describes *"the new [business] leader [as] a facilitator, not an order giver"* (p. 209; Naisbitt's emphasis). The overall philosophy now in what amounts to greater participatory democracy in the business world is that "if you can develop the skills of facilitating people's involvement in decision-making processes, you can become a very effective leader in your community and in your work" (p. 209).

Another concern is with the quality of work life (QWL). Many companies employ trained personnel, often with master's degrees in counseling, to develop employee leadership and participatory skills as well as organizational structure. One approach in many companies involves Quality Circles, where workers meet regularly in small groups to discuss all aspects of a company's activities and operations, often resulting in changes of company policies and practices.

Employee Assistance Programs (EAPs) are another example of business and industrial involvement with the field of counseling. Troubled employees are more of a liability than an asset in the workplace; however, employers have discovered that in many cases it is better to offer help to such employees, rather than fire them and have to hire and train new personnel. Therefore, employers are contracting with developers of formal programs designed to help employees resolve their problems without having their work affected and before physical and/or psychological debilitation occurs. Such programs employ a number of people trained in counseling.

In general, then, the world of business and industry has become more open to the knowledge, skills, and abilities of professionally trained counselors. Even though employment in this sector is subject to fluctuations in the economy, the value of human resource development personnel is increasingly acknowledged, and such employees are not as likely to be the immediate victims of economic declines as has often been the practice.

Community Opportunities

A great number of potential employers of counselors exist in each community. Most human service agencies, whether public or private, are prospective employers. Such agencies include publicly supported mental health centers, counseling centers supported by religious institutions, vocational rehabilitation and employment counseling agencies, hospitals, youth service bureaus, hospice organizations, correctional institutions, mental health societies, Planned Parenthood, the American Cancer Society, and welfare departments.

In most areas, the local mental health center is one of the largest potential employers. Community mental health centers were developed in the early and mid-1960s and were supported in large part by the federal government. When federal funding was reduced in the late 1970s, these agencies had to become aggressive in developing programs that would be self-sustaining. Thus, health service providers had to be able to qualify for insurance payments. Because mental health counselors have only recently been able to qualify for such coverage, and even now on a limited basis, the market for master's level counselors has been restricted.

The opportunities for employment in other community social service agencies depend on a number of factors. First, governmental regulations may regulate the employment of counselors (e.g., certain positions in nursing homes may be filled only by candidates with an MSW). Second, because of insurance company limitations, some agencies will employ only professionals who can be reimbursed directly by third parties. Third, the influence of the hierarchical order is often felt, in which psychologists will often try to employ only psychologists and social workers will hire only other social workers. The professionally trained counselor does have to develop a great deal of credibility when relating to other professionals.

These barriers, however, are increasingly being broken down. Initially, this happens in areas in which professional counselors receive their education and their work becomes known. Also, as counselor licensure and national counselor certification gain increasing acceptance, the process will be accelerated. A recent survey of mental health counselors found that counselors were being successful in collecting third-party reimbursements (Kegan, 1987).

Bills have been introduced into Congress to make it legal for certified counselors to receive third-party payments from governmental sources such as Medicare and Medicaid. CHAMPUS, a federal government insurance program, has recently approved all certified clinical mental health counselors (CCMHC) for third-party payments.

Because of the variety of community service agencies it is difficult to enumerate all of the types of employment that are or will become available to certified counselors. A partial listing of community positions includes caseworkers, mental health counselors, substance abuse counselors, probation officers, and nurse-counselors.

Overall, counseling opportunities in community agencies provide an excellent source of further employment for the professional counselor. Because the field is new and relatively wide open, counseling students doing practica and internships at various community agencies are often able to help create new positions and even be hired to fill them.

Wholistic Health/Wellness

Mental health service providers have been pursuing a major new movement in the direction of more outreach work, particularly in the area of prevention. Most of this work has been done under the label of wholistic health/wellness. The wholistic health movement dates back to the concerns over nutrition and exercise in the 1960s and 1970s. "Wholistic health means dealing with the body, mind and emotions as a whole" (Naisbitt, 1984, p. 150). This movement is considered part of one of the megatrends described by Naisbitt—that of moving from institutional help to self-help. In this case the movement is away from reliance on the medical establishment. The new paradigm of wellness emphasizes preventive medicine and wholistic care: care for the whole person as opposed to the medical model that involves drugs, surgery, and the treatment of specific symptoms (Naisbitt, 1984, p. 147). A major element in the wholistic health movement has been a redefinition of health from being "the mere absence of disease to the existence of a positive state of wellness in the [total] person" (p. 150). Wholistic/wellness concepts have become an integral part of the wholistic approach to counseling and psychotherapy (see chapter 11).

Institutional help to increase personal responsibility for one's own health (self-help) is a major focus of many corporations. Firms such as Pepsico, Exxon, and Johnson & Johnson promote disease prevention and personal wellness with their own in-house fitness centers.

Community mental health centers have been increasing their number of outreach programs, offering programs in areas such as nutrition and aerobics. They have been joined in this effort by hospitals and medical centers also offering preventive programs. In South Bend, Indiana, one hospital has established a separate Health and Lifestyle Center, which is devoted almost exclusively to promoting positive wellness for the whole person. Such centers are now becoming commonplace throughout the country. They employ dietitians and physical fitness experts; these centers also employ behavioral specialists who offer programs such as stress management training and developmental counseling.

Private Practice

Some students enter the counseling field thinking of eventually going into private practice. A survey conducted by the AACD between 1982 and 1984 found that the number of counselors entering private practice had increased by 68 percent. (*Guidepost,* 1985, p. 4). Counselors in schools and agencies may develop part-time private practices distinct from their full-time position. In many cases, such practices may become sufficient to become full-time. As licensing and credentialing become more of a factor for counselors, increased numbers will likely enter private practice.

Developing and maintaining a private practice are not easy. In addition to attaining a high level of counseling skill, a counselor entering private practice requires managerial talent, financial acumen, and marketing ability. Counselors in private practice may find themselves spending as much time or more managing the business as practicing counseling. Partnerships are often established to help share the financial risks and the managerial duties. Also, a typical master's degree program in counseling does not provide the specialized training in all the areas necessary to establish a private practice; so partnerships can make available practitioners with different specialized interests and training.

Currently, the market for private practitioners appears to be poor, with a glut of counselors in many areas. In 1987, there were more than 5,300 private practitioners in Los Angeles County alone (Gelman, 1987). Melinkoff (1987) reported similar conditions in other parts of the country. Marketing skills have become essential for the private practitioner, and many counselors hire marketing consultants to develop and maintain their practice.

PROFESSIONALISM

Becoming a professional counselor is an involved, enriching process. It includes developing a high level of competence in six major areas:

1. An overall understanding of the scope of the field, its historical heritage, its purpose, and its organizational structure.
2. Active participation in the profession, through organizational work, lobbying, research, and writing.
3. Development of a professional attitude.
4. Knowledge and understanding of ethical codes and principles.
5. Extensive knowledge of relevant subject matter.
6. A diversity of supervised clinical field experiences.

This book provides a strong foundation in the first five areas. Participation in an entire counselor education program should result in developing a high degree of mastery in all six areas.

When Does Professional Life Begin?

Participation in the world of the professional counselor begins with the first course of a given program. Student memberships are available for virtually all appropriate organizations. Membership in a professional organization generally includes at least one journal subscription and a newsletter. All professional conventions have special student registration fees and usually have a number of activities geared directly to the graduate student. Students are usually invited to all regular sessions and business meetings. Generally, there is also an opportunity for students to make presentations either individually or in collaboration with other students or professors. Many journals publish student contributions. Workshops, seminars, institutes and conferences, with few exceptions, are also open to students, usually at reduced rates.

As stated in chapter 1, counseling is a way of life; total involvement in the field should begin with the first course. The better the student understands the nature of the work, including the expectations and demands of the field, the more likely a sound personal choice will be made with regard to commitment to it. To make a decision not to pursue a career in this field because it does not fit your expectations is much wiser than to complete a degree and be unhappy in the work. Being unfulfilled or unhappy in your work may still occur, but if you were initially happy with the field of counseling, subsequent problems may be remediated (see chapter 8 on burnout).

Professional Organizations

The major professional organization in the United States for counselors is the American Association for Counseling and Development (AACD). This organization, with roots in the vocational guidance movement of the early part of this century, was created in 1952 as the American Personnel and Guidance Association (APGA) and changed to its current name in 1983. In 1990, the organization had more than 55,000 members and 16 subdivisions representing the broad spectrum of the field.

The AACD publishes the *Journal for Counseling and Development* bimonthly and *Guidepost,* a biweekly newspaper. Most subdivisions also publish journals related to their areas of specialization. The organization is concerned with professional issues at all levels. It has developed a general code of ethics for the field as well as specialized codes of ethics (e.g., for group workers). The Association has developed and now maintains accreditation and certification procedures as described earlier in this chapter.

The AACD lobbies with Congress and state legislatures on issues related to the field of counseling. In addition to holding annual conventions, it sponsors training programs and publishes and distributes books, movies, audio and video cassettes, and other educational material. The Association also offers placement services for members through its newsletter and at the annual convention. The Association's regional and state organizations also hold meetings and sponsor workshops on a regular basis.

A counselor cannot be a member of a division without being a member of AACD itself. There are student rates for membership. Figure 6.1 lists and describes the 16 divisions of AACD.

Another major professional organization is the American Psychological Association (APA). Its membership is restricted to psychologists, but much of its work often finds its way into the counseling literature. The APA has 40 divisions that publish journals, several of which are of direct interest to counselors. Other professional organizations include the American Association of Marriage and Family Therapists (AAMFT), the American Society for Training and Development (ASTD), and the National Association of Social Workers (NASW).

What Does It Mean to Be a Professional Counselor?

The field of counseling is a professional occupation. Sociologically speaking, a profession has six basic features:

Division 1: American College Personnel Association (ACPA)

ACPA is the collective voice of the college student profession—teachers, counselors, deans, department heads, researchers. ACPA is committed to a program of professional and student development. Publications: *The Journal of College Student Personnel; ACPA Developments Newsletter.*

Division 2: Association for Counselor Education and Supervision (ACES)

ACES emphasizes the need for highly skilled guidance and personnel workers in efforts to improve counselor education and supervision at all levels of education, rehabilitation and employment settings. Publications: *Counselor Education and Supervision; ACES Newsletter.*

Division 3: National Career Development Association (NCDA)

NCDA is concerned with the lifelong use of people's knowledge, abilities, and skills. NCDA seeks to gain recognition and status for the profession of counseling and to improve skills, systems, and standards of service in counseling. Publications: *The Career Development Quarterly; NCDA Newsletter.*

Division 4: Association for Humanistic Education and Development (AHEAD)

AHEAD seeks to provide a forum for the exchange of information about humanistically oriented educational practices and to promote changes in education that reflect the growing body of knowledge about human development and potential. Publications: *The Humanist Educator: Infochange Newsletter.*

Division 5: American School Counselor Association (ASCA)

ASCA works to define and advance the role of the school counselor at all educational levels, elementary through postsecondary, and to achieve national recognition for this important function in education. Publications: *The School Counselor; Elementary School Guidance and Counseling; ASCA Newsletter.*

Division 6: American Rehabilitation Counseling Association (ARCA)

The rehabilitation counselor works with physically, mentally, or emotionally handicapped people. ARCA links the practitioner with a nationwide community of rehabilitation counselors. Publications: *Rehabilitation Counseling Bulletin; ARCA Newsletter.*

Division 7: Association for Measurement and Evaluation in Counseling and Development (AMECD)

AMECD members plan, administer and conduct testing programs; provide test scoring services; interpret and use test results; and develop evaluation instruments.

(continued)

FIGURE 6.1 National Divisions of the American Association for Counseling and Development. (Divisions of AACD. Reprinted by permission of American Association for Counseling and Development, publisher and copyright holder).

FIGURE 6.1 Continued

They also teach college-level courses or conduct research in this area of interest. Publications: *Measurement and Evaluation in Counseling and Development; AMECD Newsnotes.*

Division 8: National Employment Counselors Association (NECA)

NECA offers professional leadership to people who counsel in an employment setting or to those employed in related areas of counselor education, research, administration or supervision in business and industry, colleges and universities, and federal and state governments. Publications: *Journal of Employment Counseling; NECA Newsletter.*

Division 9: Association for Multicultural Counseling and Development (AMCD)

By seeking to eliminate prejudice and discrimination and by defending those human and civil rights that have been secured by law, AMCD is dedicated to the insurance of equality as regards the treatment, advancement, qualification, and status of individuals of color in personnel and guidance work. Publications: *Journal for Multicultural Counseling and Development; AMCD Newsletter.*

Division 10: Association for Religious and Value Issues in Counseling (ARVIC)

ARVIC seeks to examine the roles of values and theological, philosophical, and ethical considerations and principles in current counseling personnel practices and to share this knowledge with colleagues. ARVIC sponsors regional workshops and programs to stimulate the personal and professional growth of its members working in schools, colleges, community, and industry. One major thrust of ARVIC is to develop competence in its members to meet new challenges in our rapidly changing society. Publications: *Counseling and Values; ARVIC Newsletter.*

Division 11: Association for Specialists in Group Work (ASGW)

This is the division of workers in education, mental health, physical health, offender rehabilitation, religion, and the human potential movement who share a common interest in group work. ASGW seeks to assist and further the interests of children, youth, and adults by seeking to provide effective services through the group medium to prevent problems, to promote maximum development, and to remediate disabling behaviors. Publications: *Journal for Specialists in Group Work; ASGW Newsletter.*

Division 12: International Association of Addictions and Offender Counselors (IAAOC)

Membership is interdisciplinary in nature and includes professionals in the related fields of addictions treatment and public offender rehabilitation. IAAOC members are involved in the such areas as drug/alcohol abuse, gambling and relationship/sexual dependency, co-dependency, and adult and juvenile offender rehabilitation. Publications: *Journal of Addictions and Offender Counseling; IAAOC Report/Newsletter.*

Division 13: American Mental Health Counselors Association (AMHCA)

This division is for professionals in mental health centers, private practice, agency counseling, and pastoral counseling. The interdisciplinary membership of AMHCA is dedicated to maintaining and improving the quality of mental health in the nation. Publications: *AMHCA Journal; AMHCA News.*

Division 14: Military Educators and Counselors Association (MECA)

MECA was formed to encourage and deliver guidance, counseling, and educational programs to all members of the Armed Services, veterans, their dependents, and civilian employees of the Armed Services. It develops and promotes standards of professional conduct among counselors and educators working with Armed Services personnel and veterans and conducts programs to enhance individual human development and increase recognition of humanistic values and goals within the Armed Services. MECA also establishes, promotes, and maintains improved communication with the nonmilitary community. Publication: *MECA Newsletter.*

Division 15: Association for Adult Development and Aging (AADA)

AADA provides leadership and information to counselors and other service providers in the helping professions, to family members, to legislators, and to community service agencies on matters related to the development and needs of adults across the life span. Publication: *AADA Newsletter.*

Division 16: International Association of Marriage and Family Counselors (IAMFC)

IAMFC was formed to meet the need to focus on the multitude of problems connected with marital and family issues. Publication: *IAMFC Newsletter.*

---

1. A profession determines its own preparation and training standards. This is being done in the field of counseling through AACD accreditation procedures.
2. A profession is recognized legally via licensure and certification using criteria defined by the members of the group. The various national certification and state licensure efforts are examples of work undertaken toward this objective.
3. A unique role for the profession in general and for each specialty within the profession must be determined by the members of the group (Ohlsen, 1983). AACD and the members of its various divisions have worked to develop these unique role definitions. This is also being done through the licensure process.
4. A profession has its own professional ethics. Ethical standards for the professional conduct of counselors have been developed and widely disseminated. AACD has a well-developed code of ethics, initially established in

1961. (See Appendix.) Divisions of AACD such as the Association of Specialists in Group Work (ASGW) have formulated supplemental codes of ethics in areas of specialization.

5. A profession has procedures for disciplining members who behave unethically. The ethical guidelines of the AACD mentioned above provide procedures for the recognition and the disciplining of practitioners who violate approved ethical principles.

6. Generally, a profession is considered a terminal occupation, where a practitioner may be gainfully and productively employed throughout his or her career.

Professional Attitude (PA)

These six criteria refer to factors that are prerequisites of a profession such as counseling. In making a commitment to become a counselor and in taking the role of counselor as a way of life, it is important to note that more than knowledge and skill are involved. Working as a professional clearly indicates more than being gainfully employed or simply having a job. An additional factor seems to be necessary: a professional attitude (PA).

Professional attitude in counseling begins with making the commitment to become a counselor. PA includes learning the content and processes so they become part of your being rather than as something to be forgotten after examinations. PA means making a commitment to continued growth both personally and professionally. This means looking for new ideas and skills on a regular basis so that you can do your work better, rather than going to a seminar because you need more continuing education units to maintain your National Counselor Certificate. Professional attitude means accepting and following the professional code of ethics even when it is difficult, such as reporting a colleague for violating it. PA means doing research necessary to help find ways to deal with challenging clients and to make appropriate referrals when you are not qualified to handle a given case.

PA includes working to improve your profession by participating in professional organizations; attending conventions; holding office; making presentations to peers; and sharing your experience, research, and ideas by writing articles or making presentations at conferences, conventions, and workshops. PA means keeping up with literature in your field—books, journal articles, newsletters, and material in the general media. Newspapers and magazines often devote space to various aspects of human behavior.

PA means being willing to devote time, energy, and money for issues that are in the best interests of the profession. This can range from signing a petition or writing letters to legislators to organizing a drive to support legislation to bring about a licensure law for counselors in your state. Because the counseling profession has direct financial and legal ties to both state and local governments, it is incumbent on the professionals in the field to monitor their relationships with those governments regularly.

One major issue in our society that affects the counseling profession is that mental health problems are still difficult for many people to talk about with a professional. A large segment of the population finds it difficult to admit that they are not able to handle their own problems and must seek help from a stranger. Many people have no difficulty seeking help for physical problems, but they are reluctant to pursue outside help for personal, emotional problems. To deal with this issue, the professional counselor has a duty to promote the field and to help overcome biases and misinformation about mental health and counseling itself. This can be accomplished by being willing to give talks, presentations, and workshops or seminars to lay groups such as the PTA, Rotary Club, and church groups. In the final analysis, professional attitude requires the fostering of your own personal growth within the field as well as supporting and encouraging the growth of the field itself.

ETHICAL AND LEGAL ISSUES IN COUNSELING

In the counseling field, as in all professions, there is a major concern that practitioners behave both in ethical and legal ways. One way to determine a profession's concern for ethics is to find out if it has a code of ethics. The AACD has a code of ethics (see Appendix), and at least six of its subdivisions also have their own set of standards. This is in addition to the codes developed by other professional organizations in the field, such as the American Psychological Association, the Association of Certified Social Workers, the American Association of Marriage and Family Therapists, and the National Board of Certified Counselors.

While there is consensus among these various sets of ethical guidelines on many issues, there are situations and circumstances that may not be covered by the various ethical codes or on which the codes are vague or even in conflict. We discuss several issues in which there is general consensus among ethical codes and then provide some principles for professionals to follow in handling situations in which the codes of ethics are not clear. This is followed by a discussion of legal concerns of interest to counselors.

Three ethical issues highlighted here are confidentiality, professional limits, and sexual conduct.

Confidentiality

For the counseling relationship to be successful, trust needs to be established and maintained. A genuine concern of clients, and one that leads them to have reservations about entering into counseling relationships, is that their personal problems may become known around the community. If prospective counselors have difficulty keeping to themselves what other people tell them, this should be acknowledged as early as possible and another career choice pursued.

However, even though confidentiality is the foundation of the counseling relationship, there are some exceptions to the rule. These exceptions include cases in which there is clear and imminent danger to the client or to other people, actual or suspected child abuse, and records of a counselor who is not covered by the legal concept of privileged communication.

Clear and Imminent Danger

One vital exception to the rule of confidentiality, which is built into the ethical standards, is when the client indicates that there is clear and imminent danger to the client or to other people. If this should occur, the counselor "must take reasonable personal action or inform responsible authorities" (Appendix). One way that such an occurrence can be dealt with to help ensure that the counseling relationship can be maintained is to follow the principle of informed consent. Informed consent means that the counselor provides clients with pertinent information regarding counseling goals, services to be provided, procedures and techniques that may be used, fees, anticipated duration of counseling, limits on confidentiality, and rights of access to files (Corey, Corey, & Callanan, 1988). The licensure laws in some states may mandate that such informed consent procedures be used.

An example of what now is referred to as the duty to warn is when a client informs the counselor that violent action of any kind is to be taken against an unsuspecting third party. In this case, the third party and others who might be identified in advance as potential victims would have to be notified directly of the imminent danger (Leslie, 1983).

Child Abuse

Another instance in which confidentiality cannot be guaranteed occurs when the issue of child abuse is raised. Today, in all states, a counselor who becomes aware of or even suspects a situation involving child abuse is required by law, as well as by ethical standards, to report such information immediately to the proper authorities.

Privileged Communication

Privileged communication is a legal concept that affords clients the right not to have their communications used in court proceedings without their consent. This concept generally applies to the patients of doctors and to lawyer's clients, but, at the present time, it rarely applies to the clients of counselors. The records of most counselors, therefore, are subject to subpoena.

Professional Limits

The AACD ethical standards state that a counselor shall neither claim nor imply professional qualifications exceeding those possessed and should only accept positions for which he or she is professionally qualified. Even though this is not necessarily an issue of immediate concern to a beginning counselor, it is important to be aware of it throughout a counselor training program. In particular, although it may seem obvious that receiving a master's degree in counseling does not certify you as proficient in all areas of counseling, an issue might arise even within a practicum or internship setting. For instance, a client might be seeking help in sex therapy and even though you have had no direct training and supervision, you need the hours this client would provide to complete your course requirements. The professional responsibility and skill in making an appropriate referral would be required here.

Sexual Conduct

The counseling relationship can be intimate. However, the codes of ethics are clear that the relationship should not include sexual intimacies. Such behavior has been determined to be harmful to the parties involved as well as to the counseling profession itself. The use of sexist language or other types of sexual harassment also is not condoned.

Ethical Principles

To have a better idea of the expectations and responsibilities of being a professional counselor, the student should read through the AACD Ethical Standards early in the training program (see the Appendix). Not everything will have direct meaning for prospective counselors. You may, however, be able to note items on which you have to work to accept (such as not to counsel close friends or relatives) and, perhaps, become aware of an area that you know probably will not change (such as keeping information confidential).

What happens, however, if a situation arises that is not covered by the codes of ethics? One limitation of a code of ethics is that it cannot anticipate every possible situation and have an appropriate guideline. To handle such situations, the counselor should refer to the basic principles on which the codes of ethics themselves are based. The circumstances should be measured against each principle, ultimately resulting in a defensible decision.

Kitchener (1984) offers five fundamental principles of counseling: autonomy, beneficence, nonmaleficence, justice, and fidelity.

- Autonomy refers to clients' right to chose their own course of action as long as it does not interfere with the rights of others. Counselors are expected to respect clients as autonomous individuals who are responsible for their own behavior.
- Beneficence, the principle of doing good for others, is a critical factor in counseling. Counselors who are incompetent or dishonest or who otherwise do not contribute to the growth and welfare of the clients cause harm to their clients and to the profession.
- A related principle is nonmaleficence, not doing harm. Included in this principle are both the avoidance of inflicting harm and the admonition to refrain

from actions that risk harming others (Van Hoose, 1989, p. 169). Counselors may be legally responsible for actions that harm other people.

- Justice and fairness are principles based on the premise that all clients are equal regardless of race, sex, and/or creed. This entails equal access to treatment as well as equivalent services within an agency.
- Fidelity refers to loyalty, faithfulness, and keeping promises. Lying and not fulfilling the counseling contract (i.e., missing appointments without notice, breaking confidentiality) are examples of violations of fidelity.

These five ethical principles provide a basis for understanding the counseling profession and the various codes of ethics and serve as guideposts for the review of ethical dilemmas not otherwise covered. However, while knowledge of codes of ethics and the principles on which they are based is vital, given the ever-increasing number and complexity of ethical issues facing the counselor, it may be as important to develop what Tennyson and Strom (1986) call moral responsibleness, or Wilcoxon (1987) labels an "ethical conscience."

To develop moral responsibleness or an ethical conscience, prospective counselors must be committed to rational thinking based on the moral principles described above. This takes place through a process of critical reflection on the meaning and consequences of their counseling goals, theoretical approach, and specific interventions. This reflection or self-confrontation can be done as part of the self-attending process described in chapter 3, as part of the review of taped counseling sessions, and as part of the counselors' ongoing journal writing.

This self-confrontation needs to be supplemented by dialogue. It requires active communication with mentors and/or professional colleagues to clarify and test the validity of personal decisions, to learn about and examine other points of view, and to become involved in mutual problem solving (Tennyson & Strom, 1986). The development of this professional dialogue directed toward developing moral responsibleness should be an integral part of a counselor education program. The lack of such an ongoing dialogue is a major drawback to the development of ethical consciousness in counselors' receiving most of their training in workshops, institutes, or poorly run counselor education programs (Wilcoxon, 1987). The development of collegial dialogues needs to be encouraged even more when the student becomes a practicing professional. The scope and nature of the ethical issues confronted do not diminish on graduation or with the receipt of certification. Further, in many settings the counselor may not have immediate access to peer dialogues such as those held in an agency as part of case conferences. The continued development of moral responsibleness is a further reason for the development and maintenance of a professional network (see chapter 8).

Legal Issues

It is not easy to separate ethical and legal issues into clearly distinct categories. Issues that may have been primarily ethical concerns often become fixed in law, such as the necessity for reporting suspected child abuse. On the other hand, counselors have been sued in court for violating ethical codes that were formulated by professional organizations but not by state or national legislative bodies.

Professional counselors must be aware of a number of issues in regard to legal matters. These issues range from the possibility of being sued for malpractice, to carrying out the requirements of specific laws, to having to testify in court on behalf of a client in a child custody case.

There are two primary ways by which a counselor's behavior is regulated by law. One is by specific laws themselves; the other is as a result of court rulings.

Some specific laws that affect the actions of counselors include the following:

- Title IX of the Education Amendments of 1972. As a result of this law, a school counselor is prohibited from cooperating with an outside agency, organization, or individual that discriminates against students on the basis of sex (Knox, 1977).
- Family Education Rights and Privacy Act–1974 (Buckley Amendment). This law provides parents of children under the age of 18 and students over 18 the right to review records related to them that are held by an institution. Most of us are familiar with this act because of our use of recommendation forms whereby we can waive the right to have access to a given recommendation.
- Education for All Handicapped Children Act–1975 (PL 94–142). This law provides guidelines for school counselors who work with handicapped children.
- All states now have laws requiring counselors and other people to report actual and suspected cases of child abuse.

Our society has become increasingly litigious. In cases involving professional counselors and psychologists, the issues have generally been related to violations of the professional ethical standards. The most significant case in recent years was *Tarasoff* vs. *The State of California,* where a psychologist (and his employer) was sued for not notifying a potential victim of imminent danger. The psychologist notified the campus police after his client threatened to do harm to a woman. The suspect was interrogated and released, but he subsequently killed the woman. The victim's family sued and won the case on the basis that the woman herself was never notified of the threat.

In terms of numbers of cases in recent years, probably the most common case—and it is not all that common—is of a client suing the therapist for sexual intimacies. Such behavior on the part of a therapist is in clear violation of the ethical standards of AACD and APA. Some therapists have claimed that sex can be therapeutic; however, such claims have not been documented, and the potential as well as actual negative ramifications of such behavior have been determined to overshadow all possible beneficial effects.

As a result of potential danger of being sued, more counselors are taking out professional liability insurance. Many insurance companies offer such policies, as do the AACD and the APA. An insurance policy can also be taken out by a student who is doing a practicum or internship course. Most agencies or institutions have insurance coverage for all of their working staff, but it would be prudent for any practicum and internship student, as well as any prospective employee, to inquire about the nature and coverage of available liability insurance plans.

Counselors may be called to testify in court on any of a number of possible situations. In effect, if a client becomes involved with the legal system, there is always the possibility that the counselor may be called in to testify about what he or she knows in relation to the case. A major issue in such cases is privileged information. Privileged information refers to the counselor's right not to have to divulge specific information gleaned as a result of the counseling relationship. State laws vary as to who does and who does not have the right of privileged information. For example, in Indiana, school counselors have the right by law, whereas mental health counselors do not.

Not having the right of privileged communication could affect the nature of record keeping. For example, being forced by a judge to reveal detailed notes of actual counseling sessions could have untold negative consequences in terms of the client-counselor relationship and the client's relationship with his or her family.

As part of the training process, then, counselor education students need to be aware of the potential legal and ethical implications of their work. The process of helping is a complex one that often affects people and institutions far beyond the individual client. These implications need to be known from the beginning of a training program.

SUMMARY

The changing nature of the field of counseling has been presented in this chapter, with the primary change being the shifting of emphasis in counselor education programs from being oriented primarily to school counseling to a more generic mental health counselor orientation. The result is that counselor education graduates are now being employed in a broad variety of helping profession occupations. This is not happening, however, without difficulty. Mental health counselors are having to establish their identity alongside the previously established mental health professionals, such as psychiatrists, psychologists, and social workers, as well as with insurance companies and governmental agencies that pay for services provided.

A major thrust in developing a strong identity for mental health counselors is occurring as a result of the credentialing process. Credentials in the form of licensure and certification are becoming increasingly available for counselors through governmental and organizational auspices. Counselor education programs and counseling service agencies are increasingly becoming accredited by professional organizations. Licensure, certification, and accreditation are not guarantors of counseling effectiveness; however, they do help to assure basic standards with regard to counselor qualifications, educational competence, and training experience.

Obtaining a degree and being licensed or certified are not sufficient. Ongoing continuing education is an expected part of this profession. To maintain most licenses and certificates, regular documentation of ongoing training and education is required. This includes specialized training programs, advanced courses in counseling, and all types of workshops and seminars. Independent reading in books and journals is also an expected activity of professionals in the field.

Employment trends for counseling generally appear bright. Employment in service occupations in general is increasing in our society. Changes in the society and in the structure of the family in particular, with more people living alone and with increased numbers of single-parent families, appear to increase the need for counseling. The extended family is generally no longer as available as a personal resource. A downward trend in the need for school counselors may be leveling off, with a possible increased demand in sight. The greatest employment prospects may be in community health agencies, in business and industry, and with wholistic health providers. The emphases in the latter two areas of employment are on prevention, training, and development. One outcome of the emphasis on licensure and certification is that an increasing number of mental health counselors are going into private practice on either a full- or part-time basis.

Being a professional in counseling requires making a career commitment to total involvement in the field. It includes nurturing a professional attitude by being an active member of local, state, and national organizations, continued striving to enhance one's own skills and education as well as helping to improve the profession as a whole. It includes a commitment to act in ethically appropriate ways; to understand legal issues in the field; to realize how much the work of a counselor is affected by the legal system; and to know how to resolve situations in which there may be no ethical or legal guidelines. Counseling is a broad, challenging field, where stringent demands are made of the professionals in it, and where the ultimate payoff comes from being able to work to help people in a variety of creative ways.

QUESTIONS AND ACTIVITIES

1. What is your present professional attitude (PA) and what, if anything, do you need to do to strengthen it? Could you ignore the factors involved in developing and maintaining a professional attitude (PA) and still be an effective counselor? If so, how?

2. Some states license more than one type of counselor (school counselors, substance abuse counselors, etc.). Find out what certification is available to you and what the requirements are. Would it be to your advantage to be licensed in more than one area/specialty?

3. Investigate rules and regulations, if any, for establishing a private practice in

your state. Interview several private practitioners and find out what they see as the problems and benefits of private practice. Would this be a direction that you might seriously consider? If so, what special training do you anticipate you may need in order to ensure success as a private practitioner?

4. From the information given, on which divisions of AACD would you be willing to spend money to join and actively participate in the division's work? Are there divisions in which you would just like to get the journal but not become an active member?

CHAPTER 7

Selected Counseling Specialties

In what areas can a counselor specialize?

Becoming a counselor involves making choices. There are a number of directions that a person could deliberately choose to take, and unexpected opportunities open up as a person progresses along the career path. This chapter gives a brief overview of some specialty areas within the profession and some issues to consider in making a decision on an area of specialization. Two additional specialty areas are described in separate chapters—family counseling (chapter 13) and career and lifestyle counseling (chapter 14).

There are a large number of areas in which a counselor might specialize. The areas represented in this chapter are those in which sizable numbers of trained counselors are now working or areas that are relatively new and have excellent potential for expanding in terms of counselor demand.

GENERALIST OR SPECIALIST

Even though master's level counselor training programs are now designed primarily for training generalists in the field, there is a question as to how viable it is to be a generalist. With the field as broad and diverse as it is, and with the relentless increase of knowledge and the attendant development of technology, effectiveness in all areas of the counseling field would be impossible. However, being too highly specialized can be restrictive. For example, being highly trained only in sex counseling could limit employment opportunities. School counselors who try to find work in public or private agencies have not always been able to find employment without upgrading their skills.

Some career choices occur by chance and some by design. Even though chance will always be a possible influence in career choices, it is helpful to have some design with which to focus attention and energy. Kottler and Brown (1985) suggest pursuing a flexible specialty. This means focusing on one or perhaps two specialty areas within the field, while continuing to become aware of other aspects of the total field. Some major specialty areas, along with occupations within each, are shown in Figure 7.1

Child Development and Counseling

Parent Education

Preschool Counseling

Early Childhood Education

Elementary School Counseling

Child Counseling in Mental Health Agencies

Counseling with Battered and Abused Children and Their Families

Adolescent Development and Counseling

Middle/High School Counseling

Psychological Education

Career-Development Specialist

Adolescent Counseling in Mental Health Agencies

Youth Work in a Residential Facility

Youth Probation Officer

Student Assistance Program Professional

The Aged

Preretirement Counseling

Nursing Home Counseling

Hospice Work

Marital/Relationship Counseling

Premarital Counseling

Marriage Counseling

Family Counseling

Sex Education

Sexual Dysfunction Counseling

Divorce Mediation

Careers/Lifestyle

Career Development

Employment Counseling

Career-Change Counseling

Vocational Rehabilitation

Occupational Therapy

Leisure Counseling

College and University

College Student Counseling

Student Activities

Student Personnel Work

Resident Hall Counselor

Counselor Educator

Drugs

Substance Abuse Counseling

Alcohol Counseling

Drug Counseling

Stop Smoking Programs

Adult Children of Alcoholics Counseling

Consultation

Agency and Corporate Consulting

Organizational Development

Industrial Psychology

Training

Business and Industry

Training and Development

Personnel

Quality of Worklife/Quality Circles

Employee Assistance Programs

Employee Career Development

FIGURE 7.1 Selected Specialty Areas in Counseling (Adapted from *Introduction to Therapeutic Counseling* by J. Kottler and R. Brown. Copyright © 1985 by Wadsworth, Inc. Reprinted by permission of Brooks/Cole Publishing Co., Monterey, CA 93940)

Health

Nutritional Counseling
Exercise and Health Education
Nurse-Counselor
Rehabilitation Counseling
Stress Management Counseling
Wholistic Health Counseling
Anorexia/Bulimia Counseling
Genetic Counseling
AIDS Counseling

Other Specialties

Affirmative Action/Equal Opportunity
  Specialist
Phobia Counseling
  Agoraphobia
Grief Counseling
Crisis Intervention Counseling
Posttraumatic Stress
  Disorder Counseling
Sports Counseling

Note that within most areas listed are opportunities for preventive, developmental, and remedial work. These specialty areas are in addition to developing skills in a given theoretical approach, such as Gestalt therapy, or the attainment of expertise in some special treatment modality such as art therapy.

GUIDELINES FOR SELECTING A COUNSELING SPECIALTY

Six guidelines to use in selecting a counseling specialty are as follows:

1. Assess personal strengths and weaknesses. As part of the process of developing self-knowledge described in chapter 1, consider how areas of personal strength and weakness relate to certain types of work settings and types of clients. For example, having feelings of discomfort when being around handicapped people might preclude working as a rehabilitation counselor. Interests also need to be considered at the same time. A person may be able to relate very well to children but have no interest in working with them professionally, preferring instead to work with adults. The more open and honest you are in this self-assessment, the less likely you are to make a disappointing career decision. Solicit feedback from instructors, peers, and other people who know you well. Do not argue with feedback that you have requested; listen, and check it out. If it fits, acknowledge it; if it does not fit, simply thank the sender.

2. Clarify values related to work and lifestyle. Examining your values early in the training process could prevent making decisions that could be quite uncomfortable and frustrating in a few years. For example, if you value a lifestyle that takes a lot of money to maintain, you may rule out most agency work.

3. Visit as many different specialty settings as possible. Reading about different types of specialization is helpful, but it can never give the full impact of the nature of the occupation that a person can receive by spending time in various settings, observing, asking questions, and, in general, testing the reality of the occupation.

4. Interview as many counselors in the field as possible. In each setting, it would be desirable to interview each of the different types of counselors that might be represented there. In a mental health center, for example, there usually is a broad variety of counselors working in a variety of ways with different populations. One strategy that can be helpful is to arrange to "shadow" a counselor during a routine work day, sitting in on activities from the beginning of the day until the counselor heads home.

5. Maximize practicum and internship experiences. When given the opportunity to choose practicum and internship sites, select sites that will give you a variety of diversified experiences and opportunities. Select a totally different site for an internship than you had for a practicum. For example, if you worked in a university counseling center for your practicum, you might choose to work with the aged in a nursing home for an internship. These supervised experiences allow you a significant amount of freedom to work extensively in different types of settings and with different types of populations without having to make a long-term commitment. Some students have discovered that doing an outstanding job in a practicum or internship has led to employment in that setting.

6. Develop a "futures" orientation. The counseling field is a continually emerging one. Students graduating this year will be employed in positions that did not exist 5 or 10 years ago. As Naisbitt has pointed out (chapter 6), this trend is here for the foreseeable future. Therefore, it behooves the student to remain cognizant of this fact and to be open to the possibility of making changes within the field as circumstances dictate (Kottler & Brown, 1985, pp. 75–76).

A major concern in selecting a specialty is that it may require additional training following the completion of the master's degree. This should be no real stumbling block, however, since being certified or licensed as a counselor already means a lifetime commitment to continuing education to maintain the credential (see chapter 6).

SELECTED SPECIALTY AREAS

The specialty areas discussed below represent areas in which large numbers of people trained as counselors are employed or in which there is an anticipated job market for such people.

Counseling in Schools and Universities

Most people have their first and in some cases their only contact with a counselor in a school setting. Although school counselors may be encountered at almost any level of education, students generally have the most direct contact with them in high school. Students attending institutions of higher education are likely to encounter personnel with counseling backgrounds in the student services area of a college or institute as well as in the housing and residence hall sectors of major campuses. A description of counseling opportunities at different levels of education follows, along with some positive and negative aspects of each level.

Elementary School Counseling

Everyone agrees on the need for counselors in the secondary school; however, the same cannot be said for counselors in the elementary school. To a great extent, having counselors in the elementary school has been viewed as a frill or a luxury rather than a necessity. This is evidenced by the fact that a large number of school districts do not employ any elementary counselors, and in districts that do, there are often not enough counselors available to have one counselor per elementary school building.

To a large extent, this lack of elementary school counselors has been a result of the underfunding of education in this country. In school districts in which there are elementary counselors, these positions are usually the first to be eliminated in the event of financial hardship.

What, then, is the case for having elementary and preschool counseling? Early views of counseling in the elementary schools stressed problem prevention and the development of human potential as primary factors in a rationale for elementary school counseling (Van Hoose, Pietrofesa, & Carlson, 1973). Recently, however, the nature of problems faced by children is better known and understood, and the problems may require remediation as well as preventive and developmental measures. A major area of concern involves children who are considered at risk in terms of possibly dropping out of school before graduation. Other areas of concern include suicide potential, incest, child pornography and other child abuse, and working with children who are dealing with divorce, alcohol and other drug abuse, two-career families, and single-parent families (latch-key children).

The National Education Association makes the following case for elementary school counselors:

> The new attitude in counseling is, the earlier the better. Or, don't wait for disaster. In the past, counseling was generally thought of as a task for the secondary school. Surely elementary students—cherubic, naive, still so young—could have no real problems, certainly none that would require professional help.
>
> Today's educators know better. The most serious problems of adolescence and even of adulthood—alcoholism, drug abuse, depressions, suicidal impulses, sexual

conflicts—are showing up in the pre-teen population. And even the very young don't seem to be immune from them.

These facts explain the new push to offer a variety of counseling services at the elementary level. There's clear evidence that behavioral problems are more easily identified, treated, and remedied in young children than in adolescents. What may be no more than a psychological bruise for a child at age 9 can, if untreated, easily become a gaping wound by age 16. (*Today's Education,* 1983–84, p. 52)

The need for elementary and preschool counselors is evident. However, until there are more of them, the role and functions of elementary school counselors will be relatively constricted. Even when working with a large number of groups, one counselor in an elementary school would have great difficulty providing counseling for all those needing it. Therefore, the five primary functions for elementary school counselors are specially prescribed by the American School Counselors Association (ASCA):

1. Provide inservice training to teachers to assist them in planning and implementing guidance interventions (preschool to 3rd grade) in order to maximize developmental benefits (such as self-esteem, personal relationships, positive school attitude, and sex-fair choices) in the hope of preventing serious problems or minimizing the size of such problems, if and when they occur.
2. Provide consultation for teachers who need assistance with understanding and assistance with incorporating developmental concepts in teaching content as well as support for building a healthy classroom environment.
3. Accommodate parents who need assistance with understanding normal child growth and development; improving family communication skills; or understanding their role in encouraging their child to learn.
4. Cooperate with other school staff in the early identification, remediation, or referral of children with developmental deficiencies or handicaps.
5. As children reach the upper elementary grades, effort is directed through the curriculum toward increasing student awareness of the relationship between school and work, especially the impact of educational choices on one's lifestyle and career development. (ASCA, 1981, p. 9)

The question then becomes not whether we should have elementary school counselors, but how to attain more of them for our schools. The good news is that there is a growing movement across the country, both at the individual school district level and at the state level, to substantially increase the number of elementary school counselors.

Middle/Junior High–Senior High School Counseling

At the middle/junior high and senior high school levels, the general desirability and need for counselors are rarely questioned. The need for counselors at this level is acknowledged in almost all school districts in the country. However, the commitment to employing a full component of counselors has been less than total. As noted above, when there are financial setbacks in a district, generally speaking, the counseling service office has been one of the first areas to be reduced. This has been evident in the public attitude toward the schools. A Gallup poll on education (1984), asking public response to where cuts should come in the event of financial problems in the schools, placed counseling second behind administrative staff and well ahead of programs such as athletics and extracurricular activities.

Counseling in the middle and junior high schools is not as firmly entrenched as at the high school level. However, as the needs of these students are increasingly recognized, there is hope that these positions will be universally accepted and filled. Some functions of middle or junior high counselors are to:

1. Concentrate efforts (through group guidance, peer facilitators, and teacher in-service training) to smooth the transition for students from the more confining environment of the lower school to the middle or junior high school where students are expected to assume greater responsibility for their own learning and personal development.
2. Identify, encourage, and support teachers (through inservice training, consultation, and coteaching) who are interested in incorporating units emphasizing preventive and developmental concepts in such curriculum areas as English, social studies, health, and home economics.
3. Organize and implement a career guidance program for students that includes an assessment of their career maturity and career-planning status; easy access to relevant career information; and assistance with processing data for personal use in schoolwork related decision-making. (ASCA, 1981, pp. 9–10)

At the high school level, counselors are relatively well established. A major concern at this level is the student load per counselor. The recommendations of ASCA are that there should be no more than 400 students per counselor. Even with this number it is understandable why counselors are not able to spend extended amounts of time counseling individual students. Another major concern is that counselors often are perceived as spending a lot of time on quasiadministrative tasks and not much time working with students. There are some cases in which school administrators have required counselors to perform administrative duties such as developing class schedules. These duties go beyond those proscribed by the profession for school counselors.

In fact, the functions delineated by ASCA are such that there is not sufficient time to accomplish them in a school year, much less take on administrative duties. Functions specific to high school counselors according to ASCA include:

1. Organize and implement through interested teachers guidance curricula interventions that focus upon important developmental concerns of adoles-

cents (identity, career choice and planning, social relationships, and so forth).

2. Organize and make available comprehensive information systems (print, computer-based, audio-visual) necessary for educational-vocational planning and decision-making.

3. Assist students with assessment of personal characteristics (e.g., competencies, interests, aptitudes, needs, career maturity) for personal use in such areas as course selection, post-high-school planning, and career choices.

4. Provide remedial interventions of alternative programs for those students showing in-school adjustment problems, vocational immaturity, or general negative attitudes toward personal growth. (ASCA, 1981, p. 10)

In addition to providing direct services to children, school counselors at all levels serve as consultants to administrators, teachers, and parents.

High school counselors in this decade will continue to have to work to reduce their administrative duties and responsibilities so they can provide the direct services advocated by ASCA. In addition to being assertive on an individual basis, the support of a professional organization may be necessary.

Because student populations have been increasing and large numbers of counselors are approaching retirement age, the number of openings for high school counselors has been increasing in recent years. This trend is expected to continue through the 1990s.

School counselors generally are eligible for at least provisional certification in the state in which they receive their degree on completion of their master's degree. Many states require that school counselors obtain additional education or experience before the level of professionally certified counselor is attained. Also, some states may require that prospective counselors have one or more years of teaching experience before attaining counselor certification.

Student Assistance Programs

Some school districts, recognizing the need for more counseling services for their students and realizing that the regular school counselors are not available to provide the in-depth attention necessary, are now contracting with outside agencies such as youth service bureaus and mental health centers to provide such services. One formal program instituted in a number of U.S. schools is the Student Assistance Program (SAP). SAPs are patterned after Employee Assistance Programs in industry (see p. 164). SAPs generally have four components: group counseling sessions for students with alcoholic parents, counseling for students using drugs and alcohol, sessions for students not known to have problems with alcohol but who are performing poorly in school, and a component bringing SAPs and parent and community groups together (Schaefer, 1989).

Some schools have hired their own special counselor to establish an in-house Student Assistance Program to supplement existing counselors. Other schools are using a team approach with existing personnel. Student Assistance Professionals have their own professional organization—the National Organization of Student Assistance Program Professionals.

Student Personnel Services—Higher Education

A variety of counseling services generally are available at postsecondary institutions, with the size of the institution often being a determinant as to limits placed on services. The most common services offered are academic advising and financial aid. Personal counseling constitutes another large area of services, usually including testing and individual and group counseling. Such counseling services are often restricted to students, faculty, and staff; at some colleges the counseling center may be open to the community. A placement center may often be connected to a counseling center to help students and graduates find employment both during their school years and after graduation.

Increasingly, college centers are reaching out, going beyond the walls of the center and offering a variety of programs to students in residence halls, in regular classrooms, and even in off-campus settings. Such programs tend to be proactive, such as assertiveness-training workshops, personal growth groups, and career and lifestyle planning seminars. Many college counseling centers also serve as crisis centers, dealing with such problems as potential suicide and drug abuse. On larger campuses, trained counselors live and work in residence halls and provide many of the above services directly to the residents with whom they are living.

The professional organization that most closely relates to the work of the college student service specialist is the American College Personnel Association, a division of AACD. "In terms of role and function, counselors make up about 25 percent of the association, with administrators (22 percent), Student Affairs workers (19 percent), and supervisor counselors (18 percent) following in number. Other categories include paraprofessionals, students, researchers, and those in private business" (Johnson, 1985, p. 409).

Substance Abuse Counseling

An area with increasing opportunity for counselors is in the specialty of substance abuse counseling. Substance abuse includes the abuse of all drugs, including alcohol, although the definition even includes foods like sugar when they are used for the purpose of altering a person's mood or psychological state, usually for the purpose of avoiding dealing with difficult situations (Schmolling, Youkelles, & Burger, 1985). Abuse often leads to addiction, psychological or physical. Because this specialty usually involves physical symptoms, many treatment centers related to different types of substance abuse are located in hospitals and clinics.

Drug abuse has become recognized as a disease by insurance companies and the federal government, and there have been substantial amounts of money available for treatment purposes. As a result, drug abuse counseling and treatment programs constitute one of the biggest growth areas in the field. However, even though substance abuse counseling is an area of specialization by itself, many people do abuse food and drugs in some form from time to time. What is likely, then, is that a client seen in any agency, at almost any age, may be a substance abuser in addition to having other problems. It is therefore important that all counselors have awareness of substance abuse, if only to help in making proper referrals.

Counseling for substance abusers can be complex because there may be other problems in a person's life in addition to chemical dependency. While there is not total agreement among professionals within the field that ingesting a given substance actually leads to acquiring a disease, having a disease label such as *alcoholism* has made it possible for some people to risk getting help and to have financial assistance through health insurance for the costs involved in doing so. In many cases the problem may be so severe that detoxification is necessary, preferably under medical supervision. Also, medication may need to be provided as part of a treatment plan.

In most cases of substance abuse, medical treatment alone is not sufficient; generally a variety of counseling services is offered. These services include group and family counseling, both of which may be extremely important in helping a person decide to change an undesirable behavior pattern and then to maintain the new behavior. For the best results, this is usually supplemented by support groups, such as Alcoholics Anonymous or Overeaters Anonymous, to help maintain the desired behavior for life. Exercise and relaxation programs are often prescribed to improve physical well being and establish positive addictions (Glasser, 1976).

Substance abuse education as part of a prevention program is particularly important in this field; research suggests that only 1 in 36 alcoholics receives treatment, recovers, and gets well (Ohlms, 1983). This treatment record is not impressive, and it emphasizes the need for preventive programs.

Substance abuse counselors often take specialized programs and in some cases can receive special certification as drug and alcohol abuse counselors. It is possible in some states such as Indiana to be certified directly as a drug abuse counselor without necessarily having a counseling degree. Marriage, family, and child counselors in California must now complete a course in substance abuse in order to be eligible for their license.

One factor that has prevailed from the earliest work with drug abuse counseling is that recovering addicts are often given preference over nonaddicts for counseling positions. This practice has occurred because presumably the addict's personal experience would make for greater empathy, and the model of being a productive recovering addict would have a positive impact on clients. The assumption that one must be a recovering addict to provide effective treatment has been challenged by research. The general conclusion is that counselors who are recovering addicts are not any more effective than counselors who are nonaddicts (LoBello, 1984).

An area of specialization related to substance abuse counseling is working with the adult children of alcoholics (ACOAs). Alcohol abuse causes problems for the abusers and their immediate families and also for the children of the abuser(s) after they have grown, regardless of whether they drink themselves. Having been part of a dysfunctional family has left the ACOAs with deficiencies in coping and in relationship skills that have a significant impact on their personal and emotional development. Counseling processes include working with grief and shame and helping clients learn to accept themselves, express their needs, and have fun without guilt (Fossum & Mason, 1986; Gravitz & Bowden, 1986; Middleton-Moz & Dwinell, 1986).

Gerontological Counseling

One area of growth in the counseling field is gerontological counseling, the counseling of older citizens. In a survey of counselor educators, Daniel and Weikel (1983) found that the primary trend identified was an increase in gerontological counseling as a specialty. This movement toward working more with the older members of our society was highlighted in 1988, when the Association for Adult Development and Aging (AADA) became a division of AACD.

With the increasing number of people aged 60 and over has been a corresponding increase in interest in working with the aged in a variety of settings (e.g., community centers, retirement centers, nursing homes, and hospice programs). Counselors working in these settings can be employed by the agency itself or be private practitioners (Tomine, 1986).

Even though the problems of the aged are not necessarily that different from those of people at younger ages, the needs of the elderly have often been overlooked in the past. This age group has recently found that it can exert a significant amount of political influence on behalf of issues of importance to people over age 60. Therefore, even though much effort has gone into expanding and improving the services offered to the elderly in a variety of settings, more can be expected in the future.

Health Counseling

Another major area opening up for trained counselors is health counseling. As Thoreson and Eagleston (1985) have stated, "Good health needs good counseling. . . . Wellness depends on the ongoing integrity of thoughts, feelings and actions" (p. 77). It is in the promotion of positive interaction of these attributes that the skills of the counselor can be most invaluable. Health counseling or behavioral health is perhaps the most predominantly preventive specialty area. Behavioral health has been defined by Matarazzo as

> an interdisciplinary field dedicated to promoting a philosophy of health that stresses individual responsibility in the application of behavioral and biomedical science knowledge and techniques to the maintenance of health and the prevention of illness and dysfunction by a variety of self-initiated individual or shared activities. (Matarazzo, 1986, p. 813)

The clients for such services may have had problems of various types, but the focus in health counseling is not to remediate old problems but to promote well-ness, prevent disease, and help people learn to "care for their own 'disease' when appropriate" (Thoreson & Eagleston, 1985, p. 77). Therefore, much more is done in the way of education and training than in therapy. Rejecting the medi-cal model that focuses on the diagnosis and treatment of disease, Thoreson and Eagleston (1985) proscribe an educational model that emphasizes training people to think, make decisions, and solve problems. These skills are deemed necessary for the ongoing prevention of disease and the maintenance of wellness. Such an approach requires an educated, informed public. Skilled counselors may be em-ployed in a variety of settings to work with health-related issues of men, women, and children of all racial and ethnic groups to assure that these skills are learned. Included in this area is the concept of wholistic counseling, an approach that looks at the total person and works to integrate the physical, psychological, and spiritual dimensions of a person's life.

Some evidence of the changes in the proactive approaches to health can be seen in most communities as hospitals and medical centers broaden the scope of their services. Instead of focusing only on remediation and treatment, hospitals are now adding health and lifestyle centers or wellness centers to their opera-tions and, in general, appear to be taking a more preventive view toward health. Subspecialty areas offered at such wellness centers include nutritional counsel-ing, exercise and health education, and stress management, and while these areas all focus on the total person, they do in some ways overlap. For example, a proper diet and a sound exercise program are considered important components of a good stress management program (see chapter 8).

Some occupations such as nurse-counselor and physician's assistant may be oriented to some degree toward remediation. Such practitioners tend to work with people who are experiencing one or more problems and need more time to be heard and to understand personal care procedures than is generally available from a physician. Nurse-counselors, in addition to working with patients, often are able to provide support to other nurses; for example, helping to work with problems of stress that could lead to burnout.

Two types of eating disorders, anorexia and bulimia, both related to using eating habits as a way of trying to enhance a person's self-image and often to control other people, are dealt with in group and family counseling settings, along with medical consultation. Weight reduction programs, a form of nutri-tional counseling, generally offer group work to provide support and encourage-ment to the participants.

Counseling AIDS victims and their families has also become an area of major concern to health professionals. They work with current cases and strive to pre-vent future occurrences.

Governmental Support

All of these health counseling approaches are being pursued with the full encour-agement of the federal government. Research into a number of areas has produced results indicating that some chronic diseases are not as inevitable as once feared. These diseases include lung cancer, heart disease, and adult-onset diabetes. The result has been the development of the Office of Disease Prevention and Health Promotion (ODPHP) for the purpose of pursuing proactive initiatives (McGinnis, 1985).

The set of national health objective developed by ODPHP in 1980 included, among other things, the need for measures to motivate behavior change in order to prevent debilitating problems (U.S. Department of Health and Human Services, 1980). Specific preventive initiatives include

> (a) working with professional organizations with an opportunity to influence the behavior of health providers operating in clinical settings; (b) working with public and private reimbursement agencies and organizations to foster their consideration of reimbursement of preventive services; and (c) support in evaluations and studies to enhance the understanding of the effectiveness of preventive services offered in a clinical setting. (McGinnis, 1985, p. 210)

Health counseling, or the behavioral health movement, "while still in its infancy, is likely to become a professional domain of major significance during the next two decades" (Ford, 1985, p. 93). It will be exciting to see the many ways that counselors will be able to apply their special areas of knowledge and skill in conjunction with other health professionals.

Rehabilitation Counseling

Rehabilitation counselors are specialists who work with disabled clients in overcoming deficits in their skills. Disabilities can manifest themselves in many different ways. Even though a major objective of a rehabilitation counselor is to help a client learn to cope with a specific mental or physical disability such as deafness, the full goal is wholistic in nature, to help the client become fully functioning in all areas in spite of any handicap or limitation.

In addition to physical handicaps such as blindness or loss of a leg, rehabilitation counseling is necessary for prisoners after release from prison, for psychiatric patients after release from mental hospitals, and for the mentally handicapped. Much substance abuse counseling might be considered rehabilitative. People who have lost their jobs after many years of employment also need to go through a rehabilitative process. In recent years many companies and unions have established counseling programs for workers who have lost their jobs as a result of plant closings.

Rehabilitation counselors generally specialize within the field itself, working with specific physical disabilities, for example. A great amount of knowledge and considerable skill are essential in working with a targeted population in that the counselor needs to understand the nature of the disability itself, be able to establish the therapeutic alliance necessary to help the person, and be aware of all the dynamics surrounding the situation. In many cases of rehabilitation counseling, the clients have incurred some kind of loss; for example, the loss of a leg or the loss of a job. The counselor's understanding of the grief process (Kubler-Ross, 1969), which accompanies any significant loss, is vital. Much rehabilitation work is vocational, requiring knowledge and skills in career counseling. Marriage and family counseling is often required, as well as sex counseling, if the disability affects sexual functioning.

Rehabilitation counseling is often associated with hospitals such as the Veterans Administration hospitals, rehabilitation centers established by insurance companies, and state and local agencies. Certification as a certified rehabilitation counselor (CRC) can be attained through the American Rehabilitation Counselors Association (ARCA), a division of AACD. Many states also have licensing requirements for rehabilitation counselors.

CONSULTATION

One major way counselors can use their skills is through the process of consultation. As noted, much of the counselor's work in the school setting is as a consultant. "The consultative process involves one person (the client) who has a problem but lacks the knowledge or skill for its solution, turning to another (the consultant) who has the requisite ability to aid in its solution" (Korchin, 1976, pp. 510–11). It should be noted that the consultative process is not that different from the counseling process, and that is why many counselors can take on the role of consultant easily. However, it is different enough to warrant concern about specific ethical issues peculiar to the consulting relationship (Robinson & Gross, 1985; Lowman, 1985; Crego, 1985; Gallessich, 1982). These issues include the consultant's having appropriate training for the services provided, proper assessment of organizational readiness for change, and the balancing of the organization's need to know with the client/employee's right to privacy (Robinson & Gross, 1985).

An important feature that distinguishes consultation from counseling is that in consultation the client is generally a professional who has particular responsibilities to other people or to an organization. An implied part of the consultative process is that the work the consultant does with the client may affect the people and the organization for which the client is responsible. The consultant's role may be an indirect one, working with what might be considered the middle level. In the long run, however, successful consultants can have a significant impact because they can reach many more people as a result of their consultations with mental health professionals, personnel officers, teachers, and administrators than they could ever reach in one-on-one settings.

Other noteworthy features of consultation include the emphasis on providing human services rather than focusing on mental health, and that consultation generally takes place in the natural environment. Consultation "is an intervention aimed at changing the social situation within which the client is embedded" (Mannino & Shore, 1985, p. 364).

Types of Consultation

Four distinct types of consultation have been described by Caplan (1970).

Client-Centered Case Consultation

In client-centered or clinical (Gallessich, 1985) consultation, a referral is made to a specialist who provides direct service to the client. The service may be in the form of an examination and diagnosis with recommendations for treatment, or the specialist may take over full responsibility for subsequent treatment of the client (e.g., a counselor referring a client to a psychiatrist for a medical evalua- tion, and the possible need for drug therapy).

Consultee-Centered Case Consultation

In this instance, the consultant works with the consultee's difficulties in working with a particular client or groups of clients. The consultant may work to resolve a very specific situation that the consultee is having with a client, expand the con- sultee's overall skill in dealing with a particular type of client, or improve the consultee skills in general. In each instance, the focus of the consultant is on the consultee's work and would rarely, if ever, involve direct service to a primary client. Because the consultee is directly involved, there is a distinct advantage in this approach. The consultee may learn information and skills that will allow him or her to work effectively with similar clients in the future without the help of consultants. This triadic arrangement is considered to be one of the "definitive orienting concepts for the field" of consulting (Mannino & Shore, 1985, p. 364). The consultant's roles include being an educator and a facilitator (Gallessich, 1985); for example, a counselor working with a teacher on classroom manage- ment skills.

Program-Centered Administrative Consultation

In this type of consultation, the focus is on working with a specific program or organizational structure and not on the consultee's difficulties with the program or structure. For instance, a consultant might be employed to make recommenda- tions to a college counseling center that is contemplating making programmatic changes. Professionals pursuing this type of consultation are often referred to as organizational consultants, concerned with organizational development (OD). Roles implemented by consultants working with organizational development in- clude teacher, trainer, diagnostician, participant-observer, coach, facilitator, and action-researcher (Gallessich, 1985).

Consultee-Centered Administrative Consultation

In this type of consultation, the consultee's difficulties in working with a pro- gram or organization form the primary objective; the various components of the program or organization are secondary. For example, a consultant might work directly with an administrator on leadership or management skills. This is more of a doctor-patient model (Schein, 1978) or prescriptive mode (Kurpius, 1978), where the consultant is to define or diagnose the problem, explore various solutions, and prescribe action. The consultant then supports the consultee as the action steps are implemented.

In practice it may be difficult to determine the exact type of consultation being used, especially when there is a continuation of the above approaches. In the initial establishment of a consulting relationship, however, it is important to be specific as to the desired objective(s). Each type of consultation generally calls for a different contract, different expectations, and different behavior. Ultimately, the determination of the effectiveness of consulting is based on the degree of success to which the contract and all objectives therein, have been met.

Basic Conditions for Human Relations Consulting

The following four conditions have been found to be important in achieving effectiveness in consulting in the area of human relations. There are some exceptions, which are noted.

1. A voluntary relationship. The consultant is chosen freely by the client, and they enter into a mutually acceptable working relationship with either party free to terminate the relationship.
2. The consultant is generally an outsider. When consultants are not an integral part of the organization with which they are consulting, they can have greater objectivity and speak more frankly about the situation being observed.
3. Each consultation is focused on a particular problem. Consultants deal with the work of their clients, not their personal lives and problems. Consultation contracts do not typically include the provision of psychotherapy, so it is important for the consultant not to violate the contract and perhaps even alienate the client by so doing. Because a client's problems so often involve emotions as well as self-defeating behaviors, this is a vital distinction between consulting and psychotherapy.
4. The consulting relationship is generally time-limited. The consultant works with a given problem, and the relationship terminates with the completion of the task. The consultant may be called in for additional consultations, but each one is discrete.

The Roles of a Consultant

Consultants may serve in one or more roles in each consulting relationship. They may be teachers and trainers, communication facilitators, and/or human relations mediators, and they may serve as catalysts, helping clients brainstorm and put ideas into action (Korchin, 1976).

As teachers and trainers, consultants function both as technical helpers and resource personnel. They bring in relevant research literature in the area of concern along with experience with comparable problems in other settings and knowledge of useful techniques relevant to the concern of clients.

As communication facilitators, consultants may work with various members within the client's agency, or between agencies, or between the client, the agency, and the larger community. When working as human relations mediators, consultants, as outsiders, can often diagnose and provide assistance to the resolution of internal conflicts that affect the work of clients. In such cases they must avoid being pushed into the role of judge or referee. Finally, as catalysts, consultants can help inspire and even rejuvenate a client, agency, or organization by helping develop new ideas as well as plan for implementation of ideas deemed desirable. The ultimate function of the consultant is to contribute to the solution of the client's problems, while at the same time developing the client's capacity to resolve future problems (Korchin, 1976, p. 512).

The Consultation Process

Like counseling, the consultation process proceeds through a series of stages. Kurpius (1978) has described nine stages, which he labels preentry, entry, gathering information, defining the problem, determination of the problem solution, stating objectives, implementing the plan, evaluation, and termination.

In the preentry stage, when the consultant is contacted by the client, the consultant needs to determine whether he or she has the skills, attitudes, and time necessary to provide the requested services effectively. If the answer is no, an appropriate referral needs to be made; if the answer is yes, the consultant and client move to the entry stage, where the basic working relationship is established. The entry stage "involves the establishment of the relationship between consultant and consultees upon which the rest of the process depends" (Korchin, 1976, p. 515).

Exploring the nature of the problem and gathering as much information as possible then ensue in order to define the problem. With the problem defined and mutually agreed on between the consultant and the client, a variety of solutions are developed, and one is selected. If the problem is sufficiently complex, there may be a number of specific objectives to be met before a total solution is attained. The solution to the plan would then be implemented and the results evaluated. The process could then be recycled, or the consulting relationship terminated.

Counseling and Consulting Compared

Overall, there probably are many more similarities than differences between counseling and consulting, as noted by reviewing the brief description of the consulting process above. Although counseling and psychotherapy have not generally been time-limited (restricted to a set number of sessions or period of time) in the past, there are now specific time-limited approaches to counseling. Also, some consulting relationships are not necessarily time limited. A psychologist, for example, may serve as an ongoing consultant with a school district, meeting weekly with school counselors to discuss difficult cases the counselors may have.

Consulting, like counseling, requires the development of an interpersonal relationship characterized by trust and respect. The actual consulting and counseling processes closely parallel each other. Perhaps the major difference between the two is that consultation generally involves working with a middle person, one who has responsibility for working with others. As a result, consultants may have the opportunity for greater general impact because their work may, in the long run, affect many more people than they might ever see as a counselor. Egan (1986) suggests that counselors who hold client self-responsibility and self-efficacy as important values may be considered consultants hired by clients to help them face more effectively problems in living.

It is important to note that a trained professional can serve both as a counselor and as a consultant. The roles are not mutually exclusive. Faust (1968) has long advocated that the elementary school counselor serve more as a consultant working with the various teachers in the school, focusing more on preventive and developmental counseling than on remedial counseling. Overall, this is seen as a much more effective use of the counselor's time than primarily providing individual and group counseling.

The school counselor as consultant does violate the general principle of having the consultant be an outsider, as do the many businesses and industries that employ psychologists or other human relations personnel to work with management and staff with training and various other problems. Such internal consultants have special problems to deal with in establishing relationships with their clients. There may be status conflicts, power issues, concerns over confidentiality, and the like, which must be resolved before they can begin working together effectively. The period of establishing trust in such cases may take a great deal more skill and time than an outside consultant might need. Generally speaking, an outsider is often much more easily accepted as an expert than an insider.

HUMAN RESOURCE DEVELOPMENT IN BUSINESS AND INDUSTRY

Lester Thurow (1985) has indicated that one major problem with U.S. business and industry is the low level of its trained workforce. To upgrade the standards of the workforce, making it more competitive internationally, on-the-job training will be required, among other things. It is in the care and training of the modern work force that increasing numbers of professionals trained in the facilitation of human growth and change are finding gainful employment. Smith and Walz (1984) note what makes the helping professional so appealing:

Counselors in the privacy of their offices have successfully worked with individuals by helping them to develop, change, cope, and grow. Many of the same techniques work successfully when applied to the corporate setting. (p. 8)

Human Resource Development

The more or less generic title given to the concept of using helping skills in an organizational setting is human resource development (HRD). HRD consists of

> a process by which the employees of an organization are helped, in a continuous, planned way, to:
>
> 1. Acquire or sharpen capabilities required to perform various functions associated with their present or expected future roles;
> 2. Develop their general capabilities as individuals and discover and exploit their own inner potentials for their own and/or organizational developmental purposes;
> 3. Develop an organizational culture in which supervisor-subordinate relationships, teamwork, and collaboration among subunits are strong and contribute to the professional well-being, motivation, and pride of employees. (Rao, 1985, p. 227)

Rao (1985) believes that HRD is needed by any organization that wants to be dynamic and growth-oriented or to succeed in a fast-changing environment (p. 227). HRD ideas and processes can be used in virtually all types of organizations including governmental bodies and fraternal organizations. The descriptions offered here focus on applications within business and industry.

Specific mechanisms that help develop the capabilities of the employees and units within an organization include career development programs, training, organizational development, employee assistance programs, and quality of worklife programs.

Career Development Programs

Business organizations do not deliberately remain static, and working from within an HRD framework, employees are not expected to, either. Career development has been defined as "a process of human development that involves self investigation, learning, information gathering, decision making and change on the part of the individual" (Smith & Walz, 1984, p. 38). Within the context of the business enterprise, the HRD professional helps keep individuals apprised of projected changes and helps plan career moves as appropriate. The basic philosophy of providing for career planning is based on the belief that employees who are working satisfactorily within their career goals and expectations are more likely to be productive.

Training and Education

The greatest growth in the field of education today is in the area of business and industry. According to Naisbitt and Aburdene (1985)

> Training and education programs within American business are so vast, so extensive, that they represent in effect an alternative system to the nations public and private schools, colleges and universities. . . . About 8 million people are learning within corporations—about the same number that are enrolled in institutions of higher learning. (p. 66)

Training includes making assessments of employee needs as far as knowledge and skills are concerned to perform specific tasks, preparing appropriate instructional materials, conducting actual training session(s), and evaluating the results of the training. As companies grow and change, and as employees move within the company and new employees are hired, there is generally a regular amount of training occurring within a moderate-to-large size company.

Organizational Development (OD)

The organization development specialist works to maintain a psychological climate within the company that is conducive to high productivity. Experts in this area also help any department or unit within a company that is having trouble with such problems as absenteeism, low production, or interpersonal conflict. The structure of the company itself, or subdivisions thereof, may also come into the purview of experts within this area (Rao, 1985, p. 231).

Employee Assistance Programs

Employee Assistance Programs (EAPs) are set up or contracted by companies to help employees who may be having personal difficulties that could be interfering with their productivity on the job. Personal difficulties could include financial, marriage, or substance abuse problems. EAP clients are generally referred to experts outside of the company to receive assistance on their particular problems, although there may be some in-house assistance provided in some programs.

EAP specialists educate all employees on the characteristics of the employee assistance plan, provide specific training to supervisory personnel so that they can help employees use the system effectively, work directly with employees who have problems and make referrals to appropriate agencies and experts, and do followup evaluations. The EAP specialist would rarely provide any direct service for an employee. Direct services are almost always provided by trained personnel external to the EAP itself.

Quality of Worklife Programs

Quality of worklife programs focus on helping make the place in which employees spend 40 hours or so a week a generally positive, attractive environment. The actual work that employees do may be tedious and monotonous, but if it is being done in a place they believe is safe and reasonably esthetic, where there may be a sense of belonging and a feeling that their opinions about working conditions will be heard, it can be said that there is a relatively high quality of worklife.

Quality of worklife specialists may work on improving physical conditions, plan recreational facilities and activities, and help improve fringe benefit packages such as educational subsidies and health and medical benefits. An overall objective is to help develop the sense of belonging and loyalty to the company that in the long run benefits all concerned (Rao, 1985).

These descriptions indicate the variety of activities presently being undertaken in various businesses and industries by personnel trained in the helping professions. Organizations that do not have the size or capital to justify employing full-time human resource development specialists may contract with a variety of external consultants who would be able to provide the various services. The need for training, development, and improved working conditions and employee services is there, and the job market for experts in this field appears to be expanding (Smith & Walz, 1984; Chalofsky, 1985).

A professional organization that specifically deals with the issues in this area is the Association of Specialists in Training and Development (ASTD). The organization publishes the *Training and Development Journal.* Specialized training for work in this field is offered by the National Training Laboratories (NTL) and University Associates (UA).

SUMMARY

One decision facing all prospective counselors is whether to be a generalist and work in almost all areas of the field or specialize in one or two areas. The general guidelines of a flexible specialty have been offered, suggesting a concentration in one or two specialty areas while continuing to maintain an awareness of techniques and developments in the total field.

Guidelines for use in selecting a counseling specialty include assessing personal strengths and weaknesses, clarifying personal values related to work and lifestyle, being in direct contact with counselors in a broad variety of specialty settings, using practicum and internship experiences as testing grounds, and being flexible and open to change.

Specialty areas in which many counselors are employed, or in which employment opportunities in the future appear promising, have been described. These include elementary, middle, and high schools, student personnel work in higher education, substance abuse counseling, rehabilitation counseling, gerontological counseling, health counseling, consultation, and personnel work in business and industry. The consultation process has been described and compared to the counseling process. Consultation is an approach that can be used as part of a specialization such as school counseling or can be sustained as a separate private practice.

Other specialties described in subsequent chapters are career counseling and family counseling. In all of these specialty areas, additional education and training beyond the master's degree level are generally required.

QUESTIONS AND ACTIVITIES

1. How are you determining whether to become a generalist or a specialist? Review the pros and cons of each and then share your conclusions with fellow students. What issues cause you the most difficulty with this decision?
2. What practicum or internship sites are available to you in your region that might afford you the opportunity to investigate in depth one or two areas of specialization that appeal to you? Check with your instructor as to the proper time and the approach to make in contacting these sites for practicum/internship placement.
3. Consider the following statement: "There is no difference between effective counseling and effective consulting in terms of process." Do you agree or disagree? Would your response to this question be of any influence in terms of a career decision you might make?

The Problems of Becoming and Being a Counselor: Stress Management and the Prevention of Burnout

Of what must I, as a counselor in training, be aware?

Since the mid 1970s, the terms *stress* and *burnout* have been used frequently to describe certain negative consequences of work in various fields. People from housewives to air traffic controllers have found application for these terms. What is of particular importance here is that these concepts and their consequences are particularly prevalent in the helping professions, including students preparing for occupations in the profession. We believe that the issues of stress management and the prevention of burnout need to be understood and behavior changes made as necessary from the first course in a counseling program.

STRESS AND BURNOUT DEFINED

Stress and burnout are not new. Stress has always been with us, and burnout may be a term used to describe what was once called a nervous breakdown. A major problem in understanding the dynamics of stress and burnout has been the failure to arrive at commonly accepted definitions (Moracco & McFadden, 1982). To add to the confusion, the terms are often used interchangeably. Therefore, a clarification of terms is necessary from the outset.

Stress is the "experiencing of external environmental or internal environmental impingements (stimuli) or stressors" (Kutash, Schlessinger, & Assoc., 1980, p. 464). A stressor is a stress-producing factor, the source of which can be either internal or external (Selye, 1980). Burnout is the depletion of physical and mental resources characterized by a loss of motivation, enthusiasm, energy, and interest as well as a significantly lower level of performance (Kyriacou & Sutcliff, 1978).

Stress is not something to avoid; in fact, it is impossible to do so. Complete freedom from stress is death (Selye, 1980). Selye distinguishes between two basic types of stress: *eustress*, which is pleasant, curative, and often motivational, and *distress*, which is unpleasant or disease-producing stress (Selye, 1980, p. 128). Some people are stress-seekers, searching for and participating in activities in which there may be a lot of stress involved, such as hang gliding, skydiving, downhill skiing, motorcycle racing, and even sedentary competitive activities such as playing duplicate bridge. People entering the field of counseling may be stress seekers, because most could probably be gainfully employed in occupations involving less personal stress and perhaps even make more money.

What may be distress to one person may be eustress to another. How a person responds to stress depends on a number of factors: the environment, the magnitude of the stressor, what has gone before, the person's perception of the situation and self-perceived ability to handle the stressor, the person's physical condition, and the person's previous pattern in dealing with the stressor (Benjamin, 1987).

Selye also adds two other characteristics to the description of the stress of life. These are "overstress" (hyperstress), where we have extended the limits of adaptability, and "understress" (hypostress), where we suffer from a lack of self-realization, such as physical immobility, boredom, or sensory deprivation (Selye, 1980, p. 141).

Figure 8.1 illustrates the relation among the various aspects of stress and burnout. A fairly high level of eustress, for example, would generally lead to a

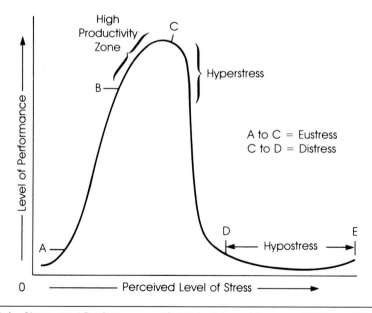

FIGURE 8.1 Stress and Performance *(Adapted from Morano, 1977, p. 23)*

high rate of productivity in most cases. However, too much stress, hyperstress, could be counterproductive. Distress could result, followed in some cases by hypostress and burnout.

Stress can be either self-imposed or situational. Some people impose stress on themselves by setting unreasonably high standards or having unrealistic expectations regarding their abilities. Situational stress is often caused by time constraints, lack of resources, threats to emotional or physical well being, interpersonal value conflicts, and overwhelming challenges.

Type A and B Personalities

Doctors Meyer Friedman and Ray Rosenman (1974) discovered a connection between certain personality traits and coronary thrombosis. They described persons who exhibit a high degree of such traits as self-control, impatience, time urgency, aggressiveness, tenseness, inability to relax, achievement orientation, and insecure status as Type A personalities. Type A personalities also appear more prone to stress-related illnesses than do Type B personalities—people who can relax without feeling guilty, who move and talk more slowly, and who have the ability to have fun for the sake of it and to play without having to win at any cost (Rice, 1987).

Type C Behavior

Further analysis of individuals with Type A behavior resulted in the finding that many of these people appear to thrive on the stress they experience, manifesting none of the debilitating results experienced by others designated as Type A. In investigating this phenomenon with people from a variety of occupations, Maddi and Kobasa (1984) discovered what they call the hardiness factor. A distress-resistant pattern was identified, consisting of three attitudes or perspectives involving challenge, commitment, and control. Hardy individuals view stress as a challenge rather than a threat; they are strongly committed to their work, their families, and their beliefs; and they believe they are able to control or influence events and their reactions to events rather than feel helpless.

A study of athletes, musicians, speakers, and other people who were able to attain peak performances while under great pressure yielded similar results (Kriegel & Kriegel, 1984). Kriegel and Kriegel also identified three basic attitudes each beginning with the letter *C:* challenge, control, and confidence. When the results of these two studies are combined, a picture emerges of the disease-resistant individual, the person who seems to thrive on stress. This individual views stress as a challenge rather than as a threat, exudes confidence rather than self-doubt, has a strong sense of commitment rather than feeling detached and alienated, and feels in control rather than helpless (Schafer, 1987). Each of these C attitudes or perspectives can be learned and strengthened.

Burnout

Burnout seems to be a dynamic process characterized by at least three distinct stages (Daley, 1979). Stage one is the alarm reaction stage in which counselors mobilize their defense mechanisms. Victims of burnout fail to respond constructively to this early warning alarm. They are not able to adapt to new or continued stressors. Burnout victims often deny that there is anything wrong. They pass off initial symptoms as minor reactions to pressures and direct their energies toward overcoming perceived obstacles. Burnout victims often place unrealistic, perfectionist demands on themselves, or they set impossible goals.

As stressors on counselors continue to persist and increase in intensity, stage two may manifest itself. Stage two is called the resistance stage. It is characterized by the diversion of energies away from personal growth and professional responsibilities and toward managing stress directly. Clients suffer when their counselors begin to feel helpless and powerless and cease to care. Counselors in this stage of burnout function at a low level, both professionally and at home, as their interpersonal relations begin to deteriorate.

Finally, failure to deal effectively with the first two stages may lead to the third stage, exhaustion. This stage is characterized by increased cynicism, inflexibility, withdrawal, illness, depression, and possible suicide (Nicholson & Golsan, 1983).

Whatever the stage, burnout can have physical, psychological, and behavioral effects on counselors. Some physical effects include ulcers, respiratory illness, headaches, hypertension, insomnia, and cardiovascular diseases. Psychological effects include depression, general anxiety, poor self-concept, confused thinking, and paranoid symptoms. Behavioral effects include absenteeism at work, poor relations with colleagues, inability to concentrate, and impaired interpersonal communication.

From this discussion we conclude that burnout results from excess levels of stress (hyperstress), involves a great amount of distress, and ultimately results in hypostress (exhaustion).

CAUSES OF BURNOUT IN COUNSELING TRAINING

Counselor burnout has many causes. It is often experienced by students in counselor training programs. Many students are initially overwhelmed by the many theories and methods presented to them in training programs. They quickly become discouraged. Students believe that they will never be able to master the complex skills and approaches or to attain the other qualities that they believe a successful counselor must have. They want to become competent and polished immediately. The students become impatient with themselves. This perfectionistic drive can also be a problem with experienced counselors. In training programs, the feelings of being overwhelmed represent a failure to see professional growth and competency as a developmental process. Students need time to assimilate ideas and integrate them. They need time to begin the development of their own theoretical positions. They also need to realize that professional growth is a continuing process that goes on long after their degrees and licenses are achieved. Continuous experience and supervision account for a great portion of one's development.

Students are often inadequately prepared to cope with negative stressors. Warnath and Shelton (1976) conclude that graduate school experiences are not positive ones for significant numbers of students and that the seeds of ultimate burnout are planted there. They point to ineffective modeling by professors who talk about the core conditions of warmth, openness, and honesty as essential characteristics for counselors, but who are themselves distant, closed, and manipulative in their contacts with students. Students soon learn to play the academic game and give their professors what they want in order to earn their degrees and credentials while putting off their own need gratifications.

Contending with Family Relationships

Students entering graduate work in the field of counseling are not always prepared for the effect this will have on family relationships. It is not surprising for graduate students to report relationship crises. Many graduate counseling programs provide opportunities for students to view and evaluate their own growth and development. Introspection is not only accepted but encouraged. This is a luxury that is generally lacking in everyday living—people rarely take the time to look at the process of their lives because they are too busy getting things done. This opportunity for individual focus can become an integrative element in students' interpsychic lives affecting their interpersonal relations.

Students often report feeling confused and unsure as they encounter themselves. Things that were previously taken for granted or accepted are now reexamined. As students begin to undergo growth and change, their relationships also begin to change. This process produces a great deal of pressure, which, if not handled appropriately, can lead to overstress, distress, and burnout.

Students who are working to make the skills of counseling a part of their way of life may make some changes in their thinking or behavior patterns that are not acceptable to families and friends. Families and friends may respond in ways that cause the student to revert to former behavioral patterns. Students may experience stressful conflicts based on the possible incompatibility of their goals: striving for personal growth while trying to please significant others.

Attempting to counsel one's family can also cause difficulties. Ethically, counselors should limit their involvement in family matters to listening and responding skills and leave in-depth counseling to qualified professionals.

The pressure and conflicts that arise in a family as a result of one member pursuing an education are not exclusive to counseling students. This phenomenon occurs in other educational settings as well, particularly when one spouse is growing educationally and the other is not. It is important to keep family members fully aware of the nature of the work and expectations of the counselor training program. Bringing family members to the campus library to study with you can be helpful in reducing some of the mystery related to your studies. It also may be possible to invite one or more family members to attend a class session or two in order to meet your instructors and your classmates.

Other Outside Pressures

For many students, the act of embarking on a course of graduate study is a transition, and transitions by their nature affect interpersonal relations. Many students must have a job while attending school. The responsibilities of work, study, and family can become difficult to balance. There is not enough time to do all that is required. Students may find it difficult to establish priorities, and this may strain relationships, especially friendships. Pressures may develop to the point at which students may feel the need to cut back on their work commitments, often causing a financial strain. Sometimes power and control issues with significant others involving support of the student's career rise to the surface. Close relationships dissolve when the people involved fail to adapt to the changes.

Family relations and friendships can also be strengthened if those involved are flexible and secure enough to adjust to the changes. Those who have established a solid personal identity and have achieved intimate relationships are able to allow others to grow and mature without barriers or restrictions.

CAUSES OF COUNSELOR BURNOUT

Striving for perfection is one cause of burnout for both the counselor in training and the counselor in service. Many counselors place unrealistic demands on themselves, interfering with their personal needs. This leads to a vicious cycle of frustration: the more accomplished, the more that remains to be accomplished. The problem is compounded when demands are not clearly defined. Sometimes the goals are unattainable, and the perfectionist counselor who equates self-worth with accomplishment is in trouble. As with academic striving, counselors must differentiate between self-defeating perfectionism and the healthy pursuit of excellence.

Work and Play

The busman's holiday syndrome is a danger in any occupation. In the counseling field, the counselors' personal and professional life merge. This causes a mind set in which there may seem to be no opportunity to be casual or to be one's own person. Everything in a counselor's existence does not need to be scrutinized from a psychological perspective. Family and friends should be counseled by someone else. Counseling should not be the only topic of discussion in relationships. Counselors need to work to live, not to live to work. When play becomes work rather than work becoming play, that is a danger signal.

Even if work is not perceived as play, if it is not what a person really wants to do and feels committed to do, the person would seem to be more vulnerable to distress. Counselors **might** benefit from regular examination of their work and career goals, and their current satisfaction with what they are doing. When people are doing what they really want to do, they are in charge of their own lives and are less likely to become burned out regardless of the pressures involved.

Counselor-Client Interaction

Being fully with a client in the therapeutic interaction can be demanding. The authors do not recommend that counselors withdraw from their clients by falling asleep when the presented material is on a superficial level, as Fritz Perls is reported to have done. Yet, as Watkins (1983) states,

> The counselor, during counseling sessions, may experience periods of phasing out with greater intensity and frequency, and the therapeutic hour can come to be regarded as just another opportunity for encounter with another human being. An ever hardening and pervasive attitude of indifference tends to develop and can have sabotaging effects on the counselor's work. (p. 208)

Phasing out, or losing contact with a client, may, of course, be due to other factors, such as a defensive reaction to issues raised by the client with which the counselor has personal troubles dealing. In any event, clients may eventually become discouraged and vent their anger toward their counselors in various nonconstructive ways. When this happens, counselors may develop an increased hostility toward clients manifested by veiled sarcasm or extreme silence.

Counselors need to learn to pace themselves during counseling sessions and to withdraw momentarily to accumulate new energy when necessary. Counselors can resort to timely, appropriate self-disclosure when appropriate (see self-attending, chapter 3). They must also seek supervision to determine whether their distortions, personal issues, and other countertransference behaviors may be impeding their presence in counseling relationships.

In chapter 1 we describe counseling as a way of life. Counseling is not a career in which counselors can successfully wear one hat in the counseling room and another outside; inevitably this can lead to conflict and distress. Counselors need to be concrete and genuine. Although clients may be troubled, they often are good crap detectors and can sense when the counselor is simply playing a role.

Another potential problem area exists when counselors assume responsibility for their clients and for the solution of their problems. It is possible for them even to feel responsible for clients' lives. Not only is this behavior unhealthy and nontherapeutic, but it also places a tremendous amount of pressure on counselors. The more we attempt to become responsible for other people, the more we cheat them out of their own selfhood and foster the possibility of dependency relationships. In effect, we fail to show respect for our clients' ability to change and grow. Perls (1969) advised counselors never to do for clients what clients are capable of doing for themselves. The help provided in such cases is, in actuality, not helpful to clients or to counselors.

Counselors also need to be aware that seeing a steady stream of troubled people over long periods of time can lead to a skewed picture of the world. It is possible to see the whole world as suffering from immense and hopeless problems from which there appears to be no escape.

Counselors in Agencies and Institutions

Counselors who work for agencies and institutions often face additional pressures. Sometimes there is no positive reinforcement on the job. Most people like to receive some recognition for work well done, but in the hectic everyday world, positive recognition is not often given. This can have a devastating effect on staff, especially when a self-support system is lacking. As counselors become more and more frustrated, they increasingly look for a reward system outside of counseling. Complicating the reward system is the difficulty of measuring tangible success with clients.

Also, financial rewards are not usually adequate for counselors, and in times of budgetary crises, jobs may be in jeopardy. There is often agency pressure to be more efficient and take on greater case loads, often at the expense of the agency clientele.

Sometimes graduate students develop unrealistic expectations regarding the future. For example, many school counselors become disappointed when they find themselves arranging bus and class schedules and assuming other management functions. A large ratio of students per counselor leaves little time for counseling. Agency counselors can also find themselves doing meaningless work and, as a result, may experience diminished job satisfaction.

Many counselors work with difficult clients who come for counseling only because they have to be there. These counselors become discouraged when they see little progress being made. There can be conflict and tension and lack of support among coworkers as well as lack of trust between counselors and supervisors. Experimentation, change, and innovation can be discouraged in institutional bureaucracy. Sometimes there is no opportunity for professional renewal, such as in-service workshops or continuing education.

Counselors are especially vulnerable to failing to preempt their maternal role professionally. Virginia Satir, the noted family therapist, reported feeling like her whole body was covered with breasts when she entered the profession. Counselors need to free their souls and take care of themselves while they are giving as much as they can give. Maslach (1982) refers to this as "balance." The key to preventing burnout according to Maslach is to maintain a balance between giving and getting, stress and calm, work and home.

STRESS MANAGEMENT—PREVENTING BURNOUT

In chapter 1, it was mentioned that the counselor needs a great amount of personal energy to perform effectively. Of concern here is that the initial reservoirs of energy are quickly depleted and then not renewed. What is needed from the onset of a career in counseling is a systematic approach to the renewal of personal energy. Figure 8.2 indicates how the deliberate recycling of energy might occur. Initial stores of energy and positive motivating stressors help provide the eustress necessary for high-level productivity. As suggested earlier, counselors may deliberately seek additional personal stressors for motivational purposes and to reenergize themselves. Within this framework, then, stress management techniques are systematically used to provide the rest and relaxation the body and mind need, as well as the renewal of personal energy necessary for continued high level work.

Fortunately, there are numerous approaches to stress management and the prevention of burnout. Counselors need to be familiar with the various ideas and methods available, not only for their own functioning, but also as tools for their clients. Some people can handle a great deal of stress and thrive on it, while others can cope with very little. As noted, stress in and of itself is not the culprit. It is the inappropriate methods used in coping with stress that lead to burnout. The emphasis here is on developing positive methods for managing stress and for developing an overall approach to personal wellness.

BREADS/LT

Some major areas of concern in the prevention and relief of burnout center around Breathing, Relaxation, Exercise, Attitude, Diet, and Support, all tempered

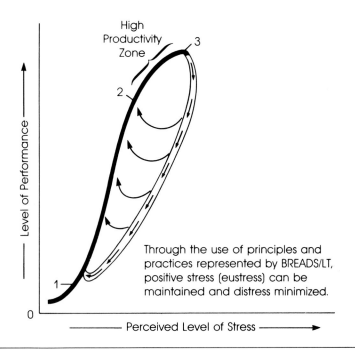

FIGURE 8.2 Positive Stress Cycle

by Laughter and structured by effective Time Management. These several approaches can be referred to by the acronym BREADS/LT and are described below.

Breathing

A common physiological response to stress or anxiety is a constriction of the muscles in the upper chest and neck. Breathing can become severely restricted. This adds up to the overall feeling of discomfort and further aggravates an already unpleasant condition.

When people are under stress their breathing becomes very shallow and fresh air seldom gets to the bottom of their lungs. They can be seen to inhale, but exhalation is difficult to detect. It is as though they were willing to take things in but not let things out.

When working with people under stress, it is often necessary to have them take some deep breaths and encourage them to exhale clearly each time before starting work on any personal issues. The awareness of breathing patterns and the practice of proper breathing before, during, and after any stressful events are important components to use when dealing with major life stressors. Effective breathing can help increase energy levels.

Relaxation and Meditation

Counselors can use private time to their advantage by engaging in various types of contemplation and meditation. The many approaches to this include Yoga, transcendental meditation (TM), biofeedback, progressive relaxation, Tai Chi, prayer, chanting, singing, and self-attending. Some are easy, some are difficult, but the result of these techniques is physical and mental rejuvenation. It often is surprising to people who do not use systematic relaxation techniques to realize how energizing they can be.

Exercise

Counseling is basically a sedentary experience, and counselors need physical outlets for their mental as well as physical well being. Certain exercises and sports can be practiced throughout life by counselors, including hiking, jogging, tennis, bowling, and aerobics. There is evidence that the body releases certain hormones during exercise that can relieve depression and increase energy.

Attitude

Negative attitudes are contagious. Counselors who have become cynical or depressed affect the people with whom they come in contact. Nicholson and Golsan (1983) state that the negativism fostered by a sense that we are not in control of our lives is a real enemy. Often negative feeling states lead to deeper problems when counselors start feeling guilty about having them. The guilt feelings compound the original negative feelings and drive the counselor further into the burnout cycle. Ironically, counselors often spend much of their time fighting the same symptoms in their clients. Counselors need to realize that they are responsible for their attitudes, and that they must learn to make growth-enhancing choices for themselves.

Diet

Proper nutrition is important. Treatment of stress is environmental, social, mental, and physical; therefore, intervention needs to be wholistic, incorporating a wide range of strategies that lead to healthy patterns of living. Just as exercise has become accepted as an integral part of our culture, proper nutrition has also become an accepted practice. More and more people are concerned with food additives, weight control, and balanced diets. The basic guidelines are to eat food daily from the four basic food groups—dairy, meat, vegetables and fruit, and cereal and grain—with an emphasis on fish and poultry over red meat. With a balanced diet, vitamin supplements are rarely needed unless a known deficiency exists.

Support Groups

Counselors, especially those who work with a regular routine of crisis counseling, need to spend time with healthy people, whether colleagues, friends, or family. Healthy people do not gossip or find fault. They are nourishing and supportive. Ironically, human service organizations often neglect human concerns within their own staff. Some organizations become so bureaucratic that their clientele also suffers. Sometimes a support group of colleagues who are more fully functioning can make all the difference. Colleagues who focus only on gossip and negative griping tend to become toxic. Having highly functioning friends and family members also helps to counter adverse working conditions. Counselors can choose to be with nourishing, supportive people. Intimate personal relationships make life richer.

Laughter

An excellent source of tension relief is laughter. Wholesome, hearty laughter has been described as the muscle of the soul. Laughter activates chemicals in the brain called endorphins, which provide a feeling of euphoria. It is extremely difficult to remain in a state of anxiety or depression when you are laughing. Humor that is self-depreciating or meant to put down other people is not appropriate. A healthy approach to stress management or the treatment of burnout requires regular (daily) doses of laughter.

Laughter has been defined as internal jogging. Watching television shows that are particularly funny to you, listening to tapes or records of favorite comedians, reading books by humorous authors, and telling jokes are all ways by which laughter can be a regular part of your life.

Time Management—Setting Priorities

Counseling students and beginning counselors often take on more than they can handle. They find themselves in over their heads. Counselors must be more selective in choosing their activities and even their clients if they can. A very discouraging situation for counselors is to end up with a full load of clients at very low levels of functioning. If clients can be selected on the basis of probability of success, high risk clients can be balanced by low risk ones, thereby reducing the potential for burnout. Counselors can also help themselves by selecting clients who fit their particular skills or areas of interest. Having areas of specialization enables counselors to focus on those areas without the additional pressures of being up on all aspects of counseling (see chapter 15).

Counselors also need to make priorities as to what they can take on and to delegate lower priority duties when possible. Sometimes establishing job exchanges with other people provides for some variety, newness, and increased interest. Counselors who are burdened with interfering noncounseling activities must take the offensive with their administration. Perhaps they must redefine their jobs and suggest alternatives so that they can be free to do more counseling. Assertive training skills such as learning to say "no" can be invaluable when employer demands are unreasonable or unrealistic.

In order for counseling students to apply themselves fully to their studies they must be aware of the necessity to set priorities. These priorities may affect friends, family, and even their work if they are employed. The affected people should be made aware of the student's priority decisions directly and not have to discover these indirectly or by accident. Directness on the part of the student is the most beneficial approach for all concerned.

Private Time.   An important consideration is that counselors have ample free time to develop nonwork activities and interests. The scheduling of enjoyable nonwork activities can enrich the professional and personal lives of the counselor. Hobbies, travel, nonprofessional reading, and play allow for personal renewal. As counselors experience their own lives more fully, they become more effective as counselors. Health demands balance in all areas of living. Overinvolvement with work can strain family relationships. Overinvolvement with family prevents family members from becoming individuals. Overinvolvement with self is narcissistic. In all cases self-growth is retarded.

One particularly good use of private time is to set aside specific time for worrying. It is not realistic to expect people not to worry, and there are occasions when worry is helpful. Worrying can, however, be overly time-consuming and induce distress. What some counselors and others have found to be helpful is to reserve time for worrying just as they have time reserved for exercise and relaxation (e.g., Wednesday evening, from 7 to 8 o'clock). Any worries throughout the rest of the week can be assigned to that time period.

The BREADS/LT components, if systematically applied to the point of becoming habitual, can be invaluable in preventing excessive distress and burnout.

The various components can also be used individually or in various combinations, whenever crisis situations and other distressing circumstances occur, to help minimize the experience of distress.

In addition to establishing your own BREADS/LT program of stress management, three positive ways of working with stress recommended by Selye (1978) can be implemented. First, he suggests choosing a level of stress that is comfortable. This includes knowing when to seek stress for stimulation and motivation, and also when to avoid additional stressors over which you have no control. Second, Selye suggests that we choose our own goals. Choices that are introjected from significant others are not our own choices. They are "shoulds" that are swallowed whole without being thought through. Counselors need to think through and clarify their own values and goals. Finally, Selye suggests developing a broad repertoire of competence in order to make ourselves invaluable to others. This altruistic egoism combats social stress by giving meaning to life.

Responsibility and Personal Therapy

Most counselors believe that we are all responsible for our behaviors. Indeed, much of what transpires in the counseling process is related to clients' taking responsibility for the part they play in their problems and for changing their attitudes and behaviors as a way of coping with those problems. Counselors must also face personal responsibility for their own wellness and discover methods for maintaining it.

At the same time, counselors must avoid assuming responsibility for others. If counselors become aware of experiencing burnout symptoms and have difficulty resolving them, personal therapy might be called for. Personal therapy can help counselors develop increased understanding and insight into themselves, their clients, and their counseling behaviors. Additionally, it can help improve intimate interpersonal relationships which almost always suffer during burnout. Egan (1986) states,

> Ideally, [helpers] are first of all committed to their own growth—physical, intellectual, social-emotional, and spiritual—for they realize that helping often involves modeling the patterns of behavior their clients hope to achieve. They know that they can help only if, in the root sense of the term, they are "potent" human beings—that is, people with both the resources and the will to act. (p. 28)

SUMMARY

Helping counselors learn how to manage stress and prevent burnout is the theme of this chapter. The different aspects of stress have been defined and described: eustress is positive stress; distress, negative stress; hyperstress is being overstressed; and hypostress, being understressed. Because eustress can be motivating, people may seek it out (stress-seekers). A fair amount of stress is needed to work at a maximum productivity level. What is necessary is to use a stress management plan to assure that the stressors do not become overwhelming, leading to hyperstress and then hypostress (the burnout syndrome). The stages of burnout resulting from poor stress management or an abundance of negative stressors have been described.

Negative stressors that could lead to burnout can occur during counselor training as a result of being overwhelmed by the material to be learned, being perfectionistic and impatient with personal progress, and experiencing relationship crises with family and friends, often as a consequence of school commitments.

Family issues also can be a factor leading to burnout in practicing counselors, in addition to other causes such as striving for perfection; setting unattainable goals; not having a balance between work and play; getting overly emotionally involved with client's problems; experiencing a lack of positive reinforcement, praise, or appreciation; and not taking care of oneself.

Basic components of a stress management program have been presented to provide for personal care, the effective management of stress, and the prevention of burnout for both counselors-in-training and practicing counselors. These components include breathing, relaxation, exercise, attitude, diet, support groups, laughter, and time management. The acronym BREADS/LT is offered to help ensure retention of the ideas. All of these components are natural, inexpensive ways that when systematically used provide the nourishment, rest, and reenergizing necessary to maintain the eustress desired for high level wellness.

An important side effect of developing a sound personal stress management plan is that it can be used in counseling. The problems of many clients involve the ineffective management of stressors. Counselors who have been able to manage their stressors successfully will be able to serve as models for their clients and help clients develop their own stress management plans.

QUESTIONS AND ACTIVITIES

1. Are you more of a stress seeker or a stress avoider? Could it be that many people who enter the field of counselor education are stress seekers? Explore this idea with members of your class and with practicing counselors.
2. Name and describe the three stages of burnout. How might a counselor recognize herself or himself as being in the first stage? How might you as a student recognize yourself as being in one of these stages? If you were in one of the stages of burnout, what would you do then?
3. Consider the acronym BREADS/LT as one way of conceptualizing major factors that need to be considered in a stress management/burnout prevention plan. Devise your own stress management plan—one to which you will be willing to make a commitment—and come up with your own acronym to

highlight the factors that are most meaningful to you. Share this plan with one or two significant others and ask them to help you monitor the plan for a given period of time.

4. How could personal counseling for a counselor or a counselor-in-training be considered an effective component of a stress management plan?

CHAPTER 9

The Responsibility of the Counselor in the Greater Society

What responsibilities if any do counselors have to social issues? Is it too much to expect counselors to get involved in outside issues when they are generally already overinvolved in their work and often underpaid?

If we as counselors are expected to empower our clients, then we might also become more assertive and empower ourselves by working toward social change. This chapter examines the responsibility of counselors to society.

THE SOCIAL CONTEXT OF CHANGE

Our society is currently moving out of the industrial age into an information/electronics age. In this continually evolving world counselors have a responsibility to examine whether their theoretical applications are responsive to society's changes.

Early reformers in mental health had a broad and comprehensive perspective. They were involved in consciousness-raising activities and promoted social legislation to deal with the social problems brought on by industrialization (Aubrey, 1980). Kelly (1989) notes that this significant role of social commitment in counseling is present and needs to be enhanced by clarifying the balance between the individual and social perspectives. As the profession of counseling developed counselors took on a narrower focus, emphasizing intrapsychic change, technology, and technique. The social context of change was for the most part ignored. As a result, during the social and political upheavals of the 1960s, the counseling profession was not able to respond to a multitude of social issues. Counselors were unable to deal with people coping with problems of civil rights, the Vietnam war, women's rights, counterculture, drugs, and alienation from the establishment value system. According to Aubrey and Lewis (1988), psychotherapeutic models failed in both perspective and application. Perspective had a narrow, intrapsychic focus, and application focused on awareness, insight, and self-discovery when what often seemed needed were both a broadening of perspective and a wider array of intervention techniques.

More recently, adherents of a multicultural perspective to counseling have been critical of traditional counseling as being nonegalitarian, office-bound, and intrapsychically focused (see chapter 16). The critics advocate that the role of a counselor must include being a change agent who works to affect the environment in which the client lives. Environmental interventions should include confronting and modifying institutional bureaucracies and working to reduce racism, sexism, and other discriminatory attitudes (Atkinson, Morton, & Sue, 1983, p. 240).

Human beings do not live in a vacuum. Each of us operates in the larger context of society. The process of self-actualization involves significant relationships with others in the world. Our feelings, attitudes, values, and behavior are influenced by interpersonal, family, local, national, and global conflicts and issues. We helping professionals must attend to the context in which behavior occurs in order to be effective. We must begin thinking more about prevention. Counselors have numerous contributions to make to the many significant issues society faces today, such as achieving peace, confronting world hunger, reducing family violence, fighting drugs, aiding the homeless, and protecting the environment. Insights into how people change their behavior, how to relate to each other in more peaceful ways, and the psychodynamics of life can be used in dealing with many of these issues.

> The consequences of growing up under the influence of a nuclear crisis seem to have direct professional implications. To explore those implications through research and case study and to develop measures appropriate to the findings for action on an individual, group or systems basis are very much the business of every intelligent and enlightened counselor. Such steps are not some extracurricular activity, not some luxury, and certainly not the radical action of an avant-garde group of counselors. On the contrary, they reflect the only direction for ethical practice at this time in the 20th century. (Schwebel, 1984, p. 74)

PRECEDENCE FOR SOCIAL COMMITMENT

Kelly (1989) argues that there is a significant role of social commitment in counseling that needs to be enhanced by clarifying the balance between the individual and social perspectives. He proposes retaining a primary emphasis on a carefully explicated balance of both social and individual dimensions.

Even Sigmund Freud, the founder of psychoanalysis, corresponded with Albert Einstein on whether future wars could be prevented. A major tenet of Adlerian psychotherapy has always been the primary concern for social interest as an innate part of a person's development. Adler believed that individuals should feel themselves to be a part of a larger social whole and contribute to the common well being. He wrote on such social issues as crime, war, and nationalism. Other theorists and practitioners who have advocated social consciousness include Abraham Maslow, Carl Rogers, Victor Frankl, Jerome Frank, Albert Ellis, B. F. Skinner, Robert Jay Lifton, David Adams, and also Erik Erikson and Harry Stack Sullivan.

Abraham Maslow's characteristics of self-actualizing persons include the belief that self-actualizing persons are concerned about discrepancies between what is and what might be, in themselves, others, and society. They also are problem-centered rather than ego-centered and focus on problems outside themselves on the basis of a sense of responsibility, duty, or obligation. Maslow also developed an extension of his self-actualization model to societal levels, calling it Politics 3. He compared the process of creating the good society with that of creating the good person and saw no difference between the goals psychotherapists had for individuals and those they should have for society.

Carl Rogers, during his later years, expanded his concept of the person-centered approach to apply to resolving conflict between adversarial groups in international seminars and workshops in such settings as Northern Ireland, South Africa, Austria, Hungary, Brazil, the U.S.S.R., Spain, and the United States. The topics included human oppressions, nuclear arms, and political and religious differences. Rogers also strongly advocated long-range training programs for leaders in politics, business, and industry so they could become facilitators of international disputes.

Victor Frankl holds that the significance of individuals and the meaning of human personality are related to community, and that the meaning of individuality comes to fulfillment in the community. Psychiatrist Jerome Frank has been actively writing and speaking about the nuclear peril. His book *Psychotherapy and the Human Predicament* (1978) deals with the place of the helping professions in social problems. Albert Ellis (1984) has theorized that although environmental threats do not directly cause emotional disturbance, people's cognitions and views about these threats significantly contribute to or influence disturbance. Ellis advocates that therapists help clients first cope with external threats and then, if feasible, ameliorate or eliminate them. B. F. Skinner's controversial fictional outline of a modern utopia, *Walden Two* (1948), conceptualizes a society in which human problems are solved by a scientific technology of human conduct.

Psychiatrist Robert Jay Lifton has spent much of his life actively crusading for world peace and was an early member of Physicians for Social Responsibility. He has written extensively on such topics as Nazi doctors, Vietnam veterans, and Hiroshima survivors. Lifton believes that the claim of professional neutrality in the face of ultimate destruction is immoral and insists that the helping professions bear a special responsibility to take a stand (Kohn, 1988). David Adams, a psychologist and peace activist, advocates a new psychology that would proclaim the values of peace and justice and promote these values in all areas of society. This stance, according to Adams, is unlike traditional psychology, which favors political neutrality and resists being involved in questions of values and purpose (Adams, 1987).

In May 1986 a group of 20 scientists from 12 nations gathered in Seville, Spain, to develop a statement on violence and human nature. The statement has since been endorsed by the American Association for Counseling and Development, the American Psychological Association, and Psychologists for Social Responsibility. The statement finds that "violence is neither in our evolutionary legacy nor in our genes." It concludes that "biology does not condemn humanity to war, and that humanity can be freed from the bondage of biological pessimism. . . . Just as 'wars begin in the minds of men,' peace also begins in our minds. The same species [that] invented war is capable of inventing peace" (UNESCO Sixth International Colloquium on Brain and Aggression, 1986). This statement rejects as scientifically incorrect the following five commonly held propositions: that people have inherited a tendency to make war from our animal ancestors; that war or any other violent behavior is genetically programmed into our nature; that in the course of human evolution there has been a selection for aggressive behavior more than for other kinds of behavior; that human beings have a violent brain; and that war is caused by instinct or any other single motivation.

OBSTACLES TO PROFESSIONAL INVOLVEMENT

The primary professional obstacle to professional involvement, the emphasis on intrapsychic change as opposed to social change, has led to an even further narrowness of focus. For example, many counselors specialize in a therapeutic modality, such as body therapy, hypnotherapy, play therapy, or art therapy. They might then emphasize group counseling, family counseling, marriage counseling, or career counseling. They may further specialize by working with specific problems such as child abuse, weight loss, depression, or midlife crisis. The more the specialization, the more counselors risk distancing themselves from social, cultural, and political ills and from other disciplines. Disciplines develop their own values, perceptions, and jargon and fail to communicate with each other. Mitroff (1988) bemoans the low level of social intercourse between the many relevant fields in universities.

> In the end, the saddest thing of all must be the way that we have so organized human knowledge that it appears to have little relevancy for people in opposing disciplines. Notice I used the word 'opposing.' They're not even opposite disciplines anymore. (p. 68)

The low level of social intercourse is compounded by a lack of consensus among experts even within disciplines about how to deal with social problems. Many social problems, such as environmental issues, are multidimensional and require input from many academic disciplines and professional specialties. Frank (1987) points out that psychologists and other helping professionals have a temptation to communicate in such a way that implies more profound insight than the lay person may have, thus antagonizing the people they are trying to influence. Blight (1988) and Mitroff (1988) each criticize the psychological community for failing to communicate in the language of the policy community, thus further alienating them from the policy makers who regard psychologists as irrelevant and beneath them.

VALUES AND PRIORITIES

Dyson (1984) and Frank (1987) believe helping professionals have values and priorities different from those of national leaders. For example, we are moved by compassion and fear, whereas these emotions have little appeal to national security managers who are concerned that such emotions undermine strength of will and that people who exhibit them are cowards or sentimentalists. There is also a difference in focus and perception between scientists and helping professionals. Most scientists by the nature of their work lack the time to examine the broad consequences of their endeavors and their own willingness to accept responsibility for the potential destructiveness of their endeavors. Counselors have much to offer in this area. Gearhart (1984) states that "although technology is complicated, the morality is not" (p. 70).

INCOMPLETE EVIDENCE

One area in which counselors and lay people alike face difficulty is their reluctance to express opinions. Counselors and helping professionals often hold back because of an absence of conclusive information, whereas the populace in general feel a lack of confidence in their ability to understand social problems that seem complex. As a result, an attitude of leaving the problems to the experts develops. However, clinicians have an advantage over scientists because the nature of clinicians' everyday work forces them to act on conclusions based on incomplete evidence (Frank, 1987). This ability can be used in dealing with social issues. Furthermore, counselors have created a strong empirical base for deriving conclusions in such areas as conflict resolution, effective communications, and pathological behaviors that can be destructive to self and country.

EMOTIONAL FACTORS

It is not surprising that the prime obstacle for professional and nonprofessional involvement relates to ourselves and our emotions. These emotions include nuclear numbing, feeling overwhelmed by issues as well as workloads (see chapter 8 on burnout), and feelings of powerlessness.

Psychiatrist Robert Jay Lifton uses the term *nuclear numbing* to describe the process of denying and repressing the thoughts about nuclear war and its consequences. The emotionality of the subject matter has made the topic unthinkable. As a result we go about our lives as if nothing has changed, while we in fact know that everything has changed. We in effect live what Lifton has labeled a ''double life.'' The prospect of arousing our feelings seems too painful and frightening. As Macy (1983) states, ''We are afraid that if we were to let ourselves fully experience our dread, we might fall apart, lose control or be mired in it permanently'' (p. 7).

A process similar to nuclear numbing is involved in other emotional problems and issues in our lives. Harry Stack Sullivan used the broad concept termed *selective inattention* to refer to an active resistance to thinking about or avoiding certain kinds of things because of their nature. The source of selective inattention is anxiety related to our self-image and in defense of it. The defense mechanisms include those described by Freud. When certain things are a threat to our self-image or to our perceptions of reality, we often put blinders on in order not to upset our equilibrium. We interpret reality to fit our self-image or perceptions. Dass and Gorman (1988) state, ''We may have a difficult time facing the suffering of others because we don't know how to deal with our own pain and fear'' (p. 12). As a result we may selectively inattend, for example, delay or fail to visit a terminally ill colleague with whom we have worked for years, because of a fear of our own death.

Macy (1983) notes other causes of repression or numbing, including fear of pain; of appearing morbid or stupid; of guilt; of causing distress; of provoking disaster; of appearing unpatriotic, too emotional, or powerless; of sowing panic; and of religious doubt; and also being conditioned to take seriously only feelings that pertain to us individually, thus letting us deny and/or discredit feelings we suffer for society itself.

The consequences to repressing our feelings are many. Macy (1983) lists several, including fragmentation, alienation, desperate pursuit of pleasure, political passivity, destructive behaviors, psychological projection, diminished intellectual performance, sense of powerlessness, burnout, and depression. Solomon (1986) believes that many novels, films, and television shows, in their attempt to raise awareness and overcome numbing, have elicited feelings of helplessness and despair.

WHAT CAN WE DO?

Macy (1983) advocates a process of working through our pain, fear, anger, despair, and powerlessness leading to empowerment. She lists five guidelines for the process.

1. *Acknowledge our pain for the world.* What is there cannot be pushed away. Like any unfinished business, it will affect our lives until we acknowledge it and take care of it. Examples of acknowledging this pain include journal writing, prayer, communicating our awareness to significant others, and undergoing therapy.

2. *Validate our pain for the world.* These feelings are healthy, normal, and ap-

propriate under the circumstances. We need to accept that and listen to these feelings in ourselves and others. Examples of validating this pain include using inner-viewing skills and not rushing in with words of cheer.

3. *Experience the pain.* We are not fragile; we will not break. By making contact with the pain, we will be better able to move through it. An example of releasing the pain includes relaxing rigid defenses and allowing these painful feelings to flow through. Art, ritual, movement, and sounds can play a cathartic role, as can psychotherapy. Catharsis leads to healing.

4. *Move through the pain to its source.* The pain is rooted in caring for all humanity. This caring can bring us in touch with our feelings of interconnectedness with other people, a feeling of oneness. An example is to allow this sense of mutual belonging to express itself in whatever words and images seem meaningful and to share them widely.

5. *Experience the power of interconnectedness.* Realizing how we are one can bring about feelings of personal security and empowerment. Macy states "There is wonder, even joy, as we come home to our mutual belonging—*and* there is a new kind of power." (p. 23)

We add a sixth guideline to this list:

6. *Act on these feelings.* It is not enough merely to realize this empowerment and then not act. If we see the necessity for immediate action and act, then we are taking care of our unfinished business and actualizing ourselves. Below are suggestions for taking action.

Having worked through our pain, fear, anger, despair, and powerlessness in a manner similar to the counseling process, there is much that we can do. Individuals can make a difference. Many movements such as the abolition of slavery, women's suffrage, and civil rights that began on the grass-roots level changed the course of history. As David South (1984) states,

> When citizens get concerned enough to participate in the political process . . . it works for them. Government policy reflects the level of consciousness of the citizens; if the citizens are asleep, the government acts out their dreams and their nightmares. (p. 31)

We can participate in the political process through recruiting, nominating, campaigning, and supporting political candidates and by contributing to political action committees (PACs). We can educate citizens about problems and encourage open and shared expressions of feelings. Many counselors are active in such organizations as Psychologists for Social Responsibility and Educators for Social Responsibility. The Executive Committee of the Association for Counselor Education and Supervision sponsored a Quest for Peace videotape film series featuring 25 prominent Americans as part of their Counselor of Tomorrow program. We can work on making a difference in ourselves (inner work) and on making a difference in our environment (outer work).

Inner Work

The place to start making a difference is in ourselves. We achieve peace within ourselves through self-knowledge and awareness. When we put an end to war in ourselves we can be more fully functioning in all areas of our lives. Below are some suggestions for inner work. They are not to be considered as a list of shoulds but as some ideas to experiment with.

> Be open to new possibilities.
> Learn to listen to yourself and others.
> Seek out, value, and appreciate differences of opinion.
> Resolve conflict without violence.
> Regularly and persistently affirm and imagine a positive goal of sustainable peace.
> Identify with humankind; do not preoccupy yourself with an enemy.
> Allow yourself to be you. Get in touch with the innermost core of your being.
> Practice what you preach on a personal level, whether it be for justice, equality, concern for the environment, or peace. Learn to take care of yourself in terms of relaxation, exercise, diet and nutrition, rest, laughter and enjoyment, and time management.

Outer Work

Sometimes people become motivated to do something about a concern in which they strongly believe, but they do not exactly know what to do. Below are some suggestions for outer work. Check off those in which you would like to engage.

_____ Be informed; read up on social/global issues.

_____ Set up study groups to discuss social/global issues and alternatives to present policies. Bring in experts. Release proceedings to the media. Or, join a group.

_____ Write a letter about a specific issue to the editor of local, regional, daily, and/or weekly newspapers.

_____ Write a letter to your legislators. Legislators consider one letter to be the voice of a hundred people.

_____ Call elected officials, national television networks, the White House, the Pentagon, and/or local radio and/or television talk shows.

_____ Ask your own club or civic group or religious group to sponsor speakers from various groups and to contribute to desired causes.

_____ Join or establish a local group of helping professionals concerned with social issues.

_____ Affiliate with a local, state, national, and/or international organization as an individual and/or as a group.

_____ Study psychological aspects of certain issues, such as the arms race or the depletion of the earth's ozone layer. Write and speak on these issues to local mainstream groups, such as the Rotary Club or the League of Women Voters.

Personal Implications

Each of us must decide for ourselves according to our own beliefs, needs, and priorities how involved we can become. We each have a responsibility by being a citizen in a democracy at least to express our convictions by voting in local, state, and national elections. We also need to take care of the necessities of our personal lives, including work, education, career, and family, and to leave room for leisure. Beyond this, most of us can occasionally find a few minutes to write a letter or make a call about an issue dear to our hearts. We can also financially contribute to the causes we espouse.

We also need to be alert as to how social issues can affect our clients. Perhaps we need to create a context, offer permission, or establish a therapeutic method for dealing with social and political subjects with our clients. Finally, there should be a place in counselor education programs for dealing with the ideas and concepts discussed in this chapter. If today's counselor educators give no importance to social responsibility, it is unlikely that future counselors will.

We all can do the necessary inner work to achieve peace within ourselves, nourish ourselves, and prevent burnout. Unless we are in the process of working on ourselves, it is difficult to do the necessary outer work. Collective change in our society is always the result of a process beginning with individual change. Without individual change, societal change cannot occur. As counselors, most of us are committed to our own personal growth. We cannot, however, be complacent; we need to follow through. Perhaps the best way we can serve our clients and students is to be an excellent model, practicing what we preach.

SUMMARY

This chapter examined the role of the counselor in the greater society and presented a rationale for social commitment in counseling.

Obstacles to professional involvement were noted, including the emphasis on intrapsychic change as opposed to social change, lack of communication between disciplines, failure to frame comunications in the language of the audience it is directed toward, differences in values and priorities between helping professionals and national leaders, and a reluctance to express opinions. The most significant obstacles are emotional ones. Of these, nuclear numbing and selective inattention, both processes of denying and repressing unthinkable thoughts, were noted as the most formidable.

In order to move into responsible social action, one must first get in touch with one's pain and repressed feelings, experience the pain, work through the pain to its source, and become empowered. Suggestions were given for making a difference in ourselves (inner work) and in our environment (outer work).

QUESTIONS AND ACTIVITIES

1. What do you think is our society's most urgent problem? the environment? drugs? nuclear war? the economy? homelessness? AIDS? Why? Discuss this question with friends and colleagues.

2. Are the issues that become salient for psychotherapeutic work determined only by the private circumstances of clients' lives? Or, are they determined also by the outside world and the cultural community that surrounds clients? What are the role and responsibility of the counselor to global issues in which life itself is threatened? Do counselors have a responsibility to help their clients care about the delicate balance of life on this planet? If so, how do counselors exercise this responsibility in the therapeutic context in a way that does not intrude their own agendas on their clients' lives? Investigate and discuss with others.

3. A significant form of commitment to an issue is making a financial contribution. On what issue do you feel most strongly about so that you are willing to contribute at least $25 to a legitimate group favoring your point of view on that issue? Affirm your conviction and send the group a check.

Foundation Areas in Counseling

CHAPTER 10

Theory in the Practice of Counseling

*Does having a theory of counseling help
or hinder the practitioner?*

Much literature in the field of counseling is related to theory. In this individualistic, idiosyncratic field, it often seems that everyone has a personal theory of counseling. This chapter discusses the nature of theories, whether we need them, four significant theoretical forces, and an emerging major theoretical formulation—general systems theory. Finally, the process for developing a personal theory is presented.

WHAT IS A THEORY?

All of us live by a different road map of the world. This map is based on all of our past and present experiences, and for us this map is reality. Our behaviors are based on this map of reality. The more structure and detail this map has, the better we are able to organize our actions. This is what a theory does. It provides a structure from which to understand what we are doing and the process of doing it. A theory is a framework on which interventions are based. It enables us to form relationships from the data we collect from our experiences and to make sense of those data. As we develop more experiences, more of the road map gets filled in.

Hansen, Stevic, and Warner (1986) refer to theory as an explanation for events that can be tested by events and that is useful only to the extent that it influences behavior. Patterson (1986) states that a formal theory has certain characteristics. These characteristics include (a) a set of stated assumptions regarding the given field; (b) a set of definitions of the ideas and concepts in the theory stated in behavioral or observational terms so that the concepts are amenable to research; (c) concepts that bear certain relationships to one another, including cause-and-effect relationships; and (d) hypotheses constructed from these assumptions, definitions, and relationships that can be tested through research and experimentation. Research outcomes may not validate predictions emanating from the theory so that aspects of the theory may have to be modified. The development of a theory, therefore, goes through a continual process of construction, testing, modification or reconstruction, and further testing. The theory thus is self-correcting and, no matter how attractive, does not need to be accepted on faith alone (Blocher, 1987).

A formal theory should deal with meaningful matters that have relevance to life. That is, however, a subjective criterion and thus difficult to evaluate. Usually, in fact, a theory and its relevance are determined by whether other professionals in the field pay attention to it. A formal theory should be clear, precise, and easily understood. Concepts should be thought out and related or connected. There should be no internal inconsistencies, and the theory should be easily related to practice.

A good theory should also be comprehensive so that it takes into account numerous events in a variety of situations. The more comprehensive a theory is, the more utility it has. A good counseling theory needs to be based in part on personality theory to provide counselors with knowledge of the development of normal and maladaptive behavior and human nature.

Currently, no counseling theories meet all of these criteria. We have more of what Blocher (1987) has labeled pseudotheories or process models. A process model prescribes a more or less clearly defined set of actions for counselors to take in pursuit of specific goals and objectives with certain types of clients (p. 67).

Counseling is still in its youth, and much work with regard to the development of theory lies ahead. We now examine some arguments for and against using counseling theories.

WHY HAVE A THEORY?

> *To function without theory is to operate without placing events in some order and thus to function meaninglessly.*
>
> Hansen, Stevic, and Warner, 1986, p. 12

> *All that is required of counselors is being real. The only value is authenticity. To achieve this, counselors must be willing to forsake all theories about how a good counselor should respond.*
>
> Bergantino, 1978, p. 290

There is considerable debate going on regarding the value of psychotherapeutic theory, especially as it is applied to practice. Brammer and Shostrom (1982) believe that the scientific clinical approach as manifested by the application of counseling theory is too difficult for counselors to use. In addition, they report a lack of strong evidence that a counselor's effectiveness in producing certain outcomes correlates with the extent and explicitness of one's theoretical foundations. However, they believe that counselors are still interested in theory as a means of enhancing their understanding of human behavior, even if this understanding does not lead to any practical results in counseling.

A case can be made both for and against the use of theory. Table 10.1 lists the main arguments for each side.

Arguments for Theory

As mentioned, a theory provides a structure or framework from which counselors can work in a systematic fashion. Hansen, Stevic, and Warner (1986) be-

TABLE 10.1 Arguments for and against the Use of Counseling Theory

Against Theory	*For Theory*
Confuses counselors because there are too many theories, many of them conflicting.	Provides knowledge from which to make choices and predictions.
Creates a false sense of certainty because there still is not enough psychological knowledge on which to base a complete theory.	Creates order.
	Provides a therapeutic road map.
	Helps counselors understand what they are doing.
Can lock counselors into rigid format, making them inflexible.	Influences what the counselor does and how she does it.
Limits creativity.	May cause counselors to miss valuable data in counseling sessions if not guided by theory.
Forces counselors to be mechanical.	
Can lead counselors to focus on the theory rather than on their own processes.	Generates new ideas and approaches for testing.
Makes the client conform to the counselor's theory.	May be impossible to not have a theory; having no theory is in and of itself a theory.
Puts the counselor in the position of being an interpreter, thus preventing him from being a person.	Cannot escape theorizing.
Cannot guarantee success as a counselor by having a strong theoretical approach.	May develop a reputation as a counselor more readily if you are identified with a given theory.
Cannot be fully committed to a theory because there currently is no theory that fully explains human behavior and behavioral changes; just approaches and techniques.	
Can counsel successfully without adhering to a specific theory.	

lieve that the counselor cannot function in a meaningful manner without being able to place events in some order. Stefflre and Grant (1973) argue that even counselors who hold an antitheoretical position are usually basing their behavior on vaguely defined but implicit theory. To them the choice between having a theory or not does not exist. The real questions are what theory or theories should counselors have and how should these theories be used?

Arguments against Theory

Many professionals in the field oppose those who favor theory. They see theory as an obstacle to being an effective therapist. For example, Carl Whitaker (1976) believes that all theories are bad and tend to constrict therapists by indoctrinating them in a narrow and rigid viewpoint. Arnold Lazarus (1981), the founder of multi-modal therapy, argues that the current state of psychological knowledge does not permit the development of an accurate theory of human functioning. Brammer and Shostrom (1982) state that there is no compelling evidence that counseling effectiveness in producing certain outcomes definitely depends on the extent and explicitness of one's theoretical foundations. Further, there is no evidence that one particular theory of psychotherapy is superior to another. Studies that have investigated the success of counseling consistently report that theoretical orientation does not correlate to success as a counselor (Smith & Glass, 1977; Lieberman, Yalom, & Miles, 1973).

Theories of counseling also have developed in large part to explain and treat maladaptive, undesirable behavior. So that even though a given theory may be of value in remediation, it is not often as useful in the preventive and developmental aspects of counseling. Probably the greatest objection cited by those who down play the value of theory is the belief that theory forces counselors to become rigid and mechanical and thus more interested in following a theoretical script than in being fully present with clients and tuning in to their own processes.

Types of Theories Related to the Field of Counseling

As if the counseling theory picture is not murky enough, we need to consider all the different types of theories associated with the counseling field. As noted in chapter 5, the field of counseling has been influenced by a number of major factors as it developed. Most of these factors have brought with them a variety of theoretical points of view that have contributed to the richness of the field but have also been confusing to both the beginning student and the experienced practitioner. You thus cannot think simply of theories of counseling; you also need to include theories of personality, theories of family counseling, and theories of career development. You then need to keep in mind that none of these are complete theories. (Many of these theories are referred to in subsequent parts of this book.) A counseling student might view all of these approaches as a special kind of smorgasbord. Here you have the ability to explore a broad variety of ways of looking at human behavior and the possible means for bringing about possible significant change.

Basic Theoretical Stances

Rather than go on record as being for or against theory in general or in particular, many counselors choose an appropriate compromise and call themselves eclectics. But what does eclecticism mean and how does it relate to other approaches to counseling theory?

Robinson (1965), who studied counseling approaches and labels, formulated four basic counseling orientations: pragmatic, eclectic, personality theorist, and the syncretic approach. A pragmatic counselor relies only on personal experience and does not adhere to any particular theory. An eclectic counselor critically selects concepts and techniques from a number of counseling approaches, taking research findings into account, and blends them together with personal ideas and adaptations into a consistent whole. The personality theorist is indoctrinated in and enamored of a particular theory and uses it exclusively with every type of client in every circumstance. Syncretism refers to the joining or merging of beliefs and ideas. A syncretic counselor uses ideas from two or more theories but makes no attempt to develop any coherent, consistent personal framework. Such a counselor may have a collection of techniques but does nothing to integrate their use in any logical or systematic format. Intuitive feel may be the only theory guiding the syncretic counselor.

Eclecticism is often used incorrectly in everyday use. For example, some counselors who call themselves eclectic in terms of theoretical orientation are often more like the pragmatic or syncretic counselor as defined here. Such counselors do not necessarily have a systematically developed, research-based, consistent approach to working with clients. Their approaches may be spontaneous and idiosyncratic, with little grounding in any theoretical or research base.

The authors believe that the answer to most objections to the use of theory lies in how one uses theoretical knowledge, particularly knowledge based on research. A counselor does not have to adopt a single theory, or allow theory to be a binding and constricting influence, or just have a big grab-bag of techniques. A counselor can use theory creatively, humanely, and spontaneously. We advocate that counselors critically examine a number of theoretical approaches, and become well-grounded in an approach they find that fits particularly well. One can then either remain with that particular approach, becoming a specialist in it, or move to a more eclectic approach, working to develop a consistent, systematic theory, keeping in mind the need for research support for theoretical constructs and techniques.

The Proliferation of Theories

At one time, Sigmund Freud's psychoanalysis was the one, basic approach to psychotherapy. Then several versions of psychoanalytic theory began fighting for dominance. By 1975, a National Institute of Mental Health survey reported more than 130 therapies striving for recognition. The *Psychotherapy Handbook* (Herick, 1980) lists more than 250 different types of therapy. Ivey with Simek Downing (1980) states that "there are almost as many approaches to the counseling process as there are counselors and therapists" (p. 187).

It seems that each year sees a succession of new psychotherapies, each claiming to be uniquely different from its rivals and each claiming an 80 percent to 100 percent success rate. Frank (1978) states that he has yet to hear of a school that has disbanded because it became convinced of the superiority of its rivals. So, although some therapies may seem to fade from the top 40 list of most popular psychotherapies, they all seem to maintain a following. This proliferation of approaches has confused clients and the general public and also students and helping professionals. How does a client or student choose? How does one really know which approach is most effective? To confuse matters even more, there are differences within each approach. For example, there are many forms of behavior therapy, and an East-coast-trained Gestalt therapist might work differently from a West-coast-trained Gestaltist.

Commonalities among Approaches

Virtually all of these approaches have a lot in common (in particular, the therapeutic relationship—see chapter 3) and there is much overlap. For example, many terms used in transactional analysis have evolved from terms used in Freudian analysis. According to Brammer and Shostrom (1982) there is a strong search for commonalities among the major therapeutic approaches today. Patterson (1986) has described commonalities related to the relationship between the therapist and the client. Brabeck and Welfel (1985), after reviewing recent surveys of practitioners, report a major shift toward a more eclectic or syncretic approach in the practice of counseling and psychotherapy.

Many theories complement each other. For example, Gestalt therapy and person-centered therapy relate to each other in many ways. Both methodologies focus on the present, or the here-and-now. Both focus on what the client is doing, emphasize positive directions and goals of living, and place responsibility on the client to formulate personal solutions. Both therapies have roots in a similar philosophic frame of reference, and both use feedback, although the person-centered approach emphasizes verbal interaction and Gestalt therapy tends to emphasize nonverbal behavior. Viewed in a different perspective, Gestalt therapy also complements transactional analysis (TA). TA provides relatively clear theoretical constructs, providing a cognitive framework for change, and Gestalt therapy provides practical approaches to help deal with the emotional aspects of change.

Goldfried (1982) cites a growing discontent among therapists of varying orientations as to the limits of their respective approaches. He posits that while there is little chance that a common ground can be achieved among theoretical stances on either a theoretical or philosophical level, rapprochement might be achieved on a clinical strategies level. For example, most therapies offer clients direct feedback and provide clients with new, corrective experiences. Goldfried continues:

> To the extent that clinicians of varying orientations are able to arrive at a common set of strategies, it is likely that what emerges will consist of robust phenomena, as they have managed to survive the distortions imposed by the therapists' varying theoretical biases. (p. 386)

Other commonalities also exist. Although the how or the means whereby may be different, all theories carry the belief that people are capable of changing or being changed. This belief gives clients a sense of hope that acts in an effort to reverse the helpless and demoralized state that leads them to seek therapy. Most theories recognize that behavior is not entirely caused by the past but is influenced by present and future elements.

Another common element, according to Patterson (1986), is the counselor's belief or confidence in the theory and method being used. Patterson states, "It might be hypothesized that success (or at least reports of success) bears a strong relationship to the degree of confidence the therapist has in his or her approach" (p. 547).

In a well-known study, Fiedler (1950) found that experienced helpers of different theoretical persuasions tended to have more in common than did inexperienced helpers of the same persuasion. These common elements included the relationship dimensions of genuineness, empathic understanding, respect, and acceptance of the client. Truax and Carkhuff (1967) described the same phenomenon in reporting on a number of studies comparing counselors using different approaches.

Lieberman, Yalom, and Miles (1973), in their study of group leadership, generally confirmed these conclusions. They analyzed leadership results in 10 different types of groups and found that no one type of leader was better than the other; that is, a Gestalt-oriented group leader was not necessarily better than a psychoanalytically oriented group leader. As they were observed, the behavior of leaders with a similar orientation varied greatly. The conclusion reached was that *"the ideological school to which the leader belonged told us little about the actual behavior of the leader"* (Yalom, 1975, p. 476, emphasis in original). Even though the leader's behavior was not predictable on the basis of his or her theoretical orientation, the effectiveness of each leader studied was a function of his or her behavior.

Patterson (1985) believes that a basic foundation of all major theories is the therapeutic relationship. After examining the research on relationship factors, he states that

> the magnitude of the evidence is nothing short of amazing. It might be ventured that there are few things in the field of psychology for which the evidence is so strong. The evidence for the necessity if not the sufficiency of the therapist conditions of accurate empathy, respect or warmth, and therapeutic genuineness is incontrovertible. (p. 244)

Ultimately, we see that all therapies have the common goals of helping clients reduce their suffering, improve their interpersonal relationships, and take action to live a more fulfilling life. Patterson (1986) believes that all counselors demonstrate a real concern for their clients. "They are interested in their clients, care for them, and want to help them" (p. 548). Smith, Glass, and Miller (1980), after an analysis of 475 studies of counseling outcomes, found that the average client who received therapy was better off at the end of treatment than were 80 to 85 percent of comparable clients who did not receive such treatment regardless of the theoretical orientation of the therapist. All therapies examined attained comparable results for the treatment of all disorders. As Ungersma (1961) stated, "all schools, given favorable conditions, achieve favorable results: the patient or client gets relief and is often enough cured of his difficulties."

More research needs to be conducted to discover whether certain theories and techniques work best with different counselor and client personality types. Meanwhile, there seem to be at least some commonalities that tend to reduce the confusion among theories, with more of an emphasis on counselor effectiveness, rather than on counselor theoretical orientation.

Differences among Approaches

Probably the greatest differences among the various approaches are in the counseling process itself. Psychoanalysis focuses on developing insight in relationships to past development through the process of skillful interpretation. Rational emotive counselors focus on present irrational thinking by convincing clients of their faulty thought processes and teaching them more effective rational structures by which to live. Person-centered counselors stress the building of a safe atmosphere through a nonjudgmental, accepting relationship, so that previously denied feelings will be accepted and experienced. Behavioral counselors emphasize removing undesirable and/or self-destructive behavior and then learning new behaviors.

Most therapies base their process on talk; the client generally decides what to talk about, and does most of the talking. Behaviorists, while using verbal interaction, base their processes on action or behavior. They are more concerned with what and how clients behave than with what they say.

MAJOR THEORETICAL APPROACHES

The prospect of preparing an overview of psychotherapy in America today is enough to make the most stout-hearted quail.

Frank, 1978, p. 1

The field of counseling and psychotherapy today is dominated by three major theoretical orientations: psychoanalytic, behavioral, and humanistic-existential. A fourth force, a transpersonal approach, is also beginning to make its presence felt, and despite its lack of historical development, it is attracting a significant following. Most all of the various approaches to counseling emanate from one or more of these perspectives. Each perspective differs significantly in terms of its view of human nature, the process of human development, the nature of psychopathology, the role of the counselor, the techniques used, and, ultimately, the goals of counseling. Table 10.2 illustrates the four major counseling forces and lists the names of counseling approaches and theorists related to each force. Note that no boundaries exist between these forces. Some counseling approaches are difficult to categorize; for example, Jung's approach is clearly related to the psychoanalytic force, but it also has much in common with the transpersonal force. A description of each of the four major forces follows.

Psychoanalytic Force

Psychotherapy, as we know it today, started toward the end of the 19th century with the work of Sigmund Freud (1856–1939). The influence of Freud's theoretical formulations and applications permeates many aspects of contemporary culture in addition to the fields of psychology and psychotherapy. The psychoanalytic approach remains the most comprehensive theory providing insights into psychopathology.

TABLE 10.2 Four Forces in Psychotherapy

Psychodynamic	*Cognitive Behavioral*	*Humanistic*	*Transpersonal*
Psychoanalysis Freud	*Behavioral* Systematic Desensitization Wolpe	Person Centered Rogers	Psychosynthesis Assagioli
Analytic Psychotherapy Jung	Operant Conditioning Skinner	Existential May	Zen Watts
Individual Psychology Adler	Modeling Bandura	Gestalt Perls	Yoga
Will Therapy Rank	*Cognitive* Cognitive Behavioral Beck	Logotherapy Frankl	Sufism
Also: Horney Fromm Erikson Sullivan Reich Janov Klein A. Freud	Reality Therapy Glasser		Biofeedback
	Rational Emotive Ellis		Imagery
	Transactional Analysis Berne		

Freud was trained as a physician and had an interest in the study of the functioning of the brain. Early work with hypnosis and awareness of a talking cure led him to look for a nonphysical structure of mental functioning.

The psychoanalytic position holds a deterministic view of persons. It sees people as being driven by unconscious instincts and sees life to a large extent as people living out unconscious wishes and conflicts. Freud established his theory on the basis of his study of the emotional disturbances of middle-class women in Vienna in the late 19th and early 20th centuries. There is no strong evidence that Freudian theory is equally applicable to other cultures.

Freud placed heavy emphasis on people's evil impulses. One major construct of his approach is that personality is a system composed of three major components: the id, the ego, and the superego. The id is likened to a pleasure principle that urges one's organism toward drive gratification and is destructive if left unchecked. Freud saw the ego as the reality principle that learned practical strategies often called defense mechanisms in reducing tensions created by the id in order to take account of reality. The superego is defined as the conscience, the moral and ethical part of the organism that strives to inhibit id drives. Freud viewed anxiety as the conflict created between id impulses, superego demands, and ego defenses. When the ego is unable to maintain the energy needed for its defenses against unacceptable instinctual impulses and is unable to deal adequately with the demands of the superego as well as of reality, pathology develops. If either the id or the superego becomes dominant over the other personality components, the resultant mental and behavioral aberrations are referred to as neuroses. Psychosis occurs when the ego loses all control.

The process of psychoanalysis is based on strengthening the ego and checking the id. Freud believed that logical thought and rationality should guide behavior. The goal of psychoanalysis is to totally reconstruct the personality. Psychoanalytic treatment acts as a second education of the adult that corrects the education of the child. The process of treatment is often compared to the peeling of an onion. Layer after layer is peeled away until the client reaches the core of his or her problems, which is based on some disturbance of the psychosexual stages of development. The peeling of the onion consists of dealing with the defenses people use to prevent change and growth, of analyzing fragments of the ego resistant to cure, and of discovering what is hidden in the id and why.

The primary approach to treatment that Freud used is called transference (see chapter 3). The therapist acted as a blank screen on which patients could project repressed feelings related to important people in the patient's life; for example, a patient might project his feelings of hate for his father onto the therapist. Working through these feelings becomes a part of the re-educative process. Freud sat in a chair outside of the patient's direct line of vision to better allow for this transference phenomenon to occur and to minimize other interaction with the patient.

Other approaches used to help uncover repressed material and bring it to the patient's consciousness include the telling of dreams; the use of free association, where the patient would simply talk about anything that came to mind during a session; and the analysis of patient forgetfulness or misstatements (Freudian slips). Freud also was interested in the symbolic nature of human communication and the meaning of symbols with regard to symptoms of abnormal behavior.

The major specific cause for neurotic behavior according to Freud was inhibited sexual development. Sexual development begins in infancy, according to Freud, and proceeds through several stages until maturity. Unresolved and repressed emotions related to the person's sexual development would manifest themselves in neurotic behavior and would have to be treated.

Several theorists have elaborated on Freud's work. Anna Freud, his daughter, elaborated on the concept of defense mechanisms the ego uses to regulate unconscious drives. Melanie Klein used the concepts of psychoanalysis in working with children. Erik Erikson extended the concept of developmental stages to cover the entire life span and included a description of tasks people needed to complete to successfully go through each life stage. The concepts of psychoanalysis were applied to the study of culture and human social development by Erich Fromm.

Strengths and Weaknesses of the Psychoanalytic Approach

Psychoanalysts are, in general, the most highly trained of all the mental health professionals. Training as a psychoanalyst is a lengthy process, and an M.D. degree is a requirement for entry into most training programs. The process of psychoanalysis itself is also lengthy and expensive, often taking several years to complete. Psychoanalysis, therefore, is practiced mostly by private practitioners and rarely in agencies or schools. Psychoanalytic theory remains the most comprehensive and detailed theory, especially in terms of psychological development.

Freud used a case-study approach toward research in his work, and over the years there has not been much comparative or experimental research related to psychoanalysis. This lack of research has been a weakness in winning acceptability by the scientific community, but it has not necessarily kept the approach from being influential in the field of counseling and psychology, not to mention in literature and the arts. Numerous counseling theories have been developed from the foundation laid down by psychoanalytic practitioners or in reaction to psychodynamic principles and procedures.

Other criticisms of the psychoanalytic stance are its inadequate and outdated view of female sexuality; its deterministic and pessimistic view of humankind; its tendency to define success in terms of the client's degree of acceptance of the therapist's view of life; its rigid theoretical process, which leaves little room for creative interpretations or synthesis (Carkhuff & Berenson, 1977); its disregard for the social, cultural, and interpersonal factors of behavior; and that it is a model based on the study of people classified as neurotics rather than as healthy individuals.

Cognitive-Behavioral Force

Behavior theory is often called the second force in psychology. Behavior theory includes a number of different clinical approaches related to different learning principles.

In strong contrast to psychoanalysis, behavior theory is empirically and experimentally based, with principles and constructs derived as a result of research. Rather than work with abstract ideas such as the unconscious, the behaviorists in the tradition of John Watson and other eminent experimental psychologists emphasize observable behavior. In focusing on observable behavior, early behaviorists believed that all that can be known about people can be gained by observing their behavior and that human behavior is useful only to the extent that it can be quantified and operationally defined.

Behavior theorists have built on the work of Ivan Pavlov in respondent or classical conditioning, of Albert Bandura in terms of social modeling, and of B. F. Skinner in operant conditioning to develop a broad variety of techniques and approaches that can help people change behavior. In addition to clinical uses, behavioral approaches have been used extensively in educational settings. Behaviorists emphasize the development of desirable behaviors (and the extinction of undesirable behaviors) and structure conditions in the environment so that the desired behaviors are learned and maintained.

Joseph Wolpe in the 1950s, like Freud, was concerned about the idea of neurotic anxiety. However, Wolpe considered it to be a classically conditioned (learned) response (Spence, Carson, & Thibaut, 1976). Because anxiety is something that can be learned, a person can unlearn it. Based on this premise, Wolpe developed the technique of systematic desensitization to help clients overcome debilitating anxieties.

Changing behavior by reinforcing approximations toward a desired behavior, called operant conditioning, was developed and promulgated primarily by B. F. Skinner (1953). Techniques developed around this theoretical approach are often classified in the category of behavior modification. Behavior modification techniques are widely used in educational and mental health settings. In such settings the basic approach is to reinforce and strengthen behaviors desired (by the client or the caretakers) and to extinguish or not reinforce behaviors deemed undesirable. The focus is on the specific behavior and the external factors, which could lead to either strengthening or weakening the target behavior. The client's/student's thoughts or feelings were not considered to be of any consequence because abnormal behavior could be understood and changed without regard to them (Spence et al., 1976). Children learn to manifest appropriate classroom behaviors when desirable reinforcers are appropriately presented. The children do not have to talk about how they think or feel about the situation.

Early behaviorists found it important to dissociate themselves from vague, generally untestable conceptualizations and processes of the insight therapies—therapies that held that behavior would change as a result of a client's understanding, or gaining insight on, the causes and consequences of his or her behavior. Beginning in the late 1960s, however, some behaviorally oriented therapists began to consider mental processes such as thinking and imagery in acquiring a better understanding of maladaptive behavior as well as in helping to develop more effective approaches for changing behavior. In effect, thoughts came to be viewed as behavior. This cognitively oriented conceptualization has given behavioral therapy a broader base of practitioners, including such approaches as Albert Ellis's (1962, 1989) rational emotive therapy and Beck's (1967) and Meichenbaum's (1977) cognitive behavioral approaches.

In most cognitive-behavioral approaches, clients are involved in defining their problems, selecting treatment objectives, and evaluating the counselor and their own success in achieving their objectives. The cognitive-behavioral clinician tends to take an approach that is didactic at times, often more in keeping with the role of a teacher than that of a counselor.

The goals of cognitive-behavioral counseling are to enable clients to function better in regard to their environment and to use more socially desirable behaviors. These goals are accomplished either through the process of changing clients' attitudes toward their environment or by teaching them more appropriate and rational ways of behaving.

Strengths and Weaknesses of the Cognitive-Behavioral Approach

The strengths of the cognitive-behavioral approach include its firm foundation in research, its applicability in a number of educational and clinical settings, the broad variety of techniques that have been developed to help people function more effectively, and the clear and well-defined criteria for measuring outcomes.

A major criticism of behavioral counseling is its deterministic stance. Because all behavior is believed to be externally determined, client and counselor alike are trapped by their stimuli and are never free to choose and transcend their conditioning. Behavioral approaches tend to be mechanical, leaving little room for creativity. In behavioral counseling, change comes about as a result of external control of environmental conditions. It can be viewed as an other-directed approach that does not involve a person's inner potential. This approach could be destructive if it were used to oppress or dehumanize other people. The recent addition of cognitive approaches to behavioral therapy have softened some of this criticism.

Humanistic Force

Humanistic theories are often called the third force in psychology. The roots of humanistic theories are philosophical and based on the works of European existentialists such as Albert Camus (1979), John Paul Sartre (1971), Martin Buber (1958), and Soren Kierkegaard (1967–78). Humanists believe that problems arise when our defenses interrupt our natural organismic growth. When this occurs we are not able to invest our full energies and capabilities to resolve those conflicts with which our defenses interfered.

Humanists such as Abraham Maslow (1954, 1970, 1971) and Carl Rogers (1951, 1980) stressed positive directions in living and the inborn tendency of all human beings to self-actualize, to develop to their full potential. This approach differs greatly from the psychoanalytic and behavioral approaches, which tend to represent mechanistic and predetermined views of the nature of people. Humanists have been influenced by researchers such as Maslow (1954), who studied the development of normal people rather than focusing on the behavior generally considered abnormal or maladaptive. The major humanistic approaches are Gestalt, person-centered (formerly client-centered), and existential.

Humanists believe that people have the ability to organize their experiences into meaningful patterns and create their own meaning of the environment in which they live. Humanists stress people's freedom to make choices and their ultimate responsibility for those choices. The goal of their counseling involves moving the clients toward self-direction, self-awareness, and improved decision making. Clients are helped to trust their own capabilities and to assume responsibility for all aspects of their lives. Humanists are strong believers in the importance of the interpersonal relationship for therapeutic success.

In emphasizing the counseling relationship, some humanistic therapists stress the importance of the counselor's personal characteristics, such as openness, warmth, and empathy, and downplay the use of techniques. Other humanists, such as Gestaltists, use techniques as the context calls for in order to achieve their goals.

Humanistic psychology is generally phenomenological in nature, emphasizing the actual experience of the client rather than inventing new theoretical constructs and systems. Phenomenology, a key concept for the humanists, is the idea that what is reality for a person is what he or she perceives. "External events are significant for individuals only insofar as they experience them as meaningful" (Brammer & Shostrom, 1982, p. 54). To know people, then, the counselor must be able to understand how clients perceive events in the environment and in themselves. In working with clients, counselors need to be in tune with clients' internal frame of reference in order to understand the nature of the clients' problem. The necessity for such depth of understanding of the clients' point of view is the major reason for the heavy emphasis humanists place on the skill of empathic responding.

A major construct emanating from the phenomenological framework is the self-concept—the person's view of self. Anxiety levels become high when a person is not acting in accord with this self-concept; for example, a person who considers himself to be extremely shy trying to give a speech to a large audience.

People whose concept of self is relatively close to their experience and who believe their behavior represents their ideals and values would be considered well adjusted or psychologically whole. When their awareness matches their experience, they would be considered congruent.

Another major factor in the humanistic approach is the importance of working with feelings. Humanists are aware that emotions can interfere with thought processes and can strongly affect behavior. An existentialist would suggest that there is no growth or change until clients have experienced the depth of personal despair in the safe immediacy of the relationship with the counselor. At that point the clients would realize that they are not alone and that their worst fears have failed to materialize.

Strengths and Weaknesses of the Humanistic Approach

The strengths of humanistic theory include its stress on self-determination and self-actualization; its more positive and optimistic view of human nature; its emphasis on interpersonal relationships, both in and out of counseling; its inclusion of affect and experience in treatment; its more wholistic view of behavior; and that it is a model based on a healthy view of personality.

The greatest criticisms of humanistic approaches revolve around the looseness of its research, with the exception of the fairly heavily researched person-centered counseling, and the vagueness of many of its concepts such as self-actualization. Other criticisms include its lack of grounding in solid theory and its tendency to downplay an individual's past history in regard to treatment.

The Transpersonal Force

The newest force in psychology (approximately two decades old) is the transpersonal approach, sometimes called the fourth force. Some transpersonal psychologists, such as Anthony Sutich, the founder of the Association for Transpersonal Psychology, resisted attempts at defining the transpersonal on the grounds that it was indefinable and should remain that way. Sutich wanted transpersonal psychology to be open-ended and felt that placing a definition on the transpersonal would limit its boundaries and possibly cause it to assume a rigid stance (Hendricks, 1982).

Hendricks's (1982) broad definition attempts to provide the essence of transpersonal psychology without limiting its boundaries. According to Hendricks, transpersonal psychology goes beyond the ego psychology of the West. It is concerned with the essence of all persons, what is beyond the purely personal, and what connects all persons. The basic assumption of transpersonal psychology is that there is more to an individual than personality. The personality is just one facet of the individual's total identity. Therefore, one therapeutic goal of the transpersonal approach is to align the personality within the total self so that it functions appropriately. This involves placing less emphasis on the personality in terms of a person's everyday activities. As this is accomplished, the overall self emerges and assumes a more dominant position. There then is more unity between mind and body because the self is freed from the restrictions of the personality. As a result, the individual is able to enjoy the world, while not being attached to it (Fadiman, 1980).

Transpersonal psychology assumes an expansionistic perspective. It incorporates the essential contributions of the first three forces and builds on them to take into account such elements as intuition, mysticism, psychic phenomena, and spirituality. It is influenced by concepts from yoga, sufism, biofeedback, imagery, Zen Buddhism, psychosynthesis, and from the works of Alan Watts, Abraham Maslow, William James, Frances Vaughn, and Carl Jung. Jung first used the term *transpersonal* in 1916.

Yoga seeks to achieve union with the universal soul through deep meditation, prescribed postures, and controlled breathing. Sufism seeks to attain self-knowledge by going beyond the limits of reason and reaching conclusions experimentally through experience. Biofeedback is used to control emotional states such as anxiety by training oneself through the use of electronic devices. Zen Buddhism (Watts, 1957) seeks enlightenment through meditation and intuition. Psychosynthesis is a therapeutic process of combining individual elements of the mind to form a whole personality (Assagioli, 1965). Imagery is used to modify behavior through the use of mental images.

Transpersonal psychology involves learning to accept and love all parts of oneself just as they are and giving oneself permission to feel whatever feelings one has without interfering with them. It strives to explore new territories that transcend the ego. Advocates of this approach maintain that the scientific study of the ultimate dimensions of human experience provides the most comprehensive means for understanding human nature and for helping people develop their full potential.

Transpersonal psychology is still in the process of being fully conceptualized. Presently, it is an abstraction of many loosely connected models, ideas, and therapeutic techniques (Capra, 1983). Developments in transpersonal psychology are occurring both in and outside of academic institutions. One source, the Institute of Noetic Sciences, founded by the former astronaut Edgar Mitchell, has helped sponsor research in such areas as mental telepathy, extended human capabilities, and the emotional characteristics of people who are in perfect health. Some of this research is being conducted at institutions such as Stanford and Harvard Universities.

Three major theorists in the transpersonal area today are Charles Tart, an experimental psychologist, Stanislav Grof, a psychoanalytically trained clinician, and Ken Wilber, a biochemist-philosopher (Fadiman, 1980). Tart (1969) coined the term *altered states of consciousness* and developed a theoretical structure and a scientific rationale for the study and explication of these states. Grof developed his ideas as a result of extensive research doing psychotherapy with LSD and other psychoactive drugs. His research led him from his original psychoanalytic perspective to a transpersonal one. As a result of some 3,000 psychedelic sessions he conducted and an analysis of almost 200 sessions by his colleagues, Grof constructed what he labeled a cartography of the unconscious. He noticed that his patients went through a certain definitive process in their psychedelic sessions in terms of the kind and content of problems that emerged.

[Grof] reported that a severely disturbed individual would first grapple with concerns usually associated with the writings of Rank, and then begin to have therapeutic sessions which would confront issues most clearly discussed by Jung. This developmental sequence—from issues of lust and aggression, through concerns with power and interpersonal relationships, to experiences of a transcendent, archetypical, or mystic nature—is in accord with the developmental sequence of personal growth described in both Buddhist and Sufi thought. (Fadiman, 1980, p. 38).

Ken Wilber has attempted to develop a comprehensive system of the entire range of consciousness. Wilber views consciousness as a continuum containing several levels. He distinguishes four levels of consciousness that are associated with corresponding levels of psychotherapy: the ego, the biosocial, existential, and transpersonal (Capra, 1983). The dynamics of the ego level deal with one's self-image, ideas dealt with in great detail in Freud's writings. The biosocial level represents aspects of a person's social environment, such as the influence of family relationships, and cultural traditions and beliefs on the individual's sense of identity. The existential level incorporates the thinking of humanistic and existential approaches and views the organism wholistically. The transpersonal level goes beyond the conventional boundaries of the organism and expands one's consciousness to include the mystical and the spiritual. At the end of the continuum is total unity with the universe (Capra, 1983).

The ideas of these three theorists are confluent. They demonstrate that there are many different and valid aspects to awareness and that healthy individuals attempt to experience more of them (Fadiman, 1980).

Strengths and Weaknesses of the Transpersonal Approach

The strengths of the transpersonal approach include its open stance and its willingness to explore new frontiers and consider all phenomena. Its greatest weaknesses are its poorly defined concepts and a weak research base. The critics of transpersonal psychology generally accuse it of being too esoteric and unscientific.

COUNSELING THEORY—A PARADIGM SHIFT

An effective theory of counseling provides a framework from which to understand what we are doing and how we are doing it. We have noted that one danger of adhering to a specific theory is that it can lock us into an inflexible position that makes us unable to accept other viewpoints. When this occurs, we forget that this is only a road map of the world and not the world itself. Kuhn (1970) stated that change in scientific thinking must often be brought about by the crisis of new data and phenomena that cannot be accommodated by current scientific models. He called the changes developing from these times of crisis *paradigm shifts* (the word *paradigm* comes from the Greek word for pattern). Kuhn believed that the concept of a paradigm was broader and more comprehensive than a theory (Caple, 1985). The shift from one paradigm to another is relatively abrupt, such as in the shift toward Darwin's theory of evolution (Lucas, 1985).

The shift encompasses a transition period characterized by confusion and overlap about the effectiveness of the old versus the new paradigm in solving problems. The new paradigm, however, produces an entirely different road map. The new paradigm requires giving up old ideas, concepts, attitudes, and perceptions for new ones, and seeing and thinking differently. Goldfried (1982), Newton (1985), Caple (1985), Lucas (1985), and Bozarth (1985) each indicate that a paradigm shift currently is taking place in the scientific community that will affect many disciplines including counseling. The shift is from mechanistic, scientific thought to a wholistic conception of reality.

The Old Paradigms

Until the 15th century, the predominant paradigm rested on the views of Aristotle and of the Church as conceptualized by Thomas Aquinas. This early paradigm was based on reason and faith and sought to understand the meaning and significance of natural phenomena from a spiritual and ethical perspective (Capra, 1983). This outlook began to change radically in the 16th and 17th centuries to a paradigm of the world as a machine. Beginning with Copernicus and his discovery that the Earth was not the center of the universe, the revised paradigm included the findings of Kepler, whose work with astronomical tables lent support to Copernicus; of Galileo, who stressed an empirical mathematical approach; and of Sir Francis Bacon, who felt that nature had to be dominated and controlled (Capra, 1983). French philosopher Réné Descartes believed that one could find absolute truth in science. His beliefs became known as Cartesian philosophy. His model of the world arranged the constituent parts of the world into causal laws (Lucas, 1985). Descartes believed that all aspects of complex phenomena could be understood in this way.

Sir Isaac Newton believed that God set the universe in motion and that it has run like a machine governed by immutable laws (Capra, 1983). Newton's laws depict events that are simple to understand and easy to picture (Zukav, 1979). Nothing could be knowable unless it could be empirically pictured and demonstrated.

The Cartesian-Newtonian model led to many of the great scientific breakthroughs of the 20th century. According to Capra (1983), Descartes's method made it possible for NASA to put a man on the moon, and Zukav (1979) states that, ''Newton's work has influenced us so forcefully.'' For example, the behavioristic view that living organisms are complex machines reacting to external stimuli is modeled after Newtonian physics (Capra, 1983). However, the Cartesian-Newtonian model also proved inadequate to explain many discoveries of the 19th and 20th centuries.

The New Paradigm

At the beginning of the 20th century, a new paradigm, called quantum theory or quantum mechanics, began to develop based initially on the pioneering work of scientists Niels Bohr, Max Planck, and Werner Heisenberg, with contributions from Albert Einstein (Herbert, 1985; Capra, 1983). Quantum theory did not replace the Cartesian-Newtonian paradigm but included it. The Cartesian-Newtonian model could not adequately explain subatomic phenomena; it did not work in the realm of the very small (Zukav, 1979).

In contrast to the mechanistic, Cartesian view of the world, quantum theory has led to a number of views of reality or models of the world. One quantum reality is that reality is an undivided wholeness (Herbert, 1985). This world view can be characterized by such words as *organic, wholistic,* and *ecological.* It might also be called a systems view in the sense of a general systems theory.

> The universe is no longer seen as a machine, made up of a multitude of objects, but has to be pictured as one indivisible, dynamic whole whose parts are essentially interrelated and can be understood only as patterns of a cosmic process. (Capra, 1983, pp. 78–79)

Table 10.3 depicts some of the differences between Newtonian physics and quantum physics.

In studying subatomic particles, quantum physicists discovered that they do not resemble the solid objects of classical physics. Subatomic units of matter were found to be abstract entities with dual aspects. They could not be pictured. Depending on how they were observed, they sometimes appeared one way,

TABLE 10.3 Newtonian versus Quantum Physics

Newtonian Physics	Quantum Physics
Can picture it.	Cannot picture it.
Based on ordinary sense perceptions.	Based on behavior of subatomic particles and systems not directly observable.
Describes things; individual objects in space and their changes in time.	Describes statistical behavior of systems.
Predicts events.	Predicts probabilities.
Assumes as objective reality "out there."	Does not assume an objective reality apart from our experience.
We can observe something without changing it.	We cannot observe something without changing it.
Claims to be based on absolute truth; the way that nature really is behind the scenes.	Claims only to correlate experience correctly.

Excerpts adapted from *The Dancing Wu Li Masters* by Gary Zukav. Copyright © 1979 by Gary Zukav. By permission of William Morrow & Company sometimes another. For example, in Newtonian physics, if one knew the position and momentum of an object at a particular time, one could calculate where it would be at some time in the future. This reasoning does not apply to subatomic phenomena in quantum physics. There, the more one knows about position, the less one knows about momentum, and vice versa. One can know both approximately, but never exactly. This principle, called the uncertainty principle, was discovered by Warner Heisenberg (Zukav, 1979; Capra, 1983). Because both position and momentum cannot be measured, specific events cannot be predicted. Only the probability that something is going to happen can be predicted. The experimenter must choose between measuring position or measuring momentum accurately because both cannot be known. Zukav (1979) states,

> Not only do we influence our reality, we *create* it . . . *we must choose* which of these two properties we want to determine.
>
> Quantum physicists ponder questions like, ''did a particle with momentum exist before we conducted an experiment to measure its momentum?''; ''Did a particle with position exist before we conducted an experiment to measure its position?''; and ''Did any particles exist at all before we thought about them and measured them?'' ''Did we create the particles that we are experimenting with?'' Incredible as it sounds, this is a possibility that many physicists recognize. (p. 28)

In effect, observers cannot be separated from what they observe.

Another great discovery, made by physicist Niels Bohr, is the principle of complementarity. This principle blurs the distinction between the knower and the known (Lucas, 1985). For example, two properties can be ascribed to light: particlelike behavior and wavelike behavior. Zukav (1979) goes on to state:

> Since particle-like behavior and wave-like behavior are the only properties that we ascribe to light, and since these now are recognized to belong (if complementarity is correct) not to light itself, but to our interaction with light, then it appears that light has no properties independent of us! To say that something has no properties is the same as saying that it does not exist. The next step in this logic is inescapable. Without us, light does not exist.
>
> Transferring the properties that we usually ascribe to light to our interaction with light deprives light of an independent existence. Without us, or by implication, anything else to interact with, light does not exist. This remarkable conclusion is only half the story. The other half is that, in a similar manner, without light, or, by implication, anything else to interact with, we do not exist! (p. 95)

Finally, in Newtonian physics there is absolute truth. Events can be predicted with certainty. In quantum physics atomic events cannot be predicted with certainty. There is only the probability of interconnections.

> Subatomic particles have no meaning as isolated entities but can be understood only as interconnections, or correlations, between various processes of observation and measurement. (Capra, 1983, p. 80)

These basic concepts underlying quantum physics bear a strong relationship to Eastern mystical thought. Capra (1985) states that Bohr's principle of complementarity is related to Chinese yin/yang philosophy whereby the yin and yang opposites are interrelated in a polar or complementary way. For example, Lucas (1985) points out that in Oriental philosophical thought there is

> a tempting conclusion that the picture of the world provided by postmodern Western science is equally well framed by the dominant trend in Oriental philosophical thought. In each no viable separation of subjectivity and objectivity is sustained. Both views hold that there is no independently existent world discoverable apart from the operations of the mind. Metaphysically speaking, sensory perceptions are illusory. Consciousness is the locus, creator, and editor of the space-time matter matrix, selecting and reifying the world from an infinite array of possible realities. Ultimately, the universe is an unbroken wholeness: that which is. (p. 167)

These discoveries have enormous although uncertain potential applications for counseling.

GENERAL SYSTEMS THEORY—APPLICATIONS FOR COUNSELING

The new paradigm according to quantum theory is based on a general systems view of life. The principles of this new paradigm emphasize relationships rather than isolated parts, inherent dynamics of relationships, process thinking, wholistic thinking, subjectivity, and autonomy (Bozarth, 1985). These principles have direct implications for counseling. (See Table 10.4.)

State of Nonequilibrium

Chapter 2 states that clients often come into counseling expecting counselors to provide a magic solution, to make it all better. If this expectation is fulfilled, the

TABLE 10.4 General Systems Theory Principles and Their Implications for Counseling

General Systems Theory	*Implications for Counseling*
State of Nonequilibrium Inherently dynamic, interrelated and interconnected	Requires an integrated, wholistic view of health that eliminates mechanistic explanations
Tendency toward Individual Autonomy and Integrative Tendency to Wholeness Self-renewal and self-transcendence	Requires a trust in the person's direction and choices
Inseparability of Observer	Requires involvement as an in-dweller with clients

J. D. Bozarth, "Quantum Theory and the Person-Centered Approach," *Journal of Counseling and Development* 3 (1985):179–182. Reprinted by permission of American Association for Counseling and Development, publisher and copyright holder.

effect is to move clients back to equilibrium. But the task of the counselor is to move the client away from equilibrium. Caple (1985) states that movement toward nonequilibrium is good mental health and movement toward equilibrium is poor mental health. Viewing mental health this way eliminates the need for mechanistic explanations and requires a wholistic way to view the relationship of physical and mental health as interdependent and interconnected. Lucas (1985) states that

> it remains unclear what specific forms therapy may assume in the future. But it can be said that the new psychological approaches now evolving mark a decisive break with the traditions of the past because they do not hinge on a single aspect or variable of human experience (e.g., sexuality, birth trauma, family dynamics, or existential encounter). [They also] do not generalize a limited dimension of the self to the total psyche. (p. 170)

With this paradigm, the client-counselor relationship would also move away from equilibrium. Bozarth (1985) believes that the counselor would be open to surprise in the relationship and would not be able to determine the specific kind of client change in advance.

Organismic Tendencies

Two principal dynamic phenomena of the general systems view are:

> Self-renewal: The ability of living systems to renew and recycle their components continuously while maintaining the integrity of structure.
> Self-transcendence: The ability to reach out beyond physical and mental boundaries in the process of learning, development, and evolution in a creative way. (Capra, 1982, p. 269)

Many theories of counseling (Adlerian, Jungian, person-centered, Gestalt, and existential) already include the self-renewal principal. It is the belief that there is an inherent organismic tendency toward growth that the counselor must tap. Furthermore, the human organism has the capacity to self-organize and transcend. This capacity is governed by the same laws of self-organization as any other system. Bozarth (1985) believes that the counselor's role is that of a catalyst that will permit the client to self-regulate and transcend. The primary ingredient is the counselor's reliance on and confirmation of the client's striving toward self-renewal and self-transcendence.

Inseparability of Observer

Chapter 2 discusses the therapeutic alliance as the most important single element in the relationship. It also speaks of the necessity of the counselor to enter the client's world and inner-view the client. The counselor must be an in-dweller with clients by demonstrating certain attitudinal qualities. These qualities include the core conditions of genuineness, positive regard, and empathy.

The Emerging Counseling Theory

We note earlier in this chapter that there is a proliferation of counseling theories and that they differed in origin and focus. Most schools of counseling tend to focus on a narrow range of psychological phenomena such as behavioral problems or family communication patterns (Capra, 1983). It may be that just as in physics, many of these approaches are limited in their attempt to be a comprehensive theory. They do not account for all human phenomena, or they view such phenomena according to a paradigm that is not appropriate or applicable.

As part of the description of the four forces in psychotherapy it was pointed out that both psychoanalytic and behavioristic approaches are deterministic. The behavioral stance sees everyone as wholly conditioned by social forces, never free to choose and transcend their conditioning. The psychoanalytical stance views people as being driven by unconscious instincts and living out their lives through unconscious wishes and conflicts. In addition, strict behaviorists have rejected dealing with any part of the human personality that could not be concretely defined and measured. Both of these psychological forces are based on the Newtonian-Cartesian orientation, and they do not address such issues as self-actualization, higher values, being, and ego-transcendence.

The first theorists to break away from Freud's psychological determinism were Adler, Jung, Karen Horney, Erikson, Sullivan, and Fromm. Of these, Capra (1983) cites Jung as probably having ideas closest to those of modern physics. Capra states that, in fact, many of Freud and Jung's differences parallel the differences between classical and modern physics. For example, Jung's concept of a collective unconscious in each individual that represents a deeper level of the psyche and is common to all humankind becomes a link that connects each individual with humanity as a whole. According to Capra (1983), this principle cannot be understood within a mechanistic framework, but it fits with a systems view of the mind. Capra believes that Jung's concepts are similar to those of contemporary physicists when they describe subatomic particles.

Humanistic theory, with its rejection of mechanistic and predetermined views, and transpersonal psychology, with its emphasis on non-ordinary, mystical, or alternate states of consciousness, are both complementary to the new paradigm from quantum physics. The evolution of family systems theory (see chapter 12) also has its roots in this paradigm. Lucas (1985) and Capra (1983) both see a multilevel approach emerging with different, though interlocking, frames of reference from divergent disciplines. This approach would be wholistic, antireductionistic, and subjective and would include paranormal phenomena.

Wrenn (1980) envisions more cooperation between health professionals such as physicians, nurses, and counselors. He perceives a trend in wholistic health in which the interrelationships among the biophysical self, the transpersonal-spiritual self, the psycho-emotional self, and the sociocultural context in which the individual lives are all taken into account. Lucas (1985) believes that the implications of this new paradigm for the field of counseling are still uncertain. However, he foresees the emergence of a "broader, richer, and infinitely more humane approach to psychological inquiry" (pp. 170–171).

DEVELOPING A PERSONAL APPROACH TO THEORY

Becoming an effective counselor is analogous in many ways to becoming an effective singer, artist, or writer. Just like artists, counselor trainees attempt to master the core skills. Their teachers become models for them, and they learn from other established counselors by way of films, audio- and videotapes, and typescripts that are part of case studies.

The first attempts of counseling students at practicing counseling are often characterized by a great deal of self-consciousness. They try to copy their models and often become good at it. We have often heard references, for example, of a singer who sounds just like Sinatra. Eventually, as trainees become more knowledgeable about theory and techniques, examine their own beliefs, and become more knowledgeable about themselves, they maintain much of the style of their models, but their own individual style begins to emerge. Finally, they give up being like their models (although some influential behaviors still remain) and become entirely themselves. The singer in our example begins to develop a personal phrasing, vocal range, and choice of songs, which perhaps still show some of Sinatra's influence, but which are particularly his own. He then spends his career on continually refining and perhaps even changing this style. Ivey, with Simek-Downing (1980) states,

> Thus, the task of each potential counselor and therapist is to enter the field as a lifetime student, fully aware that a final answer to the questions which engage counseling and therapy may ultimately be unanswerable. Yet, paradoxically, the very asking of questions and the systematic study leading to answers inevitably does two things: 1. it suggests what can be done, and 2. it simultaneously opens newer and more complex questions needing further study and examination. (p. 436)

Adopting an existing theory or developing one's personal theory involves a great amount of study and effort and an inquiring, creative mind, as well as ongoing, practical experience.

Passons (1975) suggests three key ingredients to the process of developing a personal theory of counseling: the counselor as a person, the existent theories, and the synthesizing processes counselors use in formulating a personal theory. To these needs to be added the important dimension of the research results regarding the effectiveness of existing theories, theoretical constructs, and techniques. All beginning counselors have already lived with themselves for many years and have formulated a system of values, beliefs, needs, and feelings. They need to bring these components to a high level of awareness. These elements then become the basis for adopting an existing theoretical approach or developing a personal theoretical stance. As counselors develop greater self-awareness and knowledge of research support for various theories, they will be better able to determine the appropriateness of any particular theory for themselves.

Chapter 11 describes some of the more influential approaches to counseling in order to give you an opportunity to begin your own understanding of how you might approach clients and to assist you further in the development of your own personal theory.

SUMMARY

The basic components necessary for a theory of counseling have been presented. They include a framework on which to base counseling interventions; a continual process of theory construction, testing, modification, and further testing; and a method of dealing with meaningful matters that have relevance to life. The purposes of theory were described as bringing organization out of chaos and enhancing one's understanding of human behavior.

The pros and cons of counseling theory were presented, and four basic theoretical stances were described: the pragmatic, eclectic, personality, and syncretic approaches. Commonalities and differences among all approaches were discussed. A format for classifying counseling theories was presented based on the four major forces on psychology—psychoanalytic, behavioral, humanistic, and transpersonal—along with an overview of each force. This discussion was followed by a description of the development of the general systems theory, an approach with excellent potential for becoming a comprehensive counseling theory. The chapter concluded with a description of the process through which counselors move as they develop their personal theoretical approach to counseling.

QUESTIONS AND ACTIVITIES

1. Do people really change? If so, how? Is change based primarily on insight? manipulation? accident? What conditions help facilitate change? Is theory needed to bring about change? If so, why?

2. Should counselors adopt an existing theory, develop their own theories, or counsel without regard to theory? Examine all sides of the issue. Share your conclusions with other students.

3. How do you think a counselor can best help another person? What should be the counselor's main goal in helping someone? Which theoretical approach most closely matches your point of view?

4. Find a friend or relative and try to explain to him or her how a paradigm shift in the field of physics can relate to the field of counseling.

5. How do you feel about transpersonal theory's being part of this new paradigm? What do you believe about the concepts of mystical experiences or altered states of consciousness? Do they really relate to the field of counseling?

CHAPTER 11

_____ FOCUS ON _____

Selected Theoretical Approaches to Counseling and Psychotherapy

If the theoretical approach a counselor assumes
makes no significant difference,
why spend any time studying different counseling
approaches?

Chapter 10 notes that there are hundreds of formal approaches to counseling and psychotherapy and many more combinations of approaches. Because success in counseling is dependent not on the type of counseling approach used but on other factors, the question can be raised as to why spend time and energy pursuing particular approaches? Actually, the nature of these approaches and in many cases their dramatic differences provide much of the attractiveness, drama, and controversy to the entire field. For many years, one way to fill a large hall at a counseling convention was to schedule debate between a behavioral therapist and a client-centered (Rogerian) therapist. More recently there has been a heated exchange between proponents of rational-emotive therapy and advocates of the transpersonal approach (Ellis, 1986, 1989a; Walsh, 1989b; Wilber, 1989).

The fact that, to date, no one approach to counseling has been universally recognized as inherently superior provides a lot of interest. Future counselors explore the variety of counseling approaches, in many cases looking for an approach that will fit them and their particular style. Future and present counselors may also dream that perhaps one day one of them might develop a counseling theory that will meet all of the qualifications stated above and be superior to all other approaches.

Also, through the study of different approaches, the student can become more involved with some major figures in the field, including Carl Rogers, B. F. Skinner, Fritz Perls, Eric Berne, Albert Ellis, and Carl Jung. Exploring the work of these pioneers helps provide a more human dimension to the field. Because each of these individuals can be considered a personality theorist as described in chapter 10, a student could pursue further study at training centers focusing on becoming expert in a given counseling approach; for example, attaining training at a Gestalt Training Center or a Jungian Institute. In many cases, special certification may be attained on the completion of a course of study in a particular approach.

This chapter describes seven current counseling approaches. The examples here illustrate the diverse nature of the field of counseling at this time. Because most university counselor education programs have one or more courses devoted specifically to the in-depth study of different counseling approaches, we present only a general description of each approach. Table 11.1 cites how the approaches described in this chapter are similar or different on a number of criteria. All approaches described here can be applied to individual, group, and family counseling. Additional approaches to family counseling are described in chapter 12.

PERSON-CENTERED COUNSELING

Background

Although there have been other early nonmedical counseling approaches such as the trait-factor approach, person-centered counseling is probably the pioneering approach that helped establish the field of counseling as we know it, and it continues to be a significant influence on the field. Carl Rogers (1902–1988), the founder of person-centered counseling, insisted that his work was original and not a reaction to Freud, or borrowed or adapted from other precursors. The primary influence in the development of his approach were Rogers's own experiences as a therapist and his belief that people are good and ultimately have the power to solve their own problems.

The theoretical rationale for change in person-centered counseling is that individuals have the capacity to understand the circumstances that cause unhappiness and can reorganize their lives accordingly. A person's ability to deal with these circumstances is enhanced if the therapist establishes a warm, accepting, and understanding relationship. Adherents of this approach believe that the quality of the interpersonal encounter is the most significant element in determining the outcome of any counseling relationship.

In person-centered counseling, the emphasis is on experiencing events in the present. Searching for and trying to understand underlying causes for problems are held to be of minor importance.

The person-centered approach is noteworthy because of its evolution over time. It is a theoretical approach that, like the clients it has served, has grown and developed since its origin. In its beginning formulation in the 1940s, this approach was referred to as nondirective counseling, with sessions conducted accordingly. The approach evolved in the 1950s to become client-centered counseling and then changed in the 1970s to person-centered counseling. The

TABLE 11.1 Comparison of Counseling Approaches

Characteristics	Person-Centered	Gestalt Therapy	Transactional Analysis
1. Nature of People	The individual is rational, good, trustworthy, moves in self-actualizing directions or toward growth, health, self-realization, independence, and autonomy.	Human beings not independent from their environment but work as a whole. Individual not sum of parts but a coordination.	Determined by childhood experiences, but can change.
2. Major Personality Constructs	Self-concept a regulator of behavior and perceptual field is reality for the individual, behavior a function of perceptions and organized with respect to self-concept.	Individual is considered a system in balance. He or she lives in a public (doing) level and a private (thinking) level. Imbalance is experienced as a corrective need. Awareness permits self-regulation and self-control.	Conceptualized as three ego states—parent, adult, child.
3. Nature of Anxiety	Incongruence between self-concept and experience, conditions of worth violated, and need for self-regard frustrated.	The gap between the now and the then; unfinished business.	Results from conflicts, concerts, or contaminations between ego states.
4. Counseling Goals	Self-direction and full functioning of client who is congruent, mature, and open to experience.	To mature, to grow up, to take responsibility for one's life, to be in touch with one's self and with the world.	Cure presenting problem, enabling people to experience freedom of choice.

Behavioral Counseling	Cognitive-Behavioral	Transpersonal	Wholistic
Depends on theorist, but human beings viewed as both producers and products of environmental events.	Human being subject to powerful biological and social forces, has potential for being rational. Can rid self of emotional difficulty by maximizing rational thinking.	All human beings have the same needs, feelings, and potentials, including being intuitive, psychic, and spiritual.	Seen as spiritual as well as physical, emotional, and mental. Having the potential for harmonious and total (wholistic) development.
Human behavior is lawful and a function of antecedent and consequent conditions.	Psychological states largely the results of thinking illogically; thinking and reasoning are not two disparate processes; human beings are rewarded or punished by their own thinking or self-talk.	Acceptance and use of altered states of consciousness, mystical insights, paranormal powers, and the human quest for contact and unity with the divine.	The focus is on multiple systems, both internal and external to the individual.
Results from faulty learning. Learned reactions to cues in certain situations operating as secondary or acquired drives, learned reactions to originally neutral stimuli.	Overgeneralizing that an event will be catastrophic.	Not recognizing that we are all one; not finding that within us which gives us freedom, wholeness, and connectedness with all.	Difficulty in personal functioning as a result of conflict within internal and/or external system.
Eliminate problem behaviors and learn more effective ways of behaving.	Elimination of anxiety and fears; the attainment of rational behavior, happiness, self-actualization.	To develop sense of personal unity with self and others; to live as totally free of distortion as possible.	A client who can identify and apply learned strategies as personal interventions when needed.

(continued)

TABLE 11.1   Continued

Characteristics	Person-Centered	Gestalt Therapy	Transactional Analysis
5. Major Techniques	Limited use of questioning, reassurance, encouragement, suggestion; technique a way of communicating acceptance, respect, understanding.	Confrontative; provide situations in which client experiences frustrations; focus attention on body posture, gestures, enactment of dreams.	Diagnosis and analysis of transactions lifescripts.
6. Use of Tests and Appraisal Devices	Extremely limited use; tends to be seen as inimical.	Limited use.	Limited use.
7. History Taking	Inimical to counseling process.	Limited use.	Limited use.
8. Diagnosis and Prognosis	Inimical to counseling process.	Limited use.	Diagnosis of ego states to determine executive power, adaptability, mentality, etc.

Behavioral Counseling	Cognitive-Behavioral	Transpersonal	Wholistic
Reinforcement, modeling, desensitization, and relaxation techniques. Assertion and social skills training, self-management, cognitive change procedures, behavioral rehearsal, and multimodal techniques.	Use of relationship techniques to establish rapport followed by teaching, suggestion, persuasion, confrontation, prescription of activities designed to rid the client of irrational ideas.	No special techniques; may use techniques from any source; likely to use imagery, intuition, meditation, dreamwork, and relaxation training.	Uses multiple approaches rather than singular strategies; techniques from any source may be used.
Informal assessment routinely used. May be used as needed to formulate treatment plan/evaluate progress in therapy.	Limited use.	Little formal use of such tools; some personality inventories may be used.	Minimal use.
Necessary to identify those factors which continue to influence behavior.	Relatively little use of historical clarification.	Taken as needed; generally little emphasis in this dimension.	Note is made of the nature of the internal and external systems of the individual and their interactions.
Necessary to conceptualize presenting problem and formulate treatment plan. Conducted in collaboration with client.	Used to uncover illogical ideas.	Diagnosis made in collaboration with client; the greater involvement on the part of the client, the better the prognosis.	Client invited to be participant in assessment, planning, intervention, and evaluation process.

(continued)

TABLE 11.1   Continued

Characteristics	Person-Centered	Gestalt Therapy	Transactional Analysis
9. Clientele	Currently no restriction placed on clientele.	No limitations stated.	No restriction noted.
10. Activity of Counselor	Counselor active in providing facilitative conditions.	Highly active.	Counselor very active.

Adapted by permission of Bruce Shertzer and Shelley C. Stone (1980). *Fundamentals of Counseling,* 3rd ed. (Boston: Houghton Mifflin Co.).
Additional sources include Hendricks, G., & Weinhold, B. (1982). *Transpersonal Approaches to Counseling and Psychotherapy.* Denver: Love; Texidor, M., Hawk, R., Thomas, P., Friedman, B., & Weiner, R. (1987). *Statement of the Holistic Counseling Special Interest Network of the American Mental Health Counselors Assn.* Washington, DC: AACD.

changes in title are not cosmetic; they have come about as a direct result of changes in perspective and approach within the structure of the system.

The person-centered approach has also changed along the way from almost exclusively focusing on a one-to-one relationship to now strongly emphasizing change within a group setting. Despite the changes in the theoretical approach over the years, some practitioners and some critics of this approach have not kept up to date with these changes. References to nondirective counseling as a contemporary approach are occasionally found in current counseling literature.

Goals

Person-centered counseling has no predetermined, explicit goals for the client. As a result of interaction with the counselor, clients develop their own individualized goals. An ultimate, implicit goal is the client's encounter with self. Some outcomes of person-centered counseling include greater self-acceptance, the dropping of masks (facades, roles), and positive behavior change.

Time Duration

The person-centered approach can be considered a moderate-term therapy, generally lasting from several months to a year or more.

Behavioral Counseling	Cognitive- Behavioral	Transpersonal	Wholistic
Clients must be committed to change and actively involved in treatment program.	No limitation but notes that psychotics rarely are completely cured.	No limitations; transpersonal concepts may work better with higher functioning clients.	No limitations.
Counselor warm and friendly but highly active.	Counselor highly active.	Therapy seen as partnership with counselor initiating activity at times and at other times facilitating the client's own work.	Counselor activity level varies from minimal to very active depending on the nature of the client's problem.

Time Orientation

The person-centered approach deals almost exclusively in the present. Even though a client's history may emerge during the counseling process, it is generally not pursued as such by the counselor. A client's description of a past incident would likely be responded to in terms of the emotions evident as the client speaks; for example, ''You are still very upset and angry about what your mother said to you years ago.''

Techniques

There are no formal techniques as such. In fact, Rogers carefully avoided using special techniques to bring about change. The development of the core conditions of empathy, genuineness, and respect as described in chapter 3 is as close to technique as is advocated by this approach. (See chapter 1 for an excerpt of a person-centered counseling session as conducted by Carl Rogers.)

Strengths

Person-centered counseling possesses a positive philosophy of the person. This approach enables the client to take responsibility for personal change, engage in behavior that actualizes and enhances the self, and become more accepting and trusting of the self.

Substantial research evidence supports the effectiveness of this approach. As much as any other approach to psychotherapy, person-centered counseling has developed as a result of research on the process and outcomes of therapy.

The principles of person-centered counseling can be applied to all types of settings and can be extended to teaching, organizational behavior, parenting, and human relations development. The approach is clearly person-centered, focusing on the client as a person rather than on the client's problem. It is not technique-centered, problem-centered, or counselor-centered. The attitudes and the personhood of the counselor become the primary influences that prompt the client to move toward a more satisfying and sustaining behavior.

Person-centered counseling can be individualized to the particular needs of a client. This is a major strength of this approach. Each individual is treated as a special case from the outset (Boy & Pine, 1982, pp. 46–56).

Weaknesses

The skills of developing the core conditions and learning to keep the focus on the client (person) are not easy to master, with the result that problem-centered, counselor-centered, or technique-centered approaches may appear more attractive to practitioners. The approach is seen as not being complete. Even though it does deal with emotional and intellectual content, it does not include the physical or spiritual domains, or environmental factors. Also, in many cases, the relationship may not be enough. Problem-solving approaches, borrowed from other systems, may be required to supplement this approach. And although there has been a significant amount of research related to the development of this system, there has been criticism about the nature and quality of the research.

GESTALT THERAPY

Background and Brief Theoretical Overview

Frederick (Fritz) Perls (1893–1970), the founder of Gestalt therapy, was trained in psychoanalysis. However, after being rebuffed when attempting to have an audience with Freud, Perls began to develop his own approach to psychotherapy. In so doing, he drew from a number of other sources, including Gestalt psychology, Jacob Moreno's psychodrama, and existentialism.

From Gestalt psychology Perl used the concept of figure and ground perceptual organization. The process of therapy involves helping individuals make contact with their environment and their selves so that they have less rigid or incomplete figure/ground relationships. Like person-centered counseling, Gestalt therapy is concerned with insight and awareness. As a result of insight learning there will be a restructuring of the client's perceptual field. A major source of anxiety is the client's store of unfinished business. Gestalt therapy uses a principle known as the Zeigarnik effect, a person's tendency to seek closure, as an important dynamic in helping bring about the restructuring of the client's awareness.

A significant part of Gestalt therapy is its focus on the present. Like person-centered counseling, it is believed that little can be gained by recounting the past. The client's present awareness is of most importance and most likely to lead to change. One approach a Gestalt therapist might use to help the client stay in the present would be to have the client relate a past event by using the present tense, telling and acting out the story as if it were happening right now.

From his Freudian background, Perls adapted such concepts as introjection, the taking onto yourself of aspects of other people, particularly parents. This led to Gestalt concepts of topdog and underdog, which might be considered akin to the superego and id. The topdog part of a personality has introjected all of the "shoulds" taught us by our parents and other sources of authority. The underdog part of the personality is childlike, demanding, rebellious, and evasive.

A Gestalt therapist might work to have the client integrate these two parts of the personality through the process of a dialogue. Using an empty chair or a pillow as a focal point, the client might first speak from the perspective of the topdog: "You're so irresponsible! You always want to see what you can get away with!" The counselor would then have the client switch places and respond from the perspective of the underdog: "You're no fun. All you want to do is work, work, work." The dialogue would be pursued with the goal of having the client become fully aware of these personality dimensions and work to have them become less polarized.

Goals of Therapy

The primary goals of Gestalt therapy are to help clients become mature, grow up, take responsibility for their lives, and be in touch with their selves and the world. A further goal is to help a person deal with and accept anxiety as part of the natural order of life.

Role of the Counselor

Gestalt counselors work to help clients overcome barriers to awareness. The counselor's responsibility is to give full personal expression to what the client is experiencing in the session, living it in the present moment, and not merely talk about it by interpreting the other's behavior. The counselor confronts actual experience in the immediate environment, striving to keep everything on an I-Thou basis, talking with and not about a person, and turning questions into statements. Emphasis is placed on becoming aware of nonverbal behavior and, in particular, on inconsistencies between nonverbal and verbal behavior.

Techniques

An intriguing aspect of Gestalt therapy is the number of dramatic techniques that have become associated with the approach. Gestalt techniques are extensions of basic theoretical concepts, only to be used as appropriate to the situation. The purposes of using techniques are to facilitate client learning and experience in interpersonal perception and communication and to bring about personal awareness.

In addition to the empty chair dialogue described above, two other Gestalt techniques include making the rounds and nonverbal activities.

1. *Making the rounds.* In a group counseling setting, the client asks each group member to tell all group members something that he or she has difficulty communicating. For example, a client who has difficulty talking in the group may go around to each member of the group completing the sentence, "I haven't spoken up in this group because . . ." After this sentence is told to each group member, the client may have some valuable awareness and may even institute some personal changes.
2. *Nonverbal activities.* Clients often communicate more accurate information nonverbally than verbally. A Gestalt counselor can help bring nonverbal behavior to clients' awareness in a number of ways, including:
   a. *Exaggeration.* A client with a whiny way of speaking can be asked to exaggerate the whine as he or she continues talking.
   b. *Dealing with inconsistencies.* Clients who smile when they say that they are angry can be asked to carry out a dialogue between the smile and the anger.

Strengths

Gestalt therapy is a confrontational approach in a positive way. Clients become aware of discrepancies and inconsistencies in their behavior in an experiential manner that often enhances the possibility for change. This approach is action-oriented in terms of helping clients experience the different aspects of their problems; just talking about problems is avoided.

As one of many experiential approaches available, this approach is open to the creativity of each counselor; there is no formula or prescribed set of techniques for the practitioner to follow. Unfinished business from the past is addressed in the context of the present.

Weaknesses

Gestalt therapy has a weak theoretical base, particularly in the area of personality development. It sometimes is combined with another approach such as transactional analysis to help compensate for this weakness.

Emotion rather than cognition is stressed, although this is being modified by contemporary Gestalt therapists. Many Gestalt techniques are powerful, implying that the counselor should be well grounded in their use and should have a high level of personal development before using them (Corey, 1986). The approach is highly focused on individual development with limited emphasis placed on the influence of the larger community and the environment. The Gestalt approach also has a weak research base.

TRANSACTIONAL ANALYSIS

Transactional analysis (TA) is appealing to many practitioners and lay people, in large part because it is not overly technical and complex. Basic concepts such as games, scripts, strokes, "I'm O.K., you're O.K.," and transactions are easily understood in the context of the helping relationship and can generally be used with children as well as adults.

Background

Eric Berne (1910–1970), the developer of transactional analysis, was trained in psychoanalysis, but like others, found that the psychoanalytic concepts were not sufficient to provide the theoretical structure that seemed appropriate for his clients. It thus is not surprising that many concepts in TA resemble those in psychoanalytic formulations. TA also has many other constructs that are significantly different.

Theoretical Rationale for Change

As children, individuals determine life plans for themselves and spend the rest of their lives following these scripts. Because the initial plans, or scripts, were chosen by the clients themselves, they can make new decisions regarding future behaviors and the future course of their lives.

The Ego States

Berne has described the human personality as consisting of three different observable ego states. The individual could be dominated or controlled by either of these stages at any given time. These states are the Parent, the Adult, and the Child (see Figure 11.1). They are similar but not identical to the concepts of Superego, Ego, and Id found in psychoanalytic theory. The basis for Berne's conceputalization of the human personality included his experience as a therapist and the neurological research of Dr. Wilder Penfield, which indicated that people can exist in different ego states simultaneously and that these states are connected to memories. These memories can be accessed in vivid detail, evoking sounds, smells, and feelings.

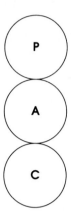

FIGURE 11.1   Ego State Structure. P represents the Parent Ego State; A represents the Adult Ego State; and C represents the Child Ego State.

The parent ego state has two parts. The critical parent includes critical, judgmental, and directive behavior, and all of the do's and don't's we have learned from our parents and other authority figures. The other part, the nurturing parent, includes the nurturing, supportive, encouraging, and protective dimensions vital for mental and physical survival. Essentially, the parent ego state consists of what is taught to us and is concerned about things that one ought to do.

The adult ego state is the thinking part of our personality. It is our data processing computer that makes decisions. It is the fact-finding, reasoning, problem-solving, and reality-testing part of our personality. In essence, the adult ego state is the cold, nonemotional, objective side of our behavior.

The child ego state is expressed in the form of feelings. It is the emotional, fun-loving, impulsive, spontaneous, sensuous, affectionate, and curious part of each of us. However, the child can also be selfish, self-centered, and rebellious and can display overly aggressive behaviors. The child ego state centers on the things one wants to do. The three ego states are generally described as three separate, unique, and independent functions and depicted as three adjacent circles.

Goals

A practitioner working within the TA framework has several major goals. One is to decontaminate any damaged ego states. Contamination occurs when there is no clear distinction between the parent and adult or the adult and child ego states. This relates to the second goal, which is to develop the capacity to use all ego states appropriately and, in particular, to develop the full use of the adult ego state. The final goal is to rid the client of poorly chosen life scripts and life position and replace them with an ''I'm OK'' position and a new, productive script.

Process

Generally, a series of progressive steps is followed in the TA approach. The first step is structural analysis, or the analysis of the person's ego states. This is done to help the individuals understand their ego state structure, to develop fully functioning ego states that are free of contamination, and to place the adult ego state in charge of life.

The second step is transactional analysis itself. This involves developing an understanding of the transactions in which the client normally engages and then working to improve communication abilities.

The third step is game analysis. Working with the knowledge of communication patterns gained through the previous step, the counselor proceeds to work with the interpretation of psychological games being played, confronting clients with the games they play and giving permission to stop playing the game(s).

The final step is script analysis. In this step, clients review the mistakes of their life script, gain social control, develop congruency, and revise life scripts as necessary.

Techniques

TA counselors have a variety of methods at their disposal, most of a conventional nature. A fair amount of teaching is involved as the counselor helps the client understand the basic TA concepts. Most TA counselors use either a chalkboard or a flipchart to illustrate such things as the ego states and different types of transactions.

An early task in transactional analysis counseling is to develop a counselor-client contract. This involves developing a specific statement of objectives to be attained by the client during the counseling process. The contract helps define the relationship, delineating the mutual responsibilities of both the client and the counselor. Establishing a contract also has the effect of letting the client know not to expect any miracle cures on the part of the counselor.

Using material presented by the client, the counselor analyzes, interrogates, confronts, offers an anecdote, simile, or comparison to clarify material, and then crystalizes—a communication at the end of therapy indicating that the client can now choose to stop game playing.

Many techniques developed by other therapists are used to great effect within the framework of transactional analysis. These include psychodrama (see chapter 5) and the broad range of Gestalt techniques.

Role of the Counselor

Transactional analysis counselors function as teachers, trainers, resource persons, and facilitators. They are skilled in the analysis of ego states, interpersonal transactions, games, and life scripts. Above all, they help clients acquire the tools necessary for change. As part of this process they provide protection, give permission, and model potency. The contractual relationship they establish results in equal status. Successful TA counselors want to conclude counseling with a client by being able to work in a game-free adult-to-adult relationship.

Time-Orientation

Transactional analysis is primarily a present-oriented therapy, although TA counselors can work with both past and future material.

Strengths

The description of personality development in TA works well with techniques and procedures associated with other counseling approaches. The concepts are easily understood, and in some cases, have become part of everyday language, such as games. The contractual approach clearly outlines the process, clarifying that the responsibility for change rests with the client, and determines when the process will be completed.

Weaknesses

The didactic nature of TA can serve to distance the counselor from the client. The counselor may become enamored with explaining concepts and diagnosing scripts and games to the point of losing the client in the relationship. The emphasis can easily become too heavily placed on the intellectual/cognitive factors to the exclusion of other dimensions of the personality. The use of TA concepts in conjunction with an affective approach like Gestalt therapy is one approach to deal with this weakness. TA also has a weak research base.

COGNITIVE-BEHAVIORAL COUNSELING

Background

As noted in Figure 5.1, behavioral counseling became a major addition to the counseling field in the 1960s, and in the 1970s the cognitive approach became influential. Table 11.1 describes how the behavioral and cognitive approaches compare with each other and with other approaches. Many behavioral counselors now tend to incorporate varying amounts of cognitive theory and methodology in their work; therefore, the two approaches are combined in this narrative. Another approach to cognitive counseling, rational-emotive therapy, is described separately.

Cognitive-behavioral counseling has evolved largely from the work emanating from university psychology departments throughout the 20th century. The earliest formulations of this constellation of approaches focused exclusively on behavioral counseling. Behavioral counseling is the application of different principles of learning theory to the changing of human behavior and problem resolution in a therapeutic setting. The basic premises to the behavioral approach are that (1) behavior is a function of current influences, (2) presenting problems should be defined specifically so that treatment and evaluation are possible, (3) treatment goals are to be described concretely, and (4) hypotheses about interventions are validated through research. The objective of the behavior counselor is to collaborate with the client in providing new learning experiences that allow the client to find more effective ways of behaving.

Learning theorists have determined that behavior is learned in three basic ways: through classical conditioning, operant conditioning, and imitation, or modeling. More recently, theorists have recognized the influence of cognitive factors on behaviors.

Aspects of Learning Theory and Their Application to Counseling

Classical (Respondent) Conditioning

Classical conditioning, made famous by Ivan Pavlov and his work with dogs, emphasizes what happens while a specific behavior is being exhibited. When a neutral stimulus is associated with a negative or positive stimulus, the previously neutral stimulus takes on positive-negative properties. An infant being presented with a white rat (neutral stimulus) at the same time that a loud noise occurs learns to fear white rats (Watson & Raynor, 1920). Such associations occur frequently in life and can be very emotional. Many cases of phobia develop in this way.

The principles of classical conditioning are used in counseling settings in such techniques as assertiveness training, systematic desensitization, and progressive relaxation. In each case, the counselor structures the setting so that positive feelings are associated with what were previously fearful ones. Some major proponents of this approach have been Joseph Wolpe (1973) and Arnold Lazarus (1971, 1981).

Operant Conditioning

Operant conditioning differs from classical conditioning in that the focus is on what happens before (antecedents) and after (consequences) the person makes a given response, rather than on responses caused by the environment. An individual can modify his or her behavior by the nature of the cues that precede problem behavior and/or the reinforcement that follows. If the environment is properly structured and reinforcement procedures are used, the desired behavior will be learned.

B. F. Skinner (1953–1990) is the best known proponent of operant conditioning. It was his belief that by reinforcing appropriate behavior, along with extinguishing maladaptive behavior, most, if not all, of our problems with learning and living could be alleviated.

This approach has been used successfully for many years systematically to modify behavior, particularly in schools, mental hospitals, and penal institutions. Applications of these behavioral techniques can also be used by parents in home settings. The operant approach tends to be most effective when the total environment can be controlled.

A number of operant conditioning techniques have been developed, including:

1. *Token economies:* the immediate presentation of tokens for desired behavior, which are then exchangeable for material goods or for privileges,
2. *Contracting:* the client and counselor agree that certain reinforcements will be forthcoming when particular behaviors occur (for many of us the reinforcement might be in the form of a paycheck), and
3. *Self-management plans:* In a self-management program, the client working with the counselor would describe the specific behavior desired, identifies the antecedent cues, selects appropriate reinforcers, and self-administers an appropriate reinforcement schedule, keeping accurate records all the while. (Mahoney, 1974)

Social Learning/Modeling

The proponents of social learning, or learning through observation and imitation, suggest that all learning that can be acquired through direct experience can also be acquired directly by observing others' behavior and the resulting consequences (Bandura & Walters, 1963). This is probably how most of us have learned to behave in a variety of social and professional settings. If we find ourselves in a new situation, we carefully try to observe the correct behavior before we do something that might be embarrassing. Examples of this approach can be seen in television commercials and sometimes as a result of television shows. There have been instances of behavior occurring in a community shortly after similar behavior was televised, suggesting that some imitative learning may have taken place. The counseling applications of social learning principles are found in play therapy, group counseling, and human relations training.

Cognitive-Behavioral Approach

Over the years one major criticism of the strict behavioral approach to counseling has been its lack of concern for the personality of the clients and its emphasis on the manipulation of the external variables related to the clients' behavior. The clients' thoughts and emotions were deemed to be essentially irrelevant. The social learning approach described here did begin to modify this approach somewhat by acknowledging that there were cognitive factors that could affect clients' behavior (Bandura, 1977, p. 345). An even more direct approach to acknowledging the individual's ability to interact on the environment eventually emerged in the form of cognitive behavior modification (Wilson, 1989).

In essence, the cognitive-behavioral approach posits thoughts as behaviors and suggests that what individuals think and in particular say to themselves influences what they do. The emphases, therefore, in this approach are to restructure how the clients think about various aspects of life and to improve the nature of self-talk.

The major cognitive-behavioral techniques involve cognitive restructuring either of irrational belief systems (Ellis, 1977), of faulty thinking styles (Beck, 1976), or of teaching problem-solving and coping skills (D'Zurilla & Goldfried, 1971). One particular technique developed by Meichenbaum (1977) is stress-innoculation training. This technique is a systematic program taught to clients to help them learn how to cope with different levels of stress.

Goals

The goals of all of the approaches to cognitive-behavioral counseling are to modify maladaptive behavior patterns and learn new functional behavior.

Role of Counselor

As with other approaches to counseling the development of a strong therapeutic relationship is a crucial factor in the cognitive-behavioral approach (Brady, 1980, p. 285). The counselor then works to eliminate specific problems and to increase the client's productive behaviors and constructive interpersonal relationships. Major tasks for the counselor are first to define the problem clearly, which includes understanding the antecedents and consequences that influence the problem, and next to collaborate with the client in formulating treatment goals and monitoring progress toward goal achievement.

Cognitive-behavioral counselors are very active. They direct client activity and reinforce goal-oriented behaviors. They teach, ask questions, give short answers, and often act as participant-observers. When working in a group setting, cognitive-behavioral counselors are generally concerned with individual rather than with group interaction.

Time Orientation

With several cognitive-behavioral techniques there is some concern about personal history in terms of the antecedent conditions related to the target behavior. Once this information has been obtained, the main focus of counseling is on the present, working to have the client learn and maintain new behaviors.

Strengths

The cognitive-behavioral approach brings specificity and explicitness to the field of counseling, focusing on the modification of observable behavior. Cognitive-behavioral counseling works with the modification of specific symptoms. It has been particularly successful with symptoms related to such things as conduct and phobic disorders.

A broad variety of powerful techniques have been used with many different populations in a variety of settings. A significant amount of research demonstrates the effectiveness of the various techniques in this approach.

Weaknesses

Cognitive-behavioral therapy is essentially a teaching or training approach rather than a comprehensive approach to counseling. Because the approach focuses on specific behaviors or thoughts, practitioners tend to ignore, avoid, or downplay certain other aspects of the human personality, such as the spiritual nature. The effectiveness of this approach may be limited to pathologies with clearly defined, overt behavioral characteristics. This latter criticism has been tempered somewhat by the recent attention being paid to cognitive and emotional dimensions.

RATIONAL-EMOTIVE THERAPY

Background

One pioneer in the field of counseling and the developer of the first cognitive-behavioral approach to counseling is Albert Ellis. Ellis began private practice in 1943 and is still counseling, writing, and lecturing. The approach he developed is called rational-emotive therapy (RET). Ellis, who was trained initially as a marriage and family therapist and then as a psychoanalyst, broke away from the analytic approach because he believed it was too slow and ineffective. He used behavioral conditioning for a while and then became convinced that it was not the person's behavior that was the essence of concern, but rather the person's thoughts about events and behaviors. He thus developed his rational, logical approach to counseling.

Ellis's approach is almost more philosophical than psychological, drawing on the work of philosophers such as Epictetus, who wrote, "Men are disturbed not by things, but by the view which they take of them" (Ellis, 1984, p. 200). In essence, this means that if people would learn to think differently about things that were disturbing them they would behave more rationally. It is not the activating event (A) that causes emotional dysfunctional consequences (C) in people, it is their interpretation of these events and their concomitant irrational beliefs (B) that cause emotional upset (Ellis, 1984, p. 198). People in effect create their own emotional disturbances or psychological disorders.

Goals

People not only have the potential to be irrational, they also have the potential to learn to be rational. The objectives, then, of RET are to help people learn to be rational, to stop using self-defeating behavior, and to acquire a more realistic, tolerant philosophy of life.

Concepts

Ellis believes that most problems people have are a result of irrational ideas that people use to indoctrinate themselves negatively. These ideas have come from our parents and our culture. Not only have we become indoctrinated by them, but we also continue to reindoctrinate ourselves on a regular basis. Ellis (1967, p. 61) has identified 11 such ideas that he believes "would seem inevitably to lead to widespread neurosis."

These ideas are as follows:

1. It is absolutely essential for an individual to be loved or approved by every significant person in his or her environment.
2. It is necessary that each individual be completely competent, adequate, and achieving in all areas if the individual is to be worthwhile.
3. Some people are bad, wicked, or villainous, and these people should be blamed and punished.
4. It is terrible and catastrophic when things are not the way an individual wants them to be.
5. Unhappiness is a function of events outside the control of the individual.
6. If something may be dangerous or harmful, an individual should constantly be concerned and think about it.
7. It is easier to run away from difficulties and self-responsibility than it is to face them.
8. Individuals need to be dependent on others and have someone stronger than themselves to lean on.
9. Past events in an individual's life determine present behavior and cannot be changed.
10. An individual should be very concerned and upset about other individuals' problems.
11. There is always a correct and precise answer to every problem, and it is catastrophic if it is not found.

Techniques

No unique techniques are used in rational-emotive therapy. A relationship is established with the client to help establish rapport. The therapist then proceeds to take an active, directive teaching stance.

> Rational-emotive practitioners often employ a fairly rapid-fire active-directive-persuasive-philosophic methodology. In most instances, they quickly pin the client down to a few basic irrational ideas. They challenge the client to validate these ideas, show how they contain extralogical premises that cannot be validated; logically analyze these ideas and make mincemeat of them; vigorously show why they cannot work and why they will almost inevitably lead to renewed disturbed symptomology; reduce these ideas to absurdity, sometimes in a highly humorous manner; explain how they can be replaced with more rational theses; and teach clients how to think

scientifically so that they can observe, logically parse, and minimize any subsequent irrational ideas and illogical deductions that lead to self-defeating feelings and behaviors." (Ellis, 1989, pp. 215–216)

The process of counseling in RET is to teach the client to think rationally. Ellis believes that the various techniques other therapists use are basically inefficient and wasteful. He believes the counselor should be direct rather than indirect.

Strengths

RET is offered as an efficient, scientific approach to behavioral change. RET generally is a short-term therapy, with a language and methodology that is fairly easily understood and practiced. Research studies indicate that it is effective with a variety of clients dealing with a wide range of disorders. The approach continues to evolve and invites scientific investigation. There is a significant amount of supporting material in the form of books, tapes, and other resource material.

Weaknesses

RET is a highly verbal, intellectual approach. The counselor takes responsibility, initially, at least, for diagnosing the client's irrational beliefs and then striving to see that the client's thought patterns are changed, raising the possibility of developing a dependency relationship. In spite of the fact that this is a cognitive approach, RET is not generally effective with clients with severe thought disorders, such as schizophrenics. Even though a fair amount of research supports the approach, questions have been raised about the methodology of some research studies (Patterson, 1986, pp. 29–30).

The personality and style of its founder, Albert Ellis, could perhaps also be cited as a weakness. Ellis is earthy and often controversial in his approach to selling his therapy. He has recently become embroiled in a heated discourse with adherents of transpersonal psychology over his perception of the dangers of their approach (Ellis & Yaeger, 1989; Wilber, 1989; Ellis, 1989a).

TRANSPERSONAL COUNSELING

Transpersonal counseling is a relative newcomer to psychotherapy; much of the literature describing this approach first appeared in the late 1960s and early 1970s. However, even though the present formulation of transpersonal ideas and methods may be new, many concepts date back to the work of Carl Jung in the early 1900s and even further with the incorporation of Eastern teachings.

Transpersonal counseling is based on the work of transpersonal psychologists who believe that there are potential cognitive, moral, and motivational stages of development beyond those reached by most adults (Walsh, 1989a). It is defined as that "aspect of therapy which goes beyond ego goals and bridges psychological and spiritual practice" (Boss, 1980, p. 161). Transpersonal counseling is "an open-ended endeavor to facilitate human growth and expand awareness beyond limits implied by most traditional Western models of mental health" (Vaughn, 1980, p. 182). The transpersonal approach brings together "the insights of the individualistic psychologies of the West with the spiritual psychologies of the East and the Middle East" (Fadiman, 1980, p. 181). Other therapies focus on emotions, behavior, and/or thoughts; transpersonal counseling adds the spiritual side of humanity as a vital dimension to be considered in fostering wellness through therapy.

Transpersonal counseling is a relatively small movement at this time for a number of reasons. First, there is no charismatic proponent of this approach to serve as a mentor or model, such as Fritz Perls in Gestalt therapy. Second, it has not been institutionalized and taught in clinical programs, as has cognitive-behavioral counseling. Third, there have been no best-selling books related to it, as in the case of transactional analysis *(Games People Play* and *I'm OK, You're OK.).* "It is an organic movement that has grown by networking, a movement that has drawn people to it who share a concern, a purpose, and a vision of what is possible for humanity. . . . It is cross-cultural and interdisciplinary; though it has roots in ancient perennial philosophy, it makes use of modern science because science, like mysticism, is a search for truth" (Vaughn, 1984, p. 25). The growth of new age literature that has in part paralleled the development of transpersonal psychology indicates a great deal of general public interest in transpersonal concepts. Some but not all of the new age literature relates to concepts found in transpersonal psychology.

There are indications that interest in the ideas that are part of the movement is growing. A review of program offerings at AACD conventions from 1987, 1988, and 1989 showed 12 content programs related to transpersonal concepts in 1987, 15 programs in 1988, and 23 programs in 1989. Some keynote speakers in 1989 dealt with transpersonal themes (e.g., Dr. Bernard Siegel). AACD now has a major content category for its conventions entitled "Spiritual, Ethical, and Moral Development."

Background

Transpersonal psychology has developed in large part as an extension of humanistic psychology. Abraham Maslow, in his study of self-actualizing individuals, discovered many healthy people from different walks of life who were going beyond the process of self-actualization (transcendence), reaching even greater fulfillment of their human potential (Maslow, 1971).

In the late 1960s, Maslow, Anthony Sutich, Stanislav Grof, and other psychologists created a new branch of psychology by combining aspects of humanistic psychology with Eastern concepts and traditions. Maslow and Sutich gave the name of *transpersonal* to this branch of psychology and in 1969 Sutich began the *Journal of Transpersonal Psychology* (Vaughn, 1984, p. 27). The concepts and processes associated with this psychology have gradually developed into a viable counseling approach.

Basic Concepts

The term *transpersonal* literally means beyond the personal, or beyond the personality. The use of this term signifies that who or what we are is not limited to being identified with our body, ego, or personality; we are and can be more than that (Vaughn, 1984, p. 26). We can, in fact, transcend to levels of which we may be unaware. Maslow (1971) has provided some 35 different meanings of the term *transcendence,* with the result that most people could recognize some aspects of transcendence in their lives. He also offered a condensed statement:

> Transcendence refers to the very highest and most inclusive levels of human consciousness, behaving, and relating, as ends rather than as means, to oneself, to significant others, to human beings in general, to other species, to nature, and to the cosmos." (p. 279)

Personality Development

The transpersonal approach builds on the idea that the human personality is formed by way of developmental stage processes as postulated and researched by Western psychologists (see chapter 15). However, transpersonal psychologists believe that the stages identified do not go far enough to detail the full potential of human nature. The levels formulated by Westerners such as Piaget, Erikson, and Kohlberg have been termed *conventional stages.* In the exploration of Eastern psychologies, transpersonal psychologists discovered that contemplative and meditative disciplines also have stages that are "sufficiently similar to suggest an underlying common invariant sequence of stages despite vast cultural and linguistic differences as well as styles of practice" (Wilber, Engler, & Brown, 1986, p. 9).

Wilbur, Engler, and Brown (1986) posit a three-level model that combines the conventional and the contemplative approaches. The first two levels, prepersonal and personal, consist of conventional development stages such as those delineated by Piaget and Erikson. The third level, transpersonal, consists of contemplative developmental stages described primarily in Eastern literature. Particular pathologies are said to be associated with the different stages; for example, the diagnosis of psychotic would tend to correlate with the prepersonal level "because this range of development involves the stages leading up to the emergence of a rational-individuated-personal selfhood" (Wilbur, Engler, & Brown, p. 12). Because transpersonal psychologists postulate a level beyond which the conventional approach leaves off, they consider a diagnosis of normalcy to be a case of developmental arrest.

Goals

The ultimate goal in transpersonal counseling is to help clients fulfill "higher needs for self-realization for full functioning at optimal levels of health," with a basic goal being to "enable each person to meet physical, emotional, mental, and spiritual needs appropriately, in accordance with individual preferences and pre-dispositions'' (Vaughn, 1980, p. 182). Additional goals include ''both traditional [goals] such as symptom relief and behavior change, and where appropriate, opti-mal work at the transpersonal level'' (Walsh & Vaughn, 1980, p. 165).

Nature of People and Anxiety

With regard to the nature of people, transpersonal counselors believe that human beings not only ''have the potential to reach eventually undreamt of levels of emotional, intellectual and ethical development'' (Grof, 1988, p. x), but they also are seen as ''seeking to enhance and surpass [themselves] in the process of self-actualization'' (Vaughn, 1980, p. 182).

Anxiety is perceived as dealing with basic human problems involving values, meaning, and purpose (Vaughn 1980, p. 161) and with the concerns of individ-uals who have already achieved a satisfactory coping level in their lives and are still unsatisfied because they intuitively seem to know that there must be more, that potentials are greater than what has already been achieved.

Techniques

Transpersonal therapists are eclectic in that they use techniques drawn from East-ern and Western psychologies to work with the mind, body, emotions, and spirit of clients. They use most of the traditional techniques noted in therapies de-scribed in this chapter and include meditation and other consciousness-raising awareness exercises and activities, such as dreamwork and imagery.

Role of Counselor

In transpersonal counseling, ''participation by therapists in all their humanity in the therapeutic relationship [and] opening themselves fully to the client's experi-ence and to their own reactions'' (Walsh & Vaughn, 1980, p. 166) is considered to be fundamental. The transpersonal perspective would add the view that thera-pists consciously use the relationship to enhance their own transpersonal growth while serving the client. Because it is known that the therapists do change as a result of being with their clients in the therapeutic relationship (see chapter 2), this conscious personal growth on the part of the counselor is performed in the context of growth through service.

> The therapist attempts to provide both an optimal environment and serve as a model for the client. Where the therapist is consciously serving the client there is no hierar-chical status accorded to being a therapist. Rather the situation is held as one in which both therapist and client are working on themselves, each in the way that is most appropriate to their development. The therapist's openness and willingness to use the therapeutic process to maximize his or her own growth and commitment to service is viewed as the optimal modeling that can be provided for the client. (Walsh & Vaughn, 1980, p. 166)

Process

Transpersonal counselors first establish the therapeutic relationship and are open to work with whatever personality or behavioral issue emerges, using given techniques if and when appropriate. If and when client concerns deal with issues of faith or go beyond what might be considered a dull, normal existence, the counselor can also work with these issues. Termination of transpersonal counseling relationship occurs when clients are functioning at levels that will provide them with the fulfillment and meaning for which they had been searching.

Strengths

Transpersonal counseling is concerned with the total person. Practitioners strive to help individuals fulfill their full potential, often going beyond levels sought by other therapies. Being free to draw from the broad range of concepts and techniques from both Eastern and Western disciplines provides a greater degree of flexibility and adaptability to client needs than do therapies that are more conceptually limited. Transpersonal counselors often consider and work with experiences and perspectives generally ignored or avoided by other approaches to therapy.

Weaknesses

Many assumptions specific to this approach have not been empirically tested. However, there is a growing body of research on the value of meditation, and there are indications that research related to other concepts is growing. A recent unsystematic sampling of doctoral dissertations from 1987 and 1988 yielded 516 dissertation titles related to transpersonal psychology (Fulton, 1989). Nevertheless, because of the relatively ambiguous nature of many constructs emphasized in this approach (e.g., levels of consciousness), the prospect for rigorous, replicable studies is not good.

The transpersonal approach would probably be more effective with clients who were already functioning at a relatively high level. Transpersonal counselors themselves, out of necessity, need to be highly functioning individuals. They need to be well-grounded in developing the therapeutic relationship, in using relevant techniques from other theoretical approaches, and in using techniques unique to the transpersonal approach. Critics of transpersonal therapy believe that some transpersonal counselors follow the teachings of extreme cults and use techniques such as "astrology, sorcery, psychic healing, [and] witchcraft" (Ellis, 1986, p. 149) in their practices. Overall, the approach is still in an early developmental stage; much more needs to be done in the formulation of theory, process, and research.

WHOLISTIC COUNSELING

Wholistic counseling can be considered the epitome of eclectic counseling. Other approaches are eclectic in that they involve systematic borrowing of concepts or techniques from different therapies. However, because the scope of these therapies is limited (e.g., focusing specifically on the cognitive realm), the amount of borrowing also tends to be limited. This is not so in wholistic counseling.

Wholistic counseling works with the total person and uses information and methodology from any source. The wholistic approach is grounded in the movement concerned with health and wellness and strives for prevention as much as if not more than remediation and cure. The wholistic approach goes beyond most other approaches to look at more than the total individual; it looks at the total environment in which the individual exists. It is a proactive as much as a reactive approach. Wholistic counseling, then, consists of working with the whole person in terms of body, mind, emotions, and spirit, in the context of the person's total environment.

Background

The counterculture and human potential movements of the late 1960s and early 1970s helped bring about awareness of a variety of problems with the nature and quality of the national health care system as well as the potential value of other approaches, including Eastern practices, in dealing with human problems. The resultant wholistic movement has developed a primary focus on wellness in reaction to medicine's focus on disease. "The wellness emphasis conveys that health is significantly more than the absence of physical symptoms and disease; it is a self-actualizing commitment to increase the quality of one's total self and one's relationship with his or her environment" (O'Donnell, 1988, p. 366).

Many health-related problems in the United States are now recognized as being self-inflicted. They are results of such things as poor behavioral choices and self-destructive attitudes, or environmental factors rather than results of germs or viruses. Therefore, the wholistic health movement has involved members of the counseling profession from the beginning along with wholistic medical practitioners, including Don Ardell (1986) and Bernie Siegel (1986).

Goals

The goals of wholistic counseling emphasize developing client independence through having clients take charge of their own well-being and helping clients reach the highest level of functioning of which they are capable (O'Donnell, 1988, p. 379). Wholistic counselors basically work to help clients attain their personal goals, and if the clients so choose, to help them move from "their presenting level of experience to the level of pure aliveness, and toward providing them with the information and skills necessary to maintain such a state" (Stensrud & Stensrud, 1984, p. 422).

Nature of People

To the wholistic counselor, people are

> seen as unitary. That is, it is not possible to divide the individual parts such as the physical, mental, psychological, cultural, and economic; these parts cannot be separated one from the other in the active and reactive life of the person. He lives, loves, works, and feels as a whole person. Arbitrary divisions of parts or functions represent but a convenient method for collecting and classifying bodies of knowledge, or organizing professions and social systems. The simplistic interpretation they reflect, however, bears little relationship to living, breathing human beings." (Goodwin, 1986, p. 30)

Human nature is perceived as being an open process that changes with the experiences of people interacting with their environment and with physical, psychological, and spiritual aspects of wellness being inextricably interrelated (Stensrud & Stensrud, 1984, p. 422; Morrison, 1986, p. 240). The wholistic counselor believes that to consider adequately any aspect of human nature requires a therapist to consider them all.

Principles

Nine basic principles or underpinnings for the wholistic health approach have been identified by O'Donnell (1988):

1. We are responsible for our health;
2. Illness is a communication from within;
3. Most healing comes from within;
4. Treatment must involve body, mind, emotions, and spirit (and in many cases, environment);
5. The [w]holistic practitioner is a consultant, facilitator, and advisor—not a miracle worker or a dogmatic authority figure;
6. Personalized caring and unconditional positive regard are essential to change and to healing;
7. Our physical and social environments greatly affect our health;
8. Nutrition and exercise are the cornerstones of good health;
9. Because clients are uniquely individualistic in their biochemistry and in their sociopsychological make-up, [w]holistic services by necessity should be eclectic and individually tailored. (pp. 366–377)

Role of Counselor

As noted in this list, a wholistic counselor is a facilitator and consultant and views the "person and his/her wellness from every possible perspective, taking into account every available skill for the person's growth toward harmony and balance . . . treating the person, not the disease . . . using mild, natural methods whenever possible" (O'Donnell, 1988, p. 366).

Wholistic counselors establish the necessary core conditions for the therapeutic relationship and then personalize their approach to the unique characteristics of their clients. The involvement of wholistic counselors in their own personal growth is important in establishing themselves as models. Wholistic counselors must be well educated. They "must have the ability to develop a total understanding of the client—physically, psychologically, spiritually, and environmentally—including the ability to intervene in any one or all of these areas" (O'Donnell, 1988, p. 379). They also have to be well grounded in any of the numerous counseling interventions available to them and ethically responsible to acknowledge when they are not qualified to make a specific intervention.

Because wholistic counselors continually consider the whole person, they have an extensive network of referral sources and may in some instances work directly with a team of interdisciplinary practitioners; for example, working as a counselor in a clinic, along with a dietician, one or more physicians, and an exercise physiologist.

Techniques

Because wholistic counseling is an eclectic approach, there are no techniques that are particularly unique to it. Wholistic practitioners draw on resources from the entire field as well as from the disciplines of nutrition, exercise physiology, medicine, and others. Because they are aware of the effects of environment in the behavior of clients, wholistic counselors generally take a systems approach (see chapter 7) to their cases.

One major strategy of wholistic counselors is their tendency to work closely with other professionals such as dieticians and physicians. Wholistic counselors are expected to be excellent role models for their clients.

Process

The therapeutic relationship as described in chapter 2 is typically developed with the counselor's being sensitive to all dimensions of the client. The nature of the client's problem determines the scope of the counselor's responses and interventions. The problem may be such that the counselor and client need only to go through the exploring and understanding stages of the process, with the client's realizing how to solve the problem. At other times, the counselor may involve the client's family and significant others in working with the problem.

The counselor is generally concerned with the physical condition of the client, referring to a physician, dietician, and/or exercise physiologist as appropriate. Whatever the extent of the counselor's involvement through the process, the relationship is concluded with the clients' having direct responsibility for their continued wellness.

Strengths

Wholistic counseling is a positive approach, focusing on the strengths of individuals and on what they can do to help themselves. All aspects of clients' lives are considered, and the broad repertoire of counseling interventions from other approaches are available to fit the needs of clients. Wholistic counseling can be seen as much as a preventive approach as it is a remedial approach.

Weaknesses

Wholistic counseling is a relatively new approach, with a diffuse theoretical base and virtually no research data specific to this total approach. Highly skilled and knowledgeable practitioners are necessary to implement this approach.

SUMMARY

A description has been provided of seven counseling approaches that are currently prominent in the field of counseling. The approaches include person-centered counseling and Gestalt therapy, which tend to emphasize working with the emotional dimension of clients; rational-emotive therapy and transactional analysis, which focus on the thoughts and beliefs of clients; the behavioral approach, which focuses on client behaviors; the cognitive-behavioral approach, which views clients' thoughts as behaviors; transpersonal counseling, which incorporates the spiritual dimensions into the counseling process; and wholistic counseling, which incorporates all of the dimensions mentioned and also works with the several environmental systems affecting clients.

Through further study of these and other approaches, students can determine which approach or approaches most closely align with their personal beliefs and development. This brief overview of the variety of counseling approaches has been presented to help make future study of counseling approaches meaningful and exciting.

QUESTIONS AND ACTIVITIES

1. Consider your philosophy of life and your view of the nature of people. Which approach described in this chapter seems to fit best with your beliefs about human nature and how people change, and with your personality? Choose to pursue further reading in that particular approach.
2. Interview one or more counselors as to their theoretical approaches. Find out why they chose their particular approaches. How closely do these counselors adhere to their chosen approaches? Did they receive any special training? If so, where and for how long?

3. Think of a problem in your life. With this problem in mind, how would you as a client react to the different approaches described in this chapter? Which approach do you believe would help you the most? Which would make you feel the most comfortable? Is the approach you think would help the same as or different from the approach you personally tend to favor for your own personal approach to counseling?

FOCUS ON
Group Work

*Can group counseling be more effective
than individual counseling?*

America is a group-oriented society. Most of us belong to many groups for a variety of reasons. Before reading this chapter, take a few moments and list all the groups that you are currently part of. This list would include family, social, academic, business, athletic, religious, and ethnic groups. Without too much difficulty, you might come up with 10 or more different ones. It is not too surprising then, that in the field of counseling, working in groups is an ever-growing dimension.

There is also a belief that the growth of therapeutic groups is an indication of our failure to provide close, meaningful relationships with our families, friends, and co-workers and a failure of people to allow emotional contact to emerge naturally and spontaneously (Starak, 1988).

This chapter considers origins of group work, the advantages and disadvantages of working in groups, types of groups, group dynamics and development, and leadership styles. Groups in schools, agencies, business and industry, and hospitals are considered here. The next chapter speaks to a special type of group work, that of family and relationship counseling.

ORIGINS

The origin of groups can be traced to the beginnings of humankind, when primitive tribes developed for survival and protection. The Greeks placed a strong emphasis on knowing oneself and examining natural phenomena, and they used the group approach as a vehicle for understanding interpersonal relations among other phenomena in the universe. Early religious sects used groups in schools, churches, and especially in monasteries in order to develop greater self-knowledge, which was more associated with religious doctrine. As society changed from rural and agrarian to industrial, intergroup cooperation became more of a necessity. Guilds, trades, and other professional groups gradually emerged. People had to work together to produce goods and trade. The pattern continues as contemporary society is composed of a multitude of groups including economic, political, family, work, and leisure groups.

Therapy Groups—Pioneers

There is a lack of agreement as to who might be the unequivocal father of group psychotherapy. Cohen and Smith (1976) list Joseph Pratt, Alfred Adler, Jacob Moreno, Trigant Burrow, and Cody Marsh as the most often cited founders of group psychotherapy. The early founders, however, did not practice group psychotherapy as we know it today. Most of them used groups to give inspirational talks or to present brief lectures to patients in hospital settings.

The onset of World War II brought on a dramatic increase in the use of group psychotherapy. In Great Britain, a group of psychiatrists at Northfield, a treatment center for psychiatric casualties, began experimenting with their patients using group psychotherapy. Some advocated an analytic group approach, looking beyond the group to the community as a whole. One approach was based on the group leader being tentative, evasive, and completely noncommittal. This methodology encouraged transference and created tension and frustration among group members, which gradually and subtly led the group to a resolution of its problems (Cohen & Smith, 1976). Alfred Adler, the founder of individual psychotherapy, was probably the first therapist to stress the importance of interpersonal relationships in mental health. Adler used interpersonal techniques in the training of therapists.

Jacob Moreno was an actor who became a therapist. He has been one of the major influences in group psychotherapy. Moreno founded a theoretical approach to groups called psychodrama, which involved creative dramatics and was based on sociometry, the measurement of social relationships among group members. In 1931, Moreno founded the first journal devoted to groups, *Impromptu*. It is currently published as *Group Psychotherapy*. He had a profound influence on Fritz Perls, the founder of Gestalt therapy, who borrowed many of Moreno's dramatic techniques.

Birth of Laboratory Training

Kurt Lewin developed a field-theory approach to groups. Field theory as defined by Lewin (1951) is a method for analyzing causal relations and of building scientific constructs. It is similar in many respects to Gestalt psychology. Lewin also advanced the concept of action research, based on democratic concepts that were advocated in the writings of John Dewey. Schmuck and Schmuck (1979) state, "If Dewey could be termed the outstanding philosopher of democracy, Lewin was surely the major theoretician or researcher of democracy among psychologists. The type of group work labeled T-group emanated directly from the work of Kurt Lewin" (p. 3). Lewin and Bradford received grants from the Office of Naval Research and the National Education Association in 1947. The National

Training Laboratories (NTL) opened in the summer of 1947 at Bethel, Maine, shortly after the death of Lewin. NTL tried to create an environment in which change could occur, especially interpersonal change through laboratory training. A major outcome of this work was the development of the T (training) group.

The Human-Potential Movement

The human potential movement that developed in the 1960s is based on the beliefs that most human beings use a very small part of their capabilities, and that through a broad spectrum of techniques this potential can be released. Collectively, the practitioners and their methods and techniques have come to be known as the human-potential movement. Its roots are based on the teachings of Moreno, Perls, Reich, Maslow, Rogers, and Schutz, among others. They include such methods as encounter groups, marathon groups, sensory awareness, and meditation.

TYPES OF GROUPS

Groups in the field of counseling can be classified in various ways. One way is according to whether they are preventive, developmental, or remedial (see chapter 5).

One major difference in types of groups is the degree of structure provided. For example, most developmental groups use a minimum of structure, and the leader works toward a shared or distributive leadership, whereas in preventive groups, there is a greater structure of the group process with many planned activities. Remedial groups are less structured than preventive groups, but the leader is the central figure.

Preventive Groups

Some preventive groups are learning groups that focus on the acquisition of specific information and knowledge. Often these groups center on career concerns such as job-seeking skills, life-planning, midlife career change, and career exploration. Child-rearing groups, topical groups such as defining sex roles, learning communications skills, and assertiveness training, and group guidance in schools are also considered preventive in nature.

Through preventive groups people can be taught how to prevent problems from occurring and how to deal with difficulties that may arise. Because most of these groups have specific behavioral goals, leaders can obtain accurate member feedback on how successful they have been and on what future changes might be made.

Developmental Groups

Developmental groups focus on personal growth of the individual members. They are intended primarily for normal people who are interested in relating better to other people, developing insights into their values, and learning to become more aware of their feelings. Developmental group members interact in the here and now with people who are relatively equal to each other. Examples of developmental groups are encounter groups, T-groups, marathon groups, and personal growth laboratories.

Encounter or Personal Growth Groups

Schutz (1980) defines encounter groups as a method of relating based on openness and honesty, self-awareness, self-responsibility, awareness of the body, attention to feelings, and emphasis on the here and now. They are designed to remove blocks to better functioning and create conditions leading to more satisfying use of human capacities. Encounter groups use techniques from a wide variety of influences, including psychodrama, Gestalt therapy, T-groups, theater, and dance. They are often referred to as personal growth groups.

T-Groups

T-groups were originally created to train managers and administrators in business and industry in human relation skills. Most often these groups are task-oriented, with the emphasis on how participants can relate better in interpersonal situations in order to improve group performance in their work environments. T-groups are developmental and growth-oriented. They deal with the here and now and not with past behavior. Participants become aware of their own functioning in groups and how to develop leadership skills.

Marathon Groups

The marathon group is basically an intensified encounter experience. The marathon group can meet anywhere from 16 hours straight to a week or more, breaking only for meals and short naps. The goals of marathon groups are to help members become aware of their masks and facades and to give these up and become more genuine. The marathon process helps participants lower their defenses and become more authentic.

Remedial Groups

Remedial groups are for members who are viewed by themselves and others as needing help. Often they are made up of psychiatric patients who have been hospitalized because of their problems and outpatients who have more severe or emotional problems. Participants are often concerned with such specific problems as phobias, depression, and sexual dysfunction. Examples of remediation groups are counseling and therapy groups.

Counseling groups focus on more conscious problems. Counseling groups are more short-term in duration and oriented toward resolution of immediate problem situations as opposed to more unconscious and deeply rooted neurotic and psychotic disorders that group therapy might include. However, just as with the distinction between individual counseling and psychotherapy, the situation becomes blurred. For example, Corey (1986) states how important it is to make clear that many private-practice therapy groups include the same type of normal individuals who make up encounter groups.

Other Types of Groups

Other types of groups of interest to prospective counselors include task-oriented groups, self-help groups, support groups, and families. We devote an entire chapter to working with families (see chapter 13).

Task groups are usually formed on the basis of need. They focus on the collaborative effort of group members around such themes as protection of the environment, conflict resolution, civil rights, improved productivity in the work place, and items of community interest such as curbside recycling or increased taxation. The emphasis in these groups is on achieving a specific goal, and not on changing group members.

Some groups deal with special populations and require different approaches from those used in preventive or developmental groups. Some examples include support groups and groups for substance abusers, victims of child abuse, and rape victims.

Self-help groups have experienced a phenomenal growth in recent years. Most are support groups such as Alcoholics Anonymous, Overeaters Anonymous, and Gamblers Anonymous, which have specific desirable changes of its group members, while at the same time providing support and encouragement. Self-help groups are unique in that they generally are leaderless.

WHY WORK WITH GROUPS?

There are many advantages to working in groups; however, as in most approaches to counseling, there are tradeoffs. The following is a summary of the positive and negative aspects of doing group work.

Advantages

Groups provide a number of safety factors that facilitate individual growth and development. Initially there is a feeling of safety because only one or two persons are the center of attention at any given time. Group members can more easily take risks as they become ready. Meanwhile there is a vicarious learning and identification process on the part of other members as a result of observing specific members in the group interact. Often group members are more willing to discuss feelings and concerns in groups of peers than in individual counseling. Learning can also be more potent in groups due to the high intensity of interactions, the support and acceptance of others, and the collective experience of group members. There usually is greater support for growth and change because of the strength in numbers, and concurrently greater acceptance and empathy. All of this gives group members a feeling of safety in order to deal with their problems and concerns.

Groups can provide a sense of belonging. Group members feel part of a social group, which satisfies needs of intimacy and relatedness. In effective groups there is immediate interpersonal feedback, which facilitates personal exploration, growth, and development.

People do not live in a vacuum—basic human needs can be met only through involvement with other human beings. The group gives meaning to each member's human existence. It provides a safe atmosphere for interpersonal risking and for trying out new behaviors that can then be incorporated into members' daily lives. The group is in itself a social milieu that parallels the milieu of group member's real world and therefore facilitates the transfer of learning more readily to the outside life of group members. Group members improve intrapersonal skills as well as interpersonal skills.

The group is an ideal place for reality-testing, to see how each member's reality matches how others perceive him or her and vice versa. It allows for group members to come out of their own concerns and reach out and become concerned for others, which is therapeutic.

Groups encompass a wide range of needs for a wide variety of age groups. They are adaptable to a broad range of helping environments and programs such as schools, colleges, mental health centers, correctional institutions, drug or alcohol treatment programs, and employment agencies. Practitioners can reach many persons in a group setting within a specific block of time, and at less cost.

Disadvantages

The group counselor has less situational control. Because there are more people, things can go wrong, and more attention must be paid to what is happening. The group counselor must also balance the need for freedom versus the need for structure. This balance becomes a paradox because to function well individuals must sacrifice themselves for the good of the group; yet for groups to function well, the needs of individuals must not be forgotten (Rutan & Groves, 1989). Each group member receives less attention in the group because less time is available for individuals.

Confidentiality is more difficult to mandate in a group than in individual counseling, and it is almost impossible to enforce. Privacy can be violated by sharing one's personal life indiscriminately. Coercion and peer pressure toward conformity are parts of every group process. Although a certain amount of peer pressure can help establish positive norms (guidelines and rules for the group), the process often referred to as group think—the forcing of group opinion on all members of the group—can curb individual initiative, autonomy, and creativity. There is a danger of group members' conforming to norms that may be distorted, inappropriate, or illogical. Shared reality can take precedence over individual perception. For example, a group norm emphasizing competition and one-upmanship can become established rather than individual perceptions that stress cooperation.

Group work is not for everyone in every situation. Groups are not advised for persons who are paranoid, brain damaged, acutely psychotic, sociopathic, suicidal, hypochondriacal, or narcissistic.

Often a group will single out certain members as scapegoats. This may be a consequence of the group counselor's failure to explore hostility directed at them and may be reinforced by the failure of the group counselor to intervene when members gang up on other members.

Group leaders or group counselors may not have the proper training to lead groups. They may fail to screen members or prepare them properly for participating in a group. They may not be able to handle the complexity of group dynamics, or destructive behaviors in a group such as angry aggressiveness, inappropriate rescuing, passivity, and monopolizing. Group leaders who are not properly trained can cause problems such as souring individuals from seeking help in the future.

Therefore, all in all, are groups a positive or negative force? According to Rutan and Groves (1989) they can be either or both, depending on their size, composition, organization, purpose, lifetime, leadership, and capacity for intimacy. Also, many disadvantages of group work can be minimized or even eliminated with the use of properly trained leaders and appropriate precautions.

THERAPEUTIC FORCES IN GROUPS

The many dynamic forces involved in groups can be called curative, healing, or therapeutic. Yalom (1985) identified 11 factors that account for change in group members, which he labeled "curative factors." According to Yalom these curative factors were applicable to all the various schools of group counseling. Yalom's factors include:

- instillation of hope
- universality (others have similar problems and concerns)
- imparting of information
- altruism
- corrective recapitulation (of one's original family group)
- development of socializing techniques
- imitative behavior
- interpersonal learning
- group cohesiveness

- catharsis
- existential factors (self-responsibility)

Corey and Corey (1982) have also identified numerous forces, which they called therapeutic factors, based on self-reports from group members. The factors are hope, commitment to change, willingness to risk and trust, caring, acceptance, empathy, intimacy, power, freedom to experiment, feedback, catharsis, meaning attribution, learning interpersonal skills, humor, self-disclosure, confrontation, and group cohesion. Corey and Corey viewed three of these factors as especially crucial to successful outcomes of groups: group cohesion, self-disclosure, and confrontation. The next section elaborates on group cohesion, confrontation, interpersonal skills, and universality as particularly important factors in group development; self-disclosure, a crucial factor as noted by Corey and Corey, is discussed in chapter 3.

Cohesion

Forsyth (1983) defined group cohesion as the strength of forces that bind members to a group. Included in this are the attractiveness of the group as a whole as well as the attraction of each member to every other member. It is a firmly established sense of we-ness characterized by high valuing commitment, diversity, and trust. Group members perceive the group as special, viable, and productive. Group members are committed not only to themselves, but also to each other. Diversity is accepted, and differences are valued. Trust has been developed during early stages of the group. Group members have weathered storms together and have not only survived but also transcended. In groups in which cohesion is lacking, group members become discouraged and frustrated with members dropping out or with poor attendance.

Universality

Often people in counseling groups perceive their problems and concerns as strange and unique. They view themselves as different and alone in their suffering. As the group process develops, members soon realize that they are not so unique and special in that sense after all. Yalom (1985) cynically refers to this phenomenon with the cliché "misery loves company." This realization becomes a strong sense of relief and lessens fears, anxieties, and feelings of alienation. Group members realize that they are human also, that other people have the same problems, concerns, fantasies, nightmares, and impulses. Yalom (1985) states that "There is no human deed or thought which is fully outside the experience of other people" (p. 8).

Interpersonal Skills

Although the focus in groups is often on intrapersonal concerns of individual members, interpersonal learning is one of the major means whereby group members grow and change. Group members know a great deal about themselves—they live with themselves 24 hours a day. Yet, this knowledge is limited. Group members have facets of themselves about which they have little or no knowledge. Sometimes other people perceive these areas accurately, but often others' perceptions are distorted and incomplete. (Note the discussion on transference in chapter 2). Harry Stack Sullivan (1953) used the term ''parataxic distortions'' to refer to peoples' tendencies to distort their perceptions of others. Parataxic distortion is similar to the Freudian concept of transference, but broader. It takes into account all interpersonal relationships and includes the distortion of interpersonal reality in response to interpersonal needs as well as the transferring of attitudes from real-life figures.

Through taking interpersonal risks by self-disclosing, giving and receiving feedback, and self-observation, group members obtain insight into and awareness of their behaviors and the impact of their behaviors on others. They realize that they are responsible for their interpersonal existence and have choices open to them as to whether to change. They also learn how to put these changes into effect. As a result, perceptions of all group members undergo change and become more objective.

Confrontation (Feedback)

Perhaps the most crucial of all interpersonal skills is confrontation, giving feedback. In groups in which there is only support and empathy, stagnation often occurs, and the developmental process of the group is impeded. Egan (1970) states that mature people learn to challenge themselves and their own productive ways of relating to others. However, because there are always areas not open to their awareness, and there are times when individuals fail to challenge themselves, mature individuals are open to constructive confrontation from others and are appreciative of such confrontation. Group members who avoid giving negative feedback in terms of how they are perceiving others and how they are affected by others cheat others from information that would be helpful for their growth. Effective feedback is a skill that must be used constructively. It does not mean putting down others in a reckless manner, attacking others and then retreating, attributing motives to other's behavior (mind reading), hurting others intentionally, or pressing others to change. Egan (1975) speaks of ''caring confrontation,'' where the personal relationship has been established and the feedback is given with genuineness and respect. (See chapter 3 for additional discussion on confrontation.)

STAGES OF GROUP DEVELOPMENT

Group counseling is a developmental process just as is individual counseling (see chapter 2). Also, just as in individual counseling, there are numerous developmental models ranging from two to four or more stages of significant periods in the group's life. Most models seem to encompass three or four stages.

A five-stage model of group development is presented here, based on Yalom (1985), Trotzer (1977), and Tuckman (1965), suitable for use in studying all types of groups. In actual practice, the stages described do not flow as neatly and orderly as presented. There is often overlap between stages. It is not uncommon for a group to remain stuck in certain stages or even to regress temporarily to an earlier stage. New conflicts can arise in any stage even after other conflicts have been resolved. Group member behavior as well as group leader behavior for each stage is presented.

Stage 1—Orientation/Forming

The first stage of group development is the coming together, or forming, stage. It is in this stage that group members become oriented to the beginning of the group process and to each other.

Group Member Behavior (Entry-Involvement)

The immediate concerns for group members usually center on the "4 I's"— Inclusion, Identity, Influence, and Intimacy (Dorsey, 1980). Group members often experience generalized anxiety over intimacy and closeness, which is characterized by tentative involvement with other group members and superficial attempts at closeness. It is difficult for most people to share those deep inner parts of themselves under any circumstances, and yet they are in a new group to do just that.

Group members often are preoccupied with how they fit in. Are they liked or not liked? How much influence do they have in the group? Will they be listened to? Will they be accepted? Can they really be themselves or must they put up a front? What are the ground rules here? Where is the jeopardy, support, or safety? Members generally need to at least partially resolve the "4 I" issues before constructive risk-taking can occur.

Members usually make some initial attempts at revealing themselves in order to see if their concerns will be attended to. They want to assure themselves that the group is indeed a safe and secure place for them to express their thoughts and feelings. The establishment of trust is the main prerequisite for further group development.

Group Leader Behavior

The core conditions that are the basis for success in individual counseling are also the basis for success in group counseling. The counselor's self—who the counselor is—becomes a crucial factor in laying the groundwork for successful group process. The counselor must model therapeutic behavior by being open, listening actively, and demonstrating acceptance, positive regard, and genuineness.

The leader must deal with group members' "4 I's" by making the group a secure and safe place. The leader must also be ready to instill a sense of hope in group members. If the leader has self-confidence in his or her ability and has faith in the group process, these attitudes are communicated to the group in verbal and nonverbal behaviors and facilitate feelings of hopefulness among group members. The group leader will generally be more task oriented than relationship oriented to help the group through the first stage.

Stage 2—Transition/Storming

Yalom (1985) refers to the major themes in the second stage of group development as those of dominance, control, and power. This is in contrast to the concerns of acceptance, approval, commitment, and search for orientation, structure, and meaning of the first stage.

Group Member Behavior

In Stage 2, group members continue to deal with Stage 1 behaviors. Usually the effect is greater, with more anxiety and ambiguity. As the group members struggle to define themselves and establish norms, conflict begins to manifest itself. Often there are verbal attacks and challenges to the leader. Some group members might attempt to provoke the leader, shock, gain approval, or wrestle power from the leader. They might closely watch the leader's reactions to all this in order to find shortcomings in the leader.

Even though group members are still concerned about safety, they also want to become more involved and committed. Group members make some tentative self-disclosures and show greater openness to discovering themselves and others. Group members seem to alternate between fight and flight, between assertiveness or aggressiveness and withdrawal or avoidance. Resistance and defensiveness are usually quite strong, and norms and cohesiveness of the group at this stage revolve around member protection and avoidance of perceived threat.

Group Leader Behavior

It is essential that in the second stage group leaders demonstrate a nondefensive attitude and allow group members to express their anxieties and resistant feelings fully. If the group leader is defensive or evasive in dealing with member confrontation, then trust will not develop, and the group process will not move forward. The group leader should help the group look at its own process here so the group has a greater awareness of exactly what is going on in the group. The group leader also needs to encourage and reinforce growth-enhancing behaviors such as acceptance and respect among members, constructive feedback, expression of disagreement, self-disclosure, and self-exploration. In this stage the leader strives to become more relationship oriented. Depending on the theoretical approach used, the task orientation of the leader may begin to fade.

Stage 3—Cohesiveness/Norming

If the problems and concerns of the second stage are successfully dealt with, group members move into the third stage of group development, cohesiveness

(Yalom, 1985). Group members demonstrate greater self-responsibility, risk taking, and openness during this stage. A greater sense of cohesiveness is experienced after intermember commitment and caring have been tested and trust established in the previous stages. During this stage, the norms or rules for how the group will continue to function become fixed.

Group Member Behavior

This stage is characterized by more self-disclosure on the part of group members. Often hard-to-express secrets are revealed. Members often meet outside the group, and there is considerable concern when any members are missing. Silent members are encouraged to interact with others.

The cohesiveness established in this stage is based on a firmly established sense of we-ness with high valuing both of members as individuals and the group as a whole. This is different from the false sense of consensus in the earlier stages of the group process. Group members become committed to helping themselves, *and* each other. There is a strong sense of interdependency. Trotzer (1977) reports a study by Lindt (1958), which found that only group members who took responsibility in the helping process benefited from their group experience. In this atmosphere of trust, acceptance, and cohesiveness, group members begin to examine their problems more closely and deeply.

Group Leader Behavior

The group leader in Stage 3 needs to facilitate deeper levels of self-exploration and help members personalize their experiences. Sometimes group members develop such a strong sense of cohesiveness here that any intermember conflict or hostility is blocked. The group leader, therefore, must demonstrate high levels of immediacy and confrontation in order to help the group move into the working stage and not stagnate into what Yalom (1985) calls a "ritualistic embrace." This stage is characterized by high relationship behaviors on the part of the leader and a relatively low number of task-oriented interventions.

Stage 4—Working/Performing

The working or performing stage is characterized by group members' willingness to experiment with new behaviors and attitudes. The group leader is seen more objectively and is no longer viewed as a threat. As a result there is less dependence on the leader for direction, and a greater egalitarian relationship among everyone in the group.

Group Member Behavior

In the working stage, group members exhibit high levels of self-disclosure, honesty, spontaneity, acceptance, and responsibility. Hostility and resentment are expressed in a constructive manner. Group members support and encourage attempts at change. Yalom (1985) refers to a group manifesting these characteristics as a "mature work group." There are occasional regressions into earlier stages, which are balanced by the present work and progress. The group has become an effective change agent.

Group Leader Behavior

The main tasks of the group leader in the fourth stage are to facilitate thorough discussion of problems and to suggest possible alternatives and examine consequences of those alternatives. At the same time, the group leader must help guide transfer of learning to the world outside the group and support and encourage experimentation, risk, and change. Because the group is functioning in a cohesive manner at this stage, the leader tends to have a low profile, having relatively few task or relationship interventions.

Stage 5—Adjourning

The final stage of group development is the adjourning, or terminating, stage. This stage may be predetermined (a group that was scheduled to meet for only eight sessions), or it may come as a result of the group's having fulfilled all of its stated purposes.

Group Member Behavior

As individual group members satisfy their present goals, the usefulness of the group becomes diminished. Although group members may even realize that the group no longer serves the same purpose as it had originally, they may still attempt to cling together because of the strong group identity and close interpersonal relationships. The main tasks of the group as well as of separate individuals are to complete unfinished business, deal with feelings of loss and separation, and make future plans for interpersonal contact. Sometimes group members will begin to distance themselves from each other as termination approaches, refusing to bring up new business or prematurely mourning their loss. Even though the end of the group is a great loss, the experience of the group, if the group has been successful, will remain with the participants forever.

Group Leader Behavior

The group leader must be able to focus the group on its feelings regarding loss and separation and help the group decide how to end. Yalom (1985) states that the task of the group leader prior to the final session is "to repeatedly call the members' attention to the impending termination" (p. 374). Since the leader is a model, he or she must be willing to self-disclose about separation feelings.

The group leader needs to provide time for allowing group members to complete any unfinished business with him or her or with each other. Although all unfinished business may not get resolved, the leader can assist group members in at least providing some means for handling their unfinished business.

Finally, for learning to be fully effective, the group leader must help group members put in meaningful perspective what has occurred in the group and also help group members carry their learning forward.

LEADERSHIP STYLES AND FUNCTIONS

It seems as though everyone has a particular style of behavior when relating to groups of people. There also are certain leadership functions, or specialized types of interventions, that individuals tend to favor when working in group settings. The timing and nature of the styles and functions group leaders use can make a significant difference in the outcomes of group work.

Leadership Styles

As early as 1944, Kurt Lewin identified what have come to be considered the three basic types of leadership styles used in group work: authoritarian, democratic, and laissez-faire. Research has attempted to determine which, if any, of these styles is clearly superior. Results from leadership effectiveness studies conducted at Ohio State University indicated that not one is inherently superior to the other two. What appears to be of most importance is the type of leadership style used at different stages of group development (Stogdill & Coons, 1957). Paul Hersey and Ken Blanchard (1972) have developed a leadership model based on the Ohio State studies.

As noted in the preceding section on the stages of group development, following Hersey and Blanchard's model, the leader's behavior varies from stage to stage. At the beginning of a group, the forming stage, it may be advisable for a leader to take somewhat of an authoritarian role, being task centered, and not to place much emphasis on developing strong relationships. As the group begins to mature through the storming and norming stages, the leader can become less task oriented and put more emphasis on developing relationships; a more democratic leadership style. Finally, as the group develops a high level of maturity, the performing stage, the leader can reduce the emphasis on relationship skills as well and use a more laissez-faire style.

This approach to group work of all types has been labeled the situational leadership model (Hersey, 1984). Becoming a situational leader means that you again have to use yourself as instrument. You have to be an astute observer of group dynamics throughout the process. You have to be very flexible and skilled in adjusting your leadership style to relate more effectively to groups as they mature. And you have to be able to share and even give up responsibility for the groups with which you would be working.

The situational leadership model is applicable in all types of group work, and it is finding a great deal of favor in group leadership programs in business and industry. In addition to being of value in group counseling, the model has also been used in parenting classes to help parents learn to cope with the development of a family.

Leadership Functions

Lieberman, Yalom, and Miles (1973) conducted the first large-scale controlled research study of the effectiveness of encounter groups. One result of the study was the identification of specific leadership functions; they identified four:

1. Emotional stimulation (challenging, confronting, intrusive modeling by personal risk-taking and high self-disclosure).
2. Caring (offering support, affection, praise, protection, warmth, acceptance, genuineness, concern).
3. Meaning attribution (explaining, clarifying, interpreting, providing a cognitive framework for change; translating feelings and experiences into ideas).
4. Executive function (setting limits, rules, norms, goals; managing time; pacing, stopping, interceding, suggesting procedures). (Yalom, 1985, p. 501)

Their findings indicated that these functions had a very clear and direct relationship to the outcome. The higher the caring and the higher the meaning attribution, the higher the positive outcome. Too much or too little emotional stimulation or executive function resulted in lower positive outcome (Yalom, 1985). The most successful group leaders demonstrated high amounts of caring and meaning attribution and moderate amounts of stimulation and executive function.

GROUP LEADERSHIP TECHNIQUES

Many group leadership techniques are identical to or only slightly different from the skills of individual therapy discussed in chapters 3 and 4. All the attending skills, responding skills, and problem-solving skills are also relevant to working with groups, and have similar aims and desired outcomes. However, because group work has a much more complex interpersonal dimension, and an added group dimension, there are a great many more intervention skills involved than in individual therapy. For example, group leaders may focus their response on the group as a whole, on an interpersonal relationship, or on one individual in the group. Also, an intervention can contain elements of all three components. Following are some selected counseling skills unique to group work.

Facilitating and Blocking Communications

Group leaders have a responsibility to facilitate open communication patterns and block destructive patterns. This is particularly crucial in the early stages of group development. Later, group members begin to take on much of this responsibility. Behaviors that are generally blocked are overuse of questions, gossiping, story telling, and other "there-and-then" behaviors, invasion of privacy, "band-aiding" or "red-crossing" (prematurely rescuing group members from working things out with each other), and mind reading. The group leader needs to model the giving of constructive feedback so that group members do not feel attacked and judged, and at the same time are able to learn how to give feedback themselves.

Mass Group Process Commentary

Often, group leaders need to provide commentary on the processes of the group rather than make an interpersonal intervention. In making a mass group commentary, group leaders will speak of "the group," "we," or "us." Some examples of mass group commentaries are:

> "The group seems to be avoiding deeper issues."
> "There seems to be a norm here that none of us confront Joe."
> "I wonder whether the group is needing a scapegoat?"
> "How does her statement affect (us) the group?"

Yalom (1985) states that the main purpose of interpretations is to get through impasses in the group process. He identifies two common impasses, anxiety-laden issues and antitherapeutic group norms. When there are anxiety-laden issues in a group, the group members often deflect their anxiety by avoiding those issues. Sometimes this is called group flight. A group member noting this might effectively deal with the phenomenon by making a mass group process commentary.

Sometimes the group may establish norms that are antitherapeutic, such as members' taking turns being in focus whether they want to or not, or keeping the focus on the first issue raised in the group even though the issue has been dealt with sufficiently. In such cases the group leader can make an effective group intervention specifically describing the behaviors and their consequences. The group leader might also imply that the group find alternative norms. In some instances, group leaders invite group members to make the commentary by stating, for example, "What's going on in the group right now?"

Directing Focus to the Here and Now

Most theoretical approaches place a strong emphasis on the here and now. In groups, progress is a result of the ongoing dynamics of the group process rather than on the expressed content of the group participants. Aliveness and change always take place in the here and now; obsession with the past and future divert energy from living in the present. It is therefore important that the group leader have various skills in the application of interventions designed to direct awareness to the here and now. The group leader should have a here-and-now awareness of self (see self-attending), of group members as individuals, of interpersonal process (transactions among members and their potential meanings), and of other factors such as the physical environment. The group leader should actively direct group focus to the here and now through asking focused questions; shifting focus of there-and-then interactions to here-and-now ones; experimentation; illumination of process (the self-reflective loop; see Figure 12.1); and the previously mentioned mass group process commentary. Here are some examples of each.

Focused Questions

"What feelings are you aware of now?"
"What do you want to happen right now?"
"What reaction do you have to what Jane just said?"
"How do you feel toward Mary right now?"
"What's missing for you right now?"
"What would you like from Jim right this moment?"

Shifting Focus

"John, you are saying that you are often shy with people—who do you feel most shy with here—and how do you demonstrate this?"
"Mary, you have said that you are an angry person—what does this mean for us here?"
"You have said you had a lot of tender warm feelings inside—if you could, who would you most want to share those with in the group?"

Experimentation

Experimentation is always a here-and-now operation because the group member is trying out new attitudes or behaviors in the present, and these attitudes or behaviors are generating some immediate internal and external reaction. For example:

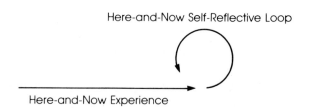

Here-and-Now Self-Reflective Loop

Here-and-Now Experience

FIGURE 12.1 Self-Reflective Loop *(From* The Theory and Practice of Group Psychotherapy by *Irwin D. Yalom. Copyright © 1985 by Basic Books, Inc., Publishers. Reproduced by permission of the publisher.)*

(To someone who has difficulty allowing others to get close and intimate with him.) "I would like you to go around to each group member and say, 'If I were to let you get close to me, then _____; or _____, I don't let you get close to me because _____.' " Have the person complete the sentence with a different ending for each group member.

After the experiment the member is encouraged to share his or her reactions and to solicit the reactions of other group members.

Illumination of Process

This strategy involves the self-reflective loop (Yalom, 1985). The leader first helps the group member focus on the here and now by being aware of his or her present behavior and then by assisting the group member in reflecting on and then getting input regarding the meaning and impact of that behavior (see Figure 12.1).

Essentially the goal is to help the group member discover or appreciate:

1. What his or her behavior is like— "What did you do (or say)?" What feelings or motives are operating at that point in time—"What are you feeling?" "What are you trying to do (or say)?" "What do you hope would happen by doing this?"
2. How does your behavior influence the opinions others have of you—"Do they like you?" "Ignore you?" "Value you?"
3. How the behavior makes others feel—"What did happen by your doing this?"
4. How does this influence the client's opinion of herself or himself—"What does all this mean to you?"

Universalizing

Group members often feel greatly relieved when they discover that they are not alone and that their concerns are similar to those of other group members. The group leader can help facilitate this universality by soliciting information from other group members when one group member has expressed a feeling or concern about a particular situation.

Susan: "I feel so strange and different in the group because of all the problems I'm having with my family."

Group leader: "I wonder if there is anyone else in the group who is having similar problems with their families, and how they feel in the group?"

Linking

Linking is a way of connecting the various feelings and concerns expressed by group members in such a way as to universalize experience. It requires the group leader to be alert to nonverbal as well as verbal behavior.

> **Group leader** (to group): "I noticed a lot of heads nodding when Joan stated how anxious she was feeling about her final examinations. I sense you really identify with Joan in regard to your finals."

GROUP APPROACHES

There are probably as many approaches to group therapy as there are to individual therapy. Most individual theories can be used in a group context and have a theoretical framework for working in groups similar to their individual theory. What is significant is that many major theoretical approaches consider the use of groups as the preferred mode of treatment. Since the late 1960s, Carl Rogers and his person-centered approach has been focused almost completely on group work in various settings. Fritz Perls, in his development of Gestalt therapy, worked almost exclusively with groups. Transactional analysis has been predominantly a group approach from its inception. William Glasser's reality therapy has been developed in large part on the work he did with groups in reformatories and the public schools. Alfred Adler was one of the first to work with the family as a group. Behaviorists use groups as a source of behavior to model and as a place to practice new behaviors and receive immediate reinforcement. Even psychoanalysts view groups as offering greater opportunities for transference to occur.

PROBLEMS AND ISSUES IN GROUP WORK

One major problem in group work deals with the training of group leaders. According to George and Dustin (1988) many counselors have received little or no specific training or supervision in leading counseling groups.

Only recently have different models for selecting and training group leaders emerged and ethical and professional standards and guidelines been developed by major group associations such as the Association for Specialists in Group Work (ASGW). Trotzer (1989) developed four basic prerequisites for an effective group leader:

> (1) Cognitive knowledge about the group process, (2) involvement as a participant in group interactions, (3) skills and techniques for use in a leadership capacity, and (4) supervised experience in the leadership role. (p. 111)

George and Dustin (1988) propose a basic information foundation including a broad understanding of group dynamics, a knowledge of the various theoretical approaches to group counseling, an awareness of the issues and techniques of leading a group, and some familiarity with the research on group practice. They also advocate supervised practice, personal participation in a group experience, and continuing education. These suggestions are in accordance with the professional standards for group counselors approved by ASGW.

Problems in Evaluation

Most group leaders shy away from evaluation of their groups. There is often a concern that the evaluations will be negative and show the leaders to be ineffective. Yalom (1985), George and Dustin (1988), and others advocate helping students learn how to evaluate their work and be open to change based on these evaluations. However, good evaluation studies of group counseling are lacking, and researchers have not advanced knowledge of the field in the last three decades despite many improvements in research methods (Bednar et al., 1987). Part of the problem is the difficulty of obtaining agreed on definitions of process and outcome so there can be meaningful evaluations. There is a lack of process and outcome instruments related specifically to group situations.

Studying a group is a more complex task than studying an individual counseling relationship. A group involves a multiplicity of communication patterns, and it is more difficult to trace the interaction among members and the impact of behaviors. It is difficult to determine whether change in groups that continue over a period of time is the result of events and relationships outside the group setting or inside the group setting.

Recently, there have been increased concern and attention to research on the effectiveness of group as well as family counseling that have similar dynamics. The next few years may see improved research methods and an increased volume of research on group work.

SUMMARY

The importance of group work as part of the helping professions has been emphasized in this chapter. A brief history of group work was presented. Reference was made to the development of laboratory training, and the human potential movement. The advantages and disadvantages of group work were presented. Among the advantages are safety, sharing, sense of belonging, social interaction, reality testing in a small safe setting, and adaptability to a broad range of environments. Among the disadvantages are less control by the group leader, less individual attention and confidentiality, danger of group members' being singled out as scapegoats, and unqualified leaders.

Three types of groups were discussed: preventive groups, developmental groups, and remediation groups. Preventive groups attempt to educate in order to prevent future problems. Developmental groups are growth-oriented and attempt to facilitate healthy development. In remediation groups, members are viewed by themselves and others as needing remedial help in order to function in everyday life. Eleven curative factors that act as therapeutic forces in groups were identified. The curative factors of cohesion, universality, interpersonal skills, and confrontation were elaborated on. Five stages of group development were presented along with appropriate group-leader and group-member behavior for each stage.

Leadership styles were noted, and the situational leadership model was described. This model suggests that a group leader's task and relationship behaviors (or style) should vary in accordance with the maturity level of the group. Four clusters of leader interventions have also been identified. These clusters, or leadership functions, are emotional stimulation, caring, meaning attribution, and executive function. The use and timing of these leadership functions has also been found to be important in conducting successful groups.

Several group leadership techniques dealing with mass group process commentary, and directing focus to the here and now were discussed. These techniques included interpretation, focused questions, shifting the focus, experimentation, illumination of process, universalizing, and linking. Finally, group theories were noted.

QUESTIONS AND ACTIVITIES

1. Study two or three group approaches in depth. Which group approach(es) appeals to you most? Why? Which appeal to you least? Why? What are some major similarities among and differences between the approaches you chose? Does your preference for an individual counseling theory strongly influence your choice of a group approach?

2. What might be some typical problem behaviors found in group members? How might a group leader deal effectively with these problem behaviors? Which problem behaviors might cause you the most difficulty as a group leader?

3. Observe a group session. Analyze the group process. What group techniques does the leader use? What nonverbal cues do you notice? Is the group cohesive? In which stage of group process is the group? What are some of the group norms?

4. Many counselors prefer to be individual counselors rather than group counselors. Assuming that you have appropriate training, would you have any reservations about initiating and leading groups? What do you believe your preference will be?

CHAPTER 13

_____ *FOCUS ON* _____

Family Counseling

If a person has a problem,
why counsel the entire family?

This chapter considers a special type of group counseling: counseling with groups that exist in the form of families. All the dynamics of working with groups apply to working with families. There is the added factor of the counselor's entering into a system that already exists. Family counseling approaches are interdisciplinary, with theories and principles being drawn from the fields of anthropology and sociology. This interdisciplinary involvement gives family counseling a special flavor. Marriage or relationship counseling, a special type of family counseling, is also described.

WHAT IS A FAMILY?

Goldenberg and Goldenberg (1985) describe a family as "a natural social system with properties all its own, one that has evolved a set of rules, roles, a power structure, forms of communication, and ways of negotiation and problem solving that allow various tasks to be performed effectively" (p. 3). All families regardless of the level of adaptivity, organization, or structure attempt to become functioning groups. Families can be traditional or nontraditional.

Individuals form families in order to satisfy some basic physical and emotional needs. Emotional needs include those of closeness and intimacy, self-expression, influence, and meaning or purpose. These needs are usually satisfied through relationships, work, and having children, which traditionally has required marriage and the formation of a family.

The traditional nuclear family structure is changing. Goldenberg and Goldenberg (1985) report that national surveys indicate drops in marriage rates and increases in divorce rates, the number of unwed mothers, and in individuals choosing to live alone. The Goldenbergs attribute the great changes in family patterns to the fact that divorce has become more commonplace than ever. However, the fact that 80 percent of those who get divorced remarry suggests how strong these physical and emotional needs are.

Families can be dysfunctional or functional. In dysfunctional families members are not able to attain their goals. According to Satir (1972) common characteristics of dysfunctional families are low self-worth; indirect, vague, or dishonest communication patterns; strict, rigid, unbending and everlasting rules; and linkages to society that are fearful, placating, and blaming. These characteristics interfere with the attainment of the needs for closeness, power, and meaning resulting in symptomatic behaviors. Common symptomatic behaviors include acting-out children, escape into long hours of work, and involvement in an affair. Dysfunctional families often experience hopelessness, helplessness, and loneliness.

In functional families, the needs of individual members are met. In highly functioning families, self-worth is high, communication is direct, clear, specific, and honest; rules are flexible, human, appropriate, and subject to change; and the linking to society is open and hopeful (Satir, 1972). Satir refers to these as vital, nurturing families. Both dysfunctional and functional families experience conflict, but functional families are willing to listen to each other, consider each other's point of view, and make compromises. Dysfunctional families are unable to accomplish this.

FAMILY LIFE CYCLE

Chapter 15 discusses the various kinds and stages of individual development, including cognitive, moral, and faith development. Families have developmental stages also. In the wholistic approach presented here and in chapter 15, all human systems are viewed as interrelating with each other. Families are social systems with unique operating principles.

Understanding the family life cycle can help counselors be more effective in dealing with family conflicts, crisis points, and tasks that need to be accomplished before moving to the next stage. Many family counselors assume a family life-cycle approach, which views problems in the family as developmental impasses that arise when the family enters transitions from one stage in the life cycle to another. The therapy is focused on resolving the developmental impasse and not on psychopathology.

Life-Cycle Models

Evelyn Duvall is credited with doing the pioneering work on family development in the early 1950s (Nichols, 1984). Duvall formulated an eight-stage model beginning with married couples establishing their relationship. Solomon (1973) modified Duvall's eight stages by condensing them to five: (1) marriage, (2) birth, (3) individuation, (4) departure of children, and (5) integration of loss.

His intent was to use the stages to aid in treatment planning. Families must deal successfully with the tasks of one stage before they can adequately deal with the next one. Carter and McGoldrick (1980) developed a six-stage model beginning with (1) the unattached young adult, (2) the joining of families through marriage, (3) the family with young children, (4) the family with adolescents, (5) launching children and moving on, and (6) the family in later life. Note that Carter and McGoldrick's model begins prior to marriage. The young adult's primary task is to accept parent-offspring separation; other tasks include differentiation of the self in relation to the family of origin, development of intimate peer relationships, and establishment of the self in work. This model takes into account previous generations of nuclear families, which they believe have had a strong impact on the family life-cycle. For example, many family attitudes, expectations, prejudices, and taboos are transmitted down through the generations (Goldenberg & Goldenberg, 1985).

Becvar and Becvar (1988) combine and update information from previous models (see Table 13.1) to arrive at their model, which begins with the unattached adult and ranges through retirement. They also include emotional issues and critical tasks for each stage. Because these models are one dimensional and do not take into account alternative family lifestyles or account for evolution and change in the future, Becvar and Becvar went a step further and conceptualized a complex dynamic process model that would be applicable to a wide variety of couples and families. Their dynamic process model integrates both individual (see Erikson, chapter 15) and family models and accounts for structural and cultural variations in families. Some of these nontraditional variations include communal families, families with cohabitive parents, and families with gay or lesbian parents. These families have many of the same issues as traditional families as well as their own requirements and special challenges. For example, a lesbian couple may have to deal with conflict over one partner's desire to be more open about their relationship than the other would like (Buhrke, 1989).

Yorburg's (1975) model also accounts for variations in the intact family by developing a typology that views the family as follows:

1. Nuclear family—complete self-sufficiency and family autonomy, no kin network influence, minimal contact outside parents and children.
2. Modified nuclear family—substantial self-sufficiency, occasional help in emergencies, weak but potential kin network with regular, but not daily contact.
3. Modified extended family—independent economic resources within nuclear family units, but daily exchange of goods and services, strong kin network with daily influence, daily contact, and geographic proximity.
4. Extended family—complete economic interdependence, common ownership of economic resources, powerful kin network providing almost all socialization, emotional support, and protection, and arbitrary, linear, intergenerational authority with daily contact. (Okun & Rappaport, 1980)

FAMILY COUNSELING

The beginnings of modern family counseling date to the early 1950s. It was influenced by the work of Sigmund Freud, Alfred Adler, and Harry Stack Sullivan (see Table 13.2). Freud was aware of the importance of family relationships, but in

TABLE 13.1 Stages of the Family Life Cycle

Stage	Emotion Issues	Stage-Critical Tasks
1. Unattached adult	Accepting parent-offspring separation	a. Differentiation from family of origin b. Development of peer relations c. Initiation of career
2. Newly married	Commitment to the marriage	a. Formation of marital system b. Making room for spouse with family and friends c. Adjusting career demands
3. Childbearing	Accepting new members into the system	a. Adjusting marriage to make room for child b. Taking on parenting roles c. Making room for grandparents
4. Preschool-age child	Accepting the new personality	a. Adjusting family to the needs of specific child(ren) b. Coping with energy drain and lack of privacy c. Taking time out to be a couple
5. School-age	Allowing child to establish relationships outside the family	a. Extending family/society interactions b. Encouraging the child's educational progress c. Dealing with increased activities and time demands
6. Teenage child	Increasing flexibility of family boundaries to allow independence	a. Shifting the balance in the parent-child relationship b. Refocusing on mid-life career and marital issues c. Dealing with increasing concerns for older generation

Stage	Emotion Issues	Stage-Critical Tasks
7. Launching center	Accepting exits from and entries into the family	a. Releasing adult children into work, college, marriage b. Maintaining supportive home base c. Accepting occasional returns of adult children
8. Middle-aged adult	Letting go of children and facing each other	a. Rebuilding the marriage b. Welcoming children's spouses, grandchildren into family c. Dealing with aging of one's own parents
9. Retirement	Accepting retirement and old age	a. Maintaining individual and couple functioning b. Supporting middle generation c. Coping with death of parents, spouse d. Closing or adapting family home

From Dorothy Stroh Becvar and Raphael J. Becvar, *Family Therapy: A Systemic Integration.* Copyright © 1988 by Allyn and Bacon. Reprinted with permission.

theory and practice he dealt with intrapsychic conflict. He was firmly opposed to working with more than one family member at a time (Goldenberg & Goldenberg, 1985). Freud's ideas were used by many of the early pioneers of family counseling such as Murray Bowen and Nathan Ackerman, who were originally trained as psychoanalysts. Alfred Adler, an early associate of Freud, provided another major influence in the development of family counseling. Adler believed that social and environmental factors played an important role in human behavior. Although Adler did not work with entire families, his awareness of the importance of the family in shaping behavior led to the development of concepts that have almost become commonplace in family counseling. These concepts include sibling rivalry, the family constellation, and the importance of birth order of children within the family.

Harry Stack Sullivan was psychoanalytically trained, but as a result of his work with schizophrenics, he noted that family relationships, especially between mother and child, were an important factor in the development of schizophrenia.

TABLE 13.2 Historical Review of Family Counseling

	Practitioners	Conceptual Antecedents	Current Theoretical Orientation	Major Concepts
Precursors	1. Sigmund Freud	Physical sciences	Psychoanalytic	Theory of instincts Psychosexual development
	2. Alfred Adler	Nietzsche, social psychology	Adlerian/Dreikursian family counseling	Family constellation Sibling birth order Style of life
	3. Harry Stack Sullivan	Psychodynamic; neo-Freudian sociology, social psychology	Psychodynamic	Interpersonal theory
First Generation First Wave	1. Nathan Ackerman	Psychoanalytic theory	Psychoanalytic family systems	Role complementarity
	2. Jay Haley Don Jackson	G. Bateson—Epistemology von Bertalanffy—General Systems theory; hypnotherapy, M. Erikson	Strategic family therapy	Double-bind homeostasis
	3. Carl Whitaker	Idiosyncratic existentialism Neo-Freudian-psychodynamic	Experiential family systems	Therapist as an active participant
	4. Murray Bowen	Psychoanalytic	Family systems	Multigenerational; Undifferentiated family ego mass
	5. R. D. Laing	Psychoanalytic/existential	Experiential family systems	Mystification
	6. J. E. Bell	Social psychology—field theory	Family group therapy	Derived from group theories

Second Wave	1. James Framo	Psychoanalytic	Object relations	Separation/individuation
	2. Paul Watzlawick	Jungian analysis G. Bateson, M. Erikson	Strategic family therapy	First and second order change; problem formulation/resolution
	3. Salvator Minuchin	Psychodynamic	Structural family therapy	"Boundaries"
	4. Virginia Satir	Psychodynamic G. Bateson	Experiential family systems	Communication skills
Second Generation	1. Norman and Betty Paul	Psychodynamics	Psychodynamic systems	Resolution of grief reactions
	2. Peggy Papp	Family systems theory	Strategic family therapy	Paradoxical prescription
	3. Richard Bandler/ John Grinder	G. Bateson, M. Erikson, V. Satir	Strategic family therapy	Neurolinguistic programming
	4. Ivan Boszormenyi-Nagy	Psychoanalytical/ existential	Intergenerational-contextual family therapy	Family ledger

He then switched from an intrapsychic to an interpersonal focus. Sullivan's ideas strongly influenced Don Jackson, who later began a school of family therapy in Palo Alto, California, which emphasized communications (Foley, 1984).

Nathan Ackerman is often referred to as the grandfather of family counseling. He was a psychoanalyst who was one of the first clinicians to work with entire families. He combined his psychoanalytical thinking with family systems concepts, although he never sacrificed his interest in individuals to one in family systems (Nichols, 1984).

During the 1950s, a number of scientific and clinical developments took place. One development was a result of the work of Gregory Bateson, Don Jackson, Jay Haley, and John Weakland (1956) dealing with families of schizophrenics. They discovered that if a schizophrenic family member got better, someone else in the family got worse. They also noted that there was a pattern in which family members encouraged and demanded that the patient not get better, but continue to show irrational behavior. The term *family homeostasis* was coined to note the obstinacy of the family to resist change.

Another development was the introduction of general systems theory, credited to biologist Ludwig von Bertalanffy (1968), which emphasized the complex patterns of behavior and ways of functioning with one another in a family (see chapter 10). The theory demonstrated how different parts of a family system are interconnected and interdependent, with changes in one part of the system effecting change in other parts. A third development was the interest in new clinical approaches, such as group counseling, further extensions of psychoanalytic theory, and child and marital counseling. Marriage, family and child counselors began to treat family members in pairs and groups as opposed to the original individual focus, and group therapy influenced family therapy by its emphasis on the developmental group process.

Family counseling is relatively new and evolving. It regards problems as resting in the family itself and not just in the individual family member. This is true even if a family member is seen individually; the focus is on the family system. In individual counseling the focus is on insight, the client-counselor relationship, and individual behavior change, whereas family counseling focuses on the communication processes, power balances and imbalances, influence processes, structures for conflict resolution, and how the family currently functions as a system. The goal of family counseling is much broader than just effecting change within the individual. It includes changing the structure of the family and the behavioral patterns among its members (Okun & Rappaport, 1980).

Family counseling has been influenced by many disciplines, from anthropology to sociology, and therefore has not had the infighting, divisiveness, and battles that have occurred with the field of individual psychotherapy. This has resulted in new perspectives on human behavior and the change process.

There seems to be a greater spirit of cooperation and eclecticism characterized by mutual appreciation among family counselors from different theoretical approaches. Most differences among theorists seem to lie in their points of emphasis rather than in their techniques. According to Nichols (1984), in the 1980s, there was a recognizable trend toward integrating concepts and methods of the various schools of family counseling.

General Systems Theory

During the first half of the 20th century, the focus of intervention in counseling was on the individual. An approach known as general systems theory resulting from the work of von Bertalanffy (1968) was one major factor in the shift to treating whole families. Von Bertalanffy provided a framework for looking at complex and seemingly unrelated patterns of behavior and seeing how they represented interrelated components of a larger system. Buckley (1967) defined a system as being composed of parts that are interconnected and interdependent with mutual causality. A change in one part of a system effects a change in other parts. Together, these parts produce a system or a whole that is greater than the sum of its interdependent parts. Each part is also related to at least some other parts, in a stable manner over time.

This view differed greatly from previous views that families were nothing more than the sum of their individual members, and thus the concentration on an individual's unresolved conflicts. For counselors, this view requires a dramatic shift in perception from that of individual counseling, as well as in the use of different intervention strategies. Counselors whose training has been geared to individual counseling may have trouble making the shift in focus. The terms *systems* and *systems theory* are often confused. Sometimes systems theory is used to refer to a particular school of family counseling, and at other times it is used to refer to this certain way of perceiving and understanding families. For our purposes we call the first, family systems approach, and the latter, general systems theory.

Systems can be closed or open. Closed systems are not open to environmental transactions. A heating system in a house is an example of a closed system. It admits no matter from outside of itself. Open systems are able to make environmental transactions. All living systems are open. Open systems have certain properties. Those properties in the context of the family system are: wholeness, feedback, and equifinality (Watzlawick, Beavin, & Jackson, 1967).

Wholeness

Wholeness refers to the fact that a system is more than and different from the sum of its parts, but includes their interaction. The family is more than just a collection of individuals; therefore, it cannot be broken down into its component parts and still be adequately understood. Each family member must be viewed in the context of his or her life, especially the relationship to other family members. The behavior of each family member is related to and dependent on the behavior of all the others (Nichols, 1984).

Feedback

Feedback refers to the process by which a system adjusts itself (Foley, 1984). Feedback can be either negative or positive. Negative feedback is the information that comes into a system and is used to maintain the status quo, thus preventing growth or change. Deviation in the system is corrected and prevented so that equilibrium is restored. An example of negative feedback is as follows. The Jones family is made up of Mr. and Mrs. Jones and three children, Maria, Carl, and Alex. Mr. Jones is treated successfully for alcoholism. Mrs. Jones suddenly transfers her anger to Maria. Maria displaces her anger toward her younger brother, Carl, and Alex, the youngest brother, begins sucking his thumb in response to Maria's aggression. Mr. Jones becomes resentful that his family is not behaving appreciatively to his going on the wagon and returns to drinking, restoring the original homeostatic balance. Mr. Jones's drinking can be labeled as negative feedback, which was needed to maintain the previous system.

Positive feedback forces a system to change. It prevents the system from returning to its previous state. It also can cause a system to self-destruct by amplifying deviation until it drives the system beyond the limit within which it can function (Steinglass, 1978). Positive feedback is often used by family therapists in order to change the family. Carl Whitaker (1975) refers to the concept of positive feedback as the "leaning tower of Pisa" approach. Rather than treating the symptom, the therapist paradoxically prescribes the symptom so as to push the problem to its limits until the leaning tower falls by its own weight. The absurdity of the symptom pushes the problem to ultimate destruction.

In order for families to stay together and function and grow in a healthy direction, they must use both negative and positive feedback. Negative feedback helps maintain the family's equilibrium in the face of developmental and environmental stresses. Positive feedback facilitates learning and growth (Nichols, 1984).

Equifinality

Equifinality means that any problem in a family, regardless of its origin, can be removed if a change is made at any time in the system (Foley, 1984). Therefore, interventions can be made effectively in the here and now to produce changes, because systems have no memories. It is not past events that perpetuate a problem but the current interaction within a system. Foley provides an example in which a man began heavy drinking because of unresolved problems with his mother and now drinks because of his present relationship with his wife. According to the concept of equifinality, the counselor can alter the interaction between the husband and wife and affect the man's drinking without dealing with the underlying causes or working with the past at all. Family counselors using the equifinality principle would not devote much time to the taking of personal and family histories, but rather would work to change dysfunctional patterns of behavior with the current family structure.

THEORETICAL APPROACHES

Attempting to classify the various approaches to family counseling is as difficult and complex as classifying theories for the counseling of individuals. Many attempts have been made to classify family theories according to different variables. We present a classification system based on the work of Foley (1984) and Goldenberg and Goldenberg (1985), which represents five major schools of family counseling in terms of a continuum ranging from object relations theory of psychoanalysis to the objective theory of strategic intervention (see Table 13.3). Although family counseling has moved from an interpersonal model to a systems concept, object relations theorists place more emphasis on past relationships than on systems thinking as opposed to those who emphasize present relationships and current systems functioning (Foley, 1984). Other important approaches to family counseling include group, behavioral, and communications counseling, which we have subsumed under these five theoretical orientations.

Object Relations

Object relations is a label given to the psychoanalytic study of the origin and nature of interpersonal relationships and intrapsychic structures that grew out of past relationships and remain to influence present interpersonal relationships. Whereas Freud identified instinctual gratification as each individual's fundamental need, the object relation theorists (Melanie Klein, Ronald Fairbairn, and others), maintain that a person's need for a satisfying object relationship constituted the fundamental motive of life (Goldenberg & Goldenberg, 1985). The term *object* in this context refers to people. The inability of an individual to make a satisfying connection with his or her family of origin carries over into later life and affects that person's new family system. The intrapsychic conflict derived from this failure to make a satisfying connection continues to be acted out or replicated with one's current relationships such as spouse and children. The individual unconsciously continues to relate to these current intimates in the same manner as in his or her distorted expectations. Current practitioners who use this framework include James Framo, Norman and Betty Paul, and Gerald Zuk (1975). Counselors who use this approach usually view the identified patient in the family as the carrier of the split-off and unacceptable impulses of other family members. Great attention is paid to past relationships during counseling sessions.

The Family Systems Approach

The family systems approach, or Bowenian approach, was developed as a result of the work of Murray Bowen (1978). Family counselors who use this approach view the dysfunctional family as trapped in repetitive, destructive games of sequences. As a result, family members are unable to free themselves from the rules

TABLE 13.3 Five Approaches to Family Counseling

Dimension	Object Relations	Family Systems	Experiential/Humanistic	Structural	Strategic Intervention
1. Major time frame	Past; history of early experiences needs to be uncovered.	Primarily the present, although attention also paid to one's family of origin.	Present; here-and-now data from immediate experience observed.	Present and past; family's current structure carried over from earlier transactional patterns.	Present; current problems or symptoms maintained by ongoing, repetitive sequences between persons.
2. Role of unconscious processes	Unresolved conflicts from the past, largely out of the person's awareness, continue to attach themselves to current objects and situations.	Earlier concepts suggested unconscious conflicts, although now recast in interactive terms.	Free choice and conscious self-determination more important than unconscious motivation.	Unconscious motivation less important than repetition of learned habits and role assignments by which the family carries out its tasks.	Family rules, homeostatic balance, and feedback loops determine behavior, not unconscious processes.
3. Insight vs. action	Insight leads to understanding, conflict reduction, and ultimately intrapsychic and interpersonal change.	Rational processes used to gain self-awareness into current relationships as well as intergenerational experiences.	Self-awareness of one's immediate existence leads to choice, responsibility and change.	Action precedes understanding; change in transactional patterns more important than insight in producing new behaviors.	Action oriented; behavior change and symptom reduction brought about through directives rather than interpretations.
4. Role of therapist	Neutral; makes interpretations of individual and family behavior patterns.	Direct but nonconfrontational; detriangulated from family fusion.	Active facilitator of potential for growth; provides family with new experiences.	Stage director; manipulates family structure in order to change dysfunctional sets.	Active; manipulative; problem-focused; prescriptive, paradoxical.

5. Unit of study	Focus on individual; emphasis on how family members feel about one another and deal with each other.	Entire family over several generations; may work with one dyad (or one partner) for a period of time.	Dyad; problems arise from interaction between two members (for example, husband and wife).	Triads; coalitions, subsystems, boundaries, power.	Dyads and triads; problems and symptoms viewed as interpersonal communications between two or more family members.
6. Major theoretical underpinnings	Psychoanalysis.	Family systems theory.	Existentialism; humanistic psychology; phenomenology.	Structural family theory; systems.	Communication theory; systems, behaviorism.
8. Major theorists and/or practitioners	Ackerman, Framo, Boszormenyi-Nagy, Zuk, Paul, Bell	Bowen	Whitaker, Kempler, Satir	Minuchin	Jackson, Erikson, Haley, Madanes, Selvini-Palazzoli
8. Goals of treatment	Insight, psychosexual maturity, strengthening of ego functioning; reduction in interlocking pathologies, more satisfying object relations.	Maximization of self-differentiation for each family member.	Growth, more fulfilling interaction patterns; clearer communication; expanded awareness; authenticity.	Change in relationship context in order to restructure family organization and change dysfunctional transactional patterns.	Change dysfunctional, redundant behavioral sequences ("games") between family members in order to eliminate presenting problem or symptom.

Reproduced by permission of the publisher, F. E. Peacock Publishers, Inc., Itasca, Illinois. From Vincent D. Foley. "Family Therapy." In Raymond J. Corsini, *Current Psychotherapies*, Third Edition 1984, p. 457, Figure 12.1.

and expectations that govern their relationships. The cornerstone of Bowen's theory is his conceptualization of the forces within the family that make for togetherness and the opposing forces that lead to individuality (Goldenberg & Goldenberg, 1985). The goal of Bowen's approach is to enable a person to individualize—to become his or her own person as differentiated from the family system (Foley, 1984). Bowen believes that family members become trapped through the family system's emotionality by each acting on an emotional basis, thus being pulled into the system. In order to avoid falling victim to the family system's emotionality and to be able to separate oneself from it, one would have to be able to differentiate between emotional and intellectual functioning and make choices based on reason and not feeling (Okun & Rappaport, 1980).

Bowen built his approach around several interlocking concepts in addition to the idea of the differentiation of the self. These concepts include triangles, nuclear family emotional system, family projection process, sibling positions, and societal regression. Triangles or triangulation refers to the tendency of two persons in the family system under stress to recruit a third person into the system, thus lowering the intensity and anxiety and gaining stability. The nuclear family emotional system is the family's way of coping with tension and maintaining stability. The family projection process is the mechanism by which parental conflicts are projected onto the children or a spouse. *Emotional cutoff* is Bowen's term for flight from an unresolved emotional attachment. The multigenerational transmission process is how family pathology is passed on to succeeding generations, usually by the child most involved in the family emotional process. Sibling position refers to Bowen's view that as the level of anxiety has increased in society in recent years, the forces leading to togetherness in the family have become more intense while the forces leading to individuation have eroded (Goldenberg & Goldenberg, 1985; Nichols, 1984). Current well-known practitioners of this approach include Philip Guerin, Elizabeth Carter, Monica McGoldrick, Thomas Fogarty, and Michael Kerr (Goldenberg & Goldenberg, 1985).

Experiential/Humanistic

Experiential family counseling emerged from the humanistic psychology of the 1960s. This approach draws heavily from Gestalt therapy, encounter groups, and existential, humanistic, and phenomenological thinking. Although it recognizes family systems concepts, its primary concern is with the individual within the system. Experiential counselors emphasize experience, encounter, confrontation, intuition, freedom, individuality, and personal fulfillment. Experiential counselors generally discourage theorizing in favor of being open and spontaneous. Outside of their existential-humanistic derivations, they are relatively atheoretical (Nichols, 1984).

Experiential counselors attempt to open individual family members to their inner experiences and unfreeze family interactions. They deal primarily with the present rather than trying to uncover the past. They believe that change resides in the growth experience, which manifests itself in the immediate therapeutic encounter between the family and an active caring counselor. This interpersonal experience becomes the primary stimulus to growth (Goldenberg & Goldenberg, 1985). Symptom relief, social adjustment, and work are considered secondary to greater freedom of choice, less dependence, expanded experiencing, and greater congruency between inner experience and outer behavior (Nichols, 1984).

This approach usually requires powerful therapeutic interventions and existential encounters. Treatment is aimed at reducing the defenses within and between family members. Leading figures in experiential family counseling have been Carl Whitaker, Walter Kempler, and Virginia Satir.

Whitaker has a reputation for being creative, intuitive, sometimes outrageous, humorous, and sarcastic. He often shocks and confuses family members by his interventions in order to move a disrupted family from its "stuckness." Walter Kempler (1981) is primarily a Gestalt counselor who deals only in the here and now. He guides family members to become aware of their defenses and self-deceptive games and to take responsibility for their behaviors. Virginia Satir (1972) was probably the most well-known of all family counselors. She emphasized the importance of good communications among family members using therapeutic interventions to achieve that purpose. Strengthening each family member's self-esteem is a cornerstone of her approach (Goldenberg & Goldenberg, 1985).

Structural

The structural approach to family counseling is associated mainly with Salvador Minuchin (1974). The basic objective of this approach is to change structures within the family, such as the realignment of alliances and the healing of splits between and among family members. The theory focuses on the ways families organize themselves through their transactional patterns. These patterns include the developing of boundaries between family subsystems, especially between parent and child (Foley, 1984). Emphasis is on present transactions and action, as opposed to insight or understanding. All behavior, including the identified patient's symptoms, is perceived within the context of family structure (Goldenberg & Goldenberg, 1985).

The major tasks of the counselor are to form a therapeutic system through joining the family as a leader; accommodating to the dysfunctional system; diagnosing, and eventually agreeing to a contract; and restructuring the family system through various intervention strategies. As a result, the family is able to challenge its current perceptions of reality, consider alternative possibilities and transactional patterns, and then develop new relationships and structures that are self-reinforcing (Okun & Rappaport, 1980).

Minuchin's interventions are active, carefully calculated, and often manipulative in order to change the dysfunctional family structures. His approach has been particularly effective with psychosomatic disorders such as anorexia nervosa (Goldenberg & Goldenberg, 1985). Nichols (1984) reports that by the late 1970s, structural family counseling had become the most influential and widely practiced of all systems of family counseling. Nichols attributes this popularity to the theory's simplicity, inclusiveness, and practicality.

Strategic Intervention

The strategic intervention approach is descended from the communications model of general systems theory. It has been variously called problem-solving therapy, brief therapy, or systemic therapy. Nichols (1984) views the strategic approach "as among the most exciting and vital of the recent developments in family therapy." Goldenberg and Goldenberg (1985) state that whereas Minuchin's structural model drew the greatest attention in the 1970s, the strategic approach took center stage in the 1980s.

The main principles of strategic intervention are that the symptom presented is the problem and serves as a metaphor for the whole family; the problem is caused by a developmental impasse arising from failure to adjust to transition points in the family life cycle; attempted solutions to the problem by family members usually have intensified the problem. The primary aim is symptom removal rather than insight and understanding. The counselor is responsible for solving the problem, and counseling is carefully planned in stages. Generally, the initial sessions are used for assessment of the family. The counselor then develops a treatment plan for solving the family's presenting problems, usually by giving directives in the form of homework assignments, advice giving, and teaching where a lack of skills might exist. The counselor's goal is to use tactics that will cause family members to behave differently (Foley, 1984).

Many tactics used in the strategic approach are in the form of therapeutic double binds or paradoxical interventions geared to changing family rules and relationship patterns (Goldenberg & Goldenberg, 1985). Paradoxical interventions prescribe the symptom by asking family members to continue to live their lives in such a manner as to make the symptom worse, not better (Foley, 1984). For example, the counselor might instruct a couple who continually engage in squabbles to set aside specific times each week to fight and to make their fights special events.

The most influential practitioner of the strategic intervention approach is Jay Haley (1963). Other important figures are Watzlawick, Weakland, and Fisch (1974), and Cloe Madanes (Madanes & Haley, 1977). Haley played an important role in formulating the concepts of general systems theory while working with families in the 1950s along with Bateson, Jackson, and Weakland. He became a student of Milton Erickson, a pioneering hypnotherapist who became well-known for his skill in tapping the unrecognized talents of his clients. Haley has also been influenced by Minuchin and takes a structural approach to family dynamics. He advocates the use of observers behind one-way mirrors who can consult with the counselor if necessary (Nichols, 1984).

Strategic intervention is an extremely powerful approach in which techniques must be carefully developed to fit each situation, based on the family counselor's clear understanding of family dynamics. Otherwise, the counselor will be ineffective and perhaps even do harm to the family (Nichols, 1984).

Comparative Analysis

The five approaches described here all view symptomatic behavior as the result of dysfunctional interaction in the family system. Object relations and family systems approaches place more emphasis on past relationships. Experiential, structural, and strategic approaches adhere more to the concept of equifinality and emphasize intervening in the present. The five approaches all have the same basic concept of the family as a system, and they all deal with communication patterns, both verbal and nonverbal. Many leading practitioners of one approach have studied with, or have otherwise been influenced by, leading practitioners of other schools. However, each approach is differentiated from the others in terms of emphasis and special viewpoints.

FAMILY COUNSELING TECHNIQUES

Many if not all the techniques of individual and group counseling (see chapters 3, 4, and 12) are appropriate to family counseling. There are also a number of specialized techniques used by family counselors. Other techniques include family sculpting, genograms, and reenactment.

Family Sculpting

Family sculpting is a nonverbal technique that examines the dimensions of closeness and power within the family. It substitutes for individual verbal descriptions, which are often difficult for family members to make. It provides a graphic representation of family structures, enabling both family members and the family counselor to understand each member's personal reality more readily, thus paving the way for change. In this procedure each family member is asked to arrange all the other family members by using space according to that person's perception of various dimensions of family relationships. The sculptor is asked to explain the completed creation, and family members are then invited to discuss it.

Genogram

The genogram is a family-assessment technique designed to provide a structural diagram of a family's multigenerational relationship system (Guerin & Pendagast, 1976). It depicts the family relationship system schematically as a family tree (see Figure 13.1). Genograms are especially used by followers of family systems theory, in which generational rules, patterns, and expectations are emphasized. The

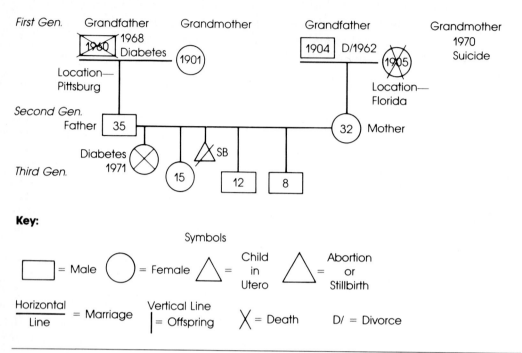

Key:

Symbols

☐ = Male   ◯ = Female   △ = Child in Utero   ▲ = Abortion or Stillbirth

Horizontal Line = Marriage   Vertical Line | = Offspring   X = Death   D/ = Divorce

FIGURE 13.1 Genogram

genogram provides a means for noting important issues within a family in a graphic manner. An example would be recognizing a pattern in which the oldest daughter in each generation gets divorced in her late thirties. It may be discovered that the oldest daughter in the current generation of the family is already expecting that her marriage will not last past her fortieth birthday.

Reenactment

Often family members describe a problem in general terms, such as a father complaining that the wife sabotages his attempts at disciplining their son. Rather than try to have the family members recall and explain their perceptions of the situation, the family counselor might ask the father to discipline the son in the session or reenact a discipline situation and ask the mother to intervene in the way that the father perceives as sabotaging his authority. This allows the counselor to see what is actually happening.

Paradoxical Interventions

Paradoxical interventions are powerful techniques. They are most often used by the strategic intervention theorists and are best used for long-standing, rigid, repetitious patterns of family interaction that do not respond to other approaches.

They encompass a variety of techniques for implementing change and are de-signed to overcome resistance by forcing family members to rebel against the counselor's directives. In doing so, they cease to act out their symptoms.

Fisher, Anderson, and Jones (1981) identified three paradoxical intervention strategies: (1) redefining the symptom by giving the behavior another meaning; (2) escalating the symptom by promoting a crisis or increasing the frequency of its expression; and (3) redirecting or changing an aspect of the symptom.

Redefinition or relabeling is an attempt to alter the apparent meaning or in-terpretation that the family places on the symptomatic behavior without chang-ing the facts. As a result the symptomatic behavior is more amenable to change. This approach usually emphasizes the positive: it is like saying that a glass is half full rather than half empty. For example, a counselor might relabel a mother's behavior as trying to be helpful rather than being possessive and overprotective, thus allowing a family to view the behavior in a more hopeful and understanding way.

Escalating the symptom is often accomplished by prescribing it, thus forcing the client to either give it up or admit that it is under voluntary control. For example, a counselor might instruct a schizophrenic client to focus on hearing voices. If the client obeys the counselor's instruction, he is complying with the counselor, thus acknowledging that the symptom is voluntary. If the client does not hear voices, then he is no longer "crazy."

Redirection and escalation both attempt to place the symptom under volun-tary control. However, in redirection, the circumstances under which the symp-tom is to occur is prescribed, and the frequency is not altered. An example of redirection with a mother who continually complains about physical symptoms for which there are no medical explanations might consist of instructing the rest of the family to listen to the mother's complaints for only 15 minutes in the evening at 6:30 P.M. The mother would then be told to approach members of the family at that time even if there were not any problems.

As stated under the strategic intervention section, these techniques require a thorough understanding of family dynamics and must be well thought out and appropriately applied. They are not intended to be used as fast and easy solutions to complex family problems.

WHEN IS FAMILY COUNSELING NEEDED?

There is no professional consensus about when family counseling is the preferred mode of treatment. Usually family counseling is called for when a problem clearly cannot be solved without the cooperation of another family member. Marital conflicts, sibling rivalry, and intergenerational conflicts are examples in which some or all of a family should be involved.

There also is little agreement as to whether to treat the family as a whole or to work with family subsystems such as the husband and the wife, or with indi-vidual family members, or with various combinations. Many family counselors refuse to see clients on an individual basis. They contend that ultimately the problem must be resolved within the family.

A common sequence according to Goldenberg and Goldenberg (1985) is for the entire family to initiate treatment, with various dyads or triads then being selected for further therapeutic work. The dyad most often selected at this point is the marital couple. In some instances, as many as three generations may be involved in family counseling at the same time.

Family counseling is usually contraindicated when the family is breaking up with little or no desire for reconciliation, or when certain members of the family need individual help before family counseling. Examples of the latter situation might be extreme emotional deprivation, or depression (Masson & O'Byrne, 1984). Generally, counselors who incline more toward a systems concept tend to view many more problems as being amenable to family counseling than those coming from a traditional psychoanalytical background.

MARRIAGE/RELATIONSHIP COUNSELING

Marriage counseling is a precursor of family counseling. It was originally developed to deal with marital relationship conflicts and emphasized the marital relationship without disregarding the value of individual counseling. Family counseling, however, began to seek alternatives to individual treatment procedures. Gradually, the two disciplines have come together. By 1970, the American Association of Marital Counseling changed its name to the American Association of Marriage and Family Therapy (Goldenberg & Goldenberg, 1985). Today, marriage and family counselors generally undergo the same training. The approaches to working with couples are pertinent to all family workers.

Even when there are children involved, a counselor may focus on the parents and their relationship rather than work with the entire family. The premise in so doing is that if things are functioning well with the parents, if they are cooperating with and supporting each other and are consistent in their dealings with the children, many if not most of the problems in the family may be resolved.

The marital dyad is not the only family relationship unit, nor is the standard reference of the typical married couple with dependent children living under the same roof the only family structure. Walsh (Walsh & Stratton, 1982) notes that fewer than one in four American families fit that description. Other important relationship units include gay couples and cohabitating couples (two unmarried persons of the opposite sex who share a nonlegal, binding living relationship). These units often require counseling and would be treated with the same procedures as the marital dyad.

Premarital counseling has also become popular, most commonly found in pastoral counseling settings. Premarital counseling is a form of preventive counseling, usually on a short-term basis (from two to eight sessions), where the basic premise is to establish a strong foundation for a long and healthy marriage.

Generally speaking, no matter what the treatment unit, marriage counseling is brief, problem-focused, and pragmatic. There is an emphasis on patterns of communication, expectations each person has of the other, role perceptions, each individual's personality, and how the couple functions together as a working unit in dealing with problems and making decisions (Cromwell, Olson, & Fournier, 1976).

Types of Marital/Relationship Counseling

There are four types of marital counseling used in working with couples. In each type, the focus is always on the couple relationship, even if the unit of treatment is the individual. The four types are concurrent marital counseling, collaborative marital counseling, conjoint marital counseling, and couples group counseling.

In concurrent marital counseling, the same counselor works separately with each partner. This method is often used when one partner has other major issues of an intrapsychic nature to resolve in addition to a problem with the relationship. The major problems of this approach are remembering what has been learned from which partner, remaining impartial, and keeping confidential the secrets one partner does not wish to be revealed to the other.

In collaborative marital counseling, each partner is seen individually by different counselors. Sometimes this occurs when one partner prefers working on the relationship, while the other partner prefers dealing with individual problems and concerns. The counselors then collaborate with each other, compare notes, and plan compatible intervention strategies. Problems with this approach include the logistics of finding counselors who would be comfortable with such a relationship and then would be able to arrange to have regular collaborative sessions between counseling sessions, and the fact that each counselor would have only a narrow and limited view of the relationship and no direct awareness of the couple interaction (Bodin, 1983).

In conjoint marital counseling, the couple is seen together by one or more counselors. This approach is often used when both partners are motivated to work on the relationship. The emphases are on understanding and modifying the relationship. This has been a popular approach among marriage and family counselors.

In couples group counseling, several couples are seen together by one or more counselors (Ohlsen, 1979). This approach is sometimes used as a supplement to conjoint counseling. It can lessen an intense emotional situation between couples since people generally tend to behave more rationally in groups than individually. It can also provide the curative factors of therapeutic groups in general (see chapter 12) and can provide troubled couples with a variety of other role models (Okun & Rappoport, 1980).

Whether or not a counselor-trainee intends to become a marriage and family counselor, a solid understanding of family development and dynamics and of the principles of marriage and family counseling can be valuable in any counseling setting. It is a rare case where a client's problem is totally separate from his or her family life.

Certification

Marriage and family counselors may be regulated by individual states. California, for example, specifically licenses marriage and family counselors on the attainment of certain requirements and standards. Nationally, a counselor can be certified as a marriage and family therapist through the Association of Marriage and Family Therapy (AAMFT).

Gladding, Burggraf, and Fenell (1987), in a survey of 274 counselor education chairpersons, reported that the respondents were unsure of what organization should accredit programs in marriage and family counseling—the American Association of Marriage and Family Therapists (AAMFT), the Association for Counselor Education and Supervision (ACES), or the Counsel for the Accreditation of Counseling and Related Programs (CACREP). They suggested that the link between types of accreditation, licensure, and employment opportunities requires further exploration. They also stated that their responses indicated that marriage and family programs in counselor education are continuing to grow in popularity.

Employment Prospects

With the increased awareness that many problems initially seen as individual problems can often be handled better through family counseling, training in family counseling is presently seen as a decided strength in pursuing employment objectives in the field of counseling. Even school counselors find that they can work more successfully with students with an awareness of family dynamics and skills in working with family groups. Receiving training and certification in marriage and family counseling would therefore be considered valuable attributes in the pursuit of employment opportunities for the foreseeable future.

Divorce Mediation

One relatively new subspecialty in this area is divorce mediation. Divorce mediation began in the United States in the early 1980s. A divorce mediator helps a couple that has already made the decision to divorce work out a mutually agreed on settlement covering all of the issues of separation including spousal and child support, custody and visitation, and the division of property, while trying to avoid or minimize bitterness, rancor, and courtroom settlements. Specialized training is available to develop the skills necessary to provide this service.

Training is provided by two rival groups, the Family Mediation Association and the Academy of Family Mediators. The process is based partly on the arbitration model of the American Arbitration Association and is usually handled by a trained team of counselors and lawyers (Goldenberg & Goldenberg, 1985).

Divorce mediation is a cognitively oriented activity based on facts rather than emotion. It has two primary goals: bringing about a working relationship between parents or spouses, and helping families overcome financial and marital dependencies (Grebe, 1986). Grebe reports that spouses who have successfully worked through mediation usually display more self-esteem and fewer signs of stress. Other benefits include lower financial costs and better postdivorce relationships between ex-spouses and children (Goldenberg & Goldenberg, 1985).

Most separating or divorcing couples are able to use mediation successfully, especially if they have at least moderate self-esteem and reasoning ability and can comprehend a range of alternatives and their possible consequences (Grebe, 1986). Divorce mediation is contraindicated if either or both partners are highly vindictive and vengeful without regard to the consequences of their behavior, or if they are alcoholic (unless in treatment), habitual liars, child abusers, spouse abusers, or victims of spouse abuse (Grebe, 1986).

The divorce mediation field is still in its infancy, but it is developing fast. Standards for practice are still in the process of development, and therefore there is as yet no required licensing or certification.

SUMMARY

Family counseling, a distinct type of group counseling that has evolved from an interdisciplinary background, has been described in this chapter. The term *family* has been defined as a natural social system with its own properties. Families can be traditional or nontraditional, functional or dysfunctional. Family life-cycle models are an aid to treatment planning. A number of models have been described.

A brief historical review of the development of family counseling has been presented. Family counseling has developed for the most part independent of individual counseling, and its goals are much broader than just effecting change within the individual. They include changing family structures and behavior patterns.

There has been a description of the dimensions of five different theoretical approaches related to family counseling. These approaches are the object relations approach, family systems theory, experiential/humanistic, structural, and strategic intervention. Several techniques used in family counseling have also been described, including family sculpting, genograms, reenactment, and paradoxical interventions.

Marriage/relationship counseling as a special type of family counseling, working with different types of couples, has also been discussed along with a description of different marriage/relationship counseling approaches. The importance of understanding relationship and family dynamics and ways of working with families is seen as an indispensable part of being a professional counselor.

Divorce mediation as a specialty within this area, working with couples who are in the process of separation and divorce, has been described as an important new field for people who have counselor training.

QUESTIONS AND ACTIVITIES

1. Consider how your family of origin dealt with the stages of the family life cycle. Write down your thoughts and memories. Share them with a family member or someone with whom you have a close relationship. What stage is your family of origin in at this time? If you have left your family of origin and have started your own family, at what stage is your present family?

2. Read more about constructing a genogram (McGoldrick & Gerson, 1985). Then construct one for your own family and consider how it might be used by a counselor in working with your family. What did you learn about your family?

3. Imagine that you are a practicing counselor. A client comes to you for help in dealing with his poor grades in college. Assuming that it was possible to involve his family, would you choose to do so? Why or why not? When would you choose to do just individual counseling and when would you insist on working with the whole family?

4. If you were to go for marriage counseling would you choose to be part of a group of other married couples or just be with your spouse and the counselor? Or perhaps have co-counselors—a male and a female?

CHAPTER 14

Career and Lifestyle Counseling

Can counseling help a person select a career?

Career counseling is one of the oldest specialties in the field of counseling. It is also one of the most creative and exciting specialties. This dynamism is the result of career counseling's evolution, its willingness to embrace changes in the conceptualization of the specialty area, advances in psychology, and the incorporation of computer technology.

We no longer think about helping clients make a single occupational choice early in life. We now think in terms of career development and view that as a "lifelong process that encompasses maturation not only in career awareness and decision-making but also in self-knowledge, life skills, and leisure pursuits" (Walz & Benjamin, 1984, p. 26). We have gone even further to consider counseling over a person's life span, including more than the world of work. We now include such things as leisure, retirement, and lifestyle counseling under the broader title of *life planning*.

This chapter describes the development of this area and its relationship to the counseling field. It also outlines the dimensions, strategies, trends, and issues that surround this specialty, one that touches each of us directly.

HISTORICAL PERSPECTIVE

Shortly after the turn of the century, Frank Parsons wrote *Choosing a Vocation* (1909), in which he coined the term *counselor* to describe the vocational guidance practitioners. As a result of his work, Parsons is recognized as the founder of systematic vocational guidance in the United States (Borow, 1984, p. 10). The groundwork established in the field of vocational guidance has fostered the development of the entire field of counseling. In 1913, the National Vocational Guidance Association (NVGA) was formed. This organization was the foundation for what is now the American Association for Counseling and Development (AACD). NVGA became one of several divisions of AACD. The first journal published in this field was *Occupations*. This journal has evolved through the years, along with the growth of the profession, becoming the *Personnel and Guidance Journal* and now the *Journal of Counseling and Development,* the official journal of AACD.

Vocational guidance as practiced by Parsons emanated from an agency he established in Boston. Since then much vocational guidance and counseling has been associated with schools. As a result, the term *counselor* itself became almost synonymous with *school counselor.* Only in the last decade or so has there been a trend for counselors to accept careers in mental health settings.

Parsons's most enduring contribution was his description of the process of vocational guidance, a procedure he called "true reasoning" (Herr & Cramer, 1984). The three steps of Parsons's approach are

> First, a clear understanding of yourself, aptitudes, abilities, interests, resources, limitations, and other qualities. Second, a knowledge of the requirements and conditions of success, advantages and disadvantages, compensation, opportunities, and prospects in different lines of work. Third, true reasoning on the relations of these two groups of facts. (Parsons, 1909, p. 5)

These guidelines are similar to modern principles of career counseling.

Parsons's conceptualization provided the basis for a major early theoretical approach to career counseling, trait-factor theory. The trait-factor approach holds that the client has certain attributes or traits and that various occupations need certain skills, aptitudes, and interests to varying degrees. The job of the counselor following this approach is to match the client with the appropriate occupation. The trait-factor approach was influential into the 1940s and was widely used in career counseling in school settings. During the 1950s and 60s, career counseling evolved from an emphasis on advice and information-giving to a form of psychological treatment relying on communication and decision-making skills (Srebalus, Marinelli, & Messing, 1982).

Career Education

During the 1970s the federal government initiated and subsidized an extensive program designed to facilitate career planning and to increase career options. This program became widely known as *career education,* a term defined in 1978 as "an effort aimed at refocusing American education and the actions of the broader community in ways that will help individuals acquire and utilize the knowledge, skills, and attitudes necessary for each to make work a more meaningful, productive, and satisfying part of his or her way of living" (Herr & Cramer, 1979, p. 37). In its implementation, this program involved people from all walks of life including farmers, executives, government employees, and educators, primarily through school counseling centers.

The career education program is an example of a proactive, preventive effort, designed to prepare people to cope with situations rather than wait until debilitation occurs. Although massive federal government funding of this program has ended, the work continues through the efforts of state agencies, business, industry, and the schools. Some important lessons were learned from this effort. It was found that no single group of people can accomplish all the goals of career education. It also became clear that the most important people were career counseling specialists (Herr & Cramer, 1984). Further, while there is no one right way to facilitate career awareness and decision making, self-awareness on the part of the individual was found to be of great importance. Self-awareness leads to self-identity so that "he knows who he is, what he is like, and he has developed a reasonably consistent internal value system" (Herr & Cramer, 1979, p. 39). Assisting students in the development of self-awareness has become a major dimension in career education; simply dispensing information on occupations and careers is not enough.

Career education approximates the counseling process in that it involves self-awareness, exploration, understanding, and the skills of decision making, along with career awareness and preparation. The basic format of enhancing and strengthening a person's self-concept through increased self-awareness and the learning of decision-making skills can be used when working with students in other areas, such as drug and alcohol or sex education.

Career education has been an important dimension of the career counselor's work. In schools the counselor often works in the role of consultant to teachers who are the primary deliverers of services to the student, encouraging and assisting teachers in the use of career information in the classroom. A key term in the career education movement has been *infusion*. A major goal of this movement has been to infuse career concepts and information into every subject area rather than to teach.career education as a separate subject.

Professional Organizations

Counselors who specialize in career and lifestyle counseling can affiliate with two divisions of AACD—the National Career Development Association (NCDA) (formerly the National Vocational Guidance Association) and the National Employment Counselors Association (NECA). In addition to holding meetings as part of the annual AACD convention, both organizations publish a newsletter and a journal. NCDA members receive *The Career Development Quarterly,* and NECA members receive the *Journal of Employment Counseling.*

TERMINOLOGY

As the field has developed, the use and even the meaning of technical terms have changed. What used to be called *vocational guidance* is now referred to as *career counseling.* Terms such as *career, occupation, job,* and *position* are often used interchangeably in the popular literature. In this chapter, the use of professional terminology is in accord with the following definitions:

Job, occupation, and vocation. These terms are used interchangeably to indicate activities of employment and employment positions (Zunker, 1990).

Career. A lifelong sequence of work, educational, and leisure experiences. "Mary's career has included teaching, counseling, graduate study, foreign travel, and many volunteer activities" (Joslin, 1984, p. 261).

Lifestyle. An individual's aspirations for social status, a particular work climate, education, mobility, and financial security (Zunker, 1990).

Career development. This term refers to "the lifelong process of developing work values, crystallizing a vocational identity, learning about opportunities, ·and trying out plans in part-time, recreational, and full-time work situations" (Tolbert, 1980, p. 31).

Career guidance. This is "an organized, systematic program to help the individual develop self-understanding, understanding of societal roles, and knowledge of the world of work . . . [career guidance] emphasizes the process of planning, decision making, and implementation of decisions" (Srebalus et al., 1982, p. 255). Career guidance has often been viewed as a teaching function. It increasingly includes more of the counseling process, to the point where the literature speaks more often of career counseling than career guidance.

Career counseling. This "includes all counseling activities associated with career choices over a life span. In the career-counseling process, all aspects of individual needs (including family, work, and leisure) are recognized as integral parts of career-decision-making and planning" (Zunker, 1990, p. 4).

Career life planning. This is "an ongoing process that allows for change of directions as individual needs change and/or situational circumstances cause change . . . [allowing for] greater opportunity for fulfillment in life" (Zunker, 1990, p. 97).

DOES CAREER COUNSELING DIFFER FROM PERSONAL COUNSELING?

In some settings, on a college campus, for example, a distinction can be made between career counseling and personal counseling. Srebalus, Marinelli, and Messing (1982) indicate that their review of the literature shows that it is difficult to make such a distinction consistently. The distinction could be based on the nature of training and experience that a counselor has, such as working predominantly with career counseling cases or working exclusively with severe psychopathology. However, making decisions about an occupation, a vocation, a lifestyle, and a career are clearly personal issues. When a 45-year-old male decides that he no longer wants to work as a salesman and wants to find an occupation that is more meaningful, that is a case of personal counseling in which a career decision needs to be made. All career counseling is personal. All personal counseling is not career counseling.

Clients may often use the need for career counseling as a safe, acceptable presenting problem (see chapter 4). This is a type of counseling that family and friends would not be likely to question. Our experience in working in a college counseling center has verified this strategy. Often when the counseling relationship has been established, the client will change the focus to another topic and may not pursue the career counseling concern again. The danger to be aware of here is to assume that all clients requesting career counseling are actually concealing a more significant problem. Legitimate career and life planning needs could be ignored.

CAREER COUNSELING THEORY

As we see in chapters 10 and 11, theory is a vital part of the counseling practice. It helps provide understanding of human behavior and offers constructs and strategies on which to base counseling decisions and interventions. It is ethically unwise to offer counseling of any type without a grounding in theory.

The practice of career counseling can fit well within the framework of the various major theoretical approaches to counseling such as psychoanalytic, person-centered, and behavioral (see Crites, 1981); however, as a counseling specialty, career counseling has had a number of specific theoretical formulations associated with it to aid in the understanding of how careers and lifestyles develop. "A theory of career development can be defined as a conceptual system that identifies, describes, and interrelates important factors affecting lifelong human involvement with work" (Srebalus et al., 1982, p. 15). Career development theory tends to be multidisciplinary, combining psychological, sociological, and even economic ideas and terms. Mention is made of several theoretical approaches, with some elaboration on the developmental theory of Donald Super. The relationship between career development theories and counseling theories is also given.

Five major types of approaches to career development have been identified by Herr and Cramer (1979, 1984):

1. The trait-factor or matching approaches. These approaches relate personal traits such as aptitudes and interests to characteristics required by a given job.
2. Decision theory. In decision theory the person chooses between vocational alternatives by using concepts unique to this approach.
3. Situational or sociological emphases. In these approaches the emphasis is on situational factors such as location in space and time, political and social factors, ethnic, religious and family beliefs, and value systems.
4. Psychological personality approaches. This perspective takes into consideration the individual's personality structure and needs.
5. Developmental approaches. Adherents of these approaches emphasize the person's long-term development.

Trait-Factor Theory

The trait-factor approach follows "the Parsonian Equation that *knowledge of self + knowledge of work + counseling = ability to choose*" (Srebalus et al., 1982, p. 96). Practitioners using this approach believed that through the identification of personal characteristics or traits of a client and the matching of these traits with factors necessary in different occupations, correct vocational decisions can be made. This approach dominated what was then called vocational counseling for more than 40 years. As more came to be known about the career development process, competing theories were developed to the point at which there are now few, if any, advocates of a pure trait-factor approach. Vestiges of trait-factor theory can still be found in almost all the current theories of career development, however (Isaacson, 1985).

Decision-Making Theory

A social learning theory of career decision-making has been developed by Krumboltz (1976). He identified the following four types of factors that influence the making of career decisions:

1. Genetic endowment and special abilities. A person's race, sex, physical appearance, intelligence, musical, and artistic abilities may all play a part in a person's career development. The characteristics may be helpful, as in the case of a 7-foot, physically coordinated male who desires a career in basketball; or they may be restrictive, as in the case of a male or female who desires a career as a musician but has only limited musical ability.
2. Environmental conditions and events. External factors that can affect a person's career choices can range from wars and depressions to earthquakes and floods, to availability of educational facilities and financial assistance, to union and government regulations.
3. Learning experiences. A person's attitudes and interests are affected by his or her previous learning experiences. Such experiences could include active involvement, such as repairing a bicycle or observing others at work.
4. Task-approach skills. Work habits, emotional responses, values, and problem-solving skills are all part of what Krumboltz calls "task-approach skills."

This approach suggests that career decision-making is more than having a good fit between personal characteristics and the requirements of a given occupation. Environmental factors, the variety and nature of personal learning experiences, and the degree of attainment of task-approach skills all need to be considered in the decision-making process.

Situational Approaches

The factors of chance, accident, and other external forces have been noted by career developmentalists. Many individuals, rather than going through some neat, orderly system of career development, have had their lives and careers directly affected by forces over which they have had little control. A major corporation moves a factory from one community to another, reducing career opportunities in one area while expanding them in another. Government regulations force the closing of a mine. A girl working in a drug store is chosen to star in a major movie. And yet, while luck or strokes of fate do seem to be involved in the career decisions of some people, the individual still can play a part. A girl may travel from New Jersey to Hollywood where she can get a job in a drug store, so that she might be discovered by a movie producer. An employee, laid off because of a plant relocation, might obtain retraining for a different occupation, which may be better than the original one.

Advocates of situational approaches to career development suggest

> that the socio-economic structure of a society operates as a percolator and a filter of information. In essence, the position a person occupies among the social strata making up the nation has much to do with the kind of information he or she gets, the alternative actions one can take, and the kind of encouragement which accrues. (Herr & Cramer, 1979, p. 84)

Because a purely situational approach to career development is not deemed sufficiently comprehensive and would render both the client and the counselor helpless, there are few practitioners who give a great deal of credence to this approach, and yet counselors cannot totally disregard these factors (Isaacson, 1985).

Psychological/Personality-Based Theory

According to theorists like Holland (1973), the major factor influencing career choices is the type of personality or behavioral style of the individual. The person's personality type is an acknowledged result of genetic and environmental factors. Four major assumptions form the core of Holland's theory:

1. There are six personality types into which most individuals can be categorized: realistic, investigative, artistic, social, enterprising, or conventional.
2. Environment can be classified into the same six categories. Each environment is dominated by people of similar personality type.
3. People search for environments in which they can comfortably express their interests, skills, and abilities and take on agreeable problems and roles.
4. A person's behavior is determined by the interaction between the personal characteristics of the individual and the characteristics of the environment.

One way to use Holland's approach is to have a client respond to an instrument like the Strong-Campbell Interest Inventory. On the basis of response patterns on the inventory he or she would be categorized according to the three most dominant personality characteristics. For example, a client might be classified as RIA (realistic, investigative, and artistic). This classification would be matched to the 456 occupations that have already been classified according to the same coding system. In this case, the occupations of architectural draftsman and dental technician have the same code. The client might then explore these two occupations and related areas using a resource such as the *Occupational Outlook Handbook,* published by the U.S. Department of Labor, along with a variety of other career education materials (Herr & Cramer, 1979).

The Developmental Approach

The developmental approach includes much of the previously mentioned approaches. It looks at career decision-making as a lifelong process with counselor interventions varying depending on the person's life stage. The most influential specific developmental approach is that of Donald Super (1957). Super developed 12 testable statements, and he devoted a major portion of his career to testing and researching these statements. These propositions are as follows:

1. Vocational development is an ongoing, continuous, generally irreversible process.
2. Vocational development is an orderly, patterned, and predictable process.
3. Vocational development is a dynamic process.
4. Self-concepts begin to form prior to adolescence, become clearer in adolescence, and are translated into occupational terms in adolescence.
5. Reality factors (the reality of personal characteristics and the reality of society) play an increasingly important part in occupational choice with increasing age, from early adolescence to adulthood.
6. Identification with a parent or parent substitute is related to the development of adequate roles, their consistent and harmonious interrelationship, and their interpretation in terms of vocational plans and eventualities.
7. The direction and rate of the vertical movement from one occupational level to another are related to intelligence, parental socio-economic level, status needs, values, interests, skill in interpersonal relationships, and the supply and demand conditions of the economy.
8. The occupational field the individual enters is related to interests, values, and needs, the identification with parental or substitute role models, the community resources used, the level and quality of educational background, and the occupational structure, trends, and attitudes of the community.
9. Although each occupation requires a characteristic pattern of abilities, interests, and personality traits, the tolerances are wide enough to allow both some variety of individuals in each occupation and some diversity of occupations for each individual.
10. Work satisfaction depends on the extent to which the individual can find adequate outlets in a job for his or her abilities, interests, values, and personality traits.
11. The degree of satisfaction the individual attains from work is related to his or her ability to implement self-concept.
12. Work and occupations provide a focus for personality organization for most

men and many women, although for some persons this focus is peripheral, incidental, or even nonexistent, and other foci such as social activities and the home are central. (Super, 1957, pp. 118–20)

Super's theory is an integrative one, which he calls a "differential-developmental-social-phenomenological psychology" (Super, 1969, p. 9) approach. It is longitudinal, with a progressive movement throughout the person's lifespan. Of vital concern to Super is the development of the person's self-concept and its influence in the making of career decisions. The basic theme stressed by Super is that "the individual chooses occupations that will allow him to function in a role consistent with his self-concept and that the latter conception is a function of his developmental history" (Herr & Cramer, 1979, p. 93). Super's approach is a wholistic one. It emphasizes four major elements:

> vocational life stages, vocational maturity, translating the self-concept into a vocational self-concept, and career patterns. According to this approach, the individual develops vocationally as one aspect of his or her total development at a rate determined in part by his or her psychological and physiological attributes and in part by environmental conditions, including significant others. (Tolbert, 1980, p. 41)

Although Super indicates that all individuals go through the various stages of career development, he has built on the ideas of those such as Havighurst (1953), who suggest that there are certain developmental tasks that need to be completed at different stages of life. Super's work incorporates developmental tasks along with the life stages (see Table 14.1).

Most people are aware of the career concerns that revolve around children. A child is always being asked, "What are you going to be when you grow up?" What has only recently come to light is the number of people who have major career concerns as adults. Some of these concerns manifest themselves in what has become known as the midlife crisis. Daniel Levinson (1977) has studied adult development and found that there are periods of stability and periods of transition, or instability, where some fine-tuning or adjustments are made to bring one's lifestyle in concert with needs and wants. This is followed by another period of stability. The midlife transition, described by Levinson, generally occurs in the late 30s or early 40s. This is a major period of evaluation, as the individuals recognize that the most productive part of their lives may be over and that goals established earlier in life may never be accomplished. Events such as children leaving home, personal illness, and having to care for elderly parents contribute to this midlife malaise.

Career counseling, in view of the developmental lifespan concept, is not just an approach to use with high school and college students to help them find the most appropriate career. It is an activity that must be pursued throughout a lifetime. Even deciding what to do after retirement is a career decision in the broadest sense.

> The developmental counselor expects that career counseling will result in the client acquiring a clearer understanding of self that results in appropriate decisions in the

TABLE 14.1 Super's Conception of Life Stages and Developmental Tasks

Growth	Exploration	Establishment	Maintenance	Decline
Birth–14 years	*14–24 years*	*24–44 years*	*44–64 years*	*64 years on*
Self-concept develops through identification with key figures in family and school; needs and fantasy are dominant early in this stage; interest and capacity become more important with increasing social participation and reality testing; learn behaviors associated with self-help, social interaction, self-direction, industriousness, goal setting, persistence. Substages: *Fantasy (4–10 years)* Needs are dominant; role-playing in fantasy is important. *Interest (11–12 years)* Likes are the major determinant of aspirations and activities. *Capacity (13–14 years)* Abilities are given more weight and job requirements (including training) are considered.	Self-examination, role try-outs and occupational exploration take place in school, leisure activities, and part-time work. Substages: *Tentative (15–17)* Needs, interests, capacities, values, and opportunities are all considered, tentative choices are made and tried out in fantasy, discussion, courses, work, etc. Possible appropriate fields and levels of work are identified. Task—Crystallizing a Vocational Preference *Transition (18–21)* Reality considerations are given more weight as the person enters the labor market or professional training and attempts to implement a self-concept. General-	Having found an appropriate field, an effort is made to establish a permanent place in it. Thereafter changes which occur are changes of position, job, or employer, not of occupation. Substages: *Trial-Commitment and Stabilization (25–30)* Settling down. Securing a permanent place in the chosen occupation. May prove unsatisfactory resulting in one or two changes before the life work is found or before it becomes clear that the life work will be a succession of unrelated jobs. *Advancements (31–44)* Effort is put forth to stabilize, to make a secure place in the world of work. For most persons these are the creative	Having made a place in the world of work, the concern is how to hold on to it. Little new ground is broken, continuation of established pattern. Concerned about maintaining present status while being forced out by competition from younger workers in the advancement stage.	As physical and mental powers decline, work activity changes and in due course ceases. New roles must be developed: first, selective participant and then observer. Individual must find other sources of satisfaction to replace those lost through retirement. Substages: *Deceleration (65–70)*

Tasks:
Developing a picture of the kind of person one is.
Developing an orientation to the world of work and an understanding of the meaning of work.

ized choice is converted to specific choice.

Task—Specifying a Vocational Preference

Trial-Little Commitment (22–24) A seemingly appropriate occupation having been found, a first job is located and is tried out as a potential life work. Commitment is still provisional and if the job is not appropriate, the person may reinstitute the process of crystallizing, specifying, and implementing a preference.

Task—Implementing a Vocational Preference

years. Seniority is acquired; clientele are developed; superior performance is demonstrated; qualifications are improved.
Tasks:
Consolidation and Advancement

The pace of work slackens, duties are shifted, or the nature of work is changed to suit declining capacities. Many men find part-time jobs to replace their full-time occupations.

Retirement (71 on)
Variation on complete cessation of work or shift to part-time volunteer, or leisure activities.
Tasks:
Deceleration, Disengagement, Retirement

From Edward L. Herr and Stanley H. Cramer, *Career Guidance through the Life Span: Systematic Approaches*, p. 95. Copyright © 1979 by Edwin L. Herr and Stanley H. Cramer. Reprinted by permission of HarperCollins Publishers.

present, compatible with client self-concept. Further, the counselor expects the client to be able to adjust or modify present decisions to fit changing circumstances in the future. (Isaacson, 1985, p. 90)

CAREER COUNSELING STRATEGIES

Career counseling, while using approaches common to other counseling specialties, also employs a number of strategies to help clients that are not often used in other counseling settings; for example, significant amounts of information giving, extensive use of computerized programs and testing, the use of placement services, and a direct emphasis on education.

Assessment

The use of tests and other assessment instruments has been linked with career counseling from its inception. The trait-factor approach required that the client's characteristics be clearly identified in order to provide a good fit with the attributes required for a given occupation. The use of assessment instruments is a major factor in career counseling, with computers assisting in the scoring, analysis, and interpretation of results. Assessment instruments generally include aptitude tests and personality and interest inventories. These types of assessment instruments are described in chapter 15.

Information Giving—Guidance

Much of the decision-making work of the career counselor falls under the rubric of information attainment and sharing. Clients often do not have the information they need to make informed decisions nor do they know how to find or use appropriate data. A significant amount of resource material and career information is available to fill the needs of clients who do not know where to turn. All major theoretical approaches use career information to some degree; however, there is a great deal of difference in emphasis. Counselors who use the trait-factor approach stress the use of career information. Person-centered counselors consider it of less importance (Crites, 1981).

A major problem with the dissemination of career information is the sheer abundance of material. More than 22,000 occupations are listed in the *Dictionary of Occupational Titles* (U.S. Department of Labor, 1983). Various amounts of published information for these are available, including books, pamphlets, audio and videotapes, films, and film strips. It is not feasible for any counselor, school, or agency to have on hand all the available resources to satisfy the needs of every prospective client; even if they were at hand, they might be overwhelming. The selection and management of career information is a major task for a career counselor.

There is a great amount of information available about occupations, but it is not always balanced. There is often an overly positive view given of occupations rather than a picture that offers negative aspects as well (Srebalus et al., 1982, p. 100). Information may also be outdated and written at the wrong level for a particular client. And so, the use of information, which seems to be a straightforward way to help people, in fact has some serious drawbacks. Further, even if the information is written at the correct level for a client and the presentation is current and balanced, simply having the information is not enough to make a lifetime decision.

Counseling—Individual and Group

Career counseling can work well in both individual and group settings. Clients receive more direct attention in individual counseling, but working in groups has valuable features. Information giving is most often done in groups for reasons of economy of time and money. Group counseling is preferred for working through the stages of counseling, for all of the reasons given in chapter 12.

Srebalus et al. (1982) suggest the incorporation of Carkhuff's three-stage model (1969), as modified by Egan (1975), into the overall scheme. These stages are exploration, understanding, and action. The components of this model fit well into the developmental approach as well as with the counseling process described in chapter 2.

1. *Exploration:* Individuals must become more aware of the broad spectrum of work. They also begin to conceptualize the relationships among occupations. As part of this conceptualization process, distortions about occupations are reduced.
2. *Understanding:* Clients differentiate among occupations according to occupational characteristics. The comparison of self to occupations is part of the process. Increased knowledge of the components of self and improved ability to differentiate among occupations permit persons to begin decision making about those occupations that meet their needs and whose requirements can be met.
3. *Action:* The active preparation for entry into the occupational world begins. Individuals eventually enter the occupational world in a more or less permanent manner during this period. Later in this stage, involvement in the maintenance and enrichment of their career occurs. (Srebalus et al., 1982, p. 103)

The movement through this process is not always sequential. The client may move from the exploration to the understanding stage and then move back to the exploration stage again before moving on to complete the action stage. The process can also be recycled, such as a client who used the exploration, understanding, action process to decide on an occupation, but then returned to go through the process again after an injury forced him or her to give up his initial occupational choice.

Teaching the Decision-Making Process

Following the understanding phase of counseling, the client may say, "Now that I've figured out what my problem really is, I now know what I have to do. Thank you very much!" In most cases, however, clients need to be assisted in the decision making necessary to implement previous learning. It is the action phase that the counselor helps the client work through a decision-making model (see chapter 3). Again, the goal of the counselor is to teach a skill that is transferable to other situations.

Placement Services

Career and employment counselors do much in the way of arranging matches between clients and employers, or between clients and colleges. This includes arranging job or college fairs, helping clients write résumés and practice interviewing, developing and maintaining placement files, and scheduling employer interviews. This service is most often found in high schools, universities, and state employment centers, but is increasingly occurring in outside agencies.

Computer Systems

Computer-assisted programs can be used at various points in the career counseling process. According to Isaacson (1985) such programs currently have their greatest value in helping clients attain occupational information and match it against various combinations of personal attributes and in relating educational and training opportunities to personal plans and characteristics. Research studies generally indicate that users of computer-assisted career guidance systems react positively, suggesting that these systems are worthwhile counseling tools that can help clients in the career exploration process.

The two basic types of computer-assisted career-guidance systems are information systems and guidance systems. Information systems provide clients with current data on subjects such as occupational descriptions and characteristics, educational institutions, and financial aid. Guidance systems generally actively involve the client in a career decision-making process, assessing values and interests, making predictions of future success, and using decision-making strategies. Some systems combine both information and guidance approaches (Zunker, 1990).

The two most popular guidance systems currently in use are SIGI (The System of Interactive Guidance and Information) and the *Discover System.* Both systems are designed to assist students in high school and college as well as older adults make career decisions.

Advantages

The advantages of using computer systems in career counseling include allowing the user to become very involved with the interactive capability of these systems.

Immediate feedback is given to responses, which enhances client motivation. The systems are designed to personalize and individualize the career exploration process, a process that can be conducted at any time access to the computer is available. The use of such a system allows for more efficient use of time with the counselor (Zunker, 1990).

Disadvantages

Some disadvantages of computer-assisted counseling include the expensive nature of both hardware and software and the cost of training personnel to use the systems. Such expenses may cause some potential users to question whether such material is cost effective as there are less expensive ways to accomplish the same objective. There also are concerns about confidentiality because many people may have access to electronic storage data. Controls have been developed to minimize this problem.

There also is a fair amount of anxiety on the part of some clients in using computer systems. Poorly motivated or inadequately prepared users can become discouraged quite easily, and a counselor may have to do directly what the computer system was expected to do. There have been some fears that computerized systems might be designed to take over the field of career counseling; however, use to date suggests that there probably will always be a need for personnel to prepare clients to use computer assisted systems, assist them when programs have several different components or stages, and to conduct follow-up sessions on completion of the programs.

TRENDS

There are several major trends within the career counseling specialty. One change, already noted, has been the evolution of terms to the point at which career development means more than merely finding a job; it involves one's entire life. Gysbers (1984) and Zunker (1990) have noted several other trends that involve changing environments and structures, increasing numbers, diversity, and quality of programs, tools and techniques, and expanding populations and settings.

Changing Environments and Structures

Our understanding of career development and the practice of career counseling are closely tied to the economic, occupational, and social environments and structures of which they are a part. Some changes under way are the following:

1. We have moved from a goods producing economic base to a service-information economy. By the year 2000, nearly 4 out of 5 jobs will be in industries that provide services. (U.S. Dept. of Labor, 1988, p. 9)

2. We are experiencing rapid acceleration in the use of high technology and automation in the workplace. This is due to the continued introduction of new highly sophisticated automated techniques, robots, and computers. Displaced workers will need retraining and/or relocation assistance.

3. We live in a world economy closely linked by fiscal policies, energy resources, multinational corporations, competition for raw materials, and the sales of goods and services.

4. We are continuing to experience population shifts that find people moving from the North and Northeast to the South and Southeast.

5. Demographic patterns in our labor force are continuing to change. There will be 139 million people in the work force in the United States by the year 2000, with significant increases in the employment of women and minorities. Proportionately, the greatest growth in the work force will be in the 25 to 54 year age bracket and not necessarily in the over-55 age bracket.

These trends should not only continue, but there is reason to believe that they also will accelerate.

Increasing Number, Diversity, and Quality of Programs, Tools, and Techniques

From being a somewhat staid, almost prosaic area of specialization in the field of counseling, career counseling has developed an exciting style. There is a great synthesis of ideas from other sectors of the field and from the study of human development. This synthesis includes working within family systems, using ideas, such as self-talk, taken from cognitive counseling, and developing counseling techniques to deal with differences in learning styles and the hemispheric functioning of the brain (Gysbers, 1984).

Related to this enriched approach to career counseling is an explosion in the number and variety of packaged programs, tests, and other diagnostic instruments, fostered by the increased use of computers. Career counseling, with its concern about self-knowledge, and the need to use and review large amounts of information about an increasing number of occupations, is very compatible with computer technology. As a result, many professionally developed programs have been created to assist in the counseling process, along with a number of other formats that are not tied to computers. As part of this trend, Gysbers (1984) notes that an increasing amount of this material is theory-based, connected to specific philosophical orientations, a feature of a maturing field.

Accurate and up-to-date information related to careers and the labor market is a vital dimension of the career counseling field. Gysbers (1984) reports that there have been significant improvements in the compilation and dissemination of such material with improved relationships between the producers and the users of career and labor market information. One of the biggest problems a career counselor has to face is keeping current with the programs and materials that will continue to become available.

To help keep track of all of these programs and material requires a systematic approach if counselors and clients alike are not to become overwhelmed. With this in mind, systems approaches to career counseling have been developed. A *system* is a sequential program that has been developed as a result of a carefully conducted and analyzed needs assessment. Within basic limits, the program needs to be fluid, responsive to changing needs, ahead of and ready for emerging needs, and flexible enough to modify particular strategies on the basis of ongoing evaluation of results (Walz & Benjamin, 1984, pp. 26–27).

Walz and Benjamin suggest that to ensure effective implementation of a systems approach to the management of career information, specialized training is required. This training could be part of the career counseling coursework offered as part of a master's degree program or as a supplemental seminar or workshop.

Expanding Populations and Settings

Gysbers (1984) says that the career development change in focus from vocational guidance for young people to a lifespan focus and the personalization of the concept of career by relating it to life roles, settings, and events means that counselors can provide programs for people of all ages in diverse settings. Career development components are increasingly found as part of agencies that primarily serve adults. These components are also becoming an integral part of personnel services in business and industry. For example, career counseling for employees who have just been laid off is available to help them find new sources of employment. Preretirement counseling can help those who are contemplating retirement and are concerned about finances, health insurance, and the satisfactory use of leisure time. The field is ever-expanding.

SUMMARY

The origin of career counseling as a specialty within the counseling profession dates back to the vocational guidance movement of the early 1900s, when the task of the counselor was to match clients with appropriate occupations. The specialty has now evolved to the point at which it is concerned with a lifelong process of career development, the learning of life skills, and the planning for leisure time.

Vocational guidance has been a major function of school counselors from the beginning of the movement. Career education programs funded by the federal government in the 1970s gave much encouragement and support to career development and counseling. The National Vocational Guidance Association has now become the National Career Development Association, a division of AACD, and offers certification as a certified career counselor. Career counselors may also affiliate with the National Employment Counselors Association (NECA).

Career counseling is considered personal counseling because it emphasizes helping people work through personal career development issues. Not all personal counseling, however, is career counseling. The five major theoretical approaches to career development are the trait-factor approach, decision theory, a focus on situational factors, the psychological approach, and the developmental approach. The premises and components of Super's developmental approach have been described.

The strategies for career counseling include assessment of client characteristics and interests, information giving, individual and group counseling, teaching the decision-making process, and the use of placement services.

Trends in career counseling include using ideas and approaches from other areas in counseling, such as incorporating aspects of family counseling, increased use of prepackaged programs, and assessment devices using computer technology. The use of computers will also lead to improvements in the compilation and dissemination of career information. Career and lifestyle counseling will continue to move from being almost exclusively aimed at children in school settings to working with people of any age in almost any setting.

QUESTIONS AND ACTIVITIES

1. How do the theories of career development relate to the theories of counseling? Are they separate and distinct or can they be successfully integrated? As you select or develop a theory of counseling, do you also have to select and/or develop a compatible theory of career development?
2. Review the processes by which you have made career decisions up to this point. What developmental theory(ies) do you seem to have followed? Interview several adults about the process they experienced in their career development. If they saw career counselors, what procedures, techniques, assessment instruments, if any, were used? Were any of these approaches helpful? Share a summary of your learnings with the class.
3. Check the local school system(s) and determine how much if anything is being done in the way of systematic career *education* in the schools. Check different types of classes as career materials might be used with a number of different courses. Is career education a strong, proactive force in your community or has it been allowed to fade from view? Have a class discussion on how counseling students can supplement existing career counseling in the schools.

General Foundations

CHAPTER 15

Human Growth and Development for Counselors

*What must counselors know about
human development?*

Relevance has always been a concern of students, and perhaps no chapter in this book is as relevant to the education of counselors as this one. First, a knowledge of one's personal development is an essential component of self-knowledge, as discussed in chapter 1; second, the topic of human growth and development is a major part of the examination to become a Nationally Certified Counselor (NCC); and third, to provide a baseline for understanding the perspective of clients, it is essential to understand the stages and processes of normal growth and development.

Because, as Ivey and Goncalves (1988) suggest, the primary goal of counseling is the facilitation of development, it is important that counselors know as much about developmental processes as possible to understand where their clients are and to make interventions appropriate to their clients' developmental levels. Taking a developmental approach to counseling means that you have to start with the client rather than with your theories. The study of human development is particularly valuable in designing preventive programs because it is possible to prevent certain types of problems by the appropriate application of current knowledge.

This chapter presents a wholistic approach to human development. All human systems are viewed as working together and influencing each other, both positively and negatively (e.g., a person who feels depressed may overeat and thereby gain weight). Our perception of our bodies can fundamentally affect our self-concepts. This chapter emphasizes how human beings are similar; the following chapter on cross-cultural approaches focuses on differences among human beings.

GROWTH AND DEVELOPMENT OF THE WHOLE PERSON

The study of human development from birth to death is a relatively recent phenomenon. Much of the early work in the field has tended to focus on child and adolescent development, where the growth processes are dramatic and easy to observe. The psychosexual stages as postulated by Freud, for example, conclude with the genital stage after puberty. Research in the last two decades indicates that we still have much to learn about all dimensions of postadolescent development.

The study of human development must include all of the multidimensional, interactional elements. Difficulties in any aspect of a person's life can lead to a need for intervention on the part of a counselor or other helping professional. Counselors working in the fields of prevention and remediation, as well as in development, need to know and understand the developmental and growth processes of the whole person.

The basic elements considered here are physical-motor, cognitive-intellectual, social-emotional, and moral-spiritual (faith). Each element interacts with and influences the others (see Figure 15.1). Physical development, for example, can affect a person's social-emotional development. A physically underdeveloped adolescent boy or girl may have difficulties in peer relationships and in feelings of self-worth. Moral development is contingent on cognitive and emotional growth. And while these interactions are occurring within the person, the person is interacting with his or her environment. These interactions are bidirectional: the person affects the environment (e.g., a 4-year-old child who is able to manipulate the members of his family), and the environment (including the family [caregivers], peers, schools, work, religion, the mass media, and major social events and influences), affects the person.

The physical motor dimension includes "body build and configuration, size, strength, rate of physical maturation, motor skill coordination, physical health and the like" (Evans & McCandless, 1978, p. 4). The cognitive-intellectual dimension includes memory, thinking, language, perception, problem solving, and academic achievement. The social-emotional category includes emotional development, temperament, and interpersonal relationship skills. The moral-spiritual dimension includes beliefs, values, morals, and faith development.

The importance of the family in the development of the person is self-evident. It is the most influential force in the development of the child for the first five years. Gradually, other external influences such as television, school, peers, and religious instruction begin to have an impact. However, the family does remain a critical factor even into adolescence. That is why high divorce rates, single-parent families, blended families (two families combined through marriage), incest, child abuse in general, as well as parent abuse (where children physically and psychologically abuse their parents) are areas of great concern in the field of human development.

The influence of peer groups begins in elementary school and continues to

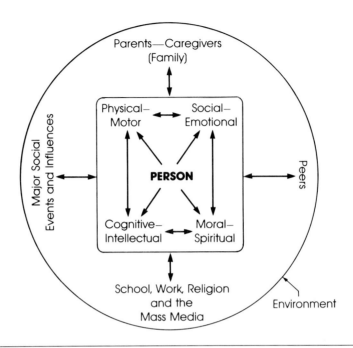

FIGURE 15.1 Factors Influencing Human Development

grow through adolescence. In some cases they may usurp the family and become the person's primary group. Schools and religious institutions influence development, but often with mixed results. The mass media, such as television, radio, and the print media, have the potential for a significant impact on a person's development because of the social learning or modeling that takes place. Viewers watch people on television and imitate their behavior. Major social events such as economic depressions or wars also have a profound influence on personal development. The total person is a highly complex structure. Many interacting elements unfold as the person grows. Some of this development is a result of genetic programming, and some is due to environmental interaction.

Some Basic Principles of Human Growth and Development

"Growth in an organism is that structural change which increases its level of functioning in specific ways, although the potential for some different but related function may be concomitantly decreased" (Wilson, Robeck, & Michaels, 1969, p. 165); for example, as a child learns language, use of baby talk declines.

Growth is a continuous, lifelong process. Beginning with the union of the ovum and the spermatozoon, and continuing until death, the final stage of growth, growth is a constant process. The rate of growth may change, but the process goes on. Our language illustrates this when we speak of growing up, growing in wisdom, or growing older.

Growth is sequential and unique. The spermatozoon and the ovum each contain 23 chromosomes. Each chromosome contains approximately 3,000 genes. When the spermatozoon and the ovum combine, a blueprint is formed that is both general to the species and unique to the individual. A child learns to sit, crawl, stand alone, and then walk, in predictable order. The timing of these progressions, however, varies. The metamorphosis from infancy, when the head size is one-fourth of body length, to adulthood, when the head size is one-eighth of body length, proceeds in an orderly fashion. The stages of growth occur at predictable times, and the result is a distinctly unique adult. Growth is the unfolding of the programmed genetic code (DNA). This unfolding will occur at the proper time, given a generally nonhostile environment. In interaction with the environment, growth includes learning and maturation and is integrative. The human organism strives to meet basic needs and in the process of interacting with the environment the child ''learns.'' If a child is hungry and cries, the child learns that crying can result in being fed. Some learning occurs best at critical or sensitive periods in the child's development (Piaget, 1972; Montessori, 1964). Growth is integrative in that all of the human systems work together: an integration of the cognitive, physical, emotional, and spiritual dimensions occurs. Each system affects the others. A child may be mentally ready to ride a bicycle, but physically might not have the strength, coordination, and balance to learn.

Growth occurs in stages. The stages are identifiable on various dimensions, but not everybody completes every stage. Also, movement through stages may be reversible. For example, a person may revert to a lower stage of moral development after having attained a higher stage at one time.

AREAS OF DEVELOPMENT

Physical and Motor Development

The most observable of the developmental processes is that of physical development. This process begins in utero on conception and is influenced by the environment provided by the mother.

In the United States, approximately 250,000 babies are born every year with birth defects. Most of these defects are preventable. Amniocentesis, the clinical examination of cells from the womb containing the fetus to determine whether genetic or environmentally caused malformations have occurred, is an increasingly used procedure. This, along with taking genetic histories of parents, has led to the development of a very specific area of counseling—genetic counseling: helping people make decisions about having children, and working with families of children who have genetic problems.

Environmental factors, including nutrition, chemical agents, disease, X-rays, and the emotional status of the mother, can play an important part in the development of the fetus. Both animal and human studies indicate that poor nutrition is closely linked to mental retardation (Smart & Smart, 1972, p. 29). Cigarette smoking during pregnancy increases the risk of stillbirths, premature birth, and low birth weight. Thirty-two percent of children born of mothers who are heavy drinkers are affected by fetal alcohol syndrome. Such children are small in size and have a low birth weight, facial abnormalities, and possible mental retardation. Other drugs appear to have equally deleterious effects. Infants born of cocaine and heroin addicts and alcoholic mothers manifest all the signs of the addiction and experience withdrawal symptoms (Evans & McCandless, 1978, p. 204; Smart & Smart, 1972, p. 34). It may be that there is no drug that is safe for the fetus.

Children born of mothers who have AIDS will have the HIV virus and have a strong possibility of developing AIDS. Diseases such as rubella, gonorrhea, syphilis, and poliomyelitis may result in a miscarriage or the birth of a mentally deficient, blind, or deaf child. Excessive doses of radiation during early pregnancy from repeated X-rays or from radium treatment for cancer have also resulted in abnormal prenatal development (Craig, 1983, p. 77). Prolonged and severe emotional stress is also associated with pregnancy complications. The mother's age can also be a problem. Older mothers, those over 35, are more likely to produce Down's syndrome children.

The Birthing Process

Giving birth to a child can be both a very exciting and a very stressful period in the lives of all concerned. Under normal circumstances the baby leaves the security of the womb and is literally forced down the narrow birth canal until born. Otto Rank (1929), a follower of Freud, suggested that the sudden change from the safety of the uterus to the bright lights and loud noises of the outside world is the first trauma in the child's life. Because it is believed that the trauma of birth instills anxiety in the neonate, Rank maintained that this trauma was the chief cause of later neuroses in adults.

To make the birthing process less traumatic, Le Boyer, a French obstetrician, developed a method in which the child is born in a quiet, dimly lit room and immediately placed on the mother's abdomen, where the child can be gently fondled and caressed. After the umbilical cord is cut, the child is bathed in warm water. Infants born in this manner do seem to cry less and respond earlier than babies born into bright light and loud noises and greeted with a vigorous slap on the buttocks. Parents involved in this experience also report feeling an exceptional interest in the child born in this manner (Craig, 1983, p. 93).

Whether the process of being born is as traumatic and as influential on later life as Rank suggested is open to debate. During the first few days after birth, infants do not appear to be very sensitive to pain and as a result may not experience the stress of birth as the painful event that many adults imagine it to be. Also, they do not appear to have the thought processes and memory developed to the point at which the significance of the event and the attendant pain can be recorded (Craig, 1983).

Birthing centers, often found in hospitals, attend to the needs of the parents as well as the child and are becoming increasingly popular. Birthing rooms provide a homelike setting with labor, delivery, and recovery taking place in the same room. Family and friends may be present as the mother desires. The father is generally encouraged to stay overnight with his partner after the child is born. Mothers are also encouraged to keep the new child with them to promote bonding rather than to have the infant in the nursery (Craig, 1983, p. 94).

Bonding

Bonding, the forming of an attachment with another person, can begin immediately after birth, forming the basis of a lifetime relationship. Skin contact, cuddling, touching, stroking, eye contact, and talking all are functions of the bonding practice. There is some evidence that the greater the length of time involved in the bonding process, the greater the chances for a strong, positive, trusting relationship in the future. This principle applies to fathers as well as mothers (Craig, 1983, p. 56).

Early Childhood

The years between birth and age 5 are most significant. The foundation for all of the child's future growth and learning become well established during that period. The child will have attained half of his or her future height by the age of 2½, and by age 4, a child's IQ will be stable enough to predict the IQ at age 17 (Hamachek, 1979, p. 74). By age 5, the child has 75 percent of his or her ultimate brain weight and 90 percent of it by age 6 (Hamachek, 1979, p. 82). From being almost immobile at birth, the 5-year-old is an active, energetic child, with the use of large muscles fairly well developed. From ages 6 to 12, physical growth slows considerably, bodily proportions continue to change, large muscle development continues, and there is greater small muscle refinement.

Adolescence

Adolescence, from a purely physical sense, begins with the prepubertal growth spurt and ends with the attainment of full physical maturity. Skeletal growth is complete, total height has been attained, and "the upper limits of genetic potential for endocrine development" (Hamachek, 1979, p. 137) have been reached. In terms of rate of biological change, the adolescent period ranks with the fetal period and the first 2 years of life. Unlike infants, however, adolescents have both the pleasure and the pain of being direct observers of the entire process. The amount of development or lack of it is a constant concern. Comparisons with peers and the prevailing ideal, plus the horror of attendant problems like acne, makes this a difficult time for adolescents and for those close to them.

During adolescence, there are several distinct periods of physical change. These are triggered by an explosion of hormones in the body. The 2 years preceding puberty are called pubescence or preadolescence. Puberty marks the onset of adolescence and is the age when secondary sex characteristics first appear and sexual organs become functional. The onset of puberty for boys is between 13 and 14. For girls, it is from about 12½ to 13 years of age. In the 19th century, when health care and nutrition were inferior to present standards, puberty for girls began between the ages of 14½ to 15½.

In addition to sexual changes in the body, a number of other changes take place. There is a growth spurt during which the individual's ultimate height is attained and where the boys are broadening at the shoulders and the girls are broadening at the hips. There is also increased activity in the sebaceous glands that can cause skin problems such as acne. While the process of going through this stage of life is standard for everyone, the times and rates at which bodily changes take place differ significantly. The result is that there are early and late bloomers in addition to those who develop on a nearly normal timetable. Early maturing boys benefit from their status, whereas there is a stigma attached to the late bloomer. The reverse seems to be true for girls, but not to the same degree. The mass media promote the idea of sexual attractiveness and conformity to certain ideals for members of both sexes.

Adulthood

Physical changes after adolescence center on the accumulation of fat. During adulthood there tends to be loss of muscle strength and endurance. This is partly due to age and partly due to a decline in activity level. With old age the process of deterioration continues. Body size shrinks and posture changes markedly. Loss of muscle strength is inevitable. In spite of all these changes, many older adults lead an active healthy life, playing tennis, jogging, and swimming, well into their sixties and seventies.

The major physiological change for females in their adult years is menopause, the time at which a woman is no longer able to conceive a child. The cessation of the menstrual cycle is brought about by a change in hormone secretions. These hormonal changes can affect the woman's total personality and result in headaches, irritability, and depression. These changes generally occur between the ages of 48 and 51 (Masters, Johnson, & Kolodny, 1982, p. 170). Menopause, or aging itself, does not necessarily lower female sexual interest or response potential (p. 170). In fact, with the fear of possible pregnancy gone, sexual interest may increase for some women.

There is no direct male equivalent to the female menopause with a major drop in sex hormone levels. Sperm production in the male, while slowing down after age 40, continues on into the eighties and nineties. A condition called the male climacteric affects about 5 percent of men over age 60. This condition results in symptoms such as tiredness, irritability, poor appetite, and impaired ability to concentrate. It is caused by decreased levels of testosterone production and can be aided by testosterone injections. The majority of men, however, do not experience this condition (Masters, Johnson, & Kolodny, 1982, p. 70).

Cognitive-Intellectual Development

The uniquely human ability to think has long been the focus of psychological investigation. These investigations have studied both the types of cognitive abilities and their rates of development.

Intelligence

When one speaks of intellectual development or intelligence, it is difficult to speak precisely. There is no commonly accepted definition of intelligence. Terman, in 1916, defined intelligence as the ability to think in abstract terms. Thorndike (1913) believed that there were three kinds of intelligence: the abstract, the mechanical, and the social. Guilford (1967), in his model of the intellect, postulates 120 factors of intelligence including many factors not currently measurable. There are many other definitions of intelligence.

Because it is probable that not all of the ways in which we are intelligent are known, it is best to make a distinction between intelligence and measured intelligence. Intelligence as a global term incorporates mental and physical processes that may or may not be measurable. Measured intelligence refers to specific mental and physical activities that have been demonstrated in a controlled testing situation. For a discussion of how mental abilities are measured, see chapter 17.

In keeping with our wholistic approach to human development, it is important to note the work of Howard Gardner (1983). After extensive research, Gardner has described seven different types of intelligence. The first two types are linguistic and logico-mathematical, which are usually thought of as the conventional types of intelligence. These types are generally measured by intelligence and aptitude tests and are the types of intelligence that generally emanate from the left hemisphere of the brain.

Two other types of intelligence identified by Gardner are more closely associated with the right hemisphere of the brain—the musical and the spatial types of intelligence. The body also has an intelligence of its own, labeled kinesthetic, most noted in the performance of dancers and athletes. Finally, there are the personal intelligences. First, there is the interpersonal or social intelligence, and the intrapersonal intelligence, or knowledge of one's self. The process of counseling could be described as the development of the client's personal intelligences.

In considering whether artificial intelligence can be developed, Frank Rose suggests that "because the computer doesn't have a body, it is missing certain valuable information. The complexity of the human body and its *interaction* with the mind, is far beyond anything artificial intelligence can yet conceive of" (Tarrytown Letter, 1985, p. 15). While each of the intelligences is unique, an interdependence factor seems to exist.

Intelligence Quotient (IQ).   Measured intelligence has usually been reported in terms of an intelligence quotient, or IQ. The IQ is an index that describes relative performance on a test. IQ test scores compare a person's performance on a given test with other persons of the same age. Table 15.1 illustrates the spread of intelligence scores on the Wechsler Adult Intelligence Scale across the range of population.

Performance on mental tests tends to correlate positively with academic and socioeconomic achievement. People who score high on such tests usually do well academically and have high income and high status occupations, and vice versa. IQ scores are often used to identify people considered mentally retarded. The third edition of the *Diagnostic and Statistical Manual* of the American Psychiatric Association (1980) (DSM-III) requires as one of the diagnostic criteria for mental retardation "an IQ of seventy or below on an individually administered IQ test" (except for infants) (p. 40).

Stability of IQ.   Although measured intelligence is generally stable throughout a person's lifetime, IQ scores have been found to increase and decrease depending on various circumstances. For example, children who are isolated and have little opportunity to interact with their environment often suffer a loss of IQ. Losses have been associated with emotional dependence on parents. IQ gains have been related to persistence in problem solving, emotional independence, curiosity, verbal aggressiveness, and competitiveness (Sontag, 1980, p. 391). Decreases in intelligence during old age are generally associated with poor health. Speed and hand-eye coordination diminish in old age, and rote learning ability also decreases.

Nature-Nurture Issue.   There is general agreement that both heredity and environment influence measured intelligence; there is, however, a continuing debate about the contribution of each. Some research suggests that measured intelligence is in large part inherited but can be affected negatively and positively by environmental influences. For example, a child with a high initial IQ raised in a sterile environment may experience a loss in measured IQ, whereas a child with a low initial IQ may experience positive change as a result of specialized experiences, such as participation in a Head Start program.

TABLE 15.1   Intelligence Classification of WAIS IQ's—Ages 16 to 75 (actual)

Classification	IQ	Percentage Included
Defective	69 and below	2.2
Borderline	70–79	6.7
Dull-normal	80–89	16.1
Average	90–109	50.0
Bright-normal	110–119	16.1
Superior	120–129	6.7
Very superior	130 and above	2.2

David Wechsler, *The Measurement and Appraisal of Adult Intelligence*, 4th ed. (Baltimore: William and Wilkins). Copyright © 1958 by David Wechsler. Reproduced by permission.

How much intellectual power a person uses at any given time is of more significance than the level of the measured IQ. Einstein estimated that he only used a small proportion of his capacity. Having a high IQ does not guarantee success any more than a low IQ assures failure. In either case, other factors such as motivation play a greater part than IQ. For this reason, among others, counselors are generally discouraged from disclosing IQ scores to individuals or their parents, unless there are exceptional circumstances.

Cognitive Development

One major component of the intellectual capacity of an individual is thinking ability. Thinking is a general category that includes such mental activities as forming concepts, making comparisons, solving problems, and reasoning. Thinking is often conceptualized as linear, sequential, and logical, a function of the left hemisphere of the brain. It can also be creative and intuitive, a function of the right hemisphere.

Jean Piaget, a Swiss genetic-epistemologist, as a result of observing young children give incorrect responses to intelligence tests, concluded that children think differently, rather than less, than adults did. These observations led to a lifelong study of the development of thinking and the cognitive processes.

Piaget's Stage Development Theory.

As Piaget worked with children, he noted their organized patterns of behavior or thought, which he labeled "schemas." He discovered how children adapted to their environment, assimilated new information into existing schemas, and accommodated new experiences by revising existing schemas. Piaget developed a theory that thinking processes develop in the same fixed sequence of stages. At fairly specific points in the developmental process, characteristic behaviors and abilities to conceptualize occur. Each stage builds on the accomplishments of the preceding one in a hierarchical fashion. Heredity, according to Piaget, has, in effect, programmed the unfolding of these stages. The physical and social environment, however, may affect the age at which specific abilities evolve, or the degree to which the abilities are developed. The following is a brief description of each cognitive developmental period. The ages for each period are meant to be taken as guidelines only.

1. *Sensorimotor stage: birth–2 years.* During the first 2 years of life, children acquire knowledge of the world primarily as a result of sensory impressions and motor activities. The development of organized patterns of behavior and thought (schemas) begins as the newborn infant explores his own body and uses his senses. It proceeds until, as a 2-year-old, the child is able to distinguish between parents and animals, has a rudimentary sense of direction and purpose, and is beginning to use representational thought.
2. *Preoperational stage: 2–7 years.* Children in the preoperational stage are able to think about their environment by using symbols such as words to represent their surroundings. Major accomplishments include the development of

language and simple conceptualizations such as being able to distinguish among types of animals. The use of imagination is also noted; for example, the use of a cardboard box as a house. A particular characteristic of this age is that it is difficult for the child to take another person's point of view. Children at this age believe that other people see things the same way that they do. Piaget labeled this characteristic "egocentrism." Along with these characteristics, preoperational children are not able to reverse actions mentally.

3. *Concrete-operational stage: 7–11 years.* Children in the concrete-operational stage are able to deal logically with objects. They are not yet able to work with abstract ideas. Using concrete objects, they are able to perform such operations as classifying, combining, separating, ordering, multiplying, dividing, substituting, reversing their thinking, and, by the end of the stage, understanding the relationship between time and speed.

4. *Formal operations stage: 11–15 years.* During the stage of formal operations children develop the skill of using abstract logic to think about the process of thinking. They are able to generalize and to formulate hypotheses and test them mentally. They are able to propose alternative solutions to problems. They can check out beliefs for logical consistency. They understand metaphors and probability, and they think about the future. They synthesize materials, creating new and unique ideas.

In 1972, Piaget extended the upper level of this stage to age 20. This indicated that everyone reaches the formal operation stage by this age. However, in spite of this modification, there are questions as to the number of people who attain this level. McKinnon and Renner (1971) found that only about 15 to 25 percent of college students used formal operational thinking. Piaget seems to have theorized about potential capacity for thinking in all individuals but has not accurately described attained results.

Implications of Piaget's Work.   Piaget was not a psychologist and therefore made little attempt to present his theory in psychological terms or to develop applications for his findings. Such transformations and applications have had to be made by others. Counselors working with preoperational children (up to second grade or so) will need to keep in mind that words have different meanings for different children. They are not generally able to perceive things from the point of view of another person.

Most children under age 12 have difficulty dealing with abstract thought. They need to work with concrete objects or their own experiences. This limits the use of highly cognitive, abstract theoretical counseling approaches. Similar concerns should be considered when working with the placement of children in schools. The child's cognitive level may be a much more accurate gauge for grade placement than chronological age.

Instead of looking at children as more or less miniature adults, as had been the practice in the 19th century, Piaget's work forces us to be aware of where children are when we are working with them. Parenting, teaching, and counseling should all be affected by a knowledge of a child's cognitive development. A fundamental effect of Piaget's work in all of these areas is to avoid presenting material to children that is beyond their cognitive level of functioning. Much that is interpreted as resistance on the part of children may be a function of material that has been presented at too difficult a level.

It has been noted that the ages given for the various developmental stages are general in nature and need to be checked out individually. It is also important to note that not all children go through the four cognitive levels. Many people may not attain the level of formal operations at any time in their lives. Others may achieve little more than a threshold level at that stage.

Social-Emotional Development

Human beings are social, emotional beings, and it is therefore not surprising that there are developmental processes that occur in this dimension as well. The work of Erik Erikson in psychosocial development is perhaps the best known. Study in the development of emotions, or affect, has, however, been rather limited.

Psychosocial Development.   Many of our ways of thinking about human behavior and the development of personality stem from the pioneering work of Sigmund Freud and his followers. Personality development was postulated as a result of a combination of external factors that affect the development of the ego, and superego, and internal factors such as biological needs and appetites represented by and affecting the id. Freud's conceptualization of personality development centered on the process of sexual energy becoming dominant in one bodily zone after another, producing developmental stages called oral, anal, phallic, latency, and genital (Coleman, Butcher, & Carson, 1980). Freud's psychosexual stages describe developmental processes up to adulthood, but provide little data for the latter stages of life.

Erik Erikson, one of Freud's followers, has been labeled an "ego psychologist." In a simplification of the Freudian approach, Erikson does not focus on the superego, but rather thinks in terms of ego development. His approach is psychosocial rather than psychosexual.

Freud believed that ego development took place as a result of conflict between the id and the superego, whereas Erikson emphasizes the interaction between the self and society. This occurs throughout a person's life, with the person in a "constant process of challenge and growth" (Corsini, 1977, p. 413). There is a regular need to make accommodations between experience with the environment and self-perception. The social milieu is particularly important in helping a person establish a personal identity.

Like Piaget, Erikson believes in epigenetic development, where the person inexorably moves from one stage to another, confronting age-specific crises along the way. Successful resolution of these conflicts results in a fully mature, emotionally healthy individual. Even though each stage is a particularly critical conflict, the issue is still present throughout life. For example, a child may establish a basic sense of trust during the first year or so of life and yet still have to deal with specific personal instances involving trust throughout life. Overall, the labels for each stage are presented as extremes. It is rare that a person resolves a conflict totally in one direction or the other (e.g., total integrity or utter despair). Erikson's stages are illustrated in Table 15.2.

Erikson's work is significant because he is one of the first to elaborate a detailed developmental life process. He also went beyond person and family to include societal impact on personality development. His emphasis on adolescence and the identity crisis described for that stage has been noted as a particularly significant contribution.

Much popular periodical literature suggests that the period of identity crisis affects young and mature adults as well. Erikson's conceptualization has provided a foundation for the increasing work in the field of gerontology.

Emotional (Affective) Development.   In contrast with the other areas of development, to date there are few elaborate theories of emotional, or affective, development. Affect development, which includes our feelings, emotions, and values, is something we all experience, yet there is little in the way of theory or research on how this process functions.

Gardner (1983), in his description of intrapersonal intelligence, describes the "core capacity at work here [as] *access to one's feeling life*—one's range of affect or emotions: the capacity instantly to effect discriminations among these feelings and eventually to label them, to enmesh them in symbolic codes, and to draw upon them as a means of understanding and guiding one's behavior" (p. 239). Gardner presents a general description of the development of personal intelligences, and relates their development to the work of Erikson, Piaget, and others.

Emotions are present and obvious from birth. From a general label of excitement at birth, Bridges (1932) has differentiated 11 emotions in infants by the age of 2 years, including fear, disgust, anger, distress, jealousy, delight, joy, elation, and affection. Some emotional states are linked to Erikson's stages, but are not necessarily associated with a stage or time of life. Despair may occur at any age, not just late in life.

Affective development has been described by Mosher (1979) as an integral part of our overall mental development. Dupont (1979) has formulated a theory of affective development which relates closely to the work of Piaget and Kohlberg. Only a portion of this theory has been confirmed by Dupont's research. Some basic tenets of this theory include

- the premise that the structural development of affect has factors in common with the structural development of cognition;
- the assumption that all thought and actions are accompanied by some change in affect; and
- the belief that there are six stages of affective development (p. 168).

TABLE 15.2 Erikson's Eight Stages of Life

Conflict at Each Stage	Emerging Value	Period of Life
Basic Trust vs. Mistrust Consistency, continuity, and comfort produce feelings of security and predictability.	Hope	Infancy
Autonomy vs. Shame and Doubt Parental firmness allows for the experience of demand fulfillment with limits that produce self-control.	Will	Early Childhood
Initiative vs. Guilt The development of the superego and cooperation with others support the growth of planning and a sense of responsibility.	Purpose	Play Age
Industry vs. Inferiority Working and learning with others produces skills, such as the ability to use tools and weapons, and feelings of self-esteem.	Competence	School Age
Identity vs. Role Confusion The physical changes of adolescence arouse a new search for sameness and continuity and the need for a coherent sense of self.	Fidelity	Adolescence
Intimacy vs. Isolation A new ability to tolerate the threat of ego loss permits the establishment of mature relationships involving the fusion and counterpointing of identity.	Love	Young Adulthood
Generativity vs. Stagnation The adult need to care for children and to guide the next generation produces the desire to leave something of substance as a legacy.	Care	Maturity
Integrity vs. Despair An accrued sense of order and meaning allows one to defend one's own life cycle as a contribution to the maintenance of the human world.	Wisdom	Old Age

From *Adolescence and Early Childhood* by Judith Stevens-Long and Nancy Cobb by permission of Mayfield Publishing Company. Copyright © 1983 by Mayfield Publishing Company.

The first stage is the egocentric-impersonal stage (0–2 years), in which children are not able to differentiate between themselves and the world around them. Contentment or discomfort and pain are the dominant affective states at this stage. Dupont believes that affective development actually begins when affect and cognition are no longer centered on the self. In the heteronomous stage (2–7 years), children differentiate between themselves and significant adults, mainly their parents. During this time they experience and learn the names for the basic feelings of fear, anger, happiness, and sadness.

In the impersonal stage (7–12 years), children evidence feelings of mutual respect and reciprocity as relationships with peers increase and those with adults diminish. The psychological-personal stage (12–15 years) is when the adolescent develops a system of values. "These values are usually concerned with universal justice, equality under a single law, patriotic conceptions of the nation or the world, and allegiance to an abstract code of ethics, laws, or religious doctrine" (Dupont, 1979, p. 178).

Dupont suggests that few people attain the last two stages: the autonomous stage and the integritous stage. In the autonomous stage, individuals become aware of and appreciate how they are personally responsible for their own behavior. As this appreciation for self-determinism develops, so does resistance to external attempts to influence this autonomous behavior. The person at the integritous stage has a fully developed philosophy of life, and integrity itself is invested with affect. Integrity refers not only to consistent conduct in accordance with principle, but also to a feeling of wholeness that the individual prizes. "Integrity may become even more valued than life itself . . . [e.g.,] Socrates, Jesus Christ, and Sir Thomas More" (Dupont, 1979, p. 180).

Dupont has created and tested educational materials based on these theoretical formulations that could be used by counselors working with children and adolescents. These are *Toward Effective Development* (ages 8–12), and *Transition* (ages 12–15).

Dumas's theory of emotion (in Stone & Church, 1973), suggests that all mild emotional arousal is pleasant. We can "enjoy the mock-fright of a ghost story or the safe terror of a roller coaster ride. As emotions become more intense, they differentiate more sharply into pleasant and unpleasant. At a still more intense level of arousal, all emotions become disagreeable so that what was pleasant at an intermediate level of arousal functioning either disintegrates or is paralyzed" (p. 72).

Although expressions of emotions are tolerated and even encouraged in young children, they are not always acceptable as the child matures. Adolescent boys learn that they should not cry. In spite of numerous attempts to add affective education to school curriculum, there has been a continuing emphasis on cognitively oriented content. A taxonomy of educational objectives for the affective domain (Krathwohl, Bloom, & Masia, 1964) has been developed, which suggests that in educational and counseling settings, it is important to be working with the first level of the affective domain, attending and awareness, before trying to work with cognitive material.

Because the institutions of society have not dealt directly with persons' affective natures, people have developed a number of ways of handling emotions—some pleasant, some unpleasant. One of Freud's major contributions was his discovery of the various defense mechanisms his patients used. Many of these mechanisms were used as a way of handling powerful emotions. Much of what a counselor does is help people cope with their emotions and learn to handle emotionally laden material. There are assertiveness training programs that deal with the differentiation among anger, aggressiveness, and assertiveness. There are stress management courses that deal with boredom and anxiety. There are clinics for phobias and depression. Much is being done for the remediation of emotional problems, but there is still little being accomplished in the area of prevention.

Howard Gardner, in describing the concept of personal intelligence, which includes emotional development, warns that when ignored and not fully developed "this kind of intelligence assumes aberrant and pathological forms. Education of the emotions clearly involves a cognitive process. The less a person understands his own feelings, the more likely he will fall prey to them and the more likely he will misunderstand the feelings and behaviors of others and fail to secure his place in the larger community." We may produce a generation that is violent and self-destructive if we do not give ourselves and our children the chance to be fully compassionate and self-aware (Tarrytown Letter, 1984, p. 6).

Moral and Spiritual Development

The moral and spiritual dimension of the human personality comes in to play quite often in counseling relationships and needs to be understood by counselors. In examining these developmental processes, it is again important to notice the interactive nature of all these dimensions, and in this particular area, the difficulty of specificity of definition of terms and measureability of concepts.

Moral Development.   In studying how children think, Piaget also included their moral development. After listening to childrens' reactions to stories containing moral dilemmas, Piaget isolated some characteristics that distinguished among different types of moral thinking (Biehler & Snowman, 1982, p. 67).

Lawrence Kohlberg, as a graduate student at the University of Chicago, built on Piaget's work. He studied verbal responses to moral dilemmas by older children. As a result of his research, Kohlberg formulated a description of seven stages of moral reasoning (see Table 15.3).

Kohlberg's model was developed from his analysis of the results of structured interviews with children in which they were asked to state how they would respond to a variety of moral dilemmas. In each instance, the child had to explain his or her reaction. Kohlberg and his colleagues also conducted longitudinal research that indicated that there is movement from one stage level to another, and that this movement is roughly correlated with age and level of cognitive development.

Some findings related to Kohlberg's work suggest that Level III, stages 5, 6,

TABLE 15.3   Kohlberg's Stages of Moral Development

Stage	*Illustrative Behavior*
Level I. Premoral	
Stage 1. Punishment and obedience orientation	Obeys rules in order to avoid punishment.
Stage 2. Naive instrumental hedonism	Conforms to obtain rewards, to have favors returned.
Level II. Morality of conventional role-conformity	
Stage 3. "Good-boy" morality of maintaining good relations, approval of others	Conforms to avoid disapproval, dislike by others.
Stage 4. Authority-maintaining morality	Conforms to avoid censure by legitimate authorities, with resultant guilt.
Level III. Morality of self-accepted moral principles	
Stage 5. Morality of contract, of individual rights, and of democratically accepted law	Conforms to maintain the respect of the impartial spectator judging in terms of community welfare.
Stage 6. Morality of individual principles of conscience	Conforms to avoid self-condemnation.
Stage 7. Meaningful solutions to moral questions are compatible with rational universal ethics; their essence is the sense of being a part of the whole of life and the adoption of a cosmic, as opposed to a universal, humanistic Stage 6 perspective.	

Kohlberg, 1958

and 7, are not attained by more than a few people. Older males tend to respond at stage 4 and women at stage 3. College students tend to have higher levels of moral judgment. This may be due to their high degree of independence and the necessity to resolve many value-laden issues as a result of being in a new environment on their own.

People do not necessarily remain at a given level. A regression effect has been demonstrated where a person who has attained a certain level may at times respond at a lower one. In fact, moral judgments may be made at two different levels within minutes of each other depending on the nature of the stimuli. In addition, there is evidence that the higher levels of moral responses can be learned through role playing and discussions (Keefe, 1975). One area of concern related to these studies is the allegation that statements of moral judgments have been investigated and not moral action. Gilligan (1978, 1982) noted that Kohlberg's research involved mainly male subjects and the use of male-dominated stories. She suggests that before accurate generalizations to both sexes can be made, more concern for the reasons women make moral judgments is necessary.

Research in the area of moral development is still new. It is seen here as a cognitive, rational process and only indirectly related to religion or spirituality. Kohlberg's theory is clearly cognitive. Few emotions are evident in any of the children's responses.

Spiritual (Faith) Development.   It is perhaps ironic that, although we are in an age in which psychology has become the secular religion and the practice of psychotherapy the new priestly rite (Kegan, 1982), there is not more attention given to the spiritual dimension of human nature in relation to personality development and to the therapeutic process. Defining the term *spirituality* has been a major concern for psychologists who prefer specific, measurable, quantifiable constructs and are faced with concepts such as hope, meaning, purpose, beliefs, values, and faith. Not being able to define precisely or measure the concept should, however, not be reason for counselors to avoid this dimension of the human personality. In many instances, the way to change a behavior or resolve a personal conflict may best be attained by working within the belief system or the faith orientation of the client.

As with the other dimensions of the human being described above, there is a developmental process associated with this area as well. James Fowler, a theologian influenced by Piaget's work in cognitive development and Kohlberg's work in moral development, has discovered and described a process that he has called "faith development."

The basic structure of the faith development process emerged as Fowler (1981) listened to the life stories of more than 200 people at the time that he was reading the work of Erik Erikson. The patterns found in the various stories led to the formulation of a six-stage process.

Faith, as defined by Fowler (1981), is "a person's way of seeing oneself in relation to others against a background of shared meaning and purpose" (p. 4). It is not always religious in its content or context. It is our way of finding coherence in and giving meaning to events in our lives.

> Our faith orientations and our corresponding characters are shaped by three major elements, the "contents" of our faiths. First, there are the *centers of value* that claim us: causes, concerns, and persons that consciously or unconsciously have the greatest worth to us. . . . Practically speaking, we worship that or those things in relation to which our lives have worth.
>
> Second, the *images of power* we hold and the *powers* with which we align ourselves to sustain us in the midst of life's contingencies. We try to align ourselves with power sufficient to sustain us and those persons and things we love.
>
> Third, the *master stories* that we tell ourselves and by which we interpret and

respond to the events that impinge upon our lives. Our master stories are the characterizations of the patterns of power-in-action that disclose the ultimate meaning of our lives. (Fowler, 1981, pp. 276–277)

According to theologians such as Reinhold Niebuhr and Paul Tillich, faith is a universal human concern. "Prior to our being religious or irreligious . . . we are already engaged with issues of faith. Whether we become nonbelievers, agnostics or atheists, we are concerned with what will make life worth living" (Fowler, 1981, p. 5).

Faith is clearly presented to be different from and not synonymous with religion and belief. "Faith can be religious faith, but it can also be centered on a career, a country, an institution, a family, money, success or even oneself" (Fowler, 1983, p. 59). Faith is not static, it is continually growing and changing.

Stages of Faith Development.   Fowler, working with the results of more than 350 carefully structured interviews, has identified a prestage and six stages of faith development.

1. *Undifferentiated (primal) faith—Infancy (0–4 years)*. The children in this stage form their basic dispositions toward the world. The beginnings of strong faith development in this stage are dependent on "the fund of basic trust and the relational experience of mutuality with the one(s) providing primary love and care" (Fowler, 1981, p. 121). The strength of this trust underlies subsequent stages of faith development. Problems develop at this level in two ways. An excessive narcissistic pattern may emerge where "the experience of being 'central' continues to dominate and distort mutuality, or experiences of neglect or inconsistence may lock the infant in patterns of isolation and failed mutuality" (Fowler, 1981, p. 122).

   The transition from the primal stage to stage 1 is facilitated by the child's use of symbols in speech and ritual play and by the concomitant development of language and thought.

2. *Stage 1. Intuitive Projective Faith—Early Childhood (2–7 years)*. Stage 1 is a period in which long-standing images and feelings, both positive and negative, in regard to faith, are produced by the child as a result of the examples and modeling of significant others (Fowler, 1981, p. 133). Imagination emerges in this stage and is its special strength. The dangers arise from the possible possession of the child's imagination by images of terror and destructiveness; or the child, wittingly or unwittingly, may use imagination in the reinforcement of taboos and moral or doctrinal expectations. The emergence of concrete operational thinking is the primary factor influencing the transition to stage 2.

3. *Stage 2. Mythical-Literal Faith (Childhood and Beyond)*. With the ability to perform concrete operations, the child begins to reconstruct earlier imaginative views of the world, taking on a more linear, cause-effect perspective to life events as a way of achieving a personal sense of order. The child increas-

ingly is able to understand the perspective of others. Much of personal meaning and belief comes through the stories, dramas, and myths of the community; meanings that are generally taken quite literally. The ability to note and reflect on conflicts and contradictions in stories marks a transition point leading to stage 3.

4. *Stage 3. Synthetic-Conventional Faith (Adolescence and Beyond).* The third stage generally corresponds to the cognitive stage of formal operations. The structure of meaning emanates from beyond the family. A personal identity is developed that is reflective of responses by others. There is a personal concern for solidarity with significant others. The person is other-directed, and has not yet attained the confidence or the ability to form and sustain an independent perspective.

    The formation of one's personal myth emerges during this stage, "the myth of one's own becoming in identity and faith, incorporating one's past and anticipated future in an image of the ultimate environment unified by characteristics of personality" (Fowler, 1981, p. 173).

    A significant change takes place as the individual moves from stage 3 to stage 4. There is an assumption of responsibility for personal commitments, attitudes, and beliefs that culminates in an overall personal lifestyle. This movement does not take place for all adults. Many remain at stage 3 or even stage 2.

5. *Stage 4. Individuative-Reflective Faith (Young Adulthood and Beyond).* For many adults, stage 4 emerges during their midthirties and early forties. In this stage one's identity or personal view of self, and one's world view become differentiated from the views and reactions of others. A personal ownership takes place. The views of others, while considered, are not necessarily accepted. This is a period of high personal tension when choices and decisions between group identification and self-actualization are being made. This is the stage for making personal commitments in relationships and for deciding on a vocation. Commitments made in earlier stages may not need to be renewed or changed during this stage.

6. *Stage 5. Conjunctive Faith (Midthirties and Beyond).* In this stage symbolic power is integrated with conceptual meanings. There is a reworking of one's past that includes dealing with material from stage 4 that may have been suppressed or unrecognized as a result of self-uncertainty. There is an appreciation for truths emanating from symbol, story, metaphor, and myths coming from all traditions. This stage's commitment is to justice. It goes beyond normal commitments to class, religion, community, or nation.

7. *Stage 6. Universalizing Faith (Midlife and Beyond).* People in this stage are grounded in a oneness with the power of being. Their visions and commitments free them for a passionate, yet detached spending of the self in love. Life is devoted to overcoming division, oppression, and brutality (Fowler, 1983, p. 58). One loves life and yet holds it loosely.

    Few people attain this stage. The person in it is quite ecumenical and is ready for fellowship with individuals from other faith traditions and from other stages of faith. Gandhi, Martin Luther King, Jr., Mother Teresa, Dag

Hammarskjold, and Buckminster Fuller are some examples of stage 6 personalities.

These latter two stages characterize a searching faith guided more by the intellect than by emotions. The few people who enter these stages tend to be found outside of organized religion since traditional religious institutions, in general, do not focus on the needs of this population.

> Faith stages are not to be understood as an achievement scale by which to evaluate the worth of persons. Nor do they represent educational or therapeutic goals toward which to hurry people. (Fowler, 1981, p. 214)

Education and preventive counseling should aim at the full realization of the potential strength of faith at each stage and at keeping changes in faith development current with the parallel transitional work in psychosocial areas. Remedial or therapeutic work is called for when the anachronism of a lagging faith stage fails to keep pace with psychosocial growth. Also, on occasion, when precocious faith develops, outstrips, or gets ahead of psychosocial growth, help may be needed in overcoming or reworking crippled psychosocial functions (Fowler, 1981, p. 114).

When considering all of these personal dimensions and the various descriptions of stages and sequences of development, it is easy to feel overwhelmed. And even more so when one realizes that there are additional sets of developmental stages formulated to describe other aspects of human development; for example, ego development (Loevinger, 1976), and vocational development [Super, 1980 (see chapter 14)]. One approach to handling all of this information might be to use an approach similar to the constructive-developmental framework of Kegan (1982). Working within this framework, the emphasis is not on the developmental stages or sequences, but rather on the developmental process itself, which could be considered a process of adaptation, or meaning-making, or evolution. The focus is therefore not on the person in a certain stage, labeled, but rather as a person evolving. This idea of personal evolution or growth can be seen in another way. Each dimension presented can be perceived as sequential spirals, each interacting with the others, and together striving to maximize the growth potential of the individual. A problem or crisis is not necessarily an illness or breakdown, but rather could be a breakthrough, or a move toward growth (Laing, 1960; Kegan, 1982). A problem affecting one spiral can affect one or more of the other dimensions; however, the other developmental areas can provide strength and support to the troubled area. The task of the counselor then is not to regard clients' disorders as sicknesses or as disasters, but rather as the pangs of their own becoming (Kegan, 1982, p. 295).

The Effects of the Environment

Much has already been noted about the effect of the environment on the development of the person. Skinner (1984) suggests that environmental influence is the most significant factor in personality development. The ingestion of toxic substances by the mother at the time of conception and afterwards has been demonstrated to have a direct effect on the child and all aspects of his or her development. The degree and type of stimulation given to a child from birth on has been found to have a marked effect on various aspects of the child's development. The influence of media, particularly television, is known to have both a positive and negative impact on the growing child as well as on the maturing adult. Other environmental factors such as air pollution and chemical pollution within the food chain can also have deleterious effects.

One purpose of schools and organized religion is to influence the development of the maturing person. Unfortunately these institutions have not been as successful in fulfilling this purpose as one might desire.

The effects of peer groups, particularly in adolescence, has been well documented, and counselors working with young people need to be aware of these dynamics. For example, it may be more successful for a counselor to work with teenagers in a group setting than individually to take maximum advantage of the interactional dynamics of this age group.

The importance of a person's work and its influence in developmental processes was recognized early by Freud. The world of work permeates a person's life. It begins with the attitudes and experiences learned by a child in the home and continues with the successes and frustrations of teenagers and young adults as they begin their life's work—the work that will provide a great deal of their identity for them. The world of work influences the midlife crises of adults and is an obvious part of the difficulties workers have in preparing for retirement and then adjusting to retired life (see chapter 14).

Environmental effects also include social and historical events. Depressions, wars, social unrest, and periods of prosperity can differentially affect a person at various formative stages of life. Living through the period of the Vietnam War had a much different effect on a person in the 18–25 year age range than it did on people in the 40–50 year age range. Adolescents and young adults are often most affected by the influence of historical events. Being aware of where a person fits in to world events can be important in understanding his or her present situation. A person who grew up during the depression is less likely to consider a job change than a young person who entered the work force during a period of prosperity. Table 15.4 illustrates different age groupings in relation to historical events. In counseling situations, awareness of these relationships may be meaningful.

Baltes, Reese, and Lipsitt (1980) suggest that over the development of a lifespan there are three fundamental factors that interact. The first is the age-graded influences that happen normally at certain specific times in a person's life, such as menopause for women. The second factor is history-graded influences. These are major historical events such as wars, epidemics, and depressions that affect most people at the same time. The third factor is nonnormative influences. These are events that do not occur at any specific time, but when they do occur, they can have a major impact on a person's life. These influences can include divorce,

TABLE 15.4 How Historical Events Affect Different Age Cohorts *

Historical Event	Year Born					
	1912	1924	1936	1948	1960	1972
1932 (The Depression)	20 years old (starting out)	8 years old (schoolchild)				
1944 (World War II)	32 (parenting/career)	20 (starting out)	8 (schoolchild)			
1956 (Postwar Boom)	44 (middle age)	32 (parenting/career)	20 (starting out)	8 (schoolchild)		
1968 (Vietnam Era)	56 (preretirement)	44 (middle age)	32 (parenting/career)	20 (starting out)	8 (schoolchild)	
1980	68 (retired)	56 (preretirement)	44 (middle age)	32 (parenting/career)	20 (starting out)	8 (schoolchild)

*Those starting out during the Depression were more affected than were schoolchildren, while those establishing a career during the postwar boom were more affected than were those nearing retirement.

Source: Grace Craig, *Human Development*, 5/e, © 1989, p. 429. Reprinted by permission of Prentice-Hall, Inc., Englewood Cliffs, New Jersey.

death in a family, loss of job, and serious illness. Generally, it is these nonnormative influences that bring a person to counseling where coping skills can be learned to deal with the nonscheduled stressors of life. However, during the latter part of the 1970s and into the 1980s, there was a significant amount of counseling related to the Vietnam war. A condition labeled posttraumatic stress disorder was identified, and numerous veterans of this war received psychological assistance.

> Each of these [environmental] influences affect people more directly at different ages. Children and those in later adulthood are often affected most by age-graded influences. Adolescents and young adults are most affected by history graded influences. While non-normative events can happen at any time, their effects on a person's life can be more significant as a person grows older. (Craig, 1983, p. 393)

SUMMARY

An overview of human development throughout the lifespan has been presented along with implications for the practicing counselor. A wholistic, integrated, interactional approach to the study of the individual has been presented with particular focus on the development of the physical, cognitive–intellectual, social–emotional, and moral–spiritual dimensions.

Physical concerns, requiring excellent prenatal, preventive counseling, begin prior to birth, during birth, and during the period of bonding after birth. As the child matures through childhood and adolescence into adulthood, physical changes can have profound effects on overall personal development. This is generally most noticeable during adolescence and after the age of 40.

In considering cognitive and intellectual development, it was stressed that intelligence can refer directly to all aspects of the person including the physical and social dimensions. Cognitive intelligence as measured by IQ has been described, along with the stability of such intelligence and the impact that heredity and environment have on it.

Piaget's theory of how children develop cognitively has been described along with counseling implications. The idea that children are not miniature adults was noted, and that counselors working with children and adolescents need to be able to relate directly to the cognitive level of the person, rather than expect the child to be at an advanced level.

The psychosocial stages of Erikson have been presented to aid in the understanding of social development. Erikson's stages, which cover life from birth to old age, are of particular importance because, among other things, they help clarify issues related to the adolescent development as well as act as a stimulus for work in gerontology. Erikson was also aware of the interaction between the person and the environment.

Emotional or affective development, although somewhat of a stepchild as far as theory and research is concerned, is nonetheless an important personal dimension. Emotional problems are a major reason for counseling, and therefore an understanding of emotions, their development, and how people try to control them is essential for counselors.

Moral development in terms of how individuals learn to deal with right and wrong and the making of moral judgments was presented in terms of Kohlberg's theory. The theory is primarily cognitive with an emphasis in research on how subjects say they would act, rather than on direct action. Faith development has been presented as a representation of the concept of spirituality. It was stressed that faith is not necessarily related to religion, and, as in the case of cognitive and moral development, everyone does not achieve the highest developmental stages.

The interaction of all of these stages as part of a wholistic growth process striving toward maximizing the growth potential of the individual has been stressed, with the counselor encouraged to focus on the process rather than a breakdown at a given stage.

The influences of the environment on human development have been considered, including the family, peers, school, work, religion, mass media, and social-historical influences. The relationship between the time when events occur and the developmental level of an individual can have a profound effect on developmental growth.

The study of human growth and development is considered essential in conjunction with the study and practice of counseling. It keeps the focus on the client and the wholistic development of both the individual and the counselor.

QUESTIONS AND ACTIVITIES

1. Growth is said to be continuous. How true is this? Outside of possibly bulging at the waistline, how much actual growth can take place in the various dimensions of human existence as you grow older? Where would the limits be?

2. List local, regional, and national events that had an effect on your development. Chart them on a time-line. Indicate the effect each event has had on you. How many of these events have been positive for you in the long run? Share your findings with your classmates.

3. Using the developmental theories of Piaget, Erikson, Dupont, Kohlberg, and Fowler, determine where you are at this time with regard to each theory. In your journal, indicate, where possible, how you were led or influenced to pass from one stage to another. Obtain feedback from others as to how they see you in accordance with each theory. Does it appear to be possible for you to move to the next stage of any of these models?

4. Consider the adage, "You cannot help a person beyond where you are." In light of your awareness of your development with regard to the various dimensions described in this chapter, where do you see yourself being able to be of the most help?

CHAPTER 16

Cross-Cultural Approaches to Counseling

Can't you use the same counseling approach with everybody?

> *Every person is like all other human beings in some ways, like others in other respects, and, finally, like no one else.*
>> Kluckholn and Murray in Lee (1984, p. 594)

The study of counseling and its application from a cross-cultural perspective provide an important vehicle for understanding the origins, concepts, values, and the generalizability of the ideas and principles studied in this text. For example, while music may be considered a universal language, the language and practice of counseling as we know it may be limited to Western culture.

More than a decade ago Carl Rogers visited China with the idea of testing in a distinctly different culture some of the person-centered concepts he had worked with during his career. His findings were profound:

> I believe the contrast in the basic philosophy of the Chinese group and that of the person-centered workshop is obvious. They are polar opposites. The Chinese approach leads to group unity, a general contentment in conformity, and satisfaction in helping to achieve the group goals. The person-centered approach leads to a sense of freedom and power, and to the anxiety and pain of being responsible for choosing one's own life. Each represents a viable philosophy, and one cannot say that one is good, the other bad. The evaluation and choice must be personal. (Rogers, 1979, p. 15)

It is not surprising that a Western approach toward interpersonal relationships and personal development is different from that of an Eastern culture. What is of greater significance for our study is that cultural differences within our own society can affect counseling success. What are the chances for counseling success with a heterosexual, middle-class, Caucasian, Catholic, female counselor and a gay, lower-class, Jewish male? What problems would an affluent, naturalized Hispanic have in working with Native Americans on a reservation? What about an upper-middle-class black Ph.D. trying to help a black elementary school dropout from Watts, a poor Los Angeles neighborhood? Do the client and the counselor have to be similar to assure effective counseling, or can a counselor learn to effectively counsel people from different cultural backgrounds? These and other questions are addressed in this chapter as we explore cultural differences and the field of counseling.

BACKGROUND

Emphasis on cross-cultural counseling grew out of the civil rights movement of the 1950s and 1960s as militant minorities demanded greater equity with all citizens, including the right to mental health care. At the same time, helping professionals began to write about the difficulties they encountered in counseling black clients. In the 1970s writers in the field were discussing how culture affected counseling and the effects of race on diagnosis.

Helping professionals were initially concerned with counseling the so-called disadvantaged, then with working with increasing numbers of international students in the United States, followed by counseling people overseas, and finally on the growing numbers of refugees from Cuba, Vietnam, Laos, and Cambodia, and the rapidly increasing Hispanic population. These groups remain underrepresented as the recipients of mental health care. Most regular mental health services are not prepared to serve them adequately (Pedersen, 1988). The majority of mental health delivery services are provided by white middle-class men whereas a great number of clients receiving these services are nonwhite, lower socioeconomic populations with different socialization and value assumptions from the counselors. These differences have resulted in culturally biased counseling with low utilization rates for mental health services by minority group members (Pedersen, 1988).

CULTURE AND CULTURAL PLURALISM

Culture has been defined as "the configuration of learned behavior and results of behavior whose components and elements are shared and transmitted by the members of a particular society" (Linton, in Atkinson, Morten, & Sue, 1983, p. 5). This definition suggests that there may be cultural differences even within racial or ethnic groups as well as across groups.

Ours is a culturally pluralistic society. Cultural pluralism exists in the United States where individual ethnic groups maintain their own cultural uniqueness while sharing common elements of the dominant American culture (Kallen, in Atkinson et al., 1983). Cultural pluralism has been likened to a cultural stew, where "the various ingredients are mixed together but rather than melting into a single mass, the components remain intact and distinguishable while contributing to a whole that is richer than its parts alone" (Atkinson et al., 1983, p. 7). An appreciation of the variety of cultural groups in our society and the contributions that these groups make to society is a vital factor in avoiding ethnocentrism.

Ethnocentrism refers to the situation where the values of the dominant culture are considered to be more important than those of minority group cultures (Atkinson et al., 1983). Differences in culture are not necessarily good or bad, better or worse. People born into a minority culture are not culturally deprived or disadvantaged; they simply have a different culture.

The term *minority* also needs some clarification because it is not always used in the most literal sense. Nonwhites in South Africa are often referred to as a minority group even though they comprise more than 80 percent of the population (Atkinson et al., 1983, p. 7). In the United States, women are often referred to as being a minority group even though statistically they make up more than one-half of the population. The term *minority,* then, includes more than a numerical base. Wirth (in Atkinson et al., 1983) defines minority as

> a group of people who, because of physical or cultural characteristics, are singled out from the others in society in which they live for differential and unequal treatment, and who therefore regard themselves as objects of collective discrimination. (p. 8)

This definition of a cultural group includes a special factor, that of being oppressed in some way by a dominant cultural group. Sue (1981) notes that "the history of minority groups in the United States is the history of oppression" (p. 11). This knowledge and awareness can be applied by a counselor working with a culturally different client when the client's problem might be, at least in part, attributable to sociopolitical circumstances rather than some personal failing on the client's part. The counselor in such a case might assume the role of an advocate on the client's behalf.

Attaining greater awareness of the differences between and similarities among people and learning how to work with these differences are the main objectives of this chapter. We describe approaches to the study of culture, barriers to cross-cultural counseling, and characteristics of culturally skilled counselors in terms of beliefs, attitudes, and values (self-awareness), knowledge, and skills. As Lee (1984) stated,

> the challenge for people wanting to be sensitive to cultural pluralism in counseling and guidance settings is to become aware of their own values, acquire knowledge of the cultural groups they are exposed to, and learn those delivery systems and helping strategies that are applicable or designed for those groups. This task is by no means an easy or quick one. It will take a certain degree of courage to venture outside of one's habitual ways of construing and interpreting events. (p. 592)

Lee (1984) has described counseling in America as "an institution created to meet the problem of individual identity and direction in a pluralistic society" (p. 595). The profession is a reflection of the dominant cultural values of our society, values such as individuality, self-direction, and personal responsibility. It also is a profession that was developed and dominated primarily by white middle-class males. When working with people from different cultural backgrounds, it is important to remember that their experiences, perceptions, values, and view of the world may be distinctly different. A counselor's task is not to be a missionary and try, for example, to convert clients to a belief in individualism if their predisposition is toward a family and group-oriented society, such as in Chinese populations.

The challenge for counselors in training is to learn to work with all types of clients. This learning begins with the awareness that

> even though our cultural structures are based on the belief that personhood is found in individual choice this is not necessarily absolute truth and normative. Nor does this belief necessarily accompany development toward modernity. Other cultures are very modern in some respects but retain what Americans consider to be old fashioned or traditional concepts in other arenas. (Lee, 1984, p. 595)

The Japanese employers' loyalty to their employees can be seen as one example of how a modern nation may have some seemingly old-fashioned ideas.

STAGES IN THE DEVELOPMENT OF CROSS-CULTURAL AWARENESS

The Five-Stage Model

At some time in the course of psychosocial development, people become aware of their position in relation to that of other people of different race or ethnicity. Christensen (1989) formulated a five-stage model for both majority and minority individuals based on the assumption that majority and minority group members go through parallel, but somewhat different stages in developing cross-cultural awareness. She identifies the five stages as unawareness, beginning awareness, conscious awareness, consolidated awareness, and transcendent awareness. The transitions from one stage to another are marked by one or more unexpected identifiable experiences or events.

Individuals in the unawareness stage have never seriously thought about cultural, racial, or ethnic differences and are unaware of their implications toward society. In the beginning awareness stage there is a growing sense of uneasiness as individuals for the first time examine issues relative to various groups. In the third stage, conscious awareness, there is a preoccupation with matters relating to injustice, inequality, and oppression. There is an incongruence with regard to handling new knowledge and feelings about racism and inequality and one's role in it. People in stage four have full knowledge and awareness of the differences in social status, life chances, and treatment of minorities. In the process, they are more accepting of themselves and dissimilar groups. Finally, in stage five individuals are able to identify with all of humankind and transcend societal dictates regarding cultural, racial, and ethnic groups. It would seem that all counselors should be striving to reach stage five.

The Etic-Emic Continuum

Two approaches to the study of culture and the developing of cross-cultural awareness are the etic and the emic approaches (Lee, 1984). In the etic approach, culture is studied and understood in terms of how it differs from or is similar to other cultures on shared dimensions such as family functions. The culture is examined from an external viewpoint. In the emic approach, a culture is studied from within the system. Comparisons are made to internal structures and not to external systems or theories. The emic approach sees culture as a phenomenon to be understood from a position within the system, whereas the etic view is that cultural differences are "really only surface variations of underlying structures shared by all people" (Lee, 1984, p. 593). A counselor, then, wishing to learn more about Native Americans could take the emic approach and become directly immersed in their culture by living on an Indian reservation. Another counselor might take the etic approach to learning about Native Americans by making a comparative study of their economic, political, social, and religious characteristics.

Lee points out that the process of

> gaining knowledge about another country is analogous to the process of getting to know a client. A counselor, rather than assuming that the categories used to make sense out of his or her experience are applicable to all people (etic) or that another person's experience and model of the world are so unique that there are no points of contact (emic), should settle somewhere in between in order to relate to another person. (p. 593)

Theoretical approaches gravitate toward different ends of the etic-emic continuum. Freudian psychoanalysis and Ellis's rational-emotive therapy tend toward the etic pole, with concepts that are postulated to apply to everybody, and neurolinguistic programming (Bandler & Grinder, 1975) favors the emic pole. In developing an allegiance to a theory of counseling, a student might want to be wary of theories that make rather firm judgments of behavior of people across all cultures.

BARRIERS IN CROSS-CULTURAL COUNSELING

Atkinson et al. (1983) suggest that the primary barrier to effective cross-cultural counseling may be the traditional counseling role itself, being nonegalitarian, office bound, and using the intrapsychic model (see description below). Feelings of helplessness and low self-esteem may only be heightened in minority clients who experience the traditional approach to counseling.

The idea that the counselor and client must have shared similar experiences to be effective does not appear to be a major barrier since there is no conclusive evidence to support this contention. "While cultural differences do result in unique experiences for both the client and the counselor, our experiences as human beings are remarkably similar" (Atkinson et al., 1983, pp. 26–27). What is of critical importance is how counselors perceive and respond to the differences. Assumptions, misperceptions, and inappropriate responses can create barriers and destroy therapeutic relationships.

The Intrapsychic Approach

A major concern in cross-cultural counseling is the predominant intrapsychic view that assumes that clients' problems are due to personal disorganization rather than to some dysfunction within the institution or the society (Belkin, 1984). An example of this is the child from a minority group who has been diagnosed as hyperactive in a traditional school classroom, but behaves normally when placed in an open, less structured classroom.

Traditional counseling approaches overemphasize intrapsychic processes, resulting "in the misperception that no matter how well a person copes or works at a problem, if the problem is not resolved, the help recipient probably could do more by assuming more responsibility for her fate" (Ohlsen, 1983, p. 214). Many clients, particularly the disadvantaged and children, generally have such environmental control over them that they are not able to change easily in constructive ways. The role of the counselor in such cases may change from that of being a facilitator assisting the client in problem solving, to that of a change agent, working to modify the environment in which the client lives. The counselor may, in the example given above, arrange to have a child moved from a traditional classroom to a classroom that is more appropriate for the child's learning style.

As a change agent, a counselor may work to confront and modify institutional bureaucracies and also work "directly with majority clients in an attempt to move them toward the goal of reducing racism, sexism, and other discriminatory attitudes toward minorities" (Atkinson et al., 1983, p. 240). A particular type of change agent is the ombudsman, a role originating in Europe, where the practitioner is paid to protect the citizens against bureaucratic policies and procedures. Some attempts to put this idea into practice in America have occurred in colleges and universities, with the practitioner being recognized as a student advocate. The idea of the counselor as an advocate for the client changes the conventional view of the counselor as a guide helping clients solve their personal problems. Judgments as to how much responsibility should be taken away from the client need to be made. One main issue in the lives of culturally different clients has been external oppression, which has left them with a feeling of helplessness. Having a counselor act on the client's behalf could continue this feeling of helplessness and may foster a sense of dependence on the counselor. Yet there are times when action must be taken, such as when any child is being physically abused by a parent.

Some additional areas of concern that can interfere with effective cross-cultural counseling include class-bound values, culture-bound values, and language. Each of these is described in turn.

Class-Bound Values

The values held within a socioeconomic class can dramatically affect the counseling relationship and result in faulty diagnoses and ineffective treatment. Lower socioeconomic class people may be less time-oriented, are often late for appointments, may be motivated more by immediate, concrete reinforcement than by delayed gratification and planning for the future. They may be more survival-oriented than searching for self-actualization. Research surveyed by Sue (1981) indicates that lower-class clients receive inferior treatment and are more likely to be diagnosed as having mental illness than middle-class clients.

Personal awareness of class-bound values may be of particular importance, since it is as difficult to counsel clients in a different socioeconomic class as it is across cultures. An upper-middle-class black person may experience frustration in trying to counsel a lower-class black who is unwilling to change self-destructive behaviors. A middle-class white counselor may have difficulty working with a white teen-aged mother who is on welfare and who is trying to find additional sources of government support. In either case, the counselors may try to have the clients adopt the more middle- or upper-middle-class values without working from within the framework of the clients' value structures. In either case, the clients may have no desire to change their values. They may just want to know how to survive more effectively within their own cultural group.

Culture-Bound Values

Cultural differences found in counseling settings include the amount of time necessary to establish a deep personal relationship, not feeling comfortable disclosing very deep personal thoughts and feelings to a virtual stranger in a temporary relationship, having different ideas of what is meant by psychological well being or mental health, and not knowing how to deal with personal problems. Most counseling theories emphasize the analytical, verbal left brain functions, which clashes with the world views and philosophies of many cultural groups. When Native Americans undergo counseling with traditional counselors, the approaches used may violate their basic philosophy of life (Sue, 1981, p. 41). Table 16.1 is an example of culturally bound differences between Native Americans and representatives of the dominant U.S. culture, labeled Anglos. Similar charts could be devised for every identifiable cultural group compared with other groups. It is not realistic to expect a counselor to be aware of the cultural differences of all the cultural groups in the United States. However, it is reasonable to expect that counselors be familiar with differences within groups that they work with on a regular basis. An Asian-American counselor working with a Hispanic community should understand and appreciate the cultural values of that particular group. In some cases, where the differences in cultural values are too great, referrals to counselors of the same cultural group may be necessary. Some advocates suggest that clients should go only to counselors with the same background. Women should go to women counselors; blacks should go to black counselors. According to Atkinson et al. (1983), there is no evidence that this practice improves counseling outcomes. One interesting approach, in terms of preventive counseling, has been the training of members of a specific cultural group such as an Indian tribe in counseling skills to use with their own people.

A major cultural barrier to counseling is that many culturally diverse groups view counseling and psychology as threats to their continued existence (Pedersen & Marsella, 1982). The fear is that the minority group will be indoctrinated

TABLE 16.1 Differences in Indian [Native American] and Anglo Values

Indians [Native Americans]	Anglos
1. Happiness—this is paramount! Be able to laugh at misery; life is to be enjoyed	1. Success—generally involving status, security, wealth, and proficiency
2. Sharing—everything belongs to others, just as Mother Earth belongs to *all* people	2. Ownership—indicating preference to own an outhouse rather than share a mansion
3. Tribe and extended family first before self	3. "Think of Number One!" syndrome
4. Humble—causing Indians to be passive-aggressive, gentle head hangers, and very modest	4. Competitive—believing "If you don't toot your own horn then who will?"
5. Honor your elders—they have wisdom	5. The future lies with the youth
6. Learning through legends; remembering the great stories of the past; that's where the knowledge comes from	6. Learning is found in school; get all the schooling you possibly can because it can't be taken away from you
7. Look backward to traditional ways—the old ways are the best ways; they have been proved	7. Look to the future to things new—"Tie Your Wagon to a Star and Keep Climbing Up and Up"
8. Work for a purpose—once you have enough then quit and enjoy life, even if for just a day	8. Work for a retirement—plan your future and stick to a job, even if you don't like it
9. Be carefree—time is only relative. Work long hours if happy. Don't worry over time: "I'll get there eventually"	9. Be structured—be most aware of time. "Don't put off until tomorrow what you have to do today." Don't procrastinate
10. Discrete—especially in dating. Be cautious with a low-key profile	10. Flout an openness—"What you see is what you get." Be a "Fonz" character
11. Religion is the universe	11. Religion is individualistic
12. Orient yourself to the land	12. Orient yourself to a house, a job
13. Be a good listener—and it is better if you use your ears and listen well	13. Look people in the eye—don't be afraid to establish eye contact. It's more honest
14. Be as free as the wind	14. Don't be a "boat rocker"
15. Cherish your memory—remember the days of your youth	15. Don't live in the past—look ahead. Live in the here-and-now
16. Live with your hands—manual activity is sacred. "Scratch an Indian—you'll find an artist." (Na-	16. Live with your mind—think intelligently. Show the teacher how well you know the answers to questions

(continued)

TABLE 16.1 Continued

Indians [Native Americans]	*Anglos*
tives are also intelligent)	he/she might ask of you. Good at books
17. Don't criticize your people	17. A critic is a good analyst
18. Don't show pain—be glad to make flesh sacrifices to the Spirits	18. Don't be tortured—don't be some kind of a masochistic nut
19. Cherish your own language and speak it when possible	19. You're in America; speak English
20. Live like the animals; the animals are your brothers and sisters	20. "What are you—some kind of an animal? A Pig or a Jackass?"
21. Children are a gift of the Great Spirit to be shared with others	21. "I'll discipline my own children; don't you tell me how to raise mine!"
22. Consider the relative nature of a crime, the personality of the individual, and the conditions. "The hoe wasn't any good anyway"	22. The law is the law! "To steal a penny is as bad as to steal 10,000! Stealing is stealing! We can't be making exceptions."
23. Leave things natural as they were meant to be	23. "You should have seen it when God had it all alone!"
24. Dance is an expression of religion	24. Dance is an expression of pleasure
25. There are no boundaries—it all belongs to the Great Spirit "Why should I fence in a yard?"	25. Everything has a limit—there must be privacy. "Fence in your yard and keep them off the grass!"
26. Few rules are best. The rules should be loosely written and flexible	26. Have a rule for every contingency. "Write your ideas in detail"
27. Intuitiveness	27. Empiricism
28. Mystical	28. Scientific
29. Be simple—eat things raw and natural. Remember your brother the Fox and live wisely	29. Be sophisticated—eat gourmet, well prepared, and seasoned. Be a connoisseur of many things
30. Judge things for yourself	30. Have instruments judge for you
31. Medicine should be natural herbs, a gift of Mother Earth	31. Synthetic medicines—"You can make anything in today's laboratories"
32. The dirt of Mother Earth on a wound is not harmful but helpful (Sun Dance, mineral intake)	32. Things must be sterile and clean, not dirty and unsanitary
33. Natives are used to small things, and they enjoy fine detail (Indian fires)	33. Bigness has become a way of life with the white society (compulsion for bigness)

Indians [Native Americans]	Anglos
34. Travel light, get along without	34. Have everything at your disposal
35. Accept others—even the drinking problem of another Indian	35. Persuade, convince and proselytize—be an evangelist/missionary
36. The price is of no concern	36. "You only get what you pay for!"
37. Enjoy simplifying problems	37. "Nothing in this world is simple."

D. W. Sue, *Counseling the Culturally Different*. Copyright © 1981 by John Wiley & Sons, Inc. Reprinted by permission of John Wiley & Sons, Inc.

to become more like the dominant cultural group. This barrier may be the most difficult one for counselors to deal with successfully.

Language Barriers

Verbal interaction is crucial in developing a therapeutic relationship as we have described it; however, it cannot be developed effectively if counselor and client are not able to understand each other. A counselor who speaks only English, no matter how well-intentioned or skilled in therapeutic techniques, will have a difficult time developing a working, therapeutic relationship with a client who speaks only Spanish. Even within languages there are great differences. A middle-class black counselor may have difficulty understanding the street talk of a lower-class black student. A Spanish-speaking person of Puerto Rican descent may have difficulty understanding a migrant Mexican-American worker in California. A deaf client using sign language will require either a translator or a counselor trained also in the use of sign language. A client's language, if not clearly understood by the counselor, may lead to erroneous interpretations, faulty diagnoses, and negative outcomes.

One reason for the emphasis on the inner-viewing process advocated in this text is that it stresses the task of the counselor to relate to clients from their frame of reference and in their language. This requires that the counselor be direct and ask a client what is meant by a given word or phrase. One of the authors was told by a Hispanic client that a relative had "bought the farm." Even though the idea seemed clear in terms of the context, the client was asked directly what he meant by that. The client responded, "My uncle committed suicide." Asking for clarification in such instances can have beneficial effects, in addition to the obvious one of mutual understanding. The counselor is presented as a person, as opposed to an omniscient, omnipotent being. When the client is able to educate the counselor, an egalitarian relationship results. This demonstrates that the client has abilities and resources and minimizes the potential development of a dependency relationship.

PROBLEMS AND ISSUES IN CROSS-CULTURAL COUNSELING

Cross-cultural counseling is still relatively new and in a state of flux. It lacks a solid identity and a coherent conceptual framework. Even though most counselor educators and practitioners seem to acknowledge its importance, there is little agreement on many issues.

Counseling Decisions Affected by Cultural Factors

Cultural differences can affect the decisions and outcomes of counseling interventions, including diagnosis and treatment. Diagnostic systems such as the DSM III-R (see chapter 17) are not readily transferable to other cultures (Ahia, 1984). They may not even be appropriate for all subcultures within our society. This is evidenced by the removal of homosexuality as a mental illness from the DSM III (American Psychiatric Association, 1980), when earlier editions had categorized it as such. Because of cultural differences in regard to self-disclosure, clients may be diagnosed as "resistant," "suspicious," or even "paranoid" when they are responding in a way that is culturally appropriate for them (Sue, 1981).

Testing is another area of concern. Tests developed in the United States to measure personality and other psychological characteristics are not necessarily transferable across cultures (Ahia, 1984). Even in our society, the results of tests used for educational placement, for example, may be invalid if the client is unable to read the language or understand the instructions and questions. Even if the language is the same, there may be differences in cultural meanings. For many years now there has been great interest in developing culture-free and culture-fair tests, but with little yet to report in the way of major breakthroughs.

Lack of Theories, Approaches, and Research

Little attention is given to the development of theories or a theory of cross-cultural counseling. Present counselors of culturally different populations use standard counseling theory geared for white U.S. residents without taking cultural factors into consideration (Jackson, 1987). The field itself is expanding rapidly, with a sharp increase in the number of articles on the subject in professional journals (Ponterotto & Benesch, 1988; Heath, Neimeyer, & Pedersen, 1988). However, there is much disagreement regarding which direction cross-cultural counseling should take and on other issues.

Pedersen (1988) reports that due to the complexity of the subject there is a lack of empirical research in the field of cross-cultural counseling. There is also a lack of consensus as to what emphasis the research should have. Much of the emphasis across cultures has been on abnormal rather than on normal behavior and on symptoms rather than on interactions among people, professional institutions, and community. The research has failed to address the practical concerns of program development, service delivery, and treatment techniques. Finally, there has not been enough interdisciplinary collaboration. Each discipline seems to be protecting its own insulated perspective.

Cross-Cultural Counselor Training

In light of growing cultural diversity that characterizes the U.S. population, increased attention has been given to the training of counselors in cross-cultural skills. In a Delphi poll that looked at the future of cross-cultural counseling (Heath, Neimeyer, & Pedersen, 1988) a panel of 53 experts in cross-cultural counseling predicted large increases in the number of cross-cultural training programs, workshops, and practica tailored specifically to cross-cultural counseling. Many writers in the field, however, remain skeptical of the quality of cross-cultural counseling provided in most counseling programs (Merta, Stringham, & Ponterotto, 1988).

Along with this increase in training programs are major criticisms leveled at cross-cultural counselor training, in addition to the criticism that present multicultural counseling approaches use standard counseling theories without making any adjustments for cultural differences. One concern is the emphasis on differences in cultural groups. Some critics argue that an overemphasis on cultural differences can create negative consequences, such as the creation of renewed forms of racism or sexism. Lloyd (1987) states, ''an approach to multicultural counseling that emphasizes the differences between groups and attempts to teach simplistic views of cultural traits, characteristics, and beliefs does not seem to be the type of instruction that should be part of teacher education or counselor education'' (p. 167). Other critics are concerned that counselors who are overly intent on focusing on the cultural characteristics of clients will forget about their humanness as individuals. Focusing on differences, some criticize, fosters a situation in which the impression is that minority clients are so different from majority counselors that only highly trained cross-cultural counselors with wisdom and patience far in excess of the ordinary or only clients from the same cultural group can counsel minority clients.

Other critics argue that focusing on differences makes counselors self-conscious and defensive and therefore likely to avoid multicultural issues and minority clients. Counselors might become overwhelmed trying to familiarize themselves with the numerous cultural groups and the many differences between and within these groups. Parker's (1987) answers to many of these criticisms could readily apply to all counselors in all settings:

> Counselors in multicultural settings need to be open and flexible and should be ready to change their approach to meet the needs of the clients they are attempting to serve. Counselors need to be cautious about taking rigid positions on the likeness versus difference dichotomy. We human beings are alike and we are different. The complexity of human beings does not always give us the luxury of taking an either-or position. (p. 180)

Many experts in the field of cross cultural counseling (e.g., Pedersen, 1988; Merta, Stringham, & Ponterotto, 1988; and Parker, Valley, & Geary, 1986) counter many of these criticisms by advocating a multifaceted approach for training students to work with ethnic minority clients. This training involves the assessment of cultural knowledge, reading ethnic literature, engaging in multicultural action planning, and making small group presentations.

Das and Littrell (1989) advance several conclusions and recommendations for counselor training programs. Among those are the belief that problems often stem from clients' sociocultural environment, and therefore knowledge of clients' cultural background should broaden counselors' awareness and increase understanding of their clients and their clients' problems. They recommend that students acquire a broad and sophisticated understanding of how culture shapes the values and behaviors of all people, not only the culturally different. One means of accomplishing this is for counselor educators to provide numerous opportunities for students to counsel clients from diverse cultures. They also advocate that students be ready to challenge the strong set of Western assumptions that permeate counseling theories and techniques when meeting clients from other cultures who may not share the counselor's assumptions, expectations, or approach to counseling. This may require modification of certain skills. For example, attending skills may not be suitable for all individuals within a culture.

A MULTICULTURAL APPROACH TO COUNSELING

In the broadest sense, counselors must think in terms of being oriented to a multicultural or pluralistic approach to working with clients. It would be virtually impossible to find a counseling position in which all clients were of the same sex, race, religion, socioeconomic level, ethnic background, and value system as the counselor. Therefore, it is important to know something about personality attributes, sociohistorical perspectives, and lifestyle characteristics of clients who have different cultural backgrounds. In effect, this means not to take anything or anybody for granted.

Cross-cultural counseling can be defined as any counseling relationship in which counselors and clients differ with respect to cultural background, values, and lifestyle. These differences and similarities may be either real or perceived. For example, white people in the United States are more culturally similar to blacks than to white Russians, although whites and blacks in the United States may not always perceive this (Jackson, 1987).

> Therefore, whether counseling is, in fact, cross-cultural depends on real and perceived cultural differences and similarities in the helping relationship. If the counselor and client perceive mutual cultural similarity, even though in reality they are culturally different, the interaction should not be labeled cross-cultural counseling. If on the other hand, the counselor and client are culturally similar but *perceive* each other as culturally different, then the interaction may be described as cross cultural. (Jackson, 1987, p. 22)

"In measurement terms, the [perceived] degree of counselor-client similarity or dissimilarity in terms of cultural background, values and lifestyles would be the key determinants in discussing cross-cultural counseling" (Atkinson et al., 1983, p. 262). A culturally skilled counselor, according to Sue et al. (1982), has certain characteristics in respect to beliefs and attitudes, knowledge, and skills.

Beliefs/Attitudes (Self-Awareness). In order to work effectively with cross-cultural clients, counselors and counselors-in-training need to be aware of "how their attitudes and personality styles may influence how they behave with [culturally different] clients" (Ohlsen, 1983, p. 220). We return here to a theme struck early in chapter 1: the counselor's having a solid base of personal knowledge. Without this personal awareness of our beliefs and biases and of how they may differ from others, we may unknowingly impose our values and standards on others and, in fact, engage in cultural oppression ourselves (Sue, 1981). False awarenesses must be changed or corrected before multicultural development can continue (Pedersen, 1988).

Culturally skilled counselors

- have moved from being culturally unaware to being aware and sensitive to their cultural heritage and to valuing and respecting differences;
- are aware of their own values and biases and how they may affect minority clients;
- are comfortable with differences that exist between the counselor and client in terms of race and beliefs; and
- are sensitive to circumstances (personal biases, stages of ethnic identity, sociopolitical influences, etc.) that may dictate referral of minority clients to members of their own culture (Sue et al., 1982).

Knowledge. An important part of the externally derived knowledge that counselors must attain as part of continued growth in the field is specific information relative to the cultural development and values of their clients.

Culturally skilled counselors in the area of knowledge

- will have a good understanding of the sociopolitical system's operation in the United States with respect to its treatment of minorities;
- must possess specific knowledge and information about the particular group they are working with; being aware, for example, of the group's approach to self-disclosure and the group's world view. It may in fact be considered unethical to work with culturally different clients without this type of knowledge (Pedersen & Marsella, 1982);
- must have a clear and explicit knowledge and understanding of the generic characteristics of counseling and therapy; and
- are aware of institutional barriers that prevent minorities from using mental health services (Sue et al. 1982).

Skills. Many skills that counselors need to work with people of different cultural backgrounds are similar to those needed for working with people of like culture.

It is important to emphasize these skills and encourage their continuous development. "Counseling interventions need to be consistent with the life experiences of our culturally different clients. . . . Different cultural groups may require different counseling goals and strategies to be helped effectively" (Sue, 1981). To use the same approach when counseling clients from different cultural backgrounds may be discriminatory.

Culturally skilled counselors

- must be able to generate a wide variety of verbal and nonverbal responses;
- are able to enter the client's frame of reference and understand the client's world view;
- must be able to send and receive both verbal and nonverbal messages accurately and appropriately; and
- are able to exercise institutional intervention skills on behalf of their clients when appropriate (Sue et al., 1982).

The Development of Multicultural Counseling Skills.   It is one thing to delineate the skills necessary for effective multicultural counseling. It is another thing to prescribe an approach that will adequately prepare counselors in all of the competencies listed. Several criteria or objectives that might be included in multicultural counselor training (Copeland, 1982) include:

1. A demonstration of success in working effectively in an environment in which ethnic and racial group problems are explored and alternatives considered.
2. Direct experiences with a variety of culturally different individuals and groups outside of university classrooms, as well as indirect experience through the literature of different groups.
3. Learning to be flexible, both with world views and with the use of traditional counseling practices; being willing to modify and adapt to meet the needs of the client.
4. Awareness and understanding of the current literature in multicultural counseling.
5. The development of attitudes and skills necessary to work with clients of diverse groups.
6. Practice in simulated cross-cultural counseling sessions, and supervision of actual cross-cultural counseling sessions.

Some of these competencies can be developed by students on their own, but there also are several ways by which a counselor education program can ensure their development. There may be a separate course offered on multicultural counseling that could include all of the above objectives. Another approach is to offer one or more areas of specialization, which may include a series of courses. Specializations could include counseling women or counseling Native Americans. A third approach is interdisciplinary, or etic, where courses in anthropology, African-American studies, comparative religions, and political science, among others, are encouraged to provide the broad educational base necessary for understanding other people. The most desirable approach is the integrative model, in which cross-cultural concepts and skills are included as appropriate throughout a counseling program. This has as its greatest advantage the assurance that all students in the program participate in such learning, since the other approaches described have, in the past, at least, tended to be options that only a small percentage of students have taken (Copeland, 1982). Because the area of cross-cultural counseling is now one of the eight areas tested on the National Certified Counselor examination, more and more counselor education programs may be requiring a course in multicultural counseling, or a very carefully developed program throughout which multiculural skills and concepts are systematically included.

Association for Multicultural Counseling and Development.   As part of the recognition of the importance of a multicultural approach to counseling, one major division of the Association of Counseling and Development is the Association for Multi-Cultural Counseling and Development (AMCD). AMCD publishes the *Journal of Multi-Cultural Counseling and Development* and a newsletter.

SUMMARY

Neimeyer and Fukuyama (1984), in their review of cross-cultural counseling literature, concluded that

> it is widely recognized that individuals differ in the cultural attitudes, values, and beliefs that comprise their unique "world views." An appreciation of these differences helps counselors move from an ethnocentric to a more pluralistic perspective, thereby enabling them to adopt more easily the client's perspective. Counselor insensitivity to the differing viewpoints of clients may serve as an impediment to effective counseling. As a result, efforts to enhance the effectiveness of cross-cultural interventions have emphasized the need for counselors to assess their clients' and their own value systems. (p. 216)

In addition to having personal and cross-cultural awareness of value systems, and being comfortable working where differences exist, it is important that counselors be able to understand and appreciate the world view of culturally different clients. Further, knowledge of sociopolitical treatment of minorities may be helpful in developing approaches for assisting clients, knowing that there may be need for some societal changes only, or in addition to personal change on the client's part. Finally, it is important to remember that there is a need for a broad repertoire of interventional skills, with no one approach being suitable for all cultural groups (Sue, 1981).

Culture has been defined to acknowledge that there are culturally diverse groups within larger racial and ethnic groups. Minority groups have been described in terms of their having a history of political oppression, rather than on the basis of group size alone. Ours is a culturally pluralistic society that includes a substantial number of minority groups.

Counselors were encouraged not to study other cultures from only a distance (the etic approach) nor necessarily to immerse themselves totally in a given culture (the emic approach). Their selection of a theoretical approach to counseling should also be selected accordingly.

Barriers to cross-cultural counseling include the traditional counseling role itself, the view that clients' problems are due primarily to something within themselves, language, and values specific to different classes and cultures within the society, including the threat to the continued existence of a given culture.

Cross-cultural counseling is still a relatively new field. There is a lack of research, direction, and a coherent conceptual framework. However, increased attention has been given to training counselors in cross-cultural skills and to major criticisms leveled at cross-cultural counselor training.

Two major counseling practices that are greatly affected by cultural factors are the diagnostic processes; in particular, the use of a standardized instrument such as the DSM III-R, and the use of standardized tests.

A multicultural approach to counseling has been presented that includes specific objectives for the culturally skilled counselor in the areas of beliefs and attitudes, knowledge, and skills. Approaches for the development of these areas of expertise have also been described.

Cross-cultural counseling is recognized as being important for all counselors and is one of the major test areas on the National Certified Counselor examination. The Association for Multi-Cultural Counseling and Development is one division of the American Association for Counseling and Development.

QUESTIONS AND ACTIVITIES

1. What are the characteristics of your own particular cultural background? When did you become aware that you were a black person, a white person, an Asian, a Native American, or Hispanic? How much influence has your racial/ethnic group membership had on you? How much have you affirmed, rejected, accepted, denied, and/or ignored your racial/ethnic identity? Do you have any mixed feelings about or unresolved conflicts with your racial/ ethnic identity?

2. What were the attitudes and feelings of your parents, friends, teachers, and other significant people in your life toward various ethnic minorities as you were growing up? What did they tell you directly? Indirectly? How did these attitudes and feelings influence your current attitudes and feelings? What generalizations do you believe other people currently make about you because of your racial/ethnic identity?

3. Think of your past and current friendships. How many of these friends are/ were ethnic minorities? In what ways, if any, were these friendships different from friendships you have established within your ethnic/racial group? What other experiences have you had with minorities? How do you believe that these experiences will influence you as you try to become the best counselor possible?

CHAPTER 17

Assessment of Individuals

What do tests have to do with counseling?

> *Perilous to us all are the devices of an art*
> *which we do not understand ourselves*
> Gandalf, the white wizard, in *The Lord of The Rings*, J. R. R. Tolkien

Gandalf might be referring to the processes of assessment and diagnosis in counseling. Assessment is one of the most controversial topics in the field. For clients it can mean being observed, tested, evaluated, and labeled in some way. For members of minority groups, it can mean being subjected to culturally biased tests. For counseling students, it can mean taking courses that are heavily laden with mathematical and statistical concepts.

Our approach to the topic of assessment is that it offers a variety of ways for counselors to better understand their clients. A full understanding of assessment concepts and practices is necessary whether we choose to use them or not in our practice. It is necessary for us to communicate with those who do use them, in case conferences, referrals, and correspondence, as well as to understand the professional literature. This chapter outlines the general philosophy and principles of assessment and diagnosis of individuals. Assessment approaches are presented from different theoretical views, followed by a description of instruments and techniques. Finally, basic guidelines for the process and practice of assessment and diagnosis are presented.

BACKGROUND

American society has had mixed attitudes toward assessment and assessment processes. There has been much concern about the possible effects of testing. Some cities, including Los Angeles, have restricted the use of intelligence tests in their schools. In the ranks of counseling professionals, there also has been a great deal of controversy related to the nature and appropriateness of assessment and diagnosis, and the practice of the art itself. Leo Goldman (1972), an expert in the use of tests in counseling, stated, ''There is increased feeling that the use of tests in counseling has been on the whole a sad disappointment and that in recent years matters have actually become worse'' (p. 213).

Sugarman (1978) found that there have been objections to the use of assessment and appraisal techniques on five different grounds:

1. It is reductionistic, reducing the complexity of the person into diagnostic categories.
2. It is artificial.
3. It ignores the quality of the relationship between the examiner and the test taker.
4. It judges people, casting a label on them.
5. It is overly intellectual, relying on complex concepts, often at the expense of a true understanding of the individual.

In 1972, the National Education Association (NEA) advocated a moratorium on the use of standardized tests. At least two states have laws regulating the use of tests (Zytowski, 1982, p. 16). However, such movements have not significantly curtailed the use of tests. In 1982, Engen, Lamb, and Prediger, reporting on the results of test use in secondary schools, found that schools continue to give tests and would do even more testing if more funds were available. The stress on excellence in schools in the early 1980s appears to have resulted in increased emphasis on testing in the schools, with a particular focus on competency testing. In 1985, the NEA reversed its earlier position and came out for competency testing for teachers as well.

Businesses and industries have used tests and inventories to varying degrees for many years, primarily as an aid in the selection of job candidates. Testing has been and continues to be a generally accepted function in mental health centers, state employment offices, and other private and public clinics and agencies.

Tests and their use have not changed significantly since objections were raised in the 1970s and before. Basically, what seems to have changed is the overall attitude of people toward tests. Gallup polls of the general public in the 1980s indicated a general acceptance of the use of standardized tests. Assessment procedures of all types are an accepted part of our contemporary society. To ensure the effective use of these procedures, practitioners in the counseling field need to be well grounded in all aspects of the assessment process.

PURPOSES OF INDIVIDUAL ASSESSMENT

In beginning the study of the assessment process, we first define the process and then indicate many purposes for using assessment procedures. We also note the context in which assessment procedures are generally studied.

Definition of Assessment

''Problem assessment consists of procedures and tools used to collect and process information from which the entire counseling program is developed'' (Cormier & Cormier, 1985, p. 146). Some of the purposes of assessment are:

1. To obtain information on the client's presenting problem and other, related problems.
2. To identify the controlling or contributing variables associated with the problem.
3. To determine the client's goals/expectations for counseling outcomes.
4. To gather baseline data that will be compared with subsequent data to assess client progress and the effect of treatment strategies. This helps the practitioner decide whether to continue or modify the treatment plan.
5. To educate and motivate clients by counselors sharing their views of the problem with them, by increasing their receptivity to treatment, and contributing to therapeutic change through reactivity. Reactivity refers to behavior change that is a consequence of the assessment procedure rather than the result of a particular change strategy.
6. To use the information obtained from the client to plan effective treatment interventions and strategies. The information obtained during the assessment process helps to answer the question: "*What* treatment, by *whom,* is most effective for *this* individual with *that* specific problem and under *which* set of circumstances?" (Paul, 1967, p. 111). (Cormier & Cormier, 1985, pp. 146–147).

It is important to note that the study of individual assessment is not a course in statistics. Many counseling students have approached courses in this area with trepidation and have, in their own mind, labeled courses in tests and measurements, or individual appraisal, as "statistics." Mathematical and statistical terms are involved in the study of assessment techniques, but a basic awareness of such concepts does not constitute an in-depth study of statistics.

The use of mathematical concepts, however, may be enough to unnerve some students who may have been attracted to the field of human services largely because of its relative freedom from mathematics. Generally speaking, there is not a significant amount of emphasis on mathematical concepts in general counseling and consulting work. It is necessary, however, for professionals in the field to know and to understand the technological aspects of the field, even if a counselor or consultant does not regularly use assessment instruments. As practitioners in the field strive to make the profession more scientifically based, it is well to consider that there will be an ever-increasing amount of rigor in terms of assessment, diagnosis, and research. Suggested guidelines for professional preparation in assessment include a basic course in measurement and evaluation; and because such a course does not emphasize statistics, there should also be a course in basic statistics. These courses would be followed by the supervised administration of assessment instruments during practicum and internship courses (Loesch, 1984).

DIAGNOSIS

An ongoing concern in the field of counseling and psychotherapy is whether to make routine, formal diagnoses of every client. Unlike the field of medicine, where such a question would be considered unthinkable, there is a concern in the field of counseling as to the validity of such a practice. In counseling and psychotherapy, the basic issue revolves around at least four different points of view or models that describe the causes of disorders. These include the medical model and the nonmedical models (the behavioristic, the humanistic, and the human services).

The Medical Model

The concept of disease or illness is fundamental to the medical model. In the practice of medicine, a clinical diagnosis of the illness is made, which includes classifying and labeling the disorder. A treatment plan is then formulated and implemented to cure the patient by dealing with the bacterial, viral, or genetic factors that have been scientifically determined to be the causative agents.

A distinction is made between organic and functional disorders. The medical model does not postulate biological or organic causes of mental or psychological disorders.

The organic disorders are caused by physical abnormalities of the brain, nervous system, and other internal systems. Epilepsy, senility, some kinds of retardation, and certain psychotic states are examples of disorders in which some physical abnormality plays a role. Organic disorders may be caused by inherited defects, chemical imbalances, viral infection, malnutrition, and various drugs and poisons. Those associated with physical damage are likely to be long standing, whereas those associated with drugs may represent temporary disorders of brain function.

The functional disorders are due to psychological factors operating within the individual. These include poorly controlled drives and impulses, unrealistic ideas, and unresolved conflicts. Addictions, antisocial tendencies, neuroses, and some psychotic reactions are classified as functional disorders. This means that the major causes are presumed to relate to the personality of the individual rather than to any physical defects. Some disorders such as alcoholism cannot be classified with great confidence because of doubt about the causes (Schmolling, Youkelles, & Burger, 1985, p. 110).

Once a diagnosis has been made and the patient's condition has been labeled, a number of treatment modalities are possible. These include drug therapy to control emotions and behavior. Drugs used may include tranquilizers and antidepressants. Other medical treatments include electroconvulsive or shock therapy and psychosurgery such as a lobotomy, the severing of nerve fibers connecting the frontal lobes from other parts of the brain. The use of tranquilizers has dramatically reduced the need for the number of lobotomies in recent years. Rehabilitation psychotherapy, occupational therapy, and psychotherapy are also used as part of the therapeutic process.

The medical model has been strongly criticized for some time now. In his book *The Myth of Mental Illness* (1973), Szasz maintains that most of what adherents of the model call mental illnesses are not illnesses at all, but rather problems in living manifested by deviations from moral, legal, and social norms. He holds that this is a form of persecution in the guise of treatment that can have the effect of excluding undesirable people from society even though they have committed no crime. Further, to label persons "sick" removes from them the responsibility for their behavior, with the result that they have little chance of recovery. In fact, they may accept the label, consider themselves sick and helpless, and pursue a life as a mental patient.

In addition to the social control that Szasz speaks of, Kovel (1980) points out that what is left out of the assessment process is the effect of environment and society itself. This includes such things as poverty, unemployment, lack of opportunity, and crime. If a person with deviant behavior is treated and cured, have we just made him or her acceptable for what may be, in fact, a sick society?

R. D. Laing, a British psychiatrist who was concerned with extreme disturbances in human communication, with different kinds of families, and with the varieties of human experiences, viewed society as being sick. He stated (1967) that society highly values normal people but that normal people are alienated, asleep, unconscious, and out of their minds. According to Laing, society educates children to become normal by losing themselves and becoming absurd. He contends that normal people have killed perhaps 100,000,000 of their fellow human beings in the period since World War I.

Diagnosis is also seen as a dehumanizing process. The diagnostic label becomes the identity of the person. These labels can actually be harmful to people, affecting their interpersonal relationships, employment opportunities, and even their civil rights. People who have been labeled *psychotic* may, in some states, be hospitalized against their will and lose their legal rights in the process.

Nonmedical Model Approaches

A number of nonmedical approaches generally share the following strategies: (1) avoiding medical terminology, such as patient, diagnosis, symptom, pathology, mental illness, treatment and cure; (2) focusing on factors other than biological ones, such as environmental factors; (3) keeping a significant amount of the responsibility for change with the client.

Some nonmedical approaches and their view of maladaptive behavior include:

1. Behaviorism: inappropriate behavior is learned and can be unlearned.
2. Humanism: abnormal behavior is the result of a lack of self-acceptance and esteem, ill-defined or unrealistic personal goals, and a failure to accept responsibility for inappropriate behaviors (Bootzin, 1980).
3. Human Services Model: society's failure to provide basic needs sometimes results in maladaptive behavior on the part of the deprived.

There are great areas of conflict between the adherents of the medical model and the nonmedical model approaches. These areas of conflict involve issues of power and turf—who can do what in the field of human services? Who can receive third-party payments? Who can be licensed by governments or governmental agencies? At present, psychiatrists have the broadest scope of power and territory in the field of human services. In varying degrees in different states, other professionals, and even paraprofessionals, are increasingly able to participate more fully in the field.

Formal diagnosis in the medical sense, then, is not a regular practice for all professionals in the field. For example, behaviorists, who are not anticipating receiving third-party payments, would generally not make a diagnosis using the diagnostic guidelines given in the *Diagnostic and Statistical Manual of Mental Disorders,* 3rd edition rev., (American Psychiatric Association, 1987), more commonly referred to as the DSM III-R. The behaviorists would focus on behaviors that need to be changed, and a mutual contract might be made between the client and the counselor to modify a given behavior. On the other hand, the use of the DSM III-R as a diagnostic tool would be routine in agencies that require a formal diagnosis and where third-party payments are involved. Behaviorists expecting third-party payments would also make a formal diagnosis. At present, insurance companies and government agencies will generally not make payments for services where a formal diagnosis using the DSM III-R has not been made. The controversial aspect of this practice is that governmental agencies and insurance companies are dictating what the actual practices of helping professionals will be. An additional concern is that third-party providers have access to the records of their clients to monitor diagnoses, treatment plans, and other records, thus jeopardizing the confidential nature of the therapeutic relationship. Only professionals who work with clients who pay their own bills may be able to avoid this dilemma. A brief description of the DSM III-R and how it is used follows.

The DSM III-R: Multiaxial Assessment

The revised version of the third edition of the *Diagnostic and Statistical Manual of Mental Disorders,* 1987, published by the American Psychiatric Association, is the basic instrument used by mental health practitioners in making and reporting formal diagnoses. It is important to be aware of the system and the vocabulary that a great percentage of the people working in the field use, even if one does not use it in practice.

The current diagnostic system is called "multiaxial" because there are five different axes, or areas of functioning, which can be considered when making assessments:

Axis I: Clinical syndromes and conditions not attributable to a mental disorder that are a focus of attention or treatment
Axis II: Developmental disorders and personality disorders
Axis III: Physical disorders and conditions
Axis IV: Severity of psychosocial stressors
Axis V: Global assessment of functioning (GAF)

Scales have been developed to help the clinician make consistent determinations of the severity of the psychosocial stressors (Axis IV) and the global assessment of functioning (GAF) (Axis V). When using the GAF on Axis V, the clinician should record a current determination and an estimate of the highest GAF for the past year.

Extensive descriptions of each syndrome or disorder are provided along with decision trees, which help the practitioner select or rule out various possible disorders. The major advantage in using this multiaxial classification system is that it "ensures that attention is given to certain types of disorders, aspects of the environment, and areas of functioning that might be overlooked if the focus were on assessing a single presenting problem" (American Psychiatric Association, 1987, p. 15).

Thus, rather than give a one- or two-word label to a diagnosed person such as "depressive neurosis," as was the practice prior to the adoption of the DSM III, the practitioner now can come up with a diagnosis such as the following:

Axis I: 296.24 Major depression, single episode; severe without psychotic features
Axis II: 301.60 Dependent personality disorder
Axis III: Diabetes
Axis IV: Psychosocial stressors: separated from spouse; conflicts with children; Severity: 3 – Moderate
Axis V: Current GAF = 44
Highest GAF past year = 55

A great deal of information is then available about a person that can lead to the development of an appropriate treatment plan and improved communication with other professionals who might be involved in the case. The information can also be used in research where associations may be found between factors on the various axes.

DIFFERENT THEORETICAL APPROACHES TO ASSESSMENT

As might be expected from the discussion in chapters 10 and 11 on theoretical points of view, the approaches of practitioners to the problems of assessment may vary significantly with regard to theoretical stance. Following are descriptions of how practitioners from different theoretical outlooks approach client assessment.

Psychoanalytic

Assessment and diagnosis play a major role in the work of psychoanalytic therapists. Such therapists are generally psychiatrists who are fully trained diagnosticians. They may use a variety of objective measures in the assessment process but tend to focus on more of the subjective types of measurement. They believe that conscious data do not tell the real story. Psychoanalysts assess the client's unconscious by techniques such as free association, dream analysis, and the use of projective instruments, such as the Rorschach and the Thematic Apperception Test (TAT). Psychoanalysts make inferences, interpretations, and diagnoses from these data and would then make interventions in line with the theoretical guidelines they follow.

Projective techniques, such as the Rorschach Diagnostic Test, require that clients respond to ambiguous stimuli. These instruments are presented with their basic purpose deliberately concealed from the client. The presupposition is that if the client is able to respond nondefensively, various responses, some of which might be considered unacceptable, can emerge to reveal unconscious aspects of the personality. The responses are then interpreted by the clinician.

Cognitive-Behavioral

Cognitive-behavioral practitioners use a variety of assessment procedures. There are the very explicit behavioral descriptions used by strict behaviorists, and then there is the strategy of assessing client characteristics and traits and making diagnoses on the basis of such data. The latter approach is represented by trait-factor theorists.

Trait-Factor

The trait-factor approach to counseling, classified as a cognitive-behavioral approach by Pietrofesa, Hoffman, and Splete (1984), among others, is the approach most likely to use a variety of assessment instruments. Trait-factor theorists believe that personality characteristics and traits can be objectively measured. At the beginning of the relationship, the counselor is an unabashed diagnostician who works to obtain as much data as is appropriate for the presenting problem, using a variety of instruments.

This counseling approach has been called "directive" because of the active role the counselor takes throughout the process (Shertzer & Stone, 1980, p. 171). Advice-giving, for example, has been one strategy used with this approach. Williamson (1972), however, sees the client as having the final responsibility when decisions are to be made.

Behavioral Counseling

The behavioral approach to assessment and counseling focuses on behaviors that can be operationally defined, observed, and measured as opposed to personality constructs or traits such as self-esteem. Assessment techniques are designed to be part of the process of behavior change.

Ways in which behavior may be measured directly include situational behavior sampling, both verbal and nonverbal, and the physiological measurement of emotional reactions. In behavior sampling, the emphasis is on detailed information concerning the onset, magnitude, and duration of the behaviors of interest and the circumstance of their occurrence. The subject himself may supply this information through various self-report techniques such as daily records, lists of problematic situations, or responses on pre-set survey scales (schedules). (Mischel, 1971, p. 200)

A behavioral counselor would work with the client's statement of the problem and strive to keep the context in behavioral terms. He or she works to have the client's objective or goal stated in terms of specific behavior. For example, a client may want to be able to make a 10-minute speech in front of a class without stuttering. The counselor generally obtains some baseline data about the present nature of the problem, by direct observation, by self-report, or by the report of others. Various approaches to change are then implemented. Some history may be taken in the assessment process to help determine the frequency of an undesired behavior. The time and circumstances of initial onset are noted along with possible events that coincide with the regular onset of the undesired behavior.

Certain behavioral techniques, such as systematic desensitization, would have the client, with the help of the counselor, construct a hierarchy of events or circumstances in a person's life that would range from pleasant (nondisturbing) to very unpleasant (highly disturbing). Most of this information is self-reported by the client. A variety of checklists or survey instruments may be used in this approach, but there is rarely any use of standardized tests.

Humanistic Approaches

In the humanistic-existential view, the clients are their own best assessors.

Research indicates that self-assessment has yielded predictions as accurate as those from more sophisticated personality tests, from combinations of tests, from clinical judgments, and from complex statistical analyses. Thus the person herself may be a good predictor of her own behavior for such diverse outcomes as success in college, in jobs, and in psychotherapy. (Mischel, 1971, p. 221)

In this approach, there is no systematic formal testing or other external measurement. There is no formal diagnosis per se. There is no attempt to learn about the client through paper-pencil tests or other external methods. There is rather an attempt to work with the client directly. Through the exploration and understanding of the client's perceptions of problems, a mutual-diagnosis is reached where both the client and the counselor acknowledge what the problem really is.

This does not preclude the use of test instruments or other devices. In discussing the client-centered approach to assessment, Patterson and Watkins (1981) suggest that when there is information the client needs and wants that might be provided by a test, tests are introduced and the client is encouraged to participate in the selection of appropriate instruments. Any of the variety of assessment instruments described below might be used as needed. In presenting test results, data must be presented as completely and as objectively as possible. The client should make the interpretations and personally ascribe any meaning to the results. The object is to keep the locus of evaluation—the place in which judgments are made—with the client. This is more likely to result in material that is understandable and usable to the client in the pursuit of personal change.

ASSESSMENT TECHNIQUES

Assessment takes place at different levels and with different techniques. Below is an overview of basic techniques used in the field of mental health.

Nonstandardized Assessment Techniques

Counselors use a variety of techniques and procedures in the process of gathering data. These can be highly structured and designed so that each time a procedure is used the process is exactly the same. This is called using a standardized format. A less rigorous but also important way of obtaining information is through the use of nonstandardized instruments. Such procedures may be idiosyncratic, specific only to a given client or set of circumstances, with a minimal chance for replication. A brief description of some nonstandardized formats follows.

Observation

The casual observation of human behavior is one of the most popular pastimes. Many people describe themselves as people watchers, and it is perhaps as a result of this that many enter the field of human services. Observation is the most fundamental assessment procedure. Highly developed skills in the use of other assessment tools are negated if the powers of observation are not well developed. Gibson and Mitchell (1981) describe casual observation and two higher levels in their discussion of the levels of observation:

> *First Level: Casual Information Observation.* The daily unstructured and usually unplanned observations that provide casual impressions. Nearly everyone engages in this type of activity. No training or instrumentation is expected or required.
> *Second Level: Guided Observation.* Planned, directed observations for a purpose. Observation at this level is usually facilitated by simple instruments such as checklists or rating scales. This is the highest level used in most counseling programs. Some training is desired.
> *Third Level: Clinical Level.* Observations, often prolonged, and frequently under controlled conditions. Sophisticated techniques and instruments are utilized with training usually at a doctoral level. (p. 111)

Problems with Observation.   The process of observation is no exception to the rule that because we do something all the time does not mean that we do it well. That is why awareness and training are necessary to be more effective observers.

We need to be aware that our observations of a person or situation may be different from those of others viewing the same scene. Movies like *Roshomon* have documented how this phenomenon can work. It is also important to note that observation can be taken too casually, and that when you may really need a particular piece of data, it isn't always available. The reader, for example, may not know the name of a particular street that is crossed regularly.

> Behavioral observation is common to all psychological approaches. It is the use that is made of the data that distinguishes between approaches. In the psychodynamic orientation behaviors serve as indirect *signs* of hypothesized underlying dispositions and motives. Behavioral approaches treat observed behavior as a *sample,* and the focus is on how the specific sample is affected by variations in the stimulus conditions. (Mischel, 1971, p. 200)

As noted in chapter 3, more than half of the message that a client communicates is nonverbal. It is particularly important that counselors be attuned to all of the nonverbal cues available and note the discrepancies and inconsistencies between these and verbal messages. Specific areas to focus on are listed in chapter 3. All of the senses are the best tools available. This includes "listening with your eyes," "seeing with your ears," "sensing with your entire body," and "listening with the third ear" (Reik, 1948). To supplement your personal "tool collection" and your total "self-as-instrument," there are a number of paper-and-pencil instruments, described below.

Observational Instruments

Formats have been developed to provide assistance in making and recording observations, checklists, rating scales and anecdotal reports. Each of these instruments makes the observations more systematic and provides a record from which changes can be measured.

Checklists.   The purpose of a checklist is to focus the observer's attention to the presence or absence of predetermined characteristics. A simple checkmark indicates whether or not the characteristic was observed. Characteristics may include: _____ 1. Is Punctual; _____ 2. Is able to carry on a sustained conversation.

Rating Scales.   A rating scale is a special kind of checklist on which the observer can note not only the presence of a given characteristic or attribute, but also the degree to which it manifests itself. Rating scales can be particularly helpful in making observations of individuals when they are in a natural setting: at school, at work, or playing in a team sport. Below is an example of an item from a rating scale that can be used in an office setting:

1	2	3	4	5
Never	Rarely	Sometimes	Usually	Always

Takes the lead in asking questions, making suggestions, raising concerns, etc.

The benefits of rating scales and checklists include having an easy-to-use approach for making objective observations. They also offer the possibility of comparing the observations of more than one observer using identical criteria. There are also some limitations in the use of such instruments, including (1) poor and unclear directions for the scales' use; (2) a failure to define terms adequately; (3) limited scales for rating; (4) items that tend to prejudice how one responds; (5) overlapping items; and (6) excessive length (Gibson & Mitchell, 1981, p. 118). Additional limitations include ratings made without sufficient observations; giving higher ratings than may be accurate; middle rating, playing it safe by giving a middle or average rating to everyone on every item; and biased ratings, where an observer's bias on an item may affect the observer's responses on other items.

In addition to being used as instruments for recording ongoing observations of clients, counselors can use checklists and rating scales for making recommendations, such as indicating a student's potential for success in graduate school, and as part of evaluations, for example, rating a counselor's ability to work with adolescent clients. This format is also used in certain types of measures of client attitudes and interests.

Anecdotal Reports.   Anecdotal reports are subjective descriptions of a client's behavior at a specific time or for a specific situation. These reports generally start out by noting the time, date, and place. This is followed by a general description of the event and the manner in which the client participated in it. It ends with observer comments that may be evaluative in nature.

Anecdotal observations made over a period of time can be helpful in providing a fuller picture of a client's behavior than can responses on a checklist or rating-scale. Because of its subjective nature, however, observer bias can be an important factor and needs to be noted and acknowledged. The more the observer is trained to note and record specific behaviors and to keep the reporting of behaviors separate from interpretations and evaluations, the more valuable the anecdotal observations.

Self-Report Instruments

In making an assessment of an individual, the most direct source of information is the client. More systematic forms of obtaining information than simply letting the clients tell stories include questionnaires, structured interviews, open-ended questions, autobiographies, and self-descriptions. Some of these forms are discussed here.

Questionnaires.   Questionnaires are a common type of nonstandardized instrument for data-gathering. They can be short enough to be filled out by a client a few minutes before the first visit to a counselor. They can be designed to provide a variety of data. Questionnaires can be used to collect vital information to determine the counseling or consulting needs of groups or organizations. This information-seeking is often included as part of a larger process called a needs assessment. Here the desired objectives or goals of a person, group, or organization are determined. Questionnaires can also be used to obtain feedback on the results of counseling and consulting.

A special form of the questionnaire format consists primarily of incomplete sentences that the client is expected to complete. The sentences can be designed, for example, to bring out affective responses, such as "When I get angry, I . . .", or "People can tell when I am happy, because . . .". Responses to such questions help a counselor compare observations with client statements and can lead to other productive areas, such as dealing with the inability to communicate emotions directly or difficulty in handling negative feelings.

Structured Interviews. A structured interview is a form of questionnaire that is read to a client by a counselor. The client is encouraged to respond as directly as possible to all questions, and the counselor has the opportunity to ask for clarification or elaboration of any question. Such an interview may be required of all first-time clients to a mental health agency as part of a case management process. One purpose is to assign the client to the staff member or program that best meets the needs of the client. Another type of structured interview focuses on a specific issue or syndrome, such as depression or alcoholism, and the questions are designed to highlight related aspects of behavior. Careful records, including tape recordings, are generally made in the case of structured interviews to be sure that all comments are noted and that nonverbal behaviors are also included.

Personal Essays and Autobiographies. More extensive written material such as having a client write a personal essay on a given topic (for example, "the kind of job that I believe I would enjoy the most") is another way to provide useful data in a short time and would generally be given as a homework assignment. A more elaborate version of the personal essay is to have the client write an autobiography. The type of material included as well as the areas not covered can provide significant data to work with in a counseling relationship.

Journals. Having a client keep a journal on a regular basis, noting new issues, changes, and so on, provides another method of obtaining self-report data on an ongoing basis. A journal is more than a diary or log of daily events. It is an opportunity to record thoughts and feelings, to make sketches, doodle, and write poems without having to worry about being evaluated. A client can share all or part of a journal at various times during therapy. Major advantages in having clients keep a journal are that it helps them become better observers of their own behavior and better communicators about issues of concern. A specialized version of the journal is a dream journal, which can be used as material to explore during a counseling session.

Standardized Assessment Techniques

The types of assessment procedures described above are labeled nonstandardized. A number of techniques were presented that were generally idiosyncratic and unsystematic. The same person using any one of these techniques would quite likely not use the technique exactly the same way each time.

There is also a need for assessment devices that can be administered in a consistent manner to a wide number of people. We now have a wide variety of tests, usually published instruments, that are standardized. A standardized test is one that has detailed, specific directions for the administration of the instrument, including the exact words with which to introduce the instrument to the client, and time limits, if any. The procedures for scoring are also specifically detailed so that all people scoring a given test will record results in the same manner. There are two basic categories of standardized tests: norm-referenced and criterion-referenced.

Norm-Referenced Tests

A further characteristic of most published instruments is that they have norms. Norms, or normative tables, are generally included in the manual accompanying published tests. These tables provide data on the performance of various groups of people taking the same instrument during the period of time when the test was being developed. The results of a newly administered test can be compared immediately to those of a peer group (for example, ninth-grade boys). Norm groups are often nationwide samples, but they can also be regional or local. A great deal of time and effort goes into the preparation of published standardized instruments. Various test items are carefully tested and analyzed before being included in the final instrument. The reliability or consistency of scores and the instrument's validity are also determined, with related data included in the manual of the published instrument. Finally, many tests are the subjects of research projects and related evaluative studies that often lead to revised editions after a period of time.

Criterion-Referenced Tests

Whereas the results of a norm-referenced test allow us to compare a client's score with an appropriate norm group, the results give little information with regard to a specific skill level. A criterion-referenced test is a test that is "used to ascertain an individual's status with respect to a well-defined behavioral domain" (Popham, 1978, p. 93). "A domain of behaviors consists of a set of skills or dispositions that examinees display when called on to do so in a testing situation. For example, a behavioral domain in the field of mathematics might consist of an individual's ability to solve a certain class of simultaneous equation problems" (p. 94). A well-constructed criterion-referenced test yields a clear description of what a client can or cannot actually do. Properly constructed competency or achievement tests can serve as examples of criterion-referenced tests. A test can be both criterion- and norm-referenced.

Types of Standardized Instruments

Assessment instruments have been developed to measure virtually all aspects of the human person. Published standardized instruments are generally catalogued and reviewed in a series of volumes entitled the *Mental Measurement Yearbook* (Buros, 1978), updated editions of which are published every few years. In this yearbook, critical reviews of the various instruments are published along with a description of each instrument. Some of the basic standardized assessment instrument classifications are achievement and aptitude (intelligence) tests, personality inventories, attitude questionnaires, interest inventories, and projective techniques.

Achievement Tests.   Achievement tests are designed to assess what a person has learned in a given subject such as music, mathematics, or German as a result of a specific curricular experience. The instrument can be designed specifically for one subject or can include a variety of subjects. Examples of the latter type of instrument are the Iowa Tests of Basic Skills and the Metropolitan Achievement Tests.

Aptitude (Intelligence) Tests.   A test used as a predictor of some future performance is called an aptitude test (Thorndike & Hagen, 1977). Aptitude tests are designed to measure the propensity to perform certain tasks that may not already be a part of a person's repertoire. Aptitude tests can be considered a form of ability testing, measuring the potential ability that a person has in a specific area. Intelligence tests can be considered measures of general ability. As discussed in chapter 15, there is no generally agreed-on definition of intelligence. However, most intelligence tests are designed to be indicators of ability to be successful in school.

Some examples of aptitude tests are the Differential Aptitude Test (DAT), the Aptitude Classification Test (ACT), and the Scholastic Aptitude Test (SAT). Examples of intelligence tests include the Stanford-Binet Intelligence Scale and the Wechsler Adult Intelligence Scale-Revised (WAIS-R).

Personality Assessment Instruments

Even though a person's personality includes everything about that person, distinctions have been made so that assessing human abilities such as aptitude and intelligence has been distinguished from the study of other dimensions of the personality. Thorndike and Hagen (1977) describe several characteristics of personality, other than abilities, that can be identified and assessed, including temperament, character, adjustment, interests, and attitudes.

- *Temperament* refers to an individual's characteristic mood, activity level, excitability, and focus of concern. It includes such dimensions as cheerful-gloomy, energetic-lethargic, excited-calm, introverted-extroverted, and dominant-submissive.
- *Character* relates to those traits to which definite social value is attached. They are the "Boy Scout" traits of honesty, kindliness, cooperation, industry, and so on.
- *Adjustment* indicates how well the individual has been able to make peace internally and with the surrounding world. The individual is considered

well-adjusted to the extent that she can accept herself and to the extent that her way of life does not get her in trouble with her social group.

- *Interests* refer to tendencies to seek out and participate in certain activities.
- *Attitudes* relate to tendencies to favor or reject particular groups of individuals, sets of ideas, or social institutions. (Thorndike & Hagen, 1977, pp. 394–395)

A variety of approaches have been used to assess each personality characteristic or dimension described above. A brief description of some of these approaches follows.

Attitude Questionnaires.   Attitude questionnaires are designed to assess the intensity of a person's sentiments with regard to a specific subject such as women's liberation, abortion, or gun control. Attitude questionnaires are relatively easy to create and as a result are probably encountered more often by the general public than are most other assessment devices. Politicians, for example, often use questionnaires to determine voter sentiment toward various political issues. The Gallup poll research organization regularly surveys the general public on a variety of issues, and the results are often published in newspapers and journals.

An attitude questionnaire generally takes the form of a series of statements related to a given topic to which the respondent is to make one of five choices: strongly agree, agree, strongly disagree, disagree, or undecided. The respondent may be asked the questions or may respond on paper to a written series of statements (see Figure 17.1).

A major limitation of questionnaires is their low reliability. The responses people make to the statements on a questionnaire may not correspond to their actions. For example, students in a school may indicate a favorable attitude to-

Attitude toward Counseling

Read each statement. Then circle the symbol that best represents your reaction to the statement according to the following scale:

        A — Strongly agree with the statement
        a — Tend to agree with the statement
        ? — Undecided. Neither agree or disagree
        d — Tend to disagree with the statement
        D — Strongly disagree with the statement

A a ? d D 1. If I had a personal problem that I wanted to talk about with someone, I would go to the school counselor.

A a ? d D 2. Counselors can be helpful to me when I need to make important decisions in my life, such as what to do after graduation from high school.

FIGURE 17.1   Example of an Attitude Questionnaire

ward counseling, and yet there may be very few self-referrals. Questionnaires can be useful research tools with the caveat noted that the responses given are those the respondents were willing to share with us at the time (Thorndike & Hagen, 1977).

Interest Inventories.   Instruments designed to determine patterns or tendencies that an individual has with regard to personal interests are called interest inventories. Interest inventories can be designed for almost any purpose—to determine interest in music, art, or athletics, for example. Many inventories have been designed for use in counseling and in particular for use in helping clients make career choices.

Interest instruments are usually constructed in the form of checklists or forced-choice questions, where the client has to select a preference from a choice of activities. For example, "Would you rather hang wallpaper, sing in a choral group, or teach young children?" One of the more popular inventories—the Strong-Campbell Interest Inventory—allows for the comparison of client interest patterns with those of people in various occupations.

Having an interest response pattern similar to that of architects, for example, does not necessarily mean that a client should pursue such a career. The client may, in fact, have no direct interest in architecture. Further, there is generally a very low correlation between interest and ability, so that having an interest in an area does not guarantee success in it. The reverse is also true. Having a high degree of ability in an area does not guarantee that a person will be satisfied with a career in that area. A person might have a great degree of musical ability, for example, but not wish to pursue a career in the field of music.

Interest inventories, then, are useful to help a client become aware of current areas of interest. Such findings in the area of career counseling, for example, can provide the basis for continued exploration on the part of the counselor and the client to determine reasonable career alternatives, combining perceived interests and abilities.

Personality Inventories.   A number of self-report instruments have been developed that are related to personal adjustment and temperament, such as the Guilford-Zimmerman Temperament Survey and the Minnesota Multiphasic Personality Inventory (MMPI). As a result of responding to such instruments, clients receive results related to such characteristics as sociability, emotional stability, and masculinity. The validity (the ability of a test to measure what it purports to measure) of such instruments, in general, is low. They involve reading and understanding the material presented, and the ability to objectively relate the material to personal behavior. They also require frank and honest answers (Thorndike & Hagen, 1977). Thorndike and Hagen (1977) conclude that in view of the facts that scores can be distorted and that there is limited validity to instruments of this nature, they should be used "very sparingly . . . and only as an adjunct to more intensive psychological services" (p. 434).

ASSESSMENT GUIDELINES

Practitioners should be aware of the basic issues involved in the use of assessment and appraisal procedures. These six issues are as follows:

1. Each person's uniqueness is to be valued. Appropriate use of individual assessment and appraisal procedures acknowledges this uniqueness.
2. Variations exist within individuals as well as between individuals.
3. Appropriate assessment procedures require the direct participation of the individual in the assessment process.
4. Accurate appraisals are limited by both instruments and personnel. All tests, for example, have some error of measurement so that any label or other diagnosis must be qualified.
5. If there are serious implications, both positive and negative data need to be evaluated and multiple sources of data used. For example, if a client obtains an IQ of 80 on the single administration of an intelligence test, it is imperative that both environmental and testing conditions be evaluated. Multiple sources of assessment need to be used, including a second administration of the original instrument, before the label "mentally retarded" is applied.
6. In each assessment case, there are specific ethical guidelines to be followed (see Ethics of the American Association for Counseling and Development [AACD] in appendix).

Using a humanistic approach, Fischer (1985) offers six interrelated principles as guidelines for an individualized approach to assessment:

1. Be descriptive. Observe behavior and provide descriptions of samples of the client's behavior "along with their meaning to the assessor" (p. 46).
2. Be contextual. Descriptions of behaviors, both in the assessment session and outside of it, need to include contextual circumstances. To paraphrase Fischer, contexts include the physical setting, the location within a period of time, the assessor's relation to the client, and what the assessor perceives as the meaning of the situation for the client. For example: "At first she smoothed the fresh paper, lined up the two pencils, and leaned back expectantly, reminding me of a student with new supplies" (p. 46).
3. Be collaborative. The client must be encouraged "to be an informed, active participant throughout the assessment, and to comment on any written document. As a co-assessor, the client is acknowledged as partly responsible for his or her past and future and as capable of participating in his or her development" (p. 47). Assessment is not a secret mystical process that is done to a client. The process is used to acquire the best possible understanding of the individual, and this can only be done with direct input from the individual.
4. Be interventional. Assessment of any type always has an impact on the client in both positive and negative ways. It is important that interventions be made as constructive as possible. "These interventions into the client's ways

of moving through situations are intended both to evaluate the client's current possibilities and to try out different ones'' (p. 47). Assessment can be an isolated process. However, with a properly developed therapeutic relationship and active client involvement, much positive therapeutic growth can occur.

5. Be structural. Behavioral events are described fully in terms of observed data in a given context and how they came into being. "What" refers to when and how, as seen through some particular behavior. The question "Why" is not usually addressed, as it generally applies to causation, which is not observable or operationally described.

6. Be circumspect. Conditions do not always allow for full assessment. Assessment instruments all have errors of measurement, and assessors have personal, professional, theoretical, historical, and cultural limitations. All of this does not negate the value and meaning of the assessment process, but it is important to remember these factors in order that results may be kept in proper perspective.

ASSESSMENT STANDARDS

Three national organizations, the American Psychological Association, the American Educational Research Association, and the National Council on Measurement, endorse the *Standards for Educational and Psychological Testing* (1985). This book assists professionals who use tests with technical and ethical recommendations regarding testing practices and procedures. *Standards* contains 16 chapters of regulations divided into 4 basic sections: technical standards, standards for test use, standards for particular applications, and standards for administrative procedures.

Standards contains a number of recommendations focusing particularly on counseling settings. Five of these are that:

1. Counselors should ensure that information gleaned from testing is presented in an appropriate and meaningful fashion.

2. Counselors should use multiple assessments so that they can arrive at informed judgments derived from many sources of test information.

3. Counselors should go beyond traditional roles in testing and advisement and should consider clients' age, sex, and ethnicity in determining the appropriateness of tests and the interpretation of results.

4. Counselors should ensure that test materials deal equitably and positively with sex, race, ethnicity, age, experiential background, and nontraditional roles.

5. Counselors must make sure that a particular combination of tests is justified and that data are reported clearly and accurately (Wagner, 1987).

According to Wagner (1987), "testing developments are ongoing, and, in a sense, *Standards* was outdated the moment it was published" (p. 203).

SUMMARY

A description of the philosophy, principles, and techniques of individual assessment has been given, beginning with the idea that such a study is not akin to a course in statistics. The study of individual assessment merely uses measurement and statistical terms in order to understand individual differences and to facilitate communication among professionals.

Even though some type of assessment and diagnosis occurs in almost every counseling relationship, there is no universal agreement as to what assessment criteria and techniques should or should not be used. The use of tests and other diagnostic procedures has been criticized on a number of grounds, in particular for their possible harmful effects.

Four approaches to diagnosis have been described: the medical, the behavioristic, the humanistic, and the human services models, each having a different focus in assessing a client's problem. A comparison of the relationship of diagnosis and assessment to different theoretical approaches to counseling has been presented.

The importance of formal diagnosis as a requirement for payment of services by insurance companies and governmental agencies has been noted as a trend that may make most discussions of diagnosis and assessment purely academic for most practitioners.

A description has been given of the diagnostic system of the American Psychiatric Association *(Diagnostic and Statistical Manual of Mental Disorders,* 3rd ed., rev.), a system almost universally used by mental health practitioners who make and report formal diagnoses. Diagnoses made with this system are designed to give information on five different dimensions rather than just provide a simple label as required in previous systems.

Specific assessment techniques have been described in two basic categories—nonstandardized and standardized approaches. Nonstandardized approaches include observation, checklists, rating scales, anecdotal reports, questionnaires, and structured interviews. Standardized techniques include achievement and aptitude tests, and attitude, interest, and personality inventories.

A listing of basic issues to be considered in assessment and a set of humanistically oriented guidelines for use in the assessment process have been presented.

QUESTIONS AND ACTIVITIES

1. Consider the theoretical stance you have tended to favor since reading chapters 10 and 11 or even before. What assessment and diagnostic approaches would be included as part of *your* adherence to this theoretical approach? How comfortable are you with the idea of using these assessment materials?
2. Arrange to take a battery of tests. Include an intelligence or aptitude test, a personality inventory, and an interest inventory. Be aware of your attitudes

and emotions as you prepare for and take the tests, and then again when you receive your results.

   a. How different might your feelings be if you were to take these or other instruments under different circumstances; e.g., in a psychiatrist's office after suffering the loss of a parent?

   b. In reviewing the results of your tests, how accurate do they seem? Were you able to interpret the results yourself or did you receive assistance from a counselor? In what ways was the counselor's behavior helpful? In what ways are the results helpful to you?

CHAPTER 18

Research in Counseling

_Why can't I just counsel and let someone else
worry about doing research?_

> _No research without action, no action without research._
>
> Kurt Lewin

The codes of ethics of the American Psychological Association and the American Association for Counseling and Development state that practitioners have a responsibility to improve their profession through research. Leading figures in the field have been urging more research in counseling and psychotherapy for many years (Rogers, 1963; Vacc & Loesch, 1984; Muro, 1984; Remer, 1981).

Research is needed to measure the effects of counseling. Does counseling really help? If so, how and with whom? Which counseling skills and theories produce desirable results? Research can also help us understand how counseling works and help us find the best ways to improve therapeutic procedures. Research can help eliminate many of our biases, prejudices, and outdated ideas so that we can perceive what we do more clearly and objectively. Research also is needed in order to help us keep pace with modern technology and use it effectively.

This chapter provides a general overview of research methodology. The problems of counseling research are examined, followed by proposals for both increasing the amount of research conducted and for using the results of research.

TYPES OF COUNSELING RESEARCH

Research in counseling can either examine the process of counseling, the outcomes of counseling, or both.

Process Research

Process research refers to behavior that occurs within the counseling session. It measures how change occurs during counseling as opposed to what results from counseling. Process research can observe counselor behaviors, client behaviors, or the interaction between the two.

Counselor variables include counselors' emotional problems, personality characteristics, sex, and the number of years of experience of the counselor, among others. Client variables include expectancy for success, intelligence, verbal skills, and social class. We refer to the YAVIS syndrome in chapter 1, in which Schofield (1964) described successful clients as young, attractive, verbal, intelligent, and successful. That study concluded that counseling was most successful with clients who were most like their counselors. Relationship variables include attitudes toward each other, expectations, and personal values. Less likely to be successful candidates for counseling have been labeled HOUNDs (homely, old, unintelligent, nonverbal and disadvantaged) and DUDs (dumb, unintelligent, and disadvantaged) (Allen, 1977).

Outcome Research

Outcome research is concerned with whether therapy works and how the various approaches compare. It assesses what has occurred as a result of counseling. Outcome research is difficult and expensive to conduct. Process research questions tend to be more amenable to research than are outcome questions. The results of outcome research are confounded by problems in the selection of measures and subjects.

METHODS OF RESEARCH

A variety of research methods are available to counselors. Each method of research has its own strengths and limitations. Which method is used is determined by the particular research question being raised.

Descriptive Research

Descriptive research is concerned with events that currently exist, such as techniques, relationships, attitudes, values, beliefs, and trends. There are several methods of conducting descriptive research. One method is survey research, which is used mostly to collect data in order to gain factual information. Surveying is done through the use of questionnaires or interviews on a representative sample of some population. Survey literature is used to learn about preferences, attitudes, and behaviors of specified groups of people (La Fleur, 1983); someone conducting a study on the effects of child abuse might survey members of Parents Anonymous. School counselors surveying the relevancy of counseling services would survey the students in their particular schools. Usually this research gathers facts that help counselors plan and evaluate services, as well as contribute to the understanding of the particular population being studied. There are a number of considerations to be aware of in survey research, including the size of the population sample being studied, the wording of questions, item selection and sequencing, the spacing of questions, and the percentage of questionnaires returned. A return of at least 70 percent is needed for data to be usable.

The case study is one of the earliest forms of counseling research. Much of Freud's writings consisted of numerous client case studies. The case study examines how information collected on one unit, the individual, family, or group, changes over time. Case study results cannot readily be generalized to other units. They can, however, help in developing questions, hypotheses, and generalizations for further investigations using different methods (La Fleur, 1983).

Other methods of descriptive research include *content analysis,* where the investigator systematically examines transcripts or documents in order to use the data according to some previously established criteria; and *participant-observer research,* where the counselor is both the researcher and a participant in the counseling process. The latter approach is used to evaluate ongoing counseling services and to conduct longitudinal and developmental studies.

Further examples of descriptive research include follow-up studies that track individuals after they leave counseling or counseling students after they graduate, or an analysis of stage theory as it applies to adult development tasks (La Fleur, 1983). Descriptive research is expensive, labor-intensive, prone to experimental biases, and liable to sampling errors (Kottler & Brown, 1985).

Experimental Research

Experimental research involves the description, comparison, and analysis of data under controlled conditions (Pietrofesa, Hoffman, & Splete, 1984). It attempts to hold some variables constant and manipulate others to predict results in controlled conditions. Experimental research uses laboratory studies, hypothesis testing, and well-controlled experimental designs. This research approach is usually used to answer questions dealing with cause-and-effect relations. The major limitation of experimental research is the difficulty in the control of variables. A high degree of control is needed to permit the counselor to make cause-and-effect conclusions about the data gathered (La Fleur, 1983). For example, in order to control all variables, experiments are performed in a laboratory in which simulated counseling situations are set up. Because the study is done in a laboratory setting, it is often difficult to generalize anything from this type of study to the way clients behave in real life (Goldman, 1976). An example of an experimental research study is an analysis of the effect of counselor-offered facilitative conditions on the depth of client self-disclosure in initial interviews (Kottler & Brown, 1985).

Evaluative Research

Evaluative research is usually done in the field. It involves delineating, obtaining, and providing useful information in order to make judgments on the merits or performances of various programs or procedures. This research approach is used to help improve decisions about competing methods or treatments (Kottler & Brown, 1985). It should be based on specific, understandable goals and objectives in order to be meaningful. An example of evaluative research is an analysis of the effect of group counseling on the self-concept and school behavior of low-achieving adolescents (La Fleur, 1983).

Historical Research

Historical research collects and examines existing information (La Fleur, 1983). Its goal is to develop future perspectives based on the examination and analysis of past information. It is often concerned with trends, causes, and effects. An example of historical research is how federal and state governments have helped mold the practice of counseling (Brown & Pate, 1983).

PROBLEMS IN ENCOURAGING RESEARCH

Originally, counseling research and counseling practice were considered to be separate disciplines and were performed by different professionals. This did not prove desirable, and mental health professionals were urged to integrate the two roles, thus creating the scientist-practitioner (Howard, 1985). This concept of the scientist-practitioner has become complex and difficult to implement. Numerous problems abound.

Few counselors either engage in research or use research findings in their practice (Howard, 1985; Vacc & Loesch, 1984; Muro, 1984; Gelso, 1979). In fact, many practitioners find that research has little relevance to their practice (Minor, 1981; Larson & Nichols, 1972; Goldman, 1976; Howard, 1985; Heppner & Anderson, 1985). Research is read mostly by other researchers rather than by practitioners (Goldman, 1976).

Graduate students do not become active and regular journal article readers (Anderson & Heppner, 1986). Counseling students, counselors, and counselor educators generally view their major role as that of helping people (Muro, 1984; Vacc & Loesch, 1984) and place a lower priority on research. Many counseling students are intimidated by the thought of having to take a research course. Winfrey (1984) states that beginning master's level students resent having to use their credits on a research or statistics course rather than on a course in their specialty.

Woolsey (1986) has grouped the practitioner-researcher split into three categories: those who fault research paradigms and methods, those who blame practitioners and/or their training, and those who focus on the lack of fit between practice and research. Those who fault research paradigms and methods believe that new research paradigms and a revised philosophy of science that addresses the concerns of the practitioners as well as those of scientists must be used. Those who blame practitioners and their training cite mathematics anxiety, lack of expertise in research methods, work environments for practitioners that are not conducive to research activities, inadequate graduate training, and failure of communication between practitioners and researchers.

The third group emphasizes the incongruencies between practice and research. Woolsey (1986) conceptualizes all the perceptions of this group as involving a conflict in values.

> A major source of counselors' alienation from research is that the value system embodied in traditional methods of research is antithetical to the value system at the heart of counseling practice. (p. 86)

PROBLEMS IN CONDUCTING RESEARCH

Some researchers (Goldman, 1976; Elmore, 1984; Howard, 1985) have responded to traditional research approaches with strong criticism and have blamed the scientific researchers for the lack of practical significance in counseling research. They have initiated a movement in counseling that attempts to create alternatives to traditional research methods in order to make counseling research more relevant. This seems to give rise to another problem, that of rigor versus relevance.

Gelso (1985) hypothesizes that the more rigorous the research, the less relevance it will have to practice. Therefore, any attempts to solve problems of low relevance create problems such as having low rigor. He called this the "bubble hypothesis." Some critics, such as Howard (1985), believe that studies can be designed that are both relevant and rigorous. Others, Heppner and Anderson (1985) and Gelso (1985), for example, call for a balance of rigor and relevance. Elmore (1984) advocates an entirely new formulation for counseling research that is not based on research paradigms of physical science, but on a wholistic model incorporating physical, mental, and spiritual development of persons to meet the demands of advanced technology and cultural diversity.

The relevance-versus-rigor debate seems to be the primary problem in conducting counseling research, but many other problems exist. Hill (1982) believes that counseling is still in too early a stage of development for researchers to be testing counseling theories. Counseling theories confound the matter by not using universally agreed on operational definitions for variables. This results in duplication among researchers with little communication among them. Hill goes on to state that theoretical bias in research leads to looking for certain phenomena rather than to being open for a multitude of factors. Howard (1985) adopts a similar position in stating that research tends to set two systems of influence at odds with each other. For example, researching whether family therapy is more effective than individual therapy in families with acting-out teenagers creates either/or thinking. Researching the effects of family therapy *and* individual therapy in order to discover their mutual influence would be more helpful to practitioners.

Goldman (1976) reports that it is extremely difficult for studies to be done in such a way as to permit any firm conclusions. The few studies that do, usually permit little generalization beyond the setting in which they were conducted and the samples that were studied. Heppner and Anderson find that because results from counseling research are presented in small pieces over time, many articles on a topic are necessary before there is enough information to be of use to counselors. Further, a considerable amount of time is necessary in order to synthesize the information.

Goldman (1976) cites additional problems in conducting research, such as failure to do replication studies, failure to choose samples properly, and failure to garner enough of a response rate from surveys. Goldman is also concerned about the failure to consider the researcher as an independent variable, the finding of answers to ambiguously worded questions, or the description of observed behaviors whose meaning is unclear.

Deficiencies in Counselor Preparation Programs

Practitioners greatly resist viewing themselves from a perspective broader than that of providing direct services (Vacc & Loesch, 1984). Much of the responsibility for this is attributed to counselor preparation programs (Muro, 1984; Heppner & Anderson, 1985; Vacc & Loesch, 1984). One criticism is that counselor educators have overemphasized the helping skills at the expense of research skills. Research is not integrated enough into the counseling curriculum, and what students learn experientially is rarely combined with research data. Muro (1984) hypothesizes that counselors and counselor educators in university settings engage in little research themselves. The large majority of studies come from master's or doctoral students. These studies tend to suffer from numerous flaws. Muro also faults them for viewing counseling theory and practice as gospel, without questioning the basis for a particular theory and whether or not it is valid. Winfrey (1984) suggests that counselor educators themselves fear change and that the research process implies a commitment to change. He believes that the cause of this fear may be the idea that counselor educators and supervisors are used to coming from a reactive, crisis stance with their clients as opposed to a proactive stance. Their clients become models for them rather than their becoming models for their clients. He also notes that counselors are typically not risk takers. They want to be liked and loved and therefore do not take leadership stances lest they offend others. Certainly, any or all of the above ideas might create interesting research projects.

Problems Specific to Counseling Practitioners

The work environment for practitioners who work in agencies, schools, colleges, and mental health centers is often not conducive to research activities. Not only do these counselors often face heavy client loads, but they also are often reinforced for carrying such loads. As a result, there is little time, if any, for counseling research (Heppner & Anderson, 1985). Heppner and Anderson suggest that many work environments may actually punish efforts at doing research. Research is often perceived as time-consuming and as reducing counselor productivity.

INCONGRUENCIES BETWEEN PRACTICE AND RESEARCH

Even if research received a greater emphasis in counselor training and in schools and agencies, most problems plaguing counseling research would still be there. According to Hill (1982) there is a disagreement about whether counseling is an art or a science. Some counselors believe that the effective ingredients of counseling are such factors as faith, hope, expectation, and motivation, which cannot be operationalized or researched because of their complexity.

Those who believe that counseling is a science maintain that counseling is a predictable and logical process and can be researched. They are primarily concerned with controlled experimental research conducted with rigor in laboratories. The core values for these scientific researchers are that only those data that can be observed, measured, studied objectively, and replicated are considered the proper data of social science (Woolsey, 1986). As a result, researchers have dismissed persons' inner experiences as subjective, private, and not meeting their core values. Hill believes that this is an artificial dichotomy because both art and science follow structure, require training, and often have unspecifiable elements.

The core values of counseling practitioners manifested in the many theories of counseling reflect mostly humanist and existential philosophies (Corsini & Wedding, 1989; Woolsey, 1986). Of the four forces in psychology (see chapter 10) only the behavioristic force appears to be congruent with scientific values. The rest seem to be in direct contradiction to the philosophical system underlying research.

Use of language is another area in which there is an incongruency. Heppner and Anderson (1985) fault many studies for their use of jargon and highly specialized language that builds a semantic wall between researchers and practitioners.

> In describing the data of counseling, researchers speak of *perceived self-efficacy, cognitive expectancies and attributions, reward-cost balancing, conceptual self-systems,* and *factors in counselor-client interactions.* Practitioners refer to the same phenomena with such phrases as *the will to power, the true self, the I-Thou versus the I-it relationship, authentic versus inauthentic self, being there,* and *caring presence.* (Woolsey, 1986, p. 90)

Before you throw your hands up in disgust or despair at this seemingly sad state of affairs, it should be stressed that research has done a great deal to enhance the practice of counseling. As Heppner and Anderson (1985) state,

> Although a practitioner may not be able to cite a specific reference, most practitioners' graduate school training was likely based on a tremendous amount of research data, all the way from personality theory to intervention strategies. The accumulation may be slow, but the data eventually advance our working knowledge of the field. (p. 545)

In fact, many of the numerous citations in almost every chapter of this book are derived from research. When one considers that counseling research has had an extremely brief history, a little more than three decades, according to Hersen, Michelson, and Bellack (1984), with the most important empirical findings only appearing since the 1960s, a great amount has been accomplished. Considering all the various issues and conflicts in the field of counseling and among counseling theories, it is not surprising to face issues and conflicts in counseling research. Future professionals can view the present state of the profession with excitement and challenge. With this idea in mind, we now look at some suggested solutions for the problems we have presented.

SOLVING THE PROBLEMS OF CONDUCTING COUNSELING RESEARCH

The solution to the problems of counseling research begins with the graduate student, who must become an active agent in making research a workable tool for the counseling profession. The first step involves the development of a spirit of inquiry. Gelso (1985) suggests that students and practitioners actively seek answers to the question, "How do these particular findings relate to my practice?" whenever encountering research studies. Goldman (1976) suggests the question, "To what populations, settings, and variables can this effect be generalized?" Nejedlo (1984) advocates asking probing questions "about the process of change, the development of potential students' programmatic needs, and the resolving of problems from the context of individuals in the societal environment in addition to an individual in his or her own environment" (p. 150). Barkley (1982) proposes six research-related competencies that graduate students should have:

1. The ability to pose good research questions.
2. The ability to use clear definitions of terms.
3. An understanding of sources of confusion and ambiguity, and how they may be controlled.
4. Awareness of problems associated with observation and measurement.
5. An understanding of the importance of documentation in the literature.
6. Knowledge about the process of research and the motivation to learn more about it throughout one's professional life.

Counselor training institutions must place a greater emphasis on research literature and techniques. Research must also be integrated more into the counseling curriculum. Counselor educators must become models in assuming a scientist/practitioner stance by taking a leadership role in the use and conduct of research. Vacc and Loesch (1984) urge that research training be embedded in the training program so that a research orientation becomes an integral part of professional behavior. This training would enable counseling students to formulate problems and issues and evaluate the results of their own work. They advocate academic courses in research, research projects in students' field experiences, and greater faculty involvement in research.

In 1976 Leo Goldman wrote an article calling for a revolution in counseling research. Numerous others have echoed his sentiments (Elmore, 1984; Gelso, 1985; Howard, 1985; Keeney & Morris, 1985; Vacc & Loesch, 1984; Woolsey, 1986). Inherent in this movement is the need to view research from a much broader perspective than the paradigms of physical science. Goldman (1976) states that "This obsession with the values and standards of the physical sciences has led us away from more meaningful, though admittedly cruder, studies of human beings and of counseling processes" (p. 545).

Goldman promotes the following changes:

1. Using macroscopic rather than microscopic research. Microscopic research focuses on very narrow topics. It examines individuals under a microscope. Macroscopic research examines the whole functioning human being, dealing with broader areas of human functioning.
2. Conduct field rather than laboratory research. Field-based research studies peoples' lives where and as they live them. It is research done in real situations such as the counseling office, or peoples' homes, or in the workplace.
3. Study individual cases rather than studying average changes in groups of persons. Combining data from groups of people usually reveals how several factors play a part in certain situations but do not help to understand the individual. For example, Goldman (1976) notes that correlations between personality measures and underachievement might reveal that social activity, excessive anxiety, or low achievement motivation play a part. However, if one were working with an individual client, the data would not deal with the complexity and interaction among these factors within the client.
4. Maintain an open arrangement with persons whose behavior is being studied. This would prevent subjects from being treated as objects and would encourage an openness in the researcher-subject relationship similar to the desired openness in counselor-client relationships.
5. Conduct more applied evaluation of programs in field settings.

Keeney and Morris (1985) suggest doing research from a "cybernetic" review of science advocated by Gregory Bateson in his "rules of thumb" for conducting research:

1. Study life in its natural setting, being careful not to destroy the historical and interactional integrity of the whole setting.
2. Think esthetically. Visualize, analogize, compare. Look for patterns and configurations.
3. Live with your data. Be a detective. Mull, contemplate, inspect. Think about, through, and beyond.
4. Don't be controlled by dogmatic formalisms about how to theorize and research. Avoid the dualisms announced as maxims by particularizing methodologists and theorists. They'll fire their shots at you one way or the other anyhow.

5. Be as precise as possible but don't close off possibilities. Look to the ever larger systems and configurations for your explanations. Keep your explanations as close to your data and experience as possible.

6. Aim for catalytic conceptualizations; warm ideas are contagious.

Keeney and Morris also suggest using research designs other than sociostatistical experimental designs including cybernetics, etiology, anthropology, and sociolinguistics. Winfrey (1984) suggests using research techniques from business and industry. For example, business uses marketing techniques in studying consumers, which would be applicable to counselors in studying their clients.

Students, as they progress through their course of study, should familiarize themselves with these alternative approaches, which would make research in counseling more relevant and at the same time offer great possibilities for advancing the profession. Ideally, students should do various types of research as an integral part of their education.

SUMMARY

The importance of research in terms of strengthening and furthering the counseling profession has been stressed in this chapter. The two basic types of counseling research, process and outcome, have been described along with four major methods of conducting research: descriptive, experimental, evaluative, and historical.

The difficulties in conducting research have been outlined, and a number of alternatives have been offered to encourage more research in counseling and to make the results more relevant. In the final analysis, any student in the field must make a commitment to becoming fully involved in the vital research component of the profession.

QUESTIONS AND ACTIVITIES

1. Read a research article on some aspect of counseling that is of interest to you. How relevant is the article to the actual practice of counseling? In what way is it relevant? What would have made it more relevant for you? Discuss your findings in class.

2. Are you approaching counseling as an art or a science? What is the implication of your answer for counseling research? Would your bias, whatever it is, affect your approach as you read about as well as conduct research? Would you consider a counselor who did not become involved in research to be a complete professional?

3. How do you feel about becoming a scientist-practitioner? What would it take for this stance to be workable for you?

The Synergistic Counselor

CHAPTER 19

Epilogue

How does all of this material fit together?

This epilogue briefly reviews our journey through the field of counseling, indicating how the various topics presented relate to the process of becoming a professional counselor. Because the field of counseling is in a process of constant growth, we also note some trends for the future.

This text approaches counseling from a wholistic, systems conceptualization. Such a conceptualization views the field of counseling as interconnected with a broad spectrum of related content areas. This approach views effective counselors as more than just knowledgeable, or skillful, or nice individuals who want to help. Each component noted is a whole in itself as well as being part of the greater totality that constitutes those who are effective counselors. Likewise, each chapter of this text is a whole in itself as well as being part of a section and of the total book.

WHO THE COUNSELOR IS

The self of the counselor is an integral part of the counselor–client–environment system. Any counseling, whether individual, group, or family, involves an interpersonal interaction between at least two people. The person of the counselor greatly impacts the counseling. As Satir (1987) points out, this involvement of the counselors' self occurs regardless of, and in addition to, the treatment philosophy or the approach.

Chapter 1 emphasizes that there is a definite correlation between the functioning level of counselors and effective counseling. The functioning level includes counselors' mental and physical well being, belief systems, and specific qualities such as empathy, respect congruence, and acceptance of self and others.

Counselors may not be able to help anyone get beyond the point that they themselves have attained. Therefore, counselors have a responsibility to monitor and evaluate their own self-actualization efforts in order to help others in their quest for self-actualization. As a major part of this process, counselors need to learn how to deal with stress and prevent burnout so that they can not only be present and effective models for their clients, but also lead fully functioning lives. Chapter 9 presents the acronym BREADS/LT (Breathing, Relaxation, Exercise, Attitude, Diet, and Support, all supplemented by Laughter and effective Time Management) to ensure the development and retention of approaches for dealing with prevention and the relief of burnout.

Counselors also need to be aware of their professional attitude and their responsibilities, including ethical behavior (see chapter 8). Counselors must be aware of their power and not use it in ways that will harm their clients or that will develop dependency relationships. Satir (1987) states that

> it is the therapist's responsibility to create a context in which people feel and are safe, and this requires sensitivity to one's own state. (p. 21)

WHAT THE COUNSELOR CAN DO

Chapters 3 and 4 especially, and parts of chapters 2, 12, 13, and 17, among others, focus on counseling skills. It is not enough to have fine personal qualities and/or to be knowledgeable. Counselors also must be able to apply these components in their work with clients.

> The most effective counselors are those who have the widest repertory of responses and can use them in a socially intelligent manner. Such a repertory enables them to respond spontaneously to the wide variety of client needs. Counseling is for the client; it is not a virtuoso performance by the helper. (Egan, 1986, p. 57)

It is through practice and experience that these skills are learned. Initially, counselor trainees often feel self-conscious and awkward. As the skills are internalized, counselor trainees feel more spontaneous and natural. They are able to put the skills together smoothly and work effectively with their clients.

WHAT THE COUNSELOR KNOWS

The remaining chapters provide a broad overview of knowledge in the field of counseling, including foundation and specialty areas, human growth and development, cross-cultural issues, and research considerations. Our objective is to provide an extensive coverage of major content areas related to the field of counseling.

The content areas presented are those covered in most master's level programs, as well as on the examination used for certifying counselors (NCC). We hope that the knowledge and experience gained as a result of your involvement with the materials presented here will enable you to make an informed decision about whether to continue your education in the field of counseling. If you do decide to continue, this book will provide a basic resource for future studies.

In today's information age, we never seem to have enough knowledge. No matter how large the book or how extensive the degree program, there will always be something additional that could have been included. What we include in this volume can be considered the basics that, if internalized, will provide students with a broad framework of knowledge for further learning and a repertoire of responses applicable to a wide variety of circumstances. We stress the importance of this approach because virtually every contact with a client brings with it the possibility of a counselor's being confronted with content for which there was no specific education.

The elements of this basic grounding include knowing the characteristics necessary for establishing an effective therapeutic relationship; the knowledge and ability to provide a broad variety of appropriate responses; the knowledge of ethical practices and the principles on which ethical decisions are made; knowledge of the full range of human development necessary to deal with issues of a developmental nature; awareness of a broad variety of theoretical approaches, with an emphasis on the wholistic, systems approach; and an awareness of the importance of preventive counseling.

Counselors, now and in the future, will face issues and problems for which they were not specifically trained. They need to know their own ethical limitations; how to find resources, including referral sources; and how to attain specialized training if desired. It is important for counselors to know that the general principles and practices espoused in this volume are applicable when they initially confront such issues as AIDS, gay and lesbian concerns, adult children of alcoholics, sexual dysfunction, child abuse, and other current or future issues. However, counselors also need to know that much additional education and experience are necessary for them to be deemed competent in working in depth in any of these areas. As the range and scope of issues that counselors deal with continue to expand, the obvious conclusion emerges: learning about this field is a lifelong pursuit. As Hershenson and Power (1987) state,

> When a physician graduates from medical school, that physician is not immediately qualified as a neurosurgeon. Further specialized learning and experience are required. Similarly, no counselor fresh out of a graduate program is an expert, advocate, consultant, or counselor. (p. 380)

SUMMARY

With a global shift from authoritarian regimes to democracy, including the sudden and rapid changes throughout the Soviet Union and Eastern Europe, humankind may be on the threshold of building a freer, healthier, wealthier, and safer world. Naisbitt and Aburdene (1990) forecast the dawn of a new era prefaced by the obsolescence of war as a means of solving problems. They predict, "The post-cold war era will see the United States and the Soviet Union collaborate on the environment and on new nonideological approaches to ending poverty" (p. 313). They view the current planetary trends as relating to and reinforcing each other to shape a new globalized world.

Who the counselor is, what the counselor knows, and what the counselor can do provide the foundation for becoming synergistic counselors prepared for working creatively and energetically with these planetary trends predicted for the 21st century. These synergistic counselors will be increasingly involved in the preventive and developmental aspects of counseling, and with groups, institutions, and communities in a consulting mode. They will develop a greater interest in the spiritual and transcendental aspects of life and will be more actively involved in affecting societal change.

Counseling is a young, vital, and dynamic field filled with countless stimulating challenges for working with the human condition in a variety of ways at a number of different levels.

ETHICAL STANDARDS of the American Association for Counseling and Development

(3rd revision, AACD Governing Council, March 1988)

PREAMBLE

The Association is an educational, scientific, and professional organization whose members are dedicated to the enhancement of the worth, dignity, potential, and uniqueness of each individual and thus to the service of society.

The Association recognizes that the role definitions and work settings of its members include a wide variety of academic disciplines, levels of academic preparation, and agency services. This diversity reflects the breadth of the Association's interest and influence. It also poses challenging complexities in efforts to set standards for the performance of members, desired requisite preparation or practice, and supporting social, legal, and ethical controls.

The specification of ethical standards enables the Association to clarify to present and future members and to those served by members the nature of ethical responsibilities held in common by its members.

The existence of such standards serves to stimulate greater concern by members for their own professional functioning and for the conduct of fellow professionals such as counselors, guidance and student personnel workers, and others in the helping professions. As the ethical code of the Association, this document establishes principles that define the ethical behavior of Association members. Additional ethical guidelines developed by the Association's Divisions for their specialty areas may further define a member's ethical behavior.

SECTION A: General

1. The member influences the development of the profession by continuous efforts to improve professional practices, teaching, services, and research. Professional growth is continuous throughout the member's career and is exemplified by the development of a philosophy that explains why and how a member functions in the helping relationship. Members must gather data on their effectiveness and be guided by the findings. Members recognize the need for continuing education to ensure competent service.

2. The member has a responsibility both to the individual who is served and to the institution within which the service is performed to maintain high standards of professional conduct. The member strives to maintain the highest levels of professional services offered to the individuals to be served. The member also strives to assist the agency, organization, or institution in providing the highest caliber of professional services. The acceptance of employment in an institution implies that the member is in agreement with the general policies and principles of the institution. Therefore the professional activities of the member are

"Ethical Standards of the AACD 3rd Revision," *Journal of Counseling and Development* 67 (9/1988):4–6. Reprinted by permission of American Association for Counseling and Development, publisher and copyright holder.

also in accord with the objectives of the institution. If, despite concerted efforts, the member cannot reach agreement with the employer as to acceptable standards of conduct that allow for changes in institutional policy conducive to the positive growth and development of clients, then terminating the affiliation should be seriously considered.

3. Ethical behavior among professional associates, both members and nonmembers, must be expected at all times. When information is possessed that raises doubt as to the ethical behavior of professional colleagues, whether Association members or not, the member must take action to attempt to rectify such a condition. Such action shall use the institution's channels first and then use procedures established by the Association.

4. The member neither claims nor implies professional qualifications exceeding those possessed and is responsible for correcting any misrepresentations of these qualifications by others.

5. In establishing fees for professional counseling services, members must consider the financial status of clients and locality. In the event that the established fee structure is inappropriate for a client, assistance must be provided in finding comparable services of acceptable cost.

6. When members provide information to the public or to subordinates, peers, or supervisors, they have a responsibility to ensure that the content is general, unidentified client information that is accurate, unbiased, and consists of objective, factual data.

7. Members recognize their boundaries of competence and provide only those services and use only those techniques for which they are qualified by training or experience. Members should only accept those positions for which they are professionally qualified.

8. In the counseling relationship, the counselor is aware of the intimacy of the relationship and maintains respect for the client and avoids engaging in activities that seek to meet the counselor's personal needs at the expense of that client.

9. Members do not condone or engage in sexual harassment which is defined as deliberate or repeated comments, gestures, or physical contacts of a sexual nature.

10. The member avoids bringing personal issues into the counseling relationship, especially if the potential for harm is present. Through awareness of the negative impact of both racial and sexual stereotyping and discrimination, the counselor guards the individual rights and personal dignity of the client in the counseling relationship.

11. Products or services provided by the member by means of classroom instruction, public lectures, demonstrations, written articles, radio or television programs, or other types of media must meet the criteria cited in these standards.

SECTION B: Counseling Relationship

This section refers to practices and procedures of individual and/or group counseling relationships.

The member must recognize the need for client freedom of choice. Under those circumstances where this is not possible, the member must apprise clients of restrictions that may limit their freedom of choice.

1. The member's primary obligation is to respect the integrity and promote the welfare of the client(s), whether the client(s) is (are) assisted individually or in a group relationship. In a group setting, the member is also responsible for taking reasonable precautions to protect individuals from physical and/or psychological trauma resulting from interaction within the group.

2. Members make provisions for maintaining confidentiality in the storage and disposal of records and follow an established record retention and disposition policy. The counseling relationship and information resulting therefrom must be kept confidential, consistent with the obligations of the member as a professional person. In a group counseling setting, the counselor must set a norm of confidentiality regarding all group participants' disclosures.

3. If an individual is already in a counseling relationship with another professional person, the member does not enter into a counseling relationship without first contacting and receiv-

ing the approval of that other professional. If the member discovers that the client is in another counseling relationship after the counseling relationship begins, the member must gain the consent of the other professional or terminate the relationship, unless the client elects to terminate the other relationship.

4. When the client's condition indicates that there is clear and imminent danger to the client or others, the member must take reasonable personal action or inform responsible authorities. Consultation with other professionals must be used where possible. The assumption of responsibility for the client's(s') behavior must be taken only after careful deliberation. The client must be involved in the resumption of responsibility as quickly as possible.

5. Records of the counseling relationship, including interview notes, test data, correspondence, tape recordings, electronic data storage, and other documents are to be considered professional information for use in counseling, and they should not be considered a part of the records of the institution or agency in which the counselor is employed unless specified by state statute or regulation. Revelation to others of counseling material must occur only upon the expressed consent of the client.

6. In view of the extensive data storage and processing capacities of the computer, the member must ensure that data maintained on a computer is: (a) limited to information that is appropriate and necessary for the services being provided; (b) destroyed after it is determined that the information is no longer of any value in providing services; and (c) restricted in terms of access to appropriate staff members involved in the provision of services by using the best computer security methods available.

7. Use of data derived from a counseling relationship for purposes of counselor training or research shall be confined to content that can be disguised to ensure full protection of the identity of the subject client.

8. The member must inform the client of the purposes, goals, techniques, rules of procedure, and limitations that may affect the relationship at or before the time that the counseling relationship is entered. When working with minors or persons who are unable to give consent, the member protects these clients' best interests.

9. In view of common misconceptions related to the perceived inherent validity of computer-generated data and narrative reports, the member must ensure that the client is provided with information as part of the counseling relationship that adequately explains the limitations of computer technology.

10. The member must screen prospective group participants, especially when the emphasis is on self-understanding and growth through self-disclosure. The member must maintain an awareness of the group participants' compatibility throughout the life of the group.

11. The member may choose to consult with any other professionally competent person about a client. In choosing a consultant, the member must avoid placing the consultant in a conflict of interest situation that would preclude the consultant's being a proper party to the member's efforts to help the client.

12. If the member determines an inability to be of professional assistance to the client, the member must either avoid initiating the counseling relationship or immediately terminate that relationship. In either event, the member must suggest appropriate alternatives. (The member must be knowledgeable about referral resources so that a satisfactory referral can be initiated.) In the event the client declines the suggested referral, the member is not obligated to continue the relationship.

13. When the member has other relationships, particularly of an administrative, supervisory, and/or evaluative nature with an individual seeking counseling services, the member must not serve as the counselor but should refer the individual to another professional. Only in instances where such an alternative is unavailable and where the individual's situation warrants counseling intervention should the member enter into and/or maintain a counseling relationship. Dual relationships with clients that might impair the member's objectivity and professional judgment (e.g., as with close friends or relatives) must be avoided and/or the counseling relationship terminated through referral to another competent professional.

14. The member will avoid any type of sexual intimacies with clients. Sexual relationships with clients are unethical.

15. All experimental methods of treatment must be clearly indicated to prospective recipients, and safety precautions are to be adhered to by the member.

16. When computer applications are used as a component of counseling services, the member must ensure that: (a) the client is intellectually, emotionally, and physically capable of using the computer application; (b) the computer application is appropriate for the needs of the client; (c) the client understands the purpose and operation of the computer application; and (d) a follow-up of client use of a computer application is provided to both correct possible problems (misconceptions or inappropriate use) and assess subsequent needs.

17. When the member is engaged in short-term group treatment/training programs (e.g., marathons and other encounter-type or growth groups), the member ensures that there is professional assistance available during and following the group experience.

18. Should the member be engaged in a work setting that calls for any variation from the above statements, the member is obligated to consult with other professionals whenever possible to consider justifiable alternatives.

19. The member must ensure that members of various ethnic, racial, religious, disability, and socioeconomic groups have equal access to computer applications used to support counseling services and that the content of available computer applications does not discriminate against the groups described above.

20. When computer applications are developed by the member for use by the general public as self-help/stand-alone computer software, the member must ensure that: (a) self-help computer applications are designed from the beginning to function in a stand-alone manner, as opposed to modifying software that was originally designed to require support from a counselor; (b) self-help computer applications will include within the program statements regarding intended user outcomes, suggestions for using the software, a description of the conditions under which self-help computer applica-

tions might not be appropriate, and a description of when and how counseling services might be beneficial; and (c) the manual for such applications will include the qualifications of the developer, the development process, validation data, and operating procedures.

SECTION C: Measurement and Evaluation
The primary purpose of educational and psychological testing is to provide descriptive measures that are objective and interpretable in either comparative or absolute terms. The member must recognize the need to interpret the statements that follow as applying to the whole range of appraisal techniques including test and nontest data. Test results constitute only one of a variety of pertinent sources of information for personnel, guidance, and counseling decisions.

1. The member must provide specific orientation or information to the examinee(s) prior to and following the test administration so that the results of testing may be placed in proper perspective with other relevant factors. In so doing, the member must recognize the effects of socioeconomic, ethnic, and cultural factors on test scores. It is the member's professional responsibility to use additional unvalidated information carefully in modifying interpretation of the test results.

2. In selecting tests for use in a given situation or with a particular client, the member must consider carefully the specific validity, reliability, and appropriateness of the test(s). General validity, reliability, and related issues may be questioned legally as well as ethically when tests are used for vocational and educational selection, placement, or counseling.

3. When making any statements to the public about tests and testing, the member must give accurate information and avoid false claims or misconceptions. Special efforts are often required to avoid unwarranted connotations of such terms as *IQ* and *grade equivalent scores*.

4. Different tests demand different levels of competence for administration, scoring, and interpretation. Members must recognize the limits of their competence and perform only those functions for which they are prepared. In particular, members using computer-based test in-

terpretations must be trained in the construct being measured and the specific instrument being used prior to using this type of computer application.

5. In situations where a computer is used for test administration and scoring, the member is responsible for ensuring that administration and scoring programs function properly to provide clients with accurate test results.

6. Tests must be administered under the same conditions that were established in their standardization. When tests are not administered under standard conditions or when unusual, behavior or irregularities occur during the testing session, those conditions must be noted and the results designated as invalid or of questionable validity. Unsupervised or inadequately supervised test-taking, such as the use of tests through the mails, is considered unethical. On the other hand, the use of instruments that are so designed or standardized to be self-administered and self-scored, such as interest inventories, is to be encouraged.

7. The meaningfulness of test results used in personnel, guidance, and counseling functions generally depends on the examinee's unfamiliarity with the specific items on the test. Any prior coaching or dissemination of the test materials can invalidate test results. Therefore, test security is one of the professional obligations of the member. Conditions that produce most favorable test results must be made known to the examinee.

8. The purpose of testing and the explicit use of the results must be made known to the examinee prior to testing. The counselor must ensure that instrument limitations are not exceeded and that periodic review and/or retesting are made to prevent client stereotyping.

9. The examinee's welfare and explicit prior understanding must be the criteria for determining the recipients of the test results. The member must see that specific interpretation accompanies any release of individual or group test data. The interpretation of test data must be related to the examinee's particular concerns.

10. Members responsible for making decisions based on test results have an understanding of educational and psychological measurement, validation criteria, and test research.

11. The member must be cautious when interpreting the results of research instruments possessing insufficient technical data. The specific purposes for the use of such instruments must be stated explicitly to examinees.

12. The member must proceed with caution when attempting to evaluate and interpret the performance of minority group members or other persons who are not represented in the norm group on which the instrument was standardized.

13. When computer-based test interpretations are developed by the member to support the assessment process, the member must ensure that the validity of such interpretations is established prior to the commercial distribution of such a computer application.

14. The member recognizes that test results may become obsolete. The member will avoid and prevent the misuse of obsolete test results.

15. The member must guard against the appropriation, reproduction, or modification of published tests or parts thereof without acknowledgement and permission from the previous publisher.

16. Regarding the preparation, publication, and distribution of tests, reference should be made to:

   a. "Standards for Educational and Psychological Testing," revised edition, 1985, published by the American Psychological Association on behalf of itself, the American Educational Research Association, and the National Council on Measurement in Education.

   b. "The Responsible Use of Tests: A Position Paper of AMEG, APGA, and NCME," *Measurement and Evaluation in Guidance*, 1972, 5, 385–388.

   c. "Responsibilities of Users of Standardized Tests," APGA, *Guidepost*, October 5, 1978, pp. 5–8.

SECTION D: Research and Publication

1. Guidelines on research with human subjects shall be adhered to, such as:

   a. *Ethical Principles in the Conduct of Research with Human Participants*, Washington, D.C.: American Psychological Association, Inc., 1982.

b. Code of Federal Regulation, Title 45, Subtitle A, Part 46, as currently issued.

c. *Ethical Principles of Psychologists*, American Psychological Association, Principle #9: Research with Human Participants.

d. Family Educational Rights and Privacy Act (the Buckley Amendment).

e. Current federal regulations and various states rights privacy acts.

2. In planning any research activity dealing with human subjects, the member must be aware of and responsive to all pertinent ethical principles and ensure that the research problem, design, and execution are in full compliance with them.

3. Responsibility for ethical research practice lies with the principal researcher, while others involved in the research activities share ethical obligation and full responsibility for their own actions.

4. In research with human subjects, researchers are responsible for the subjects' welfare throughout the experiment, and they must take all reasonable precautions to avoid causing injurious psychological, physical, or social effects on their subjects.

5. All research subjects must be informed of the purpose of the study except when withholding information or providing misinformation to them is essential to the investigation. In such research the member must be responsible for corrective action as soon as possible following completion of the research.

6. Participation in research must be voluntary. Involuntary participation is appropriate only when it can be demonstrated that participation will have no harmful effects on subjects and is essential to the investigation.

7. When reporting research results, explicit mention must be made of all variables and conditions known to the investigator that might affect the outcome of the investigation or the interpretation of the data.

8. The member must be responsible for conducting and reporting investigations in a manner that minimizes the possibility that results will be misleading.

9. The member has an obligation to make available sufficient original research data to qualified others who may wish to replicate the study.

10. When supplying data, aiding in the research of another person, reporting research results, or making original data available, due care must be taken to disguise the identity of the subjects in the absence of specific authorization from such subjects to do otherwise.

11. When conducting and reporting research, the member must be familiar with and give recognition to previous work on the topic, as well as to observe all copyright laws and follow the principles of giving full credit to all to whom credit is due.

12. The member must give due credit through joint authorship, acknowledgement, footnote statements, or other appropriate means to those who have contributed significantly to the research and/or publication, in accordance with such contributions.

13. The member must communicate to other members the results of any research judged to be of professional or scientific value. Results reflecting unfavorably on institutions, programs, services, or vested interests must not be withheld for such reasons.

14. If members agree to cooperate with another individual in research and/or publication, they incur an obligation to cooperate as promised in terms of punctuality of performance and with full regard to the completeness and accuracy of the information required.

15. Ethical practice requires that authors not submit the same manuscript or one essentially similar in content for simultaneous publication consideration by two or more journals. In addition, manuscripts published in whole or in substantial part in another journal or published work should not be submitted for publication without acknowledgement and permission from the previous publication.

SECTION E: Consulting

Consultation refers to a voluntary relationship between a professional helper and help-needing individual, group, or social unit in which the consultant is providing help to the client(s) in defining and solving a work-related problem with a client or client system.

1. The member acting as consultant must have a high degree of self-awareness of his/her own values, knowledge, skills, limitations, and needs in entering a helping relationship that involves human and/or organizational change and that the focus of the relationship be on the issues to be resolved and not on the person(s) presenting the problem.

2. There must be understanding and agreement between member and client for the problem definition, change of goals, and prediction of consequences of interventions selected.

3. The member must be reasonably certain that she/he or the organization represented has the necessary competencies and resources for giving the kind of help that is needed now or may be needed later and that appropriate referral resources are available to the consultant.

4. The consulting relationship must be one in which client adaptability and growth toward self-direction are encouraged and cultivated. The member must maintain this role consistently and not become a decision maker for the client or create a future dependency on the consultant.

5. When announcing consultant availability for services, the member conscientiously adheres to the Association's Ethical Standards.

6. The member must refuse a private fee or other remuneration for consultation with persons who are entitled to these services through the member's employing institution or agency. The policies of a particular agency may make explicit provisions for private practice with agency clients by members of its staff. In such instances, the clients must be apprised of other options open to them should they seek private counseling services.

SECTION F: Private Practice

1. The member should assist the profession by facilitating the availability of counseling services in private as well as public settings.

2. In advertising services as a private practitioner, the member must advertise the services in a manner that accurately informs the public of professional services, expertise, and techniques of counseling available. A member who assumes an executive leadership role in the organization shall not permit his/her name to be used in professional notices during periods when he/she is not actively engaged in the private practice of counseling.

3. The member may list the following: highest relevant degree, type and level of certification and/or license, address, telephone number, office hours, type and/or description of services, and other relevant information. Such information must not contain false, inaccurate, misleading, partial, out-of-context, or deceptive material or statements.

4. Members do not present their affiliation with any organization in such a way that would imply inaccurate sponsorship or certification by that organization.

5. Members may join in partnership/corporation with other members and/or other professionals provided that each member of the partnership or corporation makes clear the separate specialties by name in compliance with the regulations of the locality.

6. A member has an obligation to withdraw from a counseling relationship if it is believed that employment will result in violation of the Ethical Standards. If the mental or physical condition of the member renders it difficult to carry out an effective professional relationship or if the member is discharged by the client because the counseling relationship is no longer productive for the client, then the member is obligated to terminate the counseling relationship.

7. A member must adhere to the regulations for private practice of the locality where the services are offered.

8. It is unethical to use one's institutional affiliation to recruit clients for one's private practice.

SECTION G: Personnel Administration

It is recognized that most members are employed in public or quasi-public institutions. The functioning of a member within an institution must contribute to the goals of the institution and vice versa if either is to accomplish their respective goals or objectives. It is therefore essential that the member and the institution function in ways to: (a) make the institution's goals explicit and public; (b) make the member's contribution to institutional goals specific; and (c) foster mutual accountability for goal achievement.

To accomplish these objectives, it is recognized that the member and the employer must share responsibilities in the formulation and implementation of personnel policies.

1. Members must define and describe the parameters and levels of their professional competency.

2. Members must establish interpersonal relations and working agreements with supervisors and subordinates regarding counseling or clinical relationships, confidentiality, distinction between public and private material, maintenance and dissemination of recorded information, work load, and accountability. Working agreements in each instance must be specified and made known to those concerned.

3. Members must alert their employers to conditions that may be potentially disruptive or damaging.

4. Members must inform employers of conditions that may limit their effectiveness.

5. Members must submit regularly to professional review and evaluation.

6. Members must be responsible for inservice development of self and/or staff.

7. Members must inform their staff of goals and programs.

8. Members must provide personnel practices that guarantee and enhance the rights and welfare of each recipient of their service.

9. Members must select competent persons and assign responsibilities compatible with their skills and experiences.

10. The member, at the onset of a counseling relationship, will inform the client of the member's intended use of supervisors regarding the disclosure of information concerning this case. The member will clearly inform the client of the limits of confidentiality in the relationship.

11. Members, as either employers or employees, do not engage in or condone practices that are inhumane, illegal, or unjustifiable (such as considerations based on sex, handicap, age, race) in hiring, promotion, or training.

SECTION H: Preparation Standards

Members who are responsible for training others must be guided by the preparation standards of the Association and relevant Division(s). The member who functions in the capacity of trainer assumes unique ethical responsibilities that frequently go beyond that of the member who does not function in a training capacity. These ethical responsibilities are outlined as follows:

1. Members must orient students to program expectations, basic skills development, and employment prospects prior to admission to the program.

2. Members in charge of learning experiences must establish programs that integrate academic study and supervised practice.

3. Members must establish a program directed toward developing students' skills, knowledge, and self-understanding, stated whenever possible in competency or performance terms.

4. Members must identify the levels of competencies of their students in compliance with relevant Division standards. These competencies must accommodate the paraprofessional as well as the professional.

5. Members, through continual student evaluation and appraisal, must be aware of the personal limitations of the learner that might impede future performance. The instructor must not only assist the learner in securing remedial assistance but also screen from the program those individuals who are unable to provide competent services.

6. Members must provide a program that includes training in research commensurate with levels of role functioning. Paraprofessional and technician-level personnel must be trained as consumers of research. In addition, personnel must learn how to evaluate their own and their program's effectiveness. Graduate training, especially at the doctoral level, would include preparation for original research by the member.

7. Members must make students aware of the ethical responsibilities and standards of the profession.

8. Preparatory programs must encourage students to value the ideals of service to individuals and to society. In this regard, direct

financial remuneration or lack thereof must not influence the quality of service rendered. Monetary considerations must not be allowed to overshadow professional and humanitarian needs.

9. Members responsible for educational programs must be skilled as teachers and practitioners.

10. Members must present thoroughly varied theoretical positions so that students may make comparisons and have the opportunity to select a position.

11. Members must develop clear policies within their educational institutions regarding field placement and the roles of the student and the instructor in such placement.

12. Members must ensure that forms of learning focusing on self-understanding or growth are voluntary, or if required as part of the educational program, are made known to prospective students prior to entering the program. When the educational program offers a growth experience with an emphasis on self-disclosure or other relatively intimate or personal involvement, the member must have no administrative, supervisory, or evaluating authority regarding the participant.

13. The member will at all times provide students with clear and equally acceptable alternatives for self-understanding or growth experiences. The member will assure students that they have a right to accept these alternatives without prejudice or penalty.

14. Members must conduct an educational program in keeping with the current relevant guidelines of the Association.

Bibliography

CHAPTER 1

Aspy, D., & Roebuck, F. (1977). *Kids don't learn from people they don't like.* Amherst, MA: Human Resource Development Press.

Baldwin, M., & Satir, V. (Eds.) (1987). *The use of self in therapy.* New York: Haworth.

Bergin, A., & Garfield, S. (Eds.). (1971). *Handbook of psychotherapy and behavioral change.* New York: John Wiley & Sons.

Brammer, L., & Shostrom, E. (1982). *Therapeutic psychology,* (4th ed.). Englewood Cliffs, NJ: Prentice-Hall.

Bugental, J. (1987). *The art of the psychotherapist.* New York: Norton.

Carkhuff, R. (1980): *The art of helping IV,* Amherst, MA: Human Resource Development Press.

Carkhuff, R. (1983). *The art of helping* (5th ed.). Amherst, MA: Human Resource Development Press.

Carkhuff, R., & Alexik, M. (1967). The effects of the manipulation of client depth of self-exploration upon high and low functioning counselors. *Journal of Clinical Psychology, 23,* 210–212.

Carkhuff, R., & Berenson, B. (1967). *Beyond counseling and therapy.* New York: Holt, Rinehart & Winston.

Carkhuff, R., & Berenson, B. (1977). *Beyond counseling and therapy* (2nd ed.). New York: Holt, Rinehart & Winston.

Carkhuff, R., & Pierce, R. (1976). *Helping begins at home.* Amherst, MA: Human Resource Development Press.

Combs, A. (1986). What makes a good helper. *Person-Centered Review, 1,* 1, 51–61.

Combs, A., Avila, D., & Purkey, W. (1971). *Helping relationships: Basic concepts for the helping professions.* Boston: Allyn and Bacon.

Cormier, W., & Cormier, L. (1985). *Interviewing strategies for helpers* (2nd ed.). Monterey, CA: Brooks/Cole.

Corsini, R., and Wadding, D. (Eds.) (1989). *Current psychotherapies* (3rd ed.). Itasca, IL: Peacock.

Egan, G. (1986). *The skilled helper.* Monterey, CA: Brooks/Cole.

Eysenck, H. J. (1952). The effects of psychotherapy: An evaluation. *Journal of Consulting Psychology, 16,* 319–334.

Ford, J. (1979). Research on training counselors and clinicians. *Review of Educational Research, 49,* 87–130.

Gibran, K. (1923). The prophet. New York: Knopf.

Hamachek, D. (1985). The self's development and age growth: Conceptual analysis and implication for counselors. *Journal of Counseling and Development, 64* (2), 136–142.

Harris, S. (1981, September 28). We must know others before knowing ourselves. *South Bend Tribune,* p. 6.

Hayes, R., & Aubrey, R. (1988). *New directions for counseling and human development.* Denver, CO: Love.

Holder, T., Carkhuff, R., & Berenson, B. (1967). The differential effects of the manipulation of therapeutic conditions upon high low functioning clients. *Journal of Counseling Psychology, 14,* 63–66.

Hulnick, H. R. (1977, September). Counselor: Know thyself. *Personnel and Guidance Journal,* pp. 69–72.

Ivey, A., & Simek-Downing, L. (1980). *Counseling and psychotherapy: Skills, theories and practice.* Englewood Cliffs, NJ: Prentice-Hall.

Jersild, A. (1952). *In search of self.* New York: Teacher's College Press.

Levitt, E. (1957). The results of psychotherapy with children. *Journal of Consulting Psychology, 21,* 189–196.

Lieberman, M., Yalom, I., & Miles, M. (1973). *Encounter groups: First facts.* New York: Basic Books.

Lilly, J. (1972). *The center of the cyclone.* New York: Julian Press.

Maslow, A. H. (1956). Self-actualizing people: A study of psychological health. In C. E. Moustakas (Ed.). *The self-explorations in personal growth* (pp. 160–194). New York: Harper & Row.

Maslow, A. H. (1968). *Toward a psychology of being* (2nd ed.). Princeton, NJ: Van Nostrand Reinhold.

Maslow, A. H. (1970). *Motivation and personality* (rev. ed.). New York: Harper & Row.

Maslow, A. H. (1971). *The farther reaches of human nature.* New York: Viking Press.

May, R. (1984, March). *The wounded healer.* Presented at American Association of Counseling and Development Convention, Houston, Texas.

Meador, B., & Rogers, C. (1984). Person-centered therapy. In R. Corsini, *Current psychotherapies* (3rd ed.) (pp. 167–168). Itasca, IL: Peacock.

Nicholson, J., & Golsan, G. (1983). *The creative counselor.* New York: McGraw-Hill.

Niebuhr, R. (1955). *The self and the dramas of history.* New York: Scribners.

Patterson, C. H. (1985). *The therapeutic relationship: Foundations for an eclectic psychotherapy.* Monterey, CA: Brooks/Cole.

Piaget, G., Carkhuff, R., & Berenson, B. (1968) The development of skills in interpersonal functioning. *Counselor Education & Supervision, 2,* 102–106.

Pietrofesa, J., Hoffman, A., & Splete, H. (1984). *Counseling: An introduction* (2nd ed.). Boston: Houghton Mifflin.

Pietrofesa, J., Leonard, G., & Van Hoose, W. (1978). *The authentic counselor.* Chicago: Rand McNally.

Powell, J. (1969). *Why am I afraid to tell you who I am?* Niles, IL: Argus Press.

Prather, H. (1970). *Notes to myself, my struggle to become a person.* Lafayette, CA: Real People Press.

Rothenberg, A. (1988). *The creative process of psychotherapy.* New York: Norton.

Rothstein, S. (1989). *Shockwave.* Carlsbad, CA: Continental Publications.

Rowe, W., Murphy, G., & DeCsipkes, R. (1975). The relationship of counselor characteristics and counseling effectiveness. *Journal of Educational Research, 45* (5), 231–246.

Satir, V. (1987). The therapist story. In M. Baldwin & V. Satir (Eds.). *The use of self.* (pp. 17–25). New York: Haworth.

Schoenberg, B. N. (1971). Personal characteristics of the successful counselor. *Canadian Counselor, 5,* 251–256.

Strong, S. R. (1968). Counseling: An interpersonal influence process. *Journal of Counseling Psychology, 15,* 215–224.

Teyber, E. (1988). *Interpersonal processes in psychotherapy: A guide for clinical training.* Chicago: Dorsey.

Traux, C., & Carkhuff, R. (1967). *Toward effective counseling and psychotherapy.* Chicago: Aldine.

Weinstein, G., & Alschuler, A. (1985). Educating and counseling for self-knowledge development. *Journal of Counseling and Development, 64* (1), 19–25.

Wolpe, J. (1958). *Psychotherapy by reciprocal inhibition.* Palo Alto, CA: Stanford University Press.

Wrenn, C. G. (1983). The fighting risk-taking counselor, *Personnel & Guidance Journal, 61* (6), 323–326.

CHAPTER 2

Albee, G. (1977). Does including psychotherapy in health insurance represent a subsidy from the rich to the poor? *American Psychologist 32,* 9. In J. Hariman (Ed.) (1984). *Does psychotherapy really help people?* (pp. 3–8). Springfield, IL: Charles C Thomas.

Bandler, R., & Grinder, J. (1979). *Frogs into princes: Neuro-linguistic programming.* Moab, UT: Real People Press.

Brammer, L. (1979). *The helping relationship* (2nd ed). Englewood Cliffs, NJ: Prentice-Hall.

Brammer, L., & Shostrom, E. (1982). *Therapeutic psychology: Fundamentals of counseling and psychotherapy* (4th ed). Englewood Cliffs, NJ: Prentice-Hall.

Brammer, L. M. (1985). *The helping relationship: Process and skills* (3rd ed). Englewood Cliffs, NJ: Prentice-Hall.

Bugental, J. (1978). *Psychotherapy and process.* Reading, MA: Addison-Wesley.

Carkhuff, R. (1983). *The art of helping* (5th ed.). Amherst, MA: Human Resource Development Press.

Egan, G. (1975). *The skilled helper.* Monterey, CA: Brooks/Cole.

Egan. G. (1982). *The skilled helper* (2nd ed.). Monterey, CA: Brooks/Cole.

Egan, G. (1986). *The skilled helper* (3rd ed.). Monterey, CA: Brooks/Cole.

Erickson, M. H. (1964). A hypnotic technique for resistant patients: The patient, the technique, and its rationale and field experiments. *The American Journal of Clinical Hypnosis, 7,* 8–32.

Frank, J. (1978). *Psychotherapy and the human predicament.* New York: Schocken Books.

Goleman, D. (1985, August 2). Switching therapists may be best. *Indianapolis News,* p. 9.

Gottman, J., & Lieblum, S. (1974). *How to do psychotherapy and how to evaluate it.* New York: Holt, Rinehart & Winston.

Grinder, J., & Bandler, R. (1975). *The structure of magic* (Vol. II). Palo Alto, CA: Science and Behavior Books.

Hansen, J., Stevic, R., & Warner, R. (1986). *Counseling: Theory and Process* (4th ed.). Boston: Allyn and Bacon.

Ivey, A. (1983). *Intentional interviewing and counseling.* Monterey, CA: Brooks/Cole.

Ivey, A., & Simek-Downing, L. (1980). *Counseling and psychotherapy: Skills, theory, and practice.* Englewood Cliffs, NJ: Prentice-Hall.

Kadushin, A. (1969). *Why people go to psychotherapists.* New York: Atherton.

Lankton, S. (1980). *Practical magic.* Cupertino, CA: Meta Publications.

Otani, A (1989). Client resistance in counseling: Its theoretical rationale and taxonomic classification. *Journal of Counseling and Development, 67,* 458–461.

Patterson, C. H. (1974). *Relationship counseling and psychotherapy.* New York: Harper & Row.

Perls, F. S. (1969). *Gestalt therapy verbatim.* Lafayette, CA: Real People Press.

Peterson, V., & Nisenholz, B. (1984). Innerviewing vs. interviewing: An approach to aid counselors-in-training develop greater empathy skills. *New Jersey Journal of Professional Counseling, 47* (1), 26–29.

Rogers, C. (1951). *Client-centered therapy.* Cambridge, MA: The Riverside Press.

Rosenblatt, D. (1975). *Opening doors.* New York: Harper & Row.

Schofield, W. (1964). *Psychotherapy: The purpose of friendship.* Englewood Cliffs, NJ: Prentice-Hall.

Teyber, E. (1988). *Interpersonal process in psychotherapy: A guide for clinical training.* Chicago: Dorsey.

Watkins, C. E. (1983). Transference phenomena in the counseling situation. *The Personnel and Guidance Journal, 12,* 206–209.

Watkins, C. E. (1985). Countertransference: Its impact on the counseling situation. *Journal of Counseling and Development, 63* (2), 356–359.

Wolpe, J. (1958). *Psychotherapy by reciprocal inhibition.* Stanford, CA: Stanford University Press.

CHAPTER 3

Baldwin, M. (1987). Interview with Carl Rogers on the use of self in therapy. In M. Baldwin & V. Satir (Eds.). *The use of self in therapy* (pp. 45–52). New York: Haworth.

Bandler, R., & Grinder, J. (1975). *The structure of magic* (Vol. I). Palo Alto, CA: Science and Behavior Books.

Blocher, D. (1987). On the uses and misuses of the term theory. *Journal of Counseling and Development, 66,* 67–68.

Bozarth, J. D. (1984). Beyond reflection: Emergent modes of empathy. In R. F. Levant, & J. M. Shlien (Eds.), *Client-centered therapy and the person-centered approach.* (pp. 27–36). New York: Praeger.

Brammer, L. (1979). *The helping relationship: Process and skills* (2nd ed.). Englewood Cliffs, NJ: Prentice-Hall.

Brammer, L. (1985). *The helping relationship: Process and skills* (3rd. ed.). Englewood Cliffs, NJ: Prentice-Hall.

Brammer, L., & Shostrom E. (1982). *Therapeutic psychology: Fundamentals of counseling and psychotherapy* (4th ed.). Englewood Cliffs, NJ: Prentice-Hall.

Buber, M. (1958). *I and thou* (2nd ed.). New York: Scribner.

Bugental, J. (1978). *Psychotherapy and process.* Reading, MA: Addison-Wesley.

Carkhuff, R. (1969). *Helping and human relations.* Vol. II: *Practice and research.* New York: Holt, Rinehart & Winston.

Carkhuff, R. (1980). *The art of helping* (4th

ed.). Amherst, MA: Human Resource Development Press.

Carkhuff, R. (1985). *The art of helping* (6th ed.). Amherst, MA: Human Resource Development Press.

Carkhuff, R. (1987). *The art of helping* (7th ed.). Amherst, MA: Human Resource Development Press.

Combs, A., Avila, D., & Purkey, W. (1978). *Helping relationships: Basic concepts for the helping professions.* Boston: Allyn and Bacon.

Combs, A. W., & Avila, D. L. (1985). *Helping relationships: Basic concepts for the helping professions* (3rd ed.). Boston: Allyn and Bacon.

Cormier, W. H., & Cormier, L. S. (1985). *Interviewing strategies for helpers* (2nd ed.). Monterey, CA: Brooks/Cole.

Danish, S., & Hauer, A. (1973). *Helping skills: A basic training program.* New York: Behavioral Publications.

Dorsey, D. (1982). Unpublished manuscript.

Egan, G. (1975). *The skilled helper.* Monterey, CA: Brooks/Cole.

Egan, G. (1986). *The skilled helper.* (3rd. ed.). Monterey, CA: Brooks/Cole.

Frankl, V. (1959). *Man's search for meaning: An introduction to logotherapy.* New York: Washington Square Press.

Gazda, G., Asbury, F., & Balzer, F. (1984). *Human relations development* (3rd ed.). Boston: Allyn and Bacon.

Glasser, W. (1965). *Reality therapy: A new approach to psychiatry.* New York: Harper & Row.

Goodman, G. (1984). SASHA tapes: Expanding options for helping intended communications. In D. Larson, (Ed.), *Teaching Psychological Skills* (pp. 271–286). Monterey, CA: Brooks/Cole.

Gordon, T. (1974). *Teacher effectiveness training.* New York: Peter Wyden.

Harman, R., & O'Neil, C. (1981). Neurolinguistic programming for counselors. *Personnel and Guidance Journal, 59* (7), 449–453.

Hendricks, G., & Wills, R. (1975). *The centering book: Awareness activities for children, parents, and teachers.* Englewood Cliffs, NJ: Prentice-Hall.

Hutchins, D. E., & Cole, C. G. (1986). *Helping relationships and strategies.* Monterey, CA: Brooks/Cole.

Ivey, A. E. (1971). *Microcounseling: Innovations in interviewing training.* Springfield, IL: Charles C Thomas.

Ivey, A. (1980). *Counseling and psychotherapy: Skills, theories, and practice.* Englewood Cliffs, NJ: Prentice-Hall.

Ivey, A. (1983). *Intentional interviewing and counseling.* Monterey, CA: Brooks/Cole.

Ivey, A., & Authier, J. (1978). *Microcounseling* (2nd ed.). Springfield, IL: Charles C Thomas.

James, N., & Jongeward, D. (1971). *Born to win.* Reading, MA: Addison-Wesley.

Lanning, W., & Carey, J. (1987). Systematic termination in counseling. *Journal of Counselor Education and Supervision, 12* (2), 168–173.

Levitsky, A., & Perls, F. (1970). The rules and games of Gestalt therapy. In J. Fagan (Ed.), *Gestalt therapy now* (pp. 140–149). Palo Alto, CA: Science and Behavior Books.

Lieberman, M., Yalom, I., & Miles, M. (1973). *Encounter groups: First facts.* New York: Basic Books.

Loughary, J., & Ripley, T. (1979). *Helping others help themselves: A guide to counseling skills.* New York: McGraw-Hill.

Mehrabian, A. (1971). *Silent messages.* Belmont, CA: Wadsworth.

Patterson, C. H. (1973). *Theories of counseling and psychotherapy* (2nd ed.). New York: Harper & Row.

Patterson, C. H. (1974). *Relationship counseling and psychotherapy.* New York: Harper & Row.

Perls, F. (1969). *Gestalt therapy verbatim.* Lafayette, CA: Real People Press.

Porter, E. H. (1950). *Introduction to therapeutic counseling.* Boston: Houghton Mifflin.

Rogers, C. (1957). The necessary and sufficient condition of therapeutic personality change. *Journal of Consulting Psychology, 21,* 93–103.

Satir, V. (1987). The therapist story. In M. Baldwin & V. Satir, (Eds.). *The use of self in therapy* (pp. 17–26). New York: Haworth.

Smith, M. C., Glass, G. V., & Miller, T. J. (1980). *The benefits of psychotherapy.* Baltimore: Johns Hopkins University Press.

Traux, C., & Carkhuff, R. (1967). *Toward effective counseling and psychotherapy*. Chicago: Aldine.

Ward, D. (1984). Termination of individual counseling: Concepts and strategies. *Journal of Counseling and Development, 63*, (1), 21–25.

Wilson, F., Lopis, J., & Radke, M. (1978). *The individual and the school*. San Diego, CA: Collegiate Publishing.

Yalom, I. (1985). *The theory and practice of group psychotherapy* (2nd ed.). New York: Basic Books.

Zaro, J., Barack, R., Nedelman, D., & Dreiblatt, I. (1982). *A guide for beginning psychotherapists*. Cambridge, England: Oxford University Press.

CHAPTER 4

Belkin, G. (1975). *Introduction to counseling*. Dubuque, IA: Brown.

Cormier, W., & Cormier, L. S. (1985). *Interviewing strategies for helpers*. Monterey, CA: Brooks/Cole.

Frank, J. (1973). *Persuasion and healing*. Baltimore: Johns Hopkins University Press.

Hackney, H., & Cormier, L. S. (1979). *Counseling strategies and objectives* (2nd ed.). Englewood Cliffs, NJ: Prentice-Hall.

Ivey, A. (1971). *Microcounseling*. Springfield, IL: Charles C Thomas.

Ivey, A. (1983). *Intentional interviewing and counseling*. Monterey, CA: Brooks/Cole.

Martin, D. (1983). *Counseling and therapy skills*. Monterey, CA: Brooks/Cole.

Patterson, C. H. (1974). *Relationship counseling and psychotherapy*. New York: Harper & Row.

Patterson, C. H. (1980). *Theories of counseling and psychotherapy* (3rd ed.). New York: Harper & Row.

Patterson, C. H. (1985). *The therapeutic relationship: Foundations for an eclectic psychotherapy*. Monterey, CA: Brooks/Cole.

Patterson, L., & Eisenberg, S. (1983). *The counseling process* (3rd ed.). Boston: Houghton Mifflin.

Perls, F. (1969). *Gestalt therapy verbatim*. Lafayette, CA: Real People Press.

Pietrofesa, J., Leonard, G., & Van Hoose, W. (1978). *The authentic counselor* (2nd ed.). Chicago: Rand McNally.

Shapiro, A., & Morris, L. (1978). The placebo effect in medical and psychological therapies. In S. C. Garfield, & A. E. Bergin (Eds.), *Handbook of psychotherapy and behavior change* (pp. 370–382). New York: Wiley.

Shertzer, B., & Stone, S. (1971). *Fundamentals of counseling*. Boston: Houghton Mifflin.

Strong, S. R. (1968). Counseling: An interpersonal influence process. *Journal of Counseling Psychology, 15*, 215–224.

Teyber, E. (1988). *Interpersonal process in psychotherapy: A guide for clinical training*. Chicago: Dorsey.

Tyler, L. (1969). *The work of the counselor*. New York: Appleton, Century, Crofts.

CHAPTER 5

Ackerman, N. (1966). *Treating the troubled family*. New York: Basic Books.

Albee, G.(1977). Does including psychotherapy in health insurance represent a subsidy from the rich to the poor? *American Psychologist, 32*, 9. In J. Hariman (Ed.). *Does psychotherapy really help people* (pp. 3–8). Springfield, IL: Charles C Thomas.

American Psychiatric Association (1980). *Diagnostic and statistical manual of mental disorders* (3rd ed.). Washington, DC: American Psychiatric Association.

American Psychiatric Association (1987). *Diagnostic and statistical manual of mental disorders* (3rd ed., rev.). Wshington, DC: American Psychiatric Association.

Conyne, R. (1983). Two critical issues in primary prevention: What it is and how to do it. *Personnel and Guidance Journal, 61* (6), 331–334.

Crookston, B. (1974). The intentional democratic community in college residence halls. *Personnel and Guidance Journal, 52* (6), 382–389.

Dinges, N., Yazzie, M., & Tollefson, G. (1974). Developmental intervention for Navajo mental health. *Personnel and Guidance Journal, 52* (6), 390–395.

Dinkmeyer, D., & Caldwell, E. (1970). *Develop-

mental counseling and guidance. New York: McGraw-Hill.

Erikson, E. H. (1963). *Children and society* (rev. ed.). New York: Norton.

Felner, R., Jason, L., Moritsugu, J., & Farber, S. (Eds.) (1983). *Preventive psychology.* New York: Pergamon Press.

Gazda, G. (1984). *Group counseling: A developmental approach.* Boston: Allyn and Bacon.

Haley, J. (1971). *Changing families.* New York: Grune & Stratton.

Havighurst, R. (1953). *Human development and education.* New York: Longman.

Health and Lifestyle Center of Memorial Hospital. brochure (1983). South Bend, IN.

Ivey, A., with Simek-Downing, L. (1980). *Counseling and psychotherapy: Skills, theories, and practice.* Englewood Cliffs, NJ: Prentice-Hall.

Johnston, C. (1974). Sexuality and birth control: Impact of outreach programming. *Personnel and Guidance Journal, 52* (6), 406–411.

Kohlberg, L. (1971). The stages of moral development as a basis for moral education. In C. Beck, B. Crittenden, & E. Sullivan (Eds.). *Moral education* (pp. 23–92). New York: Newman Press.

Krumboltz, J. D. (Ed.) (1966). *Revolution in counseling.* Boston: Houghton Mifflin.

Minuchin, S. (1974). *Families and family therapy.* Cambridge, MA: Harvard University Press.

Morrill, W., Oeting, E., & Hurst, J. (1974). Dimensions of counselor functioning. *Personnel and Guidance Journal, 52* (6), 354–359.

Ohlsen, M. M. (1979). *Marriage counseling in groups.* Champaign, IL: Research Press.

Parsons, F. (1909). *Choosing a vocation.* Boston: Houghton Mifflin.

Patterson, C. H. (1974). *Relationship counseling and psychotherapy.* New York: Harper & Row.

Patterson, C. H. (1986). *Theories of counseling and psychotherapy* (4th ed.). New York: Harper & Row.

Piaget, J. (1952). *The origins of intelligence in children* (Trans. M. Cook). New York: International Universities Press.

Pietrofesa, J., Hoffman, A., & Splete, H. (1984). *Counseling: An introduction.* Boston: Houghton Mifflin.

Rogers, C. R. (1942). *Counseling and psychotherapy.* Boston: Houghton Mifflin.

Satir, V. (1967). *Conjoint family therapy* (rev. ed.). Palo Alto, CA: Science and Behavior Books.

Sheehy, G. (1976). *Passages: Predictable crises of adult life.* New York: Dutton.

Watzlawick, P. (1966). A structured family interview. *Family Process, 5,* 256–271.

Whiteley, J. M. (1984). *Counseling psychology: A historical perspective.* Schenectady, NY: Character Research Press.

Yalom, I. (1975). *The theory and practice of group psychotherapy* (2nd ed.). New York: Basic Books.

CHAPTER 6

Corey, G., Corey, M., & Callanan, P. (1988). *Issues and ethics in the helping professions.* Pacific Grove, CA: Brooks/Cole.

Dienhart, J. W. (1982). *A cognitive approach to the ethics of counseling psychology.* Washington, DC: University Press of America.

Edwards, R. B. (Ed.) (1982). *Psychiatry and ethics.* Buffalo, NY: Prometheus Books.

Engelkes, J., & Vandergoot, D. (1982). *Introduction to counseling.* Boston: Houghton Mifflin.

Gelman, D. (1987). Growing pains for the shrinks. *Newsweek, 110* (14), 70–72.

Guidepost. (1985). Membership moving toward private practice. *27* (12), 4.

Hollis, J., & Wantz, R. (1986). *Counselor preparation 1986–89.* Muncie, IN: Accelerated Development.

Kegan, A. (1987). Survey explores third-party payment procedures. *Guidepost, 29* (12), 4.

Kitchener, K. S. (1984). Intuition, critical evaluation and ethical principles: The foundation for ethical decisions in counseling psychology. *Counseling Psychologist, 12* (3), 43–55.

Knox, H. (1977). *Cracking the glass slipper: Peer's guide to ending sex bias in your school.* Washington, DC: The NOW Legal Defense and Education Fund.

Leslie, R. (1983). Tarasoff decision extended. *California Therapist,* Nov./Dec., p. 6.

McDonough, P. (1985). My view. *Guidepost, 27* (12), 4.

Melinkoff, E. (1987). Therapists learning to cope with a glut. *Los Angeles Times,* A.27, 1, 14.

Messina, J. (1985). The national academy of certified mental health counselors: Creating a new professional identity. *Journal of Counseling and Development, 63* (10), 607–608.

Naisbitt, J. (1984). *Megatrends.* New York: Warner Books.

Ohlsen, M. (1983). *Introduction to counseling.* Itasca, IL: Peacock.

Stone, L. (1985). National board for certified counselors: History, relationships, and projections. *Journal of Counseling and Development, 63* (10), 605–606.

Tennyson, W. W., & Strom, S. M. (1986). Beyond professional standards: Developing responsibleness. *Journal of Counseling and Development, 64* (5), 298–302.

United States Department of Labor (1983). *Dictionary of occupational titles.* Washington, DC: United States Government Printing Office.

United States Department of Labor (1988). *Occupational outlook handbook, 1988–89 edition.* Scottsdale, AZ: Associated Book Publishers.

Van Hoose, W. H. (1989). Ethical principles in counseling. *Journal of Counseling and Development, 65* (3), 168–169.

Wilcoxon, S. A. (1987). Ethical standards: A study of application and utility. *Journal of Counseling and Development, 65,* 510–511.

CHAPTER 7

ASCA Governing Board (1981). ASCA role statement. The practice of guidance and counseling by school counselors. *The School Counselor, 29* (1), 7–12.

Belkin, G. (1981). *Practical counseling in the schools* (2nd ed.). Dubuque, IA: Brown.

Caplan, G. (1970). *The theory and practice of mental health consultation.* New York: Basic Books.

Chalofsky, N. (1985). HRD careers update. *Training and Development Journal, 39* (5), 64–65.

Chartrand, J., & Lent, R. (1987). Sports counseling: Enhancing the development of the student athlete. *Journal of Counseling and Development, 66* (4), 164–167.

Crego, C. (1985). Ethics: The need for improved consultation training. *Counseling Psychologist, 13* (3), 473–476.

Daniel, R., & Weikel, W. (1983). Trends in counseling: A Delphi study. *Personnel and Guidance Journal, 61* (6), 327–330.

Egan, G. (1975). *The skilled helper.* Monterey, CA: Brooks/Cole.

Egan, G. (1986). The skilled helper (3rd ed.). Monterey, CA: Brooks/Cole.

Faust, V. (1968). *The counselor-consultant in the elementary school.* Boston: Houghton Mifflin.

Ford, D. (1985). The behavioral health movement. *Counseling Psychologist, 13* (1), 93–104.

Fossum, M. A., & Mason, M. J. (1986). *Facing shame: Families in recovery.* New York: W. W. Norton.

Gallessich, S. (1982). *The profession and practice of consultation.* San Francisco: Jossey-Bass.

Gallessich, S. (1985). Toward a meta-theory of consultation. *Counseling Psychologist, 13* (3), 336–354.

Gallup, G. (1984). The 16th annual Gallup poll of the public's attitudes toward the schools. *Phi Delta Kappan, 66* (1), 23–38.

Glasser, W. (1976). *Positive addiction.* New York: Harper & Row.

Gravitz, H., & Bowden, J. (1986). Therapeutic issues of adult children of alcoholics: A continuum of developmental stages. In R. J. Ackerman (Ed.), *Growing up in the shadow: Children of alcoholics* (pp. 187–207). Pompano Beach, FL: Health Communications.

Johnson, C. S. (1985). The American College Personnel Association. *Journal of Counseling and Development, 63* (7), 405–410.

Korchin, S. (1976). *Modern clinical psychology.* New York: Basic Books.

Kottler, J., & Brown, R. (1985). *Introduction to therapeutic counseling.* Monterey, CA: Brooks/Cole.

Krumboltz, C., & Eagleston, J. (1985). Counseling for health. *Counseling Psychologist, 13,* 1, 15–87.

Kubler-Ross, E. (1969). *On death and dying.* New York: Macmillan.

Kurpius, D. (1978). Consultation theory and process: An integrated model. *Personnel and Guidance Journal, 56* (6), 335–338.

LoBello, S. (1984). Counselor credibility with alcoholics and non-alcoholics: It takes one to help one? *Journal of Alcohol and Drug Education, 29* (2), 58–66.

Lowman, R. (1985). Ethical practices of psychological consultation: Not an impossible dream. *Counseling Psychologist, 13* (3), 466–472.

Mannino, F., & Shore, M. (1985). Understanding consultation: Some orienting dimensions. *Counseling Psychologist, 13* (3), 363–367.

Matarazzo, J. (1986). Computerized clinical psychological test interpretations: Unvalidated plus all mean and no signs. *American Psychologist, 41* (1), 14–24.

McGinnis, J. M. (1985). Recent history of federal initiatives in prevention policy. *American Psychologist, 40* (2), 205–212.

Middleton-Moz, J., & Dwinell, L. (1986). *After the tears.* Pompano Beach, FL: Health Communications.

Naisbitt, J., & Aburdene, P. (1985). *Reinventing the corporation.* New York: Warner.

Ohlms, D. (1983). *The disease concept of alcoholism.* Belleville, IL: Gary Whitacker.

Pietrofesa, J., Hoffman, R., & Splete, H. (1984). *Counseling: An introduction.* Boston: Houghton Mifflin.

Rao, T. V. (1985). Integrated human resource development systems. In L. Goodstein & J. P. Pfeiffer (Eds.), *The 1985 Annual: Developing Human Resources* (pp. 227–237). San Diego, CA: University Associates.

Robinson, S., & Gross, D. (1985). Ethics of consultation: The centerville ghost. *Counseling Psychologist, 13* (3), 444–446.

Schaefer, C. (1989). Student assistance programs follow lead of industry's EAPs. *Guidepost, 32* (4), 1, 3, 14.

Schein, E. H. (1978). The role of the consultant: Content expert or process facilitator? *Personnel and Guidance Journal, 56* (6), 346–350.

Schmolling, P., Youkelles, M., & Burger, W. (1985). *Human services in contemporary America.* Monterey, CA: Brooks/Cole.

Smith, R., & Walz, G. (1984). *Counseling and human resource development.* Ann Arbor, MI: ERIC Counseling and Personnel Services Clearinghouse.

Thoreson, C., & Eagleston, C. (1985). Counseling for health. *The Counseling Psychologist, 13* (1), 15–87.

Thurow, L. (1985). More growth ahead in '87. *Time 126* (26), 62.

Today's Education. (1983–84). Journal of the National Education Association Annual edition. Washington, DC: National Education Association, p. 52.

Tomine, S. (1986). Private practice in gerontological counseling. *Journal of Counseling and Development, 64* (6), 406–409.

U.S. Department of Health and Human Services. (1980). Promoting health/preventing disease: Objectives for the nation. DHHS Publication No. 80-3316999. Washington, DC: United States Government Printing Office.

Van Hoose, W., Pietrofesa, J., & Carlson, J. (Eds.). (1973). *Elementary school guidance and counseling: A composite view.* Boston: Houghton Mifflin.

CHAPTER 8

Benjamin, L. (1987). Understanding and managing stress in the academic world. *Highlights: An ERIC/CAPS digest.* Ann Arbor: The University of Michigan, ERIC Clearing House on Counseling and Personnel Services.

Daley, M. R. (1979). Burn out: Smoldering problem in protective services. *Social Work, 24,* 375–379.

Egan, G. (1986). *The skilled helper.* Monterey, CA: Brooks/Cole.

Friedman, M., & Rosenman, R. (1974). *Type A behavior and your heart.* New York: Knopf.

Kriegel, R., & Kriegel, M. (1984). *The C zone: Peak performance under pressure*. New York: Anchor/Doubleday.

Kutash, T., Schlessinger, L., & Associates (1980). *Handbook on stress and anxiety*. San Francisco: Jossey-Bass.

Kyriacou, C., & Sutcliff, J. (1978). A model of teacher stress. *Educational Studies, 4*, 1–6.

Maddi, S., & Kobasa, S. (1984). *The hardy executive*. Homewood, IL: Dow-Jones.

Maslach, C. (1982). *Burnout: The cost of caring*. Englewood Cliffs, NJ: Prentice-Hall.

Moracco, J. C., & McFadden (1982). The counselor's role in reducing teacher stress. *The Personnel and Guidance Journal*, May, 549–552.

Morano, R. A. (1977). How to manage change or reduce change. *Management Review, 66* (11), 21–25.

Nicholson, J., & Golsan, G. (1983). *The creative counselor*. New York: McGraw-Hill.

Perls, F. (1969). *Gestalt therapy verbatim*. Lafayette, CA: Real People Press.

Rice, P. (1987) *Stress and health: Principles and practice for coping and wellness*. Monterey, CA: Brooks/Cole.

Schafer, W. (1987). *Stress management for wellness*. New York: Holt, Rinehart & Winston.

Selye, H. (1978). On the real benefits of eustress. *Psychology Today, 2* (10), 60–64.

Selye, H. (1980). The stress concept today. In T. Kutash, L. Schlessinger, & Associates, *Handbook on stress and anxiety* (pp. 127–143). San Francisco: Jossey-Bass.

Warnath, C. F., & Shelton, J. L. (1976). The ultimate disappointment: The burned out counselor. *The Personnel and Guidance Journal*, Dec., 172–175.

Watkins, C. E., Jr. (1983). Burnout in counseling practice: Some potential professional and personal hazards of becoming a counselor. *The Personnel and Guidance Journal, 61* (5), 304–308. Copyright AACD.

CHAPTER 9

Adams, D. (1987). *Psychology for peace activists*. New Haven, CT: The Advocate Press.

Atkinson, D. R., Morten, G., & Sue, D. W.

(1983). *Counseling American minorities: A cross-cultural perspective* (2nd ed.). Dubuque, IA: Brown.

Aubrey, R. F. (1980). Technology of counseling and science of behavior: A reproachment. *Personnel and Guidance Journal, 58*, 318–327.

Bakan, D. (1988). Some thoughts on reading Blight's article: 'Can society reduce nuclear war?' *Journal of Humanistic Psychology, 28* (2), 61.

Blight, J. G. (1988). Can psychology help reduce the risk of nuclear war? Reflections of a "Little Drummer Boy." of nuclear psychology. *Journal of Humanistic Psychology, 28* (2), 7–58.

Carkhuff, R. R., & Berenson, B. G. (1977). *Beyond counseling and therapy*. New York: Holt, Rinehart & Winston.

Dass, R., & Gorman, P. (1984). *How can I help?* New York: Knopf.

Ellis, A. (1984). The responsibility of counselors and psychologists in preventing nuclear warfare. *Journal of Counseling and Development, 63* (2), 75–76.

Frank, J. (1978). *Psychotherapy and the human predicament*. New York: Schocken Books.

Frank, J. (1987). The drive for power and the nuclear arms race. *American Psychologist, (42)* 337–344.

Gale, R. F. (1974). *Who are you?: The psychology of being yourself*. Englewood Cliffs, NJ: Prentice-Hall.

Gearhart, J. (1984). The counselor in a nuclear world: A rationale for awareness and action. *Journal of Counseling and Development, 63* (2), 67–72.

Harmon, W. W. (1984). Peace on Earth: The impossible dream becomes possible. *Journal of Humanistic Psychology, 24* (3), 77–91.

Kelly, E. W., Jr. (1989). Social commitment and individualism in counseling. *Journal of Counseling and Development, 67* (6), 341–344.

Kohn, A. (1988). Make love, not war. *Psychology Today, 22* (6), 34–39.

Macy, J. (1983). *Despair and personal power in the nuclear age*. Philadelphia: New Society Publishers.

Mack, J., & Medmont, J. E. (1989). On being a

psychoanalyst in the nuclear age. *Journal of Humanistic Psychology, 29* (3), 338–355.

Maslow, A. (1977). Politics 3. *Journal of Humanistic Psychology, 17* (4), 5–20.

Mitroff, I. (1988). Comments on Blight's article. *Journal of Humanistic Psychology, 78* (2), 67.

Most, S., & Grasberg, L. (Eds.) (1988). *Broken circle: A search for wisdom in the nuclear age.* Palo Alto, CA: Consulting Psychologists Press.

Schwebel, M. (1984). Growing up with the bomb. *Journal of Counseling and Development, 63* (2), 73–74.

Skinner, B. F. (1948) *Walden Two.* New York: Macmillan.

Solomon, L. N. (1986). Building the image of peace. *Journal of Humanistic Psychology, 26* (4), 108–115.

South, D. (1984). Notes for a final exam. *Journal of Humanistic Psychology, 24* (3), (5–38).

Stevens, J. O. (1971) *Awareness: Exploring, experimenting, experiencing.* Moab, UT: Real People Press.

UNESCO (1986) Sixth International Colloquium on Brain and Aggression, Seville, Spain.

White, R. K. (1988). The stream of thought, the lifespace, selective attention, and war. *Journal of Humanistic Psychology, 28* (2), 73–86.

Whitely, J. M. (1984). The social ecology of peace: Implications for the helping professions and education. *Journal of Counseling and Development, 63* (2), 77–85.

CHAPTER 10

Assagioli, R. (1965). *Psychosynthesis.* New York: The Viking Press.

Bergantino, L. (1978). A theory of imperfection. *Counselor Education and Supervision, 17* (4), 286–291.

Blocher, D. (1987). On the uses and misuses of the term theory. *Journal of Counseling and Development, 66* (2), 67–68.

Bozarth, J. D. (1985). Quantum theory and the person centered approach. *Journal of Counseling and Development, (3),* 179–182.

Brabeck, M., & Walfel, E. (1985). Counseling theory: Understanding the trend toward eclecticism from a developmental perspective. *Journal of Counseling and Development, (63)* 6, 343–348.

Brammer, L., & Shostrom, E. (1982). *Therapeutic psychology: Fundamentals of counseling and psychotherapy* (4th ed.). Englewood Cliffs, NJ: Prentice-Hall.

Buber, M. (1958). *I and thou* (2nd ed.). New York: Scribner.

Camus, A. (1970). *Lyrical and critical essays* (ed. with notes by P. Thody; trans., E. Kennedy). New York: Vintage.

Caple, R. B. (1985). Counseling and the self-organization paradigm. *Journal of Counseling Development, 64,* 173–178.

Capra, F. (1983). *The turning point: Science, society and the rising culture.* Toronto: Bantam Books.

Carkhuff, R., & Berenson, B. (1977). *Beyond counseling and psychotherapy.* New York: Holt, Rinehart & Winston.

Ellis, A. (1989). Rational-emotive therapy. In R. Corsini (Ed.), *Current psychotherapies* (4th ed.) (pp. 197–238). Itasca, IL: Peacock.

Fadiman, J. (1980). The transpersonal stance. In M. Mahoney (Ed.), *Psychotherapy process: Current issues and future directions* (pp. 35–54). New York: Plenum Press.

Fiedler, F. (1950). A comparison of therapeutic relationships in psychoanalytic, non-directive and Adlerian therapeutic relationships. *Journal of Counseling Psychology, 14,* 436–445.

Frank, J. (1973). *Persuasion and healing* (rev. ed.). Baltimore: Johns Hopkins University Press.

Frank, J. (1978). *Psychotherapy and the human predicament.* New York: Schocken Books.

Goldfried, M. (1982). Toward the delineation of therapeutic change principles. In M. Goldfried (Ed.), *Converging themes in psychotherapy* (pp. 377–393). New York: Springer.

Goldfried, M. R., & Davison, G. C. (1976). *Clinical behavior therapy.* New York: Holt, Rinehart & Winston.

Hansen, J., Stevic, E., & Warner, R. (1986). *Counseling theory and practice* (4th ed.). Boston: Allyn and Bacon.

Hendricks, G. (1982). An overview. In G. Hendricks & B. Weinhold (Eds.). *Transpersonal approaches to counseling and psychotherapy* (pp. 3–22). Denver: Love.

Hendricks, G., & Weinhold, B. (1982). *Transpersonal approaches to counseling and psychotherapy.* Denver: Love.

Herbert, N. (1985). *Quantum reality.* Garden City, NY: Anchor/Doubleday.

Herink, R. (Ed.). 1980. *The psychotherapy handbook.* New York: New American Library.

Ivey, A., with Simek-Downing, L. (1980). *Counseling and psychotherapy: Skills, theories, and practice.* Englewood Cliffs, NJ: Prentice-Hall.

Kierkegaard, S. (1967–78). *Soren Kierkegaard's journals and papers.* H. Hong & E. Hong (Eds. & trans.). Bloomington: Indiana University Press.

Kuhn, T. S. (1970). *The structure of scientific revolutions* (2nd ed). Chicago: University of Chicago Press.

Lambert, M. J., Christensen, E. R., & Dejulio, S. S. (Eds.) (1983). *The assessments of therapy outcome.* New York: Wiley.

Larson, D. (Ed.). (1984). *Teaching psychological skills.* Monterey, CA: Brooks/Cole.

Lazarus, A. (1981). *The practice of multimodal therapy.* New York: McGraw-Hill.

Lieberman, M., Yalom, I., & Miles, M. (1973). *Encounter groups: First facts.* New York: Basic Books.

Lucas, C. (1985). Out at the edge: Notes on a paradigm shift. *Journal of Counseling and Development, (3),* 165–172.

Maslow, A. (1954). *Motivation and personality.* New York: Harper & Row.

Maslow, A. (1970). *Motivation and personality* (rev. ed.). New York: Harper & Row.

Maslow, A. (1971). *The farther reaches of human nature.* New York: Viking Press.

Newton, F. B. (1985). Promise or mirage: A summary. *Journal of Counseling and Development, 11,* 216–217.

Nicholson, J., & Golsan, G. (1983). *The creative counselor.* New York: McGraw-Hill.

Passons, W. (1975). *Gestalt approaches in counseling.* New York: Holt, Rinehart & Winston.

Patterson, C. H. (1973). *Theories of counseling and psychotherapy.* New York: Harper & Row.

Patterson, C. H. (1986). *Theories of counseling and psychotherapy* (4th ed.). New York: Harper & Row.

Patterson, C. H. (1985). *The therapeutic relationship: Foundations for an eclectic psychotherapy.* Monterey, CA: Brooks/Cole.

Perls, F. (1969). *Gestalt therapy verbatim.* Lafayette, CA: Real People Press.

Robinson, F. (1965). Counseling orientations and labels. *Journal of Counseling Psychology, 12,* 338.

Rogers, C. (1951). *Client-centered therapy.* Boston: Houghton Mifflin.

Rogers, C. (1980). *A way of being.* Boston: Houghton Mifflin.

Sartre, J. P. (1971). *The age of reason.* New York: Knopf.

Skinner, B. F. (1953). *Science and human behavior.* New York: Macmillan.

Smith, M. L., & Glass, G. V. (1977). Meta-analysis of psychotherapy outcome studies. *American Psychologist, 32* (9), 752–760.

Smith, M. L., Glass, G. V., & Miller, T. I. (1980). *The benefits of psychotherapy.* Baltimore: Johns Hopkins University Press.

Spence, J., Carson, R., & Thibaut, J. (Eds.) (1976). *Behavioral approaches to therapy.* Morristown, NJ: General Learning Press.

Stefflre, B., & Grant, W. H. (1973). *Theories of counseling.* New York: McGraw-Hill.

Sullivan, H. S. (1953). *The interpersonal theory of psychiatry.* New York: Norton.

Tart, C. (Ed.). (1969). *Altered states of consciousness.* New York: John Wiley & Sons.

Truax, C., & Carkhuff, R. (1967). *Toward effective counseling and psychotherapy.* Chicago: Aldine.

Ungersma, A. J. (1961). *The search for meaning.* Philadelphia: Westminster.

Watts, A. (1957). *The way of Zen.* New York: Vintage.

Whitaker, C. (1976). The hindrance of theory in clinical work. In P. J. Guerim, Jr. (Ed.), *Family therapy: Theory and practice* (pp. 154–164). New York: Gardner Press.

Wrenn, C. G. (1980). Observations on what counseling psychologists will be doing the next 20 years. *The Counseling Psychologist, 8,* 32–35.

Yalom, I. (1975). *The theory and practice of group psychotherapy.* New York: Basic Books.

Zukav, G. (1979). *The dancing Wu Li masters.* New York: Wm. Morrow.

CHAPTER 11

Ardell, D. (1986). *High-level wellness: An alternative to doctors, drugs, and disease.* Berkeley, CA: Ten Speed Press.

Bandura, A. (1977). *Social learning theory.* Englewood Cliffs, NJ: Prentice-Hall.

Bandura, A., & Walters, R. (1963). *Social learning and personality development.* New York: Holt, Rinehart & Winston.

Beck, A. T. (1976). *Cognitive therapy and emotional disorders.* New York: International Universities Press.

Beck, A. T., & Weishaar, M. (1989). "Cognitive therapy." In R. J. Corsini & D. Wedding (Eds.), *Current psychotherapies* (4th ed.) (pp. 285–320). Itasca, IL: Peacock.

Boorstein, S. (Ed.) (1980). *Transpersonal psychotherapy.* Palo Alto, CA: Science and Behavior.

Boss M. (1980). "Transpersonal psychotherapy." In R. Walsh & F. Vaughn (Eds.), *Beyond ego: Transpersonal dimensions in psychology* (pp. 161–164). Los Angeles: J. P. Tarcher.

Boy, A., & Pine, G. (1982). *Client-centered counseling: A renewal.* Boston: Allyn and Bacon.

Brady, J. P. (1980). In M. Goldfried (Ed.), "Some views of effective principles of psychotherapy." *Cognitive Therapy and Research, 4,* 271–306.

Corey, G. (1986). *Theory and practice of counseling and psychotherapy* (3rd ed.). Monterey, CA: Brooks/Cole.

Deliman, T., & Smolowe, J. (1982). *Holistic medicine—harmony of body, mind, spirit.* Reston, VA: Reston Publishing.

Dusay, J. M., & Dusay, K. M. "Transactional analysis." In R. J. Corsini & D. Wedding (Eds.), *Current Psychotherapies* (4th ed.), (pp. 405–453). Itasca, IL: Peacock.

D'Zurilla, T., & Goldfried, M. (1971). Problem solving and behavior modification. *Journal of Abnormal Psychology, 78,* 107–116.

Ellis, A. (1962). *Reason and emotion in Psychotherapy.* New York: Lyle Stuart.

Ellis, A. (1984). Rational-emotive therapy (RET) and pastoral counseling: A reply to Richard Wessler. *Personnel and Guidance Journal, (62),* 266–267.

Ellis, A. (1986a). An emotional control card for inappropriate and appropriate emotions in using rational-emotive imagery. *Journal of Counseling and Development, (65),* 205–206.

Ellis, A. (1986b). Fanaticism that may lead to a nuclear holocaust: The contributions of scientific counseling and psychotherapy. *Journal of Counseling and Development, (65),* 146–151.

Ellis, A. (1989a). Dangers of transpersonal psychology: A reply to Ken Wilber. *Journal of Counseling and Development, (67),* 336–337.

Ellis, A. (1989b). Rational-emotive therapy. In R. Corsini & D. Wedding (Eds.), *Current psychotherapies* (4th ed.) (pp. 197–238). Itasca, IL: Peacock.

Ellis, A., & Yeager, R. (1989). *Why some therapies don't work: The dangers of transpersonal psychology.* Buffalo, NY: Prometheus.

Fadiman, J. (1980). "The transpersonal stance." In R. Walsh & F. Vaughn (Eds.), *Beyond ego: Transpersonal dimensions in psychology,* (pp. 175–181). Los Angeles: J. P. Tarcher.

Fulton, P. R. (1989). "Recent transpersonal dissertations." *Common Boundary (Nov./Dec.),* 29–31.

Goodwin, L. (1986). "A holistic perspective for the provision of rehabilitation counseling services." *The Journal of Applied Rehabilitation Counseling, 17* (2), 29–35.

Grof, S. (Ed.) (1988). *Human survival and consciousness evolution.* Albany: State University of New York Press.

Hendricks, G., & Weinhold, B. (1982). *Transpersonal approaches to counseling and psychotherapy.* Denver: Love.

James, M. & contributors (1977). *Technique in*

transactional analysis. Reading, MA: Addison-Wesley.

Jung, C. (1964). *Man and his symbols.* New York: Delta Books/Dell Publishing.

Lazarus, A. (1971). *Behavior therapy and beyond.* New York: McGraw-Hill.

Lazarus, A. (1981). *The practice of multimodal therapy.* New York: McGraw-Hill.

Mahoney, M. (1974). *Cognition and behavior modification.* Cambridge, MA: Ballinger.

Maslow, A. (1971). *The farther reaches of human nature.* New York: Viking Compass Book.

Meichenbaum, D. H. (1977). *Cognitive and behavior modification.* New York: Plenum.

Morrison, Douglas A. (1986). "A holistic and relational model of health and holiness." *Studies in Formative Spirituality: The Journal of Ongoing Formation, VII* (2), 239–251.

O'Donnell, John (1988). "The holistic health movement: Implications for counseling theory and practice." In R. Hayes, & R. Aubrey (Eds.), *New directions for counseling and human development* (pp. 365–382). Denver: Love.

Ornstein, R., & Ehrlich, P. (1989). *New world, new mind: Moving towards conscious evolution.* New York: Doubleday.

Patterson, C. H. (1986). *Theories of counseling and psychotherapy.* New York: Harper & Row.

Pelletier, K. (1979). *Holistic medicine: From stress to optimum health.* New York: Delacorte Press/Seymour Lawrence.

Raskin, N. J., & Rogers, C. R. (1989). Person-centered therapy. In R. J. Corsini & D. Wedding (Eds.), *Current psychotherapies* (4th ed.) (pp. 155–194). Itasca, IL: Peacock.

Roberts, T. (Ed.) (1975). *Four psychologies applied to education: Freudian, behavioral, humanistic, transpersonal.* Cambridge, MA: Schenkman.

Shertzer, B., & Stone, S. (1980). *Fundamentals of counseling* (3rd ed.). Boston: Houghton Mifflin.

Siegel, B. (1986). *Love, medicine and miracles: Lessons learned about self-healing from a surgeon's experience with exceptional patients.* New York: Harper & Row.

Skinner, B. F. (1953). *Science and human behavior.* New York: Macmillan.

Stensrud, R., & Stensrud, K. (1984). "Holistic health through holistic counseling: Toward a unified theory." *The Personnel and Guidance Journal, (March 1984),* 421–424.

Tart, C. (1975). *Transpersonal psychologies.* Garden City, NY: Doubleday.

Texidor, M., Hawk, R., Thomas, P., Friedman, B., & Weiner, R. (1988). *Statement of the Holistic Counseling Special Interest Network of the American Mental Health Counselors Association.* Washington, DC.

Vaughn, F. (1980). "Transpersonal psychotherapy: Context, content, and process." In R. Walsh & F. Vaughn (Eds.), *Beyond ego: Transpersonal dimensions in psychology* (pp. 182–189). Los Angeles: J. P. Tarcher.

Vaughn, F. (1984). "The transpersonal perspective." In S. Grof (Ed.), *Ancient wisdom, modern science,* (pp. 24–31). Albany: State University of New York Press.

Walsh, R. (1989a). "Asian psychotherapies." In R. J. Corsini & D. Wedding (Eds.), *Current psychotherapies* (4th ed.) (pp. 547–559). Itasca, IL: Peacock.

Walsh, R. (1989b). "Psychological chauvinism and nuclear holocaust: A response to Albert Ellis and defense of nonrational emotive therapies." *The Journal of Counseling and Development, 67,* 338–339.

Walsh, R. & Vaughn, F. (Eds.) (1980). *Beyond ego: Transpersonal dimensions in psychology.* Los Angeles: J. P. Tarcher.

Watson, J. B., & Raynor, R. (1920). Conditioned emotional reactions. *Journal of Experimental Psychology, 3,* 1–14.

Wilber, K. (1980). *The Atman Project: A transpersonal view of human development.* Wheaton, IL: Theosophical Publishing House.

Wilber, K. (1981). *No boundary: Eastern and Western approaches to personal growth.* Boston: Shambhala.

Wilber, K. (1989). "Let's nuke the transpersonalists: A response to Albert Ellis." *The Journal of Counseling and Development, 67,* 332–335.

Wilber, K., Engler, J., & Brown, D. (Eds.)

(1986). *Transformations of consciousness: Conventional and contemplative perspectives on development.* Boston: New Science Library.

Wilson, G. (1989). "Behavior therapy." In R. J. Corsini & D. Wedding (Eds.), *Current psychotherapies* (4th ed.) (pp. 241–282). Itasca, IL: Peacock.

Wolpe, J. (1958). *Psychotherapy by reciprocal inhibition.* Stanford, CA: Stanford University Press.

Wolpe, J. (1973). *The practice of behavior therapy* (2nd ed.). New York: Pergamon.

Yontef, G. M., & Simkin, J. S. (1989). Gestalt therapy. In R. J. Corsini & D. Wedding (Eds.), *Current psychotherapies* (4th ed.) (pp. 323–361). Itasca, IL: Peacock.

CHAPTER 12

Antony, E. J. (1972). The history of group psychotherapy. In H. I. Kaplan, & B. J. Tadock (Eds.), *Sensitivity through encounter and marathon* (pp. 1–26). New York: E. P. Dutton.

Bednar, R. L., Corey, G., Evans, N. J., Gazda, G., Pistole, M. C., Stockton, R., & Robison, F. F. (1987). Overcoming obstacles to the future development of research on group work. *Journal for Specialists in Group Work, 12,* 98–111.

Cohen, A. M., & Smith, D. R. (1976). *The critical incident in growth groups: Theory and technique.* San Diego: University Associates.

Corey, G. (1986). *Theory and practice of group counseling* (2nd ed.). Monterey, CA: Brooks/Cole.

Corey, G. (1990). *Theory and practice of group counseling* (3rd ed.). Pacific Grove, CA: Brooks/Cole.

Corey, G., & Corey, M. S. (1982). *Groups: Process and practice* (2nd ed.). Monterey, CA: Brooks/Cole.

Egan, G. (1970). *Encounter: Group process for interpersonal growth.* Monterey, CA: Brooks/Cole.

Egan, G. (1975). *The skilled helper.* Monterey, CA: Brooks/Cole.

Egan, G. (1986). *The skilled helper* (3rd ed.). Monterey, CA: Brooks/Cole.

Forsyth, D. R. (1983). *An introduction to group dynamics.* Monterey, CA: Brooks/Cole.

George, R. & Dustin, D. (1988). *Group counseling: Theory and practice.* Englewood Cliffs, NJ: Prentice-Hall.

Hansen, J. C., Warner, R. W., & Smith, E. J. (1986). *Group counseling: Theory and process* (2nd ed.). Boston: Houghton Mifflin Co.

Hersey, P. (1984). *The situational leader.* New York: Warner.

Hersey, P., & Blanchard, K. (1972). *Management of organizational behavior: Utilizing human resources* (2nd ed.). Englewood Cliffs, NJ: Prentice-Hall.

Lewin, K. (1944). The dynamics of group action. *Educational Leadership 1,* 195–200.

Lewin, K. (1951). *Field theory in social science.* New York: Harper.

Lieberman, M., Yalom, I., & Miles, M. (1973). *Encounter groups: First facts.* New York: Basic Books.

Lindt, H. (1958). The nature of therapeutic interaction of patients in groups. *International Journal of Group Psychotherapy, 8,* 55–69.

Luft, J. (1984). *Group process: An introduction to group dynamics* (3rd ed.). Palo Alto, CA: Mayfield.

Rolf, I. (1980). Structural integration. In R. Herink (Ed.), *The psychotherapy handbook* (pp. 639–640). New York: New American Library.

Rutan, J. S., & Groves, J. E. (1989). Making society's groups more therapeutic. *International Journal of Group Psychotherapy, 39,* 3–16.

Schmuck, R. A., & Schmuck, P. A. (1979). *Group processes in the classroom* (3rd ed.). Dubuque, IA: W. C. Brown.

Schutz, W. (1980). Encounter therapy. In R. Herink (Ed.), *The psychotherapy handbook* (pp. 177–178). New York: New American Library.

Shapiro, J. L. (1978). *Methods of group psychotherapy and encounter: A tradition of innovation.* Itasca, IL: Peacock.

Starak, Y. (1988). Confessions of a group leader. *Small Group Behavior, 19,* 103–108.

Stogdill, R. M., & Coons, A. E. (Eds.) (1957). *Leader behavior: Its description and measure-*

ment (Research Monograph No. 88). Columbus: Ohio State University.

Sullivan, H. S. (1953). *Conceptions of modern psychiatry*. London: Tavistock.

Trotzer, J. P. (1977). *The counselor and the group: Integrating theory and practice*. Monterey, CA: Brooks/Cole.

Trotzer, J. P. (1989). *The counselor and the group* (2nd ed.). Muncie, IN: Accelerated Development.

Tuckman, B. (1965). Developmental changes in small groups. *Psychological Bulletin (63)*, 384–399.

Yalom, I. D. (1985). *The theory and practice of group psychotherapy* (3rd ed.). New York: Basic Books.

CHAPTER 13

Bateson, G., Jackson, D., Haley, J., & Weakland, J. (1956). Toward a theory of schizophrenia. *Behavioral Science, 6,* (1) 251–264.

Becvar, D. S., & Becvar, R. J. (1988). *Family therapy: A systemic integration*. Boston: Allyn and Bacon.

Beels, C. C., & Ferber, A. (1969). Family therapy: A view. *Family Process, 8,* 280–332.

Bertalanffy, L. von (1968). *General systems theory: Formulations, development, applications*. New York: George Braziller.

Bodin, A. M. (1983). *Family therapy*. Unpublished manuscript.

Bowen, M. (1978). *Family therapy in clinical practice*. New York: Jason Aronson.

Buckley, W. (1967). *Sociology and modern systems theory*. Englewood Cliffs, NJ: Prentice-Hall.

Buhrke, R. A. (1989). Incorporating lesbian and gay issues into counselor training: A resource guide. *Journal of Counseling and Development, 68,* 77–80.

Carter, E. A., & McGoldrick, M. (1980). The family life cycle and family therapy: An overview. In E. A. Carter & M. McGoldrick (Eds.), *The family life cycle: A framework for family therapy* (pp. 16–34). New York: Gardner Press.

Cromwell, R. E., Olson, D. H. L., & Fournier, D. G. (1976). Diagnosis and evaluation in marital and family counseling. In D. H. L. Olson (Ed.), *Treating relationships* (pp. 96–108). Lake Mills, IA: Graphic.

Fisher, L., Anderson, A., & Jones, J. (1981). Types of paradoxical interventions and indications/contraindications for use in clinical practice. *Family Process, 20* (3), 25–35.

Foley, V. (1974). *An introduction to family therapy*. New York: Grune and Stratton.

Foley, V. (1984). Family Therapy. In R. Corsini (Ed.), *Current psychotherapies* (3rd ed.) (pp. 447–490). Itasca, IL. Peacock.

Gladding, S. T., Burggraf, M., & Fenell, D. L. (1987). Marriage and family counseling in counselor education: National trends and implications. *Journal of Counseling and Development, 66,* 10.

Goldenberg, I., & Goldenberg, H. (1985). *Family therapy: An overview* (2nd ed.). Monterey, CA: Brooks/Cole.

Grebe, S. H. (1986). Mediation in separation and divorce. *Journal of Counseling and Development, 64,* 2.

Guerin, P. (Ed.) (1976). *Family therapy*. New York: Gardner Press.

Guerin, P., & Pendagast, E. (1976). Evaluation of family system and genogram. In P. Guerin (Ed.), *Family therapy* (pp. 450–464). New York: Gardner Press.

Gurman, A. S. (1979). Dimensions of marital therapy: A comparative analysis. *Journal of Marital and Family Therapy, 5,* 5–18.

Haley, J. (1963). *Strategies of psychotherapy*. New York: Grune and Stratton.

Kaslow, F. W. (1980). History of family therapy in the United States: A kaleidoscopic overview. *Marriage and Family Review, 3,* 77–111.

Kempler, W. (1981). *Experiential psychotherapy with families*. New York: Brunner/Mazel.

L'Abate, L., & Frey, J. III. (1981). The E.R.A. model: The role of feelings in family therapy reconsidered: Implications for a classification of theories of family therapy. *Journal of Marital and Family Therapy, 7,* 143–150.

Madanes, C., & Haley, J. (1977). Dimensions of family therapy. *The Journal of Nervous and Mental Disease, 165,* 88–98.

Masson, H. C., & O'Byrne, P. (1984). *Applying family therapy*, Oxford, England: Pergamon Press.

McGoldrick, M., & Gerson, R. (1985). *Genograms in family assessment*. New York: Norton.

Minuchin, S. (1974). *Families and family therapy*. Cambridge, MA: Harvard University Press.

Nichols, M. (1984). *Family therapy: Concepts and methods*. New York: Gardner Press.

Ohlsen, M. (1979). *Marriage counseling in groups*. Champaign, IL: Research Press.

Okun, D. F., & Rappaport, L. J. (1980). *Working with families: An introduction to family therapy*. North Scituate, MA: Duxbury Press.

Russell, C., Atilano, R., Andersen, S., Jurich, A., & Bergen, L. (1984). Interviewing strategies. *Journal of Marital and Family Therapy, 7*, 245–246.

Satir, V. (1972). *Peoplemaking*. Palo Alto, CA: Science and Behavior Books.

Solomon, M. A. (1973). A developmental conceptual premise for family therapy. *Family Process, 12*, 179–188.

Steinglass, P. (1978). The conceptualization of marriage from a systems theory perspective. In T. J. Paolino, Jr., & B. S. McCrady (Eds.), *Marriage and marriage therapy: Psychoanalytic, behavioral, and systems theory perspectives* (pp. 17–36). New York: Brunner/Mazel.

Walsh, F., & Stratton, H. (1982). Conceptualizations of normal functioning. In F. Walsh (Ed.), *Normal Family Processes* (pp. 113–131). New York: Guilford Press.

Watzlawick, P. A., Beavin, J. H., & Jackson, D. D. (1967). *Pragmatics of human communication*. New York: Norton.

Watzlawick, P., Weakland, J., & Fisch, R. (1974). *Change: Principles of problem formation and problem resolution*. New York: Norton.

Whitaker, C., & Napier, A. (1978). *The family crucible*, New York: Harper & Row.

Whitaker, C. A. (1975). Psychotherapy of the abused: With a special emphasis on the psychotherapy of aggression. *Family Process, 14*, 1–16.

Yorburg, B. (1975). The nuclear and extended family: An area of conceptual confusion. *Journal of Contemporary Family Studies, 6*, 1.

Zimmerman, J., & Sims, D. (1983). Family therapy. In C. E. Walker, & M. C. Roberts (Eds.), *Handbook of clinical child psychology* (pp. 178–193). New York: Wiley.

Zuk, G. H. (1971). Family therapy: 1964–1970. *Psychotherapy: Theory Research and Practice, 8*, 90–97.

Zuk, G. (1975). *Process and practice in family therapy*. Haverford, PA: Psychiatry and Behavioral Science Books.

CHAPTER 14

Borow, H. (1984). The way we were: Reflections on the history of vocational guidance. *Vocational Guidance Quarterly, 33*, 5–14.

Carkhuff, R. (1969). *Helping and human relations. Vol. I: Selection and training*. New York: Holt, Rinehart & Winston.

Crites, J. O. (1981). *Career counseling*. New York: McGraw-Hill.

Egan, G. (1975). *The skilled helper: A model for systematic helping and interpersonal relating*. Monterey, CA: Brooks/Cole.

Gysbers, N. (1984). Major trends in career development theory. *Vocational Guidance Quarterly, 33*, 1, 15–25.

Havighurst, R. (1953). *Human development and education*. New York: Longmans, Green.

Healy, C. (1982). *Career development*. Boston: Allyn and Bacon.

Herr, E., & Cramer, S. (1979). *Career guidance through the life span*. Boston: Little, Brown.

Herr, E., & Cramer, S. (1984). *Career guidance through the life span* (2nd ed.). Boston: Little, Brown.

Holland, J. (1973). *Making vocational choices: A theory of careers*. Englewood Cliffs, NJ: Prentice-Hall.

Isaacson, L. (1985). *Basics of career counseling*. Boston: Allyn and Bacon.

Joslin, L. (1984). Strictly speaking, vocationally.

The Vocational Guidance Quarterly, June, 260–263.

Krumboltz, J. D. (1976). A social learning theory of career selection. *Counseling Psychologist, 6,* 71–80.

Levinson, D. (1977). *Seasons of a man's life.* New York: Alfred A. Knopf.

Parsons, F. (1909). *Choosing a vocation.* Boston: Houghton Mifflin.

Srebalus, D., Marinelli, R., & Messing, J. (1982). *Career development.* Monterey, CA: Brooks/Cole.

Super, D. (1953). A theory of vocational development. *American Psychologist, 8,* 185–190.

Super, D. (1957). *The psychology of careers.* New York: Harper & Row.

Super, D. (1969). The natural history of lives and of vocations. *Perspectives on Education, 2,* 13–22.

Tolbert, E. (1980). *Counseling for career development.* Boston: Houghton Mifflin.

U.S. Department of Labor (1986). *Dictionary of occupational titles.* Washington, DC: United States Government Printing Office.

U.S. Department of Labor (1988). *Occupational outlook handbook* (1988–89 ed.). Scottsdale, AZ: Associated.

Walz, G., & Benjamin, L. (1984). A systems approach to guidance. *Vocational Guidance Quarterly, 33,* 26–34.

Weinrach, S. (Ed.) (1979). *Career counseling.* New York: McGraw-Hill.

Zunker, V. (1981). *Career counseling.* Monterey, CA: Brooks/Cole.

Zunker, V. (1990). *Career counseling.* (2nd ed.). Monterey, CA: Brooks/Cole.

CHAPTER 15

American Psychiatric Association. (1980). *Diagnostic and statistical manual* (3rd ed.). Washington, DC: American Psychiatric Association.

Baldwin, J. (1906). *Social and ethical interpretations in mental development.* New York: Macmillan.

Baltes, P. B., Reese, H. W., & Lipsitt, L. P. (1980). Life-span developmental psychology. *Annual Review of Psychology, 31,* 65–110.

Biehler, R., & Snowman, J. (1982). *Psychology applied to teaching* (4th ed.). Boston: Houghton Mifflin.

Bridges, K. M. B. (1932). Emotional development in early infancy. *Child Development, 3,* 324–341.

Coleman, J. C., Butcher, J., & Carson, R. (1980). *Abnormal psychology and modern life.* Glenview, IL: Scott, Foresman.

Corsini, R. (1977). *Current personality theories.* Itasca, IL: Peacock.

Craig, G. (1986). *Human development.* (4th ed.). Englewood Cliffs, NJ: Prentice-Hall.

Davidoff, L. (1980). *Introduction to psychology.* New York: McGraw-Hill.

Dewey, J. (1909). *Moral principles in education.* New York: Philosophical Library.

Dupont, H. (1979). Affective development: Stage and sequence. In Mosher, R. (Ed.). *Adolescent development and education: A Janus knot* (163–183). Berkeley, CA: McCurhan.

Erikson, E. (1963). *Childhood and society.* New York: Norton.

Evans, E., & McCandless, B. (1978). *Children and youth* (2nd ed.). New York: Holt, Rinehart & Winston.

Fowler, J. (1981). *Stages of faith: The psychology of human development and the quest for meaning.* New York: Harper & Row.

Fowler, J., with Lawrence, L. (1983). Stages of faith. *Psychology Today,* Nov., 59.

Gardner, H. (1983). *Frames of mind.* New York: Basic Books.

Gilligan, C. (1978). In a different voice: Women's conception of the self and of morality. *Harvard Education Review, 47,* (4), 481–517.

Gilligan, C. (1982). *In a different voice.* Cambridge MA: Harvard University Press.

Guilford, J. P. (1967). *The nature of human intelligence.* New York: McGraw-Hill.

Hamachek, D. (1979). *Psychology in teaching, learning, growth* (2nd ed.). Boston: Allyn and Bacon.

Ivey, A., & Goncalves, (1988). Developmental

theory: Integrating developmental processes into clinical practice. *Journal of Counseling and Development, 66* (9), 406–413.

Keefe, D. (1975). A comparison of the effect of teacher and student led discussion of short stories and case studies on the moral reasoning of adolescents using the Kohlberg model. *Dissertation Abstracts, 3605.* 2734–3735A.

Kegan, R. (1982). *The evolving self.* Cambridge, MA: Harvard University Press.

Kohlberg, L. (1958). *Stages of moral development* (unpublished doctoral dissertation). University of Chicago.

Krathwohl, D. R., Bloom, B. S., & Masia, B. B. (1964). *Taxonomy of educational objectives: Affective domain.* New York: David McKay.

Laing, R. D. (1960). *The divided self.* New York: Pantheon.

Langiman, J. (1975). *Medical embryology* (3rd ed.). Baltimore: Williams and Wilkins.

Loevinger, J. (1976). *Ego development: Conceptions and theories.* San Francisco: Jossey-Bass.

Masters, W. H., Johnson, V. E., & Kolodny, R. C. (1982). *Human sexuality.* Boston: Little, Brown.

McKinnon, J. W., & Renner, J. (1971). Are colleges concerned with intellectual development? *American Journal of Physics, 39,* 1047–1052.

Mead, G. H. (1934). *Mind, self and society: From the standpoint of a social behaviorist.* Chicago: University of Chicago Press.

Mosher, R. (Ed.) (1979). *Adolescents' development and education: A Janus knot.* Berkeley, CA: McCurhan.

Montessori, M. (1964). *The Montessori method.* New York: Schocken.

Piaget, J. (1972). Intellectual evolution from adolescence to adulthood. *Human Development, 15,* 1–12.

Rank, O. (1929). *The trauma of birth.* New York: Harcourt, Brace & World.

Skinner, B. F. (1984). The shame of education. *American Psychologist, 39* (9), 947–954.

Smart, M., & Smart, R. (1972). *Children* (2nd ed.). New York: Macmillan.

Stevens-Long, J., & Cobb, N. (1983). *Adolescence and early adulthood.* Palo Alto, CA: Mayfield.

Stone, L. J., & Church, J. (1973). *Childhood and adolescence* (3rd ed.). New York: Random House.

Super, D. E. (1980). A life-span, life-space approach to career development. *Journal of Vocational Behavior, 16,* (3), 282–298.

Tarrytown Letter. (1984). Six new thinkers about thinking. *Tarrytown Letter, 36/37.*

Tarrytown Letter. (1985). Mind over matter: The artificial intelligence debate. *Tarrytown Letter, 45.*

Thorndike, E. (1913). *Educational psychology.* New York: Teacher's College Press.

Walker, L. (1980). Cognitive and perspective-taking pre-requisites for moral development. *Child Development, 51* (1), 131–139.

Wechsler, D. (1980). *The measurement and appraisal of adult intelligence.* Baltimore: Williams and Wilkins.

Wilson, J., Robeck, M., & Michaels, W. (1969). *Psychological foundation of learning and teaching.* New York: McGraw-Hill.

CHAPTER 16

Ahia, C. (1984). Cross-cultural counseling concerns. *Personnel and Guidance Journal,* Feb., 339–341.

American Psychiatric Association (1980). *Diagnostic and statistical manual of human disorders* (3rd ed.). Washington, DC: American Psychiatric Association.

American Psychiatric Association (1987). *Diagnostic and statistical manual of human disorders* (3rd ed., rev.). Washington, DC: American Psychiatric Association.

Atkinson, D. R., Morten, G., & Sue, D. W. (1982). *Counseling American minorities.* (2nd ed.). Dubuque, IA; Brown.

Bandler, R., & Grinder, J. (1975). *The structure of magic* (Vol. I). Palo Alto, CA: Science and Behavior Books.

Belkin, G. (1984). *Introduction to counseling.* Dubuque, IA: Brown.

Copeland, E. (1982). Minority populations and traditional counseling programs: Some alternatives. *Counselor Education and Supervision, 21,* 187–193.

Christensen, C. P. (1989). Cross-cultural awareness development: A conceptual model. *Counselor Education and Supervision, 28,* 270–289.

Das, A. K., & Littrell, J. M. (1989). Multicultural education for counseling: A reply to Lloyd. *Counselor Education and Supervision, 29,* 7–15.

Fisch, R., Weakland, J., & Segal, L. (1984). *The tactics of change: Doing therapy briefly.* San Francisco: Jossey-Bass.

Heath, A. E., Neimeyer, G. J., & Pedersen, P. B. (1988). The future of cross-cultural counseling: A Delphi poll. *Journal of Counseling and Development, 67* (9), 27–30.

Jackson, M. L. (1987). Cross-cultural counseling at the crossroads: A dialogue with Clemmont E. Vontress. *Journal of Counseling and Development, 66* (9), 20–23.

Lee, D. (1984). Counseling and culture: Some issues. *Personnel and Guidance Journal, 62,* 592–597.

Lloyd, A. P. (1987). Multicultural counseling: Does it belong in a counselor education program? *Counselor Education and Supervision, 26* (3), 164–167.

Merta, R. J., Stringham, E. M., & Ponterotto, J. G. (1988). Simulating culture shock in counselor trainees: An experiential exercise for cross-cultural training. *Journal of Counseling and Development, 66* (1), 242–244.

Neimeyer, G., & Fukuyama, M. (1984). Exploring the content and structure of cross-cultural attitudes. *Counselor Education and Supervision, 23,* 216–224.

Ohlsen, M. (1983). *Introduction to counseling.* Itasca, IL: Peacock.

Parker W. M. (1987). Flexibility: A primer for multicultural counseling. *Counselor Education and Supervision, 26* (3), 176–180.

Parker, W. M., Valley, M. & Geary, C. (1986). Acquiring cultural knowledge for counselors in training: A multifaceted approach. *Counselor Educator and Supervisor, 26* (1), 61–71.

Pedersen, P. (1988). *A handbook for developing multicultural awareness.* Alexandria, VA: American Association for Counseling and Development.

Pedersen, P., & Marsella, A. (1982). The ethical crisis for cross-cultural counseling and therapy. *Professional Psychology, 13* (4), 492–500.

Ponterotto, J. G., & Benesch, K. F. (1988). An organizational framework for understanding the role of culture in counseling. *Journal of Counseling and Development, 66* (1), 237–240.

Rogers, C. (1979). Groups in two cultures. *Personnel and Guidance Journal, 58,* 11–15.

Runion, K., & Gregory, H. (1984). Training Native Americans to deliver mental health services to their own people. *Counselor Education and Supervision, 23,* 225–233.

Sue, D. W. (1981). *Counseling the culturally different: Theory and practice.* New York: Wiley.

Sue, D. W., Bernier, T. E., Durran, A., Feinberg, L., Pedersen, P., Smith, E. T., & Vasquez-Nuttall, E. (1982). Position paper: Cross-cultural counseling competencies. *The Counseling Psychologist, 10* (2), 45–52.

CHAPTER 17

American Psychiatric Association. (1987). *Diagnostic and statistical manual of human disorders* (3rd ed., rev.). Washington, DC: American Psychiatric Association.

Bootzin, R. (1980). *Abnormal psychology* (3rd ed.). New York: Random House.

Buros, O. R. (Ed.) (1975). *The eighth mental measurement yearbook.* Lincoln: University of Nebraska.

Cormier & Cormier, L. S. (1985). *Interviewing strategies for the helpers.* Monterey, CA: Brooks/Cole.

Edwards, R. D. (Ed.) (1982). *Psychiatry and ethics.* Buffalo, NY: Prometheus.

Engen, H. B., Lamb, R. R., & Prediger, D. J. (1982). Are secondary schools still using standardized tests? *Personnel and Guidance Journal, 60,* 287–290.

Fischer, C. (1985). *Individualizing psychological assessments.* Monterey, CA: Brooks/Cole.

Gibson, R., & Mitchell, M. (1981). *Introduction to guidance.* New York: Macmillan.

Goldman, L. (1972). Tests and counseling: The marriage that failed. *Measurement and Evaluation in Guidance, 4,* 213–220.

Goldman, L. (1982). Assessment in counseling: A better way. *Measurement and Evaluation in Guidance, 15* (1), 70–73.

Kovel, J. (1980). The American mental health industry. In D. Ingleby (Ed.), *Critical psychiatry* (pp. 72–100). New York: Pantheon Books.

Laing, R. D. (1967). *The politics of experience.* New York: Pantheon Books.

Loesch, L. (1984). Professional preparation guidelines: An AMECD imperative. *Measurement and Evaluation in Counseling and Development, 17* (3), 153–157.

Mischel, W. (1971). *Introduction to personality.* New York: Holt, Rinehart & Winston.

Patterson, C. H., & Watkins, C. E. (1981). Some essentials of a client-centered approach to assessment. *Measurement and Evaluation in Guidance, 15* (1), 102–106.

Paul, G. L. (1967). Strategy of outcome research in psychotherapy. *Journal of Consulting Psychology, 31,* 109–118.

Pietrofesa, J. J., Hoffman, A., & Splete, H. (1984). *Counseling: An introduction.* Boston: Houghton Mifflin.

Popham, W. J. (1978). *Criterion-reference measurement.* Englewood Cliffs, NJ: Prentice-Hall.

Reik, T. (1948). *Listening with the third ear.* New York: Farrar, Straus.

Rosenthal, R., & Jacobsen, L. (1969). *Pygmalion in the classroom: Teacher expectations and pupils' intellectual development.* New York: Holt, Rinehart & Winston.

Schmolling, P., Youkelles, M., & Burger, W. R. (1985). *Human services in contemporary America.* Monterey, CA: Brooks/Cole.

Shertzer, B., & Linden, J. (1979). *Fundamentals of individual appraisal.* Boston: Houghton Mifflin.

Sugarman, A. (1978). Is psychological diagnostic assessment humanistic? *Journal of Personality Assessment, 42,* 11–21.

Szasz, T. (1973). *The Myth of Mental Illness* (rev. ed.). New York: Harper & Row.

Thorndike, R., & Hagen, E. P. (1977). *Measurement and evaluation in psychology and education* (4th ed.). New York: John Wiley.

Wagner, E. W. (1987). A review of the 1985 standards for educational and psychological testing: User responsibility and social justice. *Journal of Counseling and Development, 66,* 202–203.

Williamson, E. (1972). Trait-factor theory and individual differences. In B. Stefflre, & W. H. Grant (Eds.), *Theories of counseling* (2nd ed.) (pp. 136–176). New York: McGraw-Hill.

Zytowski, D. (1982). Assessment in the counseling process for the 1980's. *Measurement and Evaluation in Guidance, 15* (1), 15–21.

CHAPTER 18

Anderson, W. P., & Heppner, P. (1986). Counselor applications of research findings to practice. *Journal of Counseling and Development, 65,* 152–155.

Barkley, W. M. (1982). Introducing research to graduate students in the helping professions. *Counselor Education and Supervision, 21* (4), 327–331.

Brown, J., & Pate, R. (1983). *Being a counselor: Directions and challenges.* Monterey, CA: Brooks/Cole.

Corsini, R., & Wedding, D. (1989). *Current psychotherapies* (4th ed.). Itasca, IL: Peacock.

Elmore, T. M. (1984). Counseling as research: On experiencing quality. *Measurement and Evaluation in Counseling and Development,* Oct., 142–148.

Gelso, C. J. (1979). Research in counseling: Methodologic and professional issues. *The Counseling Psychologist, 8* (3), 7–35.

Gelso, C. J. (1985). Rigor, relevance, and counseling research: On the need to maintain our course between Scylla and Charybdis. *Journal of Counseling and Development, 63* (9), 551–553.

Goldman, L. (1976). A revolution in counseling research. *Journal of Counseling Psychology, 23,* 543–552.

Heppner, P. P., & Anderson, W. P. (1985). On the perceived non-utility of research in counseling. *Journal of Counseling and Development, 63,* 545–547.

Herson, M., Michelson, L., & Bellack, A. S. (Eds.) (1984). *Issues in psychotherapy research.* New York: Plenum Press.

Hill, C. (1982). Counseling process research: Philosophical and methodological dilemmas. *The Counseling Psychologist, 10* (4), 7–20.

Howard, G. S. (1985). Can research in the human sciences become more relevant to practice? *Journal of Counseling and Development, 63,* 539–544.

Ivey, A., with Simek-Downing, L. (1983). *Counseling and psychotherapy: Skills, theory, and practice.* Englewood Cliffs, NJ: Prentice-Hall.

Keeney, B. P., & Morris, J. (1985). Implications of cybernetic epistemology for clinical research: A reply to Howard. *Journal of Counseling and Development, 63* (9), 548–552.

Kottler, J. A., & Brown, R. W. (1985). *Introduction to therapeutic counseling.* Monterey, CA: Brooks/Cole.

La Fleur, K .N. (1983). Research and evaluation. In J. A. Brown & R. H. Pate (Eds.), *Being a counselor* (pp. 147–172). Monterey, CA: Brooks/Cole.

Larson, J., & Nichols, D. (1972). If nobody knows you've done it, have you? *Evaluation, 1,* 39–44.

Minor, B. J. (1981). Bridging the gap between research and practice. *Personnel and Guidance Journal, 59* (8), 485–486.

Muro, J. J. (1984). Counselor education—Quo Vadis? *Measurement and Evaluation in Counseling and Development,* Oct., 137–138.

Nejedlo, R. (1984). The counselors of tomorrow and research. *Measurement and Evaluation in Counseling and Development,* Oct., 149–152.

Pietrofesa, J., Hoffman, A., & Splete, H. (1984). *Counseling: An introduction* (2nd ed.). Boston: Houghton Mifflin.

Remer, R. (1981). The counselor and research, Part I. *Personnel and Guidance Journal, 59* (9), 621–627.

Rogers, C. (1963). Psychotherapy today or where do we go from here? *American Journal of Psychotherapy, 17* (1), 5–16.

Schofield, W. (1964). *Psychotherapy: The purchase of friendship.* Englewood Cliffs, NJ: Prentice-Hall.

Vacc, N. A., & Loesch, L. C. (1984). Research as an instrument of professional change. *Measurement and Evaluation in Counseling and Development,* Oct., 124–131.

Winfrey, J. K. (1984). Research as an area of renewal for counselor educators and supervisors. *Measurement and Evaluation in Counseling and Development,* Oct., 139–141.

Woolsey, L. K. (1986). Research and practice in counseling. A conflict in values. *Counselor Education and Supervision, 12,* 84–94.

CHAPTER 19

Egan, G. (1986). *The skilled helper* (3rd ed.). Pacific Groves, CA: Brooks/Cole.

Hershenson, D., & Power, J. (1987). *Mental health counseling.* New York: Pergamon.

Naisbitt, J., & Aburdene, P. (1990). *Megatrends 2000.* New York: Morrow.

Satir, V. (1987). The therapist story. In M. Baldwin & V. Satir (Eds.). *The use of self in therapy* (pp. 17–25). New York: Haworth.

Author Index

Aburdene, P., 163, 393
Ackerman, N., 111
Adams, D., 184
Ahia, C., 350
Albee, G., 25, 106
Alexik, M., 5
Alschuler, A., 13
Anderson, A., 289
Anderson, W. P., 381, 384
Ardell, D., 245
Asbury, F., 47
Aspy, D., 5
Assagioli, R., 210
Atkinson, D. R., 183, 341–342, 344–346
Aubrey, R. F., 182
Avila, D., 4, 8, 12, 47

Baldwin, M., 55
Baltes, P. B., 336
Balzer, F., 47
Bandler, R., 54, 344
Bandura, A., 236
Barack, A., 81–82
Barkley, W. M., 385
Bateson, G., 278
Beavin, J. H., 279
Beck, A. T., 237
Becvar, D. S., 273, 275
Becvar, R. J., 273, 275
Bednar, R. Z., 269
Belkin, G., 89, 345
Bellack, A. S., 385
Benesch, K. F., 350
Benjamin, L., 168, 295, 311
Berenson, B., 5–6, 9, 14, 19, 205
Bergantino, L., 196
Bernier, T. E., 353–354
Bertalanffy, L. von, 278–279
Biehler, R., 330
Blanchard, K., 263
Blight, J. G., 185
Bloom, B. S., 329
Bodin, A. M., 291
Bootzin, R., 361
Borow, H., 295
Boss, M., 240
Bowen, M., 281
Boy, A., 228
Bozarth, J. D., 212, 215–216
Brabeck, J., 200
Brammer, L., 30, 42, 44, 47, 73, 196, 198, 200, 208
Bridges, K. M. B., 327
Brown, D., 242
Brown, J., 381

Brown, R., 145–146, 148, 380–381
Buber, M., 72, 207
Buckley, W., 279
Bugental, J., 12, 34
Buhrke, R. A., 273
Burger, W., 153, 360
Burggraf, M., 292
Buros, O. R., 371
Butcher, J., 326

Caldwell, E., 107
Callanan, P., 138
Camus, A., 207
Caplan, G., 159
Caple, R. B., 212, 216
Capra, 210–214, 216–217
Carey, J., 82
Carkhuff, R., 4–6, 14, 16, 19, 30, 47, 49, 51, 54, 60, 65–66, 70, 201, 205, 307
Carlson, J., 149
Carlson, R., 206, 326
Carter, E. A., 272
Chalofsky, N., 165
Christensen, C. P., 343
Church, J., 329
Cobb, N., 328
Cohen, A. M., 251
Cole, C. G., 63
Coleman, J. C., 326
Combs, A., 4, 6, 8, 12, 20, 47
Conyne, R., 106
Coons, A. E., 263
Copeland, E., 354–355
Corey, G., 138, 231, 251, 257, 269
Corey, M., 138, 257
Cormier, L., 9, 11–12, 16, 52, 86–87, 90, 358–359
Cormier, W., 9, 11–12, 16, 52, 86–87, 90, 358–359
Corsini, R., 326, 384
Craig, R., 319–320, 337–338
Cramer, S., 296–297, 299, 301–303, 305
Crites, J. O., 299, 306
Cromwell, R. E., 291
Crookston, B., 117, 119

Daley, M. R., 170
Danish, S., 47
Das, A. K., 352
Dass, R., 187
DeCsipkes, R., 5–6
Dinges, N., 117–118
Dinkmeyer, D., 107
Driblatt, I., 81–82

Dupont, H., 327, 329
Duran, A., 353, 354
Dustin, D., 268–269
D'Zurilla, T., 237

Egan, G., 11, 16, 28, 30, 47–50, 58–59, 66–67, 71–72, 162, 179, 258, 307, 392
Ellis, A., 184, 207, 220, 237–240, 244
Elmore, T. M., 382, 386
Engen, H. B., 358
Engler, J., 242
Erickson, M. H., 40
Erikson, E. H., 107
Evans, E., 316, 319
Eysenck, H. J., 4

Fadiman, J., 209–211, 241
Faust, V., 162
Feinberg, L., 353–354
Fenell, D. L., 292
Fisch, R., 286
Fischer, C., 374
Fisher, L., 289
Foley, V., 278, 280–281, 283–286
Ford, J., 6
Fournier, D. G., 291
Forsyth, D. R., 257
Fowler, J., 332–335
Frank, J., 23, 284–286, 200, 202
Frankl, V., 61, 64
Friedman, B., 226
Friedman, M., 169
Fukuyama, M., 355
Fulton, P. R., 244

Gallessich, S., 159
Gallup, G., 151
Gardner, H., 322, 327
Gazda, G., 47, 107, 269
Gearheart, J., 186
Geary, C., 351
Gelman, D., 131
Gelso, C. J., 381–382, 385–386
George, R., 268–269
Gibran, K., 13
Gibson, R., 366, 368
Gilligan, C., 332
Gladding, S. T., 292
Glass, G. V., 47, 202
Glasser, W., 80
Goldenberg, H., 271, 273, 275, 281, 284, 286, 290, 292–293
Goldenberg, I., 271, 273, 275,

281, 284, 286, 290, 292–293
Goldfried, M., 200–201, 212, 237
Goldman, L., 357, 380–383, 385–386
Goleman, D., 25
Golsan, G., 170, 176
Goodman, G., 57
Goodwin, L., 246
Gordon, T., 79
Gorman, P., 187
Gottman, J., 38
Grant, W. H., 198
Grebe, S. H., 293
Grinder, J., 54, 344
Grof, S., 243
Groves, J. E., 255–256
Guerin, P., 287
Guilford, J. P., 322
Gysbers, N., 309–310

Hagen, E. P., 371–373
Haley, J., 111, 278, 286
Hamachek, D., 13, 15, 320
Hansen, J., 30, 195–197
Harman, R., 54
Harris, S., 15
Hauer, A., 47
Havighurst, R., 107, 303
Hawk, R., 226
Heath, A. E., 350–351
Hendricks, G., 209, 226
Heppner, P., 381–384
Herbert, N., 213
Herink, R., 200
Herr, E., 296–297, 299, 301–303, 305
Hersey, P., 263
Hershensen, D., 393
Herson, M., 385
Hill, C., 382, 384
Hoffman, A., 10, 108, 364, 380
Holder, T., 5
Holland, J., 301
Hollis, J., 121
Howard, G. S., 381–382, 386
Hulnick, H. A., 13, 15
Hurst, J., 104–107, 109–110
Hutchins, D. E., 63

Isaacson, L., 300–301, 306, 308
Ivey, A., 16, 23, 30, 36, 47, 56, 64, 90, 200, 218, 315

Jackson, D., 278–279
Jackson, M. L., 350, 352
James, N., 51
Jersild, A., 12
Johnson, V. E., 321
Johnston, C., 118–119
Jones, J., 289

Jongeward, D., 51
Joslin, L., 298

Kadushin, A., 24
Keefe, D., 331
Keeney, B. P., 386–387
Kegan, A., 129
Kegan, R., 332, 335
Kelly, E. W., Jr., 182–183
Kempler, W., 285
Kitchener, K. S., 139
Knox, H., 141
Kobasa, S., 169
Kohlberg, L., 107, 331
Kohn, A., 184
Kolodny, R. C., 321
Korchin, S., 160–161
Kottler, J., 145–146, 148, 380–381
Kovel, J., 361
Krathwohl, D. R., 329
Kriegel, M., 169
Kriegel, R., 169
Krumboltz, J. D., 300
Kurpius, D., 160–161
Kutash, T., 167
Kyriacou, C., 167

La Fleur, K. N., 379–381
Laing, R. D., 335, 361
Lamb, R. R., 358
Lankton, S., 23
Lanning, W., 82
Larson, J., 381
Lazarus, A., 198, 235
Lee, D., 340, 342–344
Leonard, G., 9–10
Leslie, R., 138
Levinson, D., 303
Levitsky, A., 74
Levitt, E., 4
Lewin, K., 251
Lieberman, M., 5, 64, 198, 200–201, 264
Lieblum, S., 38
Lilly, J., 13
Lindt, H., 261
Lipsitt, L. P., 336
Littrell, J. M., 352
Lloyd, A. P., 351
Loesch, L., 359, 378, 381, 383, 385–386
Loevinger, J., 335
Lopis, J., 76
Loughary, J., 51
Lucas, C., 212, 215–217

Macy, J., 187–188
Madanes, C., 286
Maddi, S., 169
Mahoney, M., 236

Mannino, F., 159
Marinelli, R., 296, 298–300, 307
Marsella, A., 346, 353
Masia, B. B., 329
Maslach, C., 174
Maslow, A. H., 6–8, 208, 241–242
Masson, H. C., 290
Masters, W. H., 321
May, R., 13
McCandless, B., 316, 319
McDonough, P., 126
McFadden, H., 167
McGoldrick, M., 272
McKinnon, J. W., 325
Meador, B., 17
Mehrabian, A., 51
Meichenbaum, D. H., 207, 237
Melinkoff, E., 131
Merta, R. J., 351
Messina, J., 124
Messing, J., 296, 298–300, 307
Michaels, W., 317
Michelson, L., 385
Miles, M., 5, 64, 198, 200, 264
Miller, T. J., 47, 202
Minuchin, S., 111, 285
Mischel, W., 365, 367
Mitchell, M., 366, 368
Mitroff, I., 185
Montessori, M., 318
Moracco, J. C., 167
Morano, R. A., 168
Morrill, W., 104–107, 109–110
Morris, J., 386–387
Morris, L., 85
Morrison, D. A., 246
Morten, G., 183, 341–342, 344–346
Muro, J. J., 378, 381, 383
Murphy, G., 5–6

Naisbitt, J., 127–128, 130, 148, 163, 393
Nedelman, D., 81–82
Nejedlo, R., 385
Newton, F. B., 212
Nichols, D., 381
Nichols, M., 272, 278–280, 284–287
Nicholson, J., 170, 176
Niebuhr, R., 15
Niemeyer, G. J., 350–351, 355
Nisenholz, B., 28–29

O'Byrne, P., 290
O'Donnell, J., 245–247
Oeting, E., 104–107, 109–110
Ohlsen, M., 111, 135, 291, 345, 353
Okun, D. F., 273, 278, 284–285, 291

Olson, D. H. L., 291
O'Neil, C., 54
Otani, A., 40

Parker, W. M., 351
Parsons, F., 295
Pate, R., 381
Patterson, C. H., 7–8, 27, 65, 68, 70–71, 86, 115, 195, 200–202, 365
Passons, W., 218
Paul, G. L., 359
Pedersen, P. B., 341, 346, 350–351, 353–354
Pendergast, E., 287
Perls, F., 37, 42, 73–74, 93, 173
Peterson, V., 28–29
Piaget, J., 5, 107, 318
Pierce, R., 5
Pietrofesa, J., 9–10, 108, 149, 364, 380
Pine, G., 228
Pistole, M. C., 269
Ponterotto, J., 350–351
Popham, W. J., 370
Porter, E. H., 75
Powell, J., 15
Power, J., 393
Prather, H., 21
Prediger, D. J., 358
Purkey, W., 4, 8, 12

Radke, M., 76
Rank, O., 319
Rao, T. V., 163–165
Rappaport, L. J., 273, 278, 284–285, 291
Reese, H. W., 336
Reik, T., 367
Renner, J., 325
Rice, P., 169
Ripley, T., 51
Robeck, M., 317
Robinson, F., 199
Robison, F. F., 269
Roebuck, F., 5
Rogers, C., 17, 41–42, 47, 61, 64–65, 102, 340, 378
Rosenblatt, D., 26
Rosenman, R., 169
Rothstein, S., 5–6, 16, 20
Rowe, H., 5–6
Rutan, J. S., 255–256

Sartre, J. P., 207
Satir, V., 12, 55, 111, 272, 285, 391–392
Schaefer, C., 152
Schafer, W., 169
Schein, E. H., 160
Schlessinger, L., 167

Schmolling, P., 153, 360
Schmuck, P. A., 251
Schmuck, R. A., 251
Schofield, W., 25, 378
Schwebel, M., 183
Schutz, W., 253
Selye, H., 167–168, 179
Shapiro, A., 85
Sheehy, G., 107
Shelton, J. L., 171
Shertzer, B., 87, 226, 364
Shore, M., 159
Shostrom, E., 42, 44, 73, 196, 198, 200, 208
Siegel, B., 245
Simek-Downing, L., 16, 23, 36, 200, 218
Skinner, B. F., 184, 206, 235, 335
Smart, M., 319
Smart, R., 319
Smith, D. R., 251
Smith, E. T., 353–354
Smith, M. C., 202
Smith, R., 163, 165
Snowman, J., 330
Solomon, L. N., 187
Solomon, M. A., 272
South, D., 188
Spence, J., 206
Splete, H., 10, 108, 364, 380
Srebalus, D., 296, 298–300, 307
Starak, Y., 250
Stefflre, B., 198
Steinglass, P., 280
Stensrud, K., 246
Stensrud, R., 246
Stevens-Long, J., 328
Stevic, R., 30, 195–197
Stockton, R., 269
Stogdill, R. M., 263
Stone, L., 124
Stone, L. J., 329
Stone, S., 87, 226, 364
Stratton, H., 290
Stringham, E. M., 351
Strong, S. R., 11, 16, 86
Sue, D. W., 183, 341–342, 344–346, 349–350, 353–355
Sugarman, A., 358
Sullivan, H. S., 258
Super, D., 302–303, 335
Sutcliff, J., 167
Szasz, T., 360

Tart, C., 210
Texidor, M., 226
Teyber, E., 94
Thibaut, J., 206
Thomas, P., 226
Thorndike, R., 322, 371–373

Thurow, L., 162
Tolbert, E., 298, 303
Tollefson, G., 117–118
Truax, C., 5, 65, 201
Tuckman, B., 259
Tyler, L., 89

Ungersma, A. J., 202

Vacc, N. A., 378, 381, 383, 385–386
Valley, M., 351
Van Hoose, W., 9–10, 140, 149
Vasquez-Nuttall, E., 353–354
Vaughn, F., 220, 241–243

Walsh, F., 290
Walsh, R., 220, 240, 243
Walters, R., 236
Walz, G., 163, 165, 295, 311
Wantz, R., 121
Ward, D., 81–83
Warnath, C. F., 171
Warner, R., 30, 195–197
Watkins, C. E., Jr., 44, 173, 365
Watts, A., 210
Watzlawick, P., 111, 279, 286
Weakland, J., 278, 286
Wechsler, D., 323
Wedding, D., 384
Weiner, R., 226
Weinhold, B., 226
Weinstein, G., 13
Welfel, E., 200
Whitaker, C. A., 280
Whiteley, J. M., 100
Wilber, K., 220, 240, 242
Wilcoxon, S. A., 140
Williamson, E., 364
Wilson, F., 76
Wilson, J., 317
Winfrey, J. K., 381, 383, 387
Wolpe, J., 27, 235
Woolsey, L. K., 381–382, 384, 386
Wrenn, C. G., 10, 217

Yaeger, R., 240
Yalom, I., 5, 64, 110, 198, 256–257, 259–260, 262, 264–267, 269
Yazzie, M., 117–118
Yorburg, B., 273
Youkelles, M., 153, 360

Zaro, J., 81–82
Zuk, G. H., 281
Zukav, G., 212–214
Zunker, V., 298, 308–309
Zytowski, D., 358

Subject Index

Accreditation, 125–126, 135
Achievement tests, 371
Ackerman, Nathan, 275, 278
Action, 77–82
Adams, David, 184
Adler, Alfred, 183–184, 217,
    251, 268, 273, 275
Adolescence, 111, 317, 320–
    321, 325, 334, 336
Adulthood, 321
Advising, 78
Affective development, 327,
    329–330
Agencies, counselors in, 174
AIDS, 156, 319
Alcoholism, 154–155
Altered states of consciousness,
    210
Ambiguity, tolerance of, 10
American Arbitration Associa-
    tion, 292
American Association for Coun-
    seling and Development
    (AACD), 100, 107, 121,
    124, 126, 130, 132, 155,
    158, 185, 295, 297, 378
  and ethics, 135, 137–139,
    141, 395–402
American Association of Marital
    Counseling, 290
American Association of Mar-
    riage and Family Thera-
    pists (AAMFT), 124, 132,
    137, 290, 292
American College Personnel
    Association (ACPA), 133
American Mental Health Coun-
    selors Association
    (AMHCA), 124, 135
American Personnel and Guid-
    ance Association (APGA),
    100, 107, 132
American Psychiatric Association
    (APA), 25, 122, 132, 137,
    141, 185, 323, 375, 378
American Rehabilitation Coun-
    seling Association (ARCA),
    133, 158
American School Counselors
    Association (ASCA), 133,
    150
American Society of Training
    and Development (ASTD),
    116, 132
Anecdotal reports, 368
Anxiety, 243
Aptitude tests, 371
Aquinas, Thomas, 212

Aristotle, 212
Artificial intelligence, 322
Art therapy, 116
Assertiveness, 87–88
Assessment, 357–359
  approaches to, 363–366
  and career counseling, 306
  guidelines for, 374–375
  of intelligence, 322–323
  of personality, 371–372
  techniques of, 366–373
  types of, 362–366
Association for Adult Develop-
    ment and Aging (AADA),
    135, 155
Association for Counselor Edu-
    cation and Supervision
    (ACES), 125, 133, 292
Association group, 105, 111–
    112
Association for Humanistic
    Education and Develop-
    ment (AHEAD) 133
Association for Measurement
    and Evaluation in Coun-
    seling and Development
    (AMECD), 133–134
Association of Mental Health
    Counselors, 121
Association for Multicultural
    Counseling and Develop-
    ment (AMCD), 134, 355
Association for Religious and
    Value Issues in Counseling
    (ARVIC), 134
Association for Specialists in
    Group Work (ASGW),
    134, 136, 268
Association of Specialists in
    Training and Development
    (ASTD), 165
Association for Transpersonal
    Psychology, 209
Attending, 27, 34–36, 48–57, 80
  to counseling process, 91–92
  physical, 49–50
  psychological, 50–54
  self–, 54–56, 94, 140
Attitude, 3, 176–177
Attitude questionnaires, 372–
    373
Attractiveness, of counselor, 87
Audiotaping, 45, 86, 89, 109,
    117, 218
Authenticity, 10–11, 16
Autobiography, 369
Autonomy, 139
Avoidance, 71

Bacon, Sir Francis, 212
Bandura, Albert, 206
Bateson, Gregory, 386
Behavior, hostile, 45
Behavioral counseling, 78, 102,
    110, 364–365
Behaviorist theory, 202, 206–
    207, 217, 268
Beneficence, 139
Berne, Erik, 231
Bibliotherapy, 109
Biofeedback, 210
Birth defects, 318–319
Birthing process, 319–320
Body therapies, 116
Bohr, Niels, 214
Bonding, mother-child, 320
Bowen, Murray, 275, 281, 284
BREADS/LT, 175–179. See also
    Stress, managing
Breathing, 176
Buber, Martin, 207
Buckley Amendment, 141
Burnout, 55, 167–170
  causes, 172–174
  in counseling training, 170–
    172
  preventing, 174–179, 190
  and stress, 168–169
Business and industry, 109, 112,
    127–128, 162

Camus, Albert, 207
Career counseling, 307
  and computers, 308–309
  origins, 295–297
  vs. personal counseling, 298–
    299
  in schools, 297
  strategies, 306–309
  theories of, 299–306
  trends in, 309–311
Career development programs,
    163
Career education, 296–297
Careers, in counseling, See
    Specialties, counseling
Cartesian philosophy, 212, 217
Case study, 380
Case-study approach, 205
Catharsis, 37, 177, 257
Certification, 123–125, 135,
    158, 292
Certified Clinical Mental Health
    Counselor (CCMHC), 124
Change, social context of, 182–
    183
Charcot, Jean Martin, 99

Checklists, 267–268
Child abuse, 138, 141
Childhood, 320, 324–330, 333
Children, 107, 109, 325
Chinese philosophy, 214–215
Classical conditioning, 235–236
Clear and imminent danger, 138
Client-centered counseling, 202, 208, 221. *See also* Person-centered therapy
Clients, 53, 54
    becoming, 24–25
    and behaviorism, 207
    changes in, 30, 32–40
    characteristics of, 23–24, 32–40
    as group member, 259–262
    and humanistic approach, 208
    selecting, 179
    as self-assessors, 365
Closing ceremony, 40
Cognitive-behavioral approach. *See* Behaviorist theory
Cognitive-behavioral counseling, 102, 234–238
Cognitive development, 324–326
Cohesion, group, 257, 261
Collective unconscious, 217
Commission on Rehabilitation Counselor Certification, 124
Commitment, obtaining, 80
Communications, 230
    facilitating and blocking, 254–265
    and family counseling, 278, 285
    privileged, 138, 142
Community, 105, 112, 128–130
Computers, 109, 308–310
Complementarity, principle of, 214
Concreteness, 68–69
Conditioning, 206, 235–236
Confidentiality, 137–138, 255, 309
Confrontation, 69–72, 258, 261
Congruence, 65–66
Consultation, 109, 116–117, 158–162, 165
Contamination, 232
Content, responding to, 59–61
Continuing education, 126
Contract, counselor-client, 233–234
Copernicus, 212
Council for Accreditation of Counseling and Related Educational Programs (CACREP), 125, 292
Counseling:

in business and industry, 162–165
vs. consulting, 158, 161–162
and cross-cultural factors, 350
crisis, 93–94, 109
developmental, 107–109, 111
development of, 182–183
ethical issues in, 137–140
family, 111, 273, 275, 278–280
goal of, 315
as helping process, 30–45
individual, 104, 110–111
legal issues in, 137, 140–142
multicultural approach to, 352–355
origins of, 99–104
preventive, 106–109, 111
vs. psychotherapy, 112–113
scope of, 100
settings for, 375
stages of, 32, 34–40
success in, 220
theories of, 198–199
wellness, 108
Counseling model, 104–109
Counseling session, 88–94
Counseling theory, 211–215, 217–218
Counselor, 295
    in agencies and institutions, 174
    belief of in theory, 201
    as catalyst, 24
    as change agent, 345
    characteristics of, 87–88
    and children, 325
    in cognitive-behavioral counseling, 237
    education of, 20, 121, 385–387
    effective, 5–19
    family, 273, 275, 278–280
    as generalist, 145
    in Gestalt therapy, 229
    high-level, 71
    market for, 127–131
    mental health, 103, 121, 123
    as part of team, 247
    personality of, 6–11
    person-centered, 73
    professional, 132, 135–136
    in a relationship, 17–19
    and research, 385–387
    responsibility of, in society, 182–190
    self of, 391–392
    skills of, 5, 16–17, 353–354, 392–393
    in TA, 233–234
    tasks of, 25–27, 36, 216, 342–345, 349, 353–354

training of, 353–355
in transpersonal counseling, 243
types of, 122
values of, 384
variables among, 379
wholistic, 245–248
Counselor-client relationship, 173–174, 216
Countertransference, 44–45
Court testimony, 141–142
Credentialing, 122–126
Criterion-referenced tests, 370
Cross-cultural awareness, 343–344
Cross-cultural counseling, 340–343, 344–346, 349, 350–353
Cues, nonverbal, 51–52
Cultural pluralism, 341–343
Cybernetics, 386–387

Davis, Jessie, 100
Decision making, teaching, 308
Decision-making theory, 299–300
Decision points, 30
Deletions, 54
Descartes, Réné, 212
Development, human, 315
    cognitive-intellectual, 322–335
    and environment, 335–336, 338
    moral and spiritual, 330–335
    motor, 318–321
    physical, 318–321
    social-emotional, 326–327, 329–330
    stages of, 107, 324–326
    and theory, 198
    of whole person, 316–318
Developmental approach, 302–303, 306
Developmental counseling, 107–109, 111–112
Developmental groups, 253
Diagnosis, 359–363
Diagnostic and Statistical Manual, 323, 362–363
Diet, and stress–management, 177
Directives, 78–79
Direct service, 108–109, 113, 116
Disorders, organic vs. functional, 360
Distortions, 54
Distress, 168, 173
Divorce mediation, 292–293
Drug abuse. *See* Substance abuse
Drug therapy, 210, 360

Dupont, H., 327, 329
Duvall, Evelyn, 272
Dysfunction, in family, 271–272, 280–281, 285, 287

Eastern philosophy, 102, 240, 242, 245, 340
Eclecticism, 199–200
Education, 20, 163–164
Education for all Handicapped Children Act (PL 94–142), 141
Educators for Social Responsibility, 188
Ego, 204, 210–211, 326
Ego states, 231–233
Elementary schools, counseling in, 149–150
Ellis, Albert, 238, 240
Emic approach, to study of culture, 344
Emotional cutoff, 284
Emotional development, 327, 329–330
Emotional factors, as obstacles, 186–187
Emotions, 327, 329–330. See also Feelings
Empathy, 28, 257–258
   advanced accurate, 66–68
   developing, 51–52
   and reflection, 61, 64–66
   responding with, 58–59
Employee Assistance Programs (EAPs), 128, 164
Empowerment, 187–188
Encounter groups, 253, 264
"Encouragers," 56–57
Energy, level of, 9, 13
Environment:
   for counseling, 85–87, 158
   effects of, 335–336, 338
   vs. heredity, 323–324
   influence of, 318–319, 324, 326
   and stress, 168
Equifinality, 280, 287
Erikson, Erik, 205, 217, 242, 326–327, 332
Escalation, 289
Essays, client, 369
Ethics, 378
   code of, 395–403
   and groups, 268
   professional, 135–142
Ethnocentrism, 341–342
Etic approach, to study of culture, 343–344, 354–355
Eustress, 168
Exercise, 176
Existentialism, in counseling

theory, 43, 55, 207–209, 228
Experiential/humanistic counseling, 284–285
Exploration, 36–37, 58–66, 82
Eye contact, 49–50

Fairness, 140
Faith, 332
Family:
   changing nature of, 127
   of counselor, 171–172
   defined, 271–272
   homeostasis of, 278
   and human development, 316
   as intervention target, 111
   life cycle of, 272–273
   as primary group, 104–105
   sculpting, 287
   and therapy, 102–103
Family counseling, 154, 273, 275, 278–280
   approaches to, 281–287
   certification in, 292
   relationships in, 171, 172
   techniques, 287–289
   when needed, 289–290
Family Education Rights and Privacy Act—1974, 141
Family Mediation Association, 292
Family systems theory, 217, 281–284
Feedback, 61, 200–201, 258, 280, 309
Feelings, 53, 60, 80, 90–91. See also Emotions
Fees, 109
Fidelity, 140
Field of counseling model, 117–118
Field theory, 251
First session, 36
"Flight to health," 37
Fowler, James, 332–333
Frank, Jerome, 184–185
Frankl, Victor, 184
Free association, 204–205
Freud, Anna, 205
Freud, Sigmund, 43, 99, 110, 183, 187, 205, 211, 217, 221, 273, 275, 281, 316, 319, 326, 330, 336, 380
Freudian analysis, 200, 203–205
Freudian therapy, 43
Fromm, Erich, 217

Galileo, G., 212
Game analysis, 233
Gardner, Howard, 322, 327, 330
Generalist, 145

Generalizations, 54
General systems theory, 215–218, 279–280
Genogram, 287–288
Genuineness, 65–66
Gerontological counseling, 155
Gestalt therapy, 39, 43, 73–74, 78, 102, 110, 200–201, 228–231, 251, 253, 268, 284–285
Glasser, William, 80, 83–84
Gordon, Thomas, 79, 83–84
Government, 156–157
   and career education, 296–297
   programs of, 122–123, 129
Grof, Stanislav, 210–211, 241
Group counseling, 154
   advantages of, 254–255
   and career, 307
   disadvantages of, 255–256
   evaluating, 269
   focus of, 266–268
   history of, 100, 102–104, 250–252
   vs. individual, 110–111
   issues in, 268–269
   preventive, 107–108, 252
   stages of, 258–263
   therapeutic forces in, 256–258
Group flight, 265
Group leaders, 256
   behavior of, 259–264
   functions of, 264–267
   standards for, 268–269
Group psychotherapy, 251
Groups, 104–105, 110–111, 252–254
Growth, 317–318
Guidance, career, 306–307

Haley, Jay, 286
Health counseling, 155–157
Heisenberg, Werner, 214
Helping, 4–5, 19–20, 32, 34–40
Here and now, 253, 265–268, 280, 285
Heredity, vs. environment, 323–324
High schools, counseling in, 150–152
Homeostasis, family, 278
Homework, 78–79, 286
Horney, Karen, 217
Hostility, 45
Humanistic approach, 207–209, 217
   and assessment, 365–366, 374
Human nature, 246
Human-potential movement, 252

Human resource development, (HRD), 162–165
Hyperstress, 168–170
Hypnotherapy, 116
Hypostress, 168–170

Id, 204
Immediacy, 72–73
Individual, as intervention target, 104, 110–111
Individual counseling, 110–111, 307
Industry. See Business and industry
Infancy, 324, 329–333
Information giving, 306–307
Informed consent, 138
Infusion, 297
Inner-view, 48, 216, 349
    environment of, 85–87
    vs. interviewing, 26–30
Inner work, 188–190
Insights, 37–38
Insight therapies, 206
Institute of Noetic Sciences, 210
Institution, 105, 112, 174
Insurance, liability, 142
Insurance companies, 122, 129, 153–154, 362
Intelligence, 322–323, 371
Intelligence quotient (IQ), 320, 322–323
Interaction, counselor-client, 173–174
Interest inventories, 373
International Association of Addictions and Offenders Counselors (IAAOC), 134
International Association of Counseling Services (IACS), 125–126
International Association of Marriage and Family Counselors (IAMFC), 135
Interpersonal skills, 257–258
Interpretatation, 73–74
Intervention, 286–287
    methods of, 108–109, 113, 116–117
    purposes of, 106–108, 112–115
    target of, 104–105, 110–112
Interview, 26–30, 369
Intimacy, 11
Intrapsychic approach, 345–346, 349
Intrapsychic conflict, 281
Introjection, 229
Involvement, professional obstacles to, 185–186

Janet, Pierre, 99
Journals, 16, 126, 132–134, 369
Jung, Carl, 203, 210, 217, 240

Kepler, Johann, 212
Kierkegaard, Soren, 207
Klein, Melanie, 205
Kohlberg, Lawrence, 330–332

Laing, R. D., 361
Language barriers, 349
Laughter, 177
Laws, 141
Lazarus, Arnold, 198, 235
Leadership, functions of, 64
Left brain, 16, 346
Legal issues in counseling, 137–142
Lewin, Kurt, 251–252, 263
Licensure, 123–125, 135
Life counseling, 107
Life-cycle, family, 272–273
Life planning, 295, 298. See also Career counseling
Lifestyle, 298
Lifton, Robert Jay, 184, 186–187
Linking, 267–268
Listening, 27, 53–54, 80

Madanes, Cloe, 286
Male climacteric, 321
Marathon groups, 253
Marriage counseling, 111, 290–293
Maslow, Abraham, 184, 208, 210, 241, 252
Mass group process commentary, 265
Media, 109, 117, 317, 336
Medical model, 360–361
Meditation, 176, 210
Menopause, 321
Mental health, 121–123, 137
    in communities, 129–130
    and physical health, 216
    reformers in, 182
Method III approach, 79
Middle/junior high school, counseling in, 150–152
Midlife crisis, 303
Milieu therapy, 116
Military Educators and Counselors Association (MECS), 155
Minority, 342–343, 346
Minuchin, Salvador, 285–286
Mitchell, Edgar, 210
Moral development, 330–332
Moreno, Jacob, 228, 251–252
Motor development, 318–321
Multiaxial assessment, 362–363

Multi-modal therapy, 198
Music therapy, 116

National Association of Social Workers (NASW), 132
National Board of Certified Counselors, 137
National Career Development Association (NCDA), 133, 297
National Council on Measurement, 375
National Counseling Certification Exam, 12
National Defense Education Act (NDEA), 102
National Education Association (NEA), 149, 358
National Employment Counselors Association (NECA), 134, 297
National Institute of Mental Health, 200
Nationally Certified Career Counselor (NCCC), 124
Nationally Certified Counselor (NCC), 124, 136, 315, 392
National Organization of Student Assistance Program Professionals, 153
National Training Laboratory, 117, 165, 251–252
National Vocational Guidance Association (NVGA), 100, 295, 297
Native Americans, 346–349
Nature vs. nurture, 323–324
Newton, Sir Isaac, 212
Newtonian physics, 213–214, 217
Niebuhr, Reinhold, 333
Nonequilibrium, 215–216
Nonmaleficence, 139–140
Norm-referenced tests, 370
Nuclear numbing, 186–187

Object relations, 281
Observation, 51–53, 366–368
Observer, inseparability of, 216
Occupations, counseling, 149–158. See also Specialties, counseling
Office, of counselor, 85–87
Office of Disease Prevention and Health Promotion (ODPHP), 157
Ombudsman, 345
Operant conditioning, 235–236
Organizational development (OD), 117, 164

Organizations, professional, 132–134
Outer work, 188–190

Pain, working through, 187–188
Paradigm shifts, 211–215
Paradoxical interventions, 286, 288–289
Paraprofessionals, 117
Parataxic distortions, 258
Parenting classes, 106
Parsons, Frank, 295–296
Pavlov, Ivan, 206, 235
Peer group, 104–105, 111, 316–317, 336
Peer pressure, 255–256
Penfield, Wilder, 231
Performance anxiety, 94
Perls, Fritz, 73, 110, 228–229, 251–252, 268
Personal growth groups, 253
Personality:
  assessment of, 371–373
  and career choice, 147–148
  and psychoanalysis, 204
  in TA, 231
  theories of, 199, 301–302
  and transpersonal counseling, 242
  types of, 169
Personalizing, 66
Personal therapy, 179
Person-centered therapy, 39, 110, 184, 200, 221, 227–228, 268, 306, 340
Phenomenology, 208
Phototherapy, 116
Physical development, 318–321
Physicians for Social Responsibility, 184–185
Piaget, Jean, 242, 324–326, 330, 332
Placebo effect, 85–86
Placement services, 308
PL 94–142, 141
Politics, and counselors, 188–189
Pragmatism, 199
Premarital counseling, 106
Preschools, counseling in, 150
Presenting problem, 92
Preventive counseling, 106–109, 112, 198, 252, 335
Primary group, 104–105, 111
Priorities, 178–179, 186
Private practice, 130–131
Private time, 178
Probing, 75
Problem solving, 77–82

Process model, 196
Professional attitude (PA), 136–137
Professionalism, 131–137
Projective techniques, 364
Psychiatry, 99, 103–104, 122
Psychoanalysis, 99, 199–200, 202–205, 217, 268, 363–364
Psychodrama, 116, 228, 233, 253
Psychological/personality-based theory, 301–302
Psychologists, 122
Psychologists for Social Responsibility, 188
Psychometry, 100
Psychosocial development, 326–327
Psychotherapy, 112–113. 183–184, 217, 251
Puberty, 321
Punctuality, of counselor, 87

Quality Circles, 128
Quality of work life (QWL), 128, 164–165
Quantum physics, 217, 231
Questioning, 27, 75–76
Questionnaires, 368–369
Questions, 75–77

Rank, Otto, 319
Rapport, 47, 89, 239
Rating scales, 367–368
Rational emotive therapy (RET), 43, 202, 238–240
Reality testing, 255
Reality therapy, 80
Redefinition, 289
Redirection, 289
Reenactment, 288
Reflection, 61, 64–66
Rehabilitation counseling, 157–158
Reinforcement, 206
Relationship:
  core conditions of, 47–48
  counselor-client, 200, 216
  dependency, 173
  enhancing, 37
  establishing, 34–36
  family, 171–172, 273, 275, 281
  terminating, 39–40
  therapeutic, 201, 244, 247
  variables among, 379

Relaxation, 50, 56, 176
Reliability, of tests, 370, 372
Remedial groups, 253–254
Remediation, 108, 111–112, 198, 335
Research, counseling:
  and counselor education, 385–387
  and government support, 156–157
  on human development, 316
  on moral development, 332
  vs. practice, 384–385
  problems in, 381–383
  rigor vs. relevance of, 382
  studies, 5, 240, 263, 322, 383
  and theory, 196, 202
  types of, 378–381
Resistance, 40–43
Respect, 65–66
Responding, 16–17, 65–66
  and attending, 56
  with concreteness, 68–69
  with confrontation, 69–72
  to content, 59–61
  with empathy, 58–59, 66–68
  with immediacy, 72–73
  using interpretation, 73–74
  using probes and questions, 74
  with self-disclosure, 69, 72
  and silence, 57–58
Right brain, 16, 322
Risk-taking, 9–10
Rogers, Carl, 102–103, 110, 184, 208, 221, 227, 268, 340

Sartre, Jean Paul, 207
Schools:
  career education in, 297
  counseling in, 107, 109, 149–153, 162
Script analysis, 233
Self-actualization, 6–8, 183–184, 209, 228, 243, 391
Self-attending, 27, 54–56, 94, 140, 176, 266
Self-awareness, 218, 297, 342, 353
Self-confrontation, 37
Self-disclosure, 10–11, 13, 15, 17, 36, 69, 72, 173, 261
Self-help groups, 111, 254
Self-knowledge, 11–16
Self-management plans, 236
Self-reflective loop, 267
Self-reliance, 83
Self-renewal, 216

Self-report instruments, 368–369, 373
Self-transcendence, 216
Seminars, 117
Sexual conduct, 139, 141
Sexuality, 118, 205
SIGI (System of Interactive Guidance and Information), 308
Silence, as response, 57–58
Specialties, counseling:
   career-lifestyle, 299–309
   choosing, 145–148, 178
   consulting, 158–162
   cross-cultural, 342–355
   divorce, 292–293
   gerontology, 155
   health, 155–157
   human resource development, 162–165
   marriage, 289–293
   preretirement, 311
   rehabilitation, 157–158
   school and university, 149–153
   substance abuse, 153–155, 157
Spiritual development, 332–335
Strategic intervention, 286–287
Situational approaches, 300–301
Skinner, B. F., 184, 206, 235
Social commitment, 183–185
Social learning, 236
Social worker, 122
Stress, 167, 170
   and burnout, 168–169
   and development, 319, 338
   management, 94, 174–179
Strong-Campbell Interest Inventory, 301
Structural approach, 233, 285–286
Structure, 36–37, 89–90
Student Assistant Program (SAP), 152–153
Substance abuse, 153–155, 157
Sufism, 210
Sullivan, Harry Stack, 187, 217, 273, 275–278
Summarization, 64–65, 91–94
Super, Donald, 299, 302–308
Superego, 204
Support groups, 177

Sutich, Anthony, 209, 241
Syncretism, 199–200
Systems, 279
Szasz, T., 360–361

TA. *See* Transactional analysis
Talk therapy, 113
Tarasoff vs. *State of California,* 141
Tart, Charles, 210
Telephone hotline, 109
Termination, 39–40, 81–83
   of group, 262–263
   of session, 93
   of transpersonal counseling, 244
Tests, 358, 369–373. *See also* Assessment
T-groups, 251, 253
Theory, 195–202
Therapeutic alliance, 25–31, 216
"Therapeutic contract," 38–39
Therapeutic relationship, 201, 244, 247
Therapy:
   effectiveness of, 4–5
   goals of, 202
   groups, 251
   multi-modal, 198
   personal, 179
Tillich, Paul, 333
Time limits, 92–93
Time management, 178–179
Token economies, 236
Topdog, 229
Training, 116–117
   and burnout, 170–172
   in business and industry, 109, 163–164
Trait-factor theory, 296, 299–300, 306, 364
Transactional analysis (TA), 200, 231–234, 268
Transference, 43–44, 204, 251, 258
Transfer of learning, 83
Transpersonal counseling, 240–244
Transpersonal force, 209–211
Transpersonal psychology, 217
Trends, 127
Triangulation, 284

Trust, 11, 36, 58, 137, 162, 257, 259, 260–161
Truth, absolute, 214

Uncertainty principle, 214
Underdog, 229
Understanding, 66–77
Unfinished business, 82
Universality, 257
Universalizing, 267
University Associates, 168

Validity, test, 373
Values, 186, 345–346, 349
Verbal interaction, 200
Videotaping, 45, 86, 89, 109, 117, 218
Vocational guidance, 100, 295–296. *See also* Career counseling
Voice, tone of, 53

Watson, John, 206
Wechsler Adult Intelligence Scale, 323
Wellness, 108, 130, 155–156, 245–246
Whitaker, Carl, 285
Wholistic counseling, 245
Wholistic health movement, 102, 129–130, 156, 217, 272, 279, 391
   and career counseling, 303
   and human development, 315, 322
Wilder, Ken, 210–211
Wolpe, Joseph, 206, 235
Women, 342, 346
Work, world of, 336
Working distance, 49
Workshops, 117

YAVIS syndrome, 25
Yin-yang philosophy, 214–215
Yoga, 210

Zeigarnik effect, 229
Zen Buddhism, 210